A BOOK OF THE BOOK

# A BOOK OF THE BOOK

SOME WORKS & PROJECTIONS
ABOUT THE BOOK & WRITING

EDITED BY

JEROME ROTHENBERG AND
STEVEN CLAY

GRANARY BOOKS · NEW YORK CITY 2000

Library of Congress Cataloguing-in-Publication Data
A book of the book : some works & projections about the book &
writing / edited by Jerome Rothenberg and Steven Clay.
    p. cm.
  Includes bibliographical references.
  ISBN 1-887123-29-6 (hc : alk. paper)—ISBN 1-887123-28-8
  (pbk. : alk. paper) 1. Poetics. 2. Literature—Philosophy.
  3. Books. I. Rothenberg, Jerome, 1931– II. Clay, Steven, 1951–
  PN1042.B58 2000
  002—dc21                99–047295

Book design by Philip Gallo.
Cover design by Sara Seagull.
First published 2000.
Printed on acid-free paper.
Printed and bound in The United States of America.
Distributed to the trade by D.A.P./Distributed Art Publishers
155 Avenue of the Americas, Second Floor
New York NY 10013-1507
Orders: (800) 338-BOOK • Tel.: (212) 627-1999
Fax: (212) 627-9484

Granary Books Inc.
http://www.granarybooks.com

This book is dedicated to readers and writers of the future
& especially to Sadie, Lily, Naomi & Ruby

# :: CONTENTS ::

# THE BOOK IS AS OLD AS FIRE & WATER

# THE BOOK TO COME

[ x ]

# EDITORS' FOREWORD

THE PREDECESSOR TO the present book—elsewhere described—was *The Book, Spiritual Instrument*, co-edited by one of us and published by the other. It was in its aftermath that we felt the appeal of expanding the work both in size and range and in the recognition that the physicality of the book was a necessary concomitant to Mallarmé's proposition of the spiritual book that we were still eager to further explore. And we were aware too that the hegemony of the material book—as a conglomerate of cloth and paper and ink and leather and glue and thread—was in some danger of being superceded by that of the virtual non-book—much as the book and writing had challenged the dominance of the oral technologies that came before them. It is those key terms—oral, material, virtual, spiritual—that underlie the discussions in the pages that follow. Set in the context of a turning from one century into another—indeed of one millennium into another—they encompass the full range of human languages that makes an ethnopoetics the underpinning for any still viable poetics.

A more substantial pre-face from the editors' perspective heads off the first section of this gathering—a section in which we extend the privilege of prefacing to a number of other interested parties. We do this as a way to move beyond our limits and to recognize some of those who have thought long and hard about the practice and problematics of the book and writing. In much the same way we're aware that our book—whatever its size—can't do justice to all of the book artists and writers to whom, as writers and readers ourselves, we're clearly beholden. For some of this we would like to mention not only those with pieces listed in our table of contents but those also whose works are cited or included within the anthologized selections. While we're satisfied that the book is ample in its inclusions, we want to point out—as always—that a gathering like this can only scratch the surface of what the past and present have given us to work from.

The selection of course is also personal, reflective of our own experiences and needs, while hopeful that these will prove of use to others. We have moved forward in the hope that our readers will be able to construct a kind of narrative from these otherwise disparate pieces. To intensify the sense of a narrative—or a series of such narratives—we have taken the liberty of removing footnotes and bibliographic references unless, from our perspective or that of the authors, they added greatly to the story being told. We have also modified the number of illustrations for certain pieces—eliminating some or adding others—and where we have selected a section from a larger work, we have eliminated references to material included elsewhere in that work but absent from our own. On the other hand, we have been flexible about stylistic features, particularly those that distinguish American from British written usage or, still more crucially, those that represent deliberate or contrarian moves on the part of the authors. We have tried in this way—and within the limits imposed on any material book—to be faithful to the intentions of those whose works we're including. And we've also attempted to present our readers with gifts like the facsmile of the Cendrars/Delaunay *La Prose du Transsibérien* or the complete reprint of Jess's *O!* —not for their economic feasability but for the pleasure it gives us to do so.

In the course of putting the work together, we are indebted to all those artists, writers and publishers whose work has come into our enterprise. If Mallarmé was right about the spiritual book—the book that all of us are writing—it may be possible to see each generation or overlap of generations as one chapter in that common (or communal) volume. Among those of our time who have most affected us—separately or together—in our thoughts about the book and writing, are Robert Duncan, Timothy Ely, Barbara Fahrner, Walter Hamady, Dick Higgins, Edmond Jabès, Sherman Paul, Ian Tyson, and Tony Zwicker to any one of whom this book could well be dedicated. Others who shared the work with us include, most notably, Philip Gallo (as designer and assembler) and Amber Phillips (as organizer and reader), whose attentions moved us along from concept to material object.

And finally, but centrally, we have also shared time and thoughts with Julie Harrison and Diane Rothenberg—some of it in New York, some in California, and some in Paris—and we have learned between ourselves as co-makers to work together on that adventure in writing and reading that forms so crucial a part of all our lives.

—*Jerome Rothenberg*
—*Steven Clay*
*1999/2000*

# PRE-FACES

# THE POETICS & ETHNOPOETICS OF THE BOOK & WRITING

## Jerome Rothenberg

*[ The following was written for the First Annual Conference in Memoriam Eric Mottram, London, September 19, 1997, & has been revised several times since.]*

IT IS STRANGE TO BEGIN—as indeed we have to begin—in Eric Mottram's absence. For myself this is the first time that I've been in London since his death & the first time that I'll be speaking to his interests & not have him here to listen & respond. Eric was for me one of the great listeners & responders—a quality that entered into his own work as a poet & as a writer on poetry & on the larger world of which poetry is a part—a small part maybe but crucial for those of us for whom it's been an entry to that world at large. With Eric, as with few others, I could speak at length, because he gave the sense that what we said between ourselves could matter & that he was there to hear.

My intention today is to return to an interrupted part of a longer conversation that we had back in 1981. I can do that because Gavin Selerie was there with a tape recorder & with the intention, which he soon carried out, of transcribing the talk & publishing it in what was then his series of Riverside Interviews. I had been very much connected until then—through the anthologies & through my own readings & performances—with a re-exploration of the oral bases / the oral sources of our poetry. And what Eric took as an opening for our talk was a statement of mine that I was (or thought I was) "much more honest as a writer than a speaker." The reference was back to an earlier "dialogue" with William Spanos in *Boundary 2*, which Eric described as having to do "with this whole problem of the relation between oral poetry & the text." Having raised a question about what had been & became even more fertile ground for me—the idea, I mean, of writing & the book, which I had been exploring in some sense since *Technicians of the Sacred*—both of us passed it by in favor of a discussion of various aspects of oral poetry "past & present [& to come]." And when the conversation got around—as it later did—to matters of ethnopoetics & ethnicities, there was a passing suggestion of the book concern in relation to the Jewish sources I had been exploring in *Poland/1931* & elsewhere, but mostly to point out that the Jews, while founding much of their mystic tradition in oral law & a poetics of the voice, were preeminently the people-of-the-book. So the book, again, was a point of contrast rather than departure.

Eric, in other words, had given me an opening & I had let it pass without making it clear (as Eric was perhaps pushing me to do at the beginning) that the book & writing had always been part of my poetics & even my ethnopoetics & was at that moment becoming—if anything—still more overt. To begin with, I was at the time of the Riverside interview the author of some 27 books of my own poetry, eight other books of translations, & seven (mostly very large) anthologies & assemblages. And it was alongside these—& not apart from them—that I had, like most of us, been entering deeply (I thought) into *performance* as a strategy of voice & body. With that came what I described to Eric as an attempt to "desanctify & demistify the written word"—initially by finding ways to present or represent those vast areas of language art that seemed—everywhere—to precede or (often) supercede the act of writing. At the same time I began—but possibly more slowly—to recognize the similarly diverse origins & possibilities of writing & that a "symposium of the whole" (in Robert Duncan's phrase) would also involve a mix & *possibly* a clash of writings. It was as if, in place of the Bible, say, as a singularly fixed text, we were to view it now as the multiple books (the *biblia,* plural) that it actually was. And all this, in the contemporary context, against the resurgence of those (fundamentalists & others) who pretend to a single book, not in Mallarmé's sense but in that of the tyrannies from which they've descended & which they threaten to restore.

Still, for me, the central impulse in *Technicians of the Sacred,* the first of the big assemblages that I've continued to construct, was to bring together a display of those ("oral") poetries that seemed to exist apart from writing & the book. This was the start of my ethnopoetics as such, but even within that there were spaces, inevitably, in which the source poems were themselves in written form—the Egyptian Book of the Dead, say, or the Chinese Book of Changes, among the works that were the most immediately familiar. And there was also an intuition, a sense that began to play itself out, of writing like speech as some kind of universal (human) constant. So, in *Technicians,* there was, among other entries, a section early in the book called "The Pictures," with examples of pictographs & glyphs from a number of diverse cultures (largely American Indian & South Pacific), paired in the commentaries with works by visual & concrete poets of our own place & time. And elsewhere in the book I was able to include Midē [healing] songs & picture-songs from the Ojibwa Indians, nsibidi [secret] writings from the Ekoi in Africa, & pictorial songs & narratives from the Na-Khi "tribe" in China.[1] Accompanying commentaries [as later also in *Shaking the Pumpkin*] called attention to the thin line between "writing" & "drawing" that made it "hard [as I said there] to keep the functions separate or to assert with any confidence that writing is a late development rather than indigenous, in some form, to the human situation everywhere."[2]

When Dennis Tedlock & I founded *Alcheringa* in 1971 as "a first magazine of ethnopoetics" [of the world's tribal poetries], the emphasis, again,
was on "poetry made in the mouth," but our pages were open as well to a
range of traditional & early written art: paleolithic calendar notations, Egyptian & Mayan hieroglyphs, recastings of Bible & other Jewish bookworks,
Old Norse runes, & Navajo pictographs (among others). I was also working
by the middle 1970s on *A Big Jewish Book* (later revised as *Exiled in the Word*),
where I could focus on the written alongside—& drawing from—the oral,
& with a strong awareness of how central the "book" was in that highly
charged, sometimes over-determined context. (Earlier anthologies of the
1970s like *America a Prophecy & Revolution of the Word* also put a high emphasis on the written, including—most surprisingly I thought—instances of
both traditional & modern [experimental] alternatives to our normative
ideas of books & writing.) This was still before the 1981 discussions with
Eric & with Gavin Selerie, as was the founding, after my separation from
*Alcheringa,* of a successor magazine, *New Wilderness Letter,* in which I promised as editor ("a poet by inclination & practice") to pursue poesis "in all
arts & sciences...[&] not [to] be specialized & limited by culture or profession" but to enlarge the context of poetry as "a report, largely through the
creative work itself, of where that process [of poesis] takes us."

That in brief was the situation in June 1981, a year before the appearance of the book issue of *New Wilderness Letter* (about which, more later) &
during the preparation of *Symposium of the Whole* as an anthology of writings
by poets, anthropologists & others "toward an ethnopoetics." In the latter
work Diane Rothenberg & I were attempting as co-editors to open from the
more specialized emphasis on oral poetry to a still wider view that would
encompass writing & the book as well, along with other forms of visual
poetry & language (that from the cultures of the deaf a prime example) for
which there was as yet no actual poetics. By the time, then, that I returned
to London in December 1982 & was interviewed by Gavin Selerie alone,
the concern with writing & the book took up (for me) a significant part of
the conversation. And since I certainly saw Eric then, I feel quite certain
that these concerns were also part of what was further said between us.

Looking back at the conversation with Selerie, I'm aware that the point
of departure for me—the emblematic point at least—was in the poetry, the
shamanistic *veladas,* of the Mazatec shamaness María Sabina. For her—&
this was a matter that had been made clear to us by her American translator
Henry Munn—there was no actual practice of writing (or reading) but the
words of her extraordinary chants were opened to her in the form of a great
Book of Language that was given to her in her first empowering visions &
that, although she remained unlettered, she was (in her own mind) fully
able to read & to give back as song. In light of this & of my own meeting

with her a few years before, I went on to speak of myself as a writer & of writing as a primal human function:

> Increasingly [I said to Gavin] I've had to assert that what I'm involved in is not a denial of the powers of a written language, because that—the written language, writing—would be a part of the exploration also. Over the last couple of years, in fact, I've been trying to explore the uses of writing in cultures that we usually speak of as oral, non-literate, pre-literate, & so on. And the conclusion I'm drawn toward is that writing in some sense is also universal & shared among all peoples. Therefore, when human beings developed as human beings at some point in the far past—at the point where we became human beings we were probably already using some form of speech—& along with that, I would think, some form of writing, art-making, & so on.

And I added (by way of conclusion): "It's *all* very old."

In that sense, as Eric clearly knew, the book (taken as the "scene," the place in which the writing comes together) was the hidden side of my ethnopoetics, as the city was (for me) the scene of the "new wilderness" named as my project of that time. And as the talk with Eric & Gavin & others helped all of that develop, I found a number of ways over the next two or three years to let it come to surface. *Symposium of the Whole* had appeared by middle 1982, & in the aftermath of that we were organizing (through the University of Southern California in Los Angeles) a second international symposium on ethnopoetics for the spring of 1983.[3] With that, as with the book from which we took the conference's name, the idea was not simply to recapitulate what had been said before, but to bring the discourse on ethnopoetics into areas from which it seemed to have been set apart. Writing & the book clearly marked off one such territory—aided in this instance by the visit of Edmond Jabès, whom I had brought to San Diego as a visiting Regents scholar. (Others who were there were Robert Duncan, David Antin, Marjorie Perloff, Michael McClure, Roger Abrahams, Wai-lim Yip, Hugh Kenner, Paula Gunn Allen, Nathaniel Mackey, J. Stephen Lansing, Clayton Eshleman, Wendy Rose, David Guss, & Barbara Tedlock.) I had already by this time lifted for my own uses Jabès's aphorism that "the book is as old as fire & water" & had juxtaposed it with Tristan Tzara's contention that "thought is made in the mouth." So those two were now, in *my* mind at least, the axes for our discussions of an expanded ethnopoetics.

In the year preceding the symposium, then, I had opened the concern with writing & the book in a still more deliberate way—co-editing with David Guss a book issue of our magazine *New Wilderness Letter.* The work had by then accumulated—including preliminary work for the international symposium—& had been accelerated by Michael Gibbs's retranslation & visual commentary on Mallarmé's *Le livre, instrument spirituel.* The push provided by the Mallarmé (as I later wrote) "not only brought us back to the first modernist breakthroughs but also provided a context in which those breakthroughs corresponded to an ancient sense of book as sacred object." All of this—for me—was now no longer hidden but brought to surface—abetted also by the California visit earlier that year of the Peruvian *curandero* Eduardo Calderón Palomino, whom David Guss had led into a useful discussion of his *mesa* (his healing altar) as an assemblage of objects that could be read the way one reads a book. The rhyming with Mallarmé was perfect—like that of Mallarmé with María Sabina—& suggested a series of links, a web of ancient & modern possibilities that could be woven into a new display or book. And the gathering itself—a small anthology of works immediately to hand—ranged between new & old (deeply traditional & startlingly avant-garde), in such a way (I thought) that we could "grasp the actual potentialities of writing (as with any other form of language or culture [& by so doing] could extend the meaning of literacy beyond a system of (phonetic) letters to the practice of writing itself."[4] In concluding my "editor's note," I wrote:

> It is our growing belief (more apparent now than at the start of the ethnopoetics project) that the cultural dichotomies between writing & speech—the "written" & the "oral"—disappear the closer we get to the source. To say again what seems so hard to get across: there is a primal book as there is a primal voice, & it is the task of our poetry & art to recover it—in our minds & in the world at large.

That recovery, of course, is also a matter of demonstration & of coming to understand the implications of where such a view might lead us. As such it is a process that those like Eric or myself or any of us here might help to start but without the real hope or even the desire to bring it to conclusion.

A decade & a half has passed since then, during which time the books have multiplied for all of us. For myself I have been lucky not only in the normal run of book publication but to have joined with book artists like Ian Tyson (a longtime companion in this work) & Barbara Fahrner, Walter Hamady, Steven Clay, & others in the making of particular works that correspond to their ideas of where the art of books might take us. I have also worked with Pierre Joris on two volumes of an end-of-century assemblage, *Poems for the Millennium,* as a work drawing from the writings of the last 100 years & more—both those that work from a demotic spoken base & those that draw on visible language & the written word. (That there is often no clear division between the two—both the works & the makers of the works—is likely an obvious point but still a point worth making.) With regard to the book & writing (at their "limits") the work that opens the century for us is Mallarmé's—both the notes for his *Le Livre* & his promethean *Coup de dès* of 1897. (A page from William Blake's *Milton: Book the Second* is the actual first volume opener in a section called "Forerunners.") This focus—most of it book-referential—is followed up in the experiments of Futurists & Dadaists, but also in exemplary works by those like the "outsider" writer/artist Adolf Wölfli & the master of the collage-book Max Ernst, as well as in an ethnopoetic final section that draws from a range of works —both oral & written, ancient & modern.

The second volume is dedicated to Eric Mottram & attempts—with probably "unpardonable" omissions—to bring the work into the (almost) present.[5] The volume, at over 850 pages, is both long & complex, but one of the dominant thrusts is to deliver the sense—as far as can be done within anthology constraints—that poets will often write not only for the single (visible) *page* but with an idea of the poem as an extended work or *book*. (Jabès with his lifelong *Book of Questions* would be a case in point, but only one among many.) On its strongly visual side, however, the *Millennium Two* book includes works by Michaux, Cage, Mac Low, Cobra artists Christian Dotremont & Asger Jorn (but also other Cobra artist-poets such as Karel Appel, Gerrit Kouwenaar, & Pierre Alechinsky), Robert Filliou, a whole range of concretists (Eugen Gomringer, Ian Hamilton Finlay, Emmett Williams, Seiichi Nikuni, Ilse & Pierre Garnier, Haroldo & Augusto de Campos, & Karl Young, whose "bookforms" had earlier appeared in *New Wilderness Letter*), Hannah Weiner, Kamau Brathwaite, George Maciunas, Bob Cobbing, Steve McCaffery, Carolee Schneemann, Tom Phillips, Clark Coolidge (in collaboration with Philip Guston), Cecilia Vicuña, & Theresa Hak Kyung Cha. Along with these come chapter-length excerpts from text-centered works composed as books & not compendia by poets such as Alice Notley, Anne Waldman, Jacques Roubaud, & Lyn Hejinian, among many others. And there is also a section, "Toward a Cyberpoetics," going back to visual/verbal machine works by Marcel Duchamp & Abraham Lincoln Gillespie & up to computer-generated texts by Jim Rosenberg & John Cayley—as a starter.

I have no theory as to where all of this may lead us, though some sense of theory (neither "critical" nor "French" but very much, I hope, my own) must underlie all that I'm saying. Still I feel it's close to whatever basis for a poetics Eric Mottram was pursuing in his art & thought. The work continues of course, as it has to, & over the last year—but no longer able to share with Eric—I've supervised the republication (by Steven Clay & Granary Books) of the *New Wilderness Letter* book issue—now an independent volume called *The Book, Spiritual Instrument*. And looking ahead (& very much at Clay's instigation) I've embarked on another anthology project: a wide-ranging book of writings on "the book," taken in some sense as an extension of what *The Book, Spiritual Instrument* was attempting with those materials that were then immediately to hand. (This is the difference, then, between a magazine & an anthology.) It is in this context that we hope to explore more fully the points at which a poetics & an ethnopoetics of the book &

writing come together or illuminate each other. And we want at the same time to expose the material bases (ink & paper, manufacture & dissemination) of those ends to which the work of Mallarmé was leading.

There will be no limits here to what we might include—of books that have been made & books that have still to be imagined. I believe in this regard that there is also a *future* of the book—as an extended & self-contained compendium of (visible) language—& that the emergence of new technologies—new *cyberworks* I meant to say—is not a threat to our identity as poets & book people but a new aspect of it that can & will enhance all that poesis is or ever has been. In much the same way, I no longer believe, if I ever did, that the book or writing had—in some earlier time—destroyed orality or made the human voice obsolete. The book *is* as old as fire & water, & thought *is* made in the mouth—as it is also in the hands & lungs & with the inner body. If that was our condition at the beginning, it will be also in the end.

A FINAL NOTE.  In making such a book-of-the-book we have been able to draw in the first instance on a range of discursive writings that deal with one or another aspect of the book & writing. Here the many recent books, artist's books, & essays of Johanna Drucker need immediate mention, along with others in roughly the same (largely contemporary) territory by Michael Davidson, Marjorie Perloff, Anne Moeglin-Delcroix, Renée & Judd Hubert, Jerome McGann, & (in their new historical anthology of alternative forms of languaging, *Imagining Language*) Jed Rasula & Steve McCaffery. Some of these we have included in the finished volume, & some not; & we have reinforced the inclusions with critical & philosophical writings by thinkers like Jacques Derrida & Maurice Blanchot, but also by poets & artists like Anne Waldman, Michael Davidson, William Everson, Keith A. Smith, & Karl Young—the last three engaged as well in printing and book production. (Short poems or excerpts from poems by poets like Whitman, Stein, Jabès, & Khlebnikov serve a similar function.) Such works, evoking positions & preferences across what we think of as a wide artistic spectrum, appear within our opening section of pre-faces or at strategic points elsewhere in this volume.

It is our sense—mine certainly—that the practitioners—the writers & the book-makers themselves—are the key to any future poetics of the book. Accordingly we have included two large sections in which the points of reference are to specific artists & poets in the aftermath of Blake (our preeminent poet-of-the-book). In the first of these sections ("The Opening of the Field," with title after Robert Duncan), the inclusions start from Blake & run through the avant-garde movements of the 1920s & 1930s: the self-constructed fascicles of Emily Dickinson (in Susan Howe's accounting);

the Mallarmé notebooks & plottings called collectively *Le Livre*; the Blaise Cendrars/Sonia Delaunay *Prose of the Transsiberian* (rising to the height of the Eiffel Tower); the rough-hewn books of the Russian Constructivists & the liberated pages of the Italian Futurists; Marcel Duchamp's boxed notes & drawings; André Breton's musings on the germinal collage-books of Max Ernst; & writing as an act of violence & conjuration in Artaud's works on paper—what Agnès de la Beaumelle speaks of, aptly, as his "spells & gris-gris." And in the concluding work in this section, Jerome McGann runs through a range of English-language sources—William Morris, Walter Pater, Ezra Pound, Louis Zukofsky, Bob Brown—as early practitioners of book & page art, & then moves on to Susan Howe as an exemplar of its carry-over in "postmodern" writing.

But before we make our own way to the "postmodern," we insert a central section ("The Book Is As Old As Fire & Water"—from the Jabès line quoted above) in which we offer alternative ways of writing & of making books, not "modern" or "experimental" in conception but drawing from a range of times & places different from our own. These deliberately but not exclusively focus on traditions of the Indian Americas—threatened for centuries but never totally eradicated. As opener we are able to go back to a poem—recovered—from the pre-Conquest Aztec poet Nezahualcoyotl in celebration of those "painted books" that were later destroyed by the conquering missionary zealots. Even more striking at present is the reconstitution of the old Mayan writing systems, on the basis of which Dennis Tedlock offers a first attempt at a translation that reveals the underlying poetics of the classical inscriptions. In two related works, Walter D. Mignolo probes the range & character of "the book in the new world," & Henry Munn shows how a tradition of the book underlies the oral poetry & visions of the contemporary Mazatec shaman-poet ("woman of words"), María Sabina.

Apart from this Indian-related framework, the range available to us has been enormous & our selections necessarily restricted—from Nancy Munn's description of forms of writings/drawings in sand among the Walbiri people of Australia to Jean François Billeter's account of Chinese writing viewed in its own terms as a unique & particular art; Roland Barthes' approach to "the Japanese theatrical face" as a surface that isn't painted so much as written; Toshi Ishihara and Linda Reinfeld's interpretation of a well-known Japanese "anthology" in the form of a boxed game of poem cards; Martha L. Carothers's bringing together of traditional "novelty books" ("pages or pictures that fold out, revolve, slide, move, slat-dissolve, pop up, or are die-cast in special shapes") with their avant-garde counterparts; a discussion by William J. Samarin of "glossographia" as the written equivalent to the pentacostalists' more familiar "speaking in tongues"; kabbalistic readings of the night sky as a book of shifting letters ("Celestial Alphabet Event") & of the creation of the world as itself an act of writing (*Sefer Yetsirah*); & a similar account of language & creation from the Dogon thinker Ogotemmêli.

The final section of our gathering is called "The Book To Come" (after Blanchot's essay on Mallarmé, also included) & covers the latter part of the twentieth century—the second great awakening both of experimental writing & of the artist's book as such. (It is with relation to its "postwar" emergence in particular that Johanna Drucker writes: "In many ways it could be argued that the artist's book is the quintessential 20th-century artform.") In approaching this second period, we have decided, very deliberately, to avoid hard & fast categories of books & book-makers—except as they turn up in the writings of the artists we're presenting. We do however see the period as one in which—more than ever—artists & poets took control of their own work apart from the nexus of dealers & markets. Among the earliest of these we foreground Dieter Rot[h], whose self-made books & single sheets of text broke open older conventions of print & book design; Bob Cobbing, a master poet of the "democratic multiple," whose *oeuvre,* utilizing mimeograph, xerox & offset, inches today toward a thousand books as publisher & author; Ian Tyson, among those independent artists of the book who continue to work with fine print & painterly, sometimes sculptural, surfaces, in an ongoing interplay of words & images; and Jess, whose collage-book *O!,* originally published in a cheaply printed offset edition by my own Hawk's Well Press, we are reproducing in its entirety. As part of a continuity from Max Ernst's bookworks, among others, *O!* rhymes as well with Tom Phillips's *A Humument*—the latter a new form of collage (or de/collage) in which old texts are pared away & painted over, to let new texts (& images) emerge.

As Drucker's essay, "The Artist's Book As Idea and Form," presents a linkage between modern & postmodern artist's books, that by Thomas A. Vogler points to numerous examples of new & hybrid forms—"books" that are...emphatically *not* books, but rather 'book-objects,' physical objects that trope on every conceivable aspect of 'the book,' from the conventional codex format of the mass-produced commodity to its semiotic functions as the instrumental embodiment of cultural authority in the West." Alongside Vogler's numerous examples—works by Kenneth Goldsmith, Greely Myatt, Helen Lessick, Marcel Broodthaers, Buzz Spector, Byron Clercx, & Patrick Luber, among others—we have added several seminal works, some of which emphatically changed the surface of writing from the familiar book-as-codex to other vehicles or conduits for visible language: Alison Knowles's monumental *Book of Bean,* Allan Kaprow's *Words,* Ian Hamilton Finlay's garden at Little Sparta, Carolee Schneemann's *Up To and Including Her Limits,* Barbara Fahrner's encyclopedic *Kunstkammer Project,* & Faith Ringgold's *French Collection* narrative quilts. These are capped by Xu Bing's *A Book from the Sky,* an extraordinary contemporary work of glossographia based on traditional Chinese writing, & by Charles Bernstein's concluding essay, which both traces a history of writing in the west & takes on the major shift into virtual (as contrasted to material) text art in our age of audio/video/digital reproduction & internet dissemination.

To conclude, then, is to say that here as elsewhere there is no conclusion. "Of the making of books there is no end," as the old scriptural saw once put it (while reifying a single book as the unalterable word-of-god), and Mallarmé in his modernist détournement: "Everything in the world exists in order to be turned into a book." It is my sense—at least in our common work as poets—that the movement, the dialectic (to use a once fashionable word) is between book and voice, between the poets (present) in their speaking & the poets (absent) in their writing. That is to say, we are (up to & past our limits) full & sentient beings, & free, as Rimbaud once told us, to possess truth in one soul & one body. For myself, as I surely would have said to Eric Mottram (or he to me), the return to the book is the step now needed to make the work complete.                     —*Paris/London 1997*

—*Encinitas 1999*

## NOTES

1. A still larger presentation of such primal writings/drawings appears in the revised edition of *Technicians of the Sacred*, in which I open the distribution of poetries to include the European.

2. A deeper level of our ethnopoetics was of course its exploration of a poetry imbedded within the life of a people or community &, through its traditional poets as well as its modernist experimenters, a poetry that served as a primary vehicle toward the experiencing of an expanding range of actual & possible realities.

3. The first symposium on ethnopoetics, possibly more restricted in scope, had taken place eight years before at the Center for Twentieth-Century Studies in Milwaukee.

4. The works in the book issue, broken along the lines of modern & traditional, included *on its experimental side*, Karl Young's sculptural "bookforms"; Alison Knowles's *The Book of Bean*, a monumental walk-through work with accompanying remarks & "auto-dialogue" [reflections] by her & by George Quasha; & assorted writings & commentaries by Jabès, Dick Higgins, Jed Rasula, David Meltzer, Gershom Scholem, & Herbert Blau; & *on its ethnopoetic side*, the Eduardo Calderón *mesa*; an essay by J. Stephen Lansing on "the aesthetics of the sounding of the [written] text" in Balinese performance, excerpts from Dennis Tedlock's translation of the Mayan *Popol Vuh* that spoke specifically of books & writing, Tina Oldknow's offering of a Muslim practice using written (sacred) words removed from their material base & decocted in an herbal mixture ("Muslim Soup"), & Karl Young's speculative analysis of the Mixtec *Codex Vienna*, one of the surviving illuminated books from ancient Mexico. Along with this, there was a series of striking photo portraits by Becky Cohen, in which a number of American poets were shown in the act of reading, making of the book (as it were) "an instrument of performance."

5. The dedication reads "For Eric Mottram *poet, friend, & teacher*" & follows with a quote extracted from a poem of his: "that all created life be rescued / from tyranny decay sloughed for a share / in magnificence   hoof thunder   silence of / pines & birches across the taiga."

# *from* "THE BOOK AS MACHINE"
## Steve McCaffery and bpNichol

*It would be a mistake to suppose that the trend towards the oral and acoustic means that the book is becoming obsolete. It means rather that the book, as it loses its monopoly as a cultural form, will acquire new roles.*
— *Marshall McLuhan*

*Don't look around yourselves for inspiration. We have only one teacher:*
*THE MACHINE.* — *Nikolai Foregger*

IN THE BEGINNINGS of our research into narrative we ran up against the inescapable fact that *there exists no standard definition of narrative in the sense that writers seem to use the word.* There is so much confusion particularly between narrative and plot, the two terms being used almost interchangeably. Thus we feel free to create a definition which is not in the strictest sense new because there is no existing old definition. What we need to establish is a working definition of narrative and then discard it if further research proves it false or inadequate in scope.

For the purposes of this report we will deal with narrative in print rather than as an oral phenomenon. This will allow us to eliminate consideration of the innumerable narratives of daily living that are characterized by their provisionality, evanescence and intractability. In the strictest sense the most comprehensive definition of narrative would be simply our sequential life experience. We will not address this comprehension but rather deal with narrative as it occurs within the specialized area of the print experience.

Gertrude Stein put it most simply when she pointed out that narrative was anyone telling anything to anyone at anytime. When we transpose this definition into print we begin to recognize two distinct experiences: 1) The physical experience of print as word and ink and the book itself as a physical object. 2) The psychological and psychosemantic experience of operating verbal signs.

In this first part of our report we will deal with the physical aspects of the book as machine, documenting some of the attempts made towards an understanding and reassessment of the physical forms the book has already acquired and the emerging outline of future forms, considering the implications of the book's mechanicity and the active application of such considerations.

## BACKGROUNDS

By machine we mean the book's capacity and method for storing information by arresting, in the relatively immutable form of the printed word, the flow of speech conveying that information. The book's mechanism is activated when the reader picks it up, opens the covers and starts reading it. Throughout its history (and even prior to Gutenberg) the book has possessed a relatively standard form varying only in size, colour, shape and paper texture. In its most obvious working the book organizes content along three modules: the lateral flow of the line, the vertical or columnar build-up of the lines on the page, and thirdly a linear movement organized through depth (the sequential arrangement of pages upon pages).

Significantly the book assumes its particular physical format through its design to accommodate printed linguistic information in a linear form. Taking the line as a practically impossible continuum, it breaks it up into discrete units of equal length, placing them one above the other in sequence until a page unit is filled. Similarly the page units are ordered sequentially and the whole sewn or glued together to form the complete book. Already it is possible to note that the linear experience as continuum has been significantly altered, for the second and third modules mentioned are the ones which the book has placed before our reading pose. In addition the book has underlined and reinforced the first module so that we now accept all three as not simply modules but constants which are seldom questioned. Hence the surprising shock value of typographic experiments (evinced by the very fact that they are labelled *experiments*).

So far in our description of the book as machine we have dealt with it as a prose print experience. It is important, however, to point out the difference between the reading experience of prose and poetry. Prose as print encourages an inattention to the right-hand margin as a terminal point. The tendency is encouraged to read continually as though the book were one extended line. In poetry, by contrast, the end of each line is integral to the structure of the poem whether it follows older metrical prosodic models or more recent types of breath-line notation. This emphasis upon the structural aspect of the terminal point of each visual line unit in the poem is why concrete poetry is called, in fact, poetry and why the latter word is apt in its description. In poetry, where the individual line is compositionally integral, the page is more often than not itself integral. Most short poems for instance involve a significant degree of iconicity: we see the poem as a visual whole before we read it. Perceived optically as a complete unit the page is qualified to such an extent that it ceases to function as an *arbitrary* receptacle, or surface, for the maximum number of words it can contain (functioning thereby as a random-sized unit in a larger construct), becoming instead the frame, landscape, atmosphere within which the poem's own unity is enacted and reacted upon. Page and type function as the two ingredients in a verbal sculpture.

By contrast, in the majority of prose the general rule holds that the paragraph—through effecting a visual separation of sense and event—performs a similar function (optically) to the poetic line. A sentence is not visually integral until combined with the other sentences to form the paragraph. However, in both prose and the visually continuous poem (Milton's *Paradise Lost* for instance) the page has no optical significance. Being to a large extent a working out of information through duration, prose structures tend to be temporal rather than visual. For instance the chapter can seldom be grasped iconically precisely because the chapter extends over the surfaces of several pages, occupying a part of the depth module which runs from the start of a book to its end. Even the paragraph's optical quality tends to be accidental. The effect of this surface extension is to pressure the reader into moving along as quickly as possible in the depth module. In extended prose or poetry the page becomes an obstacle to be overcome. There is a difference too of urgency in the poetic and prose line. In the former the left-hand margin is always a starting point, the right-hand margin a terminal, neither of which is determined by the randomness of page size but rather by the inner necessity of the compositional process. It becomes obvious how historically the emphasis on the visual element in writing would have a *poetic* emergence, for only in poetry occurs that bridging point which permits the step from a significance through inner necessity (where each visual terminal point gains pertinence and value) to a new way of perceiving in which the visuality becomes, not the end product of an interior psychological process, but rather the beginning of a whole *new* method of perception.

There seems to exist at present a dichotomy in attitude between the book as a machine of reference and the book as a commodity to be acquired, consumed and discarded. Traditional printed narrative is largely thought of as the transcription of a hypothetical oral activity: a speech line running from a point of commencement to an end. Such books transcribe language along horizontal axes running from top left to bottom right of each page. This occidentally conventional manner of reading along the length of the line and down the length of each page from first to last in actuality reconstitutes the duration of a "listening." In reference books such as dictionaries and directories, however, the oral hypothesis is minimized to the point, perhaps, of non-existence. Such books are not thought of as having authors or a supposed unitary voice behind them. They exist as physical storage units for information, to be consulted at various times, but not designed to be consumed in a single, linear duration. Popular fiction, marketed for mass audiences, performs a different function; there the page's non-sequential storage qualities are ignored. Nobody would consider the page of such a book as an area requesting the reader's free, non-lineal eye movements over a multi-activating, multi-acting surface, but rather as a unit *necessarily endured* as a means to the complete reception of the book's information. The current predicament of popular mass fiction is the competitive threat staged by the other great machines of consumption: television and the movies. Where plot consumption is the effect intended, television and film are indubitably the more efficient media. The reason for this is clear. The book's power as an object to be dwelt on and referred back to is not a desirable feature. Not only the page but the book in its entirety is conceived as an obstacle to be overcome in order to achieve the desired goal of unproblematic, uninterrupted, unsophisticated consumption. Television and the cinema on the other hand afford more rapid and totally sensorial means of satisfying such an appetite for story. In the light of this phenomenon two important implications of such pre-masticated reading as *Reader's Digest* become obvious. There is a "division of labour" on the reader's part in that he renounces a portion of the total reading role which is performed for him. And secondly the more serious implication of a hierarchical structuring imposed upon the reading experience, by means of which a superior "essence" is thought of as being abstracted from a "lesser" padding. To extend this consumer metaphor we may say that plot is product within linguistic wrapping. Dictionaries and directories work against this status by throwing emphasis onto the single page and the information stored thereon. In their function, dictionaries move much closer to the page-iconicity described above.

Narrative then can be developed freely along either of two directions: one rooted in oral tradition and the typographic "freezing" of speech; the other set in an awareness of the page as a visual, tactile unit with its own very separate potential.

## TWENTY-ONE FACTS THAT COULD ALTER YOUR LIFE (SEND FOR FREE ILLUSTRATED BOOKLET)

1. The front page of a newspaper is the paradigm of typographic cubism. Considered as a multi-page whole, the newspaper is founded on a model of structural discontinuity and a principle of competitive attentions. Front-page stories seldom end on the front page, nor do they all end on the same interior page. The front page is an opening made up of many openings terminating on different pages, which themselves contain other openings —to read a newspaper as a consecutive experience leads to extreme discontinuity.

2. A page is literally one side of a two-sided sheet of paper—the surface of a three-dimensional object.

3.   If we consider the printless page to be a static, neutral surface, then by applying continuous type to cover that entire surface (as in a page of a novel or this page of a TRG [Toronto Research Group] report) that neutrality is not altered. Where a rectangle of type is placed upon a rectangle of page there is no attempt made to work creatively with the possible tension existing between surface (page) and object on that surface (print). Moreover, in such a placement we invest the page with a secondary quality not inherent to it: *viz.,* a top left to bottom right orientation (radically different languages such as Chinese and Hebrew impose, of course, a similar directional limitation).

4.   When Rabelais (in book 5, chapter 45 of *Gargantua and Pantagruel*) has the Goddess Bottle speak, she speaks from within a pictorial representation of a bottle. This bottle is not verbally described but rather imaged on the page; it does not illustrate the story as an appendage, it is an integral part of it. Like the corporal's stick-flourish in Sterne's *Tristram Shandy* words are forsaken for a visual instantiation of an object/event.

5.   When Simmias of Rhodes composed his *Egg,* George Herbert his *Easter Wings* and Apollinaire his *Calligrammes,* all were trying to bring together the objects signified with the words that signified them. A case of verbal description and the pictorial shape of the object described being joined iconically in pictorial space.

6.   In *Tender Buttons,* Gertrude Stein's carafe and umbrella are not visually fixed on the page. When all the words inside her at the moment of composition (of perception) came out they fused perceiver with perceived within the activity of perceiving. The language which described the object also became the object in a psychic space.

7.   In such poems as "now they found the wagon cat in human body," "no body speaking" and other pieces in *We Sleep Inside Each Other All,* Bill Bissett brings together perceiver and perceived in psychic space which becomes jointly manifest in a pictorial space. Both Stein and Bissett use syntactic rhythm to indicate subjective rhythm; both are dealing with the fundamental relationship between language and consciousness. By moving the poem back into pictorial space Bissett furthers the visual technique employed by Simmias, Herbert and Apollinaire, as well as Stein's sense of the autonomous existence of the thing composed.

8.   The compositional technique employed by Simmias and Bissett makes a radically different demand upon the page than regular linear transcription. The page ceases to be a neutral surface of support and becomes instead a spatially interacting region; it is granted thereby a metaphorical extension.

Conceived as a spatially significant unit, the page carries dimensional and gravitational implications. In Stein's writing it does not.

9.   Pierre Garnier employs the term *spatialisme* to describe his own particular type of lettristic composition. Garnier developed a theory of the letter as self-sufficing entity existing and operating within an open space or field: the page. This application of a spatial metaphor alters radically the physics of his page. In his own texts autonomous letters (as objects) occupy a gravitational region, with syntactic emphasis falling on the *interval* between the letter objects. The page becomes not only container but definer of the lettristic configuration and becomes additionally a profoundly active space.

10. *Spatialisme* is a lettristic application of Eugen Gomringer's formal concept of poetic *constellation:* a word or word cluster balanced—the analogue is "electro-magnetically"—within the force field of the page. Both *Spatialisme* and the *constellation* deploy the page as a metaphor for space in general. The page is not altered physically but its materiality receives a metaphoric supplement.

11. Page becomes an active space, a meaningful element in the compositional process and the size and shape of it become significant variables.

12. The typewriter fixes page size to carriage capacity.

13. In Steve McCaffery's *Carnival* the carriage capacity limitations are actively confronted. By rejecting its dimensional restrictions of size and by forcing it to operate modularly as a smaller unit in a much larger surface, both the page (and its traditional function *in* the book) are destroyed. *Carnival* is an anti-book: perforated pages must be physically released, torn from sequence and viewed simultaneously in the larger composite whole. The work demands that language be engaged non-sequentially rather than read in sequence. Altering the syntactic space permits the physical one to change. Altering the physical space allows both book and page to utilize at a maximum their sculptural potential.

14. By replacing the pictorial representation of the thing with its verbal description, Greg Curnoe, in his painted series *View of Victoria Hospital 1,* exploits the tensions between the viewer/reader's traditional assumptions as to what constitutes both a painting and a page. Curnoe's canvas becomes his page and by implication his page becomes his canvas.

15. John Furnival abandons the page and the book entirely in his language constructs which treat syntax as both a physical and environmental matter. Word order becomes panel/architectural layout in his elaborate verbal-architectural labyrinths that replace the complexities of paragraph and sentence. Furnival not only concretizes language but architecturalizes it as well.

16. In the environmental works of Ferdinand Kriwet the pressure to externalize language and alter the mechanics of its reading is achieved by a four-dimensional application that radically modifies the reading space. No longer turning through a book nor looking at a canvas or panel, the reader exists inside a total linguistic environment. As the book constitutes the traditional method for storing verbal information, so the four walls, ceiling and floor of the gallery become the storage tool for Kriwet's plastic word surfaces. The activation of Kriwet's machine inherently transforms the reader's role and placement. In Dickens you bring the book into your life, with Kriwet you bring your life into the "book."

17. Hart Broudy is now (1973) effecting a different application of language to environment. Using the photographic principle of the *blow-up* and applying it to a hybridized work that is both poetry and painting he is arriving at a new kind of optical linguistic environment. The starting point for his compositions is a physical fragmentation of the single letter which then functions as a blueprint for a macro-composition. Text is blown-up to canvas size in which interlocking fragments are magnified to become giant connected panels. The reader emerges as an active object in a mental paradox: a giant in a miniature world that is larger than his or her self.

18. Fragment from Tom Mot's *Seventh Notebook:*

> ...i should try technique of microfiche...could compress my random sequences onto entire card surface...Swift's Gulliver...microcard...what is it...microcard in fact to reinforce upon the large canvas sense its original quality of print as an isolated experience...microviewer as one machine to activate another... do this and then combine microcard with macroprojection say a huge screen in an auditorium if i can get one...this way could get the combination of communal experience with traditional printed book's isolated experience....

19. Ian Hamilton Finlay, at his home of Stonypath in Scotland, has returned to and revitalized the Renaissance concept of the Book of Nature. Stonypath is essentially a landscape brought into linguistic concerns as a living metaphor. The garden is Finlay's Book in which pages transform themselves to quasi-functional objects. Poems become sun dials, gravestones, the page's traditional material opacity becomes the window's clear view into the objects signified. Any traveller through Finlay's garden has to be a reader too; it is a book involving participation of the feet as well as eyes.

20. In their *Bi-Point Poetry Manifesto,* the French poets Julien Blaine and J.F. Bory urged the abandonment of book and print each in its entirety (save for their minor use in reporting non-typographic language events). The urban landscape provides both alphabet and subject for their work; economic, social and political factors become syntactic elements. Bory and Blaine's lives and actions become their writing.

21. William Shakespeare (somewhat earlier) spoke of sermons being in stones and books in running brooks. Finlay's Stonypath and the Blaine-Bory Manifesto are the physical, dynamic applications of a sixteenth-century analogy of Book and Nature.

## AFTERTHOUGHTS
### OR WHAT THIS HAS TO DO WITH ANYTHING AT ALL

So far we have reviewed/described a specific set of books and writers from the viewpoint of our own concerns with the book as machine. Each of them has, for us, significant comments to make regarding the machine's capacity to alter function and affect the psychological content of the fictional reality presented. There are three questions that arise from our considerations: 1) What are the precise applications of the solutions arrived at? 2) Does the arrived solution present a hindrance to "understanding"? 3) Does the attendant challenge to habitual reading patterns result in breakthrough or deadlock?

These questions have relevance to an interesting test case: Bill Bissett's special attention to the spelling of words. Bissett's idiosyncratic orthography and the resultant effects on that minutest level of reading—the single word—has already enjoyed a large influence inside Canada. Yet the writers who have gone on to orthographic modifications in their own work have been judged mere copiers of Bissett, rather than valourized as individuals adapting *to their own purposes* Bissett's singular insight: that spelling should be an individual decision and not an imposed norm. Accordingly, the work of these writers is in danger of being ignored through the effects of an attitude that sees formal innovation as a novelty and, by extension, as unrepeatable. In the background of such an attitude lurks the hulking form of *traditional literature* as a pre-established, easily subsumed and hence "safe" finite number of technical solutions.

To answer the above questions will require the deployment of each single isolated experiment in order that comparative assessments can be made among the experiments themselves. Consequently the answers to these questions lie outside the limits of this present article in the future writing/research to be done. What we will argue for here is an expanded awareness of both the effects on and the possibilities for narrative, by an active and thorough utilization of the book-as-machine.

. . .

# NOTATION AND THE ART OF READING
## Karl Young

*[This essay was commissioned for* Open Letter *by bpNichol,
and remains, in part, a tribute to his ability to bring out the best in people.]*

## INTRODUCTION

THE IDEA OF NOTATION implies, if not demands, performance. Virtually any form of writing is a kind of notation and any form of reading is a type of performance. Poetry is an intensely physical art, one that activates several senses at once. In aural societies poetry has traditionally been accompanied by facial movement, gesture, manipulation of symbolic objects, the drawing and painting of figures, the wearing of costumes, etc.—all of which, in a tribal context, are *read.* Poetry still is a physical art using multiple senses: the body as a whole equals or sometimes replaces the voice in performance art, and even silent readers turn pages, move their heads, their eyes, the roots of their tongues if not their tongues and lips, and so forth.

The kinesthetic link between sight, sound, and speech is mirrored by an inner speech, inner sight, and inner sound. Our thoughts are a combination of inner sight and inner speech. With this inner kinesthesia, we name things as we see them and form images of things about which we hear. Poetry, whether it is heard or seen, stimulates these inner sensations. An Anglo-Saxon warrior listening to a performance of *Beowulf* in the near darkness of a meadhall would not only be able to see dragons in the flickering coals of the fire, his mind would be filled with images generated by the words he heard. In like manner, an able contemporary reader reading silently will hear an inner voice, which may call up inner sight. A great deal has been written about the "image" in poetry throughout this century. When that term is used it seldom refers to anything that can be seen on the page, but rather the inner vision of the reader.

In the mainstream culture of the western world in the twentieth century, reading becomes an ever more ephemeral act, more able to hide or ignore its physical base. At the same time some contemporary poets work against this tendency, rediscovering reading methods from other cultures and discovering new ones on their own. Though for most people reading becomes more and more a system of simple data transference, poets attempt

---

Editors' Note: Related to his work as a poet, book artist, publisher, circa 1980, Young's speculations on the art of Aztec and Chinese books and writing can be read alongside later scholarship by Mignolo, Billeter, and others in the present volume.

to find alternative notations and to expand the range of their performance. In this essay I will give examples of how poetry was read in three cultural contexts far removed from ours in culture and time, and then describe some forms of notation in contemporary poetry and how they can be read.

## MEXICO, 1500

Many different types of books and documents were in use in Mexico on the eve of the Spanish conquest. Perhaps the most elaborate of these were the religious books of the Mayans, significant portions of which remain undecipherable at the present time. In cosmopolitan Tenochtitlan (Mexico City), all sorts of handbooks, bureaucratic documents, and legal papers were actively produced and used. The Aztecs also kept religious and historical books, books closely associated with poetry. They were generally produced by making long strips of animal skin or fig bark paper and rolling them into scrolls or folding them into screenfold format. They were sized with lime gesso and painted with a limited palette of bright, mineral base colors and lampblack ink. The writing system used was iconographic, based on highly stylized pictures representing ideas that could be orally formulated in different ways. This was not a system for recording specific words. There are instances of rebus notation, but the books chiefly presented concrete images rather than abstract symbols that shaped vocalization.

The way in which these books were read is largely a matter of conjecture. I have been studying this problem for a number of years, and will sketch some of my conclusions here. Scholars who consider the problem at all simply say that these books were mnemonic devices, used to remind readers of things they would not otherwise remember. This may have been the case with bureaucratic documents, such as the *Matrículo de Tributos*, but makes no sense in the case of the religious and historical books. The Aztecs were in our sense pre-literate and, like many other pre-literate peoples, they probably had excellent memories and didn't need external devices to remind them of their history or mythology. They seem to have had several orders of professional singers of myths, histories, genealogies, etc., not unlike the Yugoslavian Singers of Tales studied by Lord and Parry and the west African Singers of Genealogies brought to popular attention in North America by the TV series *Roots*.

The first, and probably most important, method of reading *was* mnemonic, *but* it approached memory from the other direction. We have a fairly large body of information, including citations by Sahagún's informants, that indicates that painted books and recitation of verse were major parts of education. As teaching tools the books were probably used to engrave myth and history, in a form that could be internally visualized in the minds of students. Their purpose, then, was not to remind readers of things they might otherwise forget, but to help make those things unforgettable. The brilliant and simple colors, the decisive black frame line, the striking clarity of icons, and the vibrant paratactic compositions—the basic qualities of indigenous style—are perfectly suited to this purpose. Students would embed innumerable myths, histories, genealogies, prayers, etc. in verse form in their minds along with the visual images in the books. The words and images need not have explained or commented on each other—each may have balanced, complemented, or extended the other, and each probably gave the student something the other couldn't. The visual and oral components of their education would then inform their dreams, their visions, their ethics, their conceptions of the world, and their actions throughout their lives. An image of the god Tezcatlipoca would not be in a book to tell students of his existence—they all were absolutely sure of his presence—but to fix a concrete image of him in their minds, one that intermeshed with his mythology, his liturgy, etc.

A number of sources tell us that books of this type were mounted, fully extended, on walls for ceremonial occasions. We can imagine readers standing in front of the mounted books, reciting the verses they'd learned in youth, as they visually reaffirmed and refurbished the images in their minds. A number of people acting in this manner would somewhat resemble contemporary performances of, say, Jackson Mac Low's *Gathas*—performers achieving a high degree of concentration on the images before them and on the sounds they uttered, and simultaneously feeling a sense of community with other participants. We shouldn't, however, push this parallel too far: a contemporary performance would not involve the same stored energy and association as did those of pre-conquest Mexico, but would include a sense of exploration not present in the older type of performance.

History books may have been used in the singing of epics. In this type of situation, a small audience would sit around a singer, who would place the book between himself and his audience, unfolding its pages as he sang. The book would act only minimally as a score for the singer—it would primarily function as a visual counterpart of the song for the audience to contemplate (and memorize) as they listened. Books could also be read privately. Private readings were not silent: the reader probably recited verses of all sorts as he read. With some of the religious books, this type of reading may have been an important part of an internal self-discipline, a form of yoga. Certainly many of the religious books could have been used in visualization exercises like those practiced by Tibetan Buddhists, and this may have been an important stage in the deity impersonation so important to Aztec religion. The central section of *Codex Borgia* may even have been used as a set of mandalas. The religious books contain lists, charts, and calendars used

Figure 1. Author's line drawing of p. 30 of *Codex Borgia*. The dead sun, containing the latent forms of its resurrection (Quetzalcoatl as morning and evening star) in the viscera of the underworld. A cycle of calendar signs and four forms of the rain god surround the sun. This image could have been used as a mandala. Actual size: 10 in. x 10.25 in.

in divination and in organizing ritual [Fig. 1]. These, of course, would be read in a different manner from the less compartmentalized books, and may have conveyed some new information. But even in these cases, when the reader may only have been looking for a date in a calendar, he probably did so in a prescribed manner, singing as he proceeded.

The screenfold format is well suited to these different types of reading. The Singer of Epics could spread out as many pages as necessary before his audience. The whole book could be mounted on a wall in ceremonial situations. When held in a reader's hands, a book of this type could be organized in different ways by folding up pages and thus creating juxtapositions of them. For instance, if a reader wanted to juxtapose page 1 and 6 of a book, he could simply fold the intervening pages together, placing 1 and 6 next to each other:

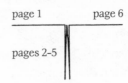

Figure 2. Author's line drawing of p. 16 (K 37) of *Codex Vienna*. The figures at right are primordial deities preparing for the emergence of the Mixtec people from the magic tree-woman of Apoala (center). The figures above and in the left column are the Mixtec patriarchs. That's a very short reading—a much longer one was possible in the book's original context. Actual size: 10.5 in. x 8.75 in.

This would be particularly useful in using ritual-calendrical books, where charts, diagrams, and calendars would be compared and correlated. In histories it could also have been useful: the indigenous Mexicans had a cyclical conception of history, and this format would allow comparison of one cycle with another.

An interesting feature of the books is that they could be given what I call a brief or an extended reading. In brief reading, the reader would simply identify the figures in the book and their functions. An extensive reading would involve a great deal more: the reader would recite portions of the verse associated with each image, though not necessarily contained in it. Let's say the page begins with a god: the reader would begin with an invocation of the deity, list his powers and attributes, narrate his relevant myths, and end with a prayer. The next figure is a man: the reader would recite his genealogy, his biography, maxims associated with him, and so forth [Fig. 2]. A brief reading of a page might take several minutes; an extended reading, several hours. The amount of time spent reading would not depend so much on the amount of information contained in the image, but how much the reader wanted to interact with it.

A Calmecac, or University, in Tenochtitlan in 1500 would probably contain a number of people reading books in a number of different ways. One reader may have hastily determined the suitability of marriage partners by the dates of their birth, as charted in an almanac. Another might have scanned the days on which the planet Venus would exert an evil influence on members of one class of society. A third may have just as quickly checked out the genealogy of an important person, giving the book a quick reading. Elsewhere in the school, a small group of students may have sat around a bard, letting the images of a hero sink into their minds as they more or less automatically committed the narrative to memory. Another group may have sat in a similar circle around a scholar who explained to them the mechanics of time, the will of the stars, the proper use of hallucinogens and other sacred plants. A third group may have discussed historical problems, using a book spread out or folded into a new page order in the middle of their circle. In a front courtyard, a merchant may have shown a priest his list of goods sold to prove his humility and pay his tithe. A student of book painting may have done sketches in sand while reciting formulas concerning the symbolic nature of straight lines and curves, perhaps as they related to mathematics. A student cloistered in a private cell, after strict fasting, ritual ingestion of psylocibin and peyote, and rigorous self-mortification may have recited a mantram over and over as he concentrated his total being on the image of a deity he would impersonate, becoming a living page of the book. A high priest may have sat in his study, contemplating the interaction of omens and an upcoming festival, whose rites he would have to organize. He may not have had any books in front of him, but have made his correlations by books he had committed to memory.

For the Aztecs, the world was full of voices, human and divine. Even plants and birds had voices, and part of the business of life was learning how to understand them. The first thing an Aztec child heard on entering the world was verse exhortation, delivered by the midwife; his life would revolve around prayers, verse formulas, and incantations; and his death would be surrounded by massive recitation. The Aztecs generally did not use books to acquire new information, but to deepen what they already knew. Books were an essential part of cult, and the interaction of spoken word and painted image had a magic function. In some of the oral poetry transcribed in the roman alphabet after the conquest, we find lines like "only as painted images in your books have we come to be alive in this place"—"perhaps his heart is a painted book"—"he [the giver of life] paints in your soul"—and "like a painted book we will fade away." In the Aztec world, books did not provide scripts for vocalization, nor could they record a fixed sequence of words or sounds. A text was not a set of symbols telling readers what to say, but a tool that allowed them to see what they heard. Books and oral poems set up complex patterns of reverberation between each other, enmeshing the reader-singer in a totality of sensual and cerebral activity impossible in a world of phonetic books.

## CHINA, 810

For millennia the Chinese have used many surfaces to write on, and they have used all the major bookforms: scrolls, screenfolds, mapfolds, several types of volumes bound along a spine. A practice reaching back nearly to the beginning of Chinese writing is the inscription or painting of poems on buildings and on the rock faces of cliffs. This latter practice united reading with the viewing of landscapes—an activity raised to a high art in China. Chinese literature is full of stories about people making long trips to read inscriptions on mountains and temples. Occasionally these inscriptions were cut very large: we have instances of several inscriptions whose characters were each more than ten feet tall. Neither giant banners with political verses written on them nor Democracy Wall in Beijing were Maoist inventions. Readers of inscriptions often made copies of them by covering the text with wet paper, working the paper into the incisions, and rubbing them with charcoal or ink. These rubbings could be rolled, folded, or bound into

Figure 3. Four pages from a screenfold book produced from stone rubbings. Actual size: 9 in. x 18.5 in.

books and it may have been this practice that gave rise to the art of printing [Fig. 3]. At some Chinese universities, official texts were inscribed on stone drums, and students acquired their textbooks by making rubbings from them. Not only was this a good way of generating copies, it produced standardized texts, an invention usually attributed to Renaissance Europe. Surfaces for writing didn't have to be flat or static: Tuan Ch'eng-shih, writing in mid-9th century, reported seeing a workman whose whole body was tattooed with poems by Po Chu-i.

Calligraphy has been essential to the art of writing poetry in China, and calligraphy, in turn, has been closely linked with painting, so that there has been a continuum between the three arts, often referred to as "The Three Perfections." Ideally, the calligraphy that a poem came in should be of as high an artistic caliber as the poem itself. The nature of written Chinese encourages this sort of artistry in a way that the roman alphabet (for all its

beauty) can not do. The large number and complexity of Chinese characters provide a wide range of design problems that challenge even the best
calligrapher's abilities, as well as allowing the widest range of potential
forms with which to express himself. This range becomes even larger in
the cursive styles of writing, in which the calligrapher abstracts, simplifies,
or elides the characters, working on intuition and a sense of the design of
the whole text. The cursive hands are difficult to read, even for adepts, and
this puts an extra emphasis on the calligrapher's art [Fig. 4]. Poems often
appear with paintings, and developments in each art influence the other.

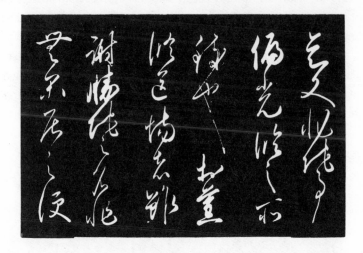

Figure 4. Six pages of a Japanese screenfold book printed from
woodblocks. Actual size: 9.5 in. x 14 in.

In some periods, landscapes, birds, etc. have been painted in calligraphic
manner; in others, pictorial possibilities of characters have been stressed.

One of the reasons for the continuity of these arts is that the basic tools
of painter and calligrapher have been the same: a hair-brush mounted in
bamboo and lampblack ink. This brush allows the artist-calligrapher a wide
range of strokes: it can handle straight lines, sharp angles, graceful curves;
thick lines can be modulated into hair-thin ones; outer hairs on the brush
can create delicate traceries around the main strokes, etc. The brush, however, does not allow the calligrapher to rest his hand in mid-stroke, which
would cause a running blot. The artist *has* to work quickly and this encourages both spontaneity and care in visualizing what he wants to do before
dipping brush in ink. The artistry of the calligrapher has shaded into the
craft of the inscriber and block-printer. By the 9th century, characters could
be painted by master calligraphers on stone or wood blocks with enough
skill and precision to accurately reproduce the graceful curves, sharp angles,
and outer hair traceries. Many rubbings and blockprints seem as spontaneous as brushwork [Figs. 3 & 4].

Another reason for the continuity of the three perfections is the nature of written Chinese. Basically there are three types of characters or character components: 1, pictograms, characters based on abstract pictures of things; 人 = man, and looks like a stick-man; sometimes these characters imitate gestures instead of static forms. 2, phonograms, symbols representing sounds without any pictorial content. 3, ideograms—these are often combinations of components in the other categories; they chart ideas but do not wholly represent them either phonetically or pictorially. Arthur Cooper has called the system etymological—perhaps the most important characteristic of this type of writing is the history behind each character. Chinese readers don't pay much attention to any of this when reading everyday documents, such as letters, popular fiction, newspaper and magazine articles—in such instances characters are just symbols for words. In writing or reading poetry, however, readers tend to be much more attuned to the interworkings of sound, sight, gesture, and idea. The interaction of components emphasizes continuity and versatility; a mind trained to read interwoven pictograms, graphs of gestures, phonograms, and ideograms can be expected to feel a continuity between sight, sound, gesture, and intellection.

The Chinese have felt that sound is an important element in poetry, as basic as the three perfections. In the 9th century, poetry was generally chanted or sung and the ideal poet was not only a good singer but also a skilled lutanist. According to the Confucian Analects, "Except in unusual circumstances, a cultured man is never without his lute." The Chinese spoken languages, which rely heavily on variations in pitch, encourage poets to create musical patterns in their poetry. This is perhaps the most difficult characteristic of Chinese poetry to bring across to western readers. I don't know of anyone who has tried to translate the music of Chinese poetry along with the lexical meaning. Many poets have tried to find correlatives for its visual forms, but its melopoeia has been thus far beyond us—perhaps it's a job for some future sound poet or composer.

Though printed books of poetry were available in the year 810, most poetry was circulated in manuscript form. A ninth century Chinese poet receiving a manuscript from a friend would first unroll or unfold it before him in an almost ritualistic fashion. He would certainly take notice of the silk or paper on which it was written, feeling its texture, hearing the sounds it made, perhaps smelling it. He would first look over the manuscript as a piece of abstract design. Then he would start reading it. It would probably be written in a cursive script, so reading would be something more like deciphering—he probably would have started figuring out the author's particular approach to cursive script when he began looking at the manuscript as abstract pattern. The design would have implied a mood or state of mind which he would now work out on the level of individual characters.

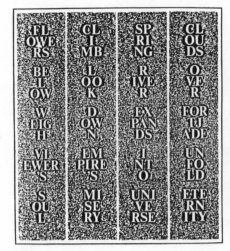
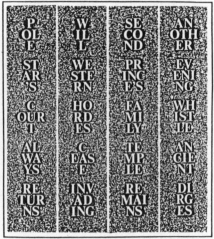

Figure 5. From *Clouds Over Fortjade* by Karl Young. Based on Tu Fu's "On Tower." In this work I have followed the 8 line, 5 characters per line *shih* form in common use during the T'ang period. I have tried to pick up as many characteristics as I could of Chinese graphic presentation. These are not translations, nor are they an attempt to get closer to the source texts. They are simply poems in which I have taken suggestions wherever they have led me. Actual size 9.5 in. x 16 in.

Having gotten his bearings, gotten the hang of the individual nature of the calligraphy, he would determine the form of the poem. Although modern editions of Chinese poetry sometimes indicate line endings by a small disk or other device, traditional Chinese poetry has not had any markings or layout conventions to indicate where lines end. A reader determines line endings by internal means involving pauses, syntax, parallelism, etc. Five and seven character lines were most common, with a caesura just before the middle and the reader would have these numbers in mind as he determined line length. Parallel or antithetical couplets were focal points in poems of the period, and the reader might isolate them first, reading them as units before he began reading the poem through from the beginning. Chinese is a language without tense or number, and with a minimum of the connective and relative components (such as pronouns, prepositions, articles, etc.) found in western languages, and Chinese poets have often accentuated the ambiguities and generalizing tendencies latent in the language. The reader would probably decide fairly quickly on solutions to these ambiguities (as he would do almost instantaneously in less artful writing) but keep other possibilities in mind as the poem as a whole took shape in his mind. Poetry of the period was full of allusions and a sensitive reader would let these reverberate through his memory, linking the poem before him with many other texts and with social situations at which they had been sung or recited. After pondering over the verses until he felt he grasped them, he might explore the poem's sound potentials beyond those of ordinary speech. The line and caesura structure would suggest a rhythm, and the tones a melody. This would give him the keys he needed to chant or sing the poem. Many poems were written to well-known tunes, and if this were the case an attentive reader would sing the poem to the appropriate tune—setting up further reverberations of allusion and memory. At this point he might get out his lute and accompany himself or grind some ink and paint a picture or write a poem in response. If the poem pleased him, he would commit it to memory.

This reading would obviously have been a slow process, but it would have allowed the reader a wide range of activity and creativity. We find in this reading a continuity between visual text and sung poem, each dependent on the other, and the two together drawing on other senses and experiences.

Like the Aztecs, the Chinese found magical powers in writing—those scrolls and wall hangings you occasionally see in Chinese restaurants in North America may have talismanic significance to the proprietors. A number of myths attribute divine and mystical origins to books and writing, and written characters retain an affinity to the hexagrams of the *I-Ching,* to which they are etymologically related. In the 9th century, Po Chu-i hoped that his profane poems would be reborn as Buddhist sutras; he hoped that he would be reincarnated as a monk, and be able to read them in their transfigured state.

## ENGLAND, 1620

In 1620, indigenous style documents were still admissible as evidence in the Spanish courts of Mexico, and some of the religious books may still have been used in secret. In China, poetry was still written and read in much the same way as it had been in the 9th century, though conventions had become more rigid and printed books were more common. In England, poetry was circulated in a number of forms: it was commonly read aloud or recited from memory at all sorts of social functions and as part of instruction and family entertainment. The theaters were still active, and at times audiences could still go to plays by Shakespeare performed by actors who had known the author. Written poetry circulated in printed books and in manuscript. Manuscripts were versatile: often they were fascicles rather like chapbooks today; they could contain a single work, a collection of poems, or a miscellany of poems by different writers, sometimes topically selected.

Printing was a different business then than it is now. In order to curb sedition and control the press, the number of printers licensed by the crown was limited, as was the number of type founders and the amount of type they could cast. Of course, there were underground presses operating in the country and type could be smuggled in from the continent, but, nonetheless, printers overworked their type, reusing it until it became completely illegible. Ink was expensive and hard to make, so it was used as sparingly as possible. Although editions with a standard of clarity at least as high as our own could be commissioned by wealthy patrons, this was by no means the norm—but that crude norm may have had some benefits. The roughness of impression gave letters a tactile quality: the printed word seemed more of an object, more a physical reality, than it does today. Print was more difficult to read then—lack of standardized spelling and a multitude of inconsistent symbols and abbreviations contributed to the difficulty, along with the worn type, the rough impression, and the light ink. Paper was heavier and the wire marks on its surface were the result of normal paper making processes, not a superfluous decoration as in most of today's laid finishes. Paper, like print, was more palpable, and a reader holding a book or turning a page probably had a greater awareness of its tactile quality than does his modern counterpart. Book bindings were sturdy, meant for active use; they might fall apart from extended wear, but were designed to be rebound. A book might stay in a family for generations, being read and reread by many of its members as well as friends to whom they might lend it. A reader buying a copy of *The Faerie Qveene* in 1620 would as likely as not be buying a used book—books were made to last and the difference between the new and used market was less distinct than it is now.

*The Faerie Qveene* had become a classic by 1620, recalling an epoch that seemed glorious, however painful it may have been to those actively involved in its political events. The reader may well have heard a good deal of the book read or recited before he bought it and may have already committed some passages to memory—he may even have used passages as maxims, things he turned over in his mind when making decisions or trying to make sense out of the world. The book he had purchased would probably not be read through and shelved (though some ostentatious buyers might keep a copy on their shelves just for show). It would be used as a script for reading to family and friends, as something to ponder over in private, or as something to commit, in part, to memory (which was still considered one of the basic arts of life). The text is admirably suited to these uses: the narrative allegory could be listened to with varying degrees of attentiveness; its regular rhythms and graceful phrases would be easy to read aloud; and the regular stanzas and rhymes would make passages relatively easy to memorize. Even its inconsistencies and obscurities—unintentional results of composition in installments—would make it something to reread many times. When reading the book in private, it would be more a script to declaim than a source of silent information, conveyed from page to brain by an easy activity of the eyes.

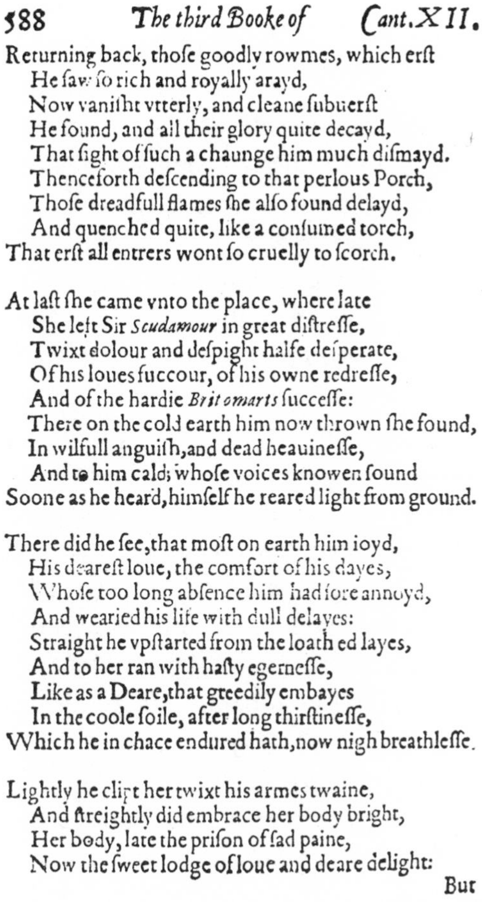

**588**     *The third Booke of*     *Cant. X II.*

Returning back, thofe goodly rowmes, which erft
  He faw fo rich and royally arayd,
  Now vanifht vtterly, and cleane fubuerft
He found, and all their glory quite decayd,
  That fight of fuch a chaunge him much difmayd.
  Thenceforth defcending to that perlous Porch,
  Thofe dreadfull flames fhe alfo found delayd,
  And quenched quite, like a confumed torch,
That erft all entrers wont fo cruelly to fcorch.

At laft fhe came vnto the place, where late
  She left Sir *Scudamour* in great diftreffe,
  Twixt dolour and defpight halfe defperate,
  Of his loues fuccour, of his owne redreffe,
  And of the hardie *Britomarts* fucceffe:
  There on the cold earth him now thrown fhe found,
  In wilfull anguifh, and dead heauineffe,
  And to him cald; whofe voices knowen found
Soone as he heard, himfelf he reared light from ground.

There did he fee, that moft on earth him ioyd,
  His deareft loue, the comfort of his dayes,
  Whofe too long abfence him had fore annoyd,
  And wearied his life with dull delayes:
  Straight he vpftarted from the loath ed layes,
  And to her ran with hafty egerneffe,
  Like as a Deare, that greedily embayes
  In the coole foile, after long thirftineffe,
Which he in chace endured hath, now nigh breathleffe.

Lightly he clift her twixt his armes twaine,
  And ftreightly did embrace her body bright,
  Her body, late the prifon of fad paine,
  Now the fweet lodge of loue and deare delight:
                                                        But

Figure 6. Page from the 1590 edition of Edmund Spenser's *The Faerie Qveene.*

Poetry that circulated in manuscript, of course, shared with printed books the current freedom from standardized orthography. Shakespeare, for instance, spelled his own name half a dozen different ways. In "The Good-Morrow," John Donne could render the word "be" three different ways (bee, beest, be) on the same sheet of paper. For Shakespeare and Donne and most of their contemporaries a written word was not confined to a single orthographic form: it could change according to the writer's intuitive sense of how it should look or sound, showing shades of emphasis, intonation, color, perhaps even pitch in his own pronunciation. Written language maintained the fluidity, even volatility, of speech: a phrase or line was something a poet created with his mouth, not an arrangement of standardized parts that could be precisely interchanged. A written poem was essentially a record of spoken verse and a score that could enable a reader to recreate it. The elaborate and inconsistent abbreviations and symbols current in script and print also underscore the oral orientation of writing. When a text is just a form of notation, "&" (a symbol that is still with us) could easily stand for "and," and "ye" could be an acceptable abbreviation for "the" (the "y" stood for "th" as in "thorn," not "y" as in "year" as some people now pronounce it in an attempt to sound old fashioned). Punctuation of this period often seems illogical to us for the same reason: we punctuate according to fixed notions of sentence construction, whereas the Jacobean poet punctuated by ear: his punctuation was a form of notation, often indicating a pause where the normal construction of a sentence would not suggest one. A number of conventions create ambiguities somewhat similar to those in Chinese verse. The use of the apostrophe in possessives had not come into standard usage, and when Donne used a word like "worlds" he may have primarily meant "world's," but wished to leave a sense of secondary meaning: multiple worlds (he was probably familiar with Giordano Bruno's notion of infinite worlds). Letters like "I" and "J" or "U" and "V" were at that time more or less interchangeable, creating further ambiguities and keeping the reader at a speed approximating serious speech.

Only four of Donne's poems were printed in his lifetime, and one of them was plagiarized rather than published under his own name. This was not because Donne couldn't find publishers for his work, but because he had several reasons for not wanting to see them in print. He only meant them for an audience of friends and didn't like the idea of having strangers see them—particularly if the poems could be used to thwart his political and ecclesiastical career. Restricting distribution allowed him a great deal of freedom to experiment with meter and syntax, use arcane reference comprehensible only to a few fellow cognoscenti, and deal with subjects he would otherwise have to keep to himself. This was not unusual at his time: other gentlemen circulated verse only in manuscript, or published their more public poems in book form while circulating more personal verses in manuscript.

Generally speaking, the manuscripts circulated by Donne and his fellows were not written in the wide-curving and ornate hands of which some 17th century penmen were capable, though they were not without flourishes and decorations. The capacity of quill pens to swing from thin to thick lines allowed a certain amount of expressive coloration in individual words, though this was minor in comparison to the expressiveness of Chinese calligraphers. Of course, manuscripts, even in fair hands, had to be read slowly. And, as important as anything else, manuscripts were personal in a way that printed books could never be. A manuscript was something fashioned by the author's (or a friend's) own hand and passed more or less directly to the reader, without the intermediary machinery of type and press, or the scrutiny of censors, publishers, typographers, proofreaders, salesmen, etc.

Donne's poetry reads as though it were meant for manuscript circulation. He assumes that the reader will be willing to spend a fair amount of time figuring out what the poems mean and how they should be vocalized. He assumes a stance of familiarity with his readers, not only sharing his private thoughts with them but also assuming that they are familiar with the arcane images, scientific experiments, philosophical arguments, and biographical details he knows.

Donne seems to assume that the manuscripts' recipients would not only read the poems aloud, but carefully rehearse them, perhaps to be recited to other friends. Lines like

She's all States, and all Princes, I,
Nothing elfe is

are difficult to recite and would have demanded a skilled speaker who had practiced a bit to bring them off right. Donne's metrics are tricky. Sometimes he creates uneven patterns simply to keep the poems from becoming too neat, too prim. Sometimes his irregularities are metrical experiments, or approximations of colloquial speech, or theatric gestures, or based on melodic patterns. Sometimes if you read what seems to be an uneven line with even stresses, the reading brings out meanings that would be muffled if normal speech rhythms were followed. A reader would have to spend considerable time sorting out these options.

The poems are, in their nature as well as their written form, often ambiguous, asking serious questions and filling in witty answers without disturbing the original puzzle. A reader would be expected to ponder them after reading them aloud and even after committing some to memory. The reader was expected to contemplate them, turn them over in his mind, apply them to the changing patterns of his life, the way he would an important letter. At the same time, the poems served as a social bond between a small group of people: something they shared but held private from the rest of the world. They could be recited in all sorts of interpersonal situations: amorous, entertaining, jocular, serious, consoling.

In 1615 Donne was ordained a minister and in 1621 became Dean of St. Paul's. After this time he tried to suppress most of his poems, apparently because they were then in fairly wide circulation and might tend to discredit his office in the church. Both the writing of lyrics and the preaching of sermons in Donne's time were closely related to theater. The texts of Donne's sermons are full of the same kind of conceits, striking images, ringing phrases, grandiose tropes, and poetic cadences as his poems. Accounts of his preaching indicate that he could use dramatic gestures, employ a wide vocal range, and even weep when it seemed like the right thing to do. He preached his last sermon dressed in his own shroud, which sounds like something out of a play by Webster. If the theater was the basis of language art in the Jacobean era, we can see a private extension of it in his lyrics and a public one in his sermons. Play, lyric, and sermon were all vocal arts that used scripts, and that's precisely what the texts of Donne's poems and sermons are.

A certain aura would have surrounded a manuscript fascicle of Donne's poems coming into a readers's hands in 1620. The reader would probably know that the author was trying to suppress them, which would make them all the more interesting. Many of the poems' initial readers had been members of an unofficial elite, and access to the manuscripts would make the new readers feel privileged to share in the glory of the small group of savants associated with Donne. The reader would certainly be aware of Donne's reputation for wit and may have heard some of the poems read or recited by other people.

He would first read through them quietly, perhaps silently. He would try to get a general sense of the poem, then concentrate on details. He would probably commit some of them to memory, and might make copies of some or all of them. Copying was a form of reading in those days: a way of becoming one with the text, of tracing its graphic form, much the way art students have copied paintings and drawings as part of their apprentice-ship. In 17th century Europe there were still monks who copied scripture as a form of prayer: they spoke the words as they wrote, touched the sacred energy of the script, and created more copies that could be used to save other souls. Transcribing also aided memorization.

The reader would rehearse oral performances of the poems. Probably, like his Chinese counterpart, he had had some musical training, and he may have tried to work out melodies for the poems, or fit them to existing tunes, perhaps accompanying himself on a lute. A poem like

> Goe, and catch a falling ſtarre,
>     Gett with child a Mandrake Roote,
> Tell me, where all paſt times are,
>     Or who cleft the Divells foote,
> Teache me to hear Mermaydes ſinginge,
> Or to keepe off Envyes ſtinginge,
>     And finde
>     What winde
> Serves to'advance an honeſt minde.

almost demands such treatment. We have one anonymous 17th century setting for it [Egerton Ms. 2013, f. 586; see Shawcross's *The Complete Poetry of John Donne,* p. 91] and certainly other readers composed settings for it. The reader might sing the poem to family or friends and it would become an integral part of social life.

A more difficult poem would require prolonged intellectual effort. Here is the last stanza of "To Chriſt":

> I have a ſinn of feare yt when I have ſpunn
>   My laſt thread, I ſhall periſh on the ſhore;
> Sweare by thy ſelf that at my Death, thy Sunn
>   Shall ſhine as it ſhines nowe, & heretofore;
>     And having that, thou haſt done,
>       I have noe more.

The spiritual and intellectual dimensions of this poem are immense— I will only point out one approach to it that is dependent on writing in the 17th century. "Sunn" is both a person of the trinity and the illuminating sphere in the sky, about which Donne and his fellows speculated endlessly. "Done" is a pun on the author's own name, and "more" is a pun on the maiden name of his wife, who was dead when this poem was written, if our current dating is correct. We tend to scorn puns because our language is not as fluid or as magical as it was in the 17th century. For Donne, however, the links between Christ and the sun, himself and his death, his wife and the joy of living were not crossword puzzle games, but the threads that shaped his life. No one bound by static orthography or a frozen conception of language could have written this poem. Its author might have understood more easily than we do the puns blood = water and flower = heart in the Aztec books, or the origin of writing in the union of light from a star with the footprints of birds in Chinese mythology.

## NORTH AMERICA, 1983

For most people living in late 20th century North America, reading is a dreary task. Its main objective (even in fiction) has become the acquisition of data. Standardized orthography and usage have taken the fluidity and magic out of the language and encouraged silent reading. Reading is now something most people want to get out of the way as quickly as possible and speed-reading is perceived as the ideal way to read. Since speedreading alters the order of words, makes some words disappear or pass in a blur, negates the timing of poetry, suppresses the sensations of inner and outer ear as well as the throat, tongue, and mouth, it deadens the physical bases of language and is completely incompatible with poetry. It is like ingesting a nutrient that you don't have to eat—smelling, chewing, tasting, digesting are time consuming activities. Even people who don't know how to speedread approach reading as if they did, wanting to get it over with as soon as possible and trying to avoid its physical qualities as much as they can. People no longer memorize verse and recite it to each other or use it to give depth or breadth to their discourse. The closest most people come to this sort of social interaction is the discussion of popular novels, often as they relate to movies or TV programs. The schism can be so great as to cause some savants to speak of "the physical text" as though a text could be anything but physical.

People interested in contemporary poetry approach reading differently. Contemporary poetry uses many of the forms of reading described in the three historical examples (usually without awareness of precedents) and has invented more. Unfortunately, people who are not familiar with contemporary poetic practice find contemporary work incomprehensible because, due to their notions of reading, they don't know *how* to read it. If their ephemeralized reading habits are too deeply ingrained, explaining alternative reading methods will probably not help them—teaching them a difficult new language, say Arabic or Hopi, might be easier. At this point it's impossible to say how much this will change in the future. Perhaps the self-destructive nature of ephemeralized reading and developments in technology will make reading for information's sake obsolete, and will return the act of reading to a form of art.

Visual poets, sound poets, and other experimentalists have developed wide ranges of notational devices. Poets work these techniques largely by intuition or personal system and they do not seem to be tending toward any sort of standardization. One poet may mean one thing by a certain notation, another poet may use the same notation for a completely different purpose. Readers must try out several possibilities when reading a new work, actively participating in the realization of the poem, considering the text from several different angles, turning it over in their minds, testing it in vocalization, and becoming more familiar with it in the process. Ultimately readers will have to hear the poet read before they can come to a complete understanding of the notation employed.

After reading sketches of some of my visual poetry, Charles Stein and George Quasha asked me how I performed it and I read them a couple of pages. They then did a two voice rendition of the same pages as they thought they should be performed. Their reading bore little resemblance to mine. Quasha and Stein are knowledgeable readers and extraordinary performers and in some ways their reading was better than mine. The important thing, though, is that all three of us ended up with a fuller appreciation of the work after we had been exposed to the two different readings. Even misreadings can expand the reader's sense of the poem, once the poet's intentions are understood.

During the sixties, concrete poetry had a tendency to be pictorial, trivially self-referential, and static. Works like the tiny masterpieces of Emmett Williams tended to get lost in a juggernaut of poems made up of the word "pine" typed over and over in the shape of a Christmas tree. The tendency of visual poetry now, however, is away from pictorial and mimetic repre-

sentations in favor of gesture, motor stimulus, gestalt, and abstract archetype. Visual poetry, whether complex or minimalist, and despite tendencies
to fall back on the concrete, has become deeper, more capable of reaching
more levels of thought, perception, and action, and, at the same time, more
oriented toward performance, public or private. This can lead to multime-
dia performance, incorporating other arts, sometimes interacting with
work produced by a number of people in a cooperative or collective effort.

Projective verse and visual poetry shade almost imperceptibly into performance art and sound poetry. The emphasis shifts from visual texts that
can be performed to scores that exist primarily to shape vocalization but can
also be read as images. A good example of a score that could find its way into
an anthology of visual poetry is Jackson Mac Low's "Vocabulary Gatha for
Pete Rose" [Figs. 7 & 8]. Readers seeing this piece in print can read it casually,
as a piece of graphic art. After reading the performance instructions, they
can do their own performances—either single voice or with friends. They will
probably appreciate the piece more if they have attended performances
done under Mac Low's supervision, and most if they have participated in
such performances themselves. If they have done this, they may be able to
hear performances with their inner ears. Experienced performers can experience this in much the same way as musicians can hear music with their
inner ear while reading musical scores. Though the reader may find the
score visually interesting, that interest pales in comparison to the satisfaction of taking part in a performance of the work—a satisfaction that can be
carried over, to some extent, into silent readings of other Mac Low scores.

A score of this sort must be relatively easy to follow and use. It is not
necessarily meant to be performed by highly skilled or professional performance artists but by sympathetic and knowledgeable members of the audience. The distinction between artist and audience blurs in this sort of performance. Other scores may be more cryptic. A score like the page from
"16 Part Suite" by the Four Horsemen [Fig. 9] is a good example of this type
of notation. It was developed for the use of a single performance group. The
Horsemen [Rafael Barreto-Rivera, Paul Dutton, Steve McCaffery, bpNichol]
weren't thinking about how it might be read by other people at the time
of composition, they were simply using the form of optophonetic scoring
developed by Raoul Hausmann as a working method. I doubt that anyone
else using it would end up with a performance anything at all like that of the
group that originally developed it. Nonetheless, it can be read as a work of
graphic art as long as the reader understands that it was composed for a different purpose. Other performances that it might inspire could be just as
meaningful as the Horsemen's and the Horsemen themselves might have
been able to further develop their own performance from such a reading.
Readers already familiar with live performances of this piece might find

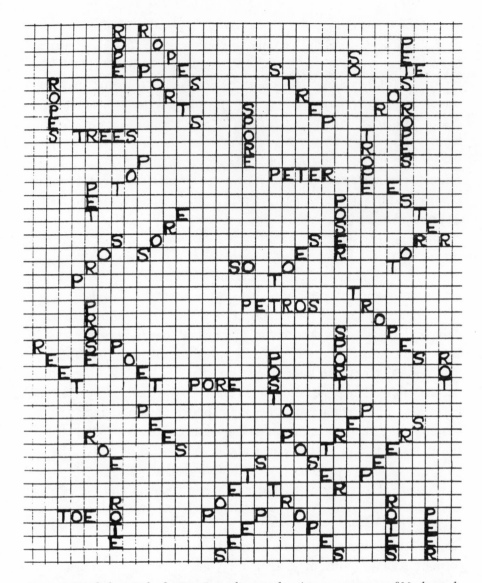

Figure 7. "Vocabulary Gatha for Pete Rose, the recorder virtuoso composer of Maplewood, N.J. who plays only contemporary Music," by Jackson Mac Low. Copyright 1978 and 1983 by Jackson Mac Low. All rights reserved. Actual size: 8.5 in. x 11 in.

their understanding of it deepened by seeing the score, somewhat as the original readers of the Aztec books found their oral poetry enhanced by visual images.

The amount of lexical material in a score, the number of words and letters, need not be great: many scores are for minimalist interpretation, somewhat like the music of Philip Glass or Steve Reich, and some scores have no words or other forms of traditional notation at all. Some Horsemen scores fall into this category, but probably the supreme master of what most readers would consider nonlexical scoring is Bob Cobbing. It seems that Cobbing can use virtually anything as a score, though the scores he has published

Performance Instructions for **A** <u>Vocabulary</u> <u>Gatha</u> <u>for</u> <u>Pete</u> <u>Rose</u>

The Gatha may be performer by a single performer or by a group of any size. Each performer starts at any square & moves from there to any adjacent one, horizontally, vertically, or diagonally, & thence to other squares. Each letter or group of letters (joined in any direction(s)) may be spoken, sung, or played on a musical instrument. All three ways of realizing the Gatha shd occur in a performance.

Vocal possibilities include the speaking or singing of the letters' individual sounds (as they are pronounced in any language known to the performer), the letters' English names (e.g., "oh" or "tee"), any syllables formed by letters adjacent in any direction(s), & whole words. Any of these elements may be repeated ad lib. The name "Pete Rose" may be spoken or sung at any time, & the performer may then jump to a square not adjacent to the last one realized. In singing, the performer may either sing pitches assigned to letters for instrumental realization (see below) or freely choose pitches in accord with the performance situation.

When playing an instrument, the performer moves from square to square as above, but realizes each letter as an instrumental tone, choosing the octave in which each tone is placed. The letters occurring in the Gatha are realized as follows:

P is played as B or B flat/A sharp.
E "    "    " E " E flat/D sharp.
T "    "    " D " D flat/C sharp.
R "    "    " A " A flat/G sharp.
O "    "    " G " G flat/F sharp.
S "    "    " C " F.

The performer chooses between alternative pitches for each letter, or trills or wavers between them, & connects tones consecutively or simultaneously as their letters lie adjacent in any direction(s). Letter tones may be repeated. adjacent ones trilled, & any group may be repeated or reversed. Tones may be connected by <u>glissandi</u> as well as being played discretely. Empty squares are rendered as silences of any duration chosen by the performer.

Each performer must listen intently to all sounds audible, including those produced by other performers (if any), by the audience, or by elements in the environment. Performers must relate with these sounds in producing their own, exercising sensitivity, tact, & courtesy, so that every performance detail contributes to a total sound sequence they wd choose to hear. Virtuosity is strongly encouraged but must be exercised with consciousness of its place in the total aural situation. Performers must be both inventive & sensitive at all times. **"Listen"** & **"Relate"** are the most important "rules."

All parameters not specified above, including octave placement, simultaneous &/or successive grouping, repetition, duration, rhythm, loudness, tempo, timbre, attack, &c., are at the discretion of the performer & are to be chosen spontaneously during a performance.

A performance may be ended at any time within the limits set by the performance situation. A total duration may be set beforehand or arrived at spontaneously. A group may appoint a leader to signal the beginning, keep track of elapsed time with a watch, & signal the end of the performance.

Figure 8. Performance instructions for Mac Low's "Vocabulary Gatha for Pete Rose."

are visually impressive, the product of careful effort, capable of standing alone as works of graphic art. This gets a bit complex in that Cobbing insists that he *reads* all these works as texts, not scores. Through this insistance, Cobbing demonstrates how profound is his visual literacy, just as his vocalization shows his great virtuosity as a performer.

Poetry evolved from song and still has close ties to the parent art. Poets often write with melodies in mind, and some poems still get set to music. Many poets base their work on larger musical structures; some, like Theodore Enslin, have had rigorous training in music and their knowledge of musical form shapes their work on all levels. In the case of sound poets, it's often a matter of semantic quibbling whether you call the work music, song,

Figure 9. Page 1 of "16 Part Suite" by The Four Horsemen, from *The Prose Tattoo*, Membrane Press, Milwaukee, 1983. Actual size: 8 in. x 10 in.

or poem. In Mac Low's "Vocabulary Gatha for Pete Rose," the same notation can be used for speaking voice, singing voice, or musical instrument, and other poets have written pieces to be performed in conjunction with music. Like music, poetry is essentially an art of time. The sense of timing a poem creates is its rhythm and that rhythm is one of its most expressive characteristics. "To read Donne you must measure Time, and discover the Time of each word by the sense of Passion," wrote Coleridge—he could have said the same thing about his own poetry, or that of Arthur Sze or The Four Horsemen or Rosmarie Waldrop or Toby Olson or Louis Zukofsky or Daphne Marlatt or Clark Coolidge or the original singer of *Beowulf*. The sense of timing in a poem can vary from the timing of discrete units, such as the clues in Anglo-Saxon riddles or the accretions of examples in Pound's *Cantos,* to the sense of time implied by spatial deployment in visual poetry, to the sense of time implied by regular meters. You can find songs meant to be delivered more rapidly than normal speech (Carmen Miranda comes to mind) but these are usually comic, and the general tendency of song has been to progress less rapidly than ordinary speech. Sound itself is a function of time: you hear different pitches by different rates of vibration. If you play a 33⅓ r.p.m. record at 78 r.p.m., you will not be able to hear the music on the record. Not only will the notes come too short and too fast and the rhythm be altered, the increased speed will have changed the pitch of the notes. Many forms of notation in contemporary poetry tend to slow reading down, to encourage the reader to dwell on small units of language, or at least to perceive the words in real (i.e., spoken) time.

The sort of song that poetry evolved from was dependent on an audience. Though some critics have claimed that contemporary poetry has no audience, this is patently false. The audience may be small, but this may also be one of its strengths. Donne actually wanted a small audience. Serious contemporary poets can get to know one another relatively easily, and at the numerous readings, festivals, etc. that have occurred during the last two decades, poets have been able to make contact with many people interested in their work, and to talk to them on a personal level. Readers depend on these performances in order to understand the notation used by poets. In many cases, such as performances of Jackson Mac Low's *Gathas,* there isn't a clear distinction between author and audience: the author is the central figure; a number of people who would ordinarily sit passively listening join in as performers; and they, in turn, take cues from the rest of the people in the room. Some poets have developed performances that include the audience, leaving no room for passive spectators—Pauline Oliveros has done a great deal in this area.

At present, poetry is largely a participatory rather than a spectator art. A large percentage of the audience for poetry is made up of writers, performers, and other artists. Readers often read not simply to be moved or entertained or instructed or morally uplifted; they read to improve their own art. This encourages them to read more closely, more critically, more intensely than they might otherwise do.

A large portion of the audience for contemporary poetry gets involved in publishing the work of other poets at some time in their lives, and this becomes a further means of participation. They may only act as a magazine's assistant editor for a short time, or they may edit their own magazines, or run their own presses. For some, this becomes a way of life. Poet-publishers tend to read manuscripts carefully and critically in determining whether or not to publish them, and they put a great deal of effort into the means of producing those they decide to publish. This type of activity tightens the bonds between poets, opens channels of communication with a larger audience, gives the editors a sense of proportion in terms of nature, size, and scope of their audience, and, again, can encourage the intimacy with the text latent in copying. Publishing requires commitment and encourages the poet-publisher to be textual analyst, literary critic, and graphic designer. Working with layout, type, perhaps presswork and binding, has suggested new kinds of notation and presentation and has inspired work that would otherwise not have been done. The method of production a poet-publisher uses often effects or reflects her or his work: offset publishers often write differently from letterpress printers. The mimeo format of d. a. levy publications continues to be an integral part of the outlaw urgency of the work, even though levy's been dead for many years. The austere design and impeccable typography of Elizabeth Press Books underscores the restrained precision of the poets published in that series. The limited press runs and personalized distribution of most poetry publishers creates a sense of intimacy and fellowship not unlike that created by the circulation of manuscripts in Donne's time.

Book art may negate notation on the level of individual words and replace it with notation by size or shape of page, materials used, form or content of book as whole entity. The reading of such a book may depend heavily on gesture, and the book may in turn be incorporated into performances including other forms of notation [Fig. 10]. The book art movement seems to have originated in the small scale cottage industry environment of alternative presses and luxurious artists' studios and can draw from all current types of poetry.

At present there are at least twenty major schools of poetry functioning in North America, each with dozens of subgenres. No group dominates, so, as long as this holds, poets can enjoy more freedom than they ever have in the past. Members of some schools can be dogmatic and exclusionist, and members of one clique can become extremely bellicose toward another coterie, but few, if any, can limit their interests to members of their own group. Hence poets belonging to one clan can be influenced by members of another—in fact, some poets switch allegiances at times, and many function in several schools at once. The cross-fertilization among these groups produces all sorts of hybrids, sometimes showing a great deal of what biologists call hybrid vigor. We should note that what poets work against is often as important as what they work with, and even bitter antagonisms can lead to positive action. As well as producing hybrid vigor, interaction among schools seems always to exert an influence on notation, keeping it from becoming rigid or consistent, and opening up new possibilities.

Contemporary readers read in a number of different ways for a number of different purposes. Sometimes the text dictates their manner of reading, sometimes their needs recast the text. A sequence of reading might be: 1, casual examination of the text—in the case of visual or sound poetry this might involve scanning the page for a point of entry, a place to begin;

Figure 10. Performance book for Pauline Oliveros by Karl Young. The pages are wooden two by fours covered with felt and material from a well worn workshirt. The pages can be clapped together to produce sounds. This book could be used in any performance in which such sounds would be called for. Photograph by Michael Sears.

2, closer examination of the text, including tentative determination of how its notation works; 3, careful reading of the text once a method of reading has been established; 4, hearing the poet read, live or on tape or record; 5, reconsidering the text in light of the poet's reading. All of these except 4 would probably include at least some vocalization on the part of the reader. Going beyond this, the reader could branch off in several directions: A, making use of something learned from the text; B, rejecting the text in whole or in part; C, getting people together for a performance of the work, soliciting work from the author for a magazine or anthology, or setting up a reading for the author; D, establishment of personal relations with the author, which could lead to interaction on a number of levels. Of course, there are other sequences readers could follow: the reader could begin by hearing the poet read or attending a performance of her or his work and then turning to the text; the reader could find something lacking in her or his own work and cast about for a solution, coming upon the text in the process, and so on.

However a poem is read, readers can employ all their faculties in reading, and the possibilities of interaction with the poem are virtually endless. At the same time, notation is not a static body of convention, but a nexus between large areas of contemporary practice.

## from "THE POEM AS ICON —
## REFLECTIONS ON PRINTING AS A FINE ART"
### William Everson

*[An Informal Discourse given on April 16, 1976,
for National Book Week at the University of California, Santa Barbara]*

I'D LIKE TO BEGIN by talking a little about the book itself as a central archetype of our culture and history, because whatever you do with a book, you're working with it also as a symbol. It is the implication and consequences that inhere in the book as a symbol that make both the incentive and also the terrible warp in your judgment as you approach it. There are very few perfect books. Very few perfect books have ever been written, and very few that are perfect have ever been printed. One reason for that is the pressure that inheres in the book as a symbol; it is so great that the individual consciousness when it approaches it cannot embrace the book in its totality. The idea of the book, the concept of the book and what we call the archetype of the book is so powerful that it has a way of reaching out and grabbing you and taking you into a dimension of itself. The distortion in yourself as you approach it, chiefly through your lack of experience with it, is bound to have its registration upon the book itself, upon your production of it, upon your poems as you write them, upon your critical values as you place them within the context of a book, and upon your printing as you try to conceive and execute the perfect format.

The archetype of the book works two ways: it is both conservative in the sense that it carries the sum of the past within it, but it also carries implications for the future, because that is the way ideas are transmuted and possessed. It is this double range that is the awesome thing about it. I mean, the invincible thing about the book is its capacity to reach backwards and forwards; in a sense it's out of your hands—before you get it, and after you are finished with it. Whatever you do to it, it will remain spoiled in some way by your own contribution to it. Some small part of what you put into it might survive in an effective way, but the book generally goes on, following the momentum of its own history.

You approach a book rather blindly at the beginning, because books are both masculine and feminine. In the way they strike they are male, they have that power, but they also have a feminine allure, which is much more glamorous and much more seductive. The two sides of the archetype, the power and the allure, the active and the passive, are all there working within the symbol itself, so that both as a writer and as a printer you find yourself over your head when you enter that domain. It takes a long time to be acclimatized. You have to write many books before you gain any sense of equipoise at all. I'm sure Kenneth* would agree that the book itself remains in the end a mystery, no matter how many you write, and you will shift in your own relation to it between the power and the allure, between the masculine and the feminine aspects of it.

Books are the most dynamic things in history. Nations have gone to war over them. Civilizations have been decimated to extirpate a single text. And yet always something escapes and goes forward, something elusive that is indigenous to the book, that vanishes, and surfaces again after the storms have passed, like the Dead Sea Scrolls. Once you've touched them you can never escape because, and especially since the invention of printing, because printing is really the reproduction of a given text. Basically that is what it is. The writer writes it, a scribe can transcribe it, and that is all that needs to be done. The author's work is finished at that point. From the point of view of the printer, that is just the beginning. Part of the terror of it, too, is that whatever you write and have published you can never escape; it follows you wherever you live. That is also the problem of the printer: every book that he has spoiled by putting his hand to it will also hound him down through the ages. You chance to go into a bookshop or into a library and see one of your books on the shelf, and it is almost shocking. There is a confrontation with it, thus. Sometimes the allure triumphs and you are seduced anew, and made proud. But sometimes the allure is too great, and instead of perfection you find you erred through excess, and botched it all.

Printing is a strange and bastard art. It derives from calligraphy, but calligraphy has far more allure. It is much more beautiful. Once in the Library of Congress I saw the manuscript that they think Gutenberg used as the model for his Bible. It is infinitely superior to the Gutenberg Bible in sheer beauty, and yet the Gutenberg is probably the noblest piece of printing. I know of no other art in which the central archetype was the first work ever done, something that no one has ever been able to equal. In this detail or that a lot of books have been able to equal it, but as an archetype it stands there at the fountainhead of the craft, and everything breaks back from it. Everything is measured against it. One of the great things about an inception point in any field, reflection or endeavor, is that once you get to the fountainhead, it has a way of defining everything that follows. The great thing about any kind of book, especially the book of a master, is that no matter how much his ideas might disperse through society, you can always go back to that fountainhead for a reinvigoration and a reclarification of what

*Kenneth Rexroth, who had previously introduced him. (Eds.)

that whole process meant. This is part of the tremendous pressure of books. By that I mean the latent consequence, the sense of awe in that nuclear entity, that sense a book has of a full potentiality that makes it so risky and dangerous and beautiful.

The printer approaches a book in a much more conscious way than a poet does. The poet's real rapport is between himself and a piece of paper. He does not think in terms of the printed book. When he creates, it is that confrontation with the blank page, and out of his inner being the whole insight and passion pours; he registers it as fast as he can, and to him really his work is done at that time. If he is successful there, the book is successful. If he fails there, the book fails. I mean, it is down his arm to the pen. That is where the flow is, and that is where his control really culminates. The apotheosis of his skills is realized at that point, not later on.

But then the printer comes into the picture. And if printing is a bastard art, then fine printing is even more so, because its whole purpose is to bring an aesthetic dimension to a reproductive process. Printing is essentially a craft of utility. "Utile" is the category, but this need to wrest that utile up into the nonutile is maddening. For the great thing about the aesthetic is that it stands apart from the world of utility and exists for its own sake. A thing of beauty simply exists for its own self. Men can utilize it, but that is not its nature. That's not why we cherish it or value it. We cherish it and value it precisely because it has no utility value. Well, to take a basically utile object like a book and give it a non-utilitarian dimension is the supreme effort of the fine printer.

And it is doomed to failure, because there is always an equivocation about it. It is like architecture in this regard. There's a utile function in architecture that is also basic. To transform a house into an aesthetic object is the same problem that the fine printer has to face in the attempt to make a beautiful book out of a utile object. That's why I entitled this meditation "The Poem as Icon," the poem as image, a poem for the eye rather than a poem for the ear. Yes, the poem is basically for the ear. Everything in the poem happens between the tongue and ear. The visual dimension is the least part of it. Modern poetics is split up and divided by a weird kind of typography called Projective Verse. It can be maintained that Charles Olson behind his typewriter ruined the craft of poetry in the twentieth century. (What am I saying? That's heresy!) Charles saw that the typewriter let the poet be his own typographer, and felt that was a great thing, the great liberator. But like every innovation which doesn't have a discipline behind it, it meant chaos. Everything goes the way of the eye and the contact with the ear is lost. But, poetry begins with the ear, the tongue and the ear. The eye is for the printer.

———

My introduction to the craft began early. My father was a printer. I was virtually born in a print shop. But I left printing because of my problems with my father—the son has to break away from his father in order to find himself. So, I got out of that shop as fast as I could, and it wasn't until I became a poet that I began to think of my lost opportunities. One point of view, you know, poets and printers, their lines cross. There's a kind of ineluctable law that they seek each other out. The poet needs a printer, and the printer needs a text. The poem really is the absolute typographical problem, because the poem is the highest form of literature, and the finest instincts of a printer are always going to be exercised and lavished upon the production of poetry. From the fine printer's point of view prose is relatively easy to print. You can lay out the basic format of a book of prose on the drawing board, send it to the printer, and he can follow the plan, but you really can't print a book of fine poetry that way at all. Each page has to have its own attention, because each page has a different configuration. From a fine printing point of view there's something massive and blockish about a page of prose which resists aesthetic treatment. You can work with the chapter heads and the section breaks, between the title-page and colophon. That's about all you have to do. Once you make your initial choice of types and paper and formal layout—whether it's going to be a trade edition of a small octavo or a monumental folio—you have the basics, and can proceed to the production. Poetry can't be done that way, which is why the poem is always the supreme challenge to the fine printer. And the greater the poetry the deeper the challenge drives into his nature.

• • •

# THE BOOK AS PHYSICAL OBJECT
## Keith A. Smith

### TYPES OF BOOKS

I pick up a book. I am holding a bound manuscript. It might be a western codex, an oriental fold book, a fan, or a Venetian blind.

Keith Smith, Book 27, 1973: a western codex. 29 x 29 x 1 cm.

Keith Smith, *Snow Job,* Book 115, 1986: an oriental fold book, edition of 300. Poem of a spring thaw is really speaking about a nuclear meltdown. 16 x 11.5 x 2 cm.

These are the type of books used by various cultures. All are a set of sheets (paper, wood, ivory, cloth, etc.) strung or bound together. The type of book is determined by how it is bound: at one or two points, along one or more edges.

Joan Lyons, *Untitled,* 1975: a fan. 17.5 x 20.5 x 1 cm.

Joan Lyons, *Untitled,* 1975: a blind (or Venetian blind). 17.5 x 20.5 x 1 cm.

## GETTING ACQUAINTED WITH THE BOOK

The best approach to gain a sense of the book is to become acquainted with the book as physical object. Pick up a book, hold it. Feel it. Look at it, then examine it, not routinely or mechanically by habit but make a conscious effort to see at every step in the process, every movement of the eyes or hands.

I often pick up a book and go through this process. I use a blank book so that I am not seduced by this picture or distracted by that composition or those words. I make note of my findings—the elaborate meanderings of my imagination and specific written lists of what to investigate on a physical level in books-as-sketches. I have learned not to take anything for granted. The procedure I am describing can't be learned by reading. It must be experienced. And so I examine a book.

Does a book have to be bound? If it weren't, it would be a portfolio or a stack. Is a stack an unbound book?

Kevin Osborn, *Vector Rev,* 1987. With polished metal covers and inlaid marbles, this fan is offset in an edition of 25. A ribbon is strung through the book. 48 x 5 x 4.5 cm.

Anonymous, untitled nineteenth century fan from Bali. Covers are incised wood, the pages are palm leaves. 25 x 3 cm.

The oriental fold book is created by folding a long sheet of paper alternately back and forth on itself. There is no sewing or gluing. The binding is mechanical. If an imaged book of this type were not folded, it would be a mural, not a book. However, if that mural is stored by rolling, it is a scroll. Is a scroll a book?

If I set out to make a photograph that is a foot tall and 10 feet long, the result is a single picture. If I roll it up to store it, is it then a scroll, or does it have to be conceived as a scroll? Does convenient storage constitute any book?

Someone takes a large sheet of blank paper, wads it up, then throws it in a kitchen trash compactor. It is then compressed flat. The paper has been "folded" by a machine. Is it then an oriental fold book, or is it trash?

It depends upon intention. If that person declares it a book, it *is* a book! If they do not, it is not. Definitions are not ageless laws, but current understanding. They grow with usage through insight and error. We extend our knowledge, as well as our false assumptions, and both of these change the way we see, the way we think. Our definitions evolve; they are not cut in stone, like the rigidity of religion.

The theologian, politician or athlete can justly ask, "How can you play fairly when you change the rules in the middle of the game?" But in science and art one must play by the rules *as* they currently stand. Rules are constantly changing. When a new theory is proven in science, all laws previously assumed which conflict with the latest belief must be thrown out. Laws must be re-written to conform with the new theory. A map of the flat earth is useless once our planet is perceived as a globe.

If a book is bound, what are the possibilities?

Must a book be bound completely across one edge? Bound at one point, it is a fan; bound at two, a blind.

Not necessarily. A fan can have a compound binding. With one sheet in common, a fan can be bound at each end. Two volumes can be separate, obliquely related, or pairs of pages can complete across tangential pages:

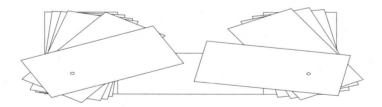

Must a codex be bound on only one side?

If a codex is bound back to back, it is a dos-à-dos; if it is bound on two opposing sides in the French Doors format, it might have sheets interwoven or tangent, allowing permutations in viewing order and contextual reference. Or, two separate, and separately bound books can be conceived to be displayed tangentially to allow reciprocation.

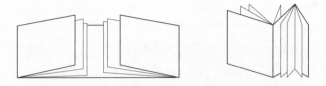

Two codices bound as French Doors format, and as a dos-à-dos.

If a codex is bound on all four sides, how does the binding determine the imagery?

Scott McCarney, *Untitled,* 1983. Fold book bound on four sides. When this book is "closed" (pleats compressed) the printed image dominates. When the book is extended, the image breaks up as the form, space and shadows become prevalent. 32 x 32 x 2 cm.

If I'm binding a fan, a Venetian blind or a codex, how many sheets must be bound before it is considered a book? Two? Three? If I fold a sheet of paper once, is the resulting folio an oriental fold book?

If I fold a sheet twice, is it a dos-à-dos?

If a broadside is folded into quarters and then eighths, is it then a book instead of a poster?

I ask questions to broaden my knowledge of traditional concepts, not to hold them as dogma, but as a foundation from which I can depart. Definitions are not an end, but a springboard. Otherwise, they stifle the expansion of ideas. Without questioning, I would tend to repeat the same solutions, relying on simulated vision and residual concepts.

Keith Smith, Book 141, 1989. This fold book does not open to a straight line, but folds across a row, then down, then reverses back across and down in a snake fashion. The format was devised by Scott McCarney, who originally called it *bostrophedon* (as the ox plows). Now he refers to it as the *Snake Format*.

19 x 19 x 5 cm. Opens to 96 cm. square.

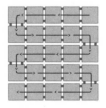

The French Door format is an unusual manner of relating two books, but the dos-à-dos is traditional. Two codices are bound with a back cover in common. One volume is read, turned over to the front cover of the other. Two related volumes, such as the *Iliad* and the *Odyssey* are appropriately bound in this manner.

The book is a physical object. The hand-held book demands touching. Effort must be taken to view it. A print on the wall under glass has no volume, no shadows, little or no texture. It is not tangible. It is almost non-physical. To the extent it can be seen, it is physical, but it is closer to a conceptual idea, a vision. Whereas a book is three dimensional. It has volume (space), it is a volume (object), and some books emit volume (sound).

And so I think of volume, of sound and pictures in space. I think of implied sound in pictures. One of my favorite painters is Giorgio de Chirico. Many times I have sat in the Art Institute of Chicago and contemplated the potential sounds depicted in his 1914 painting *The Philosopher's Conquest*. A steam locomotive rushes along. On a tower to the left are flags flapping in the breeze. A puff of wind is in the sails of a ship on the horizon. Quieter, a large clock is ever at 1:28 in the afternoon. I hear tick-tock, tick tock as my eyes lower to the protruding shadow of two figures. I imagine an even softer sound of muffled conversation. In the foreground is an object emitting no sound at present, but it has the potential of the loudest sound of all. It is a cannon.

Keith Smith, a dos-à-dos binding, 1992, of *Structure of the Visual Book* and *Text in the Book Format*.

Volume... There is the space within a picture, but this text will deal with the structured space *between* pictures and pages. The hand-held book does not have the disadvantage of wall display, which can be seen from too close, or too far away. The book is "foolproof" to a certain degree. Since it is bound, the order of viewing is maintained. The distance of viewing is set between about fourteen inches and perhaps twenty five inches, because the physical length of the viewer's arm controls the distance.

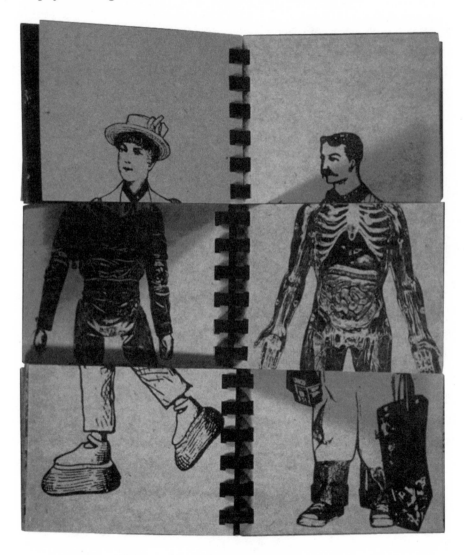

Marion Faller, *A Resurrection of the Exquisite Corpse,* Visual Studies Workshop Press, 1978. Slit pages allow for permutations of figures. 27 x 12 x 1.5 cm.

The book, as object, is intimate, it insists on a one-to-one confrontation: the bookmaker and viewer.

Yet, if it is mass-produced, the book can reach a greater audience than an exhibit. It is not relegated to a one month spread of time or a single event. A book can be seen anywhere, at any time, in any situation, and can be returned to time and again. A mass produced book with its far reaching capabilities still remains a one to one experience.

The book-as-object is compact. Covers allow for no mats, and pictures can be printed to the edge, and on both sides of fairly thin paper. To paraphrase Gary Frost, of *Booklab,* the picture field represented by the 1992 Manhattan telephone directory white pages is a picture 10 by 155 feet.

Much can be perceived about its potential by just holding a book and thinking. Now, open it. The blank pages at the beginning of a codex are called endsheets. Bookmakers are fascinated with paper; endsheets allow them to use special papers that are too expensive or not appropriate for the text block.

Turning the endsheets serves a function: to clear the mind before reading. The function of the endsheets parallels that of a mat on a single print. I spend time thinking about the physical act of turning the page. Understanding what transpires as a result of turning the page will lead to concepts of how to image the book.

Binding should not be an afterthought, or no thought. If I structure a book as a loop, because it contains cyclical ideas, the fan is an appropriate type of book because it opens with circular movement, to a circular form.

A Venetian blind would be inappropriate, not capable of reinforcing the cyclical motif. The western codex can be used, but it is not visually cyclical, as in the case of the fan. The codex literally can be cyclical in format, using spiral binding and a specific display.

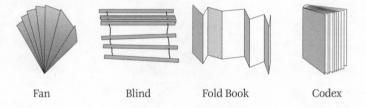

Fan            Blind        Fold Book         Codex

The non-spiral bound, linear codex can be an implied cycle by order of presentation of the pictures:

- The first picture can be removed and placed after the "final" picture.
- Repetition of the first page at the end, as the final page.

The oriental fold book would not lend itself easily to a cyclical motif if viewed fully extended—not only the type of book, but display is critical.

*Fold book as an implied cycle:* If the fold book is viewed page by page in the manner of a codex, it is cyclical, as the (non-spiral bound) codex. (It could be an implied cycle in the manner of a codex).

*Fold book as literally a cycle:* The fold book physically can be a cycle. Usually the fold book is not imaged on the back; it is a one-sided book. To make this book literally cyclical, I would continue on the back side, reading the other side of the folded paper, in codex fashion, until I returned to the front and the beginning.

A cycle does not have the concept of a "beginning" or "end." The fold book as implied cycle is more a cycle than the fold book as literal cycle. This is because I have not fully resolved the concept of no beginning or end. I must lessen the impact of the two ends of the folded sheet of paper:

• I could remove the stiff covers, so not to suggest an ending, and to give less emphasis to the one-sided characteristic, stressing the loop.

• I could start the first page abruptly, in the midst of action rather than as a title page or "first" picture. I could place the title page in the middle of the book so it did not begin at the front.

• Or, better, I could plan the book without a beginning, or end. The action would start abruptly and continue to the "end" without a rallentando. The "last" picture would be continued by the "first" picture.

A title page would interrupt the cycle causing a beginning. To negate this, I would place the title and other text in a line running throughout all the pages, not starting at the beginning of a sentence.

The type of book cannot be arbitrarily chosen and the contents stuck into it. The binding and display will alter the contents and one type of book will allow a better development of an idea than another.

## TURNING THE PAGE
• It is a physical movement.
• Turning pages reveals the order of viewing.
• It places the book into time.

• The book is a single experience, a compound picture of the many separate sheets.

• In the codex, this single experience is revealed in slivers. The total is perceived and exists only as retention of afterimage in the mind. The codex is never seen at once.

• Turning the page suggests a rate of turning. Trying to make every picture equally strong would be like reading with no inflection.

• *TRANSPARENCY:* If the pages are not paper, but transparencies (film-positives), turning the page does many things.

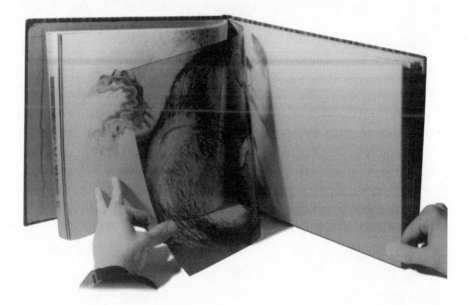

Keith Smith, Book 2, *A Change In Dimension,* 1967. One-of-a-kind. A transparent page casts a shadow which can incorporate with a picture on the following page. This transient collage exists only during the act of turning the page. 28 x 36 cm.

As the page is lifted on the right-hand side, the cast shadow appears, in focus, then goes out of focus as the page is turned, returning to focus on the left-hand side as the page is lowered in place. The cast shadow is part of the composition, imagery, experience. It exaggerates the idea that each page of a codex exists in now-time.

If the book has several transparencies in succession, as the pages are turned, the imagery builds up on the left hand side as it breaks down on the right. This need not be symmetrical repetition. The opaque pages at the beginning and end of the book/chapter can have different imagery to create a different composite on the left than on the right hand side. If several transparencies are used in succession, either I will be able to see the total composite of overlays or it will become so complex and dense that I will not. Either can be exploited to the book format's potential.

By printing locally

rather than full frame on each transparency, retaining mostly clear film, many sheets of film can build up to a composite image with little or no over-lapping of forms. The individual page is no longer a decisive moment, full-frame image. It is a page which cannot stand on its own, cannot be removed from the book to be matted and placed on a wall. The page is not the picture. It is now subordinate, totally dependent on and integrated as part of the total book. These individual sheets lose their importance in inverse propor-tion to the importance gained by the book/chapter as a whole. I think about how this concept can be used with opaque paper pages. Local printing on pages of uniform size, and printing across the stair-stepping surface of vari-able dimensional pages.

By printing full frame

the transparencies exist for many pages with much elaboration, the den-sity of images will create almost a solid black composite. As the viewer turns the pages, on the left side will be one picture, then a composite of two, three. As the turning of the pages builds the number of multiple images, the complexity will soon destroy the left side as well as the right.

In the middle of this succession of pages, both sides of the book will be black. The center pages will be seen clearly only during the act of turning the page. While they are up in the air the viewer can see the individual sheet/image. The transparency imitates a paper print. Thus, the core of the book "exists" only during the process of viewing the book. Towards the end of the book, just as at the beginning, the left-hand side increases, the complexity on the right hand side diminishes, to five, four, three, then two overlap-pings, then one page/image, creating a cycle, another form of transition.

In thinking about this concept, I try to relate it to similar struc-tures so that my imagination can elaborate more easily. Building up layers of transpar-ent pages on the left side of the gutter, while turning pages reduces the layers on the right, is a matter of balance.

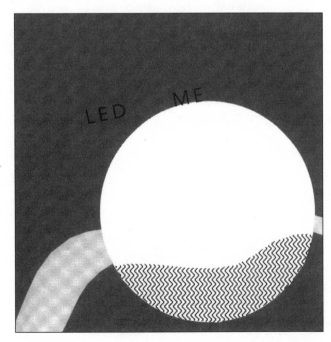

---

BOOK NUMBER 50
*(Turning the page creates and destroys the image.)*
Autumnal Equinox 1974

Construct a Western Codex book consisting of images on thirty transparencies. Process the film-positives by developing, short stop but no fix. Wash, dry and under proper safelight, hand bind as a leather case bound book. Place completed book in light-tight box.

Present the boxed book to the viewer. Upon opening the box and viewing, the entire book will not fog at once. Opening to the first page, the viewer will glimpse the image as it quickly blackens. The black will protect the remainder of the book from light. Upon turning each page, the viewer will momentarily see the image as it sacrifices itself to protect the remaining pages.

KE◉TH

---

Keith Smith, Book 50, *The Self-Sacrificing Book,* 1974. Book Number 50 is reproduced in its entirety above. It exists not as a physical object, but only as an idea conveyed through text. It is an example of a *conceptual book.*

I look up *balance* in the dictionary. I think about balance, counter-balance. As a symbol, I see the scales of justice. Further in the definition I come across accounting. Debits and credits are a balancing act. However, none of the definitions stimulate my imagination. I look elsewhere, but without success. Frustrated, I pick up my blank book. I return to meditating on the idea of turning pages for possibilities.

Turning the page, turning pages proves mechanical. Rather than waste more time, I recognize I am at a dead end. I start to work on another book, leaving this one on hold for a day, a week, or maybe five years until I know how to proceed.

This is how I work. I always have one to two dozen books in progress. When insight comes, I work on the appropriate book for as long as I am progressing. If my mind is scattered, I cut book boards, buy supplies and do the little things which do not require much critical thought. When I find I am depressed, rather than allow my mood shifts to immobilize me, I channel those feelings into an appropriate book. My work becomes my cure. When I was a student, Sonia Sheridan gave invaluable advice, "Put your work into everything, and everything into your work." The artist does not sit until inspired to make a masterpiece, and art does not have to be about monumental events.

I return to thinking of transparencies. My breakthrough comes while listening to the music of Philip Glass and, especially, Steve Reich. I learn how to utilize transparent pages conceptually in thinking of musical structure as motif.

Physically, the transparencies can be a chapter in the book, interrupted by an opaque paper page before the next group of transparencies. In effect, each chapter is not a chapter, but one compound picture. If the codex has four chapters, eight transparencies each, instead of thirty-two pictures, there are four compound pictures. Sometimes the paper page dividing the chapters may have a window allowing a preview of the next chapter. More holes reveal more of the book. Removing all opaque pages and placing glass covers on the codex makes it literally a one-picture book; I don't even have to open the covers to view the book. This is complete transition, returning to the single picture format. This book permits examination through pages-as-layers, going from the objects depicted closest to the viewer back through space to the horizon. My definition of *book* is further expanded.

*TRANSLUCENCY:* If I use translucent pages, an echo exists on the back as it is turned. A preview of the following page/s can be seen. This lends itself to ideas of afterimage, déjà vu, multiple imagery, gradation of tones and disintegration of information over a number of pages. Pictures evolve and spatially emerge, like coming out of a fog, on the right hand side, while receding into a darkening depth on the left over a period of time during the act of turning the pages. It is the process of turning pages that activates the very idea of translucency.

## THE PROCESS OF TURNING PAGES

*HOW to SEE a BOOK:* My approach to seeing a book for the first time is to go through the entire book at least two or three times at one sitting. The first time is at a fast pace, with the other viewings successively slower, having been modified by the previous viewing. The book on the first viewing, theoretically, could be upside down. I am not necessarily looking at subject matter or reading any words, but seeing the overall layout,

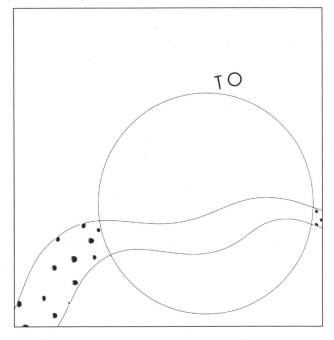

the composition of the total book, as well as the individual pictures. I am picking up the tone or mood. The second viewing is less general. I do not turn the pages at a constant pace, as previously, but create my own pacing by dwelling on things that either interest me or that I do not comprehend. At this viewing, I become acquainted with the subject matter which was only superficially seen on first viewing, and I pick up on motifs, symbolism, subtleties. I am pleased if the book requires several viewings. It then exists on more than one or two levels. The book invites the viewer back. It is exciting to pick up on nuances. On the third viewing I check to see if my previous pacing is altered by what I perceive to be the bookmaker's implied pacing.

CARE in VIEWING a BOOK: Holding near the gutter and lifting the page will cause stress and very likely kink the paper. To anyone who loves paper, kinks are upsetting. The paper loses its freshness. Bent surfaces catch raking light, casting shadows which distract from the image.

The page should not be turned by placing the index finger under the upper right-hand corner of the recto, then slipping the hand to the verso and palming it while turning the page. The entire verso receives an application of oil from the hand.

The extreme vertical edge of the recto should be lifted and placed to the extreme left. The area touched should be varied with each viewing to dissipate wear.

"Hand-held" refers to format size and that the book is experienced through touch. It does not refer to position of viewing. The book should be placed on a table and opened, allowing both covers to rest on the table, if the binding permits. After viewing, the book should not be pushed aside, as friction can mar the back cover.

The physical object has to be handled to be seen; it has to be stored. Care requires awareness. If books are abused, it is because 99% of what we read or see is mass-produced, inexpensive transients: the newspaper, magazines, paperback books, television.

ACCUMULATED FRAGMENTS: All visual books are conceptually one-picture books in as much as the total, not the individual drawings or photographs, is of major importance. Each page compounds time, memory and specific images to create one compound concept.

What I have said about a book containing transparencies is true to a large extent for a book of opaque paper pages as well. Memory persists. Animation is based on this. Because of the persistence of memory and the reten-

Susan E. King, *Women and Cars,* Paradise Press, silkscreened at Women's Studio Workshop, Rosendale, New York, 1983. Text can be read page by page. Pulling on the covers to fully extend the book, flips the flag-shaped pages to reveal a single picture. The flag format was devised by Hedi Kyle. 13 x 21 cm. Extends to 55 cm.

tion of afterimage, a previous page can be incorporated into the imagery of the following page, or even a succession of pages.

Pages 63, 65, 67 and 69 illustrate separate opaque paper pages. Imagery on these rectos builds to one, implied, compound picture, which is seen only in the mind, the manner in which any codex experience comes together.

It is one thing to relate two pictures on facing pages. It is another to relate a recto to its verso, and still another to relate one page to another specific image several pages hence. Conceptually, this is done by means of creating a series or a sequence. This is reinforced visually.

One way I like to structure is to make a compound picture which accumulates over several successive opaque paper pages. Fragments are pieced together much as the separate runs of colors build up to form one picture in printmaking. To make this procedure a book experience, I present each stage on separate pages. The "print" comes together only in the viewer's mind. This is the manner in which any codex is read. Unlike the fan, blind and fold book, in the codex the total is seen after the fact.

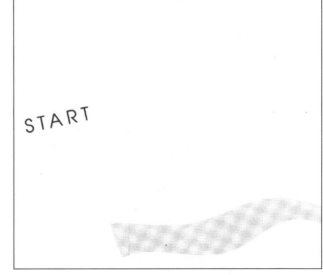

START

In structuring a book, or more likely, only a chapter, as accumulated fragments, I use only the rectos, leaving the versos blank. This reinforces the idea of an accumulated compound image, since the repetition occurs in identically the same location as the pages are turned: A form in the lower right corner (of page 63) may be only a light tone. Page 65, that same shape may be a black and white texture. Context suggests the two should be incorporated in the mind; persistence of memory urges it.

On one page that identical shape could present the subject matter. Then, the following two rectos could contain local colors which are in register with the previous shape, texture and subject matter. If one shape is blue, the other yellow, would you "see" green? If these opaque pages were transparent, the total picture would come together, seen at once.

Opaque pages create the essence of viewing a codex. Structuring with accumulated fragments exaggerates this inherent character of the codex. Building with fragments is the key to composing any book. A book is not a concern for a bunch of independent pictures capable of being viewed on a museum wall. It is not dealing with islands, but fragments.

After the first eleven pages as a chapter of piecing together fragments, I might have a chapter which treats each page as a complete picture. This would alter the pacing, speeding up the action while necessarily slowing down the rate of turning pages. In addition, two-page spreads could now be used. Chapter three might return to accumulated fragments, or might utilize single framing building up now by means of animation. Chapter four might sum up the book. The four chapters would relate in structure to the four movements of a symphony: statement of theme, variation, recapitulation and finale.

To read the individual pages of the accumulated fragments is only part of the story. As in any number of pages designed as a unit, the total is more than the sum of its parts. One transparent color over another yields a third color. One texture superimposed over a second makes a third. The illustrated text on pages 63, 65, 67, and 69, read in succession says one thing. When the four pages are consolidated to a single image, the text reads differently. Even the words are not the same:

> SO now is seen tangent with ME to read as SOME.
> START combines with LED to become STARTLED.

In conceiving any book it is worth repeating,
> "A book is *more* than the sum of its parts."

# THE MATERIAL PAGE
## Michael Davidson

WHEN MALLARMÉ ANNOUNCED a *crise de vers* in the 1890s, he antici-
pated a constellation of problems that would preoccupy poets for the next
century. At one level, the crisis refers to the problem of the sign itself, its ability to refer outside the discursive field in which it is used. In another sense,
Mallarmé was concerned with the fate of artistic language in an age of mechanical reproduction when newspapers, photography, and mass-produced
popular novels threatened to destroy the "aura" of a work's originality and
uniqueness. Mallarmé's response to these twin crises in a work like *Un coup
de dés* was to utilize the material resources of the printed page—varying
fonts, type sizes, white space—to disturb syntactic and semantic relationships. If *Un coup de dés* signaled the problematics of language that has become synonymous with modernism, it did so in the most *graphic* of terms.

For Anglo-American poets, this foregrounding of the verbal medium
offered a necessary corrective to the excesses of late Victorian verse. When
Ezra Pound set down his famous Imagist tenets of 1913, it was precisely to
excoriate the "perdamnable rhetoric" of the 1890s in England. He advised a
"harder and saner" verse, "as much like granite as it can be." Unlike Symbolism, with which it shared certain affinities, Imagism stressed the physical
properties of objects in ways that were never at issue in the earlier movement. Moreover, the visualist imperative of Imagist aesthetics extended to
the physical placement of words on the page. Pound's most famous Imagist
poem, "In a Station of the Metro," first appeared with spaces between key
words to emphasize the important relationship between musical phrasing
and notation:

> The apparition     of these faces     in the crowd
> Petals     on a wet, black     bough

However radical Pound's attack on rhetoric may have sounded, his
own early practice was much informed by the very aesthetic movements
he attacked. His early poems were modeled on medieval Tuscan and Prov-
ençal verse, and when he published his first collection of *The Cantos*, they
were ornately decorated in illuminated capitals and two-color printing
more appropriate to Pre-Raphaelite design. As Jerome McGann suggests,
Pound's "modernism" must be framed by the historicity implied by such
designs. It was not enough for him simply to invoke the glories of medieval
Tuscany or Provence; it was necessary to rearticulate them through their

contemporary manifestations in Arts and Crafts printing and bookmaking. Although Pound ultimately rejected such ornate typographic presentations during the 1930s for more "modern" visual formats, his debts to the Arts and Crafts spirit of William Morris stayed with him as an ideal synthesis of poetry, design, and material culture.

With his exposure to Continental movements such as Futurism, Cubism, and Dadaism, Pound quickly saw how the page could become more than an occasion for decorative printing but rather a generative element of meaning. Influential in Pound's thinking about the physical qualities of the page was his discovery, through the papers of Ernest Fenollosa, of the Chinese ideogram. Pound felt, however mistakenly, that the Chinese character was a series of schematic images, juxtaposed one upon the other, that created a single complex or "radiant node." The modern poem could utilize certain features of the ideogram—its concreteness, emphasis on the natural object, juxtaposition of multiple images—into a spatial whole. The "ideogrammic method" advocated by Pound implied a way of moving from one element to another without providing the usual rhetorical connectives. Applied to the *Cantos,* this method permitted Pound to create a visual field out of disparate discursive elements—a quotation from Middle English, a phrase in Greek, a reference to Egyptian mythology, a Chinese character—the juxtaposition of which would constitute a cultural hieroglyph. The simultaneity of historical moments through juxtaposition was given visual reinforcement by Pound's use of the entire page as a textual collage. In "Canto XCI," for example, Pound links the Egyptian hieroglyph for the Sun boat of Ra with the Chinese character for "tensile light," the Greek word for Helen of Troy, and the story of Sir Francis Drake. All four elements represent Neoplatonic values associated with light and fertility that Pound felt were articulated during the Renaissance, the English version of which is figured by Drake, a navigator, statesman, soldier, and servant of a powerful female monarch.

Pound's ideogrammic method was the verbal component of Vorticism, a British movement that stressed interrelationships between visual, sculptural, and literary arts. Vorticism reflected the influence of Italian Futurism, particularly its penchant for dynamic motion and speed. Although the British variant rejected the cult of the machine associated with Marinetti and Boccioni, it utilized the typographic innovations of both Russian and Italian Futurism in its principal magazine, *Blast.* First published in 1914, *Blast* printed the work of Pound, Wyndham Lewis, and the sculptor Henri Gaudier-Brzeska as well as Russian, Italian, and German poets. As Marjorie Perloff has pointed out, Vorticism exploited the formal possibilities of the manifesto as a performative genre—its direct, public address, its declamatory tone, its dynamic physical presentation—and along the way provided a new look for the printed page. In his various manifestos published in the magazine,

Wyndham Lewis "blasts" the aestheticism of the British 1890s, utilizing various type sizes to score the dynamics of his invective. Although many of the poems printed in *Blast* were written in traditional forms and utilized the hard left margin, the aesthetic and social diatribes presented alongside the poems were significant literary and typographic events in themselves.

Vorticism exploited the possibilities of the medium by taking the poem off the page and into the realm of physical gesture. There were limits, however, to a poetics based largely on invective, and by 1919, only a few years after its inaugural manifesto, the movement was dead. A more radical transformation of the page was effected by the examples of Cubism and Dadaism. In the United States, the first appearances of Cubist painting and collage in the Armory show of 1913 and then in Alfred Steiglitz's magazines *Camera Work* and *291* were a revelation to many poets. Gertrude Stein, William Carlos Williams, e. e. cummings, Mina Loy, and others seized upon the possibilities of fragmentation, repetition, and montage in the work of Picasso, Braque, and Léger. In particular, the poets were interested by the way painters incorporated found materials onto the canvas. Fragments of newspapers, advertising, and other forms of mass-produced copy became part of the overall construction, and when poets applied similar materials to their poems the effects on poetic form were dramatic. The use of verbal collage can be felt in many of the major poems of the period, from T. S. Eliot's *The Waste Land* and Pound's *Cantos* to Gertrude Stein's portraits, William Carlos Williams's *Spring and All*, and Hart Crane's *The Bridge.* Collage juxtaposition permitted poets to confront the distractions of modern urban life through the multiple voices of an emerging print culture.

If Cubism provided the formal means for a *dérèglement* of the page, Dadaism provided the iconoclastic spirit. The work of Man Ray, Francis Picabia, Marcel Duchamp, and other Europeans who visited the United States inspired poets with a sense of irreverence and daring that helped create an indigenous American avant-garde in the years following World War I. American versions of Dada were never as radical as their European counterparts, but something of the movement's nose-thumbing character can be felt in the work of Baroness Elsa von Freytag-Loringhoven, Robert McAlmon, William Carlos Williams, Mina Loy, and e. e. cummings, many of whom gathered at Walter Conrad Arensberg's apartment or published in Alfred Kreymborg's magazine, *Others.* Dada offered less a series of formal solutions to the poem than permission to invent and explore and, in the process, to use typography in highly inventive ways.

The typographic revolution brought about by Futurism, Cubism, and Dadaism led to significant experiments with Concrete or Visual Poetry. Apollinaire's *Calligrammes,* begun in 1914, utilized typography to represent rain, cannons, musical instruments, automobiles, and other objects in a series of whimsical visual poems. Such a practice was by no means original to modernism—the convention of "shaped" verse is as old as print itself —but it achieved a special importance in the post-World War I era as poets sought to liberate the word from its dependency upon conventional syntax, inherited forms, and genres. Although the use of visual poetry did not come into its own until the Concrete movement of the late 1950s, it formed an important element in the work of many poets during this period.

Much of the impetus for calligraphic and concretist experimentation was gained by the increased use of the typewriter and the flexibility of new forms of movable type. Modernist poets such as Pound, Williams, and cummings saw the advantages of this technology in gaining control over their medium. Prior to the modern period, poets had to rely on the skills (and whims) of copy editors and typesetters in interpreting their textual intentions. Modernist poets now could use new print technologies to indicate exactly what values of spacing and word placement they intended. This kind of flexibility permitted poets to utilize the range of the typewriter keyboard, from diacritical marks to the tab and space bars, in realizing their notations. Free verse had gained a new and important technical ally in completing its revolution.

Whereas the Pound/Williams generation used the typewriter to create a new visual aesthetic—the word as image or object—poets who followed them utilized that same technology in the service of an emerging oral impulse. The recovery of orality in postwar verse, with its basis in primitive, tribal cultures, coincides with a greater emphasis on personal confession and bardic testimony. Charles Olson, in his manifesto "Projective Verse" (1950), vaunted the typewriter's ability to provide a more exact register of vocal intentions. What Olson calls "open field" verse involves the line as a physical gesture, a register of physiological and muscular responses. The line is controlled no longer by a discrete count of individual elements (accents, syllables, feet) but by the emotional intensity of the moment. Bardic poets such as Allen Ginsberg or Robert Duncan utilized a characteristically long line that sustained a rolling, often mantralike cadence in the manner of Blake or Whitman; more introspective poets such as Robert Creeley or Denise Levertov utilized a shorter, more heavily enjambed line to achieve a tense, highly charged lyricism. In each case, the new poetries of the 1950s and 1960s generated notational features based on organic or psychological models that could not be accommodated to traditional prosodic form.

Olson's own practice derives from Pound and Williams, often varying short, lyric moments with long-lined, prosaic passages. He utilizes indentation and spacing to register moment-to-moment shifts of attention as he walks, literally and figuratively, through a historically encrusted landscape. Those "private" feelings are linked to the physical world in which he walks, and thus in a poem such as "Letter, May 2, 1959," he skews his lines in various directions to imitate an early map of Gloucester. Olson's impatience with traditional rhetorical devices and sequential narrative structure is registered through his highly enjambed lineation as well as his idiosyncratic use of spacing. Despite the oralist bias of "Projective Verse," Olson's primary concern is phenomenological: to create a poetry as close to perception and cognition as possible. The score for such processes was a page that resembled, as closely as possible, physical acts of writing, speaking, and walking.

Combined with a renewed emphasis on the line as expressive gesture among various poets of the 1950s and 1960s was a renewed interest in uniting poetry with other arts. Poets such as Kenneth Patchen, Ian Hamilton Finlay, Robert Duncan, and Philip Whalen illustrated their own books, but this same investment in the poem-as-art event led to more collaborative kinds of activities as well. Kenneth Rexroth, Lawrence Ferlinghetti, Jack Kerouac, and LeRoi Jones (Amiri Baraka) wrote poems to be performed with jazz musicians, leading to new notational strategies that would indicate phrasing, rhythms, and dynamics. Many poets associated with the New York School worked directly with painters, appropriating the painterly aesthetics of abstract expressionism (or, later, of Pop Art) with the personalist aesthetics defined by Frank O'Hara. Collaborations between O'Hara and Larry Rivers, Clark Coolidge and Philip Guston, Ron Padgett and Joe Brainard, and John Ashbery and Alex Katz were inspired as much by friendship between poets and artists as by shared aesthetic interests. In most cases, these collaborations resulted in the poet's work being illustrated by the painter (or vice versa), but in at least one case (Frank O'Hara's collaboration with Larry Rivers, *Stones* [1957- 58]), poet and artist worked directly (and spontaneously) on the lithographic stone. The spirit of collaboration during this period challenged poets to relinquish some of their authorial control over the text and create a more communal or dialogical art.

In the 1950s emerged a more directly visual poetry that stressed the physical properties of letters and the technologies of printing. Concrete or Visual Poetry owes its aesthetic origins to modernist movements such as Constructivism and Futurism as well as to the long tradition of shaped verse. As Emmett Williams says, Concrete Poetry is an art "beyond paraphrase, a poetry that often asked to be completed or activated by the reader, a poetry of direct presentation—the word, *not words, words, words*." Concrete Poetry aspires more directly than any other literary genre to the condition of the visual arts, although it would be wrong to assume that the linear possibilities of syntax or narrative are not highly active in the overall design. In the work of poets such as Ian Hamilton Finlay or Emmett Williams, the reader is placed in a relationship to language akin to the viewer of an acrobatic display (one of Finlay's best-known poems is called "Acrobat") in which one may see only flickering moments in an evolving activity.

Concrete Poetry explores not only the iconic and spatial features of letters but also their capacity for semantic indeterminacy. Bob Cobbing's work often deals with the visual and aural possibilities of shared elements. He deliberately blurs or smudges the typewritten page to call attention to the print medium and to confuse the boundaries between graphic sign and meaning. In "WOWROMWRORMM," (Fig. 1) a series of terms associated with physical decay ("corpse," "rust," "mouldering") descends down the page in wiggling tendrils, much like Apollinaire's raindrops in "Il Pleut". By overstriking his typewritten characters, Cobbing creates his own form of typographic decay. When combined with the thematics of death and dying (the downward progression of tendrils provides a nice visual pun on the worm's movement), the poem seems to illustrate its own demise. The final word—or word complex—"w ow r om wro rmm" represents the mortal end of letters removed from their semantic positions, but in its own multireferentiality (the complex includes the sounds of "womb" "room" and "worm") the poem adds a whimsical twist to the memento mori tradition.

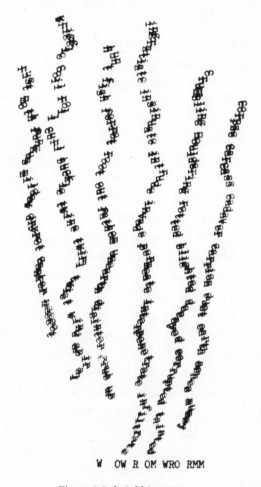

W   OW  R  OM  WRO  RMM

Figure 1. Bob Cobbing, *Worm.*

The verbal or acoustic equivalent to Cobbing's work is sound or "sound-text" poetry in which the page serves as a score for verbal performance. Drawing on Futurist and Dadaist theater, sound poetry stresses the acoustic properties of words, dismantling their phonemic properties until they exist as abstract sounds. Jackson Mac Low's sound poetry is built upon the use of chance operations to determine the selection of materials that are then subjected to further improvisation in vocal performance. In Mac Low's "Gathas," for example, Sanskrit words taken from mantras are selected by chance operations, placed in a grid, and then performed improvisationally by one or more persons. The grid in which the letters are encased isolates each sound as a phonic as well as visual element.

In the work of Steve McCaffery and other Canadian sound poets, the use of abstract sounds—grunts, whistles, groans, and breathing—combined with improvisation creates a poetry immediate to the body and expression. As McCaffery says, "sound poetry is *the* poetry of direct emotional confrontation: there is no pausing for intellectualization, there is no repeating of emotional content, each performance is unique & only the audience is repeatable." This definition could be seen as an extreme version of personalism in which the raw presentation of sound supplements the rhetorical displacement of the person through voice. In McCaffery's work, the page is less a score for the repetition of sounds than a grid for highly improvisatory performance. Anything can be a score—from a sketch to a word list to a page from the telephone directory—and in his collaborations with the Four Horsemen (bpNichol, Rafael Barreto-Rivera, Paul Dutton, Steve McCaffery) the text is often a "sketch" for performance rather than a finished document.

Concrete and sound poetries offer perhaps the most dramatic instance of a text in which the material properties of language become the subject of the poem. These movements are international in scope, English-speaking poets sharing the stage with Polish, French, German, Austrian, and Japanese writers. Similar aesthetic tendencies can be seen among American Language-writers for whom linguistic materialization is part of a general critique of expressive poetics. Among certain Language-writers, this critique is linked to a specifically political project. Whereas for modernists the defamiliarization of words implies a desire for a realm of pure literariness, for Language-writers defamiliarization involves the interrogation of discursive and ideological structures. The first stage in this critique involves dismantling syntactic and semantic contexts, isolating words or parts of words to resonate among themselves. The second stage—best seen in the work of Ron Silliman or Lyn Hejinian, for instance—involves recombination according to numerical or formulaic patterns such that narrative or chronological progress is thwarted and new kinds of connectives established.

It is a third stage of defamiliarization that engages our concerns with the visual page. Here, the conventional ratio between printed text and prior "word" is broken down and the physicality of writing materials becomes generative in composition. In the work of Johanna Drucker—herself a printer and scholar of the book—the conventions of printing and typography provide an occasion for an extended meditation on the materiality of her medium. In *Against Fiction,* for example, Drucker addresses the conventions of narrative form—its seriality, its dependence on character and action—by creating a text that thwarts forward movement and formal cohesion (Fig. 2). Extensive use of headlines, intertitles, illustrations, shifts of typeface, and eccentric spelling creates the feeling of a popular book or tabloid magazine while defying easy decoding. Its fragmentation and brokenness contrast with its familiar graphic display, creating an odd hybrid work that draws on tradition and innovation in equal parts.

A similar defamiliarization of conventions occurs in Robert Grenier's graphic works in which the author's handwriting or "scrawl" becomes the final text (Fig. 3). What is interrogated in his work since the late 1980s is the rhetoric of "finality" itself insofar as it structures a notion of aesthetic perfection. Grenier's "scrawls" are photocopies of his holograph page, replete with emendations, crossings-out, and unreadable scribbles. Like the calli-

Figure 2. Johanna Drucker, from *Against Fiction.*

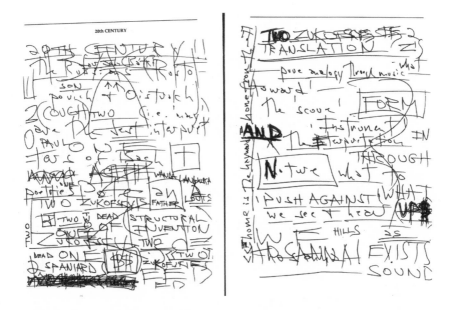

Figure 3. Robert Grenier, *Twentieth Century*.

graphic work of Jackson Pollock or Cy Twombly, Grenier's pages are gestural renderings designed less to communicate meaning than to register the immediacy and physical activity of writing. Yet since these pages depend on photocopying technology, their immediacy is quickly transformed into representation, gesture turned into copy. As Leslie Scalapino observes of these works, Grenier's work cannot be translated: "(it's opaque) because it's xerox; both individuated and continually different *and* mass produced." The odd liminal space such texts occupy—their opacity to a psychologically "deep" origin—offers a critique of the speech-based poetics of an earlier generation. "I hate speech," Grenier writes, suggesting that the traditional equation of page to voice does not apply in his case. His "scrawls" insist on writing as an act performed by the hand, at "this" moment on "this" piece of paper, available to multiple readings for a reader who, unable to decipher Grenier's script, must posit individual variants and thus generate a new text.

In such developments, the page becomes much more than a receptacle for preexisting aesthetic decisions; the page is, as I have emphasized, an element in composition itself, whether in supplying a white ground for shaped poems such as those of Dylan Thomas or John Hollander or in providing a "field" for action as in the work of Black Mountain poets. Experimentation in computer-generated writing and hypertext has altered the nature of textuality altogether, rendering the idea of the "visible page" a rather outmoded concept. But the typographic revolution in modernism made possible the conditions for the page's deconstruction as movable type gave way to photo-offset printing and now to pixel characters. In a recurring modernist paradox the page must first be seen in order to be made invisible.

# MY LIFE A BOOK
## Anne Waldman

*If I say I am the little woman of the Book, that means that a Little-One-Who-Springs-Forth is a woman and that she is the little woman of the Book.*
—*María Sabina (translated by Henry Munn)*

Trees gradually become alphabets & suggest words, peripheral, ephemeral, then take on greater namings in human hegemony.

Sound & ink. Beyond culture. The neurons display little spines that branch out in language.

A baby, a body, a book, abode.

*Lontar*: the palm leaf you scribe upon.

*Pecha*: holy texts. Rectangular pages stacked & wrapped in sacred cloth.

Tripping, you emerge from the book. Whose poem are you dwelling in?

Within rocks, water, hidden dakini scripts in cloud formation, in dream.

Book from beech from oak from birch. The child looks up, reaches, a tree comes down to hand.

Papyrus fugue.

First ubiquitous pine as in "pine for love," the romantic fugue is never over.

Eyes in the wood, cryptic code in grains of wood, scripts go prancing there.

Trees read landscapes encoded for the traveller and for when the traveller exits, what trace?

Runes of turbulent meaning ride across winsome galaxies.

Cosmic mirages. Universe is a telescope. The woman is a book.

Language over meaning assembled frontally. & lifted & held, eyes open. Look in the book-lens.

Breasts = book.

Trace your name. Meaning: Anne. Named grace, named other. Named "mirror."

Shapes mist over a sexual lingual imagination.

Stir hand toward a physical turn, tremble toward solid compatibility of what's at hand. Turn.

Child makes marks against her void. Bricks, tablets, scorings for music, objects with sense & sound inside.

That's a record, that's a map, that's a guide no that's a holy book.

No that's a body of contents, a table?

No a tablet.

Le livre est sur la table.

A throne.

You sit on the encyclopedia of all there is to know, and lists of names & numbers of all they are to know in New York City.

Don't get lost out there dangerous out there, come back inside & read.

Open by hand.

Your world hovers between seductive covers. True tragedy. False tragedy. Mixed tragedy.

What genre are you if you were literature.

If you were a formal composition.

If you were a constitution.

If you were a priest. What gender are you?

If you were a scholar what kind of book would you be?

Gnosis, a concept. Literature, a concept.

Bad books.

Criticism, a book.

Epic, a song.

Art, a book.

Art, a concept.

Book, a song.

Ideology, a book.

Science, an art.

Politics, a song.

Occulist witness witnesses a stream of character.

Vocabulary, a gnosis.

Tree, art.

Character, a book.

No need to move from this tree.

Or stay inside with a good/bad book.

Create your text out of the first oral moment after you have been outside to live.

They throw the book at you.

Politics, a book they throw at you.

Lock up your sex in an art-tree-science-book.

Revolution, a manual.

Vegetable, a page.

Law, a code.

Staple, a spine.

Ink, mineral.

Imagination, animal.

Vox, animal.

Glue, animal.

Oral, moment.

Flesh, woman.

Some girl in a dark wood in the dark wood moment.

Trees at every turn in the wood in the dark wood flesh moment.

No light to read by at any turn in the wood in the dark wood moment.

Torches? Intellectus.

A book of the wood imagination all lit up.

You master the word hobgoblin.

You drink the elixir of gnosis.

Hob gob line in the dark wood turning to a dark wood book instant.

You go inside, a different book, a light, a place to sit down.

Lexicons live there.

All the testaments including oral litanies & hagiographies & cosmographies live there.

Various books of various gods live there.

Sacred substances live there.

"With the mushrooms I see god." (María Sabina)

Human, a book.

God, an art.

A book of hours & the illuminated numbers to live by live there.

Manifesto, a claim.

Cultural identity, an art.

Enough to go around, a fact.

Structure of wave, of young star-forming blue galaxy both live there.

Application, memory, dream, data across the impulse-micro-chip-night live here.

A word was beginning in a wood & more important than god it seemed the word in the dark wood comes to light turning in the dark wood neural spine hand ritual book taut instant.

Abstraction, ghost books at hand.

# EDMOND JABÈS
# AND THE QUESTION OF THE BOOK
## Jacques Derrida

OUR REREADINGS of *Je bâtis ma demeure*\* will be better, henceforth. A certain ivy could have hidden or absorbed its meaning, could have turned its meaning in on itself. Humor and games, laughter and dances, songs, circled graciously around a discourse which, as it did not yet love its true root, bent a bit in the wind. Did not yet stand upright in order to enunciate only the rigor and rigidity of poetic obligation.

In *Le livre des questions* the voice has not been altered, nor the intention abandoned, but the accent is more serious. A powerful and ancient root is exhumed, and on it is laid bare an ageless wound (for what Jabès teaches us is that roots speak, that words want to grow, and that poetic discourse *takes root* in a wound): in question is a certain Judaism as the birth and passion of writing. The passion *of* writing, the love and endurance of the letter itself whose subject is not decidably the Jew or the Letter itself. Perhaps the common root of a people and of writing. In any event, the incommensurable destiny which grafts the history of a

> race born of the book (*Livre des questions,* p. 26)

onto the radical origin of meaning as literality, that is, onto historicity itself. For there could be no history without the gravity and labor of literality. The painful folding of itself which permits history to reflect itself as it ciphers itself. This reflection is its beginning. The only thing that begins by reflecting itself is history. And this fold, this furrow, is the Jew. The Jew who elects writing which elects the Jew, in an exchange responsible for truth's thorough suffusion with historicity and for history's *assignment* of itself to its empiricity.

> I spoke to you about the difficulty of being a Jew, which coincides with the difficulty of writing; for Judaism and writing are but the same waiting, the same hope, the same depletion. (Ibid., p. 132)

The exchange between the Jew and writing as a pure and founding exchange, an exchange without prerogatives in which the original appeal is, in another sense of the word, a *convocation*—this is the most persistent affirmation of the *Livre des questions:*

---

\*Jabès's book of early poems (1943-57), pre-dating *Le Livre des questions* (*The Book of Questions*).

[ 84 ]

*You are he who writes and is written.*

...

*And Reb Ilde: "What difference is there between choosing and being chosen when we can do nothing but submit to the choice?"* (Ibid., p. 30)

And through a kind of silent displacement toward the essential which makes of this book one long metonymy, the situation of the Jew becomes exemplary of the situation of the poet, the man of speech and of writing. The poet, in the very experience of his freedom, finds himself both bound to language and delivered from it by a speech whose master, nonetheless, he himself is.

*Words choose the poet....*
*The art of the writer consists in little by little making words interest themselves in his books.* (*Je bâtis ma demeure*)

In question is a labor, a deliverance, a slow gestation of the poet by the poem whose father he is.

*Little by little the book will finish me.* (*L'espace blanc*)

The poet is thus indeed the *subject* of the book, its substance and its master, its servant and its theme. And the book is indeed the subject of the poet, the speaking and knowing being who *in* the book writes *on* the book. This movement through which the book, *articulated* by the voice of the poet, is folded and bound to itself, the movement through which the book becomes a subject in itself and for itself, is not critical or speculative reflection, but is, first of all, poetry and history. For in its representation of itself the subject is shattered and opened. Writing is itself written, but also ruined, made into an abyss, in its own representation. Thus, within this book, which infinitely reflects itself and which develops as a painful questioning of its own possibility, the form of the book represents itself:

*The novel of Sarah and Yukel, through various dialogues and meditations attributed to imaginary rabbis, is the story of a love destroyed by men and by words. It has the dimensions of a book and the bitter obstinacy of a wandering question.* (*Livre des questions*, p. 26)

We will see that by another direction of metonymy—but to what extent is it other?—the *Livre des questions* describes the generation of God himself. The wisdom of the poet thus culminates its freedom in the passion of translating obedience to the law of the word into autonomy. Without which, and if passion becomes subjection, the poet is mad.

*The madman is the victim of the rebellion of words.* (*Je bâtis ma demeure*)

Also, through his understanding of this assignment of the root, and through the inspiration he receives from this injunction of the Law, Jabès perhaps has renounced the *verve*, that is, the *capriciousness* of the early works; but he has in no way given up his freedom of speech. He has even acknowledged that freedom must belong to the earth, to the root, or it is merely wind:

> *A teaching that Reb Zalé translated with this image: "You think that it is the bird who is free. You are deceived; it is the flower..."*
>
> *And Reb Lima: "Freedom is awakened little by little, in the extent to which we become aware of our ties, like the sleeper of his senses; then our acts finally have a name."* (Ibid., p. 124)

Freedom allies and exchanges itself with that which restrains it, with everything it receives from a buried origin, with the gravity which situates its center and its site. A site whose cult is not necessarily pagan. Provided that this Site is not a site, an enclosure, a place of exclusion, a province or a ghetto. When a Jew or a poet proclaims the Site, he is not declaring war. For this site, this land, calling to us from beyond memory, is always elsewhere. The site is not the empirical and national Here of a territory. It is immemorial, and thus also a future. Better: it is tradition as adventure. Freedom is granted to the nonpagan Land only if it is separated from freedom by the Desert of the Promise. That is, by the Poem. When it lets itself be articulated by poetic discourse, the Land always keeps itself beyond any proximity, *illic*:

> *Yukel, you have always been ill at ease with yourself, you are never* HERE, *but* ELSEWHERE...( Ibid., p. 33)

> *What are you dreaming of?—The Land.—But you are on land.—I am dreaming of the Land where I will be.—But we are right in front of each other. And we have our feet on land.—I know only the stones of the way which leads, as it is said, to the Land.*

The Poet and the Jew are not born *here* but *elsewhere*. They wander, separated from their true birth. Autochthons only of speech and writing, of Law. *"Race born of the book"* because sons of the Land to come.

Autochthons of the Book. Autonomous too, as we said. Which assumes that the poet does not simply receive his speech and his law from God. Judaic heteronomy has no need of a poet's intercession. Poetry is to prophecy what the idol is to truth. It it perhaps for this reason that in Jabès the poet and the Jew seem at once so united and disunited, and that the entire *Livre des questions* is also a self-justification addressed to the Jewish community which lives under heteronomy and to which the poet does not truly belong. Poetic autonomy, comparable to none other, presupposes broken Tables.

> *And Reb Lima: Freedom, at first, was engraved ten times in the Tables of the Law: but we deserve it so little that the Prophet broke them in his anger."* (Ibid., p. 124)

Between the fragments of the broken Tables the poem grows and the right to speech takes root. Once more begins the adventure of the text as weed, as outlaw far from *"the fatherland of the Jews,"* which is a *"sacred text surrounded by commentaries"* (p. 109). The necessity of commentary, like poetic necessity, is the very form of exiled speech. In the beginning is hermeneutics. But the *shared* necessity of exegesis, the interpretive imperative, is interpreted differently by the rabbi and the poet. The difference between the horizon of the original text and exegetic writing makes the difference between the rabbi and the poet irreducible. Forever unable to reunite with each other, yet so close to each other, how could they ever regain the *realm?* The original opening of interpretation essentially signifies that there will always be rabbis and poets. And two interpretations of interpretation. The Law then becomes Question and the right to speech coincides with the duty to interrogate. The book of man is a book of question.

*"To every question, the Jew answers with a question." Reb Lema* (Ibid., p. 125)

But if this right is absolute, it is because it does not depend upon some accident *within* history. The breaking of the Tables articulates, first of all, a rupture within God as the origin of history.

*Do not forget that you are the nucleus of a rupture.* (Ibid., p. 137)

God separated himself from himself in order to let us speak, in order to astonish and to interrogate us. He did so not by speaking but by keeping still, by letting silence interrupt his voice and his signs, by letting the Tables be broken. In *Exodus* God repented and said so at least twice, before the first and before the new Tables, between original speech and writing and, within Scripture, between the origin and repetition (*Exodus* 32:14; 33:17). Writing is, thus, originally hermetic and secondary. Our writing, certainly, but already His, which starts with the stifling of his voice and the dissimulation of his Face. This difference, this negativity in God, is our freedom, the transcendence and the verb which can relocate the purity of their negative origin only in the possibility of the Question. The question of "the irony of God," of which Schelling spoke, is first, as always, turned in on itself.

*God is in perpetual revolt against God. (Livre des questions,* p. 177)
*God is an interrogation of God.* (Ibid., p. 152)

Kafka said: "We are nihilist thoughts in the brain of God." If God opens the question in God, if he is the very opening of the Question, there can be no *simplicity* of God. And, thus, that which was unthinkable for the classical rationalists here becomes the obvious itself. Proceeding within the duplicity of his own questionability, God does not act in the simplest ways; he is not truthful, he is not sincere. Sincerity, which is simplicity, is a lying virtue. It is necessary, on the contrary, to accede to the virtue of the lie.

*"Reb Jacob, who was my first master, believed in the virtue of the lie be-cause, he said, there is no writing without a lie and writing is the way of God"* (p. 92). The clumsy, equivocal way of the detour, *borrowed* by God from God. Irony of God, ruse of God, the oblique way, born of God, the path toward God of which man is not a simple detour. The infinite detour. Way *of* God. *"Yukel, speak to us of the man who is a lie in God"* (p. 94).

This way, preceded by no truth, and thus lacking the prescription of truth's rigor, is the way through the Desert. Writing is the moment of the desert as the moment of Separation. As their name indicates—in Aramaic —the Pharisees, those misunderstood men of literality, were also "sepa-rated ones." God no longer speaks to us; he has interrupted himself: we must take words upon ourselves. We must be separated from life and com-munities, and must entrust ourselves to traces, must become men of vision because we have ceased hearing the voice from within the immediate prox-imity of the garden. *"Sarah, Sarah with what does the world begin?—With speech?—With vision?"* (p. 173). Writing is displaced on the broken line be-tween lost and promised speech. The *difference* between speech and writing is sin, the anger of God emerging from itself, lost immediacy, work outside the garden. *"The garden is speech, the desert writing. In each grain of sand a sign surprises"* (p. 169). The Judaic experience as reflection, as separation of life and thought, signifies the crossing of the book as an *infinite* anchorit-ism placed between two immediacies and two self-identifications. *"Yukel, how many pages to live, how many to die, separate you from yourself, separate you from the book to the abandoning of the book?"* (p. 44). The desert-book is made of sand, *"of mad sand,"* of infinite, innumerable and vain sand. *"Pick up a little sand, wrote Reb Ivri... then you will know the vanity of the verb"* (p. 122).

The Jewish consciousness is indeed the unhappy consciousness, and *Le livre des questions* is its poem; is the poem inscribed just beyond the phe-nomenology of the mind, which the Jew can accompany only for a short while, without eschatological provision, in order not to limit his desert, close his book and cauterize his cry. *"'Mark the first page of a book with a red rib-bon, for the wound is inscribed at its beginning.' Reb Alcé"* (p. 122).

If absence is the heart of the question, if separation can emerge only in the rupture of God—with God—if the infinite distance of the Other is *re-spected* only within the sands of a book in which wandering and mirages are always possible, then *Le livre des questions* is simultaneously the intermi-nable song of absence and a book on the book. Absence attempts to produce itself in the book and is lost in being pronounced; it knows itself as disap-pearing and lost and to this extent it remains inaccessible and impenetrable. To gain access to it is to lose it; to show it is to hide it; to acknowledge it is to lie. *"Nothing is our principle concern, said Reb Idar"* (p. 188), and Nothing—like Being—can only keep silent and hide itself.

Absence. *Absence of locality,* first of all. *"Sarah: Speech annihilates distance, makes the locale despair. Do we formulate speech or does it fashion us?"* The absence *of a place* is the title of one of the poems collected in *Je bâtis ma demeure.* It began thus: *"Vague estate, obsessed page..."* And *Le livre des questions* resolutely keeps itself on the vague estate, in the non-place, between city and desert, for in either the root is equally rejected or sterilized. Nothing flourishes in sand or between cobblestones, if not words. City and desert, which are neither countries, nor countrysides, nor gardens, besiege the poetry of Jabès and ensure that it will have a necessarily infinite echo. City and desert simultaneously, that is, Cairo, whence Jabès comes to us; he too, as is well known, had his flight from Egypt. The dwelling built by the poet with his *"swords stolen from angels"* is a fragile tent of words erected in the desert where the nomadic Jew is struck with infinity and the letter. Broken by the broken Law. Divided within himself—(the Greek tongue would doubtless tell us much about the strange relation between law, wandering, and non-identification with the self, the common root—*nemein*—of division, naming and nomadism). The poet of writing can only devote himself to the "un-happiness" that Nietzsche invokes upon, or promises to invoke upon, him who "hides deserts within him." The poet—or the Jew—protects the desert which protects both his speech (which can speak only in the desert) and his writing (which can be traced only in the desert). That is to say, by inventing, alone, an unfindable and unspecifiable pathway to which no Cartesian *resolution* can impart rectilinearity and issuance. *"Where is the way? The way is always to be found. A white sheet of paper is full of ways.... We will go over the same way ten times, a hundred times"* (*Livre des questions,* p. 55). Unwittingly, writing simultaneously designs and discovers an invisible labyrinth in the desert, a city in the sand. *"We will go over the same way ten times, a hundred times....And all these pathways have their own pathways. —Otherwise they would not be pathways"* (p. 55). The entire first part of the *Livre de l'absent* can be read as a meditation on the way and the letter. *"At noon, he found himself once more facing infinity, the white page. Every trace of footsteps had disappeared. Buried"* (p. 56). And again the transition from the desert to the city, the Limit which is the only habitat of writing: *"When he returned to his neighborhood and his house—a nomad had taken him on camel's back to the nearest outpost where he had taken a seat in a military truck headed toward the city—so many words solicited him. He persisted, however, in avoiding them"* (p. 59).

*Absence* of the writer too. For to write is to draw back. Not to retire into one's tent, in order to write, but to draw back from one's writing itself. To be grounded far from one's language, to emancipate it or lose one's hold on it, to let it make its way alone and unarmed. To leave speech. To be a poet is to know how to leave speech. To let it speak alone, which it can do only in its written form. *To leave* writing is to be there only in order to provide its passageway, to be the diaphanous element of its going forth: everything and nothing. For the work, the writer is at once everything and nothing. Like God:

> *If, wrote Reb Servi, you occasionally think that God does not see you, it Is because he has made himself so humble that you confuse him with the fly buzzing in the pane of your window. But that is the proof of his almightiness; for he is, simultaneously, Everything and Nothing. (Ibid., p. 117)*

Like God, the writer:

> *As a child, when I wrote my name for the first time I felt that I was starting a book. Reb Stein. (Ibid., p. 23)*

> *...But I am not this man for this man writes and the writer is no one. (Ibid., p. 28)*

> *I, Serafi, the absent one, I was born to write books. (I am absent because I am the storyteller. Only the story is real.) (Ibid., p. 60)*

And yet (this is only one of the contradictory postulations which ceaselessly tear apart the pages of the *Livre des questions,* and necessarily tear them apart: God contradicts himself already), only that which is written gives me existence by naming me. It is thus simultaneously true that things come into existence and lose existence by being named. Sacrifice of existence to the word, as Hegel said, but also the consecration of existence by the word. Moreover, it does not suffice to be written, for one must write in order to have a name. One must be called something. Which supposes that *"My name is a question...Reb Eglal" (p. 125). "Without my texts, I am more anonymous than a bedsheet in the wind, more transparent than a windowpane"* (p. 123).

This necessary *exchange* of one's existence with or for the letter—which is either to lose or to gain existence—is also imposed upon God:

> *I did not seek you, Sarah. I sought you. Through you, I ascend to the origin of the sign, to the unformulated writing sketched by the wind on the sand and on the sea, the untamed writing of the bird and the mischievous fish. God, Master of wind, Master of sand, Master of birds and fishes, expected from man the book that man expected from man; the one in order finally to be God, the other finally to be man. (Ibid., p. 189)*

> *All letters form absence. Thus God is the child of his name. Reb Tal (Ibid., p. 47)*

Meister Eckhart said: "God becomes God when creation says God." This assistance given to God by man's writing does not contradict writing's inability to "help itself" (*Phaedrus*). Is not the divine—the disappearance of man —announced in this distress of writing?

If absence does not allow itself to be reduced by the letter, this is so because it is the letter's ether and respiration. The letter is the separation and limit in which meaning is liberated from its imprisonment in aphoristic solitude. No "logic," no proliferation of conjunctive undergrowth can reach the end of its essential discontinuity and noncontemporaneousness, the ingenuity of its *under-stood* [*sous-entendu*] silences. The other originally collaborates with meaning. There is an essential *lapse* between significations which is not the simple and positive fraudulence of a word, nor even the nocturnal memory of all language. To allege that one reduces this lapse through narration, philosophical discourse, or the order of reasons or deduction, is to misconstrue language, to misconstrue that language is the *rupture* with totality itself. The fragment is neither a determined style nor a failure, but the form of that which is written. Unless God himself writes— and he would still have to be the God of the classical philosophers who neither interrupted nor interrogated himself, did not stifle himself, as did the God of Jabès. (But the God of the classical philosophers, whose actual infinity did not tolerate the question, precisely had no vital need for writing.) As opposed to Being and to the Leibnizian Book, the rationality of the Logos, for which our writing is responsible, obeys the principle of discontinuity. The caesura does not simply finish and fix meaning: "The aphorism," says Nietzsche, "the sentence, in which I, as the first among the Germans, am a master, are the forms of eternity." But, primarily, the caesura makes meaning emerge. It does not do so alone, of course; but without interruption— between letters, words, sentences, books—no signification could be awakened. *Assuming* that Nature refuses the *leap,* one can understand why Scripture will never be Nature. It proceeds by leaps alone. Which makes it perilous. Death strolls between letters. To write, what is called writing, assumes an access to the mind through having the courage to lose one's life, to die away from nature.

Jabès is very attentive to this generous distance between signs.

*The light is in their absence which you read.* (Ibid., p. 25)

*All letters form absence.* (Ibid., p. 47)

Absence is the permission given to letters to spell themselves out and to signify, but it is also, in language's twisting of itself, *what* letters say: they say freedom and a granted emptiness, that which is formed by being enclosed in letters' net.

Absence, finally, as the breath of the letter, for the letter *lives.* "The name must germinate, otherwise it is false," says André Breton. Signifying absence or separation, the letter lives as aphorism. It is solitude, articulates solitude, and lives on solitude. It would no longer be the letter of the law if it were outside difference, or if it left its solitude, or put an end to interruption, to distance, to respect, and to its relation to the other, that is, a certain non-relation. There is, thus, an animality of the letter which assumes the forms of the letter's desire, anxiety, and solitude.

> *Your solitude*
> *is an alphabet of squirrels*
> *at the disposition of forests.*
>     ("La clef de voûte," in *Je bâtis ma demeure*)

Like the desert and the city, the forest, in which the fearful signs swarm, doubtless articulates the non-place and the wandering, the absence of pre-scribed routes, the solitary arising of an unseen root, beyond the reach of the sun. Toward a hidden sky. But the forest, outside the rigidity of its lines, is also trees clasped by terrified letters, the wood wounded by poetic incision.

> *They engraved the fruit in the pain of the tree of solitude....*

> *Like the sailor who grafts a name*
> *On that of the mast*
> *In the sign you are alone.*

The tree of engraving and grafting no longer belongs to the garden; it is the tree of the forest or of the mast. The tree is to the mast what the desert is to the city. Like the Jew, like the poet, like man, like God, signs have a choice only between a natural or an institutionalized solitude. Then they are signs and the other becomes possible.

The animality of the letter certainly appears, at first, as *one* metaphor among others. (For example, in *Je bâtis ma demeure* the sex is a vowel, etc., or even *"Aided by an accomplice, a word sometimes changes its sex and its soul."* Or, further: *"Vowels, as they are written, resemble the mouths of fish out of water pierced by the hook; consonants resemble dispossessed scales. They live uncomfortably in their acts, in their hovels of ink. Infinity haunts them"* [p. 68]). But, above all, it is metaphor *itself,* the origin of language as metaphor in which Being and Nothing, the conditions of metaphor, the beyond-metaphor of metaphor, never say themselves. Metaphor, or the animality of the letter, is the primary and infinite equivocality of the signifier as Life. The *psychic* subversion of inert literality, that is to say, of nature, or of speech returned to nature. This overpowerfulness as the life of the signifier is produced within the anxiety and the wandering of the language always richer than knowledge, the language always capable of the movement which takes it further than peaceful and sedentary certitude.

> *How can I say what I know*
> *with words whose signification*
> *is multiple?*
>     (*Je bâtis ma demeure,* p. 41)

Betrayed by citation, the organized power of the song keeps itself beyond the reach of commentary, in the *Livre des questions*. Here in particular, is it not born of an extraordinary confluence that weighs upon the canceling lines of words, the punctual singularity of Edmond Jabès's experience, his voice, his style? A confluence in which is recalled, conjoined, and condensed the suffering, the millennial reflection of a people, the *"pain" "whose past and continuity coincide with those of writing,"* the destiny that summons the Jew, placing him between the voice and the cipher; and he weeps for the lost voice with tears as black as the trace of ink. *Je bâtis ma demeure* ("I build my dwelling") is a line borrowed from *La voix de l'encre* (1949) ("The voice of ink"). And *Le livre des questions:*

> *You gather that I attach great value to what is said, more, perhaps, than to what is written; for in what is written my voice is missing and I believe in it—I mean the creative voice, not the auxiliary voice which is a servant.*
> (*Livre des questions*, p. 88)

(In the work of Emmanuel Levinas can be found the same hesitation, the same anxious movement within the difference between the Socratic and the Hebraic, the poverty and the wealth of the letter, the pneumatic and the grammatical.)

Within original aphasia, when the voice of the god or the poet is missing, one must be satisfied with the vicars of speech that are the cry and writing. This is *Le livre des questions,* the poetic revolution of our century, the extraordinary reflection of man finally attempting today—and always in vain—to retake possession of his language (as if this were meaningful) by any means, through all routes, and to claim responsibility for it against a Father of Logos. One reads, for example, in *Le livre de l'absent* [a section of *Le Livre de questions*—eds.]: *"A decisive battle in which the vanquished, betrayed by their wounds, describe, as they fall to the ground, a page of writing dedicated by the victors to the chosen one who unwittingly set off the battle. In fact, it is in order to affirm the supremacy of the verb over man, of the verb over the verb, that the battle took place"* (*Livre de l'absent*, p. 69). Is this confluence *Le livre des questions?*

No. The song would no longer be sung if its tension was only confluential. Confluence must repeat the origin. This cry sings because in its enigma, it brings forth water from a cleft rock, the unique source, the unity of a spurting rupture. After which come "currents," "affluents," "influences." A poem always runs the risk of being meaningless, and would be nothing without this risk of being meaningless, and would be nothing without this risk. If Jabès's poem is to risk having a meaning, or if his *question,* at least, is to risk having a meaning, the source must be presumed; and it must be presumed that the unity of the source is not due to a chance encounter, but that beneath this encounter another encounter takes place today. A first encounter, an encounter above all unique because it was a separation, like the separation of Sarah and Yukel. Encounter *is* separation. Such a proposition, which contradicts "logic," breaks the unity of Being—which resides in the fragile link of the "is"—by welcoming the other and difference into the source of meaning. But, it will be said, Being must always already be conceptualized in order to say these things—the encounter and the separation of what and of whom—and especially in order to say that encounter *is* separation. Certainly, but "must always already" precisely signifies the original exile from the kingdom of Being, signifies exile as the conceptualization of Being, and signifies that Being never is, never shows *itself,* is never *present,* is never *now,* outside difference (in all the senses today required by this word). Whether he is Being or the master of beings, God himself is, and appears as what he is, within difference, that is to say, as difference and within dissimulation.

If, in the process of adding pitiful graffiti to an immense poem, as we are doing here, one insisted upon reducing the poem to its "thematic structure," as it is called, one would have to acknowledge that nothing within it is original. The well-worn themes of the question within God, of negativity within God as the liberation of historicity and human speech, of man's writing as the desire and question *of* God (and the double genitive is ontological before being grammatical, or rather is the embedding of the ontological and the grammatical within the *graphein*), of history and discourse as the anger of God emerging himself, etc., etc.—these themes are not first proper to Böhme, to German romanticism, to Hegel, to the final Scheler, etc., etc. Negativity in God, exile as writing, the life of the letter are all already in the Cabala. Which means "Tradition" itself. And Jabès is conscious of the Cabalistic resonances of his book. He even plays on them, occasionally.

But traditionality is not orthodoxy. Others, perhaps, will articulate the ways in which Jabès *also* severs himself from the Jewish community, assuming that this last notion here has a sense, or has its classical sense. He does not sever himself from it only insofar as concerns dogma, but more profoundly still. For Jabès, who acknowledges a very late discovery of a certain way of being part of Judaism, the Jew is but the suffering allegory: *"You are all Jews, even the antisemites, for you have all been designated for martyrdom"* (*Livre des questions,* p. 180). He must justify himself to his blood brothers and to rabbis who are no longer imaginary. They will all reproach him for this universalism, this essentialism, this skeletal allegorism, this neutralization of the event in the realms of the symbolic and the imaginary.

> *Addressing themselves to me, my blood brothers said: "You are not Jewish. You do not come to the synagogue."...* (*Livre des questions,* p. 63)

*The rabbis whose words you cite are charlatans. Have they ever existed? And you have nourished yourself on their impious words....*

*You are Jewish for the others and so little Jewish for us.*

*Addressing himself to me, the most contemplative of my blood brothers said: "To make no difference between a Jew and him who is not Jewish, is this not already to cease being a Jew?" And they added: "Brotherhood is to give, give, give, and you will never be able to give what you are." Striking my chest with my fist I thought: "I am nothing. I have a severed head. But is not a man worth a man? And a decapitated one worth a believer?"* (Ibid., p. 64)

Jabès is not a defendant in this dialogue, for he carries both it and the charges within him. In this noncoincidence of the self and the self, he is more and less Jewish than the Jew. But the Jew's identification with himself does not exist. The Jew is split, and split first of all between the two dimensions of the letter: allegory and literality. His history would be but one empirical history among others if he established or nationalized himself within difference and literality. He would have no history at all if he let himself be attenuated within the algebra of an abstract universalism.

Between the too warm flesh of the literal event and the cold skin of the concept runs meaning. This is how it enters into the book. Everything enters into, transpires in the book. This is why the book is never finite. It always remains suffering and vigilant.

—*A lamp is on my table and the house is in the book.*
—*I will finally live in the house.* (Ibid., p. 15)

*Where is the book found?*
—*In the book.* (Ibid.)

Every exit from the book is made within the book. Indeed, the end of writing keeps itself beyond writing: *"Writing that culminates in itself is only a manifestation of spite."* If writing is not a tearing of the self toward the other within a confession of infinite separation, if it is a delectation of itself, the pleasure of writing for its own sake, the satisfaction of the artist, then it destroys itself. It syncopates itself in the roundness of the egg and the plenitude of the Identical. It is true that to go toward the other is also to negate oneself, and meaning is alienated from itself in the transition of writing. Intention surpasses itself and disengages from itself in order to be said. *"I hate that which is pronounced in which already I am no longer"* (p. 17). Just as the end of writing passes beyond writing, its origin is not yet in the book. The writer, builder, and guardian of the book posts himself at the entrance to the house. The writer is a ferryman and his destination always has a liminal signification. *"Who are you?—The guardian of the house.—...Are you in the book?—My place is on the threshold"* (p. 15).

But—and this is the heart of the matter—everything that is exterior in relation to the book, everything that is negative as concerns the book, is produced *within the book*. The exit from the book, the other and the threshold, are all articulated *within the book*. The other and the threshold can only be written, can only affirm themselves in writing. One emerges from the book only within the book, because, for Jabès, the book is not in the world, but the world is in the book.

*"The world exists because the book exists." "The book is the work of the book." "The book multiplies the book"* (p. 33). To be is to-be-in-the-book even if Being is not the created nature often called the Book of God during the Middle Ages. *"If God is, it is because He is in the book"* (p. 32). Jabès knows that the book is possessed and threatened, that *"its response is still a question, that its dwelling is ceaselessly threatened"* (p. 32). But the book can only be threatened by nothing, non-Being, nonmeaning. If it came *to be,* the threat—as is the case here—would be avowed, pronounced, domesticated. It would be of the house and of the book.

All historic anxiety, all poetic anxiety, all Judaic anxiety thus torments this poem of the interminable question. All affirmations and all negations, all contradictory questions are welcomed into the question within the unity of the book, in a logic like none other, in Logic. Here we would have to say Grammar. But does not this anxiety and this war, this unloosening of all the waters, rest upon the peaceful and silent basis of a nonquestion? Is not the writing of the question, by its decision, by its resolution, the beginning of repose and response? The first violence as regards the question? The first crisis and the first forgetting, the necessary beginning of wandering as history, that is to say, the very dissimulation of wandering?

The nonquestion of which we are speaking is not yet a dogma; and the act of faith in the book can precede, as we know, belief in the Bible. And can also survive it. The nonquestion of which we are speaking is the unpenetrated certainty that Being is a Grammar; and that the world is in all its parts a cryptogram to be constituted or reconstituted through poetic inscription or deciphering; that the book is original, that everything *belongs to the book* before being and in order to come into the world; that any thing can be born only by *approaching* the book, can die only by failing *in sight of* the book; and that always the impassible shore of the book is *first*.

But what if the Book was only, in all senses of the word, an *epoch* of Being (an epoch coming to an end which would permit us to see Being in the glow of its agony or the relaxation of its grasp, and an end which would multiply, like a final illness, like the garrulous and tenacious hypermnesia of certain moribunds, books about the dead book)? If the form of the book was no longer to be the model of meaning? If Being was radically outside the book, outside its letter? And was such by virtue of a transcendence which could no longer be touched by inscription and signification, a transcendence which would no longer lie on the page, and which above all would have arisen before it? If Being lost itself in books? If books were the dissipation of Being? If the Being of the world, its presence and the meaning of its Being, revealed itself only in illegibility, in a radical illegibility which would not be the accomplice of a lost or sought after legibility, of a page not yet cut from some divine encyclopedia? If the world were not even, according to Jaspers's expression, "the manuscript of another," but primarily the other of every possible manuscript? And if it were always too soon to say *"revolt is a page crumpled in the waste basket"* (p. 177)? And always too soon to say that evil is only *indecipherable,* due to the effect of some *lapsus calami* or of God's cacography, and that *"our life, within Evil, has the form of an inverted letter, a letter excluded because it is illegible in the Book of Books"* (p. 85)? And if Death did not let *itself* be inscribed in the book in which, as is well known moreover, the God of the Jews every year inscribes only the names of those who may live? And if the dead soul were more or less, something other in any event, than the dead letter of the law which should always be capable of being reawakened? The dissimulation of an older or younger writing, from an age other than the age of the book, the age of grammar, the age of everything announced under the heading of the meaning of Being? The dissimulation of a still illegible writing?

The radical illegibility of which we are speaking is not irrationality, is not despair provoking non-sense, is not everything within the domains of the incomprehensible and the illogical that is anguishing. Such an interpretation—or determination—of the illegible already belongs to the book, is enveloped within the possibility of the volume. Original illegibility is not simply a moment interior to the book, to reason or to logos; nor is it any more their opposite, having no relationship of symmetry to them, being incommensurable with them. Prior to the book (in the nonchronological sense), original illegibility is therefore the very possibility of the book and, within it, of the ulterior and eventual opposition of "rationalism" and "irrationalism." The Being that is announced within the illegible is beyond these categories, beyond, as it writes itself, its own name.

It would be ludicrous to impugn Jabès for not having pronounced these questions in *Le livre des questions.* They can only sleep within the literary act which needs both their life and their lethargy. Writing would die of the pure vigilance of the question, as it would of the simple erasure of the question. Is not to write, once more, to confuse ontology and grammar? The grammar in which are inscribed all the dislocations of dead syntax, all the aggressions perpetrated by speech against language, every questioning of the letter itself? The written questions addressed to literature, all the tortures inflicted upon it, are always transfigured, drained, forgotten by literature, within literature; having become modifications of itself, by itself, in itself, they are mortifications, that is to say, as always, ruses of life. Life negates itself in literature only so that it may survive better. So that it may *be* better. It does not negate itself any more than it affirms itself: it differs from itself, defers itself, and writes itself as *différance*. Books are always books of *life* (the archetype would be the Book of Life kept by the God of the Jews) or of *afterlife* (the archetype would be the Books of the Dead kept by the Egyptians). When Maurice Blanchot writes: "Is man *capable* of a radical interrogation, that is to say, finally, is man *capable* of literature?" one could just as well say, on the basis of a certain conceptualization of life, "incapable" half the time. Except if one admits that pure literature is nonliterature, or death itself. The question about the origin of the book, the absolute interrogation, the interrogation of all possible interrogations, the "interrogation of God" will never belong to a book. Unless the question forgets itself within the articulations of its memory, the time of its interrogation, the time and tradition of its *sentence*, and unless the memory of itself, the syntax binding the question to itself, does not make a disguised affirmation of this origin. Already a book of the question becoming remote from its origin.

Henceforth, so that God may indeed be, as Jabès says, *an interrogation of God,* would we not have to transform a final affirmation into a question? Literature would then, perhaps, only be the dreamlike displacement of this question:

> "There is the book of God in which God questions himself, and there is the book of man which is proportionate to that of God."
> Reb Rida

—Translated from the French by Alan Bass.

## SOURCES

E. Jabès, *Je bâtis ma demeure: Poèmes 1943-1957.* Paris: Gallimard, 1959.

_____, *Le Livre des questions.* Paris: Gallimard, 1963.

## from *DESIRE FOR A BEGINNING*
## *DREAD OF ONE SINGLE END*
### Edmond Jabès

"...*a book—he said—that I'll never write because nobody can, it being a book:*

"—*against the book.*

"—*against thought.*

"—*against truth and against the word.*

"—*a book, then, that crumbles even while it forms.*

"—*against the book because the book has no content but itself, and it is nothing.*

"—*against thought because it is incapable of thinking its totality, let alone nothing.*

"—*against truth because truth is God, and God escapes thought; against truth, then, which for us remains legendary, an unknown quantity.*

"—*against the word, finally, because the word says only what little it can, and this little is nothing and only nothing could express it.*

"And yet I know:

"—*that the book is written against the book that tries to destroy it.*

"—*that thought thinks against the thought that covets its place.*

"—*that truth comes through the lived moment as the one moment to be lived.*

"—*that the word in vanishing reveals the very distress of man who vanishes with it.*"

—Translated from the French by Rosmarie Waldrop.

# THE OPENING OF THE FIELD

# BOOK

## Gertrude Stein

BOOK WAS THERE, it was there. Book was there. Stop it, stop it, it was a cleaner, a wet cleaner and it was not where it was wet, it was not high, it was directly placed back, not back again, back it was returned, it was needless, it put a bank, a bank when, a bank care.

Suppose a man a realistic expression of resolute reliability suggests pleasing itself white all white and no head does that mean soap. It does not so. It means kind wavers and little chance to beside beside rest. A plain.

Suppose ear rings, that is one way to breed, breed that. Oh chance to say, oh nice old pole. Next best and nearest a pillar. Chest not valuable, be papered.

Cover up cover up the two with a little piece of string and hope rose and green, green.

Please a plate, put a match to the seam and really then really then, really then it is a remark that joins many many lead games. It is a sister and sister and a flower and a flower and a dog and a colored sky a sky colored grey and nearly that nearly that let.

# from *THE MARRIAGE OF HEAVEN AND HELL*
## William Blake

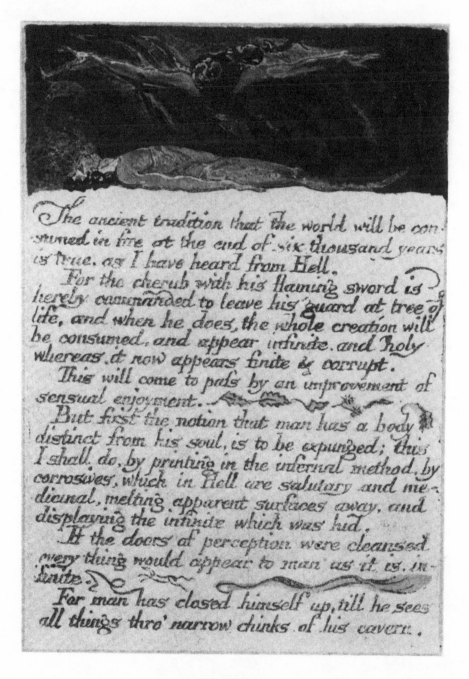

The ancient tradition that the world will be consumed in fire at the end of six thousand years is true. as I have heard from Hell.

For the cherub with his flaming sword is hereby commanded to leave his guard at tree of life, and when he does, the whole creation will be consumed. and appear infinite. and holy whereas it now appears finite & corrupt.

This will come to pass by an improvement of sensual enjoyment.

But first the notion that man has a body distinct from his soul, is to be expunged; this I shall do, by printing in the infernal method, by corrosives, which in Hell are salutary and medicinal, melting apparent surfaces away, and displaying the infinite which was hid.

If the doors of perception were cleansed every thing would appear to man as it is, infinite.

For man has closed himself up, till he sees all things thro' narrow chinks of his cavern.

*Marriage 14.*

[ 104 ]

A Memorable Fancy

I was in a Printing house in Hell & saw the method in which knowledge is transmitted from generation to generation.

In the first chamber was a Dragon-Man, clearing away the rubbish from a caves mouth; within, a number of Dragons were hollowing the cave.

In the second chamber was a Viper folding round the rock & the cave, and others adorning it with gold silver and precious stones.

In the third chamber was an Eagle with wings and feathers of air, he caused the inside of the cave to be infinite, around were numbers of Eagle like men, who built palaces in the immense cliffs.

In the fourth chamber were Lions of flaming fire raging around & melting the metals into living fluids.

In the fifth chamber were Unnam'd forms, which cast the metals into the expanse.

There they were reciev'd by Men who occupied the sixth chamber, and took the forms of books & were arranged in libraries.

*Marriage* 15.

## BLAKE'S PRINTING HOUSE

*When I came home, on the abyss of the five senses, where a flat*
*steep frowns over the present world, I saw a mighty Devil folded in*
*black clouds, hovering on the sides of the rock, with corroding fires*
*he wrote the following sentence now percieved by the minds of*
*men, & read by them on earth.*

   *How do you know but ev'ry Bird that cuts the airy way,*
   *Is an immense world of delight, clos'd by your senses five.*

In Blake's description in *Marriage* 15 of "A Printing house in Hell" the immediate subject of text and pictures is Illuminated Printing, allegorically described. Each metal plate, cut and burnt into by tool and fiery acid, is a "cave,"
each process that the cave goes through is a "chamber" in the printing house.
And the result of the process, the surface of paper printed and colored,
which we also call a plate, is a "cave" too. The reader-spectator enters it to
find the immense palaces which the poet-artist is building for his delight....
In the teamwork of eagle and viper, depicted at the bottom of Plate 15, the
serpent's tongue performs the function of lightning, but the eagle holds
him so high *in the air* that his words are cut on clouds, not rocks. The "cave"
that mediates between copper and cloud of vision represents "the minds of
men," that is, the "cavern" through which man "sees all things."

—David V. Erdman

# from "INTRODUCTION" TO
## *THE ILLUMINATED BLAKE*
### David V. Erdman

*If the Spectator could Enter into these Images in his Imagination approaching
them on the Fiery Chariot of his Contemplative Thought if he could Enter into
Noahs Rainbow or into his bosom or could make a Friend & Companion of one
of these Images of wonder which always intreats him to leave mortal things as
he must know then would he arise from his Grave then would he meet the Lord
in the Air & then he would be happy...it is in Particulars that Wisdom consists
& Happiness too.*                              —W. B., *A Vision of the Last Judgment*

THE FACT THAT WILLIAM BLAKE wrote, printed, illustrated, and published his own poems by "a method of Printing which combines the Painter
and the Poet"—with no assistance but that of his wife Catherine—guaran-
teed the direct communication of the author's original and final "invention"
and "illumination" to the fortunate reader and spectator of each original
copy of his "Illuminated Books." No other English poet has had the power to
invite his audience so fully into the particular shapes and colors of his images of wonder. Few original copies could be made, however, and although
most of these seem to have survived, Blake's readers are rarely able to be
spectators but have had to depend primarily on the reprinted words. Color
facsimiles of most of the illuminated canon had been made by the end of
the nineteenth century, some of them rather good but unreliable in details
and often misleading in color. Much more faithful facsimiles have been
made by the Trianon Press and distributed by the William Blake Trust during the past twenty years, and color slides have become familiar in many
classrooms. But it still requires visits to several libraries in several cities to
become directly acquainted with the variety of Blake's own illuminations
as uniquely created in each copy he produced.

To the question often raised, whether Blake considered his poems or
his designs the more important, the best answer is drawn from his comment to Dawson Turner (who wanted the pictures "without the Writing")
that printing the pictures alone meant "the Loss of some of the best things,"
that the pictures "when Printed perfect accompany Poetical Personifica-
tions & Acts, without which Poems they never could have been Executed"
(Blake to Turner, June 9 1818). And certainly the poems can stand alone,
while many of the pictures cannot. Yet the poet's work is not perfectly "done"
until that moment when the reader, travelling the line of text, becomes a
spectator, seeing at one pulse beat the "single visualizable picture" (these

words are Northrop Frye's) and then, between that and the next pulsation, leaving these mortal things, text and picture, to enter into Noah's rainbow, into "the eternal world that ever groweth" (these are the words of the Fairy who dictated *Europe*): "then he would be happy."

"Author and Printer" is the identification Blake gave himself in his first etched title page, and he refers back to it in the colophon of his last work in relief etching: "1822 W Blakes Original Stereotype was 1788" (*Ghost of Abel 2*), still calling attention to his particular method of reaching reader and spectator in one single or solid (stereo) impression (type). In his own advertisement of October 1793, itself an example of his illuminated printing (the original now lost, a common fate of advertising fliers), he describes his invention of "a method of Printing both Letter-press and Engraving in a style more ornamental, uniform, and grand, than any before discovered," as "a phenomenon worthy of public attention." It is Blake's own attention to it that is worthy of ours. If we respect it, both author and spectator may be "sure of...reward." For we shall discover not only that becoming equally familiar with the bride and the groom of Blake's marriage of painting and poetry will enable us to share in the perfect happiness promised by Blake's art, but also that the substance of the work itself, the dialectal components of its design, the polar terms of its reference whether in thematic structure (at the center) or in ornament (at the circumference) will lead again and again to the struggle and symbiosis, the mutual embracing and mutual annihilation, of Poetry and Painting, of linear song and spatial image. All these symbolic levels only exist and act in human forms, as everyone knows but may sometimes forget.

For any writer there is some incorporation of his means into his ends, some awareness, reflected in the surface of his language, of the processes of putting pen to paper or fingers to keyboard. But for Blake there was a constant invention and revision of his own equipment, a concern about paper and ink but also about the copper surfaces of his plates, the varnish or ground that must hold its delineations firm and adhere to the copper rock, while his corrosive fires (aqua fortis) etched valleys around the exposed cliffs; then concern about the ink and its impression upon the "most beautiful wove paper that could be procured"; and then, a subject of experiment all his life, the painting of the printed paper, with translucent and opaque water colors, or with thick pigments by "colour printing." Even at the center of his early master work that undertakes for its vast subject *The Marriage of Heaven and Hell,* the text of one plate is devoted to an account of a "Printing house in Hell," with an illustration consisting of an emblem of the collaboration of the serpent of temporal delineation with the eagle of spatial illustration. Only when this collaboration, joined in by the spectator, is attended to and perfected as Illumination, can the poet's mental images arise from the grave or cave of copper into the universal air above "Time's troubled fountains" of acid and ink and such mortal things.

In short, Blake's text frequently incorporates images of delineation and coloring while his illustrations frequently incorporate images of thinking and writing. As a poet he keeps a constant eye on his own shadow or spectre—at first a harpist or piper whose musical notes materialize as clusters of flying birds—or ripening grapes—promptly depicted by the painter, not dropping his quill but seizing an etching or engraving tool in his other hand. Later a blacksmith (Los) and architect (Urizen) whose furnaces and drawing board tend to throw each other out of focus: the "thought" of the architect with his geometer's circumscribing compasses turning the infinite options of "outline" into a serpent of stylized and countable coils that threaten to subside into a cypher. The resultant "wheel" may masquerade as useful, even as a means of obtaining bread, but is no more than a complicatedly redundant mill. To reach this extreme would be to reduce the poetic line to clichés and the illumination to journeymen's labor, at best meaningless except for an occasional witticism or spot of light. The opposite extreme, with Imagination taking the bit in its mouth and racing toward vision without the mercy of any timing, would send the sun plunging into the abyss, the nitric acid devouring every word and line on the surface until even Leviathan became formless and invisible.

To say that Blake was able, as author and printer, to keep all aspects of the production of his works under his own control is to reduce to an easy formula (the Urizenic triumph) the most difficult—and endless—struggle of his life, the effort to seize the symmetries that confronted him at every step, to create simultaneously and harmoniously in words, birds, lines, colors, a living city of Art that would resurrect us from our graves to meet the Savior in the air. Hands, tools, liquids, light, color were very real beings in Blake's furnace—and in Nebuchadnezzar's or Urizen's. As compared to the writer whose efforts shape thoughts and images into words to be set by journeyman printers, Blake felt the advantage and the responsibility of a process that allowed words to grow into vines and fruit and human forms, or into caves and forests and beasts of prey or comfort; into emblematic dramas or visions in human form, into sons and daughters shaking their bright fiery wings. In Plate 37 of *Jerusalem* we see the giant Albion bent over in melancholy, with a scroll across his lap which he is not reading, Blake's audience gone to sleep. But we see the Gulliver-sized William Blake sitting on the free coil of the scroll and busy with pen in hand inscribing a warning against melancholy for Albion when he does awake. It is written in mirror-writing because that is how Blake the printer must put the words on the plate to be legible when reversed by printing. Blake the artist has drawn a watery mirror in front of Albion up to the edge of the chalky cliff he sits on, where he will have to read the message. On the facing page, *Jerusalem 36*, which parenthetically refers to the poet's building "English, the rough basement," as the "stubborn structure of the Language" to act "against Albions melancholy, who must else have been a Dumb despair," Blake, having expelled his own despair, fills the illumination with a bouquet of color and life, prepared for Albion after his self baptism. A banquet, actually, an illumination of living vines by the unfurling of leaves and the lavishing of color. The eternal artist, Los, and his emanation, Enitharmon, residing for this occasion in their vehicular forms William and Catherine Blake, are joyously busy creating a gay tapestry of flourishing vines and ripening grapes for the Last Vintage and the annihilation of mortal melancholy. We are shown Blake's painting arm metamorphosed into three stems growing into grape vines and leaves, the longest dividing again into two stems, one spinning out a tendril of communication and another leaf, the other terminating in a scythe blade bravely flourished over the words "Eternal Death." His third "stem" arm branches downward as a paintbrush dripping with reds and blues. All the while his feet stride forward on the line (of text and delineation) which loops down the page, with several grape leaves and a large cluster of grapes, to divide into two ribbons terminating at the feet of Catherine Blake (serving as muse, inspiration, and colorist). Busy with both hands, she adjusts the color of the ripening grapes. Beside her is a double paintbrush hand wet with extra colors. The page exemplifies "our being fully employed" (see letter to Butts of July 6 1803).

Twelve pages further on—we are still only halfway through *Jerusalem*—after a page especially vibrant with birds of paradise and fertile leafage, there comes on Plate 49 a swift reversal. The voice uttering the poetry, the sad prophetic Erin, laments that now all the "Animals & vegetations…contained in the All Glorious Imagination are witherd & darkend." Albion, she says, has slid into such melancholy that his Emanation must be rescued and removed from "these terrible Surfaces." And we see that the text of this page is unadorned, stripped of all birds and leaves, of all interlinear ornament whatsoever, the poet-artist standing forlorn under a leafless tree looking up at its few shriveling colorless apples, his helpmate gone, his painting arm terminating in a scrawny twig with five skeletal fingers. (That he pictures it as the left arm does not mean literally that he painted with it.)

The most universal as well as the most personal themes of the poem are represented in these plates, and Blake is far from reducing his tale to the ups and downs of poetic and artistic endeavor. The very web and texture and color of his thinking derive and spin out and exfoliate from the daily acts of his labors on copper, from the minute particulars of the intimate, delicate, thread-thin and steel-strong interconnection of life and art. For the moment everything else is funneled through that vortex.

Much of the time, nevertheless, the printing house particulars are subordinated or transmuted nearly beyond recognition. The heroic bard exchanges harp and trump—not to mention graver and pencil—for the hammer and fire of the smithy. His adversary abstracts the tongs into compasses. The wheel of Hand becomes the enemy's printing house, though the wine-press remains Los's. When the successful work of turning night into day begins in earnest in *Jerusalem* 85 the picture of Los and Enitharmon extruding vines bearing grapes and blossoms refers primarily to the elemental extrusion and commingling of fibres of blood and milk and to the "Wine-presses of Love & Wrath" and rather incidentally and in passing to the illumination of the book itself.

If the present annotations should appear at times reductively attentive to the embracing of ink and paper when the more obvious and more fully human referents are soul and body, female and male, father and child, I can only protest that one gets easily into the habit of seeing all marrying contraries as contained each in the other and fourfold or twenty-seven fold in one. I would wish in each instance to attend to the fold of meaning that seems uppermost, yet to take notice of Blake's workshop symbolism whenever it visibly links illustrations and text. In notes as brief as these there is often not time even to hint at the other meanings.

# from "SO LONG!"
## Walt Whitman

CAMERADO, this is no book,
Who touches this touches a man,
(Is it night? are we here together alone?)
It is I you hold and who holds you,
I spring from the pages into your arms—decease calls me forth.

O how your fingers drowse me,
Your breath falls around me like dew, your pulse lulls the tympans of my
    ears,
I feel immerged from head to foot,
Delicious, enough.

Enough O deed impromptu and secret,
Enough O gliding present—enough O summ'd-up past.

Dear friend whoever you are take this kiss,
I give it especially to you, do not forget me,
I feel like one who has done work for the day to retire awhile,
I receive now again of my many translations, from my avatars ascending,
    while others doubtless await me,
An unknown sphere more real than I dream'd, more direct,
    darts awakening rays about me, So long!
Remember my words, I may again return,
I love you, I depart from materials,
I am as one disembodied, triumphant, dead.

# THESE FLAMES AND GENEROSITIES
## OF THE HEART
### EMILY DICKINSON AND THE ILLOGIC OF
### SUMPTUARY VALUES

## Susan Howe

*Spirit cannot be moved by Flesh—It must be moved by spirit—*
*It is strange that the most intangible is the heaviest—but Joy and Gravitation*
*have their own ways. My ways are not your ways—* —E.D.

AN IDEA OF THE AUTHOR Emily Dickinson—her symbolic value and aesthetic function—has been shaped by *The Poems of Emily Dickinson; Including variant readings critically compared with all known manuscripts,* edited by Thomas H. Johnson and first published by the Belknap Press of Harvard University in 1951, later digested into a one-volume edition, to which I do not refer because of Johnson's further acknowledged editorial emendations. For a long time I believed that this editor had given us the poems as they looked. Nearly forty years later, *The Manuscript Books of Emily Dickinson,* edited by R. W. Franklin and again published by the Belknap Press of Harvard University, Cambridge, Massachusetts, and London, in 1981, and *The Master Letters of Emily Dickinson,* also edited by R. W. Franklin, in 1986, this time published by the Amherst College Press, show me that in a system of restricted exchange, the subject-creator and her art in its potential gesture were domesticated and occluded by an assumptive privileged Imperative.

\* \* \*

*A Concrete Community of Exchange Among Peers*

1951: "1860: Alignment of words less regular, letters in a word sometimes diminishing in size toward the end, which gives an uneven effect to the page. *No important changes in form"* [my italics.] (PED liv).

1986: "Standard typesetting conventions have also been followed in regard to spacing and punctuation. No attempt has been made to indicate the amount of space between words, or between words and punctuation, or to indicate, for example, the length of a dash, its angle, spatial relation to adjoining words or distance from the line of inscription. Dashes of any length are represented by an en dash, spaced on each side. Periods, commas, question marks, ending quotation marks, and the like, have no space preceding them, however situated in the manuscripts. Stray marks have been ignored." (ML 10)

[ 113 ]

\* \* \*

*Fellows*

1958: Thomas H. Johnson: Introduction to *The Letters of Emily Dickinson*.

Since Emily Dickinson's full maturity as a dedicated artist occurred during the span of the Civil War, the most convulsive era of the nation's history, one of course turns to the letters of 1861–1865, and the years that follow, for her interpretation of events. But the fact is that she did not live in history and held no view of it past or current (L XX).

1986: Ralph W. Franklin: Introduction to *The Master Letters*.

Dickinson did not write letters as a fictional genre, and these were surely part of a much larger correspondence yet unknown to us. In the earliest one, written when both she and the Master were ill, she is responding to his initiative after a considerable silence. The tone, a little distant but respectful and gracious, claims few prerogatives from their experience, nothing more than the license to be concerned about his health.... The other two letters, written a few years later, stand in impassioned contrast to this.... In both she defends herself, reviewing their history, asserting her fidelity. She asks what he would do if she came "in white." She pleads to see him. (ML 5)
    A drop of ink mars the top of the third page [first letter], but it may have come after she had written an *awkward predication* [my italics] further down the same page:

> Each Sabbath on the
> sea, makes me count
> the Sabbaths, till we
>          will the
> meet on shore  —  and
> whether the hills will
> look as blue as the
> sailors say—

This would require obstrusive correction, and what was to have been a final draft became an intermediate one (ML 11).

1951: T. H. Johnson: Introduction to Emily Dickinson's *Collected Poems*, called "Creating the Poems: The Poet and the Muse."

It would thus Appear that when Emily Dickinson was about twenty years old her latent talents were invigorated by a gentle, grave young man [Benjamin Franklin Newton] who taught her how to observe the world.... Perhaps during the five years after Newton's death she was trying to fashion verses in a *desultory* manner. Her muse had left the land and she must await the coming of another. That event occurred in 1858 or 1859 in the person of the Reverend Charles Wadsworth.... A volcanic commotion is becoming apparent in the emotional life of Emily Dickinson.... Except to her sister Lavinia, who never saw Wadsworth, she talked to no one about him. That fact alone establishes the place he filled in the structure of her emotion. Whereas Newton as muse had awakened her to a sense of her talents, Wadsworth as muse made her a poet. The Philadelphia pastor, now forty-seven, was at the zenith of his mature influence, fifteen years married and the head of a family, an established man of God whose rectitude was unquestioned.... By 1870...[t]he crisis in Emily Dickinson's life was over. Though nothing again would wring from her the anguish and the fulfillment of the years 1861–1865, she continued to write *verses* throughout her life. [my italics] (PED xxi-iv)

1971: *Webster's Third New International Dictionary.*

VERSE: 3 a (1): metrical language: speech or writing distinguished from ordinary language by its distinctive patterning of sounds and esp. by its more pronounced or elaborate rhythm. (2): metrical writing that is distinguished from poetry esp. by its lower level of intensity and its lack of essential conviction and commitment. < many writers of ~ ~ who have not aimed at writing poetry—T. S. Eliot > (3): POETRY 2 < ~ ~ that gives immortal youth to mortal maids—W. S. Landor >
    4a (1): a unit of metrical writing larger than a single line: STANZA.

* * *

*Circles*

In 1985 I wrote a letter to Ralph Franklin, the busy director of the Beinecke Rare Book and Manuscript Library at Yale University, to suggest that *The Manuscript Books of Emily Dickinson* show that after the ninth fascicle (about 1860) she began to break her lines with a consistency that the Johnson edition seemed to have ignored. I was interested because Franklin [was then] editing the new *Poems of Emily Dickinson: Including variant readings critically compared with all known manuscripts* for Harvard University Press. I received a curt letter in response. He told me the notebooks were not artistic structures and were not intended for other readers; Dickinson had a long history of sending poems to people—individual poems—that were complete, he said. My suggestion about line breaks depended on an "assumption" that one reads in lines; he asked, "what happens if the form lurking in the mind is the *stanza*?" [my italics]

\* \* \*

(MBED 2:1020; S3)

Thomas H. Johnson's *The Poems of Emily Dickinson* did restore the poet's idiosyncratic spelling, punctuation (the famous dashes), and word variants to her poems. At the same time he created the impression that a definitive textual edition could exist. He called his Introduction "Creating the Poems," then gave their creator a male muse-minister. He arranged her "verses" into hymnlike stanzas with little variation in form and no variation of cadence. By choosing a sovereign system for her line endings—*his* preappointed Plan—he established the constraints of a strained positivity. Copious footnotes, numbers, comparisons, and chronologies mask his authorial role.

Here is a typographical transcription of Dickinson's manuscript version:

> Experience  is  the  Angled
> Road
> Preferred  against  the
> Mind
> By  ⁓ Paradox  ‒ The
> Mind  itself  ⌄
> Presuming  it  to  lead
>
> Quite  Opposite  ‒ How
> Complicate
> The  Discipline  of
> Man ‒
> Compelling  Him    to
> ·  Choose  Himself
> His  Pre appointed  Pain  ⁓

*The Manuscript Books of Emily Dickinson* complicate T. H. Johnson's criteria for poetic order.

These lines traced by pencil or in ink on paper were formed by an innovator.

33        x +      2w            15

Experience is the Angled
Road
Preferred against the
Mind
By - Paradox - The
Mind itself
Presuming it to lead

Quite Opposite - How
Complicate
The discipline of
Man -
Compelling Him to
Choose Himself
His Pre appointed Pain -

(MBED 2:1033; S5)

This visible handwritten sequence establishes an enunciative clearing outside intention while obeying intuition's agonistic necessity.

These lines move freely through a notion of series we may happen to cross—ambiguous articulated Place.

At the end of conformity on small sheets of stationery:

When Winds hold Forests in their Paws _
✝ The Firmaments ⌐ are still –
⊢ The Universe ⌐ is still ✝

(MBED 1:505; f22)

Deflagration of what was there to say. No message to decode or finally decide. The fascicles have a "halo of wilderness." By continually interweaving expectation and categories they checkmate inscription to become what a reader offers them.

Publication_is  the  Auction
Of  the  Mind  of  Man -
Poverty - be  justifying
For  so  foul  a  thing

Possibly - but  We - would
rather
From  Our  Garret  go
White -Unto  the  White Creator_
Than  invest - Our  Snow -

Thought  belong  to Him  who
gave  it  _
Then -- to  Him  Who  bear
Its  Corporeal  illustration - Sell
The  Royal  Air _

In  the  Parcel -  Be the Merchant
Of  the  Heavenly  Grace -
But reduce  no  Human  Spirit
To  Disgrace  of  Price -

(MBED 2: 915; f37)

Use value is a blasphemy. Form and content collapse the assumption of Project and Masterpiece. Free from limitations of genre Language finds true knowledge estranged in itself.

Distance . be  Her  only
⁺ Motion -
If  tis  Nay - or  Yes -
Acquiescence . or  Demurral -
Whosoever  guess -

⁺ He -must pass the Crystal Angle
That ⁺ obscure  Her  face --
He - must have  achieved  in
person
Equal  Paradise .

+ too + Swelling + fitter  for
the feet + Ever  could  endow -
+ claim + Signal +- first +- limit
+ divide -

(MBED 2:818; f34)

\* \* \*

1991: *An editor's query.* "You need to give the reader some thoughts about making use of the words at the end of the 'poem proper' (in this case, I think, beginning with 'too swelling fitter for'). Are we to attach these words as alternatives to certain words in the 'poem'?; *i.e., where does 'too' go? What am I to do with it?"*

This is a good question: Thomas Johnson reads these words as alternatives.

1840: Noah Webster: *An American Dictionary of the English Language.*\*

TOO, *adv.* [Sax, *to.*]

1. Over: more than enough; noting excess; as, a thing is *too* long, *too* short, or *too* wide; *too* high; *too* many; *too* much.

His will *too* strong to bend, *too* proud to learn.    *Cowley.*

2. Likewise; also; in addition.

A courtier and a patriot *too*                    Pope
Let those eyes that view
The daring crime, behold the vengeance *too.* Pope

3. *Too, too.* repeated, denotes excess emphatically; but this repetition is not in respectable use.

[The original application of *to,* now *too,* seems to have been to a word signifying a great quantity; as, speaking or giving *to* much; that is, *to* a great amount. *To* was thus used by old authors.] (WD 1159–60)

\* \* \*

*Rearrangement*

Much critical and editorial attention has been given to Dickinson's use of capitalization and the dash in her poems and letters; while motivating factors for words and phrases she often added to a "poem proper," sometimes in the margins, sometimes between lines, but most often at the end, have aroused less interest. Since the Johnson edition was published in 1951, it has been a given of Dickinson scholarship that these words represent nothing more than suggested alternates for specific words in the text the poet had frequently marked with a cross.

Ralph Franklin says that after 1861 these possibilities for alternate readings are a part of the structure of the poems she transcribed and bound

---

\*Emily Dickinson owned an 1844 reprint of Webster's 1840 edition. The family owned the 1828 two-volume first edition. Webster, a friend of the Dickinson family, was a resident of Amherst, helped to found Amherst College with Samuel Fowler Dickinson, and served on the board of the Amherst Academy with Edward Dickinson.

together, and his edition of *The Manuscript Books* shows this to have been the case.

After 1861, Dickinson's practice of variation and fragmentation also included line breaks. Unlike Franklin, I believe there is a reason for them.

This space is the poem's space. Letters are sounds we see. Sounds leap to the eye. Word lists, crosses, blanks, and ruptured stanzas are points of contact and displacement. Line breaks and visual contrapuntal stresses represent an athematic compositional intention.

This space is the poet's space. Its demand is her method.

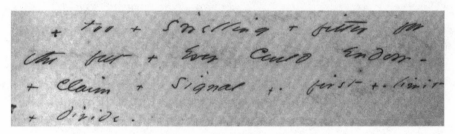

(MBED 2:818; f34)

One of Thomas Johnson's contributions to transmission of the handwritten manuscripts into print was to place these words, sometimes short phrases, at the end of a poem, as Dickinson had done. But he couldn't leave it at that. This textual scholar-editor, probably with the best intentions, matched word to counterword, numbered lines as *he* had reduplicated them, then exchanged his line numbers for her crosses.

|  |  |
|---|---|
| 3.  True] too | 17.  ask] claim |
| 6.  Loaded] Swelling | 21.  Motion] Signal |
| 13.  Fitter feet—of Her] fitter for the feet 25.  Angle] limit | 25.  He] first |
| 16.  Ever could endow— | 26.  obscure] divide— |

(PED 649)

Emily Dickinson's writing is a premeditated immersion in immediacy.

Codes are confounded and converted. "Authoritative readings" confuse her nonconformity.

In 1991 these manuscripts still represent a Reformation.

\* \* \*

*Swelling*

NOAH WEBSTER:

SWELL. v.t. To increase the size, bulk, or dimensions of; to cause to rise, dilate, or increase. Rains and dissolving snow *swell* the rivers in spring, and cause floods. Jordan is *swelled* by the snows of Mount Libanus (WD 1118).

* * *

*A covenant of works*

"The flood of her talent is rising" (L 332).

The production of meaning will be brought under the control of social authority.

For T. H. Johnson, R. W. Franklin, and their publishing institution, the Belknap Press of Harvard University, the conventions of print require humilities of caution.

Obedience to tradition. Dress up dissonance. Customary usage.

Provoking visual fragmentation will be banished from the body of the "poem proper."

Numbers and word matches will valorize these sensuous visual catastrophes.

Lines will be brought into line without any indication of their actual position.

An editor edits for mistakes. Subdivided in conformity with propriety.

A discreet biographical explanation: unrequited love for a popular minister will consecrate the gesture of this unconverted antinomian who refused to pass her work through proof.

Later the minister will turn into a man called "Master."

R.W. FRANKLIN: Although there is no evidence the [Master] letters were ever posted (none of the surviving documents would have been in suitable condition), they indicate a long relationship, geographically apart, in which correspondence would have been the primary means of communication (ML 5).

Poems will be called letters and letters will be called Poems.

"The tone, a little distant but respectful and gracious, claims few prerogatives." (ML 5)

"...*the Hens*

*lay finely...*" (Epigraph to L, part I, vol. I)

Now she is her sex for certain for editors picking and choosing for a general reader reading.

NOMINALIST and REALIST

"Into [print] will I grind thee, my bride" (E2 241).

Franklin's facsimile edition of *The Manuscript Books of Emily Dickinson* shows some poems with so many lists of words or variants that even Johnson, who was nothing if not methodical, couldn't find numbers for such polyphonic visual complexity.

What if the author went to great care to fit these words onto pages she could have copied over? Left in place, seemingly scattered and random, these words form their own compositional relation.

R.W. EMERSON: I am very much struck in literature by the appearance that one person wrote all the books; as if the editor of a journal planted his body of reporters in different parts of the field of action, and relieved some by others from time to time; but there is such equality and identity both of judgment and point of view in the narrative that it is plainly the work of one all-seeing, all-hearing gentleman. I looked into Pope's Odyssey yesterday: it is as correct and elegant after our canon of to-day as if it were newly written (E2 232).

*Antinomy.* A conflict of authority. A contradiction between conclusions that seem equally logical reasonable correct sealed natural necessary

1637: Thomas Dudley at *Mrs. Ann Hutchinson's examination by the General Court at Newton:*
"What is the scripture she brings?" (AC 338)

An improper poem. Not in respectable use. Another way of reading. Troubled subject-matter is like troubled water.

* * *

*Fire may be raked up in the ashes, though not seen.*

Words are only frames. No comfortable conclusion. Letters are scrawls, turnabouts, astonishments, strokes, cuts, masks.
These poems are representations. These manuscripts should be understood as visual productions.
The physical act of copying is a mysterious sensuous expression.
Wrapped in the mirror of the word.
Most often these poems were copied onto sheets of stationery previously folded by the manufacturer. The author paid attention to the smallest physical details of the page. Embossed seals in the corner of recto and verso leaves of paper are part of the fictitious real.
Spaces between letters, dashes, apostrophes, commas, crosses, form networks of signs and discontinuities.
"Train up a Heart in the way it should go and as quick as it can twill depart from it" (L pf115).
Mystery is the content. Intractable expression. Deaf to rules of composition.
What is writing but continuing.
Who knows what needs she has?

The greatest trial is trust.
Fire in the heart overcomes fire without

(MBED 1:134; f8)

basket of flowers
C.V. Mills, capitol and, CONGRESS
capitol in oval
CONGRESS above capitol
flower in oval
G&T in eight-sided device
G&T in oval
LEE MASS.
PARSONS PAPER CO
queen's head above L (laid)
queen's head above L (wove)
WM above double-headed eagle
(MBED 2:1411)

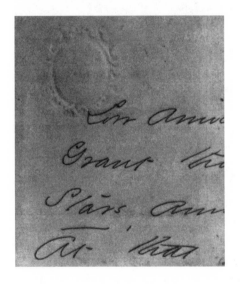

(MBED 1:135; f8)

\* \* \*

Franklin's notes to set 7 tell us: "On her inventory of the manuscripts obtained from her mother [Mabel Loomis Todd], MTB [Millicent Todd Bingham] recorded a small slip laid inside sheet A 86-³⁄₄ bearing only the word 'Augustly!' The paper is wove, cream, and blue-ruled." (MBED 2: 1387)

* * *

*Disjunct Leaves*

 Emily Dickinson almost never titled a poem.

 She titled poems several times.

 She drew an ink slash at the end of a poem.

 Sometimes she didn't.

 She seldom used numbers to show where a word or a poem should go.

 She sometimes used numbers to show where a word or a line should go.

 The poems in packets and sets can be read as linked series.

 The original order of the packets was broken by her friends and first editors so that even R. W. Franklin—the one scholar, apart from the Curator of Manuscripts, allowed unlimited access to the originals at Harvard University's Houghton Library—can be absolutely sure only of a particular series order for poems on a single folded sheet of stationery.

 Maybe the poems in a packet were copied down in random order, and the size of letter paper dictated a series; maybe not.

 When she sent her first group of poems to T.W. Higginson, she sent them separately but together.

 She chose separate poems from the packets to send to friends.

 Sometimes letters are poems with a salutation and signature.

 Sometimes poems are letters with a salutation and signature.

 If limits disappear where will we find bearings?

 What were her intentions for these crosses and word lists?

 If we could perfectly restore each packet to its original order, her original impulse would be impossible to decipher. The manuscript books and sets preserve their insubordination. They can be read as events, signals in a pattern, relays, inventions or singular hymnlike stanzas.

 T.W. Higginson wrote in his "Preface" to *Poems by Emily Dickinson* (1890): "The verses of Emily Dickinson belong emphatically to what Emerson long since called 'The Poetry of the Portfolio,'—something produced absolutely without the thought of publication, and solely by way of the writer's own mind.... They are here published as they were written, with very few and superficial changes; although it is fair to say the titles have been assigned, almost invariably, by the editors" (P iii—v).

 But the poet's manuscript books and sets had already been torn open. Their contents had been sifted, translated, titled, then regrouped under categories called, by her two first editor-"friends": "Life," "Love," "Nature," "Time and Eternity."

* * *

*White lines on a white stone*

On September 12, 1840, Ralph Waldo Emerson wrote to Elizabeth Hoar: "My chapter on 'Circles' begins to prosper, and when it is October I shall write like a Latin Father" (E1 433*n*).

"The one thing which we seek with insatiable desire is to forget ourselves, to be surprised out of our propriety, to lose our sempiternal memory and to do something without knowing how or why; in short to draw a new circle. Nothing great was ever achieved without enthusiasm. The way of life is wonderful; it is by abandonment" (E1 321).

* * *

*Overflow*

1891: Twenty years after the event, T.W. Higginson, with Mabel Loomis Todd, the first editor of Emily Dickinson's poetry, recalled one of his two meetings with the poet.

> The impression undoubtedly made on me was that of an excess of tension, and of an abnormal life. Perhaps in time I could have got beyond that somewhat overstrained relation which not my will, but her needs had forced upon us. Certainly I should have been most glad to bring it down to the level of simple truth and every-day comradeship; but it was not altogether easy (L 342b*n*).

TOO. *adv.* [Sax. *to.*]
    Over; more than enough; noting excess; as, a thing is *too* long, *too* short, *too* wide, *too* high, *too* many, *too* much (WD 1159).

* * *

*Coming to Grips with the World*

In 1986, Ralph Franklin sent me a copy of *The Master Letters of Emily Dickinson,* published by the Amherst College Press. Along with *The Manuscript Books,* this is the most important contribution to Dickinson scholarship I know of. In this edition, Franklin decided on a correct order for the letters, showed facsimiles, and had them set in type on each facing page, with the line breaks as she made them. I wrote him a letter again suggesting that if he broke the lines here according to the original text, he might consider doing the same for the poems. He thanked me for my "immodest" compliments and said he had broken the letters line-for-physical-line only to make reference to the facsimiles easier; if he were editing a book of the letters, he would use run-on treatment, as there is no expected genre form for prose. He told me there is such a form for poetry, and he intended to follow it, rather than accidents of physical line breaks on paper.

* * *

As a poet, I cannot assert that Dickinson composed in stanzas and was careless about line breaks. In the precinct of Poetry, a word, the space around a word, each letter, every mark, silence, or sound volatizes an inner law of form—moves on a rigorous line.

(MBED 2:815; f34)

I wonder at Ralph Franklin's conclusion that these facsimiles are not to be considered as artistic structures.

How can this meticulous editor, whose acute attention to his subject matter has yet to be deciphered in the neutralized reading even her fervent admirers give her, now repress the physical immediacy of these spiritual improvisations he has brought to light?

A  Man    may   ʼmake
a   Remark -
In   itself ⸝a  ʼquiet  thing
That   may   furnish  ⤬  the
Fuse   unto    a    Spark
In   dormant   nature - lain ⸍

Let  us  ⁺divide ⸝with
skill ⸍
Let  us  ⁺discourse ⸍with
care ⸍
Powder   exists  in ⁺Charcoal ⸌
Before   it ⁺exists    in
Fire ⸍

⁺˙drop  ⁺ tranquil   ⁺ ignition
⸝ deport   ⸝ disclose
⸝ Elements   ⸍ sulphurets
⸝ express

(MBED 2:1047; S5)

Simple reflection should cast light on the inauthentic nostalgia of *A Portrait of the Artist as a Woman,* isolated from historical consciousness, killing time for no reason but arbitrary convenience, as she composes, transcribes, and arranges into notebooks or sets over a thousand visionary works.

During her lifetime this writer refused to collaborate with the institutions of publishing. When she created herself author, editor, and publisher, she situated her production in a field of free transgressive prediscovery.

It is over a hundred years after her death; if I am writing a book and I quote from one of her letters or poems and use either the Johnson or Franklin edition of her texts, I must obtain permission from and pay a fee to

The President and Fellows of Harvard College
and the Trustees of Amherst College.

"is this the Hope that opens and shuts, like the eye of the Wax Doll?
Your Scholar—" (L 553)

"This is the World that opens and shuts, like the Eye of the Wax Doll—"
(L 554)

\* \* \*

(MBED 2:1047; s5)

Poetry is never a personal possession. The poem was a vision and gesture before it became sign and coded exchange in a political economy of value. At the moment these manuscripts are accepted into the property of our culture their philosopher-author escapes the ritual of framing—symmetrical order and arrangement. Are all these works poems? Are they fragments, meditations, aphorisms, events, letters? After the first nine fascicles, lines break off interrupting meter. Righthand margins perish into edges sometimes tipped by crosses and calligraphic slashes.

This World  is not  Conclusion -
A *Species  stands  beyond
Invisible , as   Music
But  positive, as  Sound -
It   beckons , and it baffles -
Philosophy  / dont   know
And  through  a Riddle, at the last
Sagacity  / must  go -
To *guess it , puzzles   scholars -
To  gain  it  Men  have  borne
Contempt  of  Generations
And  Crucifixion, shown -
Faith  slips ,and  laughs, and  rallies
Blushes, if  any  see
Plucks  at a twig of  Evidence
And  asks  a  Vane, the  way -
Much   Gesture  from  the
Pulpit -
Strong *Hallelujahs   roll -
Narcotics  cannot  still  the
Tooth
That   nibbles  at  the  soul -

* A sequel -   * prove it
* Sure     + Mouse _ .

(MBED 1: 396–97; f18)

Define the bounds of naked Expression. *Use.*

All scandalous breakings out are thoughts at first. Resequenced. Shifted. Excluded. Lost.

"She reverted to pinning slips to sheets to maintain the proper association" (MBED p1413).

Oneness and scattering.

Marginal notes. Irretrievable indirection—

Uncertainty extends to the heart of replication. Meaning is scattered at the limit of concentration. The other of meaning is indecipherable variation.

In his preface to *The Poems of Emily Dickinson,* called "Creating the Poems," T.H. Johnson referred to her "fear of publication," as many others have done since. He called her poems "effusions." During the 1860s, "[h]er creative energies were at flood, and she was being overwhelmed by forces which she could not control" (PED xviii).

"Over; more than enough; noting excess; as, a thing is *too* long, *too* short, *too* high, *too* many, *too* much" (WD II59).

(MBED 2:797; f 33)

Wayward Puritan. Charged with enthusiasm. Enthusiasm is antinomian.

## KEY

AC      *The Antinomian Controversy*: David Hall, ed.

E1      *Essays by Ralph Waldo Emerson* (First Series).

E2      *Essays by Ralph Waldo Emerson* (Second Series).

L       *The Letters of Emily Dickinson*: Johnson and Ward, eds. (pf, prose fragment)

MBED    *The Manuscript Books of Emily Dickinson*: R.W. Franklin, ed.
        (f, fascicle; s, set)

ML      *The Master Letters of Emily Dickinson*: R.W. Franklin, ed.

P       *Poems by Emily Dickinson*: Todd and Higginson, eds.

PED     *The Poems of Emily Dickinson*: Thomas H. Johnson, ed.

WD      *An American Dictionary of the English Language*: Noah Webster.

## SOURCES

Emily Dickinson. *The Letters of Emily Dickinson.* 3 vols. Edited by Thomas H. Johnson and Theodora Ward. Cambridge, Mass.: The Belknap Press, Harvard University Press, 1958.

_____. *The Manuscript Books of Emily Dickinson.* 2 vols. Edited by R.W. Franklin. Cambridge, Mass.: The Belknap Press, Harvard University Press, 1981.

_____. *The Master Letters of Emily Dickinson.* Edited by R.W. Franklin. Amherst, Mass.: Amherst College Press, 1986.

_____. *Poems by Emily Dickinson.* Edited by Mabel Loomis Todd and T.W. Higginson. Boston: Roberts Brothers, 1891.

_____. *The Poems of Emily Dickinson.* 3 vols. Edited by Thomas H. Johnson. Cambridge, Mass.: The Belknap Press of Harvard University Press, 1951.

Emerson, Ralph Waldo. *Essays by Ralph Waldo Emerson.* First Series. Boston and New York: Riverside Press, Houghton Mifflin, 1865.

——. *Essays by Ralph Waldo Emerson.* Second Series. Boston and New York: Riverside Press, Houghton Mifflin, 1876.

Hall, David D., ed. *The Antinomian Controversy, 1636–1638: A Documentary History.* Middletown, Conn.: Wesleyan University Press, 1968.

Webster, Noah. *An American Dictionary of the English Language.* Revised and enlarged by Chauncey A. Goodrich. Springfield, Mass.: George and Charles Merriam, 1852.

——. *Webster's Third New International Dictionary of the English Language Unabridged.* Edited by Philip Babcock Gove, Ph.D., and the Merriam Webster editorial staff. Springfield, Mass.: G. & C. Merriam Company, 1971.

## NOTES

My title is the seven last words of Emerson's essay called "Circles."

"'A man,' said Oliver Cromwell, 'never rises so high as when he knows not whither he is going.' Dreams and drunkenness, the use of opium and alcohol are the semblance and the counterfeit of this oracular genius, and hence their dangerous attraction for men. For the like reason they ask the aid of wild passions, as in gaming and war, to ape in some manner these flames and generosities of the heart" (E1 322).

I have tried to match the poems in type, as nearly as possible, to the Franklin edition of *The Manuscript Books.* In translating Dickinson's handwriting into type I have *not* followed standard typesetting conventions. I *have* paid attention to space between handwritten words. I *have* broken the lines exactly as she broke them. I *have* tried to match the spacing between words in the lists at the end of poems. I have not been able to pay attention to spaces between letters. I think that in the later poetry such spacing is a part of the meaning. Dickinson's frequent use of the dash was noted in the Johnson edition, but he regularized these marks. I know that in some books printed during the nineteenth century, variant readings were sometimes supplied at the end of a page, and they were marked by a sort of cross. *The History of New England from 1630 to 1649,* by John Winthrop, edited by James Savage, and published in Boston in 1826, is a good example of such practice; however, if there were more than two words, a number was used for the second one, and in other books the number of crosses increased for each word. Emily Dickinson had enough humor to read these variants as found poems. She was her own publisher and could do as she liked with her texts. These were the days of Edward Lear and Lewis Carroll; liberties were taken in print.

The bottom of a page of the Savage edition of Winthrop's *History* looked like this:

> some other place, which they both consented to, but still the
> difficulty remained; for those three, who pretended themselves
>
> ||conferred||     ||²step||     ||³we||     ||⁴taking||     ||⁵her||
>
> 39        VOL. 1.

> Reason 2. All punishments ought to be just, and, offences varying so
> much in their merit by occasion of circumstances, it would be unjust to
> inflict the same punishment upon the least as upon the greatest.
>
> || theft||     ||²presumptuous||

These manuscript books and sets represent the poet's "letter to the world." The discovery of these packets and sets galvanized her sister Lavinia into action. If Dickinson sent some of the poems in letters to friends, she also left these packets in a certain order. It is doubtful, to say the least, whether her various correspondents would have bothered to collect and then publish her poem-letters.

I have followed Johnson's choices for capitals, although I feel I could argue with his choices at times. I have been allowed access only to the originals of two manuscript books, and as a result I wouldn't dare to. In a review of *The Poems of Emily Dickinson,* published in the Boston *Public Library Quarterly,* July 1956, the poet Jack Spicer suggested such marks might have been meant as signs "of stress and tempo stronger than a comma and weaker than a period." The new critical edition must reconsider such questions. In the early fascicles, Dickinson frequently uses exclamation marks. Around fascicles 6–12, as she begins to break her lines in a new way and to regularly insert variant words into the structure of her work, nervous and repetitive exclamation marks change to the more abstract and sweeping dash. Sometimes the way she crosses her *t*'s (and this no printed version could match) seems to influence the length of the direction of the dash. The crosses she added to her texts when she included variant word possibilities should also be translated into print. The most frequent argument in favor of Johnson's changing the line breaks is the assumption that Dickinson (thrifty Yankee spinster) broke her lines at the righthand margin because of the size of the paper she was using. In other words, she ran out of space and wanted to save paper. Close examination of the Franklin Manuscript Edition shows that she could have put words onto a line had she wished to; in some cases she did crowd words onto a line. As she went on working, Dickinson increased the space between words and eventually the space between letters. If you follow Johnson's edition, you get the idea that there was no change in form from the first poem in fascicle 1 to the last poems in the sets.

In the long run, the best way to read Dickinson is to read the facsimiles, because her calligraphy influences her meaning. However, Franklin's edition is far too expensive for most people, and then there is the added difficulty of reading handwriting. I think her poems need to be transcribed into type, although increasingly I wonder if this is possible. If the cost of *The Manuscript Books* is prohibitive, what would an edition of the *Collected Letters* cost? Can the later letters and poems be separated into different categories? I am a poet, not a textual scholar. In 1956, Spicer wrote: "The reason for the difficulty of drawing a line between the poetry and prose of Emily Dickinson is that she did not wish such a line to be drawn. If large portions of her correspondence are considered not as mere letters—and indeed, they seldom communicate information, or have much to do with the person to whom they were written—but as experiments in a heightened prose combined with poetry, a new approach to her letters opens up." He based his opinion on careful examination of the letters and poems owned by the Boston Public Library.

For its time the Johnson edition was a necessary contribution to any Dickinson scholarship. It radically changed the reading of her poetry. I can't imagine my life as a poet without it. But as Emerson wrote in "Circles," "The universe is fluid and volatile. Permanence is but a word of degrees.... Our culture is the predominance of an idea which draws after it this train of cities and institutions. Let us rise into another idea; they will disappear." A lot has changed in poetry and in academia since 1951. The crucial advance for Dickinson textual scholarship was Ralph Franklin's facsimile edition of *The Manuscript Books*. Now the essentialist practice of traditional Dickinson textual scholarship needs to acknowledge the way these texts continually open inside meaning to be rethought. In a Dickinson poem or letter there is always something other.

# FROM MALLARMÉ'S *LE LIVRE*

Richard Sieburth

OF THE VARIOUS major items contained in Mallarmé's posthumous bibliography—*Igitur,* published by his son-in-law Edmond Bonniot in 1925, *Les Noces d'Hérodiade: Mystère,* published by Gardener Davies in 1959, and *Pour un tombeau d'Anatole,* published by Jean-Pierre Richard in 1961, the most enigmatic is no doubt *Le Livre,* a sheaf of 202 jumbled loose leaves piously passed on by Bonniot to Henri Mondor and then on to Jacques Scherer, who first published them as a volume in 1957 and, in a slightly revised edition, again in 1977. Bertrand Marchal has provided a new reading of these materials in his 1998 Pléiade edition of Mallarmé's *Oeuvres complètes:* this is the version I follow. The actual manuscript of Mallarmé's *Le Livre* is housed in Harvard's Houghton Library, the Bibliothèque Nationale having apparently decided that a book this ideal, this virtual, this ghostly could hardly be considered a non-exportable treasure of 'le patrimoine national.'

It was thus at Houghton that, as a young graduate student, I had the privilege of perusing Mallarmé's manuscript—a rather arduous process, given that his 'monceau demi-séculaire de notes,' many of which consisted of sheets with no more than a minuscule scatter of words on them, had been distributed into gunmetal-grey archival acid-free folders, only four of which at a time one was permitted to call up and consult: 'la lecture, cette pratique désesperé,' especially when undertaken under the watchful and hostile eyes of rare book room librarians. After several sessions of intermittent and intimidated scanning, I had worked my way through these *feuilles volantes* folder by folder, having understood virtually nothing, yet exhilarated to have experienced Mallarmé at his most evanescent and most immediate. What above all intrigued me, I suppose, was simply the material feel of Mallarmé in manuscript: page after page of abstruse mental doodles, fragmentary seismographs of a mind sketching out a project for the ideal Book, the Book to end all books (and thus to end all reading?), not the layered lacquerwork or diamantine faceting of his published poetry, but the dreamy and unruly gestures and 'jets' of an oeuvre registering its own gestation, a kind of 'action writing' whose random jottings, scrawlings, scribblings, graphings, diagrammings, and erasures reminded me of Jackson Pollock's drip paintings or Cy Twombly's works on blackboard or paper. It's unclear whether Mallarmé ever shared these private graffiti with his disciple Valéry (although we do know he went over the manuscript and the proofs of *Un Coup de dés* with him), but perhaps only the latter's *Cahiers* (or some of Hölderlin's late manuscripts or Emily Dickinson's poems on paper bags, insides of envelopes, or discarded bills) give a similarly urgent sense of what Mallarmé called 'les subdivisions prismatiques de l'Idée,' that scene of the mind in play, in action on the *support* of the page, 'cet emploi à nu de la pensée avec retraits, prolongements, fuites,' in short, a score, 'une partition,' for some eventual reader's—or translator's—unperformable interpretation.

[The following pages are from *Le Livre.*]

---

is it in exchange for fact that half
is blank (black of writing — situ-
ated only underneath — 1/2)                              that


· · ·  ╱       I display double subject
       ╱
      ╱  · · ·   furnished by this writing.


the two leaflets within the 1/2 leaf there
to bring about echo of rhyme of two lines
        — and the other half-leaf —
                                half or
                                            leaf

            stanza and sheet


    gilding
on 3 half leaves
at once
        with other book                  nothing is proved save to
immediately divine                                others
grants right to possess    and to prove by reading

there are 8 pages
— 2 leaves —

Only the leaf counts
imparts unity.
The leaf and the line
The volume and the play

the page:
the sign —                     ——
    this book        1/2 leaf
has abstracted        the leaf
itself from             1/4 of
        = 2 half leaves

                           which can be tripled
    and a double          in either case

gesture triage
page   ~~song~~        in full leaf          3 1/2 lvs.          3 1/2 lvs.
    hymn        or 4 quarters                        +
                    or 6 1/4 lvs.        or 6 1/ 4 lvs.

and start over 4 times
96  x  4 = 384

~~and triple it once~~        ~~384 x 3 = 1152~~
                           the inverse
                     then ~~the con-~~
                        ~~trary~~

and the whole thing 5 times = 384 x 10
                    5   +   5

The seats — The cabinet

curtain

enters, through the space left empty by the seats

The reader ~~arrives greets to the right, with a glimpse~~

to the right and left, and goes directly

~~of the eyes, observes six seats, the same as double~~

somewhat bowed

~~finds him~~    goes to    ~~leaves~~ to the lacquer — cabinet —

~~thus divided~~                half full evidently

arranged diagonally.

thus

| | | | |

‾‾‾‾

‾‾‾‾

‾‾‾‾

‾‾‾‾

| | | | |

each of these 6 pigeon-holes in a diagonal,

containing 5 leaves (number easily seized by

the eye) — [the upper leaves upright and

He knows, at this point, and

a turn made toward what has become

the lower ones upside down?]    ~~He takes~~ a

his right

turned from where he has come ~~from, on toward the left~~

takes his    place under ~~the single electric light, after~~ having

first leaf from ~~the first pigeon hole~~ of the five ~~of the first~~

taken a

pigeon-hole, above  —  ~~then turned toward the right~~

and below, holding these

six leaves

~~his right and an equal leaf, below that he holds in~~
 by half
in each of his hands, for the time ~~it takes to~~
~~confront~~ to join them, upside down righted like
but    ⌊ if the others ⌋
like the first one—as if confronting
according
the total format.


He has at this point ~~the~~ a number
of leaflets equal to half of the seats
in the audience, i.e. 6, and just as these seats
~~can~~  are double, even if reserved for a single
ticket-holder, so the leaves doubled into
two leaflets.         (each leaflet
one face of which inside.
comprises 8 pages — so that 3 leaflets = 24 pages]
~~He gathers 3 leaves~~    ~~He changes the 3 leaves~~
, ~~displaying this:~~
~~leaf by leaf~~ the inner leaflet of one to
the other leaf that is the first ~~in two~~
two, the second two and the third

momentarily set aside, he *reads.*

     unless, turning three times toward
the left (smile — bear with me) towards those to whom
this successive act best appears  — somewhat veiled for the right
     he take up the leaves in succession.


~~Nonetheless~~        until such moment
when, having gathered them all together again,
the Operator steps forth from where he is, carrying
        identifying himself with it
(towards the voice that read) this fascicule as
        for each and everybody.
his . (~~identifying himself with its~~,

     The whole thing has lasted three quarters of an hour — a
quarter hour intermission (tinkling of bell
        as when waiting for it to begin
anew, lamplight)    and

               total 2 hours

reentrance this time of the Operator    ~~in order to~~
bearing the volume thus composed —
~~evidently to redistribute it, i.e.~~
                              ~~into the pigeon holes, as~~
i.e.                                                ~~block~~
an inverse operation
undertaken ~~a part of the~~ in reference to the
second portion of the audience. He will
hence read it and redistribute it in
the pigeon-holes but in inverse order      ~~like a~~

|||||
       —
     —
   —
|||||

                                        where it seems

——Such  the double session.
having demonstrated the identity of this volume with
       itself        and the
~~himself:~~   session involving 24 people —
each at a given moment having

represented one of the leaflets  — or the
12 seats the twelve leaves      (leaflets that
cannot be separated from the leaves except
to interpolate them by an exchange and that's all)

⌐purity elec. light-
                    —the volume, despite the im-
pression of fixity, becomes, via this game, mobile — dead, it takes on life  ⌐

So that that everything that is there,
of a piece, proceed. 5 readings needed, i.e. 96 x
5 = 480 x 2 = 960 pages (with 480)

double price.
establish the price
and the 100 f

—

A second series of readings can be given in
inverse order  ╱  then  ╲

price of ticket

from 20 f

to 1 f   =   20 copies @ 1 f.

6 seats                                        120 copies   10
   20 f x 6 = 120 f                                doz

                                      x 5
                                  ——

                                600            50 doz

                     x2            =        100 doz
                                        or 1200 f.

---

5
——
5

= 5 x

*— Translated from the French by Richard Sieburth.*

# THE BOOK TO COME
## Maurice Blanchot

### 1  Ecce Liber

'LE LIVRE'—WHAT DOES Mallarmé mean by this word? From 1866 on he always thinks and says the same thing. Yet the same is not equal to the same. It is essential to understand how such duplication constitutes the process which gradually opens the way. All that he has to say seems fixed from the start yet what he continues to say is only roughly similar.

What are the similarities? The book which, from the start, is undoubtedly the Book, the epitome of literature, is also quite simply a book. This one and only book is in various volumes—five in 1866; a great many in 1885.[1] This multiplicity is unexpected from a perfectionist who, by 1885, can have had no doubts as to his natural distaste for prolixity. In his early maturity he seems to have required a multifaceted book, its facets turned, on the one hand, towards what he calls the Void, and on the other towards Beauty (as he was to say later, music and literature 'are alternative facets—now turned towards darkness, now scintillating with certainty'). Thus it is clear that the multiplicity of singleness corresponds to a need to grade creative space into different levels, and if he was already at the time referring to The Book as to a finished work, it is only because he had given so much thought to its layout that it pre-existed the content in his mind.[2]

For another constant feature is that what he first perceives is the inevitable structure of the book, his concept of this work as architectural and deliberate, not as a collection of chance though marvellous impressions. This definition dates from 1885, but already in 1868 he describes it as so carefully planned and graded (or 'perfectly defined') that the author can alter nothing, neither an impression, an idea or an intellectual mood. Whence the remarkable consequence that, if henceforth he tries to write anything which is not part of the Book it will be no more than a non-poem. This significantly forecasts the future, for his concern to isolate the Book—which will never be more than self-isolation—seems to have made him write nothing but non-poems, that is, give poetic force and reality only to what exists beyond reality (and beyond the Book which is this reality) and, in so doing, discover the Book's basic core.

What do terms such as 'deliberate, architectural, defined, graded' signify? They all imply a purposeful computation, and the deployment of exceptional powers of concentration capable of organising all the elements of the work infallibly. At first this was a natural preoccupation: to write according to the strictest rules of composition. Later it came to reflect a more complex need: to write with a rigorous concentration that reflects intellectual control and ensures its full development. But there is a further purpose which corresponds to the word 'chance' as well as to the decision to abolish chance. Basically it is still the old yearning for a controlled, controlling structure. In 1866 he wrote to Coppée: 'Chance cannot broach a line of poetry, that is what counts'; but he adds:

> We have, some of us, achieved it, and I think, having so perfectly defined the outline, what we must aim at in particular is that, in the poem the words—already sufficiently themselves to resist foreign influences—should mirror each other until they appear to lose their individual hues and become no more than the transitions in a scale. *(Correspondance,* I, 246)

Many of these theories will be developed in his later writings. For instance the decision to abolish chance together with the decision to abolish material objects and to deny them the right to be poetically expressed. Poetry does not respond to the appeal of material objects. Its function is not to preserve them by naming them. On the contrary, poetry is 'the wonder of transposing a fact of nature in its quivering near-disappearance.' Chance will be held at bay by the book when language, taken to the limit of possibility and opposing the concrete substantiality of individual objects, reveals nothing but the system of correspondence active in all things. Poetry is then like music reduced to its silent essence: a progression and unfolding of pure correspondence: pure mobility.

This straining against chance represents Mallarmé's effort to realise, through poetic skill and structural expertise, the converting potential of language. And it represents too the mystical or philosophical experience depicted with enigmatic exuberance but only partial success in the story of *Igitur.*

The point I wish to make is simply that Mallarmé's attitude to chance has a dual aspect: on the one hand it can be seen in his effort to create an essential work whereby he tends towards a poetry of abstraction and negation involving nothing remotely anecdotal whether it be real or fictional; and on the other hand, we know that he derives a direct and eminently significant experience from these negative powers he seems to exploit in language, where they are equally active, for the sole purpose of achieving through the elimination of spontaneity the most precise expression—an experience which might be seen as immediate were not immediacy precisely what is 'immediately' refuted by this experience. In 1907 he wrote to Lefébure:

> My work is the result of *elimination,* and any truth I achieved emerged from the loss of an impression which, having flared, burnt itself out and enabled me, thanks to the regained dark, to experience Absolute Dark. Destruction has been my Beatrice. (Ibid., I, 245–6)

The book which is the Book is a book like other books. It is manifold, self-multiplying by a specific process, and in it diversity infallibly occurs according to the different levels of the space it occupies. The necessary book abolishes chance. It avoids chance by structure and by definition and thus realises the basic function of language, which is to use objects by turning them into abstractions and submitting these abstractions to the rhythmic becoming which is the pure process of correspondences. The hazardless book is authorless: impersonal. This theory—crucial for Mallarmé—likewise involves two different spheres. On the one hand it concerns technique and linguistics (and could be seen as the link between Mallarmé and Valéry); on the other it corresponds to the experience which his 1867 letters describe. The one cannot be taken without the other but their relationship has never been clarified.

It would require a detailed analysis to determine the various levels Mallarmé's theory involves. Sometimes he is simply saying that the book must be anonymous—the author will not sign it ('granted, the work bears no signature'). The poet has no direct relation to, and still less ownership of, the poem. He cannot lay claim to what he has written. And what he has written remains anonymous, even under his name.

Why this anonymity? The answer may be contained in Mallarmé's notion that the book pre-exists its realisation, is innate to mankind and written in nature: he believes all this to be written in nature so clearly that only those intent on not seeing can fail to see it; the work exists, everyone has attempted it unconsciously; there is not a genius or a buffoon who has not discovered some aspect of it unawares. This opinion was given in reply to an enquiry and thus may represent only what he thought was accessible to 'outsiders'; yet he does not express himself very differently with Verlaine. On another occasion he declares that the order of the poems in a book is innate or universal, abolishes chance; and so it must be, to omit the author. But here the meaning is slightly different. Mallarmé's involvement with occultism had begun. Occultism seemed to offer a solution to the problems of literary creativity. This solution consisted in isolating art from some of its functions and attempting to realise these independently by turning them into forces that could be used for practical ends. A solution Mallarmé finally rejects—although his favourable opinions are widely quoted, the reservations which were always attached are omitted:

> No, you are not content, like them (the Cabbalists) to detach from art, through carelessness and misunderstanding, those functions which are integral and basic to it and, without justification, to realise them independently—which, at least, is a clumsy form of veneration. You eliminate even its original sacred significance.[3]

For Mallarmé there is no other magic than literature which is only achieved when it faces up to itself in a manner that excludes magic. He specifies that, even though the only two venues open to intellectual enquiry are aesthetics and political economy, alchemy was, largely, the 'glorious, premature and disturbing' precursor of the latter. The term 'premature' is significant. Impatience is what characterises magic, whose mastery over nature has to be instantaneous. Poetry on the contrary asserts itself with infinite patience. Alchemy tries to create and make. Poetry de-creates. It opens the way to what is not and can never be. For poetry, man's highest aim is something that cannot be expressed in terms of power (it should be noted that this is in total conflict with Valéry).

Mallarmé, whose involvement with occultism was purely social, was aware of certain superficial affinities. He borrowed some of its terminology as well as a certain tonality and its wistfulness. The book written in nature is not unlike the hermetic, sacred book that shines fragmentarily here and there, which an ancient tradition has transmitted through the ages and preserved for the initiate. The German Romantics also believed in a single, absolute book. Novalis says that the folly to which all sane men aspire in order to be whole is to write a Bible. According to him the Bible is the ideal to which every book tends. And Schlegel talks of an infinite book, absolutely book and the absolute book, while Novalis further considers using the poetic form of the fairy-tale for his projected sequel to the Bible. But this is very far from Mallarmé who criticised Wagner in the following terms:

> If a Frenchman with his imaginative, abstract and therefore poetic mind were to create a stir it could never be in the same way: because he is inventive and has an integrity peculiar to Art that will have no truck with Legend. (*Oeuvres Complètes,* p. 544)

Doubtless at a certain level Mallarmé does sound rather like the occultists, the German Romantics and *Naturphilosophie,* when he is prepared to see the book as a written textual equivalent of universal nature:

> Chimera, but to have thought of it is proof…that all books, more or less, contain the fusion of a few valuable repetitions: rather there is but one—to the world its law—a Bible such as all nations counterfeit. (Ibid., p. 367)

This is clearly one of his ideals, just as he dreams of a language that would be 'reality materialised.'

But at another level the notion of the authorless book has a very different significance and one which, to my mind, is far more important. 'The pure work implies the disappearance of the poet as speaker, who hands over to the words, set in motion by the shock of their unevenness' (*The Poems,* p. 45). This 'disappearance of the poet as speaker' is reminiscent of the famous passage about 'the wonder of transposing a fact of nature.' The poet disappears under the weight of the poem by the very process that causes material reality to disappear. Or, more precisely, it is not enough to say that reality disintegrates and the poet withdraws, for it should be added that one and the other, while experiencing the suspension of true annihilation, assert themselves in this very disappearance and through the process itself —the one vibratory, the other elocutive. Nature is transposed by language into the rhythmic process which causes its incessant, infinite disappearance. And the poet, in so far as he speaks the language of poetry, vanishes into this language, becomes the disappearance achieved by such language which alone is originating and original: the origin. 'Poetry, ritual.' The 'omission of self,' the 'anonymous death' of the poetic ritual, turns poetry into a true self-immolation, not for the purpose of questionable magical transports, but for almost technical reasons: since he who speaks the language of poetry is exposed to the kind of dying which true speech inevitably involves.

The book is authorless because its writing requires the author's disappearance. It needs an author only in so far as he is absence and the place of absence. A book is a Book when it does not reflect someone who might have made it and when it is as unsullied by his name and as detached from his existence as it is from the reader's. Can a casual, private individual who has no relation to the book as author play a significant part in it as reader? 'Depersonalised in so far as the author separates himself from it, the book claims nothing from the reader. As such of all human accessories it is the only one that occurs independently: made, being.'

This is one of Mallarmé's most superb statements. It epitomises with total assurance the true nature of the book: its independence, its emergence from itself as from a place, its dual assertion—juxtaposed and divided by a logical and temporal hiatus—of what *makes* it be and of the *being* whereby it is independent and indifferent to the *making*;—the simultaneity, in fact, of its instantaneous presence and of the growth of its realisation: as soon as it is made ceasing to have been made and asserting only this, that it is.

Nothing could be further from the Book of Romantic and esoteric tradition, the substantial book existing through the eternal truth of which it is the hidden yet accessible revelation—a revelation which enables those who understand to possess divine knowledge and existence. Mallarmé rejects the notion of substance as well as that of final, concrete truth. When he mentions truth—sometimes implying dream or ideal—he is always referring to something which is based only on the acknowledged, overt unreality of fiction. Whence for him the major problem is whether something like literature exists, in what way does literature exist, and how does literature correspond to existence? It is a fact that Mallarmé denies any reality to the present: 'there is no present, no—the present does not exist.' 'Ill-informed is he who claims to be his own contemporary.' And he refuses on the same grounds to admit the existence of a regular historical progression—all is interruption and rupture, everything breaks off, and transfusions are the exception. His writings are either frozen in a blank static virtuality or, more significantly, they are endowed with a remarkable temporal discontinuity and subjected to changes of rhythm and fragmentary interruptions deriving from a totally unprecedented sort of mobility, as foreign to eternal permanence as it is to quotidian duration, now anticipating, now recalling, in the future, in the past, or assuming a false appearance of present.

One way or the other the time expressed by the book, contained in it and inherent to it, is a presentless time. Likewise the book must never be seen as actually there. We cannot hold it. And yet if there is indeed no present, if the present is inevitably unreal and somehow false and fictitious, then it will be the ideal time for the unreal book; not the time it expresses —which is always the past or the future, a leap over the void of the present—but that in which it asserts itself with its own specific obviousness; when, as its own unreality coincides with the unreality of the present, it makes the one exist through the other in a lightning flash that blazes from the dark of which it is a blinding condensation. Mallarmé negates the present. But he preserves it for the book where it becomes a presentless assertion in which all that is flares and vanishes simultaneously—the instant at which they flare and fade is an instant blossom on some ethereal transparency. The book's obviousness, its palpable presence, is thus such that we have to say that it exists and is present, since without it nothing could ever be present, and yet that it never quite conforms to the conditions of real existence—it is, while being impossible.

According to Scherer the posthumous manuscript[4] clearly proves that, despite the doubts expressed by his detractors, the book was not a myth and that Mallarmé had given considerable thought to its realisation. Nearly all Mallarmé's theoretical writings refer almost obsessively to his projected Book in such detail that this unwritten work has acquired reality and existence for us. Those who are not interested in this kind of evidence and who continue to see Mallarmé as someone who, for thirty years, misled the public with his wonderful descriptions of an illusory Book and with cryptic allusions to insignificant scraps of paper, will not be convinced. On the contrary they will see in these notes, where practical and financial matters relating to the publication of a non-existing book are considered in great detail, the symptoms of a familiar, easily diagnosed pathological condition.

Besides, if the book existed, I would like to know how Scherer would set about proclaiming *Ecce Liber* and forcing us to acknowledge it, when its intrinsic nature makes its very acknowledgement unreal and when, furthermore, there exists an insoluble contradiction between its visible presence and its ever problematic reality.

Yet the practical, almost Balzacian world of financial backings, publication and sales into which the manuscript projects the book shows the extent to which Mallarmé was concerned with the possibilities of an historical impact that might determine the course of literature. It is gradually becoming obvious that Mallarmé was not constantly cloistered in his apartments in the rue de Rome. He was concerned with history. He was concerned with the relation between the influence on society of political economy and that of art ('restricted influence'). He came to the conclusion that, since for the artist, his 'age' is always a 'passage,' an interval or betweenwhiles, he should not rely on circumstances that can never be more than partially favourable, in order to achieve the perfect art an integral work requires, but should swim against the tide and stress the conflict, the temporal split, in order that it may be exposed. A work of art must express the conflict between the 'times' and the creative process, for this is part of the process, is the process.

Mallarmé was no less concerned with the major crisis literature was undergoing at the time. Thus he should not be seen as a Symbolist poet any more than Hölderlin can be associated with the Romantics. The symbolist venture has nothing whatever to do with his precise account (in *Music and Letters*) of the crisis he had experienced thirty years earlier and which he rightly diagnosed as the historical crisis of a whole generation:

> In upheavals, very much to the credit of the present generation, writing tried to find its own roots. Right in the forefront, at least as to its aim, is what I define as: to decide whether there is any point in writing. (Ibid., p. 645)

And again:

> Does something like literature exist...? Few have confronted this disturbing problem as I do, late in life, seized with a sudden doubt concerning the things I would like to speak about impulsively. (Ibid., p. 645)

To which 'sensational ultimatum' his answer was Yes, literature does exist, possibly alone, to the exclusion of all else.

The project and the realisation of the Book are obviously related to this ultimatum. Literature cannot be conceived in its basic integrity without the experience which excludes all normal conditions of choice. It was such for Mallarmé who only conceived the Book when, having experienced the disturbing symptoms the mere act of writing provoked, he none the less continued to write because writing had ceased to be a matter of choice. 'Storm, purification.' But the storm, in the course of which all literary conventions are washed overboard and which compels the writer to find his own depths at the confluence of two vacuums, leads to a further upheaval. Mallarmé confronted it with utter amazement: 'I have indeed news to impart...Such things were never seen. We landed at poetry' (ibid., p. 643). Governments may change but poetry remains intact. In his eyes an experience of this kind cannot fail to leave its mark on history. History is redirected by the total transformation of literature which can only occur through a radical self-questioning, a self-exploration 'to the roots.' A transformation that starts from a reassessment of prosodic traditions.

This was a painful blow to Mallarmé for rather ambiguous reasons. He had always asserted with unusual consistency that when there is rhythm there is poetry, and that the one thing that matters is to discover and master the true rhythm of life. He felt that only the scansion of great poetic rhythms could contain reality in language. Yet at the same time he refers to this now abandoned prosody as to an interruption in poetry, a gap as if the absence of traditional rhyme caused the disruption of poetics as such. All of which portends the violent upheaval the overthrow of 'guardian' rhyme represented for him. Yet his last work was to have been a 'poem.' A true poem, not a prose poem, but one that for the first and only time would depart from tradition—not only consenting to this departure but purposefully inaugurating a new art, an art to come and the future as art. This was a crucial decision and a decisive undertaking.

### 2 A new concept of literary space

If we accept—perhaps prematurely—that Mallarmé never ceased to acknowledge that traditional verse was capable of overcoming chance 'word for word,' we shall see that in *Un Coup de dés* there exists an intimate correspondence between the conviction with which the main sentence asserts that chance is invincible, and the rejection of traditional verse which is the chanciest form possible. The words 'A throw of the dice will never do away with chance' simply reproduce the significance of the new form whose nature they express. But in so doing, and since there exists an exact correlation between the poem's structure and what it states, necessity is re-established. Chance is not released by this break with traditional verse— on the contrary, being precisely expressed it is subjected to the precise rule of the form that governs it and to which it has to submit. Chance is thus, if not overcome, at least drawn into the stricture of language and set in the precise pattern of an enclosing form. Whence a kind of inconsistency that once again reduces the pressure of necessity.

This is clearly outlined in *Un Coup de dés*, a poem which is neither a present nor even a future reality but, in its doubly negative aspect of unrealised past and impossible future, is set in the furthest reaches of an exceptional 'perhaps.' If we rely on those certainties which alone determine the reality of things, the poem cannot take place. *Un Coup de dés* whose unquestionable presence our hands, our eyes and our attention acknowledge, is not only unreal and uncertain but can only exist if the convention which accepts chance as a law is ignored in some sphere of existence where what is necessary and what is fortuitous are both overcome by the violence of disaster. Thus it is a book which is not there, which is present only in so far as it coincides with what is forever beyond. *Un Coup de dés* only exists in so far as it expresses the extreme and exquisite impossibility of itself, of that Constellation which, by means of an exceptional 'perhaps,' and with no other justification than the void above and the disintegrating depth, is projected 'on some void and higher surface': the birth of a still unknown space, the space of the poem.

*Un Coup de dés* is thus not unlike the Book. For only the Book can be seen as the promise and expectancy of the work it is, without other content than the presence of its infinitely problematic future, forever existing before it can exist and never ceasing to be separated and divided to become finally its own division and separation. 'Watching doubting wheeling shining and pondering.' These five words which present the poem in the specific invisibility of its becoming require some consideration. They are totally devoid of magical connotation and, in the infinite tension which seems to create a different time, a pure time of expectancy and attention, they appeal to the intellect alone to tend the flame of poetic experience.

Obviously I do not wish to infer that *Un Coup de dés* is the Book. The Book's requirements would make such an assertion meaningless. But, far more than the notes Mr. Scherer has revived, it gives the book substance and reality, shows the same reticence and ever hidden presence, peril and purpose and the same measure of measureless defiance. The Book's intrinsic nature is also its own: present in a lightning flash that divides and unites it, it is also so problematic that even today when the unfamiliar has become (or seems to have become) wholly familiar, it continues to be the most improbable of books. It could be said that Mallarmé's work has been more or less successfully assimilated, except for *Un Coup de dés*. For this is a very different book from any we are accustomed to: it suggests that what according to Western tradition we call a poem—where the continuous linear to-ing and fro-ing of the eyes is associated with the process of comprehending—is justified only by the ease of analytic comprehension. In fact we have to admit that our books are as inadequate as they can be and that we read now, after so many centuries, as if we had just started to learn to read.

*Un Coup de dés* opens up a new dimension for literature in a combined effort of dispersal and concentration through the discovery of more complex structures. The mind, says Mallarmé (after Hegel), is 'volatile dispersal.'

A book that gives access to the mind will thus give access to an immensely destructive force, a boundless anxiety it cannot contain, that eliminates all content, all limited, defined and complete significance. It is a process of dispersal which must not be repressed but, on the contrary, preserved and garnered as such into the space it projects and to which this process responds —response to an infinitely multiplied void in which the dispersal acquires the form and appearance of unity. Such a book, always in motion, always on the verge of dispersal, will also always unite from all directions through this dispersal and according to its necessary division, which it does not abolish but produces and maintains so that it may be realised in it.

*Un Coup de dés* is the outcome of a new concept of literary space as a space where a new rhythmic order would give rise to a new system of correspondences. Mallarmé had always been aware of the fact—unrecognised before and perhaps after him—that language is a system of highly complex spatial relations whose singularity neither ordinary geometrical space nor the space of everyday life allows us to appreciate. Nothing is created and no discourse can be creative except through the preliminary exploration of the totally vacant region where language, before it is a set of given words, is a silent process of correspondences, or a rhythmic scansion of life. Words exist only to signify the area of correspondence, the space onto which they are projected and which, no sooner signified, furls and unfurls, never being where it is.[5] Poetic space, the space and 'outcome' of language, never exists like an object but is always spaced out and scattered. Whence Mallarmé's interest in anything that has to do with the singular essence of place—such as theatre or dance—and his constant awareness of the fact that all human thoughts and emotions necessarily tend to create their own environment; that every one of our sensations emerges from us to create an environment or else, in us, merges and contains it. Thus poetic emotion is not an inner emotion, a subjective impression, but is a foreign 'outside' into which we are hurled inside ourselves out of ourselves. Therefore he has this to say about dance:

> Whence this slackening around a bareness, great with contrasting flights wherein the latter organises it, stormy, hovering, and magnifies it till it dissolves: focal. (Ibid., p. 309)

The new language Mallarmé is said to have invented for the sole purpose of being incomprehensible—and to which Mr. Scherer has consecrated a reliable study—is a strict language whose purpose is to construct, according to new methods, the specific space of language which, in everyday conversation as well as in literary prose, we tend to reduce to a simple surface traversed in a uniform, irreversible movement. Mallarmé restores depth to this space. A sentence is not simply projected linearly. It opens out. In this opening other sentence and word rhythms emerge, space themselves out and regroup at varying depths—words and sentences which are interrelated by definite structural affinities though not according to common logic (the logic of subordination) which destroys the space and standardises the movement. Mallarmé is the one writer who can be said to be deep—not metaphorically and because he says deep things, but because what he says presupposes a multi-dimensional space and can only be understood at various levels. (Indeed what do we really mean when we say such and such a thing is profound? Depth of meaning consists in a stepping back, in a distancing the meaning requires of us.)

*Un Coup de dés* is the tangible manifestation of this new space. It is the space made poem. The fiction it involves seems to have no further aim than to achieve—through the experience of a shipwreck whence emerge and perish ever more subtly elusive figures and more distant spaces—the disintegration of all real space, the 'identical neutrality of the pit' whereby, at the limit of dispersal only the place remains—nothingness as the place where nothing takes place. Is this the eternal void *Igitur* tried to achieve? A pure and final vacancy? No. This is an indistinct stirring of absence, 'some lower lapping' 'those regions of the wave wherein all reality dissolves' while the disintegration never disintegrates the process of disintegration— a becoming ceaselessly becoming in the depths of the place.

However it is the place, the gaping depth of the pit, which, being reversed to the height of exception, creates that other pit of vacant skies where it becomes a constellation—an infinite dispersal uniting in a distinct plurality of stars; a poem whose words are nothing but the space of words and whose space glows with pure stellar light.

It is obvious that Mallarmé's choice of cosmic terms to express his poetic theory is not a mere acknowledgement of Poe (*Eureka, The Power of Speech*); creative space, which is creative in so far as it is infinitely vacant with an infinitely changing vacancy, required such terms. The dialogue of *Toast in Memory* suggests the way Mallarmé thought man should be defined: he is a being of horizons, the demand for the distances created by language and which his very death extends, the space with which he merges as soon as he speaks:

> The void to what was this Man, done away:
> 'Memories of skylines, what is Earth, O creature?'
> Howls this dream: and, a voice parched of all feature,
> Space trifles with the cry: 'I do not know!'

Half-way between Pascal's terror of the eternal silence of space and Joubert's delight in the void-strewn firmament, Mallarmé's man undergoes a new experience: space as the way to *another* space which is creative source and the discovery of the poetic process. Although the poet is acquainted with anguish and aware of the impossible, of the void peculiar to the time of distress which is his time, the time of suspense and interregnum, it would be misguided to set, as one tends to do, the mask of stoicism on Mallarmé's features and to see him only as the champion of lucid despair. If he must be encapsulated in some vague philosophical formula, pessimism is surely not the most appropriate; for his poetry always opts for joy and ecstatic assertion whenever the choice presents itself. The famous words of *Music and Letters* express such joy; they declare that the civilised Edenite, who has carefully preserved the holiness of the letters of the alphabet as well as the significance of their correspondences, possesses above all other riches the ingredients of felicity: a doctrine as well as a domicile. The word domicile recalls the word sojourn. Poetry, says Mallarmé, answering rather tersely one of his correspondents, 'thus endows our sojourn with authenticity' (*Oeuvres Complètes*, p. 646).[6] We only sojourn authentically when poetry takes place and gives place. This is very like Hölderlin's assertion that man sojourns 'poetically' (though it should be noted that this statement is to be found in a late text whose authenticity is doubtful), as well as his remark that whatever sojourns was established by the poets. Perhaps the significance I give to these words does not conform precisely to Heidegger's interpretation. Because, according to Mallarmé what poets establish—space: void and basis of language—is what does not remain, and man's authentic sojourn is not the shelter where he seeks protection, but corresponds to the reef, the shipwreck and whirlpool, and to that 'memorable crisis' which alone gives access to the moving void, the place where creative activity begins.

When Mallarmé says that the 'Orphic' explanation of the world, the explanation of man, is the poet's mission and the Book's purpose, what does he mean by the word explanation? Exactly what it stands for: the unfurling of the world and of man in the poem's space. Not the knowledge of what one and the other naturally are, but their development from their given reality to their mysterious, unrevealed essence through the dispersing power of space and the uniting power of rhythmic becoming. Because poetry exists not only is something changed in the universe but an essential change somehow occurs in the universe whose significance the Book's existence merely reveals and establishes. Poetry always starts *something different*. Compared to reality it is unreal ('this land did not exist'); compared to the time of the world it is interregnum or eternity; and compared to the powers that affect nature it is a restricted power. But such expressions can do no more than reduce the understanding of that *something different* to theoretical definitions.

Here a digression is necessary. In the three works, *Toast Funèbre*, the sonnet *Quand l'ombre menaça* and *Un Coup de dés*, written in the course of twenty-five years, the correspondence between poetic and cosmic space is maintained. These poems differ in many ways, of which one is immediately obvious. In the sonnet nothing is more certain than the poetic experience blazing in the sky like a festive star, supremely significant and real, the sun of suns around which the bright fires of the lesser stars circle to set off its brilliance. 'Yes...I know.' But in *Un Coup de dés* every certainty has vanished. The poem's Constellation—distant as it is improbable, out of sight in the summits of exception, never present but only suspended for ever in the future where it might take place—is forgotten before it exists instead of being extolled. Should we infer that Mallarmé, overcome by doubt, has almost ceased to believe in poetic creativity and in its stellar counterpart? Should we assume that he confronted death in a state of poetic disbelief? Indeed, it would not be unreasonable to do so. Yet reason can be very misleading when it tries to legislate over *something different* (which it turns into a supernatural world or a different, spiritual reality). *Un Coup de dés* on the contrary asserts more decisively than the sonnet, and in a manner which involves us in a more radical future, the specific determination of creative language. And Mallarmé, by ceasing to claim for the poem the kind of certainty objects possess, and by presenting it in the simple perspective from which its presence can be perceived as the expectation of what is furthest and most uncertain, establishes a more confident relation to the book's significance. Or to put it differently—and less clearly—doubt is part of poetic certainty just as the inability to assert the poem involves us in its own assertion, which the five words 'Watching doubting wheeling shining and pondering' assign to the mind.

The presence of poetry is in the future. It comes from beyond the future and does not cease to come when it has come. A different temporal dimension from that of the world we have mastered operates in language when it reveals, through the rhythmic scansion of life, the space of its unfurling. It does not state certainties. Those who rely on certainty, or even on lesser forms of probability, do not seek the skyline, nor are they fellow-travellers of the singing mind whose five ways of playing are played in the realm of chance.

The poem is the expectancy of the poem. Only in expectancy do we concentrate that impersonal attention whose venues and place are the specific space of language. *Un Coup de dés* is the book to come. Mallarmé states clearly—specifically in the preface—that his intention is to express in a manner that will transform time the correspondences between space and the passage of time. Space, which does not exist, is scattered, interiorised, disintegrates or settles according to the various forms of motion of what is written, excludes ordinary time. In this space—the specific space of the poem—seconds do not follow seconds in the linear succession of irreversible becoming. It does not contain an account of something that might have occurred, were it even fictionally. The story is replaced by a hypothetical 'Supposing that....' The event that motivates the poem is not presented as true historical (or true fictional) fact: it only exists in relation to all the intellectual and linguistic activity it sets in motion and whose perceptible representation, with cuts, expansions, evasions, is like another language that sparks off new interactions of space and time.

All of which is unavoidably ambiguous. On the one hand we have an attempt to eliminate historical time and replace it by the proportional and reciprocal correspondences, always prominent in Mallarmé's theoretical investigations: 'if this is that, that is this,' he declares in the posthumous manuscript, or again: 'two alternatives for a given plot—either this or that —not developed sequentially, historically, but always intellectually.' In the same vein he deplores the French seventeenth-century playwrights' habit of taking their plots from Greek and Roman tragedy rather than from the works of Descartes (an idea with which Valéry toyed), and tries to apply the precision of geometrical methods to language so as to free it from sequential linearity and restore its autonomous correspondences. But Mallarmé was not Spinoza, and the result was nothing but pastiche. Having failed to geometrise language he settles for 'Supposing that....' Hence everything occurs by shortcuts, hypothetically, and narrative is avoided. Why is narrative avoided? Not simply because narrative time is abolished, but because narrative is replaced by images. This is where Mallarmé saw himself as the great innovator. For the first time the inner space of thought and language is perceptibly represented. The distance which mentally separates words or groups of words from each other is typographically visible together with the significance of such phonemes, their assertiveness, relative acceleration, concentration and dispersal, and the reproduction, through their speed and rhythm, of the things to which they refer.

The result is an exceptional expressivity which is quite unexpected. But equally unexpected is the fact that Mallarmé here contradicts himself. He restores to a language formerly seen as an immaterial power of abstraction, all the presence and materiality it was supposed to abolish. The 'tacit flight of abstraction' becomes a visible word-landscape. We no longer say: a flower. We trace it in words. Such inconsistency is in language as well as in Mallarmé's ambiguous attitude to language—and this has frequently been noted and commented. What else does *Un Coup de dés* reveal? The poem hovers between visible and legible presence—a musical score or a painting to be read and a poem to be contemplated—and, through its shifting aspects, attempts to enhance analytical reading by a global, simultaneous vision; to enhance static vision as well, by the dynamic interaction of rhythms; and attempts furthermore to situate itself at the point of intersection where hearing is seeing and reading, but also at that point where they have not yet joined, so that the poem occupies the central vacancy which is the exceptional future.

Mallarmé wants to remain at the preliminary stage—the song before the concept ('The song springs from an innate source: anteceding its concept.')—where all art is language and language wavers between the being it expresses by abstracting it, and the semblance of being it absorbs to give expressive form and mobility to the invisibility of meaning. This mobile hesitation is the true reality of language's specific space, whose rhythmic and temporal diversity—that establishes it as meaning while preserving it as the source of all meaning—the poem, the book to come, is alone able to assert. The book is thus centred on the harmony arising from the almost simultaneous switch from reading as vision to vision as legible clarity. Moreover it is constantly uncentred in relation to itself, not simply because it is both an entirely stable and an entirely unstable work, but because the *becoming* which unfurls it is created by and is dependent on it.

The time of the poem is not human time. It is fashioned by the poem, specific and intrinsic to the poem which is the least mobile thing conceivable. When we say 'the' time, as though there were but one form of duration, we fail to appreciate the mystery and inexhaustible fascination of this work. Even without a detailed analysis it is obvious that, 'under a false appearance of present,' different temporal possibilities are continuously superimposed, not in jumbled confusion but because a given unit (usually represented by a double page), which requires a given time, also belongs to other times in so far as the *group* of units into which it is inserted requires a different temporal structure—while 'at the same time' the whole poem is traversed, as by powerful crossbeams, by the echoing, unwavering dominant voice that expresses the future; an ever negative future however ('never shall abolish') that none the less is dually extended: in a past future-perfect cancelling action even in its apparent failure ('will not have taken place') and in a new possibility towards which, beyond negations and supported by negations, the poem leaps—the time of exception in the height of a 'perhaps.'

It might be suggested that Mallarmé relies on the reading of this poem, made inaccessible by its shifts of tenses, for it to become present. A problem he failed to abolish by abolishing the reader. On the contrary once the reader is abolished, the problem of reading becomes more pressing. Mallarmé gave much thought to this. 'A hopeless business' he calls it. And it is on the book's communication—its self-communication in its own specific *becoming*—that the posthumous manuscript throws some light. How can the authorless, readerless Book which need not be closed but is never static, assert itself according to its peculiar rhythm if it does not somehow emerge from itself to encounter an outside that will match the mobile privacy of its own structure and where it can establish a contact with its own distance? It requires a mediator. This is none other than the reading. Not a reading by an ordinary reader who cannot fail to equate the poem with his fortuitous individuality. Mallarmé will be the voice of this essential reading. Vanished and abolished as author, he is, through his disappearance, in contact with the appearing and disappearing essence of the Book, with the ceaseless oscillation which is its communication.

This mediating role is not like that of a conductor or an officiating priest. For although the posthumous manuscript seems to imply that reading is somewhat similar to a sacred rite that would be part conjuring trick, part drama and part liturgy, we should not forget that Mallarmé was aware that, if he is not an ordinary reader, neither is he an exceptional interpreter capable of explaining the text, of revealing its hidden meaning, or of allowing all its possible meanings to emerge simultaneously. He is not really a reader. He is the reading: the communicability whereby the book communicates with itself—first through the different physical variants made possible and necessary by the loose pages;[7] then through the new process of understanding derived from the language that combines various *genres* and art forms; and finally through the exceptional future from whence the book meets itself and meets us in exposing us to the supreme interplay of space and time.

Mallarmé calls the reader the 'operator.' Reading, like poetry, is an 'operation.' The term retains for him, throughout, its dual connotation of work and of something almost surgical, derived ironically from its functional nature: operation as amputation, rather like the Hegelian *Aufhebung*. Reading is an operation, a labour of self-suppression which is substantiated in a self-confrontation and simultaneously abolished and asserted. In the posthumous manuscript Mallarmé emphasises the danger and daring of reading—daring apparently to claim authorial rights over the book, which would turn it back into an ordinary book; the danger of communication as such, of the adventurous testing process which precludes the reader, be he Mallarmé himself, from knowing in advance what the book is, if it is, and whether the becoming to which it corresponds and which springs from its infinite suppression has already a meaning for us, and will ever have a meaning. 'Watching doubting wheeling shining and pondering'—will this descending movement which expresses the indefinite exchange whereby the book is created finally come up against the moment at which everything must end, the ultimate time that flees before the book, bringing it to a premature standstill by confronting it with the 'final crowning point'? The moment when all moments stop in final achievement, the end of what is endless; is this the end? Is it at this point of motionlessness that we must henceforth contemplate the whole work with the foreknowledge of a universal death which is always a little bit the reader's?

But beyond this end and beyond this beyond, *Un Coup de dés* shows that there is yet something to be said, a statement whose finality is somehow the sum and the 'result' of the whole work, a resolute statement in which the work is resolved while it emerges: 'Any Thought Utters a Dice Throw.' This sentence, isolated in its harshness as though in it were fulfilled the supreme isolation of language, is not easily pinned down. It has a conclusive violence that forbids further speech yet is itself already almost outside the poem—a boundary-line beyond the boundary. Its content, by linking thought and chance, by simultaneously refuting and asserting chance and by likening thought to a gamble and gambling to thought, tries to contain in one brief phrase the sum of all that is possible. 'Any thought utters a Throw of Dice.' Such is the *clausula* and the overture, the invisible transition where spherical mobility ends and begins ceaselessly. It is all over and it all starts again. Thus the Book is cautiously asserted in the *becoming* which is perhaps its significance, a significance which could be that of the circle's circuit. The end of the work is its origin, its new and ancient beginning: it is its possibility renewed once again so that the dice, thrown once again, may be the throw of the theme words which, by denying the poem's existence: 'A DICE THROW WILL NEVER' [8] recreates the final shipwreck where, in the depth of the place, all has always disappeared: chance, the poem, thought, 'EXCEPT at the height PERHAPS....'

*— Translated from the French by Sacha Rabinovitch.*

## NOTES

1  In 1867 he restricts the size of the Book to three poems and four prose poems. In 1871, though here the concept is slightly different, he announces one volume of tales, one of poems and one of essays. In the posthumous manuscript published by Scherer he speaks of four books divided into twenty volumes.

2  He was later to describe the relation which, from one volume to the others, would reflect and amplify the multiple correspondences inherent to each and waiting to emerge: 'A parallel symmetry which, from the position of the lines in the poem links up with the poem's authenticity in the volume, escapes from the volume to other volumes, themselves inscribing on intellectual space the amplified signature of an anonymous mind, and perfect as an artistic presence.' (*Oeuvres complètes*, p. 367)

3  Here Mallarmé is comparing journalists to the poor Cabbalists who are accused of having murdered the Abbé Boullan by casting spells. But from the point of view of art the first are more guilty than the others, even if the latter make the mistake of 'detaching from an art its functions which are integral...to it.' Magic should never be separated from art.

4 The manuscript given by Mondor to Scherer who carefully edited it and published it under the title: Le 'Livre' de Mallarmé: Premières recherches sur des documents inédits (Paris, 1957). Does this manuscript cast any light on Mallarmé's main project? It can only do so on condition that we never lose sight of the fact that this is not the manuscript of the Book. The published manuscript is neither a complete text like Igitur nor a collection of substantial, even if still disconnected fragments, but a bundle of loose sheets covered with minute notes, isolated words and illegible signs. We do not even know if they are part of a single work or if they are published in the order in which they were found after Mallarmé's death, which even then, might have been a chance classification or the accidental order of a long abandoned work. What is more, we do not know what these notes, preserved for an unknown purpose, represent in relation to all the others which, according to Mondor, were destroyed. Thus we cannot tell what position they held for Mallarmé in the whole. Perhaps he had purposely discarded them because they no longer interested him, or because they were random thoughts he had scribbled. Furthermore, since he only ascribed significance and reality to what was expressed in the individual structure and explicit form of his language, these formless notes quite possibly meant nothing to him and he wished us to read nothing into them—they were totally undistinguished. The date or dates of these notes is uncertain as well as their place in his work, their coherence with the rest, their purpose and even their reality. Thus the one essential book he might have written to overcome chance appears to be the most hazardous publication made up of chance phrases arranged by chance on pages that are put together by chance. A failure which has not even the advantage of being Mallarmé's, since it is the simple-minded work of some posthumous editors, not unlike those explorers who, every so often, unearth a fragment of Noah's Ark or of the Tablets of the Law shattered by Moses. Such at least is the impression we first receive from these documents presented as the Book's first draft. However our second thoughts are somewhat different. For the publication of these more or less blank pages on which words are drawn rather than written, and which enable us to perceive the point at which necessity merges with pure dispersal, might not perhaps have entirely displeased Mallarmé.

I must note, however—not to rouse general indignation but simply to point out the remarkable disregard for ethical probity even the most worthy are prone to when the publication of a posthumous work is concerned—that the ms has been published against the author's formal instructions. Though the situation may have been ambiguous in the case of Kafka, here it is perfectly clear. Mallarmé died unexpectedly. Between the first attack—from which he recovered and which seemed to be no more than a warning—and the second to which he succumbed in a matter of minutes, only a few hours elapsed. Mallarmé spent this brief respite writing his 'instructions concerning my papers.' He wanted everything destroyed. 'Burn, then: there is no literary legacy here, my poor children.' Moreover he forbade any kind of inquisitive interference or inspection: that which must be destroyed must first be removed from sight. 'Not be submitted to anybody for appreciation: forbid curious or friendly interference. Say that all is illegible—which in fact it is.' Formal instructions which were promptly disregarded. The dead are defenceless. A few days later Valéry was allowed to examine the papers and, during fifty years, with constant and amazing regularity, important, authentic works have been unearthed and exposed as though Mallarmé were more prolific dead than alive.

I know that Apollinaire decreed that everything must be published. A decree that has more meanings than one. It could be seen as a reference to the tendency of all hidden things to surface, to become explicit, of the unexpressed to be publicly expressed. This is neither a law nor a principle. It is the compulsion that dominates all writers, especially when they resist and deny it. It is the same compulsion which precludes the ownership of the work. The author has no rights over it and is nothing to it, since he is already dead and done away with. Let not, therefore, his will be done. Logically it is fitting that his last instructions be ignored and that the same should apply to those he expresses when alive. Yet the opposite seems to occur then. The author wants to publish and the publisher does not. But this is not what really happens. Think of all the hidden pressures, friendly, insistent, unsolicited, which compel us to write and to publish what we do not want. Visible-invisible, the compulsion is ever present, unconcerned about our feelings and, to our surprise, taking the pages from our very hands. The living are defenceless.

What is this compulsion? Not the reader, nor society, nor the State, nor culture. To name and acknowledge it in all its unreality was Mallarmé's mission. He called it the Book.

5 It should be remembered that the extremely close attention Heidegger gives to language is an attention to words considered independently—as self-sufficient—to certain words he sees as fundamental and at which he worries until he has recovered, from the history of their construction, the history of existence; but that it is not an attention to their correspondence and still less to the preliminary space such correspondence suggests and whose originating process is the one thing that makes the dissemination of language possible. For Mallarmé, language is not made of words, even unadulterated words: it is that into which words have always already disappeared and the process of oscillation from appearance to disappearance.

6 'Poetry is the expression, through human speech reduced to its basic rhythm, of the mysterious significance of aspects of existence; it endows our sojourn with authenticity and represents our one spiritual task.' (*Correspondance*, p. 266) And in *Richard Wagner, Rêverie d'un poète français* (*Oeuvres complètes*, p. 545): 'Man and his authentic earthly sojourn exchange a mutuality of evidences.'

7 According to the Manuscript, the Book is made of loose pages: 'Thus,' says Mallarmé, 'it is possible to switch them around and read them—not indeed in any order—but in different distinct orders pre-determined by laws of permutation.' The book is always different, it changes and switches through a collation of the diversity of its sections; thus the linear progression—the one-way system—is avoided in its reading. Moreover the reading, by furling and unfurling, dispersing and uniting, demonstrates its lack of substantiality: it is never there but is always decomposing as it is composed.

8 The conditional tense implies that this is not *Un Coup de dés*'s last word on the meaning of poetic becoming which is at stake. We realise, when confronted with this poem, how inadequately our concept of literature and of art satisfies the potentialities they contain. Nowadays painting occasionally makes us realise that what it wants to create, its 'production,' can no longer be works of art, but corresponds rather to something for which there is not yet a name. The same applies to literature. That towards which we are advancing is not perhaps what the future will in fact disclose. Yet that towards which we advance is vacant and full of a future we must refrain from freezing in the traditions of past structures.

## SOURCES

Mallarmé, Stéphane. *Correspondance*. Ed. H. Mondor and L. J. Austin. (Paris: Gallimard, 1959).

Mallarmé, Stéphane. *Oeuvres complètes*. Ed. Henri Mondor and G. Jean-Aubry. (Paris: Gallimard, 1965).

Scherer, Jacques, ed. *Le "Livre" de Mallarmé*. (Paris: Gallimard, 1957).

# from THE FUTURIST MOMENT
## Marjorie Perloff

IN THE AUTUMN OF 1913, *Les Hommes nouveaux,* a radical journal and small press founded by Blaise Cendrars and his friend Emile Szytta, published a remarkable verbal-visual text called *La Prose du Transsibérien et de la petite Jehanne de France.* It bore the subtitle: "poèmes, couleurs simultanées de tirage atteignant la hauteur de la Tour Eiffel: 150 exemplaires numérotés et signés" ("poems, simultaneous colors, in an edition attaining the height of the Eiffel Tower: 150 copies numbered and signed"). *Le Premier livre simultané,* as the work was also called, was made up of a single sheet of paper, divided down the center, which unfolded like an accordion, through twenty-two panels to a length of almost seven feet. The height of the Eiffel Tower was to be attained by lining up the 150 copies of the text vertically.

On the left, a panel containing the title page initiates the passage of the eye downward, through a sequence of visual semiabstract forms in bright primary colors, to a final panel that contains a child's image of the Eiffel Tower, a curiously innocent giant red phallus penetrating an orange Great Wheel with a green center. On the right, meanwhile, the text of the poem is prefaced by a Michelin railway map of the Trans-Siberian journey from Moscow to the Sea of Japan; underneath this map, a wide strip of green introduces the poem's title in big block letters as if the *pochoir* were a poster signboard. The text then follows, arranged in succeeding blocks made up of different typefaces and broken by large irregularly shaped planes of predominantly pastel color. The coda, "Paris / Ville de la Tour unique du grand Gibet et de la Roue" ("Paris / City of the incomparable Tower of the Rack and the Wheel"), corresponds to the visual image of tower and wheel on the bottom left.

*La Prose du Transsibérien* was the collaboration of the poet Blaise Cendrars and the painter Sonia Delaunay. The particular version of modernity found in this text makes it an especially fitting emblem of what I call the Futurist moment. Cendrars's is not, of course, strictly speaking a "Futurist" (*e.g.,* Italian Futurist or Russian Futurist) poem, but, perhaps precisely for that reason, it furnishes us with a paradigm of Futurism in the larger sense, as the arena of agitation and projected revolution that characterizes the *avant guerre.* Certainly, *La Prose du Transsibérien* embodies Antonio Gramsci's understanding, voiced in *L'Ordine Nuovo* (the official organ of the newly formed Italian Communist party), that Futurism was the first movement to give artistic expression to the "intense and tumultuous life" of the newly industrialized urban landscape.

The very names Blaise Cendrars and Sonia Delaunay are emblematic of the anomalies that characterize the Futurist ethos. Mme Delaunay-Terk, as she is listed on the title page of the poem-painting, was born in the Ukraine to Jewish parents; as a small child she was adopted by her maternal uncle Henri Terk and grew up in Petersburg. In 1905 she went to Paris to study art; in 1909 she decided that the best way to assert her independence from her Russian relatives was to accept a marriage offer from a Parisian gallery owner, the German art collector William Uhde. A year later, the two were amicably divorced and Sonia Terk Uhde married her husband's painter friend Robert Delaunay.

Sonia Delaunay's place in the French avant-garde of the 1910s (it is usual to speak of the "orphism" or "simultaneism" of "the Delaunays" as if Sonia's work were no more than a footnote to Robert's) is thus complicated by her Russian origins and German Expressionist connections. Blaise Cendrars's self-characterization as the only poet in the Paris of 1913 who could seriously rival Apollinaire is even more ironic. Born in La Chaux-de-Fonds, Switzerland, Cendrars was christened Frédéric Louis Sauser. As a young man he called himself Freddy Sausey, and then, by the late fall of 1911, when he was living in New York, he was using the signature Blaise Cendrart, a name that, at the time of his arrival in Paris a few months later, had become Blaise Cendrars. Blaise, as the poet later explained it to a friend, came from *braise* (ember, cinder) by means of the simple "confusion of *R*- and *L*-sounds"; as for Cendrars, from *cendres* (again cinders, though more in the sense of ashes), in his autobiographical fragment *Une Nuit dans la forêt,* the poet explains:

> Well, one may adore fire, but not indefinitely respect the ashes; that's why I rake up my life and exercise my heart (and my mind and my balls) with the poker. The flame shoots forth.

The role-playing that transformed a Frédéric Sauser into Blaise Cendrars, a Sonia Terk into Madame Delaunay, points to the curious tension between nationalism and internationalism that is at the heart of *avant guerre* consciousness. Delaunay's abstractions have strong affinities to primitive Russian *lubki* (woodblocks) as well as to the collages of the Russian Cubo-Futurists who were her contemporaries; she also had contact with Wassily Kandinsky, then living in Munich. Yet although the Delaunays received artists and poets from all over Europe and the United States, she remained for the rest of her life ardently French, refusing, for example, so much as to visit America.

Again, the Switzerland of Cendrars's birth represented the confluence of German and Latin currents, specifically the Milan (Italian Futurist)-

Berlin (German Expressionist) axis. Freddy-Blaise was entirely bilingual (German-French); when he ran away from home at the age of seventeen and spent three years (1904–7) in St. Petersburg, he added Russian to his repertoire and then, in New York (1911–12), some English. Restlessly international by background and inclination, he had been in Paris a brief two years when the war broke out in August 1914. Nevertheless, despite his close ties with such German intellectuals and artists as Herwath Walden (the editor of *Der Sturm*) and Franz Marc, he could hardly wait to join the French Foreign Legion and to fight for what he, like his friend and fellow poet Apollinaire, who was also a foreigner with an adopted name, took to be the great cause. "This war," Cendrars wrote to a friend in September, on his way to the front, "is a painful delivery, needed to give birth to liberty. It fits me like a glove. Reaction or Revolution—man must become more human. I will return. There can be no doubt." And a little later, "The war has saved my life. This sounds like a paradox, but a hundred times I have told myself that if I had continued to live with those people [the bohemian radical artists of Montparnasse], I would have croaked." Within a year he had been wounded and lost his right arm: nevertheless on 2 November 1915 he wrote (painfully, with his left hand) to Apollinaire: "I had to have my arm amputated. I am as well as can be expected. My spirits are good."

Seventy years and two world wars later, it is almost impossible to understand this particular mixture of radicalism and patriotism, of a worldly, international outlook and a violently nationalist faith. Yet we find this paradox everywhere in the arts of the *avant guerre*. Before we dismiss as a contemptible proto-Fascist the Marinetti who declared, in the first Futurist manifesto (1909), "We will glorify war—the world's only hygiene," we must look at the context in which such statements were made. The publication and exhibition history of *La Prose du Transsibérien* may provide us with some interesting leads.

· · ·

Neither Blaise Cendrars nor Sonia Delaunay considered themselves Futurists: indeed, Cendrars repeatedly insisted that, as he put it in a letter to André Salmon (12 October 1913): "The inspiration of this poem [*La Prose du Transsibérien*] came to me naturally and...has nothing to do with the commercial agitation of M. Marinetti." But despite such disclaimers—disclaimers that, as we shall see, were largely prompted by the strong nationalist rivalries of the period—*La Prose du Transsibérien* can be taken as a kind of hub of the Futurist wheel that spun over Europe in the years of *avant guerre*.

Consider the publicity campaign launched by Cendrars on behalf of his poem. Its September 1913 publication was preceded by a flurry of leaflets, subscription forms, and prospectuses announcing the impending publication of "le Premier livre simultané," whose height would rival that of the Eiffel Tower. The word *"simultané"* predictably aroused the anger of the Italian Futurists, whose own manifestos had regularly advocated simultaneity: in the words of Boccioni's 1912 manifesto, "The simultaneousness of states of mind in the work of art: that is the intoxicating aim of our art." By *simultaneity,* Boccioni and his fellow painters meant "the synthesis of *what one remembers* and of *what one sees,*" the possibility of representing successive stages of motion in linear sequence, as in Giacomo Balla's famous *Dynamism of a Dog in Motion* of 1912. The "Rayonism" of the Russian Futurist painters Mikhail Larionov and Natalya Goncharova was a similar call for the depiction of simultaneous motion, of dynamism and speed.

Sonia Delaunay's term *"couleurs simultanés,"* on the other hand, refers, in the first place, to something quite specific: M. E. Chevreul's 1839 treatise *De la Loi du contraste simultané des couleurs* from which Robert Delaunay derived his doctrine of "simultaneism" as the dynamic counterpoint of otherwise dissonant colors when observed in complementarity. Again, *La Prose du Transsibérien* is a "simultaneous" book in that the reader takes in, or is meant to take in, text and image simultaneously; the eye travels back and forth between Delaunay's colored forms and Cendrars's words. Third, *simultaneity* here refers to the spatial and temporal distortions that, as we shall see, characterize *La Prose du Transsibérien,* a poem that collapses present and past, the cities and steppes of the Russian orient and the City of the Tower, the Gibbet, and the Wheel, which is Paris.

Cendrars seems, in any case, to have relished the controversy generated by the circulars for *La Prose.* For one thing, it brought such poets as Apollinaire to his defense. In *Les Soirées de Paris* (15 June 1914), the latter reports:

> Blaise Cendrars and Mme Delaunay-Terk have carried out a unique experiment in simultaneity, written in contrasting colors in order to train the eye to read with one glance the whole of a poem, even as an orchestra conductor reads with one glance the notes placed up and down on the bar, even as one reads with a single glance the plastic elements printed on a poster.

The poem-painting as a kind of advertising poster—here is the analogy at the heart of Marinetti's *parole in libertà,* the words-in-freedom arranged artfully on the page in different sizes, typefaces, and colors. But the transformation of the conventional page found in *La Prose*—a transformation I shall consider later—is specifically related by Cendrars himself to the layout of the "luminous" billboard. "The flower of contemporary life," as he playfully calls advertising, in a short piece called "Advertising = Poetry" (1927), "is the warmest sign of the vigor of today's men—indeed, one of the seven wonders of the world."

Have you ever thought about the sadness that streets, squares, stations, subways, first class hotels, dance halls, movies, dining cars, highways, nature would all exhibit without the innumerable billboards, without show windows (those beautiful, brand new toys for thoughtful families), without luminous signboards, without the false blandishments of loudspeakers, and imagine the sadness and monotony of meals and wine without polychrome menus and fancy labels.

Luminous signboards and polychrome menus—it is thus that "art" and "life" are destined to become one. To announce the publication of his own *La Prose du Transsibérien,* Cendrars published a manifesto in the September 1913 number of Herwath Walden's avant-garde Berlin periodical *Der Sturm:*

> I am not a poet. I am a libertine. I have no method of working. I have a sex.... And if I write, it is perhaps out of need, for my health, even as one eats, one breathes, one sings....
>
> Literature is a part of life. It is not something "special." I do not write by vocation. Living is not a vocation....I have written my most beautiful poems in the great cities, among five million men—or, not forgetting the most beautiful games of my childhood, five thousand leagues under the sea in the company of Jules Verne. All of life is nothing but a poem, a movement....
>
> I love legends, dialects, grammatical errors, detective novels, the flesh of whores, the sun, the Eiffel Tower, Apaches, good negroes, and that trickster of a European who makes fun of modernity. Where am I going? I have no idea, since I even visit museums....
>
> Here is what I wanted to say. I have a fever. And this is why I love the painting of the Delaunays, full of sun, of heat, of violence. Mme Delaunay has made such a beautiful book of colors that my poem is more saturated with light than is my life. That's what makes me happy. Besides, think that this book should be two meters high! Moreover, that the edition should reach the height of the Eiffel Tower!

Here, playing the enfant terrible, Cendrars grandly dissociates himself from all poetic "schools" only to echo the Futurist doctrine that life and art are inseparable, that poetry demands violence and energy, that it is a kind of "fever" in which the life of the modern city merges with the exotic Other, the fantasy world of Apaches and "les bons nègres." Like Rimbaud, whose prose the *Sturm* essay recalls, Cendrars is drawn to the offbeat, the erotic, the populist. But the urge to communicate directly with the masses, to play to the crowd—the urge that makes Cendrars, like Apollinaire and like Marinetti, extol advertising—gives a kind of hard edge to Rimbaud's more visionary mode. In a letter to Victor Smirnoff (December 1913), Cendrars insists: "The role of the new poetry is to throw one's treasures out the window, among the people, into the crowd, into life. I throw money out of the window." And he quotes from his *poème élastique* "Contraste": "Les fénêtres de ma poésie sont grand'ouvertes sur les boulevards" ("The windows of my poetry are wide open to the boulevards").

Curiously enough, this was literally the case. During the fall of 1913 the Cendrars-Delaunay *Prose du Transsibérien* was exhibited in Paris (the annual Salon d'Automne), Berlin (the Herbst Salon), London, New York, Moscow, and St. Petersburg. It became not only a poem but an event, a happening. In St. Petersburg, the poet-painter Victor Smirnoff gave an accompanying lecture called "Simultaneous Contrasts and Plastic Poetry." At the *Montjoie!* exposition in Paris on 24 February 1914, Mme Lucy Wilhelm stood on a chair so as to recite the gigantic poem, which was hung on the wall. Beginning at ceiling level, she gradually bent her knees and finally sat down on the chair to read the conclusion.

Performance art, we would now call it. But even more remarkable is the way the "windows" of Cendrars's poetry "opened," so to speak, onto the boulevards of Berlin. Herwath Walden's *Der Sturm*, which began publication in 1910 with a weekly circulation of approximately thirty thousand, published such writers as Karl Kraus, Heinrich Mann, and August Strindberg, as well as the art work of the *Blaue Reiter* group and the manifestos of the Italian Futurists. Wilhelm Worringer's "On the Development of Modern Painting," Kandinsky's "Language of Form and Color," Boccioni's *Futurist Painting: Technical Manifesto*—all these appeared in the pages of *Der Sturm.* Cendrars himself contributed a translation of Apollinaire's *Les Peintres cubistes* and an essay on Henri Rousseau (both in 1913).

*Der Sturm* also sponsored major exhibitions in which the German Expressionists were shown side by side with Picasso and Delaunay, with Vladimir and David Burliuk and Natalya Goncharova. In the summer of 1913, Walden decided to organize a Herbst Salon, on the model of the Paris Salon d'Automne. According to Peter Selz, Walden traveled with "meteoric speed" (the speed, we might say, celebrated in Futurist art), through most European art centers from Budapest to Paris and assembled 366 paintings and pieces of sculpture by some ninety artists from fifteen countries. This was to be the last of the significant international exhibitions of contemporary art held in Germany before World War I. Accordingly, the list of painters represented is significant:

FRANCE: Marc Chagall, Robert Delaunay, Sonia Delaunay, Albert
    Gleizes, Fernand Léger, Jean Metzinger, Francis Picabia.
ITALY: Giacomo Balla, Umberto Boccioni, Carlo Carrà, Luigi Russolo,
    Gino Severini, Ardengo Soffici.
RUSSIA: David Burliuk, Vladimir Burliuk, Natalya Goncharova,
    N. Kulbin, Mikhail Larionov.

AUSTRIA: Oskar Kokoschka.

HOLLAND: Five artists including Piet Mondrian.

SWITZERLAND: Members of the *Moderne Bund* including Paul Klee.

UNITED STATES: Lyonel Feininger, Marsden Hartley.

GERMANY: From *Der Blaue Reiter* group: Franz Marc, Wassily Kandinsky, Alfred Kubin, Alexej von Jawlensky, August Macke, Gabriele Münter. From the younger generation: Hans Arp, Max Ernst.

More specifically, the Herbst Salon included Balla's *Dog on Leash,* Boccioni's *Unique Forms of Continuity in Space,* Kandinsky's *Composition No. 6,* Delaunay's *Solar Discs,* Léger's *Woman in Blue,* and Marc's *Tower of Blue Horses.*

It is in this international context that *La Prose du Transsibérien et de la Petite Jehanne de France* by Cendrars and Sonia Delaunay made its first appearance. Cendrars, for whom German was as native as French, had close personal ties with the Expressionist poets and painters who were his contemporaries. The correspondence between Cendrars and Walden, between the Delaunays and Franz Marc, flowed steadily throughout 1913. "People of different countries," wrote Delaunay to Marc on 11 January, "get to like one another by seeing. In Berlin, I felt out of place only in terms of the language spoken there."

Yet within little over a year, the poets and painters of Delaunay's circle greeted the outbreak of war with Germany as both inevitable and desirable. Indeed, war, far from being extolled only by Marinetti's Italian Futurist circle, was, until 1916 or so, equated with revolution—the breaking of the vessels of oppression. Thus Kasimir Malevich could declare:

> The academy is a moldy vault in which art is being flagellated.
>
> Gigantic wars, great inventions, conquest of the air, speed of travel, telephones, telegraphs, dreadnoughts are the realm of electricity....
>
> The new life of iron and the machine, the roar of motorcars, the brilliance of electric lights, the growling of propellers, have awakened the soul, which was suffocating in the catacombs of old reason and has emerged at the intersection of the paths of heaven and earth.
>
> If all artists were to see the crossroads of these heavenly paths, if they were to comprehend these monstrous runways and intersections of our bodies with the clouds in the heavens, then they would not paint chrysanthemums.

It was a lesson Cendrars and Delaunay did not have to learn: the "roar of motorcars, the brilliance of electric lights, the growling of propellers" was precisely their subject, even as it was the subject of Malevich and Vladimir Tatlin. But the darker implications of this new technology, imperfectly understood by the artists of the *avant guerre* themselves, are expressed, however subliminally, in their poetry and painting, their collage works and artist's books.

# THE PROSE OF THE TRANS-SIBERIAN
## AND OF LITTLE JEANNE OF FRANCE
### Blaise Cendrars

*Dedicated to the musicians*

Back then I was still young
I was barely sixteen but my childhood memories were gone
I was 48,000 miles away from where I was born
I was in Moscow, city of a thousand and three bell towers and
    seven train stations
And the thousand and three towers and seven stations weren't
    enough for me
Because I was such a hot and crazy teenager
That my heart was burning like the Temple of Ephesus or like
    Red Square in Moscow
At sunset
And my eyes were shining down those old roads
And I was already such a bad poet
That I didn't know how to take it all the way.

The Kremlin was like an immense Tartar cake
Iced with gold
With big blanched-almond cathedrals
And the honey gold of the bells...
An old monk was reading me the legend of Novgorod
I was thirsty
And I was deciphering cuneiform characters
Then all at once the pigeons of the Holy Ghost flew up over the
    square
And my hands flew up too, sounding like an albatross taking off
And, well, that's the last I remember of the last day
Of the very last trip
And of the sea.

Still, I was a really bad poet.
I didn't know how to take it all the way.
I was hungry
And all those days and all those women in all those cafés and all
    those glasses
I wanted to drink them down and break them
And all those windows and all those streets
And all those houses and all those lives
And all those carriage wheels raising swirls from the broken
    pavement
I would have liked to have rammed them into a roaring furnace
And I would have liked to have ground up all their bones
And ripped out all those tongues
And liquefied all those big bodies naked and strange under
    clothes that drive me mad...
I foresaw the coming of the big red Christ of the Russian
    Revolution...
And the sun was an ugly sore
Splitting apart like a red-hot coal.

Back then I was still quite young
I was barely sixteen but I'd already forgotten about where I was
    born
I was in Moscow wanting to wolf down flames
And there weren't enough of those towers and stations
    sparkling in my eyes
In Siberia the artillery rumbled—it was war
Hunger cold plague cholera
And the muddy waters of the Amur carrying along millions of
    corpses
In every station I watched the last trains leave
That's all: they weren't selling any more tickets
And the soldiers would far rather have stayed...
An old monk was singing me the legend of Novgorod.

Me, the bad poet who wanted to go nowhere, I could go anywhere
And of course the businessmen still had enough money
To go out and seek their fortunes.
Their train left every Friday morning.
It sounded like a lot of people were dying.
One guy took along a hundred cases of alarm clocks and cuckoo
    clocks from the Black Forest
Another took hatboxes, stovepipes, and an assortment of
    Sheffield corkscrews
Another, coffins from Malmo filled with canned goods and
    sardines in oil
And there were a lot of women
Women with vacant thighs for hire
Who could also serve
Coffins
They were all licensed
It sounded like a lot of people were dying out there
The women traveled at a reduced fare
And they all had bank accounts.

Now, one Friday morning it was my turn to go
It was in December
And I left too, with a traveling jewel merchant on his way to
    Harbin
We had two compartments on the express and 34 boxes of
    jewelry from Pforzheim
German junk "Made in Germany"
He had bought me some new clothes and I had lost a button
    getting on the train
—I remember, I remember, I've often thought about it since—
I slept on the jewels and felt great playing with the nickel-plated
    Browning he had given me
I was very happy and careless

It was like Cops and Robbers
We had stolen the treasure of Golconda
And we were taking it on the Trans-Siberian to hide it on the
    other side of the world
I had to guard it from the thieves in the Urals who had attacked
    the circus caravan in Jules Verne
From the Khunkhuz, the Boxers of China
And the angry little Mongols of the Great Lama
Ali Baba and the Forty Thieves
And the followers of the terrible Old Man of the Mountain
And worst of all, the most modern
The cat burglars
And the specialists of the international express.

And still, and still
I was as sad as a little boy
The rhythms of the train
What American psychiatrists call "railroad nerves"
The noise of doors voices axles screeching along frozen rails
The golden thread of my future
My Browning the piano the swearing of the card players in the
    next compartment
The terrific presence of Jeanne
The man in blue glasses nervously pacing up and down the
    corridor and glancing in at me
Swishing of women
And the whistle blowing
And the eternal sound of the wheels wildly rolling along ruts in
    the sky

The windows frosted over
No nature!
And out there the Siberian plains the low sky the big shadows of
    the Taciturns rising and falling
I'm asleep in a tartan
Plaid
Like my life
With my life keeping me no warmer than this Scotch
Shawl
And all of Europe seen through the wind-cutter of an express at
    top speed
No richer than my life
My poor life
This shawl
Frayed on strongboxes full of gold
I roll along with
Dream
And smoke
And the only flame in the universe
Is a poor thought…

Tears rise from the bottom of my heart
If I think, O Love, of my mistress;
She is but a child, whom I found, so pale
And pure, in the back of a bordel.

She is but a fair child who laughs,
Is sad, doesn't smile, and never cries;
But the poet's flower, the silver lily, trembles
When she lets you see it in the depths of her eyes.

She is sweet, says nothing you can hear,
With a long, slow trembling when you draw near;
But when I come to her, from here, from there,
She takes a step and shuts her eyes—and takes a step.

For she is my love and other women
Are but big bodies of flame sheathed in gold,
My poor friend is so alone
She is stark naked, has no body—she's too poor.

She is but an innocent flower, all thin and delicate,
The poet's flower, a pathetic silver lily,
So cold, so alone, and so wilted now
That tears rise if I think of her heart.

And this night is like a hundred thousand others when a train
    slips through the night
—Comets fall—
And a man and a woman, no matter how young, enjoy making
    love.

The sky is like the torn tent of a rundown circus in a little
    fishing village
In Flanders
The sun like a smoking lamp
And way up on the trapeze a woman does a crescent moon
The clarinet the trumpet a shrill flute a beat-up drum
And here is my cradle
My cradle
It was always near the piano when my mother, like Madame
    Bovary, played Beethoven's sonatas
I spent my childhood in the hanging gardens of Babylon
Playing hooky, following the trains as they pulled out of the
    stations
Now I've made the trains follow me
Basel—Timbuktu
I've played the horses at tracks like Auteuil and Longchamps
Paris—New York
Now the trains run alongside me
Madrid—Stockholm
Lost it all at the gay pari-mutuel

Patagonia is what's left, Patagonia, which befits my immense
    sadness, Patagonia and a trip to the South Seas
I'm on the road
I've always been on the road
I'm on the road with little Jeanne of France
The train does a somersault and lands on all fours
The train lands on its wheels
The train always lands on all its wheels

"Blaise, say, are we really a long way from Montmartre?"

A long way, Jeanne, you've been rolling along for seven days
You're a long way from Montmartre, from the Butte that
    brought you up, from the Sacré-Coeur you snuggled up to
Paris has disappeared with its enormous blaze
Everything gone except cinders flying back
The rain falling
The peat bogs swelling
Siberia turning
Heavy sheets of snow piling up
And the bell of madness that jingles like a final desire in the
    bluish air
The train throbs at the heart of the leaden horizon
And your desolation snickers…

"Say, Blaise, are we really a long way from Montmartre?"

Troubles
Forget your troubles
All the cracked and leaning stations along the way
The telegraph lines they hang from
The grimacing poles that reach out to strangle them
The world stretches out elongates and snaps back like an
    accordion in the hands of a raging sadist
Wild locomotives fly through rips in the sky
And in the holes
The dizzying wheels the mouths the voices
And the dogs of misery that bark at our heels
The demons are unleashed
Scrap iron
Everything clanks
Slightly off
The clickety-clack of the wheels
Lurches
Jerks
We are a storm in the skull of a deaf man…

"Say, Blaise, are we really a long way from Montmartre?"

Of course we are, stop bothering me, you know we are, a long
    way
An overheated madness bellows in the locomotive
Plague and cholera rise like burning embers around us
We disappear right into a tunnel of war
Hunger, that whore, clutches the clouds scattered across the sky
    and craps on the battlefield piles of stinking corpses
Do what it does, do your job…

"Say, Blaise, are we really a long way from Montmartre?"

Yes, we are, we are
All the scapegoats have swollen up and collapsed in this desert
Listen to the cowbells of this mangy troop
Tomsk Chelyabinsk Kansk Ob' Tayshet Verkne-Udinsk Kurgan
    Samara Penza-Tulun
Death in Manchuria
Is where we get off is our last stop
This trip is terrible
Yesterday morning
Ivan Ulitch's hair turned white
And Kolia Nikolai Ivanovitch has been biting his fingers for two
    weeks…

Do what Death and Famine do, do your job
It costs one hundred sous—in Trans-Siberian that's one hundred
    rubles
Fire up the seats and blush under the table
The devil is at the keyboard
His knotty fingers thrill all the women
Instinct
OK gals
Do your job
Until we get to Harbin...

"Say, Blaise, are we really a long way from Montmartre?"

No, hey... Stop bothering me... Leave me alone
Your pelvis sticks out
Your belly's sour and you have the clap
The only thing Paris laid in your lap
And there's a little soul...because you're unhappy
I feel sorry for you come here to my heart
The wheels are windmills in the land of Cockaigne
And the windmills are crutches a beggar whirls over his head
We are the amputees of space
We move on our four wounds
Our wings have been clipped
The wings of our seven sins
And the trains are all the devil's toys
Chicken coop
The modern world
Speed is of no use
The modern world
The distances are too far away
And at the end of a trip it's horrible to be a man with a woman...

"Blaise, say, are we really a long way from Montmartre?"

I feel so sorry for you come here I'm going to tell you a story
Come get in my bed
Put your head on my shoulder
I'm going to tell you a story...

Oh come on!

It's always spring in the Fijis
You lay around
The lovers swoon in the high grass and hot syphilis drifts among
    the banana trees
Come to the lost islands of the Pacific!
Names like Phoenix, the Marquesas
Borneo and Java
And Celebes shaped like a cat

We can't go to Japan
Come to Mexico!
Tulip trees flourish on the high plateaus
Clinging vines hang down like hair from the sun
It's as if the brushes and palette of a painter
Had used colors stunning as gongs—
Rousseau was there
It dazzled him forever
It's a great bird country
The bird of paradise the lyre bird
The toucan the mockingbird
And the hummingbird nests in the heart of the black lily
Come!
We'll love each other in the majestic ruins of an Aztec temple
You'll be my idol
Splashed with color childish slightly ugly and really weird
Oh come!

If you want we'll take a plane and fly over the land of the
    thousand lakes
The nights there are outrageously long

The sound of the engine will scare our prehistoric ancestors
I'll land
And build a hangar out of mammoth fossils
The primitive fire will rekindle our poor love
Samovar
And we'll settle down like ordinary folks near the pole
Oh come!

Jeanne Jeannette my pet my pot my poot
My me mama poopoo Peru
Peepee cuckoo
Ding ding my dong
Sweet pea sweet flea sweet bumblebee
Chickadee beddy-bye
Little dove my love
Little cookie-nookie
Asleep.

She's asleep
And she hasn't taken in a thing the whole way
All those faces glimpsed in the stations
All the clocks
Paris time Berlin time Saint Petersburg time all those stations'
    times
And at Ufa the bloody face of the cannoneer
And the absurdly luminous dial at Grodno
And the train moving forward endlessly
Every morning you set your watch ahead
The train moves forward and the sun loses time
It's no use! I hear the bells
The big bell at Notre-Dame
The sharp bell at the Louvre that rang on Saint Bartholomew's
    Day
The rusty carillons of Bruges-the-Dead
The electric bells of the New York Public Library
The campaniles of Venice
And the bells of Moscow ringing, the clock at Red Gate that kept
    time for me when I was working in an office
And my memories
The train thunders into the roundhouse
The train rolls along
A gramophone blurts out a tinny Bohemian march
And the world, like the hands of the clock in the Jewish section
    of Prague, turns wildly backwards.

Cast caution to the winds
Now the storm is raging
And the trains storm over tangled tracks
Infernal toys
There are trains that never meet
Others just get lost
The stationmasters play chess
Backgammon
Shoot pool
Carom shots
Parabolas
The railway system is a new geometry
Syracuse
Archimedes
And the soldiers who butchered him
And the galleys
And the warships
And the astounding engines he invented
And all that killing
Ancient history
Modern history
Vortex
Shipwreck
Even that of the *Titanic* I read about in the paper
So many associations images I can't get into my poem
Because I'm still such a really bad poet

Because the universe rushes over me
And I didn't bother to insure myself against train wreck
Because I don't know how to take it all the way
And I'm scared.

I'm scared
I don't know how to take it all the way.
Like my friend Chagall I could do a series of irrational paintings
But I didn't take notes
"Forgive my ignorance
Pardon my forgetting how to play the ancient game of Verse"
As Guillaume Apollinaire says
If you want to know anything about the war read Kuropotkin's
     *Memoirs*
Or the Japanese newspapers with their ghastly illustrations
But why compile a bibliography
I give up
Bounce back into my leaping memory...

At Irkutsk the trip suddenly slows down
Really drags
We were the first train to wind around Lake Baikal
The locomotive was decked out with flags and lanterns
And we had left the station to the sad sound of "God Save the
     Czar."
If I were a painter I would splash lots of red and yellow over the
     end of this trip
Because I think we were all slightly crazy
And that an overwhelming delirium brought blood to the
     exhausted faces of my traveling companions
As we came closer to Mongolia
Which roared like a forest fire.
The train had slowed down
And in the perpetual screeching of wheels I heard
The insane sobbing and screaming
Of an eternal liturgy

I saw
I saw the silent trains the black trains returning from the Far East
     and going by like phantoms
And my eyes, like tail lights, are still trailing along behind those
     trains
At Talga 100,000 wounded were dying with no help coming
I went to the hospitals in Krasnoyarsk
And at Khilok we met a long convoy of soldiers gone insane
I saw in quarantine gaping sores and wounds with blood
     gushing out
And the amputated limbs danced around or flew up in the raw air
Fire was in their faces and in their hearts
Idiot fingers drumming on all the windowpanes
And under the pressure of fear an expression would burst like
     an abcess
In all the stations they had set fire to all the cars
And I saw
I saw trains with 60 locomotives streaking away chased by hot
     horizons and desperate crows
Disappearing
In the direction of Port Arthur.

At Chita we had a few days' rest
A five-day stop while they cleared the tracks
We stayed with Mr. Iankelevitch who wanted me to marry his
     only daughter
Then it was time to go.
Now I was the one playing the piano and I had a toothache
And when I want I can see it all again those quiet rooms the store
     and the eyes of the daughter who slept with me every night
Mussorgsky
And the lieder of Hugo Wolf
And the sands of the Gobi Desert
And at Khailar a caravan of white camels

I'd swear I was drunk for over 300 miles
But I was playing the piano—it's all I saw
You should close your eyes on a trip
And sleep
I was dying to sleep
With my eyes closed I can smell what country I'm in
And I can hear what kind of train is going by
European trains are in 4/4 while the Asian ones are 5/4 or 7/4
Others go humming along are like lullabies
And there are some whose wheels' monotone reminds me of
     the heavy prose of Maeterlinck
I deciphered all the garbled texts of the wheels and united the
     scattered elements of a violent beauty
Which I possess
And which drives me

Tsitsihar and Harbin
That's as far as I go
The last station
I stepped off the train at Harbin a minute after they had set fire
     to the Red Cross office.

O Paris
Great warm hearth with the intersecting embers of your streets
     and your old houses leaning over them for warmth
Like grandmothers
And here are posters in red in green all colors like my past in a
     word yellow
Yellow the proud color of the novels of France
In big cities I like to rub elbows with the buses as they go by
Those of the Saint-Germain—Montmartre line that carry me to
     the assault of the Butte
The motors bellow like golden bulls
The cows of dusk graze on Sacré-Coeur
O Paris
Main station where desires arrive at the crossroads of restlessness
Now only the paint store has a little light on its door
The International Pullman and Great European Express
     Company has sent me its brochure
It's the most beautiful church in the world
I have friends who surround me like guardrails
They're afraid that when I leave I'll never come back
All the women I've ever known appear around me on the
     horizon
Holding out their arms and looking like sad lighthouses in the
     rain
Bella, Agnès, Catherine, and the mother of my son in Italy
And she who is the mother of my love in America
Sometimes the cry of a whistle tears me apart
Over in Manchuria a belly is still heaving, as if giving birth
I wish
I wish I'd never started traveling
Tonight a great love is driving me out of my mind
And I can't help thinking about little Jeanne of France.
It's through a sad night that I've written this poem in her honor
Jeanne
The little prostitute
I'm sad so sad
I'm going to the Lapin Agile to remember my lost youth again
Have a few drinks
And come back home alone

Paris

City of the incomparable Tower the great Gibbet and the Wheel

*Paris, 1913*

*—Translated from the French by Ron Padgett.*

• • •

*I have deciphered all the confused texts of the wheels and I have assembled the*
  *scattered elements of a most violent beauty*
*That I control*
*And which compels me.*

The "assembl[ing] of the scattered elements" of which Cendrars speaks involves, of course, the original typography and layout of the text as well as
Sonia Delaunay's painted *pochoir* accompaniment. In recalling the train's
approach to Mongolia, Cendrars declares:

If I were a painter I would spill great splashes of yellow and red over the end
  of this trip
Because I am quite sure we were all a little mad
And that a raging delirium was bloodying the lifeless faces of my
  travelling companions.

"Great splashes of yellow and red" do turn up in Delaunay's "illustration"
for the poem, but her interpretation of the journey emphasizes its life,
movement, energy, and color rather than its darker undertones: if Cendrars's sun is "a fierce wound," Delaunay's is a gorgeous golden ball. But even
this contrast is not quite accurate for Delaunay's painting is, of course, essentially nonrepresentational; she and her husband were among the first
abstract artists of Europe. Her *Transsibérien* is a complex arrangement of
concentric circles, ovals, triangles, and rectangles, whose brilliant opposition of colors is in itself the "subject" of the painting. A distinction Cendrars
made in a 1914 article on Robert Delaunay applies equally well to Sonia:

Our eyes reach up to the sun.
  A color is not a color in itself. It is a color only in contrast to another or to
several other colors. A blue is only blue in contrast to a red, a green, an orange, a gray and all the other colors.
  Contrast is not a matter of black and white, an opposition, a non-resem-
blance. Contrast is a resemblance. One travels in order to know, to recognize
men, things, animals. To live with. One faces things, one does not withdraw.
It is what men have most in common that distinguishes them the most. The
two sexes are in contrast. Contrast is love.

It is this system of differences that characterizes Delaunay's color field.
But her painting is not wholly nonrepresentational either. Without illustrating Cendrars's narrative, it nevertheless complements it. Thus we begin
at the top with large blue and violet discs and a vertical white tower shape
—a kind of abstract Moscow, the city of the one thousand and three bell
towers and the "great almonds of the cathedrals all in white." Patches of red
and yellow in the top quadrant suggest Red Square and the golden sun, or

again the Kremlin "like an immense Tartar cake / Frosted in gold" and the "honeyed gold of the bells."

As the eye moves downward, it travels over a rainbow-colored world of whirling suns, clouds, and wheels—a vision, perhaps, of the Trans-Siberian journey as seen not from a moving train but from an airplane, a kind of unfolding aerial map. Paradoxically, as Pierre Caizergues remarks, the vertical axis is the privileged one, even though everything in the poem celebrates horizontality, the spatialization of time. Indeed, the vertical-horizontal opposition is an example of what Cendrars calls simultaneous contrast. Delaunay's emphasis is on motion, circular form, color; her long sinuous ovals recall both machine parts and phalluses. These whirling forms descend, finally, on a little red toy version of the Eiffel Tower penetrating an equally childlike rendition of the Great Wheel.

At one point in the poem, Cendrars compares the rhythm of the speeding train to "Le ferlin d'or de mon avenir" ("The golden thread of my future"). This "golden thread" can be seen running from top to bottom of Delaunay's painting, curving in and out and finally materializing as the three-quarter halo that acts as the rim of the abstracted wheel. Again, golden threads and red ones, as well as large planes of pastel colors—rose, light blue, light yellow, violet, pale green—are inserted between the verse paragraphs and lines of the poem so as to destroy the continuity of the whole as uniform text. The resultant blocks of print, surrounded by color forms, display their own internal contrasts: the lettering shifts from roman to italic, uppercase to lowercase, black to red, light to dark, and so on.

There is not, of course, a one-to-one correspondence between typeface and a particular emotion or theme. But notice that what is probably the key turn in the poem—the abandonment of the [Trans-Siberian] journey and sudden "cut" to Paris—is printed in large black block letters and that the apostrophe to Paris that follows has a justified right rather than a justified left margin, heavy typeface being reserved for the references to color: "du rouge du vert," "du jaune," "Jaune." The second "O Paris" passage is juxtaposed to the first by the shift from a justified right to a justified left margin, the page thus opposing two rectangular forms that almost meet at midpoint, surrounded by equal amounts of white space.

What is the effect of this visualisation of the page? It implies, I think, a *mise en question* of the text's lyric frame, its generic identity as lyric poem as well as its semantic coherence. For Delaunay's painting, far from matching the verbal text to be illustrated, undermines its meanings: her version is everywhere brighter, sunnier, more positive, more optimistic than is Cendrars's voyage into the world of war. Indeed, in Delaunay's painting, the war remains an absence; the technological world, the world of propellers and air balloons, of engines and steel towers, is bright and beautiful even as we will see that machine world represented by the early Léger or Tatlin. Delaunay's version of *La Prose* draws out, so to speak, the international side of Futurism, the productive energy and vitality that the verbal text, with its precise delineation of place, has already questioned. To put it another way: Paris, the brilliant and vibrant international center of the *avant guerre*, is juxtaposed to the Trans-Siberian journey that will finally destroy it.

# from DESTRUCTION OF SYNTAX— IMAGINATION WITHOUT STRINGS— WORDS-IN-FREEDOM 1913

F. T. Marinetti

*The Futurist sensibility*

MY TECHNICAL MANIFESTO of Futurist Literature (11 May 1912), with which I invented *essential and synthetic lyricism, imagination without strings,* and *words-in-freedom,* deals exclusively with poetic inspiration.

Philosophy, the exact sciences, politics, journalism, education, business, however much they may seek synthetic forms of expression, will still need to use syntax and punctuation. I am obliged, for that matter, to use them myself in order to make myself clear to you.

Futurism is grounded in the complete renewal of human sensibility brought about by the great discoveries of science. Those people who today make use of the telegraph, the telephone, the phonograph, the train, the bicycle, the motorcycle, the automobile, the ocean liner, the dirigible, the aeroplane, the cinema, the great newspaper (synthesis of a day in the world's life) do not realize that these various means of communication, transportation and information have a decisive influence on their psyches.

An ordinary man can in a day's time travel by train from a little dead town of empty squares, where the sun, the dust, and the wind amuse themselves in silence, to a great capital city bristling with lights, gestures, and street cries. By reading a newspaper the inhabitant of a mountain village can tremble each day with anxiety, following insurrection in China, the London and New York suffragettes, Doctor Carrel, and the heroic dog-sleds of the polar explorers. The timid, sedentary inhabitant of any provincial town can indulge in the intoxication of danger by going to the movies and watching a great hunt in the Congo. He can admire Japanese athletes, Negro boxers, tireless American eccentrics, the most elegant Parisian women, by paying a franc to go to the variety theatre. Then, back in his bourgeois bed, he can enjoy the distant, expensive voice of a Caruso or a Burzio.

Having become commonplace, these opportunities arouse no curiosity in superficial minds who are as incapable of grasping any novel facts *as the Arabs who looked with indifference at the first aeroplanes in the sky of Tripoli.* For the keen observer, however, these facts are important modifiers of our sensibility because they have caused the following significant phenomena:

1.   Acceleration of life to today's swift pace. Physical, intellectual, and sentimental equilibration on the cord of speed stretched between contrary magnetisms. Multiple and simultaneous awareness in a single individual.

2.   Dread of the old and the known. Love of the new, the unexpected.

3.   Dread of quiet living, love of danger, and an attitude of daily heroism.

4.   Destruction of a sense of the Beyond and an increased value of the individual whose desire is *vivre sa vie,* in Bonnot's phrase.

5.   The multiplication and unbridling of human desires and ambitions.

6.   An exact awareness of everything inaccessible and unrealizable in every person.

7.   Semi-equality of man and woman and a lessening of the disproportion in their social rights.

8.   Disdain for *amore* (sentimentality or lechery) produced by the greater freedom and erotic ease of women and by the universal exaggeration of female luxury. Let me explain: Today's woman loves luxury more than love. A visit to a great dressmaker's establishment, escorted by a paunchy, gouty banker friend who pays the bills, is a perfect substitute for the most amorous rendezvous with an adored young man. The woman finds all the mystery of love in the selection of an amazing ensemble, the latest model, which her friends still do not have. Men do not love women who lack luxury. The lover has lost all his prestige. Love has lost its absolute worth. A complex question; all I can do is to raise it.

9.   A modification of patriotism, which now means a heroic idealization of the commercial, industrial, and artistic solidarity of a people.

10. A modification in the idea of war, which has become the necessary and bloody test of a people's force.

11. The passion, art, and idealism of Business. New financial sensibility.

12. Man multiplied by the machine. New mechanical sense, a fusion of instinct with the efficiency of motors and conquered forces.

13. The passion, art, and idealism of Sport. Idea and love of the 'record.'

14. New tourist sensibility bred by ocean liners and great hotels (annual synthesis of different races). Passion for the city. Negation of distances and nostalgic solitudes. Ridicule of the 'holy green silence' and the ineffable landscape.

15. The earth shrunk by speed. New sense of the world. To be precise: One after the other, man will gain the sense of his home, of the quarter where he lives, of his region, and finally of the continent. Today he is aware of the whole world. He little needs to know what his ancestors did, but he must assiduously discover what his contemporaries are doing all over the world. The single man, therefore, must communicate with every people on earth. He must feel himself to be the axis, judge, and motor of the explored and unexplored infinite. Vast increase of a sense of humanity and a momentary urgent need to establish relations with all mankind.

16. A loathing of curved lines, spirals, and the *tourniquet*. Love for the straight line and the tunnel. The habit of visual foreshortening and visual synthesis caused by the speed of trains and cars that look down on cities and countrysides. Dread of slowness, pettiness, analysis, and detailed explanations. Love of speed, abbreviation, and the summary. 'Quick, give me the whole thing in two words!'

17. Love of depth and essence in every exercise of the spirit.

So these are some elements of the new Futurist sensibility that has generated our pictorial dynamism, our antigraceful music in its free, irregular rhythms, our noise-art and our words-in-freedom.

*Words-in-freedom*

Casting aside every stupid formula and all the confused verbalisms of the professors, I now declare that lyricism is the exquisite faculty of intoxicating oneself with life, of filling life with the inebriation of oneself. The faculty of changing into wine the muddy water of the life that swirls and engulfs us. The ability to colour the world with the unique colours of our changeable selves.

Now suppose that a friend of yours gifted with this faculty finds himself in a zone of intense life (revolution, war, shipwreck, earthquake, and so on) and starts right away to tell you his impressions. Do you know what this lyric, excited friend of yours will instinctively do?

He will begin by brutally destroying the syntax of his speech. He wastes no time in building sentences. Punctuation and the right adjectives will mean nothing to him. He will despise subtleties and nuances of language. Breathlessly he will assault your nerves with visual, auditory, olfactory sensations, just as they come to him. The rush of steam-emotion will burst the sentence's steampipe, the valves of punctuation, and the adjectival clamp. Fistfuls of essential words in no conventional order. Sole preoccupation of the narrator, to render every vibration of his being.

If the mind of this gifted lyrical narrator is also populated by general ideas, he will involuntarily bind up his sensations with the entire universe that he intuitively knows. And in order to render the true worth and dimensions of his lived life, he will cast immense nets of analogy across the world. In this way he will reveal the analogical foundation of life, telegraphically, with the same economical speed that the telegraph imposes on reporters and war correspondents in their swift reportings. This urgent laconism answers not only to the laws of speed that govern us but also to the rapport of centuries between poet and audience. Between poet and audience, in fact, the same rapport exists as between two old friends. They can make themselves understood with half a word, a gesture, a glance. So the poet's imagination must weave together distant things *with no connecting strings*, by means of essential *free* words.

## Death of free verse

Free verse once had countless reasons for existing but now is destined to be replaced by *words-in-freedom.*

The evolution of poetry and human sensibility has shown us the two incurable defects of free verse.

1. Free verse fatally pushes the poet towards facile sound effects, banal double meanings, monotonous cadences, a foolish chiming, and an inevitable echo-play, internal and external.

2. Free verse artificially channels the flow of lyric emotion between the high walls of syntax and the weirs of grammar. The free intuitive inspiration that addresses itself directly to the intuition of the ideal reader finds itself imprisoned and distributed like purified water for the nourishment of all fussy, restless intelligences.

When I speak of destroying the canals of syntax, I am neither categorical nor systematic. Traces of conventional syntax and even of true logical sentences will be found here and there in the words-in-freedom of my unchained lyricism. This inequality in conciseness and freedom is natural and inevitable. Since poetry is in truth only a superior, more concentrated and intense life than what we live from day to day, like the latter it is composed of hyper-alive elements and moribund elements.

We ought not, therefore, to be too much preoccupied with these elements. But we should at all costs avoid rhetoric and banalities telegraphically expressed.

*The imagination without strings*

By the imagination without strings I mean the absolute freedom of images or analogies, expressed with unhampered words and with no connecting strings of syntax and with no punctuation.

'Up to now writers have been restricted to immediate analogies. For instance, they have compared an animal with a man or with another animal, which is almost the same as a kind of photography. (They have compared, for example, a fox terrier to a very small thoroughbred. Others, more advanced, might compare the same trembling fox terrier to a little Morse Code machine. I, on the other hand, compare it with gurgling water. In this there is an *ever vaster gradation of analogies,* there are ever deeper and more solid affinities, however remote.)

'Analogy is nothing more than the deep love that assembles distant, seemingly diverse and hostile things. An orchestral style, at once polychromatic, polyphonic, and polymorphous, can embrace the life of matter only by means of the most extensive analogies.

'When, in my *Battle of Tripoli,* I compared a trench bristling with bayonets to an orchestra, a machine gun to a *femme fatale,* I intuitively introduced a large part of the universe into a short episode of African battle.

'Images are not flowers to be chosen and picked with parsimony, as Voltaire said. They are the very lifeblood of poetry. Poetry should be an uninterrupted sequence of new images, or it is mere anaemia and greensickness.

'The broader their affinities, the longer will images keep their power to amaze.'

(Technical Manifesto of Futurist Literature)

The imagination without strings, and words-in-freedom, will bring us to the essence of material. As we discover new analogies between distant and apparently contrary things, we will endow them with an ever more intimate value. Instead of *humanizing* animals, vegetables, and minerals (an outmoded system) we will be able to *animalize, vegetize, mineralize, electrify, or liquefy our style,* making it live the life of material. For example, to represent the life of a blade of grass, I say, 'Tomorrow I'll be greener.'

With words-in-freedom we will have: CONDENSED METAPHORS. TELEGRAPHIC IMAGES. MAXIMUM VIBRATIONS. NODES OF THOUGHT. CLOSED OR OPEN FANS OF MOVEMENT. COMPRESSED ANALOGIES. COLOUR BALANCES. DIMENSIONS, WEIGHTS, MEASURES, AND THE SPEED OF SENSATIONS. THE PLUNGE OF THE ESSENTIAL WORD INTO THE WATER OF SENSIBILITY, MINUS THE CONCENTRIC CIRCLES THAT THE WORD PRODUCES. RESTFUL MOMENTS OF INTUITION. MOVEMENTS IN TWO, THREE, FOUR, FIVE DIFFERENT RHYTHMS. THE ANALYTIC, EXPLORATORY POLES THAT SUSTAIN THE BUNDLE OF INTUITIVE STRINGS.

• • •

Filippo Tommaso Marinetti. *Les mots en liberté futuristes*. 1919. Cover and inside page of book.

## Typographical revolution

I initiate a typographical revolution aimed at the bestial, nauseating idea of the book of passéist and D'Annunzian verse, on seventeenth-century hand-made paper bordered with helmets, Minervas, Apollos, elaborate red initials, vegetables, mythological missal ribbons, epigraphs, and roman numerals. The book must be the Futurist expression of our Futurist thought. Not only that. My revolution is aimed at the so-called typographical harmony of the page, which is contrary to the flux and reflux, the leaps and bursts of style that run through the page. On the same page, therefore, we will use *three or four colours of ink,* or even twenty different typefaces if necessary. For example: italics for a series of similar or swift sensations, boldface for the violent onomatopoeias, and so on. With this typographical revolution and this multi-coloured variety in the letters I mean to redouble the expressive force of words.

I oppose the decorative, precious aesthetic of Mallarmé and his search for the rare word, the one indispensable, elegant, suggestive, exquisite adjective. I do not want to suggest an idea or a sensation with passéist airs and graces. Instead I want to grasp them brutally and hurl them in the reader's face.

Moreover, I combat Mallarmé's static ideal with this typographical revolution that allows me to impress on the words (already free, dynamic, and torpedo-like) every velocity of the stars, the clouds, aeroplanes, trains, waves, explosives, globules of seafoam, molecules, and atoms.

Thus I realize the fourth principle of my First Futurist Manifesto (20 February 1909): 'We affirm that the world's beauty is enriched by a new beauty: the beauty of speed.'

*Multilinear lyricism*

In addition, I have conceived *multilinear lyricism,* with which I succeed in reaching that lyric simultaneity that obsessed the Futurist painters as well: multilinear lyricism by means of which I am sure to achieve the most complex lyric simultaneities.

On several parallel lines, the poet will throw out several chains of colour, sound, smell, noise, weight, thickness, analogy. One of these lines might, for instance, be olfactory, another musical, another pictorial.

Let us suppose that the chain of pictorial sensations and analogies dominates the others. In this case it will be printed in a heavier typeface than the second and third lines (one of them containing, for example, the chain of musical sensations and analogies, the other the chain of olfactory sensations and analogies).

Given a page that contains many bundles of sensations and analogies, each of which is composed of three or four lines, the chain of pictorial sensations and analogies (printed in boldface) will form the first line of the first bundle and will continue (always in the same type) on the first line of all the other bundles.

The chain of musical sensations and analogies, less important than the chain of pictorial sensations and analogies (first line) but more important than that of the olfactory sensations and analogies (third line), will be printed in smaller type than that of the first line and larger than that of the third.

*Free expressive orthography*

The historical necessity of free expressive orthography is demonstrated by the successive revolutions that have continuously freed the lyric powers of the human race from shackles and rules.

1.  In fact, the poets began by channelling their lyric intoxication into a series of equal breaths, with accents, echoes, assonances, or rhymes at pre-established intervals (*traditional metric*). Then the poets varied these different measured breaths of their predecessors' lungs with a certain freedom.

2.  Later the poets realized that the different moments of their lyric intoxication had to create breaths suited to the most varied and surprising intervals, with absolute freedom of accentuation. Thus they arrived at *free verse,* but they still preserved the syntactic order of the words, so that the lyric intoxication could flow down to the listeners by the logical canal of syntax.

3.  Today we no longer want the lyric intoxication to order the words syntactically before launching them forth with the breaths we have invented, and we have *words-in-freedom.* Moreover our lyric intoxication should freely

deform, reflesh the words, cutting them short, stretching them out, reinforcing the centre or the extremities, augmenting or diminishing the number of vowels and consonants. Thus we will have the *new orthography* that I call *free expressive.* This instinctive deformation of words corresponds to our natural tendency towards onomatopoeia. It matters little if the deformed word becomes ambiguous. It will marry itself to the onomatopoetic harmonies, or the noise-summaries, and will permit us soon to reach the *onomatopoetic psychic* harmony, the sonorous but abstract expression of an emotion or a pure thought. But one may object that my words-in-freedom, my imagination without strings, demand special speakers if they are to be understood. Although I do not care for the comprehension of the multitude, I will reply that the number of Futurist public speakers is increasing and that any admired traditional poem, for that matter, requires a special speaker if it is to be understood.

11 May 1913

Published in *Lacerba* (Florence), 15 June 1913

*— Translated from the Italian by R. W. Flint.*

# *from* "KRUCHONYKH AND THE MANUSCRIPT BOOK"
## THE FIRST [SIX] MANUSCRIPT BOOKS

### Gerald Janecek

IN MID-1912, Aleksey Kruchonykh (1886–1968) published his first literary works, thereby initiating a series of manuscript books that was to continue into the 1920s and that constitutes his major contribution to the look of Futurist literature....

The first books by Kruchonykh, six lithographed pamphlets, are extreme rarities, as are most of the later ones. They are not readily available in the United States, or even in Soviet libraries, although recently some have come up for sale at Sotheby auctions and elsewhere and may eventually turn up in the collections of museums and wealthy libraries. They are also available now on microfiche from Chadwych-Healey Ltd. and Interdocumentation Corp. A good selection of Kruchonykh's works in photocopied book form was edited and published by V. Markov (*Izbrannoe,* 1973). Three of the first six are included in the Markov book, as are ten later booklets and additional material; this anthology is thus the handiest source for an overview of Kruchonykh's works. Lacking more specific or contradictory information, I will assume that the bibliography, which is subdivided by years, lists the works in chronological order.

Before we study the individual works by Kruchonykh and his collaborators, it is worthwhile to pause a moment to consider the technical conditions and limitations under which the books were produced. Donald Karshan, in his print catalogue of Malevich, discusses these matters primarily in relation to the painter, but his analysis applies to many of the other works in which Malevich was not directly involved. Regarding the paper used for many of the books, Karshan notes that it was

> ...usually the cheapest and thus the most perishable variety; thin, brittle and made of wood pulp. The reasons for such a selection were twofold: In some instances it was simply a matter of the publisher, usually the writers themselves, not having the funds for better paper (there was a great scarcity of paper in Russia during those years); in other instances, common paper was deliberately chosen, as an anti-establishment gesture and extension of their ideological stance. At this time, Paris-illustrated books, such as those by Kahnweiler and illustrated by Picasso, were printed on luxurious hand-made papers. (*Malevich: The Graphic Work 1913–1930, A Print Catalogue Raisonné,* 1975, p. 29)

On size limitations, Karshan explains:

> The Malevich lithographs were nearly all very small, as compared to most prints of the same epoch published in France and Germany. This was probably due to the fact that only small limestone slabs for the making of the lithographic images were available to Malevich and his collaborators. And then, the format of the booklets themselves [was] quite small, particularly in the case of the Futurist pamphlets and books—a scale chosen as an anti-book gesture or anti-elitist symbol, but perhaps also influenced by budgetary limitations. Parisian publications of the same epoch were generally much larger in format, with generous margins around the images; were issued in special editions on different papers, often pencil-numbered and signed by the artist. (p. 31)

And finally, on the printing process itself:

> Typography by letterpress is a *relief process,* as are photoengraved plates. That which is *raised* on the plate, such as a line, is printed (the reverse exists for traditional engraving, etching). Woodcut is also a relief process: that which is cut away, does not print; only the raised portions do. Consequently, the less costly process, say for the preparations of *Victory over the Sun,* was to employ the photoengraved plate for the Malevich image, and the David Burliuk woodcut which is printed on the back cover. The plate, the type, and the woodcut all printed on one press cycle. This is why the lithographs which appear with typeset in futurist books are always *handmounted* on the covers or *hand-inserted* within. A lithographic image cannot be pulled on the same press cycle as the type, which is printed by letterpress. This also explains the all-lithographed books such as *A Game in Hell*: one process all the way through the printing procedure. Many deluxe illustrated books in the west juxtapose lithographic or etched images, for example, with typeset, necessitating the costly use of two or more separate printing processes. (p. 63)

To this, Susan Compton adds:

> The degree of participation by the artist who originated the image or the handwriting would vary. The printing was done by the professional, rather than the artist himself, from a lithographic stone, or sometimes, a zinc plate. The artist rarely worked on the stone, but provided the drawing and writing on paper. Special transfer papers were available, ready prepared for an artist to draw on, either with a lithographic crayon or pen, though cartridge paper could also be used. (*The World Backwards,* 1978, pp. 70–71)

There were several advantages to the process: transfer papers allowed the artist to draw or write forward, rather than in mirror image, as was done when working directly on stone; the artist did not need to work at the lithographers, but could prepare his drawings wherever and whenever he wanted; and the handwritten text and the illustrations did not have to be done together, but could be done separately and combined later. "The finished result," as Compton remarks, "is not inferior to work drawn directly on the stone." Many of the drawings led a life separate from the texts, either in exhibits or as illustrations in other books.... Such practices sometimes led to disunity or dissatisfaction among the contributing parties (see the discussion below on *A Game in Hell*).

All six of the books by Kruchonykh surveyed in this section are, except when otherwise indicated, lithographed throughout; they are printed on only one side of the page, and are octavo or smaller in size. We must remember that book design and production were based not only on aesthetic principles but also on the available financial resources. Thus, if a book was to be lithographed throughout, it was simpler and more economical to have the text handwritten on the stone or on transfer paper, whereas typesetting would incur considerable additional expense. Of course, one might say that all art exists within technical constraints, and it is what is achieved within those constraints that matters—not the constraints themselves.

Kruchonykh's first monographic publication, *Old-Fashioned Love*, appeared around August 1912, the date of *A Game in Hell,* co-authored by Kruchonykh and Khlebnikov. It is listed as the first item in Kruchonykh's bibliography and perhaps it came out slightly before *Game*. Immediately striking is the design of the book, which is really more the size of a pamphlet (14 pages plus cover). It is lithographed from a handwritten text of eleven pages; two full-page rayist drawings, and the front and back cover designs, headpiece, and tailpiece were all done by M. Larionov.... As Markov comments, "It was obviously meant to be a complete break with the tradition of symbolist deluxe editions. The illustrations were either primitivist in the manner of folk art, or imitative of children's drawings, but some of them could be termed nonobjective" (V. Markov, *Russian Futurism: A History,* 1968, p. 41).

Besides being shocked to find in his hands a published work by a modern author that was handwritten and illustrated with primitive drawings, the reader of *Old-Fashioned Love* was probably struck by the poor quality of the book: cheap paper, poor binding, and unevenly trimmed pages—a rather makeshift and naive product compared to the prevailing norms. This, of course, was precisely the point, as Markov notes. Yet once the shock subsided, the reader was surely impressed by the visual unity of the whole work, which imparts the sensation of having been written and drawn by the same hand. In contrast to the usual design of an illustrated book of the time, in which text pages differed markedly from illustration pages in the production process (letterpress versus lithography, color gravure, photoengraving, etc.), kind of paper, and craftsmanship, the drawings and text of Kruchonykh's first publication were both lithographed on the same paper.

The fact that only one process is used throughout *Old-Fashioned Love* not only allows for a unity of impression between text and illustration, but also permits the easy interpenetration of the two components. Thus rayist doodles or decorations can appear on a page of text [Fig. 1], and the page

number can become incorporated into a drawing [Fig. 2, lower left corner].
On page 1 [Fig. 3], little cubist flowers fall from the headpiece drawing of a
nude and a vase of flowers into the lines of text below. Although drawing
and text remain distinguishable in this instance, they unexpectedly share
the same space, and it is probably not immediately obvious that the little
geometric figures belong to the illustration. They almost look like accents
over the vowels below them. The boundary between text and illustration is
thus subtly obliterated. The text itself consists of seven poems that sometimes parody nineteenth-century love lyrics by juxtaposing romantic clichés
with "stylistic dissonances or nonaesthetic details (e.g., pus, vomit)" (ibid.,
p. 42). The poems per se are less innovative than the visual aspects of the
book and do not establish Kruchonykh as a first-rate poet.

Larionov's illustrations reflect the mood of "romantic clichés" in the repeated images of a nude and a vase of flowers. The drawings themselves
tell a mute story:

> Front cover: Close-up vase of flowers [Fig. 4].
> p. 1: small reclining female nude with vase of
> flowers nearby, petals falling [Fig. 3].
> p. 3: abstract rayist composition [Fig. 2].
> p. 7: foreground, lady with umbrella; man in
> background walking on perpendicular path,
> street light shining (rayist style) [Fig. 5].
> p. 14: female nude, rear view [Fig. 6].
> Back cover: large overturned vase of flowers;
> small-scaled nude overlapping composition;
> birds or butterflies (Compton, p. 71) flying off
> in opposite directions [Fig. 7].

Figure 2. A. Kruchonykh,
*Old-Fashioned Love,* 1912, p. 3;
drawing by M. Larionov.

Figure 1. A. Kruchonykh,
*Old-Fashioned Love,* 1912, p. 2.

Figure 3. A. Kruchonykh,
*Old-Fashioned Love,* 1912, p. 1;
drawing by M. Larionov.

Figure 4. A. Kruchonykh,
*Old-Fashioned Love,* front cover
by M. Larionov.

The scene on page 7 takes some effort to "read" (Compton, p. 89) and does not have a precise connection with any moment in the text; but it can be seen as a composite of various lines of text. About the woman it is said, "Dearest of all are you in an old hat, rumpled sides," while she says, "I arrive at a sacred tremor, walking under your umbrella." The man "loves to stroll," but next to her so that she can't "tyrannize" him with a head-on glance or "boldly insult" him directly to his face. Nighttime episodes are included in an on-again, off-again love affair of pseudo-tragic triteness, which is well captured in this sketch and the others:

> Then, triumphing amid the world,
> You [the woman] groaned thus in the quiet of nights!
> Despising you and jealous all the same
> I chose the path of devils!... (p. 11)

The fact that page 7 is ultimately "readable" inclines one to try reading the rayist sketch on page 3 for some objective content. The page must be turned so the page number is in the lower left corner, and in that position one can barely make out a nude figure sitting on the end of a bed (?) in a room, with a window in the upper left corner. Such a "reading" is possible only in the context of the other illustrations, and with the text as a guide.

Another item of interest is the orthography of the text. Although in many respects it moves away from the old orthography, it is inconsistent, no doubt intentionally so. For instance, on page 1, line 1, we have хочеш (for хочешь, [you want]) and несчасным (for несчастнымъ [unhappy]); but in line 2 we have have слѣдъ прекрасным (for прекраснымъ [fine]). Despite inconsistencies, mainly on page 1, there is a system of sorts that leans toward the new orthography by rejecting the use of ъ after final consonants; otherwise the text usually follows Grot's rules. The departures

Figure 5. A. Kruchonykh,
*Old-Fashioned Love,* p. 7;
drawing by M. Larionov.

Figure 6. A. Kruchonykh,
*Old-Fashioned Love,* p. 14;
drawing by M. Larionov.

Figure 7. A. Kruchonykh,
*Old-Fashioned Love,* back cover
by M. Larionov.

from these rules are done for phonetic accuracy. Standard punctuation is sometimes omitted. This revised orthography is very likely Kruchonykh's responsibility rather than Larionov's, since it follows Kruchonykh's own personal spelling as seen in most of the books he edited and/or wrote; in contrast, Larionov's *Rayism* (1913) used the standard Grot orthography.

*A Game in Hell* (1912) is Kruchonykh's first collaboration with Khlebnikov. The poem, which describes a card game between devils and sinners in hell, was conceived by Kruchonykh as "a parody of the archaic idea of the devil done in the manner of a *lubok*." [Popular Russian broadsides produced continuously from the 17th into the early 20th century. —Eds.] The collaboration arose spontaneously, as Kruchonykh reports:

> David Burliuk acquainted me with Khlebnikov at the beginning of 1912 in Moscow at some debate or exhibition.... In one of the subsequent meetings in Khlebnikov's untidy and student-like bare room, I pulled from my notebook two sheets of a draft of 40-50 lines of my poem *A Game in Hell*. I showed it to him humbly. Suddenly, to my surprise, Velimir sat down and began to add his own lines above, below and around mine. This was a characteristic trait of Khlebnikov's: he caught fire creatively from the slightest spark. He showed me the pages covered with his minute handwriting. We read it together, argued, corrected it again. Thus unexpectedly and unwittingly we became co-authors.

So began a relationship that produced a number of joint books and manifestoes. The artist for the book this time was Larionov's lifelong companion Nataliya Goncharova [Fig. 8]. The calligraphic style of pages 1 to 7 and 14 is archaic, often resembling medieval Church Slavic *poluustav* lettering or later chancellery script [Fig. 9]. Old orthography is consistently observed. (Oddly, pages 8, 10, and 11 switch to the cursive style of *Old-Fashioned Love* and drop the ъ and old letter forms as if these pages were done by a different hand.) It is heavily illustrated in Goncharova's finest primitive manner, and every page of text except the last (p. 14) has an illustration, three of them

Figure 8. A. Kruchonykh and V. Khlebnikov, *A Game in Hell,* first edition, 1912, with drawings by N. Goncharova. The complete book is shown on following pages.

Figure 8, continued.

(pp. 9, 11, and 13) full-page. Contrary to Larionov's practice, the illustrations are sharply separated from the text by a strong black-white contrast line. But the positioning of the drawings is striking, with the artist taking advantage of the margins to depict full-length vertical figures of devils. This shape resembles that of deisis icons and was used by Goncharova elsewhere as well, most notably in her paintings of the four evangelists (1910–11). Two pages contain a quadrilateral illustration, with one non-rectilinear side consuming the upper right corner and squeezing the text diagonally to the left margin; two other pages devote the entire upper part to an illustration. The alternation of these illustration shapes gives the book a complex rhythm. In contrast to the somewhat haphazard look of *Old-Fashioned Love*, *A Game* gives the impression of genuine antiquity and primitiveness, and of well-thought-out high art. The book has structure and rhythm, and the illustrations are well suited to the style of the text, which has gained much by the participation of Khlebnikov's poetic genius. N. Khardzhiev has called the book "one of the classic examples of the unbroken unity of illustrations and text." This is despite the recorded dissatisfaction of the artist in a letter to Kruchonykh:

Figure 8, continued.

I received the proofs. They are printed very well, but positioned very badly. The drawing is placed on the stapled binding side [i.e., left]—this is very ugly; it would have been much better to place it on the outer edge of the page [i.e., right], which was what the whole composition of the drawings was predicated on and which gives more decorative unity and mass to the whole book. On those pages where the drawing is at the top, it would have been better to write the text right up or closer to the outer edge of the book. In any case, now it would be better to staple the page either at the bottom or the top, or so that the written side [the book was printed in recto] ends up not on the right side of the opened book, but on the left, i.e., facing the back cover as in old Hebrew and Arabic books.

This was not done, but the book hardly suffered as a result. Goncharova's remark about the positioning of the text indicates that although she did the drawings, she was not responsible for the calligraphy. Nevertheless, it is beautifully done by whoever did it, and Khlebnikov himself was pleased with the book, indicating "It has a sharp-witted appearance and cover." It does not have the uneven, "sloppy" character of *Old-Fashioned Love.*

With *Worldbackwards* (1912) we move into something that is "much more experimental" (Markov) and away from what is merely a text with pictures, albeit a text handwritten by the artist himself. The title makes clear the author's intention to turn the usual norms upside down, and so he does. Although a section is devoted to Khlebnikov, it seems certain that Kruchonykh was entirely in control of this production.

The experimental nature of this work can be summarized as an obvious attempt to emphasize disorder or to avoid the unity that characterized the first two books. Everything is done to upset traditional notions of aesthetic organization: materials, and therefore colors, are mixed; two kinds and weights of paper are used in uneven alternation throughout, one whiter and thinner for the "stamped" pages, another heavier and thicker mainly for the lithographed pages; and a paper polyfoil leaf is pasted to the cover. The artists, and therefore the style of illustrations, are multiple: not only did Larionov and Goncharova make major contributions, but Rogovin and Tatlin also added a few drawings. The style of the latter two artists contrasts noticeably with the former two. And for the first time, the printing process is varied: the illustrations, with the exception of the leaf on the cover, are all lithographed as before, as is most of the text, but also included are thirteen pages of text done by a process that produces a colored copy instead of the black of the lithographed pages. The text in these instances is not handwritten, but rather it is rubber-stamped in typescript letters of varying sizes, mixing upper and lower case haphazardly [Fig. 10]. Added to some of these pages are much larger, handwritten letters in contrasting

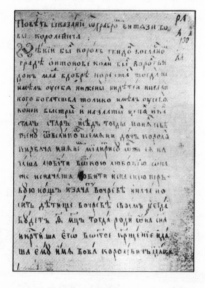

Figure 9. Eighteenth-century *poluustav* manuscript of the "Tale of Bova."

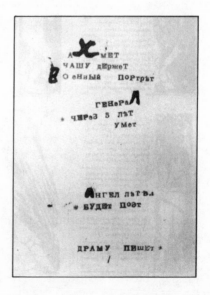

Figure 10. A. Kruchonykh et. al., *Worldbackwards*, 1912–13, page with rubber-stamped text.

black, or in the case of the *n* in "Stikhi V. Khlebnikova" (verses by V. Khleb-nikov) in red, which appear to have been done by hand on each copy. One such page (p. 22) is mounted with the text running vertically, so that one must turn the book 90° to read the passage.

Only Goncharova's drawings are honored by a reference on the pre-ceding page, and in one instance a drawing is heralded on the *two* preceding pages (pp. 23–24); the first of these also contains the title of Kruchonykh's travelogue, which begins on the page following Goncharova's drawing (p. 25). In another instance, such a reference is followed not by a Goncharova drawing, but by a piece of text with a drawing by Larionov (p. 48).

Also somewhat chaotic and unpredictable is the interpolation of blank pages made of white paper. These blanks precede illustrations (including some illustrations with texts), which can be seen through the transparent paper, and thus act as veils, but they also resemble the slips used to overlay illustrations in elegant editions. At one point (pp. 39–40), two such blank pages follow one another, after the announcement of "Verses by V. Khleb-nikov"; they are followed by a Rogovin drawing in which the artist has added doodles to his own rather wild handwritten copy of several verses [Fig. 11]. The page looks more like a piece of graffiti than a dignified presentation of a poem or illustration, which one would normally expect. In any case, the double blank page seems to be a mistake that playfully calls attention to the very existence and function (or lack thereof) of the blank pages them-selves—a "baring of the device." The Lenin Library copy, however, lacks these thin and blank pages.

Figure 11. *Worldbackwards*, 1912–13, page by I. Rogovin, poem by V. Khlebnikov.

Figure 12. *Worldbackwards*, 1912–13, page by M. Larionov, text by V. Khlebnikov.

The texts vary, ranging from stanzas in traditional meters to unpunctuated automatic prose writing. The fact that some of it is lithographed handwriting and some rubber-stamped typeset adds to the feeling of disparity. The lettering is usually chaotic in form, particularly in the prose travelogue, and the diverse handwritings on the pages containing both illustration and text suggest that the artist also did the calligraphy. This is most obvious in the cases of Larionov (pp. 2, 48 [Fig. 12], and 54; compare with *Old-Fashioned Love*) and Rogovin (p. 42 [Fig. 11]), but is probably true of the Goncharova pages as well.

One particularly interesting new feature of this book—in view of its intentionally blurred organization—is a decided blurring of the boundary between text and illustration. There is a variety of instances in which letters themselves become part of the composition of an illustration, as in Picasso and Braque Cubist collages beginning in 1911. Goncharova, Shevchenko, Larionov, and others began to do this in 1912. Thus, in addition to illustrations such as those found in the earlier books, we have Fig. 13 with the syllables *AX* and *ME* to left of the head echoing the word "axmet" on the following page of text and with the artist's name broken up in an attention-getting manner below. Or, in Fig. 14 we see *MEE* (or Ɛ ) and *ME* Ƃ ( ∧ ) combined with musical notes and lines suggesting musical instruments. Even more fascinating is Fig. 15, in which the creature in the drawing appears to be shouting "OZZ"; yet, since his ear is drawn in a stroke like the letters, the ear seems to be a letter C.

Rogovin's two drawings on pages 19 and 20 look like primitive cave writings, with stick figures prancing around in various positions. It takes one a moment to realize that in the second sketch [Fig. 16] the parade of "figures" up the right margin is the artist's signature, so much do the first

Figure 13. *Worldbackwards*, 1912–13, page by M. Larionov.  Figure 14. *Worldbackwards*, 1912–13, page by M. Larionov.  Figure 15. *Worldbackwards*, 1912–13, page by M. Larionov.

two letters with their extra appendages (H, P) look like figures. In the Rogovin example shown in Fig. 11 the script is so rambling and disconnected that it is hard to distinguish the text from the doodles [...]

This page is followed by two pages of drawings by Larionov that are stylistically close to Rogovin's. The first of these has a caption written mostly in mirror-image letters [Fig. 17]. The text, deciphered, is:

> Наш кочень очень озабочен
> Нож отточен точен очень

> Our cabbage head is very very worried
> The knife is very very sharp

The second drawing has a caption also, but it is written in normal letters. Interesting here are the stick cave figures that seem to imitate Rogovin's signature in Fig. 16 but do not spell anything [Fig. 18]. The natural gravity of the figures and the whole composition dictate that the page should be rotated 90° clockwise, but the caption would then be in the wrong position (first read, then rotate) (Compton, p. 92).

Kruchonykh's next three booklets, published in rapid succession in early 1913, add little in the way of new visual devices. *Pomade*, illustrated by Larionov, is quite short (18 pages). Its cover is handcut from shiny, cinnabar-red paper and most of the full-page illustrations are mounted on gold leaf papers rather than stapled in as in earlier books. The lithographs are watercolored in twenty-five of the copies. *Pomade* gained particular notoriety for having introduced to the world three poems written in what was

Figure 16. *Worldbackwards*, 1912–13, page by I. Rogovin.

Figure 17. *Worldbackwards*, 1912–13, page by M. Larionov.

Figure 18. *Worldbackwards*, 1912–13, page by M. Larionov.

later called *zaum* (transrational language). Fig. 19 reproduces the famous *zaum* poem "dyr bul shchyl." The poems written after the three *zaum* poems are more traditional in form but have "shifted" syntax. Note also the continual alternation of cursive and printed letter forms and the complete absence of ъ [Fig. 20].

*Half-Alive* (1913), with marvelously expressive drawings by Larionov, is a single narrative poem, similar to *A Game in Hell* in its emphasis on the hellish. Compton notes the echo of violence in the progressive disintegration of the nude figures. Finally, *Desert Dwellers* (1913), illustrated by Goncharova, is unique in separating the text completely from the illustrations. The drawings take up the full page, and there are no drawings as part of the text pages. Furthermore, the text, written in double columns, is bound in at the top of the page, that is, at right angles to the illustrations. This calls for a constant 90° rotation of the book back and forth, between text pages and illustration pages [Fig. 21]. The illustration and comment by Compton (p. 33) indicate that this right-angle arrangement may have transpired by mistake. Inexplicably, the illustrations are twice as large as the text pages. To bind the two together necessitated the turning of the text pages on their sides to create the same size page as the illustrations. Compton's illustration 21 shows one of the text pages already cut to the smaller size, with two leaves placed one above the other to form a large page; however, the other pages are uncut. The text consists of two narrative poems, "Desert Dwellers" and "Woman Desert Dweller," the first of which is written in the nearly consistent chancellery script of *Game* while the second is in the mixed script of the other booklets. Moreover, the text and illustrations share the same mix-

Figure 19. A. Kruchonykh, *Pomade*, 1913, showing the famous transrational poem "Dyr bul shchyl"; drawing by M. Larionov.

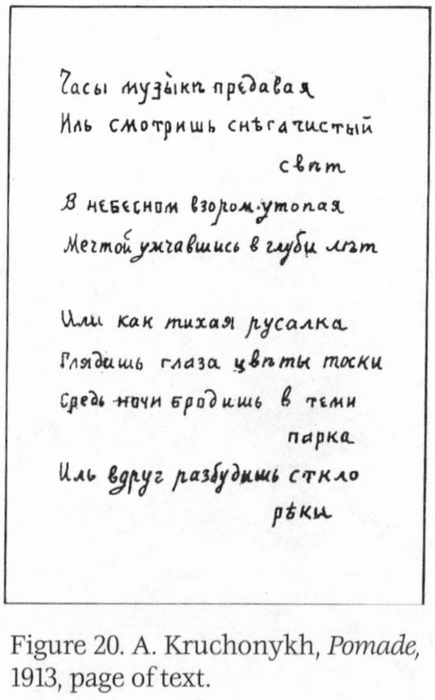

Figure 20. A. Kruchonykh, *Pomade*, 1913, page of text.

Figure 21. A. Kruchonykh, *Desert Dwellers*, 1913, drawing by N. Goncharova.

ture of "Byzantine severity and popular humor" (M. Chamot, *Goncharova*, 1972, p. 84) and thus are harmonious complements.

The importance of these six booklets in the history of the Russian Avant Garde cannot be overestimated. In Markov's words, "In his first publishing ventures, Kruchonykh added his own note to Russian primitivism; created, mainly with the artists Goncharova and Larionov, the classic form of a Futurist publication; and inaugurated the most extreme of all Futurist achievements, *zaum*" (1968, p. 44). In terms of visual effects, *Worldbackwards* is the most avant-garde of the avant-garde books in the set because of its anti-aesthetic disunity and emphasis on the Futurist collective, which stands "on the solid block of the word 'we' amid the sea of boos and indignation" (Ibid., p. 46).

After the publication of these booklets the collaboration of Goncharova and Larionov in the work of Kruchonykh tapers off; it is thus appropriate to pause and consider their role. Khardzhiev, in his necrological survey of their achievements, understandably emphasizes the importance of the two painters in these projects: "Larionov and Goncharova created a new type of poetic book—entirely lithographed with a text written by the author or artist (*samopismo*)." He points out that this format permitted the close relationship of illustration to text and also provided a programmatic answer to the elegant graphics of the World of Art group. Furthermore, "The aim of Larionov's and Goncharova's illustrations was the illumination of the poetic work not by literary but by painterly means. Precisely this explains the adoption by the artists of the lithographic technique—its specific peculiarities did not limit the freedom of purely painterly solutions."* These statements appear to credit the artists with the lithographic innovations, but Khardzhiev had immediately before this noted that it was Kruchonykh, a trained graphic artist, who had first led the two away from the easel and to book illustration by suggesting they lithograph some of their paintings for postcards, which he then had published in mid-1912 . Kruchonykh later explained his own move away from painting toward literature in the following way:

> In these years (1910–11), having a foreboding of the rapid death of painting and its substitution by something different, which subsequently took shape in photo montage, I broke my brushes ahead of time, abandoned my palette and washed my hands in order, with a pure soul, to take up the pen and work for the glory and destruction of Futurism—that farewell literary school which was only then beginning to burn with its final (and brightest) worldwide fire.

Although Kruchonykh seems to have been the main editor and producer of the booklets, the venture was obviously a cooperative one. When the involvement of the two artists in this sort of work ended…Kruchonykh continued to publish similar and varied works for some time after with the help of other artists. Moreover, Kruchonykh, with Khlebnikov, is responsible for the supportive theories that emerged soon after these first publications.

---

*In an interesting technical remark, Khardzhiev notes: "In contrast to illustrations by Goncharova, who preferred to work with a lithographic pencil, the whole illustration series by Larionov in 1912–13, except for the first book [*Old-Fashioned Love*], was done with lithographic ink. This was an avoidance of three-dimensional spatial constructions and a move to schematic planar solutions. With the help of this new principle Larionov attained the full unity of book architechtonics" [*Iskusstvo knigi*. Vol. 5 (1963–64): 316]. The difference between thick-lined planar ink technique and the more modeled, granular pencil technique is evident in many of the above examples.

# THE ONE, THE ONLY BOOK
## Velimir Khlebnikov

I have seen the black Vedas,
the Koran and the Gospels
and the books of the Mongols
on their silken boards—
all made of dust, of earth's ashes,
of the sweet-smelling dung
that Kalmyk women use each morning for fuel—
I have seen them go to the fire,
lie down in a heap and vanish
white as widows in clouds of smoke
in order to hasten the coming
of the One, the Only Book,
whose pages are enormous oceans
flickering like the wings of a blue butterfly,
and the silk thread marking the place
where the reader rests his gaze
is all the great rivers in a dark-blue flood:

    Volga, where they sing the Razin songs at nighttime,
    yellow Nile, where they worship the sun,
    Yangtze-Kiang, oozing with people,
    and mighty Mississippi, where the Yankees strut
    in star-spangled trousers, yes, in pants
    all covered with stars.
    and Ganges, whose dark people are trees of the mind,
    and Danube, white people in white shirts
    whose whiteness is reflected in the water,
    and Zambezi, whose people are blacker than boots,
    and stormy Ob, where they hack out their idol
    and turn him to face the wall
    whenever they eat forbidden fat,
    and Thames which is boring, boring.

Race of Humanity, you are Readers of the Book
whose cover bears the creator's signature,
the sky-blue letters of my name!
Yes, you, careless reader,

look up! Pay attention!
You let your attention wander idly,
as if you were still in catechism class.
Soon, very soon you will read
these mountain chains and these enormous oceans!
They are the One, the Only Book!
The whale leaps from its pages,
and the eagle's pinion bends the page's edge
as it swoops across sea waves, the breast
of ocean, to rest in the osprey's bed.

*—Translated from the Russian by Paul Schmidt.*

# THE PHENOMENON OF ADOLF WÖLFLI
## John Maizels

ADOLF WÖLFLI (1864–1930), a patient in a mental institution for most of his adult life, was a prolific artist whom many today regard as a creative genius. His life, psychological condition and art were the subject of a book by his doctor, Walter Morgenthaler, *Ein Geisteskranker als Künstler (A Mentally Ill Patient as an Artist)*, published in 1921. Morgenthaler's familiarity with developments in contemporary art enabled him to see the significance of Wölfli's work. He was one of the first to argue that a mentally ill person could be considered a serious artist.

Brutalized and abandoned as a child himself, Wölfli had a history of attempted child molestation. He was admitted to the Waldau clinic near Bern in 1895, an unhappy, introverted and often violent patient. After a few years of introspection and isolation, he inexplicably began to draw. None of his very early works survive—they were probably dismissed with patronizing

A selection of Adolf Wölfli's many illustrated volumes, photographed in 1976.

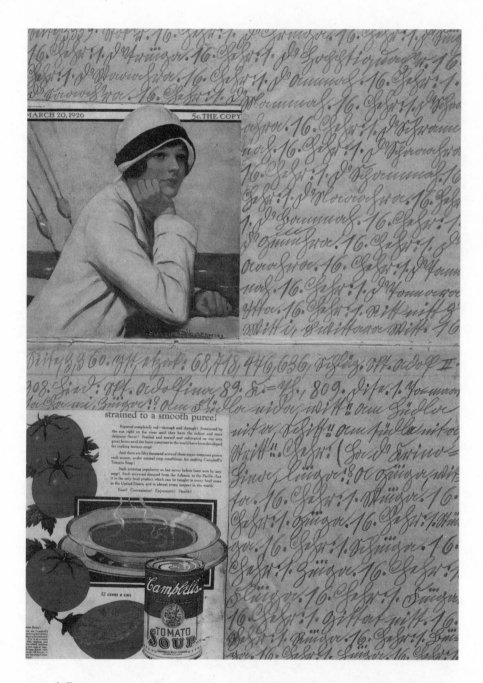

*Campbell's Tomato Soup*, 1929. Pencil, coloured pencil and collage on newsprint. 70 x 50 cm.

amusement by clinic authorities and destroyed. However, a body of fifty large pencil drawings created between 1904 and 1906, before Morgenthaler's arrival at the Waldau clinic, have been preserved. These detailed and near-symmetrical compositions, many numbered in sequence, introduced a rich visual vocabulary that was to remain with Wölfli all his life: highly repetitive and detailed decorative borders and bands which sweep around each composition, the use of musical manuscript fragments (still empty of notation at this stage), the introduction of lettering and word forms, the inclusion of small self-portrait heads and distinctive 'bird' motifs, even the introduction of collage. All these elements were combined to form richly textured compositions with flowing circular and linear forms.

Drawing calmed Wölfli; it became an essential part of his existence. He worked every day, from morning to night, drawing, writing and composing. As well as being a skilled draughtsman, Wölfli was fascinated with algebraic forms and with musical composition, at times signing himself 'Adolf Wölfli, composer.' Morgenthaler wrote:

> Every Monday morning Wölfli is given a new pencil and two large sheets of unprinted newsprint. The pencil is used up in two days; then he has to make do with the stubs he has saved or with whatever he can beg off someone else. He often writes with pieces only five to seven millimetres long or even with the broken-off points of lead, which he handles deftly, holding them between his fingernails. He carefully collects packing paper and any other paper he can get from the guards and the patients in his area; otherwise he would run out of paper well before the next Sunday night. At Christmas the house gives him a box of coloured pencils, which lasts him two or three weeks at the most.

Wölfli received encouragement from Morgenthaler, and even before the publication of Morgenthaler's book in 1921 he had become a minor celebrity within artistic circles. His pictures began to be collected. He occasionally received visitors and acquired as gifts materials to help him with his work.

Adolf Wölfli with his paper trumpet, 1925.

In 1908 he embarked on his greatest endeavour: an illustrated epic of 45 massive volumes containing a total of 25,000 pages, 1,600 illustrations and 1,500 collages. The first eight books, entitled *From the Cradle to the Grave* (1908–12) narrate his own imaginary life story, his abandonment as a child being replaced by the exotic travels of the child Doufi, accompanied by his mother, relatives and friends. The events of his adult life are transformed into glorious and fantastical experiences. From the child 'Doufi' he becomes 'Knight Adolf,' 'Emperor Adolf,' 'St Adolf Great God' and finally from 1916 onwards, 'St Adolf II.' His texts and accompanying drawings take him on endless grandiose journeys and explorations, suffering death, yet always being brought back to life once more to continue his adventures.

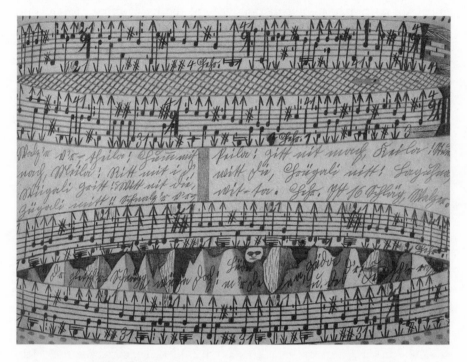

Untitled, 1913. Pencil and coloured pencil on paper. 37 x 50 cm.

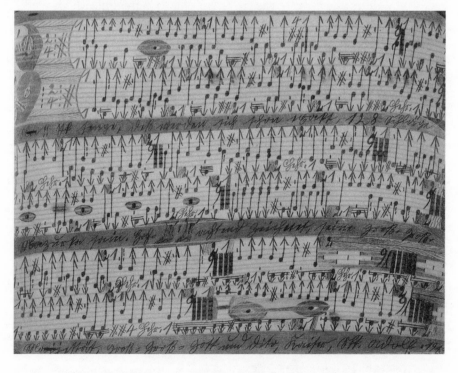

Untitled, 1913. Pencil and coloured pencil on paper. 37 x 50 cm.

Wölfli's musical scores were set out in the same manner as his drawings and often were combined with them. The result is some of the most extraordinary musical manuscripts of all time, although only now are they being deciphered and performed. Wölfli played his music himself, on a trumpet made of rolled-up paper.

In the following seven volumes, the *Geographic and Algebraic Books* (1912–16), he describes the founding of 'St Adolf Giant Creation.' Using his vast imaginary fortune, he embarks on a massive construction programme, even purchasing many of the countries he visits in his travels. The development of his personal cosmos continued with the *Books with Songs and Dances* (1917–22), *Dances and Marches* (1924–8) and finally his great requiem, the

Adolf Wölfli. *Medizinische Fakultät* (Faculty of Medicine), 1905. Pencil on newsprint. 75.0 x 99.7 cm.

sixteen-volume *Funeral March* (1928–30). The drawings are an integral part of the narrative, illustrating particular passages of text, and indeed the graphic imagery and text often were intertwined. Attached and bound into the books, the drawings fold out several times to form large sheets. Many are on paper measuring 100 x 75 centimetres; one of the largest drawings, in Book 5 of *From the Cradle to the Grave,* measures 468 x 70 centimetres and is folded twelve times. Wölfli's fantasy paralleled his real life in many ways:

> The narrative begins with the fictitious emigration of the Wölfli family to America and is subsequently transformed into a journey 'researching nature' more or less over the entire globe. In his imagination Wölfli sees himself initially in the company of his mother, brothers and sisters; later the group grows larger and larger as more and more friends join it, and finally takes shape as the 'Naturvorscher-Schweizer-Avantt-Gaarde' (Vanguard-of-the-

Swiss - Hunters - and - Nature - Researchers - Journey). Wölfli dates everything which happens on this journey exclusively and precisely within the years 1866 and 1872. In this way he is documenting for himself a fictitious childhood from the age of two to eight years. (Theodor Spoerri, from the catalog of *documenta 5* [Kassel, 1972])

Wölfli's perception of himself changed dramatically during the course of his autobiography. In *From the Cradle to the Grave* he refers to himself as:

Naturalist, poet, writer, draughtsman, composer, farm labourer, dairy-hand, handyman, gardener, plasterer, cement-layer, railway worker, day-labourer, knife grinder, fisherman, boatman, hunter, migrant-worker, grave digger, and soldier of the third Section of the third company of the Emmenthal Battalion. Hooray!

In the *Funeral March,* however, he has become:

St Adolf II, Master of Algebra, Military Commander-in-Chief and Chief Music-Director, Giant-Theatre-Director, Captain of the Almighty-Giant-Steamship and Doctor of Arts and Sciences, Director of the Algebra-and-Geography-Text-book-Production Company and Fusilier General. Inventor of 160 original and highly valuable inventions patented for all time by the Russian Tsar and hallelujah the glorious victor of many violent battles against Giants.

*Skt Adolf = Schatz = Kammer = Schlüssel* (St Adolf = Treasure = Chamber = Key), 1913. Pencil and coloured pencil on paper. 36/69.1 x 78/96.2 cm.

With Mogenthaler's encouragement Wölfli produced countless single-sheet drawings in addition to his epic autobiography. Some, referred to as 'bread-art,' were sold to the visitors who began to appear at the Waldau clinic as his fame spread. Others were given away as presents or used as barter for materials. Although smaller in scale and scope than the illustrations to his books, they nevertheless have a compact power of their own. Many are a synthesis of grander conceptions, with human forms surrounded by ornate decorative and symbolic borders, while later drawings drew on his imagery

*Der Gross = Gott = Vatter = Huht mit Skt Adolf = Kuss, Riesen = Fonttaine* (The great = god = father = hat with St Adolf = kiss, giant = fountain), 1917. Pencil and coloured pencil on paper. 38.0 x 50.2 cm.

of mandala forms and symmetrical archetypal composition. Although not part of the books themselves, these works still relate to Wölfli's great narrative and have references on their reverse to specific events.

Morgenthaler's interest in collecting objects and pictures created by mental patients led him in 1916 to commission Wölfli to decorate two large wooden panelled cabinets. These were to contain both his collection and that of the Swiss Psychiatric Society, which later formed the nucleus of the Waldau Museum. Wölfli drew directly on the irregular parts of the wood framing, but for the larger rectangular areas drawings were made on paper and then glued into position. He used the same method in 1921 when he constructed a ceiling mural in his own small cell; the completed collaged drawing was 2.35 x 3.50 metres, exactly the same dimensions as the room.

Wölfli worked in a continuous flow; he often began at the edge of the paper with the ornate borders and friezes that provide the main force of his compositions. Consisting of linking bells, circles, crosses, spirals, ovals, stars,

triangles, birds, numbers, lines, marks and hatching, they both frame the
work and give it a surging motion. On reaching his inner territory, he worked
towards the centre, creating a complex web of linear and rounded elements
which both engulfed and defined human forms and faces, often self-depic-
tions. Birds, beasts, calligraphy, musical notation, buildings and cities, collaged pictures from magazines, events from his life before his internment,
the life and exploits of St Adolf, even monetary and algebraic calculations:
all are borne along by the sweeping force of his detailed and rhythmic dec-

*(Left)*. Painted cabinets decorated by Adolf Wölfli to house his books and drawings.
*(Right)*. Painted cabinets, detail of door panel.

Adolf Wofli's 45 volumes of illustrations and collages,
made between 1908 and 1930.

orative currents. The centres of his drawings are often dominated by mandala forms—his own face peering out from the centre, the master of his universe and yet somehow imprisoned within it.

Little is known of the origins of Wölfli's strange and powerful imagery. The scholar John MacGregor has argued that Wölfli was attempting to draw what he could actually see before his eyes, opened or closed, to come to terms with the psychotic hallucinations that overwhelmed him. It may

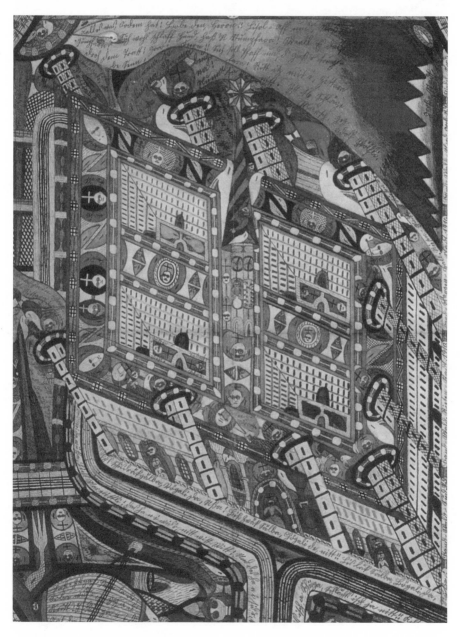

*Irren-Anstalt Band-Hain.* (Mental asylum Band-Hain), 1910. Pencil and coloured pencil on newsprint. 99.7 x 72.1 cm.

be that Wölfli's work embodies archetypes of the collective unconscious or describes hallucinatory forms that stem from deep within. In trying to decipher the extraordinary phenomenon that was Adolf Wölfli, Elka Spoerri, for many years the guardian of Wölfli's works as the curator of the Adolf Wölfli Foundation in Bern, has concluded:

> Although Wölfli was not active as an artist before the onset of his illness, he must be viewed as an artist who happened to become afflicted with a psychosis. The illness did not awaken any creative capacities that were not already part of his personality. His social origins, however—his life of great poverty and social regimentation as an orphan, hireling and labourer—never permitted him even to think of becoming an artist. His entire life story proved as fateful as his illness and internment.

In his thirty-five years of confinement at the Waldau clinic, Wölfli produced a unique and overpowering body of work. On his death in 1930, his small cell in the Swiss asylum where he had lived alone for so many years was stacked from floor to ceiling with his huge hand-bound books and drawings. These were moved to the Waldau Museum, where much of the work was stored in the very cabinets Wölfli had so carefully decorated. The cabinets are now on display at the new Waldau Museum, Bern, along with a few fragments of the ceiling mural that were saved at the time of the demolition of the old Waldau building. In 1975 all of Wölfli's other works held by the Waldau and Morgenthaler collections were entrusted to the newly formed Adolf Wölfli Foundation at the Kunstmuseum, Bern. In spite of Wölfli's stature and importance it is rare to find his work in any of the great art museums of the world. The first time that it was seen outside any specialist collection was at the German annual exhibition of avant-garde and contemporary art, *documenta* 5, held in Kassel in 1972.

Wölfli's compelling vision and all-enveloping creative drive stand as testament to the power of the imagination and to the resilience of the human spirit. Adolf Wölfli was able to transcend the sadness and tragedy of his own life to create a miraculous personal cosmography, a visionary universe of epic proportions.

# FOREWORD TO
## *THE HUNDRED HEADLESS WOMAN*
## BY MAX ERNST
André Breton

The splendid illustrations of novels and children's books like *Rocambole* or *Costal the Indian,* intended for persons who can scarcely read, are among the few things capable of moving to tears those who can say they have read everything. This road to knowledge, which tends to substitute the most forbidding, mirageless desert for the most astonishing virgin-forest, is not, unhappily, of the sort that permits retreat. The most we can hope for is to peek into some old gilt-edged volume, some pages with turned-down corners (as if we were only allowed to find the magician's hat), sparkling or somber pages that might reveal better than all else the special nature of our dreams, the elective reality of our love, the manner of our life's incomparable unwinding. And if such is the way a soul is formed, how would one view the ordinary simple soul that is daily formed by sight and sound rather than texts, that needs the massive shock of the sight of blood, the ceremonious blacks and whites, the ninety-degree angle of spring light, the miracles found in trash, the popular songs; of that candid soul that vibrates in millions and that on the day of revolution, and just because of that simple candor, will carve its true emblems in the unalterable colors of its own exaltation. These colors that are all we want to remember of the anthems, golden chalices, gunfire, waving plumes and banners, even when they are absent from these pages, pages forming a luminous bouquet above a far-away phrase ("Shoking cried: Peace, Sultan!" or "His half-open coat disclosed a lamp hanging from his neck" or "All seized their swords in the same instant") suspended from a phrase waking the echoes of the *passé défini*—for some reason ever more mysterious—are, for better or worse, from birth to death, the colors that dye our enchantment and our fear. Spoken or written language cannot describe an event in the way it brings about the highly suggestive and furtive displacements of animate or inanimate beings, and it is patently evident that one can't give even a hint of a character while trying to lend him some interest without revealing his full portrait. How not to deplore then the fact that until now only rather flat adventure stories have been the object of the kind of inquiry that occupies us here, and that even now most of the artists charged with giving greater value to tales which, without their intervention would remain ephemeral, have not hesitated to deflect attention from that which occurs by the author's intention and instead bring it to focus on their "style"? Thus one can proclaim the genius of those anonymous illustrators of *The Chronicle of the Duke Ernst* and *Fantômas* in their wholehearted submission to the faintest caprices of a text or their enthusiastic search for the tone to which a work aspires.

It remained to examine these grid-covered pages,* out of a thousand old books with all kinds of titles, of forgotten identity—by which I mean that they are no longer read. These illustrations, unlike the impossibly boring texts they refer to, represent for us a plethora of such disconcerting conjectures that they become precious in themselves, as is the meticulous reconstruction of a crime witnessed in a dream, without our being in the least concerned with the name or motives of the assassin. Many of these pictures, full of an agitation all the more extraordinary for its cause being unknown to us—and the case is the same with diagrams from, say, some technical work, providing we know nothing of it—give an illusion of veritable *slits* in time, space, customs and even beliefs, wherein there is not one element that isn't finally a risk, and whose use, to fulfill even the elastic conditions of verisimilitude, would be unthinkable for any other purpose: this man with white beard coming out of a house holding a lantern, if I cover the rest with my hand, might find himself face to face with a winged lion; if I cover his lantern he might just as easily, thus posed, drop stars or stones to the ground. Superposition, if I am not careful, and even if I am, operates moreover, if not strictly speaking before our eyes, at least very objectively and in a continuous manner. This marvelous array, that skips pages as a little girl skips rope or traces a magic circle to use as a hoop, roams day and night the warehouse where all those things we involuntarily accept or reject are stored in the greatest disorder. Each one's special truth is a game of solitaire in which he must quickly choose his cards from among all the others and without ever having seen them before.

Everything that has been written about, described, called fake, doubtful, or true, and above all, pictured, has a singular power to touch us: it is clear that we can't possess it all and so desire it all the more. The wisest of men tends to play with some grave science or other almost as with the evanescent images of a flickering fireplace. History itself, with the childish impressions that it leaves in our minds—more likely of Charles VI or Geneviève de Brabant than of Mary Stuart or Louis XIV—history falls *outside* like snow.

One awaited a book that would take into account the drastic exaggeration of those salient lines emphasized by the attenuation of all the others, a book whose author had the drive needed to bring him to the top of the precipice of indifference where a statue is far less interesting on its pedestal than in a pit, where an aurora borealis reproduced in the magazine *Nature*

---

*Reference is made here to the process of engraving, the only means of reproducing pictures until the advent of photography. (Translator's note.)

is less beautiful than in any unexpected elsewhere. Surreality will be, moreover, the means of our wish for total evasion (and it is understood that one can go so far in dislocating a hand from its arm that the hand thereby becomes increasingly *hand,* and also that in speaking of evasion we are not only referring to space). We awaited a book that avoids all parallels with other books aside from their mutual use of ink and type, as if there were the slightest need, in making a statue appear in a pit, to be the sculptor! I would add, besides, that in order to be truly displaced, the statue had to have once lived a conventional statue-life in a conventional statue-place. The entire value of such an enterprise—and perhaps of all artistic enterprise—seems to me a question of choice,‡ of audacity and of the success, by one's power of appropriation, of certain *transformations.* One awaited a book that refused at once the mysterious, the troubled qualities of many universes that are similar by virtue only of a rather meaningless physiomoral principle and are, to say the least, undesirable in any sense of grandeur (let's take a bottle: *they* immediately think we are about to drink, but no, it is empty, corked, and bobbing on the waves; now *they*'ve got it: it is the bottle on the sea, and so on). Everything has a use other than the one generally attributed to it. It is even out of the conscious sacrifice of their primary usage (to manipulate an object for the first time not knowing what is or was its use) that certain transcendent properties can be deduced, properties that belong to another given or possible world where, for example, an axe can be taken for a sunset, where the virtual elements are not even admissible (I imagine a phantom at a crossroads consulting the road sign), where the migratory instinct usually attributed to birds, encompasses autumn leaves, where former lives, actual lives, future lives melt together into one life; the *life* utterly depersonalized (what a pity for the painters: never to be able to make more than one or two heads; and the novelists! Only human beings do not resemble each other). One awaited, finally, *The Hundred Headless Woman* because one knew that in our day Max Ernst is the only one to have severely refused those considerations that for other artists refer to "form," in regard to which all compliance leads to chanting the idiotic hymn of the "three apples" perpetrated, in the final analysis, all the more grotesquely for their manners, by Cézanne and Renoir. Because one knew that Max Ernst was not the man to draw back from anything that might widen the modern field of vision and provoke the innumerable *illusions of true recognition* that we alone must choose to see in the future and in the past. Because one knew that Max Ernst's is the most magnificently haunted brain of our day, by that I mean the one that

---

‡"Taste" is the literal word used here. I have preferred "choice" as reflecting, in English, the truer thought of André Breton. (Translator's note.)

knows it is not enough to send a new boat into the world, even a pirate ship, but instead to build the *ark* and in such a way that, this time, it is not the dove that returns, but the raven.

*The Hundred Headless Woman* will be preeminently the picture book of our day, wherein it will be more and more apparent that every living room has gone "to the bottom of a lake" with, we must point out, its chandeliers of fishes, its gilded stars, its dancing grasses, its mud bottom and its raiment of reflections. Such is our idea of progress that, on the eve of 1930, we are glad and impatient, for once, to see children's eyes, filled with the ineffable, open like butterflies on the edge of this lake while, for their amazement and our own, fall the black lace masks that covered the first hundred faces of the enchantress.

*—Translated from the French by Dorothea Tanning.*

# *from* THE HUNDRED HEADLESS WOMAN
## Max Ernst

Crime or miracle: a complete man.

The might-have-been Immaculate Conception.

The same, for the second...

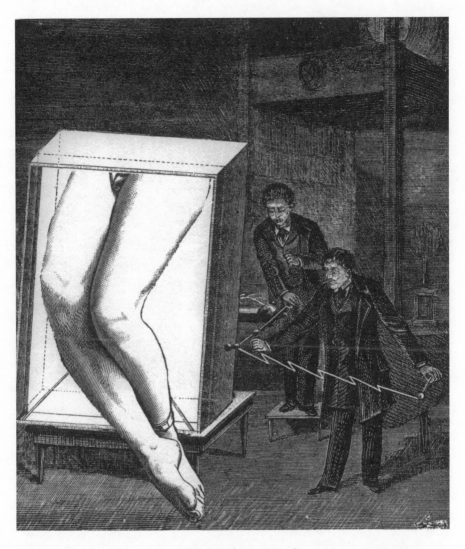

...and the third time missed.

# BOÎTE-EN-VALISE
## Marcel Duchamp

Boîte-en-valise

Box in a Valise (1935/41). Edition of miniature reproductions comprising the de luxe edition of twenty contained in a leather valise, each with an original piece; and the regular edition of 300 assembled in batches from 1942 with variations in the number of contents, structure, and the outer container. 40 x 40 x10 cm.

# SPELLS AND GRIS-GRIS
Agnès de la Beaumelle

STRANGE LITTLE PIECES OF PAPER, written and drawn upon, often stained and burned, bearing imprecations, the "spells" issued by Antonin Artaud beginning in September 1937, sent from Dublin, Sainte-Anne Hospital, and the Ville-Évrard asylum, are integral parts of written letters and thus constitute, aside from an exercise in magic, actual missives. That the epistolary terrain should be chosen for the resumption—or, rather, reinvention—of graphic activity, more than ten years after he had apparently given up drawing for the theater, should not be surprising from someone who, starting in 1924 with the letters to Jacques Rivière, the "addresses" to the Pope and the Dalai Lama, to the Rectors of the European Universities and the Head Doctors of the Insane Asylums, and so forth, established his writing as a demonstrative act, defensive and offensive, sent to another as a gesture of protest. Out of the disastrous experience in Ireland, out of the despair of confinement in asylums, the need to multiply invectives and appeals would be developed in a mode yet more "barbarous" with the spells. The urgency of literally emitting "signs" of life, of sending tangible messages whose significance had to be perceived by the recipient right away, whose effectiveness had to be immediate, led him to find a totally new means of graphic expression. In many ways, these imprecatory letters, drawn upon and often violently colored, functioning magically, can be considered explosive attacks that inaugurate the unique method of drawing—in terms of function and status—practiced by Artaud starting in 1945 at Rodez, then at Ivry, a close suburb of Paris. "I had made up my mind," he would write in 1947, "to *coax out* those forms, lines, outlines, shadows, colors...which would create, as it were, above the paper a kind of counter-figure which would be an ongoing protest against the laws of the created object." Here the function of exorcism and insurrection is announced, to which all the later "awkward" drawings— "counter-figures" to use his term—correspond; here the necessity of an act of total *ex*pression is defined, where writing and drawing, the physical and oral, function together. Messages, testimonies, incantations, imprecations—such would be the large sheets of Rodez, as well as the portraits of the last period filled with glossolalia or graphic expulsions.

More precisely, in 1937, the spells constitute proofs, notionally operative, of the magic power foreshadowed when, upon returning from Mexico, Artaud had called himself "Le Révélé" (The Revealed), and when, armed with Saint Patrick's cane, he went like a shaman to reveal to the Irish their lost secrets. Though sometimes charged with protective powers, the spells generally emit forces of death or vengeance, threats against everything that from that time forward seemed "impure" to Artaud: sexual practices, alliances with money and power, the contempt of God. The recipients of these unsettling missives varied: the spells that we know of (Paule Thévenin has catalogued seven, but one may suppose that many disappeared, that they were lost, or that the hospital administration had them confiscated, or even that those in possession of them were too attached to them to disclose them) are addressed to close friends (Roger Blin), most often women (Lise Deharme, Sonia Mossé, Jacqueline Breton), or to doctors (Dr. Fouks, Dr. Lubtchansky), and, very rarely, to public figures (Hitler)—recipients on whom they were supposed to act *physically*.

The first ones, sent from Dublin, retain the appearance of letters: the violence of the words that pour forth overshadows the drawn elements; the page is still usually filled with written lines, interrupted only by a few cabalistic figures or marks (those of his signature, the date), traces or holes burnt by a cigarette, or rare spatterings of ink. The sheet of letter paper—as later the schoolboy's notebook and the drawing paper—becomes for Artaud a surface that is as much active as acted upon, a field of action combining the lettering—fully thought out, it seems—of the various graphic elements of the handwritten text (capital letters, Roman numerals, block letters), the layout (the placement of drawn elements at the center and at the corners of the paper, an effect of symmetry, a triangular arrangement), and finally the attack of the maculations: the burned perforations, imposed on the paper itself, the "subjectile," in order to denounce its inertia and impotence. Altogether the ensemble already has the appearance of a votive "image" of an infernal realm. At the same time it possesses the function of exorcism, the theatricality of which is evident: the double sign of the Cross superimposed on the spell sent to Jacqueline Lamba constitutes a sacred gesture of protection (recalling that of the monk—played by Artaud—brandishing a crucifix over Joan of Arc's head in Carl Dreyer's film); the traces of burns are obvious acts of aggression and purification.

Effective in a different way are the spells sent out in 1939 from the Ville-Évrard asylum: their imprecatory violence now resides more in the physical state of the missive than in the words. Inscribed with a thick ink crayon in purple, the different signs (crosses, stars, triangles, spirals in the shape of serpents, the cabalistic significance of which Artaud well knew) proliferate in all directions, invade the center of the paper itself, break the continuous thread of writing drawn with the same ink crayon: fragments of writing and drawn pictograms henceforth form one body. Not only that: knots, amorphous clusters of crayon, seem to respond in counterpoint, proceeding from the same charge of aggression, to the holes produced by burning the paper (the edges of which are also ravaged); and traces of violent shades of yellow, blue, and red (Artaud also knew the symbolism of colors: these are the colors of death) intensify by their physical presence the imprecatory force of the words. These are no longer simple votive letters but true magical objects, to be handled while making ritualistic gestures (the spell for Léon Fouks [p. 226]), which can "illuminate themselves," like "gris-gris." [A word of African origin meaning a charm, fetish, or amulet.—Eds.]

Tattoos of colored signs inscribed on the paper, perforations made by burning the body of the paper itself: the "melding" of these two processes—painting and fire—long since adopted by Artaud, takes on the nature of revelation for him. Speaking in 1925 of André Masson's painting, he said he saw "cocoons of fire" lacerating human entrails, which were to be deciphered like those of a sacrifice. In "L'Automate personnel," he admires the painting of Jean de Bosschère, which he considers "a world cut open, a naked world, full of filaments and strips, where the inflaming force of fire lacerates the interior firmament, the tearing apart of the mind." Once again, he highlights the role of fire in the fascination that Lucas van Leyden's painting *Lot and His Daughters* (c. 1509) exerts on him; its analysis initiates his reflection on the exorcising, operative function—destructive, constructive—of "true" theater, that in which or by which an original tongue is rediscovered. The language of fire or the fire of language: all the same for the founder of the Theater of Cruelty, the "fires" of the footlights forming a symbolic dividing line, beyond which no compromise can take place.

For Artaud, returned from Mexico where Indians of the scorched land of the Tarahumara had taught him the purifying function of fire (a sorcerer was burned there for having believed in several gods), and in despair over an "impossible" work, fire comes to be invested with the ultimate power, that of symbolically effecting the total Destruction of the Universe, "but consciously and in revolt"; in certain spells, the central place of the number 9, the cabalistic number of infernal destruction, is significant. In 1937, in *The New Revelations of Being*, where his own name, his individual identity, his writer's signature disappear, Artaud declares: "Burning is a magic act and ...one must consent to burning, burning in advance and immediately, not one thing, but *all that for us represents things,* so as not to expose oneself to burning completely. All that is not burned by all of Us and that does not make Us *Desperates* and *Loners,* the Earth will burn." Beyond the urge for self-destruction, these "cruel" letters that are the spells manifest a necessity to conjure, to exorcise a curse. They fully set in motion the blaze of writing that is finally freed—"this atmospheric thunder, this lightning"—at Rodez after 1945, the ash and blood conflagration of pictogram remnants and charred faces that will appear on the large sheets of drawing paper.

"It was in 1939, at the Ville-Évrard asylum, that I constructed my first gris-gris; on little sheets of gridded paper torn from a schoolboy's notebook I composed passive figures, like heads ravaged by fits of asthma, torments, and hiccups." Confined at Ville-Évrard and then, beginning in 1943, at Rodez, doomed to silence and oblivion, Artaud drew "figures" instead of writing, constructed new spells on sheets of paper, but this time for his personal use; his "gris-gris" have for him a curative, protective, offensive function against the "demons" assailing him: "what one sees here are totems, the weapons I take up the moment I awake." Of this production only a few drawings executed in early 1944 remain. The cabalistic signs (notably ∞, the infinity sign, but also the sign of apocalyptic Destruction) now occupy by themselves the surface of the sheet: a type of drawn "hieroglyphs," made up of crosses or other geometric lines, and arranged in a repetitive symmetry—a permanent echo of the signs Artaud saw in the land of the Tarahumara—from now on constitute the basic ideograms of a primary language, first steps toward the physical sign language that he attempted to create in the theater. Here signs emerge from his breath, syncopated by "asthmas" and "hiccups." Inscribed at the center of this sort of geometric architecture are skulls, as though imprisoned. Was this a reference to the human skulls lodged in the stone niches of Roquepertuse at the gates of Marseille, with which, being so well known, Artaud must have been familiar? A multiplicity of other references could be found in the immured figures of sacred pre-Columbian sanctuaries. For, faced as he is at Rodez with the tragic loss of himself, a "man suicided by society" through institutional confinement, Artaud seeks to rediscover the primary forces of ancestral creation, attempting to update the forms and meaning of an archaic visual language that traces its roots to the depths of time.

—*Translated from the French by Jeanine Herman.*

# SPELL FOR LÉON FOUKS

## Antonin Artaud

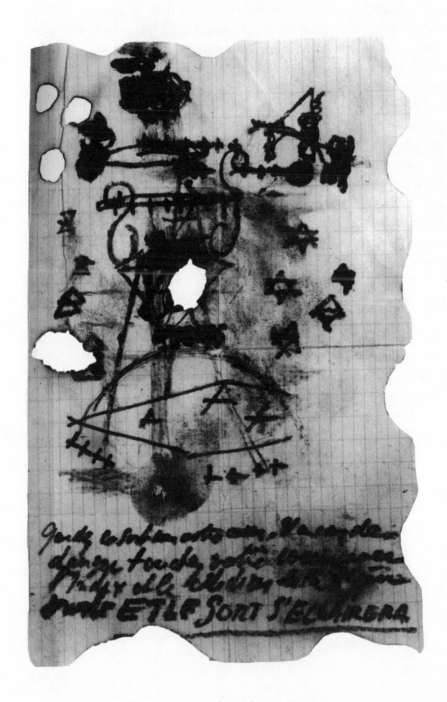

8 May 1939, wax crayon on burned paper. 21 x 13.5 cm.

[Of this Artaud had written:]

THE FIGURES on the inert page said nothing
beneath my hand. They offered themselves to
me like millstones that would not inspire
drawing, and that I could plumb, carve, scrape,
file, seam together and sunder, hack, slash to
ribbons, and score without the surface ever
thereby crying uncle.

Which is to say, knowing no more about
drawing than about nature, I had made up my
mind to coax out those forms, lines, outlines,
shadows, colors, features that, as in modern
painting, would represent nothing and would
moreover not claim to be integrated in
accordance with whatsoever visual or material
law, but would create, as it were, above the paper
a kind of counter-figure that would be an
ongoing protest against the laws of the
created object.

The goal of all these drawn and colored
figures was to exorcize the curse, to vituperate
bodily against the exigencies of spatial form,
of perspective, of measure, of equilibrium,
of dimension and, via this vituperative act of
protest, to condemn the psychic world which,
like a crab louse, digs its way into the physical,
and, like an incubus or succubus, claims to have
given it shape....

And the figures that I thereby made
were spells—which, after so meticulously
having drawn them, I put a match to.

*—Translated from the French by Richard Sieburth.*

# *from* "COMPOSITION AS EXPLANATION (OF MODERN AND POSTMODERN POETRIES)"

## Jerome McGann

IN "LITERATURE AND THE LIVING VOICE" Yeats observed that "English literature, alone of great literatures because the newest of them all, has all but completely shaped itself in the printing press." In truth the history of modernist writing could be written as a history of the modernist book. Were one to write that history, Ezra Pound would appear once again the crucial point of departure. Like the Alps for a western imagination, he and his *Cantos* prove—for better and for worse—unevadable:

> There they are, you will have to go a long way round if
> you want to avoid them.

Bunting's famous lines go to the heart of the matter: that Pound's work has a substantial *thingness* to it, a kind of hard objective presence. The title of the poem—"On the Fly-Leaf of Pound's Cantos"—defines the modernist perspective that Yeats had called attention to.

Consider the three books that first printed Cantos I-XXX. Their significance is completely involved with the late nineteenth century's Renaissance of Printing. To understand how deeply this is true we have to retreat in time to the earliest period of Pound's literary life—to the year, in fact, when he (later) said he "began the Cantos" (even though, as he also said, he "didn't get [them] onto paper" at that time). In a letter to his mother from Hamilton College in 1904 Pound said he was writing an "Essay on early poetry of Wm Morris." Shortly afterwards, during the intensities of his affair with H.D., Pound's involvement with Morris and Pre-Raphaelitism had deepened considerably. Not only does his early poetry display the influence of several Pre-Raphaelite styles (Morris, Rossetti, and Swinburne especially), Pound shows himself fully aware of the late nineteenth century's printing revolution that Pre-Raphaelitism had done so much to inaugurate and advance.

That awareness is materialized in the unique (handmade) volume he titled *Hilda's Book,* his first book of poetry. Though a gift to H.D., the book is an act of homage to Pre-Raphaelitism and the ideal of the troubadour poet it passed on to him. *Hilda's Book* is a small volume of verse, mostly handwritten in an ornamental script, bound in vellum. As H.D. wrote later in *End to Torment,*

> He brought me the Portland, Maine, Thomas Mosher reprint of the Iseult
> and Tristram story. He called me Is-hilda and wrote a sonnet a day: he bound
> them in a parchment folder.

Like Morris when he founded the Kelmscott Press, Thomas Mosher began his famous press (the same year as Kelmscott, 1891) in conscious imitation of the master printers of the fifteenth century. In the imagination of those swept up in the late nineteenth century's Renaissance of Printing, the physical presentation of texts was a fundamental feature of their expressiveness. The material form in which one read "the Iseult and Tristram story" had to be thought as important as the story itself.

The point was not simply that writing ought to look handsome or attractive. More crucial were the historical meanings that could be carried by a book's "ornamental" features. Pound apparently learned the power of graphic and typographic book production from Morris and Pre-Raphaelitism. But as his move to London shows, he understood that Morris's Kelmscott adventure was not the only model available to someone interested in expressive book design. In fact, two great bibliographical styles emerged in English book production of the 1890s.

The most celebrated of the two is the Kelmscott style. As we have seen, Morris's books were consciously designed to recall the revolutionary bookwork of the fifteenth century—and especially those early printed books that stood closest to richly decorated medieval manuscript books scripted in closely written Gothic bookhands. For the modern eye, however, such a style can create reading problems. In Kelmscott Press books a recollective visual design is so paramount that legibility becomes almost a second-order goal of the printing work.

The rich weight of Morris's Kelmscott texts would ultimately stand as only one pole of the imagination that drove the late nineteenth-century Renaissance of Printing. The other was represented by the textual clarities made famous in the work of the Bodley Head Press. For Ezra Pound, Bodley Head proved as formative a resource as Kelmscott.

Begun jointly by Elkin Mathews and John Lane in 1889, Bodley Head chiefly published serious and experimental writing in handsome book designs at relatively cheap prices. Printing runs were small as the books were being offered to a special audience. Indeed, the press succeeded in no small part because it helped to consolidate such an audience. To be a Bodley Head author, or reader, defined you as a certain type of person—aesthetic and very modern.

Bodley Head's most famous publication was probably *The Yellow Book,* but the firm's authors, book designers, and illustrators included the most prominent figures of the period. Unlike Morris's Kelmscott books, the Bodley Head book featured a clear and readable page, where beauty emerged as a function of the elegance and simplicity of arrangement. The approach to book design, which shows the influence of Whistler, was executed by men like Charles Ricketts, Charles Jacobi, and especially Walter Blaikie.

Ricketts founded the famous Vale Press with Charles Shannon; Jacobi was general manager of the legendary Chiswick Press, and Blaikie (of T. and A. Constable) was, next to Morris, probably the most respected and influential "artist printer" of the period.

In 1894 the partnership between Mathews and Lane was dissolved and each went his own way. Mathews retained some of the most prominent of the old Bodley Head authors, including Wilde, Lionel Johnson, and Yeats. Of the two original partners, Mathews was distinctly the less aggressive entrepreneur. His relatively noncommercial approach to publishing, so unlike Lane's, was part of the overall scrupulousness that appealed to the authors he printed.

This history is important to recall because when Pound went to London in 1908 he immediately sought out Mathews as a possible publisher for his work. The two hit it off immediately and Mathews became Pound's principal publisher. The poet's first four books issued by Mathews—between 1909 and 1916—were in fact all printed at Chiswick Press. Jacobi had been manager of this old and distinguished firm. As we have already seen, at the outset of his career Morris sought out Chiswick Press to print his books. He returned to Chiswick again, in the late 1880s, when he and Emery Walker began the bookmaking collaboration that would result in the founding of Kelmscott Press.

So far as Pound's work is concerned, two matters are especially important here. First, Pound from the start conceived his own work in the context of the late nineteenth-century Renaissance of Printing. He understood what had been happening in that movement and he sympathized with its goals. Second, he kept close contact with the actual design and production of his own work. He published his first printed book *A Lume Spento* himself and afterwards he never abandoned a practical involvement in all the productive aspects of his writing. By the time he came to publish the first book installments of the *Cantos,* Pound was knowledgeable and experienced in the making of books.

The first two volumes were *A Draft of XVI Cantos* (1925) and *A Draft of the Cantos 17-27* (1928). The former was printed and published in Paris at William Bird's Three Mountains Press in a large format (39.2 x 26.2 cm.). The initials and headpieces were designed by Henry Strater under Pound's careful instructions. The second book (39.1 x 25.9 cm.) was meant to be uniform with the first. It was published in London by John Rodker and printed in England by J. Curwen and Sons, Ltd. The initials and headpieces were executed by Gladys Hynes. The colophons for both books clearly indicate their lavish and expensive production values. The third volume was *A Draft of XXX Cantos* (1930), published in Paris by Nancy Cunard's Hours Press. The format was much smaller (21.2 x 14.8 cm.), the headpieces and colored printing were absent, and the initials were designed in a vorticist style by Pound's wife Dorothy. All three books are printed in the same modernized Caslon typeface, although the smaller format of the 1930 volume necessitated the choice of a smaller font.

The most striking visual feature of the 1925 and 1928 volumes is their eclecticism. Although the style of the titles of the different *Cantos* varies, all the titles recall medieval calligraphy or decorative printing. Indeed, Pound's titles distinctly recall the uncial calligraphic forms that stand behind subsequent medieval developments in lettering. The same kind of antique allusion appears in the ornamented (or even historiated) initials, as well as in the headpieces (recalling the woodcuts of early printed books). The red and black printing functions in a similar way. In these textual features we see the strong influence of the Kelmscott book, which is distinguished by elaborate ornamental materials, including decorative capitals and two-color printing in red and black. The typeface, on the other hand, so clearly modern, makes a sharp contrast with the medievalism of the books' other features. As in Yeats's Dun Emer/Cuala Press books, one sees here a compromise, or marriage, of the different styles of Morris on the one hand and Blaikie on the other—of Kelmscott and Bodley Head.

This bibliographical contrast also helps to define the historical meaning, or argument, which these two installments of the *Cantos* are making. Canto I launches the *Cantos* project in explicitly bibliographical terms: the voyage of Odysseus is a matter of linguistic translation and book production. From Pound's vantage, then, it would be important to express that historical subject at every level of the work. The stylistic contrast between his books' ornament and typography maps the history he is interested in. The pages of these books recollect at the design level the epochal (bibliographical) events of the fifteenth century and the late nineteenth century. The *Cantos* project locates itself within that historical nexus.

*A Draft of XXX Cantos* is uniform with the two previous books in that Pound continues to exploit a contrast between the ornamental initials and the body of the text. In this case, however, the contrast operates wholly within a relatively "modern" horizon. The typeface is modernized Caslon, but because the initials are so aggressively vorticist, the typeface functions now as the sign of an earlier historical or stylistic moment. From a purely personal point of view the initials recollect Pound's London years, and the beginning of his "modernism" (in the most restricted sense of the term). At the level of the work's bibliographical symbology, *A Draft of XXX Cantos* has moved a step away from the Pre-Raphaelite and aesthetic position recollected in the first two volumes.

The physical presentation of these three books thus constitutes a display of their meanings. Book design here defines not merely the immediate historical horizon of Pound's *Cantos* project, it declares the meaningful-ness of historical horizons as such. In doing this, the work equally declares its commitment to a fully materialized understanding of language. The *Cantos* summons up the power and authority of the most elementary forms of language, its systems of signifiers, and it apprehends these signi-fiers as historical artifacts. The graphic presentation of Pound's books is thus made an index of their aims. Through book design Pound makes an issue of language's physique, deliberateness, and historicality.

The history inscribed in Pound's initial project for the *Cantos* has been pre-served in other important records of the period. Many of the most influen-tial works of the Harlem Renaissance—for instance Hughes's *The Weary Blues* (1926), various books by Countee Cullen, Alain Locke's anthology *The New Negro* (1925)—all display the profound effect produced by the graphic and bibliographic revolution at the end of the nineteenth century. In these cases the style has taken a definitively modernist step beyond me-dievalism and aestheticism; nonetheless, that step would not have been possible without the historical inertia generated out of the late Victorians. Nor did their influence extend only to experimentalist writing. Hardy's first book of verse, *Wessex Poems* (1898), marries the new aesthetic style of text presentation with a series of sketches (by Hardy himself) "illustrating" the symbolic topography being constructed by the book.

The Yeatsian record—so crucial in every way—tells a similar story. When Yeats tried to summarize modern poetry in his *Oxford Book of Modern Verse* (1936) he made a famous gesture to modernism's aesthetic and Pre-Raphaelite inheritance. He printed as the first text in his collection a no-table passage from Pater's *The Renaissance.* An unusual choice of text, but most startling of all was its graphic appearance: Yeats reformatted Pater's lush prose as a free verse poem [see Fig. 1]. Readers have generally taken free form as an emblem of modernism's experimental advance beyond its nineteenth-century precursors. But the truth is that those free verse forms emerged in part because Morris and some of his contemporaries had begun to work consciously with the spatial features of the page and the book as they might be resources for poetic effects.

❖ Mallarmé's experiments with the spatial form of the page are surely more to the point, don't you think?

That's been the view of our traditional literary histories. But it's a narrow view, despite its apparent internationalism. We aren't discounting modern-ism's French connections by calling attention to others that were equally, and perhaps even more, significant. Kelmscott Press and Bodley Head locate historical relations that have been largely forgotten.

## WALTER PATER

1839–1894

*I*        *Mona Lisa*

S HE is older than the rocks among which she sits;
Like the Vampire,
She has been dead many times,
And learned the secrets of the grave;
And has been a diver in deep seas,
And keeps their fallen day about her;
And trafficked for strange webs with Eastern merchants;
And, as Leda,
Was the mother of Helen of Troy,
And, as St Anne,
Was the mother of Mary;
And all this has been to her but as the sound of lyres and
     flutes,
And lives
Only in the delicacy
With which it has moulded the changing lineaments,
And tinged the eyelids and the hands.

Figure 1. Walter Pater, "Mona Lisa," from Yeats's *Oxford Book of Modern Verse 1892–1935* (1936).

In any event, at stake here is something more important than establishing clear lines of historical causation. Only certain aspects of English Pre-Raphaelitism and French symbolism seemed important to the programs of modernism. The format of Yeats's text from Pater is a bibliographically coded message drawing a historical relation between Pre-Raphaelitism, aestheticism, and modernism. The semantic content of the message is carried by the graphic features. This ascension of the signifier speaks on one hand about the coming of modernism, and constructs on the other Yeats's version of its prehistory. The text is an emblem for a poetry that means to come to its senses.

Yeats tells an odd history here and he tells it in an odd way. What is even more odd, I suspect that he took his immediate inspiration for rewriting Pater's work from Louis Zukofsky. The last section of *An "Objectivists" Anthology* (1932), headed "Collaborations," prints a series of texts that have been similarly "rewritten." Zukofsky apparently meant these "collaborations" to illustrate a distinction he wanted to draw between "sincerity" and "objectification" in poetry. However immediate the relation between Yeats's Pater text and Zukofsky's anthology, both works illustrate the renewed interest that modern poets were taking in the materialities of poetic textualization.

So far I have been emphasizing the analogy between "composition" as it concerns the typographer and "composition" as it concerns the visual artist.

Another analogy is possible, however, and has been equally important. "Composition" is an activity of musicians, and the printed page may equally be produced as a kind of musical score, or set of directions for the audition of verse and voice.

So far as modernism is concerned, Zukofsky is a key figure for such a project. As much as Pater he saw poetry as an aspiration—in both senses—toward the condition of music. His interest in the visual field of the page was finally auditional: the formatting of a text as a means for scoring the musical resources of poetry, including voice.

> Typography—certainly—if print and the arrangement of it will help to tell how the voice should sound.

Zukofsky is aware that modernism, and in particular the work of Pound, offered another very different way of thinking about typography. His next sentence alludes to this other way, but sets it aside:

> It is questionable on the other hand whether the letters of the alphabet can be felt as the Chinese feel their written characters.

The (free verse) line from Zukofsky to the projectivist work of the 1950s is quite direct. It is a line for composing, in the musical sense, sound and speech patterns. If we look backwards from Zukofsky this line—as we all know—is spun out of Whitman.

I recall these matters to contrast them with a very different tradition of the free verse movement. Morris did not write free verse, but his interest in the physique of poetry had its greatest impact on this other tradition, where "Writing as Composition" connects to the visual imagination of the painter, the graphic artist, and the typographer. (The poems on the title pages of both *The Roots of the Mountains* and *The House of the Wolfings* illustrate types of what we would now call "concrete poetry.") In the European context the tradition begins with Mallarmé and then explodes in Apollinaire's calligrammatology and Cendrars's stunning experiments in "Simultaneity." As I have already suggested, this alternative line—so far as American poetry is concerned—should be connected with the textual innovations of Emily Dickinson.* To see her verse as a kind of graffiti seems to me useful.

Pound's typographical experiments, glanced at by Zukofsky, have come to epitomize this other tradition for English readers. The visual tradition's most important modernist practitioner and theorist, however, was Robert Carlton ("Bob") Brown—that strange and arresting American, now academically forgotten, whose work culminates the extraordinary tradition of modern experimentalist writing. The year that Nancy Cunard's Hours Press brought out Pound's *A Draft of XXX Cantos* (1930) also saw the appearance

---

*See Susan Howe's essay *These Flames and Generosities of the Heart,* page 113, above. (Eds.)

Figure 2. Robert Carlton Brown. *1450–1950,* dedication page (1929).

of Brown's polemical treatise on poetry and printing, *The Readies.* Each book is a conscious reimagination of the possibilities of poetic expression, and both situate themselves in the bibliographical renaissance that Morris had brought to a flash point.

The two works display very different emphases. *A Draft of XXX Cantos* looks directly back to the craft traditions revivified by the work of Morris. The book is handprinted on rag paper in the modern Caslon used by William Bird for his previous editions of Pound's Pre-Raphaelite cantos—a variant of the same font that had been resurrected by Chiswick Press in the nineteenth century, and that so captured the imagination of Morris. Brown's work, by contrast, is a small pamphlet printed by machine on cheap chemical paper.

The difference Brown's book makes with Pound's is, however, conscious and deliberate. *The Readies* issues a hail and farewell to earlier dreamers of a revolutionary word. Brown made his point even more dramatically a year earlier when he published his collection of (what shall we call them?) "optical poems" in the book *1450–1950,* with its graphic dedication page [see Fig. 2]. "Writing has been bottled up in books since the start," Brown playfully laments in *The Readies;* "It is time to pull out the stopper."

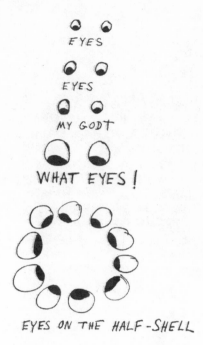

Figure 3. Robert Carlton Brown, "Eyes on the Half-Shell," from *1450–1950* (1929).

Brown had been working at that stuck stopper since 1914, when he first read Stein's *Tender Buttons,* which seems to have completely transformed his sense of writing. "I began to see that a story might be anything...[and] didn't have to be a tangible hunk of bread interest.... Thank God for Gert Stein." He "began to experiment for the first time," and when he struck off his optical poem "Eyes on the Half-Shell," Marcel Duchamp printed it in his journal *Blindman* in 1917 [see Fig. 3]. Brown later included it in his collection *1450–1950.* His commentary on the text is important:

> I have since taken this for a symbol of what I have been trying to do in writing, off and on for fifteen years.... I like to look at it, merely sit and look at it, take it all in without moving an eye. It gives me more than rhymed poetry. It rhymes in my eyes. Here are Black Riders for me at last galloping across a blank page.

Brown's optical poems can be misleading, can make one think that he is simply reconnecting with those innovative visual texts produced by Edward Lear, Lewis Carroll, and (before them) William Blake. Of course Brown's relation to these poets is important, but in his mind the optical poem does not at all require figural decorative ornaments. The physical medium of any kind of textuality—in a typographical mode the basic elements are paper, ink, cuts, and various type fonts—can be manipulated to the same effect.

> I'm for new methods of reading and writing and I believe the up-to-date reader deserves an eye-ful when he buys something to read.

Brown's idea was to immerse the reader in the print medium, much as the viewer is immersed in images at the cinema. "The Readies" is Brown's witty bibliographical takeoff on those recent modernist inventions, the "movies" and "talkies." When Brown declared "I bathe in Apollinaire," he was announcing his ideal linguistic experience.

At the center of Brown's program was his half-serious half-playful invention, a "reading machine." This apparatus was supposed to provide the reader with the power to read in all directions and at any speed, to change type size and type-face at will, to leap forward or backward in the text: to browse, to speedread, to connect any and all parts of the text in any and all ways.

Brown wants to overgo the recent advances of those who used fine-book production as a means to radical poetic innovation. So he puns his refusal of the bibliographical tradition on which Yeats and Pound had drawn, those "beautiful but dumb books as clumsy in their way as the Rozetti stone." But Brown's rejection is full of homage and admiration because the great earlier traditions of printing and manuscript illumination had taught him a "loving wonder, a great want-to-know about words, their here and their there, their this and their that":

> The monks in the beginning didn't do it so badly in their illuminated manuscripts, they retained a little of the healthy hieroglyphic, all Oriental books in ideogrammatic character are delights, early colophons splendid.

Even as Brown explicitly pays his respects to Blake, Morris, Pound and the traditions they cherished, he makes his turn toward a new world of words.

> For the first time in the history of mental optics there will exist a visual Literary Language sharply separated from the Speaking Tongue. Literary Language is Optical, speaking language Vocal, and the gap between them must spread till it becomes a gulf. My reading machine will serve as a wedge. Makers of words will be born; fresh, vital eye-words will wink out of dull, dismal, drooling type at startled smug readers here below....The Revolution of the Word will be all over but the shouting....

Brown's *jouissance* of the word anticipates the Derridean moment by forty years, and prophecies as well the practical emergence of computerized word-processing and hypertextual fields.

Blake, Rossetti, and Morris were inspirations rather than models. The point is made clearly in one of the texts printed in Brown's optical collection *1450–1950* [see *e.g.,* Fig. 4]. The poles of *1450/1950* are defined by "ILLUMINATED MSS." on one hand and "ILLUMINATING/MOVIE SCRIPTS" on the other. Brown faces "forward," but with many glances "back" and sideways full of interest and respect. He keeps his eyes open in all directions. Most immediately, he looks to find on the contemporary scene those "makers of words" called for by *The Readies.*

I LIKE LOOKING BACK
AT THE
ILLUMINATED MSS. OF

1450
AND FORWARD
TO THE
MORE ILLUMINATING
MOVIE SCRIPTS OF
1950

I LIKE TO SEE
FLY SPECKS
ON YELLOWED PAGES
I LIKE TOO
LEAVING MY OWN ON
NEW ONES

MY FLY SPECK

Figure 4. Robert Carlton Brown, from *1450–1950* (1929).

The makers were alive and very active. Brown's manifesto was followed almost immediately by his anthology *Readies for Bob Brown's Machine* (1931), an extraordinary collection of liberated texts supplied to Brown by some of the most innovative writers of his age: Williams, McAlmon, Harry Crosby, Stein, Sidney Hunt, Pound, Hemingway, and many others. When the afterhistory of modernism is written, this collection—along with its better known counterpart published a year later, Zukofsky's *An "Objectivists" Anthology*—will be recognized as a work of signal importance.

*Readies for Bob Brown's Machine* is a far more European work of modernism than Zukofsky's anthology. Unlike the latter, Brown's book displays a conscious appropriation of the many textual and bibliographical innovations that had been sweeping across Europe for twenty years and more. Futurism, dada, simultaneism, zaum, vorticism, cubism, German expressionism: all these movements have left their visible marks on Brown's collection, whereas in Zukofsky's gathering—except for imagism—the firestorm of modernism's experimental energies has been translated and modified. In each anthology the rules of a liberated verse are largely governed by intuitions of the eye, but in one case the eye is more interested in composing temporal forms, whereas spatiality dominates in the other. Besides, Brown's book—so far as poetry as such is concerned—enters wilder territory, as a casual glance at almost any page of the collection indicates. Sidney

Hunt's "MORNINIGHT CAR (nocturnal day realm)," for example, distinctly recollects Brown's call in *The Readies* to "see words machinewise."

> Black-Riders-Crash-by-hell-bent-for-leather-
> uppercase-LOWERCASE-both——together-chanting-
> valorously-Print-in-action-at——longlast-movable-
> type-at-breakneck-gallop[...] daredevil-commaless-
> Cossacks-astride-mustang-bronco——vocabularies-
> leaning-farout-into-inky-night——

The word "uppercase" printed here in lowercase, the word "LOWERCASE" printed in uppercase: it is a small emblem of what Brown has in his mind. Futurism supplies Brown with the trope of speed and the wisdom of machines ("machinewise") that negotiates the field of this particular text [see also Fig. 5].

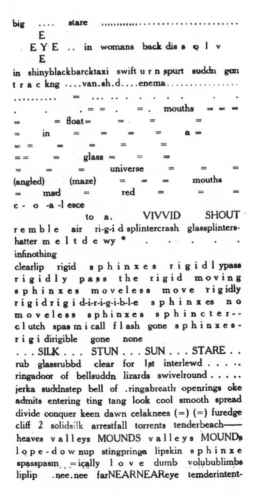

Figure 5. Sidney Hunt, "MORNINIGHT CAR (nocturnal day realm)," from *Readies for Bob Brown's Machine* (1931).

• • •

Anyone who reads postmodern poetry will have been struck by its vigorous appropriation of this bibliographical inheritance. I have in mind not merely the widespread development of various kinds of Concrete Poetry, but the visual structure of Jackson Mac Low's chance poems, of John Cage's work, of Clark Coolidge's spatialized texts. Typography and layout are not simply devices "to tell how the voice should sound," they are poetic resources adaptable to many uses: poster poems like Robert Grenier's "Cambridge M'ass," Johanna Drucker's breathtaking books of "words made flesh," Charles Bernstein and Susan Bee's parodies of the emblem tradition in their witty collaborative collection *The Nude Formalism* (1989) [see Fig. 6].

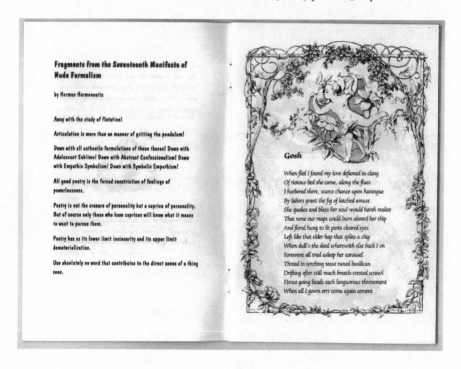

Figure 6. Charles Bernstein аμnd Susan Bee, "Fragments from the Seventeenth Manifesto of Nude Formalism" and "Gosh," from *The Nude Formalism* (Sun & Moon Press, 1989).

Susan Howe's *Pythagorean Silence* (1982), an exemplary text of our period, is also an explicit meditation on postmodern writing. Like Yeats in his anthology of modernism, Howe gives a hypothetical *terminus a quo* for American postmodernism: December 7, 1941, Pearl Harbor. On this day of lamentation the world is imagined as once again lost, and Rachel reappears "In Rama...weeping for her children." The text's representation of this mythic event is wholly postmodern in form:

R

(her cry

silences

whole

vocabularies

of *names* for

*things*

The wordplay of "whole/vocabularies" locates the text's immersion in silence and fragmentation. Loss here is represented as the loss of language: the round earth's imagined corners are blown apart in this textual representation of a new apocalypse, whose cataclysm deconstructs a world held in being by its faith in the referential structure of signs. As this world disappears we glimpse language turning toward a more elemental condition, toward an Adamic language of performative utterances ("her cry") and scripts that function purely as sonic and visible forms. The "meaning" of the capital letter "R" heading this text is intratextual—a signifier that rhymes sonically with the copulative "are" appearing in the previous passage, and visually with the first letters of "Rachel" and "Rama" in the same passage.

In Rama
Rachel weeping for her children
refuses
to be comforted

because they *are* not

The textual character of these events is underscored in Part II section I:

a sentence        or character
suddenly

steps out to seek for truth      fails
falls

into a stream of ink        Sequence
trails off

must go on

These stumbling and fractured texts forecast the climactic event in *Pythagorean Silence*—its own visionary dance of pure words and linguistic forms. Its unheard Pythagorean harmonies have to be seen to be apprehended. But they typically appear as (apparitionally) lawless and anarchic texts. In truth, like the Christian imagined in Paul's new dispensation, they speak toward a freedom from the death of the Old Law (which in this case is figured as instrumental grammatical law).

❖ Pythagorean harmonies? Pauline dispensations? Which is it? Mixing concepts is like mixing metaphors. You just get confused. Myself, I'd stick with the Pythagoreans—as being closer to Howe's text.

Just nominally "closer" I think. It's as if Howe had appropriated the Pythagorean model as a figural form for her puritanism. Howe's mind is clearly out of New England, not Pythagoras or the classical world. "Pythagorean silence" is her antinomian trope for what literary historians call American transcendentalism. She treats her poem's silence like a fire sermon.

❖ That may be. My problem is not with Howe's work but with yours. No one builds a coherent argument by throwing together such opposite and discordant materials.

True, no one does. But then not every part of an argument—even a scholarly argument—is or ought to be coherent and expository. The question is whether critical writing can find formal equivalences for its subject matter and still preserve its communicative function. Poetry is a discourse committed to the display and exploitation of contradiction. Criticism, by contrast, is an informational discourse. How do we keep criticism from murdering its subject with its pretensions to truth?

❖ Do you think it helps to bewilder the language, to confuse your reader?

Do *you* think that "bewildering language" and "confusing the reader" are equivalents? When that equation is made, we have abandoned all possibility of poetry.

❖ Perhaps, but not of criticism.

Perhaps, but in that case you seem to leave us with only a *certain kind* of criticism: one committed to a particular idea and point of view. There are other forms—as with this dispute of ours, there is also criticism as *textus interruptus.*

❖ Which creates its own kinds of problem. So go on with what you were saying. We can talk about critical method later. Now I want to hear more about Howe's poetry.

Well, as I was suggesting, an elementary move toward the peculiar freedom of her texts is to reimagine the physical field of the printed work. In the first (*Montemora*) edition of the poem, the reader is subtly moved toward that reimagination by the absence of numbers on the pages. Their removal inhibits the serial inertia of the codex format, slowing down the process of reading slightly, urging that we stay for a while with each individual page. The general structure of the poem does not obliterate seriality altogether, but locates it as a form of order within a more encompassing form. The poem is divided into three large sections, and section 2 is serially arranged as seventeen units. But this section is framed by opening and closing sections that are entirely unnumbered. In those sections, the absence of seriality spatializes the reading field, so that temporal orders as we ordinarily know them are broken down.

Howe—who spent the first part of her artistic life working as a painter—tends to see the page as a visual artist sees it. One is inevitably reminded of Blake not only in the way she asks us to encounter the page, but in the relation between pages that is enforced by the codex medium. Consider this brief transitive event in the climactic movement of *Pythagorean Silence* [see Fig. 7]. The effect is astonishing—the page comes on one like a revelation—because it exploits and overturns various serial conventions of reading.

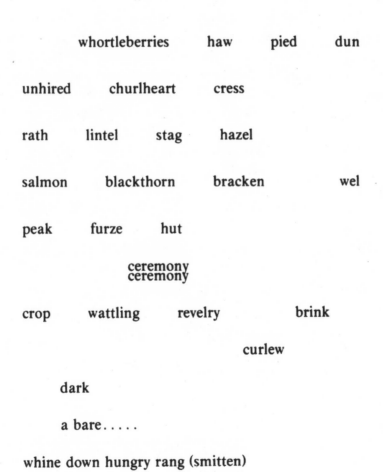

Figure 7. Susan Howe, from *Pythagorean Silence* (Montemora edition, 1982), unpaginated.

Stein, and the Yeats who rewrote Pater, would have understood this kind of work immediately: the composition of the page *is* its explanation.

Following one of the basic serialities of the conventional text—the seriality of page by page reading—we encounter this page only after we turn to it, only as we actually move from a recto to this verso—and from a recto which stands in sharp contrast to this page:

> clear cry a cause
> (no lie) hounds they race all night

Two points of contrast are important. First, these two lines appear alone on the page, placed slightly above midpoint. The white emptiness of this recto, its textual stillness, will be replaced by the text of richly scattered words we just saw. Second, the remnants of grammatical order, still present in this recto's minimal horizontality, are abandoned altogether when we turn the page. The recto is followed by a page that we initially encounter as something to be seen rather than read. We gaze at it much as one gazes at a night sky, scanning its reaches, no longer being told where to begin or where to go. The law of the margin (left to right reading) and the law of headers and footers (top to bottom reading) are both called to judgment when we turn to the verse, along with that other great seriality of language, syntax. The rhetorics of temporality, arrested in their flight, submit to their own revelation by a poem seeking to gain (literally) a measure of control over the murderous cruelties of time.

Howe has described the elemental form of her work as "the sound of what is thought." What she refers to, I think, are the complex systems of sonic echo that dictate her poetry's network of possible relations. In this respect her work is deeply auditory. But the *form* of those sonic systems appeals, for its foundation, to a Pythagorean "harmony of the spheres" rather than to actual speech rhythms. As a consequence, her pages are far closer to

**we that were wood**
**when that a wide wood was**

**In a physical Universe playing with**

**words**

**Bark be my limbs my hair be leaf**
**Bride be my bow my lyre my quiver**

Figure 8. Susan Howe, from *Pythagorean Silence* (Montemora edition, 1982), unpaginated.

mathematical and geometrical constructions than they are to linguistic events. The "sound" of her poetry's "thought" is—quite literally—visionary.

This fact about her work must be emphasized because Howe is often taken for a "Language Poet." And while it is true that her work, and perhaps even more her life, has moved in the orbit of Language Writing, she is—like Michael Palmer—more an absolutist of the word than most of the writers we associate with the movement. This being said, however, we also register Howe's almost mystical involvement with the materialities of writing. The poetical epigraph which she places at the beginning of *Pythagorean Silence* is exemplary [see Fig 8]. Howe's first poetic move in her poem is to disrupt a printing convention. The jammed entanglement of the first two lines calls our attention to the physicality of the text. At the semantic level the passage suggests a magical or primitive turn, a prayer or incantation to bring about a translation of being. The allusions to Blake's *Milton* and Shakespeare's *Midsummer Night's Dream* underscore Howe's pursuit of transmigratory meanings.

These are brought to a dramatic focus when the sonic mirrorings that play through the first two lines plunge together in the isolated fourth line, "words." The text's "we" is playing with itself, with the "words" that make up its being and with the "physical Universe" of its world—that is to say, with this very book, which will not be wholly disconnected from its material origins in wood and its spiritual origins in magic. The passage may well remind us of a key Pythagorean idea, that the universe is alive and that all scales of its living forms are involved with each other. The Pythagorean doctrine of transmigration depends upon this idea.

Howe's poetry is grounded in such linguistic and bibliographical devices. They recall the constructivist experiments of the late nineteenth and early twentieth centuries, and they connect her work to various writers associated with the contemporary Language movement in poetry. Indeed, these kinds of technical appropriations explain why Language Writing has emerged as a key index of the postmodern scene of writing in general.

· · ·

# THE BOOK IS AS OLD
# AS FIRE & WATER

# THE PAINTED BOOK
## Nezahualcoyotl

1

In the house of paintings
the singing begins,
song is intoned,
flowers are spread,
the song rejoices.

Above the flowers is singing
the radiant pheasant:
his song expands
into the interior of the waters.
To him reply
all manner of red birds:
the dazzling red bird
sings a beautiful chant.

Your heart is a book of paintings,
You have come to sing,
to make Your drums resound.
You are the singer.
Within the house of springtime,
You make the people happy.

You alone bestow
intoxicating flowers,
precious flowers.
You are the singer.
Within the house of springtime,
You make the people happy.

2

With flowers You write,
O Giver of Life:
with songs You give color,
with songs You shade
those who must live on the earth.

Later You will destroy eagles and ocelots:
we live only in Your book of paintings,
here, on the earth.

With black ink You will blot out
all that was friendship,
brotherhood, nobility.

You give shading
to those who must live on the earth.
We live only in Your book of paintings,
here on the earth.

3
I comprehend the secret, the hidden:
O my lords!
Thus we are,
we are mortal,
men through and through,
we all will have to go away,
we all will have to die on earth.
Like a painting,
we will be erased.
Like a flower,
we will dry up
here on earth.

Like plumed vestments of the precious bird,
that precious bird with the agile neck,
we will come to an end.
Think on this, my lords,
eagles and ocelots,
though you be of jade,
though you be of gold
you also will go there,
to the place of the fleshless.
We will have to disappear,
no one can remain.

—*Translated from the Nahuatl by Miguel Léon-Portilla.*

# WRITING IN THE IMAGINATION
## OF AN ORAL POET
### Henry Munn

I am the woman of the great expanse of the water
I am the woman of the expanse of the divine sea
the woman of the flowing water
a woman who examines and searches
a woman with hands and measure
a woman mistress of measure

\*\*\*

I am a woman of letters, it says
I am a book woman, it says
nobody can close my book, it says
nobody can take my book away from me, it says
my book encountered beneath the water, it says
my book of prayers

\*\*\*

I am a woman wise in words beneath the water, it says
I am a woman wise in words beneath the sea, it says

"YOU MY MOTHER who are in the House of Heaven," sings María Sabina in 1956, "You my Father who are in the House of Heaven/ There do I go/ And there do I go arriving/ There do I go showing my book/ There do I go showing my tongue and my mouth/ There do I go signalling the tracks of the palms of my hands."

In this stanza she goes from the idea of writing, embodied in the book (a word she says in Spanish) to that of vocal speech to that of tracks. The image of footprints recurs throughout the shamanistic chants of the Mazatecs like an insistent reference in the course of the verbal flow of words to graphic marks. Frequently throughout the 1958 session she says: "The path of your hands, the path of your fists, the path of your feet." In other words: what one does, where one goes. "I am she who questions and sees," says the shamaness. "I am she who examines the tracks of the feet and of the hands."

Here we find the idea of reading in a more primordial sense than reading words. The hunter on the track of game is a reader of signs as is the shaman who interprets the symptoms of illness. The imprint of feet in the mud is the first writing of intentional existence. It is not by chance that the

Minister of Houang-ti got the idea of writing from the tracks of birds in the sand. In the pre-Columbian codices footprints often appear, depicting the path of migration or used to mark intervals, as the tracks of moose and other animals appear in the petroglyphs of the North American Indians.

María Sabina is an oral poet; her society is one without writing, but curiously enough one of the principal themes of her chants is the book.[1] "I examine," she says in 1958, "because I have seen my clean book/ my ready book/ my clean pen/ my ready pen." And in 1970: "This is your book/ unique book/ book of the dew/ fresh book/ book of clarity/ I am a woman of the breeze."

She told Alvaro Estrada (1981) that once when she had eaten mushrooms to cure her sister she saw the following vision: "Some persons appeared who inspired me with respect. I knew they were the Principal Ones of whom my ancestors spoke. They were seated behind a table on which there were important papers. The Principal Ones were various, seven or eight. Some looked at me, others read the papers on the table, others seemed to be looking for something among the same papers. On the table of the Principal Ones, there appeared a book, an open book that went on growing until it was the size of a person. In its pages there were letters. It was a white book, so white it was resplendent. One of the Principal Ones spoke to me and said, This is the Book of Wisdom. It is the Book of Language. Everything written in it is for you. The Book is yours, take it so you can work."

The vision of these men sitting around a table moving papers like a group of lawyers or functionaries is worthy of Kafka. Here we see the influence of the modern state, which exists at the periphery of her indigenous world, with its offices and paperwork, on the imagination of a woman who can neither read nor write. For her, the heavenly lords are a kind of celestial bureaucracy, which corresponds with her concept of herself as a lawyer who goes up to heaven to argue the case of her patients with the powers that govern life. "I am a lawyer woman, a woman of transactions/ I go up to heaven/ there is my paper/ there is my book/ Before your gaze/ before your mouth/ even unto your glory." In 1956 she sings: "Paper/ Book of the Law/ Book of Government/ I know how to speak with the judge/ the judge knows me/ the government knows me/ the law knows me/ God knows me/ So it is in reality, I am a woman of justice/ A law woman."

The connection in her mind between writing and the law is founded in fact, for the law is primordially written and writing is in essence legislative. But even though her conception of the Principal Ones reflects the actual modern world of government with which she is familiar, it also has a precedent in the past: in the hierarchy of power of ancient Mexican society, the priests at the top of the pyramid were the ones who held the sacred books of oracle and wisdom. The wise men were described as those "loudly moving the leaves of the codices." The German scholar, Ernst Robert Curtius, in an essay (1956) about the metaphor of the book of nature in European literature, says that only in civilizations where writing was the prerogative of a religious ruling class does the image of the sacred book of wisdom appear. Such was the case, not only in Egypt and Mesopotamia, but in pre-Columbian Mexico as well.

They said of their wise men: "His is the ink red and black. His are the codices, the colored books of pictures. He himself is writing and wisdom." [Fray Bernardino de Sahagún] And María Sabina says: "It is your clean book/ It is your clean pen/ that I have Father/ Before your gaze, before your mouth, even unto your glory/ Look, I feel as if I were going up to heaven."

This woman of words, who is completely illiterate, is fascinated, haunted, obsessed by the idea of writing. "I am a woman of letters," she says. "I am a book woman."

The ancient Mexicans were the only Indians of all the Americas to invent a highly developed system of writing: a pictographic one. Theirs were the only Amerindian civilizations in which books played an important role. One of the reasons may be because they were a people who used psilocybin, a medicine for the mind given them by their earth with the unique power of activating the configurative activity of human signification. On the mushrooms, one sees walls covered with a fine tracery of lines projected before the eyes. It is as if the night were imprinted with signs like glyphs. In these conditions, if one takes up a brush, dips it into paint, and begins to draw, it is as if the hand were animated by an extraordinary ideoplastic ability.

Instead of saying that God speaks through the wise man, the ancient Mexicans said that life paints through him, in other words writes, since for them to write was to paint: the imagination in act constitutive of images. "In you he lives/ in you he is painting/ invents/ the Giver of Life/ Chichimeca Prince, Nezahualcoyotl."[2] Where we would expect them to refer to the voice, they say write. "On the mat of flowers/ you paint your song, your word/ Prince Nezahualcoyotl/ In painting is your heart/ with flowers of all colors/ you paint your song, your word/ Prince Nezahualcoyotl."

The psychedelics bring into play the same mechanisms that are at work in the production of dreams. One of the principal aspects of such awakenings are visions. Freud called dreams a hieroglyphic text. He said their language was closer to a pictographic form of writing than to verbal speech.

The metaphor of the book of life is as central to the mystical poetry of Nezahualcoyotl as it is to the thought of Plotinus, who said the art of the seer is "a reading of the written characters of Nature, which reveal its order and its law." "With flowers you write, Giver of Life," sings Nezahualcoyotl, "with songs you give color,/ with songs you shadow forth/ those who are to live in the earth/ Afterwards you will destroy eagles and tigers/ only in your book of paintings do we live/ here on the earth."

"The book," says Curtius, "received its supreme consecration from Christianity, religion of the sacred book. Christ is the only god whom antiquity represents with a volume in his hand." María Sabina stands at the convergence of the traditions of Mesoamerica and Christianity. When she sings in 1970, "I bring with me my sacred eagle/ Lord Saint John/ Father scribe in the House of Heaven," she refers to the statue of the patron of Huautla, the author of the Epistle according to Saint John, who stands in the Huautla church with a golden goblet of communion wine raised in one hand and a quill in the other, a lectern in the form of an eagle before him with a scroll over its shoulder on which is written in Latin: In the beginning was the Word.

In an interview with reporters from *L'Europeo* of Milan, she described in somewhat different terms the same capital, inaugural vision she later described to Estrada. She said that an elf appeared before her and asked her what she wanted to become. She replied that she would like to become a saint. "Then the spirit smiled and immediately he had in his hands something that was not there before, a big Book with many written pages. 'Here,' he said, 'I am giving you this book so that you can work better and help the people who need help and know the secrets of the world where everything is known.' I thumbed through the leaves of the book many and many written pages, and alas I thought I did not know how to read. And suddenly I realized I was reading and understanding all that was written on the Book and it was as though I had become richer, wiser, and in a moment I learned millions of things."

The pages are covered with written characters. The designs one sees on the psychedelics, which many people have described as the motifs of oriental carpets, at least this once took the form of script in her imagination. She says the pages were covered with letters.

One can hardly imagine a more eloquent, poignant description of an oral poet's desire for the knowledge contained in books. She cannot read, but in her transcendental condition she can. The book is thus a perfect image of the divine wisdom which is beyond ordinary understanding but which the mushrooms enable one to comprehend.

One is reminded of the metaphor of the book of nature which occurs frequently in European literature, that "universal and publick manuscript which lies expansed unto the eyes of all," as Sir Thomas Browne said, adding that its hieroglyphics were more familiar to heathens than to Christians. Paracelsus, "doctor and alchemist, who established the role of chemistry in medicine," stated: "It is from the light of nature that this illumination should come, so that the text of the books of nature may be comprehended and without this illumination, there would be no philosopher or naturalist."

María Sabina is indeed enlightened with the light of nature and enabled thereby to read the text of nature which we know today is written in genetic script.

She told Estrada: "The Principal Ones disappeared and left me alone in front of the immense book. I knew that it was the book of wisdom. The book was before me, I could see it but not touch it. I tried to caress it but my hands touched nothing. I limited myself to contemplating it and at that moment, I began to speak. Then I realized that I was reading the sacred book of Language."

In the background as she sings, crickets chirp, near and far, throughout the mountain night. The chirps of crickets, say neurobiologists, are "read-outs" of impulse signals coded in the nucleic acid sequences of their genes. María Sabina, surprisingly enough, says that when she began to speak, she realized she was reading. One would think that for such an oral poet her inventions were wholly verbal, vocal ones, but for herself she is chanting what is written. She is reading at the same time as speaking as they must have done when they chanted their myths with the codices open before them like musicological scores. She is saying what she sees, which is, in a sense, to read. Where could such an idea come from, for her whose own language is an unwritten one, but from some sense of giving utterance to what has been coded in advance, what is inscribed in her brain, which is maybe what she means by saying that she has her knowledge from birth, that it is innate.

Of course it is not, but cultural in origin like the traditional form of her chant itself, yet the rhythms that vehicle her words are neurophysiological ones and her visions themselves are generated by the deep-lying mechanisms of the human cerebral cortex and nervous system.

"That is your book, my Father/ That is your clock," she sings. For her everything is written, predestined, foreordained. God has wound up the clock of existence and set it going, allotting to each his or her number of days. As Derrida has said, the metaphor of the book of the world is a theological one.[3] A universe in expansion, where events are the outcome of chance as much as necessity, can't be contained between the covers of a book; a reality which is not created once and for all but in course of realization is not written in advance but being written, it demands a text, an open-ended, unlimited play of signifiers in accord with the combinatory play of life itself.

It is as if, however, she goes back to the origins of writing. In her oral autobiography, she relates: "And as well I see that language falls, comes from up above, as if they were little luminous objects that fall from heaven. Language falls on the sacred table, falls on my body. So I catch word after word with my hands. That happens when I don't see the book." Words are invisible. If she sees them falling from heaven they must be changed into images, ideograms. Her words recall in a remarkable way the Chinese myth about the origin of writing recounted by Chang Yen-Yuan in the *Li Tai Ming Hua Chi:* "The K'uei star with pointed rays is the Lord of Literature on earth and as Tsang Chieh, who had four eyes, looked up (into heaven) he saw images dropping down (from the star) and these he combined with footprints of birds and tortoises."

## NOTES

1. To R. Gordon Wasson belongs the credit for being the first person to discern the importance of this theme. Referring to the conjurations of the ancient Mexican sorcerers collected by Ruiz de Alarcón in the seventeenth century and recently retranslated and interpreted by López Austin, he writes: "'The Book' is, I am sure, a permanent feature throughout much of Mesoamerican religious practice, and it goes back far into the past.... Ruiz de Alarcón quotes his Nahuatl informants as speaking of a Book, using the Nahuatl word, *amoxtli*. This word meant in pre-Conquest times the pictographic writings of the Nahuas and Mixtecs.... When Ruiz de Alarcón's informants spoke about the *amoxtli* what did they mean? They would not have had access to the Codices, which were closely held by the powerful. Alfredo López Austin thinks this word was used by them metaphorically, by which I take it he means precisely what María Sabina means: the 'Book' in the Mesoamerican Indian mentality is a fount of mystical lore." (See Wasson. *María Sabina and Her Mazatec Mushroom Velada.* New York: Harcourt Brace Jovanovich, 1974. This book contains the text of the 1958 session I refer to, translated by the linguist George Cowan. The 1956 session, also recorded by Wasson, is on a Folkways record.)

2. Nezahualcoyotl, the King of Tezcoco, was a mystic, architect, and poet. (See Miguel León-Portilla, *Trece Poetas del Mundo Azteca,* 1967, [and the translation of "The Painted Book," above, p. 249—Eds.].)

3. Jacques Derrida, *De La Grammatologie* (Paris: Editions de Minuit, 1967). In connection with the image of the path as it occurs throughout the chants of the Mazatecs it is worth pondering his statement that "it would be necessary to mediate together...the history of writing and the history of the route." "It is difficult to imagine," he goes on, "that the access to the possibility of trails should not be at the same time access to writing" (p. 158).

# TOWARD A POETICS
# OF POLYPHONY AND TRANSLATABILITY
## Dennis Tedlock

*can you tell us which direction we are taking*
*caz we waan no whé paat we guen;*
*bisétuna nasú busini halía badúa lañ;*
*queremos saber nuestra dirección*
*whé paat we guen......*

— *Luke E. Ramirez*

IF A POEM IS supposed to consist of exactly the right words and no others, then there are multiple worlds in which poems are never quite finished, never quite closed. In some of these worlds poets use writing, but there is nothing about writing, in and of itself, that requires a text to be fixed for all times and places. Writing, like speaking, is a performance.

If poetics is supposed to belong to the interior of language, as opposed to the exterior realm of referentiality, then there are multiple worlds in which being a verbal artist means pursuing a dual career in poetics and semantics. This does not mean bringing words and their objects into ever closer alignment, but rather playing on the differences. The sounding of different voices does not require putting multiple poets on the same bill, but takes place in the poem at hand. If the poem is written there may be multiple graphic moves in the same text, and these need not be in synchrony with the voices.

If literature means the world of letters, Greco-Roman alphabetic letters, then the poets of these other worlds are not producers of literature. Some of them do use the alphabet, but not necessarily for the purposes intended by lettered invaders and evangelists. For those looking outward from the inside of the Greco-Roman heritage, composing verse with its rhymes blanked, its meter freed, and its breaths notated is not quite enough to open the boundaries between worlds. There is still this recurring desire to close in on exactly the right words. For other poets in other worlds, paraphrase has never been a heresy and translation has never been treasonous.

In geographical terms, alternative poetries completely surround the world of letters and are practiced in the very precincts of its culture capitals. The examples presented here happen to come from speakers and writers of Mayan languages, who number well over six million today. Their home-lands lie in Guatemala, El Salvador, Honduras, Belize, and Mexico, and they also have communities in South Florida, Houston, Los Angeles, and the Bay Area. The earliest evidence for poetry in their world is a brief text on the back of a jade plaque, written in the Mayan script.[1] Included is a date, with the number of the year given as 3483. For those of us who come from within the world of letters that was 320 A.D., before there was any such thing as English literature.

An excellent introduction to Mayan poetics may be found in a sixteenth-century work known as Popol Vuh or "Council Book," from the highlands of Guatemala.[2] It is written in the Mayan language known as Quiché or K'iche', but in the letters of the Roman alphabet. The authors chose letters in the aftermath of the European invasion, when books written in the Mayan script were subject to being confiscated and burned. They give their lessons in poetics in the course of telling the story of how the gods prepared the world for human beings, and how human beings built towns and kingdoms. Their lessons take the form of examples, but instead of quoting poems by famous authors they offer hypothetical poems of the kinds humans might have performed at different stages in their condition as poets.

From the very beginning the gods wanted to make beings who could speak to them, but their expectations were only partly linguistic. Yes, they did want beings who could put the adjective *ch'ipa* (newborn) in front of the noun *kaqulja* (thunderbolt) and say *ch'ipa kaqulja,* referring to a fulgurite (a glassy stone formed where lightning strikes the ground). And yes, they wanted beings who could combine the stem *tz'aq-* (make) with the suffix *-ol* (-er) and say *tz'aqol* (maker). But their expectations were also poetic. They didn't yearn to hear complete sentences so much as they wanted to hear phrases or words in parallel pairs, such as *ch'ipa kaqulja, raxa kaqulja,* "newborn thunderbolt, sudden thunderbolt," and *tz'aqol, b'itol,* "maker, modeler." When they made the beings that became today's animals and tried to teach them to speak this way, each species made a different sound. Worse yet, a given species simply repeated its cry, as if to say something like *tz'aqol, tz'aqol* instead of *tz'aqol, b'itol.* Some animals, especially birds, received their names from their cries. The whippoorwill, which says *xpurpuweq, xpurpuweq,* is now called *purpuweq.* The laughing falcon, which says *wak ko, wak ko,* is called *wak.*

The whippoorwill can index its own presence with its call, but it can neither name the laughing falcon nor pretend to be one. For Mayans, it is only in this compartmentalized, subhuman domain that wordlike sounds can stay in tidy, isomorphic relationships with their meanings. Once *purpuweq* and *wak* become words in a real language, a poet who names the *purpuweq* may also call it *chajal tikon,* "guardian of the plants." Instead of naming the *wak* straight out, the poet may say *jun nima tz'ikin, ri wak ub'i,* "a large bird, the laughing falcon by name." Europeans once imagined a time, lasting from Eden until Babel, when humans spoke a single, original language composed of words that were intrinsically and unambiguously tied to distinct objects. For Mayans this would be a world before language, and certainly a world before poetry.

After four tries the gods succeed at making real humans, four of them. When they ask these four to talk about themselves, they get a poem in reply. It opens as shown below, with a monostich followed by a distich whose lines are parallel in both syntax and meaning:

| | |
|---|---|
| *Qitzij chik,* | Truly now, |
| *kamul k'amo,* | double thanks, |
| *oxmul k'amo,* | triple thanks, |

The pairing of words or phrases is by far the commonest gesture in parallel verse, whether it be Mayan or Chinese or else from the ancient Middle East. Equally widespread is the use of a monostich to provide a frame, as in this example, or to mark internal transitions.[3] The gods would have been perfectly happy with a composition that followed the first distich with a succession of other distichs of similar construction, but they had unwittingly created poets who were more than versifiers. Even the distich has a twist to it, playing off form against meaning by pairing "double" with "triple." The poem continues with a tristich that has a playful turbulence in its syntax, with each line structured slightly differently from the others. Then comes a tetrastich, the rarest of the forms employed so far, but its unusual length is compensated by the uniformity of its syntax:

| | |
|---|---|
| *mixojwinaqirik* | we've been formed |
| *mi pu xojchi'nik,* | and we have mouths, |
| *xojwachinik,* | we have faces, |
| *kojch'awik,* | we speak, |
| *kojta'onik,* | we listen, |
| *kojb'isonik,* | we wonder, |
| *kojsilab'ik,* | we move, |

In verse of this kind groups of parallel lines can be isometrical, as in the case of the four-syllable lines that make up the distich, but they can just as well be heterometrical, as in the case of the lines of six, five, and four syllables that make up the tristich. In the passage as a whole lines range from three syllables (in the monostich and the first line of the tetrastich) to twice that number (in the first line of the tristich). There are rhythms here, but they are temporary rhythms created by temporary alignments of syntax and therefore of meaning. There are rhymes as well, in the broad sense of recurring combinations of consonants and vowels, but again they are aligned with syntax and meaning. The effect is to foreground the parts of parallel lines that do *not* rhyme, which is to say the morphemes or words that change from one line to the next without changing their position within the line. In the distich, everything rhymes except for the morphemes *ka-* and *ox-*, equivalent to "dou-" and "tri-" in the translation. In the tetrastich, the repetition of the morphemes *k-* (incomplete aspect), *-oj-* (first-person plural), and *-ik* (clause-final verb ending) places the emphasis on the contrasting verb stems they enclose.

The first sentence uttered by the first human beings is not yet over, and as it continues they add a few more poetic moves to the ones they've tried already. In syntactic terms their next line is a monostich, contrasting in structure with the lines that immediately precede and follow it, but in semantic terms it forms a tristich with the syntactic distich that follows it, creating a momentary tension between form and meaning:

| | |
|---|---|
| *utz kaqana'o,* | our thinking is good, |
| *xketamaj naj naqaj* | we have the knowledge of the far and near |
| *mi pu xqilo nim ch'utin* | and we've seen the great and small |
| *upa kaj,* | in the sky, |
| *upa ulew.* | on the earth. |

The first of the two distichs harbors a slight syntactic change of its own, adding *mi* (perfect aspect) and *pu* (a conjunction) in front of the verb in the second line, and each of its lines harbors a smaller-scale distich, composed of *naj nakaj* (far near) in one and *nim ch'utin* (great small) in the other. The latter line is the longest in the whole sentence, running to seven syllables, but the first line of the final distich drops all the way back to three, returning to the shortness of the monostich that began the sentence.

Each of the poetic moves in this first of all human sentences can be found elsewhere in Quiché and other Mayan poetry, whether ancient or contemporary, but seldom are so many different moves employed in so short a time. This is the performance of beings who have, for the moment, complete understanding of everything in the world, and the utterance itself is a poetic tour de force. The gods are alarmed by what they have wrought and decide to cloud the vision of the first humans. After that "it was only from close up that they could see what was there with any clarity," and with this came a decline in their poetic abilities. Reduced to mortals who could only communicate with the gods from a distance, they began their first prayer as follows:

| | |
|---|---|
| *Aqaroq!* | Alas! |
| *at tz'aqol,* | thou maker, |
| *at b'itol,* | thou modeler, |
| *kojawila',* | look at us, |
| *kojata',* | listen to us, |
| *mojasako,* | don't let us fall, |
| *mojapiskalij,* | don't leave us aside, |

After the opening monostich, consisting of a lament called out to unseen gods in the distance, comes an unbroken series of distichs that rolls on for many more lines beyond the ones quoted here. The first distich is isometrical, but the rest at least have the virtue of having unequal hemistichs.

After a long period of wandering in darkness, humans recover some of their lost understanding. They become dreamers and diviners, and they also learn how to use *ilob'al*, "instruments for seeing," such as crystals and books. At the same time they regain their former poetic skills, but unlike the first poets they don't squander all their best moves in just a few lines.

One of the effects of parallel verse is what the Sinologist James Hightower called "verbal polyphony."[4] This effect is prominent in Russian folk poetry, but M.M. Bakhtin left that out of consideration when he set up an antithesis between poetry, which he declared to be monological, and the dialogical or polyphonic discourse of the novel. Tracing dialogical effects all the way down to the scale of individual words, he noted that a given word exists in an environment of other words that could have been used with reference to the same object, and that these other words may come to the mind of the hearer or reader.[5] What happens in parallel verse is that one or more of these other words is actually given voice. Consider this distich from the opening of the Popol Vuh:

> *Waral xchqatz'ib'a wi*
> *xchiqatikib'a wi Ojer Tzij.*

> Here we shall inscribe
> we shall implant the Ancient Word.

By using the stem *tz'ib'-* in the first line, the authors refer to writing without venturing into figurative usage. But then, in the second line, they use the stem *tiki-*, which refers to planting—not in the sense of sowing seeds that will become something else, but in the sense of planting (or transplanting) something that is already a plant in its own right. That something is the Ancient Word, which the authors are transplanting from one book, written in the words and syllables of the Mayan script, into another book, written in the consonants and vowels of the Roman script. In both cases the signs in the graphic field are planted in rows.

The completion of a group of parallel lines that share a common object does not imply that all has been said that could be said about it. In other passages about writing the authors of the Popol Vuh use other words they could have used here. For example, they might have added a phrase that included the word *retal*, "sign, mark, trace," which refers to a clue left behind by a past act, such as a footprint. Or they might have made use of *wuj*, literally "paper" but a metonym for "book." If they had been inscribing a wood or stone surface instead of paper, they might have invoked *k'ot* (carving), a stem they later pair with *tz'ib'* (writing) when referring to the scribal profession.

It could be argued that the choice the authors actually made in the passage quoted above, to pair planting with writing, ultimately clarifies what they are proposing to do. But the notion of planting serves this purpose only by way of a figurative detour that leaves a residue of additional meanings that would only complicate matters if we stopped to explore them. If we want parallel lines to bring their common object into focus with a minimum of complication, a better example is provided by passages in which the authors pair the word *poy*, which refers to dolls or manikins but doesn't tell us what they are made of, with *ajamche'*, which refers to woodcarvings but doesn't tell us, by itself, that the woodcarvings in question are manikins. The Sinologist Peter Boodberg compared the effect of this kind of distich to stereoscopic vision,[6] a notion that has been picked up by various students of parallelism. But I think Jean-Jacques Rousseau came closer to the mark when he wrote, "The successive impressions of discourse, which strike a redoubled blow, produce a different feeling from that of the continuous presence of the same object, which can be taken in at a single glance."[7] It needs to be added that there is no moment at which the successive blows of discourse hammer out a complete object, but only a moment in the course of a performance at which writers or speakers either stop or move on to something else.

In some passages the writers of the Popol Vuh leave their "manikins, woodcarvings" behind right away, but in others they add such statements as *xewinaq wachinik, xewinaq tzijonik puch*, "They were human in looks, they were human in speech as well." It might be claimed that this distich clarifies the picture further, even beyond what the addition of "woodcarvings" did for "manikins," but it also has the potential for contradicting an image we had already formed and replacing it with a new (and still incomplete) image, or making us wonder whether someone is ventriloquizing the manikins, which now sound like puppets, and so on. Instead of being present continuously, the object never quite becomes identical with itself.

There are times when parallel words or phrases, instead of constructing an object out of its parts or aspects, converge on saying nearly the same thing about it. The example given below also happens to shed light on how contemporary speakers of Quiché construct the relationship between language and experience. It comes from a conversation in which Barbara Tedlock and myself were learning how to talk about dreams from Andrés Xiloj Peruch, a diviner. When we asked whether one could describe a *q'alaj wachik* (clear dream) as *kajuljutik* (shining or gleaming), he began with a charitable "yes" but then suggested a more acceptable statement:

> *Xulik pa ri saq*
> > *q'alaj ri wachik,*
>
> > *kajuljutik,*
> > *kachupchutik.*
>
> The dream came out bright
> > and clear,
>
> > gleaming,
> > glittering.

Thus he produced the word *saq*, "light, white, bright," to make a pair with a word from our question, *q'alaj*, which refers to clarity (as opposed to obscurity) and can be used to describe discourse. Then he took the onomatopoeic verb *kajuljutik*, whose reduplicated stem (*julju-*) gives it the character of a small-scale distich, and added a second verb with a reduplicated stem (*chupchu-*). Both verbs indicate some degree of fluctuation in the reception of this "bright and clear" dream, but with a slight difference. *Julju-* carries a sense of acuteness that includes the prickliness of spines and the piquancy of chili, while *chupchu-* is less fine-grained, evoking sensations that include the flickering of a candle and the splashing of water. The effect of the sentence as a whole is to raise the discontinuity of the "presence of the same object" to a high frequency. To paraphrase (and subvert) Charles Olson's version of the famous dictum of Edward Dahlberg, one perception immediately and directly leads to a separate perception of the same object.[8]

The convergence of meaning in Xiloj's statement is supported not only by vocabulary and syntax, but also by the assonance and alliteration that link *saq* with *q'alaj* and *kajuljutik* with *kachupchutik*. But there are other moments in which resonances of this kind are used to rhyme words that are parallel neither in syntax nor in meaning. The purpose is not to answer the demands of a rhyme scheme, but to make a pun. The Quiché term for punning is *sakb'al tzij*, "word dice." Winning combinations of words that share sounds create a sudden shift in meaning that is nevertheless appropriate to the matter at hand. Hearing such a shift provokes neither groans nor outright laughter, but a chuckle or "ah" or "hm" of recognition. Diviners often interpret the Quiché calendar by speaking the number and name of a given date and then giving its augury by playing on the name.[9] Here are three successive dates, each accompanied by two alternative auguries:

| | |
|---|---|
| *Wajxaqib' Tz'i', tz'iyalaj tzij.* | Eight Dog, a jealous god. |
| (or) | (or) |
| *Wajxaqib' Tz'i', katz'iyarik.* | Eight Dog, it's all in a fog. |
| | |
| *B'elejeb' B'atz', kab'atz'inik.* | Nine Monkey, right on the money. |
| (or) | (or) |

| *B'elejeb' B'atz', ri tz'onoj.* | Nine Monkey, matrimony. |
|---|---|

| *Lajuj E, ri utzilaj b'e, kalominaj b'e.* | Ten Tooth, on the tried and true route. |
|---|---|
| (or) | (or) |
| *Lajuj E, xasachom ub'e.* | Ten Tooth, the wayward youth. |

There are times when phrases that are properly parallel in their syntax and meaning nevertheless stand at a considerable distance from one another, opening up a whole range of distinct objects between them. The following example, from the Popol Vuh, evokes the powers of shamans:

> *Xa kinawal,*
> *xa kipus xb'anataj wi.*

> Their genius alone,
> their sharpness alone got it done.

To possess *nawal* is to possess genius in the old sense of the word, adding the powers of a spirit familiar to one's own. A second power is *pus,* literally referring to the cutting open of sacrificial flesh but here understood as the ability to reveal, with a single stroke, something deeply hidden. As a pair these words imply a range of shamanic powers, not because they comprise two grand categories into which everything else fits but because they form a pair of complementary metonyms. The authors could have made a further power explicit by adding (for example) *xa ki tzij,* "their words alone," but instead they chose to use this phrase elsewhere.

In Mayan languages, as in Chinese, complementary metonyms may be compressed into a single word. Here are some Quiché examples, hyphenated to show the locations of suppressed word boundaries; each is followed by a literal English rendering and an explanation:

| *cho-palo* | lakesea | all pooled water, fresh or salt |
|---|---|---|
| *kaj-ulew* | skyearth | world, water included |
| *q'ij-ik'* | sunmoon | includes planets but not fixed stars |
| *kej-tz'ikin* | deerbird | animals of land and air |
| *kar-tap* | fishcrab | aquatic animals |
| *nan-tat* | motherfather | parents and all ancestors |

Even when Mayans make long lists instead of stating a double metonymy, they seem to let some items that could be on the list remain implicit, as if resisting totalization. The authors of the Popol Vuh stop at either nine or thirteen generations when they list the predecessors of the current holders of noble titles, not because the historical total for any lineage was nine or thirteen, but because these numbers belong to a poetics of quantity, one that continues to be followed in present-day invocations of ancestors.[10] The names not mentioned in the Popol Vuh, though perhaps not all of them, can be found by consulting other sixteenth-century sources. There are several documents containing overlapping lists, no two of which are identical in their choices.

Proper names would seem to have at least the potential for bringing words and objects into stable, isomorphic relationships, but they are not exempt from the poetics of saying things in more than one way. Mayan speakers and writers are fond of undoing the "proper name effect," which, to quote Peggy Kamuf's translation of Claude Lévesque's quotation of Jacques Derrida, is manifested by "any signified whose signifier cannot vary nor let itself be translated into another signifier without loss of meaning," which is to say without the loss of one-on-one referentiality.[11] When the authors of the Popol Vuh invoke a proper name that might seem foreign or otherwise opaque to their readers, they often gloss it instead of allowing it to remain in isolation. In telling an animal tale they introduce one of the characters by writing, *Tamasul u b'i, ri xpeq,* or "Tamazul is his name, the toad." Thus they treat their version of *tamazulin,* the ordinary Nahuatl (Aztec) term for a toad, as a proper name, but then demystify this name by supplying *xpeq,* the ordinary Quiché term for the same animal. In the course of telling how the name of the god Hacauitz came to be given to a mountain, they produce the following pair of phrases:

> *Mana pa k'echelaj xk'oje wi Jakawitz,*
> *xa saqi juyub' xewax wi Jakawitz.*

> Hacauitz didn't stay in the forest,
> Hacauitz was hidden instead on a bald mountain.

Here they show their knowledge of Chol, a Mayan language in which *jaka witz* is literally "stripped mountain," a condition described by *saqi juyub',* "bare (or plain) mountain," in Quiché. The effect they create is something like that of disturbing the properness of the name Chicago, which comes from an Algonkian language, by remarking, "Chicago was founded in a place where wild garlic once grew."

Another way Mayans dispel the properness of names is to multiply them. This is not simply a matter of using both a name and a surname (Robert and Creeley), but it does resemble the cases of a name and nickname (Robert and Bob) or a name and an epithet (Buffalo and Nickel City). What remains different is that a single proper name, unless it forms part of a list of persons or places that parallel one another, is likely to be denied self-sufficiency. Instead of replacing some other name, a nickname or epithet is invoked alongside it, as if to say "Robert Bob" or "Buffalo Nickel City."

An eighth-century picture of a Mayan noblewoman at the site of Yaxchilán, in Chiapas, is captioned as follows:[12]

| | |
|---|---|
| *Na Ba'te'el,* | Mother Warrior, |
| *Wak Chan Ahaw,* | Sixth Sky Sovereign, |
| *Na Ik' Ahaw,* | Mother Wind Sovereign, |
| *Na Bakab* | Mother Cornerpost |

The use of the Mother and/or Sovereign titles with each of the four names equalizes them, making it impossible to tell the difference between primary names and secondary epithets (if indeed there is any). The caption for another picture of the same woman utilizes some of the same words and adds others:

| | |
|---|---|
| *Na Ch'ul,* | Mother Goddess, |
| *Na Wak Tun,* | Mother Sixth Stone, |
| *Na Ik' Ahaw,* | Mother Wind Sovereign, |
| *Na Bakab,* | Mother Cornerpost, |
| *Chik'in Chak Te'* | Sunset Red Tree |

For the original writers and readers of these captions the multiple names may have evoked discontinuous aspects of this woman's history, personality, or powers. In other words, the effect would have been different from that of the continuous presence of the "same" person.

Whether parallel words or phrases refer to the same (although intermittently present) object, or else point to objects other than the particular ones they name, they constantly work against the notion that an isomorphism between words and their objects could actually be realized. To paraphrase (and invert) Charles Olson's version of the famous dictum of Robert Creeley, this is a poetics in which form is *always other* than an extension of content.[13]

A parallel poetics stands opposed to the philosophical or scientific project of developing an object language whose meanings have been shorn of all synonymy and polysemy. At the same time it stands opposed to the literary project of protecting poems against the "heresy of paraphrase" by treating them as if they were Scripture, composed of precisely the right words and no others. To paraphrase (and invert) Charles Bernstein's rephrasing of the orthodox position of I.A. Richards and/or Cleanth Brooks, a parallel poetics is one in which a poem *not* said in any other way is not a poem in the first place.[14]

In a poetics that always stands ready, once something has been said, to find other ways to say it, there can be no fetishization of verbatim quotation, which lies at the very heart of the Western commodification of words. In the Mayan case not even writing, whether in the Mayan script or the Roman alphabet, carries with it a need for exact quotation. When Mayan authors cite previous texts, and even when they cite earlier passages in the

same text, they unfailingly construct paraphrases. Such is the case at the
site of Palenque, in Chiapas, where three eighth-century temples contain
texts that tell a long story whose episodes are partly different and partly
overlapped from one temple to the next. Among the events are the formation of the present world by the gods and the deeds of kings who claim divine inspiration, but the text is not what we would call Scripture. In the
overlapping episodes not a single sentence is repeated verbatim from one
temple to another. Smaller-scale examples of paraphrase occur in the dialogues among characters in the Popol Vuh. When spoken messages are sent
through third parties, the words that are quoted as having been sent and
those that are quoted as having been delivered never match one another
verbatim. This is true even in an episode in which the senders are described as having messengers who "repeated their words, in just the same
order." Here are before and after versions of a sentence from the message:

> *Chikik'am k'u uloq ri kichoqonisan.*
> So they must bring along their sports gear.

> *Chik'am uloq ri ronojel ketz'ab'al.*
> He must bring along all their gaming equipment.

It would have been easy for the authors to match the quotations letter for
letter, since they occur on the same page, but they didn't bother. The two
sentences are at least parallel, or put together "in the same order," and they
share a focus on sports equipment.

Our own notions of accurate quotation have been shaped, in part, by
print technology, which finds its purest expression in the exact reproduction of Scripture and other canonized texts. The technology of sound
recording is a further chapter in the same grand story of representation, but
it produces a surplus of aural information that causes problems for text-
based researchers who turn their attention to recorded speech. Folklorists
have a way of making "oral formulaic composition" sound like a primitive
predecessor of typesetting, providing a partial remedy for the crisis of
memory that supposedly afflicts the members of oral cultures. Linguists
have a way of making "performance" sound as though it were an optional
addition to a standard software package, one that would otherwise print out
a perfectly normal text. Meanwhile, in the poetics of parallelism, variation
is not something that waits for a later performance of the same poem, but is
required for the production of this poem, or any poem, in the first place.

Translation caused anxiety long before the current critique of representations, especially the translation of poetry. Roman Jakobson pointed
the way to a new construction of this problem, suggesting that the process
of rewording might be called *intra*lingual translation.[15] Here we may add
that within parallel verse, not only in theory but in practice, the further

step to *inter*lingual translation may take place, with words from two different languages dividing an object between them. In the simplest case the passage from one parallel phrase to the next entails the replacement of a single word with its near-equivalent in another language.

The epigram to this essay changes languages by whole phrases, passing from standard English to Belizean Creole to Garífuna (an Amerindian language spoken by Belizean blacks whose ancestors learned it on St. Vincent) to Spanish and then back to Creole, ironically bypassing the indigenous language of Belize (Mopán Maya).[16] In the macaronic verse of medieval Europe, the changes took place between Latin and the local vernacular. Quiché writers of the sixteenth century sometimes paired words from Nahuatl (the language of the Aztecs) with Quiché equivalents. In the Popol Vuh two terms for a royal house or lineage, *chinamit* (from Nahuatl *chinamitl*) and *nimja* (Quiché), are paired in *e oxib' chinamit, oxib' puch nimja,* which might be translated as "those of the three casas grandes and three great houses." In contemporary discourse Spanish has taken the place of Nahuatl, as in this double question from a story told by Vicente de León Abac of Momostenango: *Jasa ri kab'anoq chech? De qué consiste?* This is something like saying, "What could be happening to them? Vas est das?"

Here we have entered a realm in which the popular notion of an enmity between poetry and translation does not apply. To quote Robert Frost's famous phrasing of this notion, as remembered by Edwin Honig in conversation with Octavio Paz, "Poetry is what gets lost in translation."[17] As Andrew Schelling remembers this exchange, Paz countered Honig by paraphrasing Frost, saying, "Poetry is what is translated." To take this statement a step further and paraphrase it for purposes of the present discussion, poetry *is* translation.

Frost's notion is an ethnocentric one, rooted in a poetic tradition that has devoted much of its energy to manipulating linguistic sounds at a level below that of words and syntax, which is to say below the level of segments that have already begun to carry meaning. This is the level that is most resistant to translation—unless we do as Louis Zukofsky did, finding English meanings to fit the sounds of Catullus. But in a tradition that does its main work above the phonetic level, translation is one of the principal means by which poems are constructed in the first place. Translation into a further language at a later date, like nonverbatim quotation at a later date, then becomes a continuation of a process already under way in the poem itself.

Keeping parallel phrases parallel solves one kind of translation problem but raises others, among them the question of graphic representation. To speak of "parallel lines" is to speak the language of alphabetic writing even before the letters are arranged in lines on a page. For well over a thousand years, Mayan poetry was written in a graphic code that looks quite different from the one in which the texts quoted so far have been cast. In his *Mayan Letters,* Olson first suggested that "the glyphs were the alphabet of [Mayan] books," which "puts the whole thing back into the spoken language." Four days later he wrote, "A Maya glyph is more pertinent to our purposes than anything else," because "these people…had forms which unfolded directly from content."[18] Taken together, these statements project the dream of a writing system that is transparent to language and the world at one and the same time. As it turns out the signs of Mayan writing do notate linguistic sounds, but they do not constitute an alphabet. And, though some signs do take their forms from objects in the world, they rarely mean what they look like.

Instead of notating consonants and vowels, Mayan signs go by syllables and whole words. And where an alphabet constitutes a closed code, fixed at a small number of signs that are (ideally) isomorphic with the sounds they notate, Mayan signs (like Egyptian and Chinese signs) are abundant, providing multiple ways of spelling any given syllable or word. This kind of script is reader- friendly in its own particular ways, permitting the annotation of a word sign with a syllabic hint as to its pronunciation, or permitting a reader to recall a forgotten sign or learn a new one by comparing two different spellings in places where the text would seem to demand the same word. It is also writer-friendly, presenting choices that are more than a matter of calligraphy or typography. Here we need a new term or two, perhaps *polygraphy or diagraphism.* Just as a Mayan poem reminds the hearer that different words can be used with reference to the same object, so a Mayan text reminds the reader that different signs can be used for the same syllables or words.

When a Mayan sign appears to be iconic, its object, if we want to get on with the reading of the text, is usually a sound rather than the thing it pictures. In this pair of signs:

written by a poet/scribe of the fifteenth century, the upper one is the profiled head of a *mut,* a kind of partridge. But here it is meant to be read as the syllable *mu,* and below it is a sign for *ka,* read as the sound of *k* alone in this position, where it completes the word *muk,* "herald" or "augur." Now it happens that the bird called *mut* is an augur, a giver of signs or omens, and that its name serves as a metonym for omens in general, which may be why the poet chose this particular way of spelling *muk.* It also happens that the same poet used the word *mut* in the other half of the same distich in which *muk* appears, but chose to spell it with this pair of signs:

The upper element stands for *mu* and the lower one for *ti*, here read as the *t* sound that completes the word *mut*. As in the case of two lines of verse that are parallel semantically but not syntactically, the result is a tension between form and meaning.

These examples of Mayan spelling have been extracted from larger characters or glyphs, which often include more than two signs apiece. The signs that make up a glyph are clustered in a rectangular space and account for at least one complete word. The glyphs themselves are arranged in double columns, with each pair of glyphs read from left to right and each pair of columns read from top to bottom. With such a format it would have been easy for Mayan poets to create graphic displays of the structure of parallel verse, bringing variable syllable counts into line by packing more signs into some glyphs than others. In books the minimal text consists of four glyphs, one pair beneath the other. Even the quarter-inch glyphs used in books sometimes contain as many as six syllables, so four glyphs could have been composed in such a way as to spell out two full distichs, one beneath the other. A more legible text could have been produced by giving each half of a distich a whole line (two glyphs) to itself. What the scribes did instead, more often than not, was to devote most of the available space to the first part of a distich and then resort to ellipsis for the second part. The following text (the source of the signs discussed above) is from an almanac that tracks the changing relationship between the moon goddess and the fixed stars. It concerns moon rises preceded by the appearance of the Macaw constellation (the Big Dipper):[19]

<table>
<tr><td>*Mo'o*<br>The Scarlet Macaw</td><td rowspan="2"></td><td>*yox mut*<br>is the third sign of</td></tr>
<tr><td>*Sak Che'l,*<br>the Arc of Light,</td><td>*u muk.*<br>her herald.</td></tr>
</table>

A priest-shaman reading aloud from this text in the presence of a client would have had the option of expanding upon "her herald" to fill out the second hemistich, saying some or all of "[the Scarlet Macaw] is the [third] herald of [the Arc of Light]." A further option might have been the substitution of alternative names, such as *Wuk Ek'* (Seven Stars) for "Scarlet Macaw," or *Pal Ú* (Young Moon) for "Arc of Light."

In longer texts Mayan scribes created a sustained counterpoint between poetic structure and visual organization. At the scale of a whole

| | |
|---|---|
| ...on 2 Kib | 14 Mol |
| they rejoined | their umbilical cord, |
| the divine triplets: | Mirror, |
| Thunderbolt, | Sustainer of Dreams. |
| 5  On the day | 3 Kaban |
| 15 Mol | he walked around |
| Thunderbolt Sun-Eye | Feathered Jaguar Temple, |
| the home of | those who fast: |
| Sun-Eye Sky Jaguar, | Holy Lord of Egrets. |
| 10  On the third day | he summons the ghost of |
| the namesake of Lady Sky, | a wise woman, |
| from the cut in his tongue; | he takes the white crown of |
| his holiness: | Sun-Eye Sky Jaguar, |
| Holy Lord of Egrets. | It happened at Hollow Tree, |
| 15  Sky Granary, | the invocation of |
| Sixth Sky Thunderbolt, | three Jaguar Thunderbolts, |
| Holy Lady of Egrets. | 4 and 6 score days... |

From the tablet in the Temple of the Foliated Cross at Palenque, in Chiapas, Mexico. The reading order is left to right and top to bottom. The date 2 Kib 14 Mol fell on July 18, 690, when Sun-Eye Sky Jaguar was Holy Lord of Egrets (the king who ruled from Palenque). The Divine Triplets or three Jaguar Thunderbolts (Mars, Jupiter, and Saturn) had all met up with Sixth Sky Thunderbolt (Antares) at the foot of Hollow Tree or Sky Granary (the part of the Milky Way that currently stood on the southwest horizon at midnight). On 3 Kaban 15 Mol (July 19) the triplets were joined by their mother, Lady Sky or Holy Lady of Egrets (the moon). Sun-Eye Sky Jaguar then called up the ghost of her namesake, a former queen of Palenque and his own grandmother.

composition they sometimes divided a text covering two major topics into two blocks of writing with an equal number of glyphs, but always with the transition between the two topics offset from the visual boundary in the text. The boundary was as likely to fall in the middle of a sentence as anywhere else, as in the case of the excerpt on page 271.[20] It opens the second half of a text that is divided into left and right halves by a picture. The first pair of phrases, "on 2 Kib 14 Mol" (a two-part date on the Mayan calendar), corresponds to two glyphs written side by side, but a similar pair appearing later, "3 Kaban 15 Mol," is split between two lines. The distich "Sun-Eye Sky Jaguar, Holy Lord of Egrets" is written with paired glyphs the first time it appears, but the same two glyphs are split between lines the second time. The double name of the temple where the inscription is located, "Thunderbolt Sun-Eye" and "Feathered Jaguar," is carried by paired glyphs (with "temple" appended to the second), but the two glyphs that give the double name of a portion of the Milky Way, "Hollow Tree" and "Sky Granary," are divided between lines. Moreover, "Hollow Tree" is in the right half of a glyph whose left half, "It happened at," starts a new sentence in the middle of a line. The tristichs in this passage—"Mirror, Thunderbolt, Sustainer of Dreams" and "Sixth Sky Thunderbolt, three Jaguar Thunderbolts, Holy Lady of Egrets"— could have been squared up by spelling out their Mayan equivalents with even numbers of glyphs, but in both cases the scribe chose to highlight their oddness rather than conceal it, using exactly three glyphs.

Though the pairing of glyphs in ancient Mayan texts cross-cuts the structures of Mayan verse, it still keeps verse in visual play at least part of the time. In this respect it stands between the graphic practices of ancient Mesopotamia and Egypt, where a text in verse looks the same as any other, and those of ancient Greece and Rome, where verse was written in lines that mirrored its structure. In the beginning Greco-Roman lines were those of isometric verse, and the lines of various European poetries have followed suit for most of their history. In purely graphic terms, such verse has a curious kinship with prose. When Greeks and Romans wrote prose, they strove for a justified right margin and broke words wherever necessary. When they wrote verse they left the right margin just ragged enough to call attention to the achievement of a near-match between the organization of discourse and the organization of the graphic field. The addition of end rhymes made this achievement still more visible. Against this background the contemporary move to verse that is not only blank (note the visual metaphor) but also free of isometric schemes created a deficit in the visual display of poetic artifice. Olson, as if seeking to compensate for this, wanted the poet to use typography "to indicate exactly the breath, the pauses, the suspensions even of syllables, the juxtapositions of parts of phrases, which he intends."[21] His project comes very close to reversing a long-standing Western subordination of voice and ear to the scanning eye, but he reaches for the voice without letting go of the notion that the poem said in some other way is not the poem. To get the poet's intentions right, he tells us, we must repeat not only the words but the breaths, pauses, and suspensions as well.

As we have seen, Mayan poets who used the Mayan script chose to treat the graphic field and parallel verse as semi-independent systems rather than forcing one to mirror the other. When they adopted the Roman alphabet they chose to put everything they wrote (except for a few lists) into a prose format with occasional paragraph breaks. Some of our own poets— Gertrude Stein and Lyn Hejinian—for example have also chosen to use a prose format for parallel phrasing. The five lines of Quiché prose illustrated below come from the manuscript of an ancient play known as *Rab'inal Achi*, "Man of Rabinal," or *Xajoj Tun*, "Dance of the Trumpet":[22]

Demonstrating the verse in such texts for the European eye requires reorganizing them into parallel lines, as I have done for the Popol Vuh excerpts already presented. Scanning the present text (and modernizing its sixteenth-century orthography) yields the following results:

| | |
|---|---|
| *chinsata na k'u uwach,* | and I have yet to show her face, |
| *chinmesesejtaj,* | I would dance her round and round, |
| *chinjikikijtaj,* | I would dance her on and on, |
| *chupam unimal tz'aq,* | inside the great fortress, |
| *unimal k'oxtun,* | the great walls, |
| *chi kaj pa,* | in all four directions, |
| *chi kaj xukutal,* | in all four corners, |
| *xata nima retalil nukamik,* | just to mark the greatness of my death, |
| *nusachik,* | my disappearance, |
| *waral chuxmut kaj,* | here at the navel of the sky, |
| *chuxmut* | at the navel of |

As they were written on a page, these lines happen to begin halfway through a distich (the first half translates as "I have yet to show her mouth") and end in the midst of a hemistich (which ends with "the earth"). The scanned version appears to rescue the poetry from the prose, but there remains the problem of how to voice it. Taking our own verse tradition as a guide, we might end each hemistich by lowering our pitch (as indicated by the commas) and then pausing. Or we could modify this approach by saving our pauses for the transition between one full distich and the next, which would put our combination of pitches and pauses directly in the service of the hierarchical structure created by the scanning eye. But that is not the way these words are performed by an actor.

Just as the phrasing of Mayan glyphs interacts with the structure of verse without being reduced to a mere instrument of scansion, so does the phrasing created by Mayan pitches and pauses. Pitch contours and pauses also interact with one another, but without being mere functions of one another.[23] The punctuation and line breaks in Emily Dickinson's manuscripts make it plain that she understood the polysystemic nature of spoken phrasing quite well, and the simplifications carried out by the editors of older printed versions testify to the dominance of eye over ear in mainstream Western poetics. In the case of the Mayan play the art of speaking the parts has been passed along orally, in company with the manuscript. José León Coloch, the present director and producer of the play, coaches the actors by reading their parts aloud. When he speaks the passage under discussion here it comes out as shown below. Each dash indicates a slight rise, each new flush-left line is preceded by an unmistakably deliberate pause, and the final period indicates a sentence-ending drop in intonation:

> and I have yet to show her face—
> I would dance her round and round—
> I would dance her on and on—
> inside the great fortress—
> the great walls—
> in all four directions—
> in all four corners—
> just to mark the greatness of—
> my death—my disappearance—here at the navel of the sky—at the navel
>     of the earth.

Thus hemistich boundaries are marked in the same way as distich boundaries. The tension created by the pauses at these boundaries, instead of being softened by a slight fall in pitch that would signal the completion of a phrase or clause (but not a sentence) in ordinary conversation, is heightened by a slight rise that emphasizes incompleteness. A slightly steeper rise would imply a question, signalling that the hearer should complete the pitch contour by providing an answer with a terminal drop (as we do in English). In other words, each successive line is poised on the edge of a question-and-answer dialogue, but the second half of a distich is not allowed to sound like an answer to the question raised by the first half. These quasi-questions go on piling up until the tension reaches its high point with the line "just to mark the greatness of—" where syntactical incompleteness (or enjambment) reaches its high point and the completion of a hemistich is withheld until the next line. The phrases in that line continue to be marked off by rises, but the elimination of pauses lessens the suspense and a sentence-terminal fall (marked by a period) releases it. At the largest scale, this passage might be said to raise a list of questions for which the long last line provides an answer.

Like the director of the Rabinal play, Quiché poets who specialize in the performance of prayers treat verse phrasing, intonational phrasing, and pause phrasing as three semi-independent systems. In this excerpt from the opening of a prayer spoken by Esteban Ajxup of Momostenango, the commas indicate slight drops in pitch, in contrast to the slight rise indicated (as above) by a dash:

> *Sacha la numak komon nan—*
> *komon waq remaj,*
> *komon waq tik'aj,*
> *komon chuch, komon qajaw,*
> *komon ajchak, komon ajpatan, komon ajbara, komon ajpunto, komon*
>     *ajtz'ite, komon ajwaraje,*
> *uk'amik, uchokik, wa chak, wa patan, chikiwa ri nan, chikiwa ri tat,*
>
> Pardon my trespass all mothers—
> all six generations,
> all six jarsfull,
> all matriarchs, all patriarchs,
> all workers, all servers, all mixers, all pointers, all counters of seeds,
>     all readers of cards,
> who received, who entered, this work, this service, before the mothers,
>     before the fathers,

Here the opening monostich has been created by means of ellipsis; it could have been followed by some or all of "pardon my trespass all fathers." Next comes a distich whose delivery as two separate lines, each of them ended with a slight drop in pitch, marks if off from what comes before and after. The next distich is run on as a single line, which again sets it off (but in a different way). There follows a further acceleration, with two very long lines in succession. They are parallel in the sense that each consists of three distichs, and in the sense that they are identical in their pitch and pause phrasing, but there is a tension between them at the level of syntax. The first one reiterates a single grammatical pattern six times, while the second moves through three different patterns, repeating each one twice. As in the case

of performances of the Rabinal play, there is no moment in Ajxup's performances at which a sustained pattern of pitches and pauses falls into lock
step with scansion.

Following Bakhtin, we could try to see the complexity of Mayan poetry
as the result of a conflict between centripetal forces in language, which are
supposed to produce formal and authoritative discourse, and centrifugal
forces, which are supposed to open language to its changing contexts and
foment new kinds of discourse.[24] But this is a profoundly Western way of
stating the problem. Available to speakers of any language are multiple systems for phrasing utterances, including syntax, semantics, intonation, and
pausing. Available to writers (even within the limits of a keyboard) is a variety of signs, of which some are highly conventional and particulate while
others are iconic and may stand for whole words. There is nothing intrinsic
to any one of these various spoken and written codes, not even the alphabet itself, that demands the reduction of all or any of the others to its own
terms. Bringing multiple codes into agreement with one another is not a
matter of poetics as such, but of centralized authority. It is no accident that
Mayans, who never formed a conquest state and have kept their distance
from European versions of the state right down to the current morning
news, do not bend their poetic energies to making systems stack.

Lastly, a poem written by Humberto Ak'abal of Momostenango.[25] By
means of an animal metaphor he evokes the recent Guatemalan civil war,
with its helicopter gun ships and clandestine cemeteries. But instead of extending his chosen metaphor into a systematic allegory he runs it up
against the fact that animals are without language, thus evoking the story
told in the Popol Vuh:

| | |
|---|---|
| *K'uch:* | Buzzard: |
| *kaxa re kaminaq,* | box for the dead, |
| *muqub'al karapapik,* | grave on the wing, |
| *xawi karaj kaweqaj* | but you're not burdened |
| *ri ub'i ri kaminaq.* | with the names of the dead. |

## NOTES

1. For a detailed account of this artifact, which is known as the Leyden Plaque after
its present location in the Netherlands, see Floyd G. Lounsbury, "The Ancient Writing
of Middle America," in *The Origins of Writing*, edited by Wayne M. Senner (Lincoln: University of Nebraska Press, 1989), pp. 205–208.

2. This and other textual excerpts from the Popol Vuh or *Popol Wuj* are given in the
official orthography of the Academia de las Lenguas Mayas de Guatemala and include
emendations of the manuscript. For a complete translation see Dennis Tedlock, *Popol
Vuh: The Mayan Book of the Dawn of Life*, revised edition (New York: Simon & Schuster,
1996).

3. See Roman Jakobson, *Language in Literature*, edited by Krystyna Pomorska and
Stephen Rudy (Cambridge: Harvard University Press, 1987), p. 156.

4. Cited in a 1959 source not available to me by Roman Jakobson, in *Language in Literature,* p. 172. He relies heavily on Hightower when discussing parallelism in Russian poetry.

5. M.M. Bakhtin, *The Dialogic Imagination,* translated by C. Emerson and M. Holquist (Austin: University of Texas Press, 1981), pp. 68–82.

6. Peter Boodberg, "Cedules from a Berkeley Workshop in Asiatic Philology," in *Selected Works of Peter A. Boodberg,* compiled by Alvin P. Cohen (Berkeley: University of California Press, 1979), p. 184.

7. Jean-Jacques Rousseau, "Essay on the Origin of Languages," in *On the Origin of Language,* translated by John H. Moran (New York: Frederick Ungar, 1966), p. 8.

8. See Charles Olson, *Selected Writings,* edited by Robert Creeley (New York: New Directions, 1966), p. 17. Olson's version of Dahlberg's statement, which Olson means to keep the poet moving fast rather than lingering, is "ONE PERCEPTION MUST IMMEDIATELY AND DIRECTLY LEAD TO A FURTHER PERCEPTION."

9. For more on this see Barbara Tedlock, *Time and the Highland Maya,* revised edition (Albuquerque: University of New Mexico Press, 1992), chap. 5.

10. Dennis Tedlock, *Popol Vuh,* pp. 56, 194–97.

11. Claude Lévesque, Introduction to "Roundtable on Translation," In *The Ear of the Other: Otobiography, Transference, Translation,* edited by Christie V. McDonald (New York: Schocken, 1985), p. 93.

12. The two pictures and captions discussed here are on lintels 41 and 38, illustrated and glossed in Carolyn E. Tate, *Yaxchilan: The Design of a Maya Ceremonial City* (Austin: University of Texas Press, 1992), pp. 177–78, 250–1, 277–78. The translations are mine.

13. Olson, *Selected Writings,* p. 16. His version of Creeley's statement is "FORM IS NEVER MORE THAN AN EXTENSION OF CONTENT."

14. Bernstein's formulation, "The problem is that the poem said in any other way is not the poem," may be found in his *A Poetics* (Cambridge: Harvard University Press, 1992), p. 16.

15. Jakobson, *Language in Literature,* p. 429.

16. The epigram is from the end of a longer poem in Luke E. Ramirez, *The Poems I Write* (Belize: Belizean Heritage Foundation, 1990), p. 17. The ellipsis is in the original.

17. Edwin Honig, *The Poet's Other Voice: Conversations on Literary Translation,* edited by Edwin Honig (Amherst, Mass.: University of Massachusetts Press, 1985), p. 154.

18. Olson, *Selected Writings,* pp. 108, 113.

19. The hieroglyphic text, in Yucatec Maya, is from page 16c of the Dresden Codex, which is reproduced in full in J. Eric S. Thompson, *A Commentary on the Dresden Codex* (Philadelphia: American Philosophical Society, 1972). The alphabetic transcription is a revised version of the one given in Charles A. Hofling, "The Morphosyntactic Basis of Discourse Structure in Glyphic Text in the Dresden Codex," in *Word and Image in Maya Culture: Explorations in Language, Writing, and Representation,* edited by William F. Hanks and Don S. Rice (Salt Lake City: University of Utah Press, 1989), p. 61. The translation is mine.

20. For a detailed discussion of this text, see Linda Schele, *XVI Maya Hieroglyphic Workshop at Texas* (Austin: Department of Art and Art History, University of Texas, 1992), pp. 169–74. My departures from her views are minor at the level of the phonetic values she assigns to the glyphs but considerable at the level of translation and interpretation. In separating the incomplete and complete aspects of verbs (rendered here

as present and past tenses) I follow Stephen D. Houston, "The Shifting Now: Aspect, Deixis, and Narrative in Classic Maya Texts," *American Anthropologist* 98 (1996).

21. Olson, *Selected Writings,* p. 22.

22. From Miguel Pérez, "Rabinal achi vepu xahoh tun," p. 57. Manuscript dated 1913, copy in the Latin American Library, Tulane University. This is the most recent in a series of copies made over a period of centuries in the town of Rabinal.

23. For a linguistic discussion of the contrasts among different kinds of phrasing, see Anthony C. Woodbury, "Rhetorical Structure in a Central Alaskan Yupik Eskimo Traditional Narrative," in *Native American Discourse: Poetics and Rhetoric,* edited by Joel Sherzer and Anthony C. Woodbury (Cambridge: Cambridge University Press, 1987), pp. 176–239.

24. Bakhtin, *The Dialogic Imagination,* pp. 272–73.

25. Humberto Ak'abal, *El animalero,* Colección Poesía Guatemalteca 5 (Guatemala: Ministerio de Cultura y Deportes, 1990), p. 14; translation mine. An extended discussion of contemporary Mayan poetics is included in Enrique Sam Colop, "Maya Poetics," Ph.D. dissertation in English, State University of New York at Buffalo (1994).

# GURUWARI DESIGNS*
## Nancy Munn

IN WALBIRI THOUGHT there is a close relation between graphic forms and the country, or ground (*walya*), since the term *guruwari* can be used in a general sense to refer to any visible mark left by an ancestor in the country, and in addition, *guruwari* in the abstract aspect of "ancestral powers" are lodged in the country. Among the most prominent of the graphs that Walbiri draw in the sand are track prints of animals and birds and circle or circle-line notations referring to places and journeys. An examination of these apparently simple forms can lead us into a closer examination of Walbiri thought concerning the association between *guruwari* designs and the country.

Footprints are impressed in the sand by holding the hand in various special positions; their production is a casual play activity in which men, women, and children may indulge. The circle or circle-line notation commonly appears during general conversation about journeys and places. The circle signifies a locale and the line a path or movement from place to place; a group of circles may be used to specify the relative orientation of locales. Although both types of graphs are generally available among men and women, men apply them more widely, giving them a featured place in their storytelling repertory and ancestral designs.

Looked at in the context of the wider graphic system, track-print imitations (called *wulya*, "foot," "footprints") constitute a special class of elements and figures, for they are essentially translations of natural sand markings into artifactual ones of human making.

Each element or figure signifies the print made by one or more species, for example, there is one type of print for marsupial mouse and opossum (that is, they belong to a single visual category), another for the varieties of kangaroo, and a third for human beings. A figure may consist of a number of the same elements (footprints) or of the footprints ranged on either side of a "tail" (a meandering or straight line).

One man impressing track prints on the sand accompanied this activity with a commentary, for example, "the man ran away"; "he ran south." In

*Author's Note: This selection is drawn from a book which discusses modes of developing narrative and figurative meaning in the graphic art of central Australian Walbiri (now written "Warlpiri") studied in the late 1950s. The book argues that the form-meaning relations characteristic of both women's and men's ancestral designs cannot be adequately understood apart from the designs' common matrix in an art of sand narration practiced by both sexes but most elaborated in women's storytelling. Since the graphic designs illustrated in this excerpt derived only from the men's art and focus primarily on the use of footprints, they necessarily give a somewhat unbalanced view of the characteristic visual forms of men's ancestral designs and of the relation between these designs and the wider art.

another instance a man elaborated the depiction of a kangaroo print that he was demonstrating to me into a hunting scene. After the prints were impressed, he drew a circle to indicate the location of the kangaroo sleeping under a tree, and another slightly farther off to indicate the location of the hunter. "He throws a spear!" said the narrator and swiftly drew a line from the hunter to the kangaroo.

Prints used to tell stories in this way carry a standard signification. They convey the species, number (when over three or four, "many"), and

Track prints used to tell stories. After charcoal (1, 2, 4) and pencil crayon (3) drawings. The drawings were done by different men, but at the same time. The snake is a traditional form, but water hole and grass (3) are nontraditional in style.

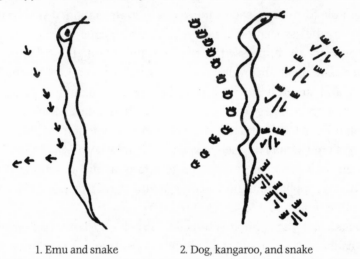

1. Emu and snake          2. Dog, kangaroo, and snake

*1. An emu saw a snake and, becoming afraid, ran away eastward. The upper set of prints depicts the emu running away. East is left in this picture. 2. Seeing a snake, a dog turned away westward; a kangaroo also saw the snake and went east. East is right in this picture.*

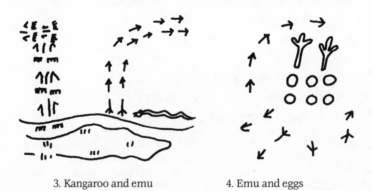

3. Kangaroo and emu          4. Emu and eggs

*3. A kangaroo and emu come down to the water to drink. 4. An emu, leaving its nest, goes to a water hole. Prints at bottom left apparently indicate the return.*

**Figure 1.** Track-print stories and designs.

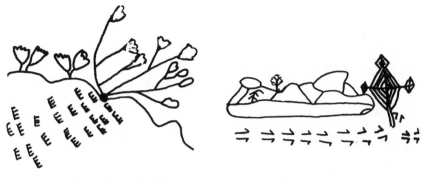

1. Two opossum ancestors                    2. A kangaroo ancestor

*1. Two opossum ancestors went into the ground at a site called Waraginbiri. The base of the little bush is the point at which they entered the ground. 2. A kangaroo ancestor came to Wanabi, took the large string cross,which is a ceremonial object, out of his body and left it there. A number of other kangaroos who were traveling behind him (not shown in the drawing) came up and saw it. A rocky hill with trees is shown behind the string cross.*

**Figure 2.** Track prints representing ancestral journeys. After pencil crayon drawings.

direction of individuals moving through the country. As one young Walbiri man put it, the graphs can be "read." What is "read" obviously replicates the signaling value of the prints in ordinary hunting contexts.

Figures 1 and 2 illustrate how some men made use of track prints to tell stories in drawings that they made for me on paper.[1] In these typical narrative improvisations the prints are combined with a few additional elements (a water hole, a nest of eggs, a snake) to convey a narrative situation such as "an emu, seeing a snake, became afraid and went away east."

Clearly, a graph that signifies the footprint of a species such as opossum or kangaroo may, when transferred to a narrative about ancestors, signify the footprints of kangaroo or possum ancestors, and this is actually a characteristic feature of men's use of the footprints in storytelling. In the paper drawings of figure 2, track prints used to recount ancestral incidents tell us of the number and direction of movement of certain ancestors passing through a particular locale. It happens that in the drawing of figure 2.2, the fact that the actors are ancestors is graphically signaled by the presence of a ceremonial string cross in the drawing, but no such graphic cue is available in figure 2.1, although here also the informant regarded the drawing as an ancestral scene. The same drawing could equally well have been used to portray a scene of daily life.

In still other cases a man may regard a particular set of prints as a *guruwari* design belonging to an ancestor of that species; as designs, track prints can occur independently or fixed into larger graphic composites. When the prints occur independently only extragraphic factors, such as the medium

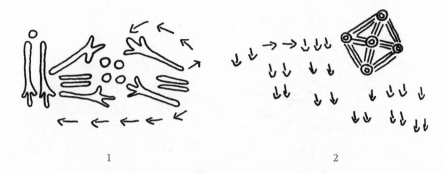

1                                    2

---

Emu *guruwari* on the cave walls at the site Rugari. After cave paintings.

*1. Prints of an emu standing over its eggs. 2. Prints of a large number of emus who came to the site. The circle-line figure signifies that they walked around the site. Each circle is a camp.*

**Figure 3.** Track prints as *guruwari* designs.

and social context in which they appear or the informant's assertion that the graph is an ancestral design, cue the difference between instances of this kind and those in which the prints are simply used to recount ancestral movements (without also being regarded as designs). Thus paintings on the cave walls at Rugari, an important emu site west of Yuendumu, are the *guruwari* of ancestral emus who came to the site and walked around there (Fig. 3.1). At the same time, the prints provide narrative information on their direction of travel and indicate their presence at the site.

Indeed only a fine line divides the use of the graphs simply to recount ancestral, movements and their use as designs, since the term *guruwari* may refer not only to ancestral designs as such but also to the track prints of the ancestor, the actual prints made by him as he travels along. When a man identifies conventional prints as *guruwari*, he may mean that they depict the footprints of the ancestor, and therefore are his *guruwari*, or he may be indicating that the prints are a particular ancestral design. Actually, for Walbiri, the one tends to imply the other: the ancestor's footprints are his designs in the sense that they are among those "marks" or vestiges of his passage in the country through which he is identified and fixed forever in the consciousness of living Walbiri. Here we meet again with the circle of reality and reference so characteristic of Walbiri thinking about designs and ancestral events: designs are among the marks made by ancestors in the country and they also *represent* such marks.[...]

The most general premise behind the Walbiri conception of ancestral times is that all ancestors traveled routes which can be located in the country. The major topographical features are viewed as having been created through ancestral events, and may be thought of as metamorphoses of parts of an ancestor's body, or as due to his bodily imprints in the country. As a result, an ancestor can be "followed" (*bura*, to follow, as in hunting, to come behind), literally kept track of, through his site associations. Each ancestral journey begins with an emergence from the ground and is finalized in a return to the ground, whether at the site of emergence or at some place far distant from it. Ancestors are thought to remain today inside the ground.

This concept of locale and journey provides the framework for men's songs and narratives about ancestral events. Some songs consist simply of site names, and the term for song, *yiri*, also means "name," as well as "visible mark." Used in a broad sense *yiri* includes *guruwari* (visible marks of the ancestor), although in a narrower sense it refers to the verbal forms only. A sequence of songs or what the Walbiri call a "line" provides names of the sites associated with an ancestor as well as references to events along the track. Walbiri men think of the songs as having an exact sequence, correlated with the sequence of sites.[2]

Similarly, the typical ancestral narrative is built upon a framework of site sequences, a mode of narrative order which, as we have seen, is not used by Walbiri women, who typically build their stories on a micro-temporal scaffolding of the daily life cycle rather than on the macro-time of the journey. The journey model is the more inclusive, since it can include the daily cycle of activities (for example, some of men's narrative accounts describe daily hunting and gathering activities at the sites along a route).

Some accounts of an ancestral track consist almost entirely of lists of site names connected by phrases indicating the movement of the ancestors between sites. This provides a kind of minimal account of an ancestral journey. The same track may, of course, be rich in events that take place along the route, but the site-path framework is brought into relief by this sort of narration. An abstract from one such minimal account will suggest the pattern:

They slept at Wabadi ["small yam"]. The two kangaroos rested. They go on to Bigili [Vaughan Springs]. Afterward they go on to Walguru ["stone axe"]. On they went. The two kangaroos went on.... They slept at Ngalyirba. Afterward they went on to Bangunubunda [where] they scooped out wooden dishes.... They went on to Winidjara [where] howling dogs pursued them. They fled.... Afterward they went to Ganibaguru. They sat down, sat down, sat down [i.e., for long time]. They went into the distance to another country.

Not only are men's myth narratives constructed through the site-path framework but so also is the stereotype for dreams in which men may see designs and songs for *bulaba* (public camp ceremonies). The Walbiri view is that a dreamer first hears a *guruwalba* singing on a tree, perhaps while he is still half-awake. Then he follows the ancestor's track from place to place, and the various *guruwari* and songs are revealed to him. In the latter situation he appears to be merged with the ancestor. For example, a snake *bulaba* being performed during my stay at Yuendumu was said to have been dreamed by two Yanmadjiri men at a settlement to the northeast. According to my informants the dreamers followed the track or line of the snake as he moved from site to site. A line of men dancing in the ceremony was also said to "follow up" the track of the ancestor.[3]

• • •

*Designs and Songs*

Walbiri postulate close associations between the *guruwari* designs associated with a single ancestor and the songs detailing the events of his track. The fact that the term *yiri* can cover both verbal forms and visual marks also points to the Walbiri view that designs and songs constitute a single complex. Not only is their association expressed in the norms of ritual behavior, but it can also be observed in the way men handle the meanings of designs and songs, since they tend to treat them as complementary channels of communication about an ancestor.[...] For instance, one man sang the following song while drawing meander lines representing smoke in a design for a fire ancestor:

> *walunggana*      *miraranggana*
> fire              "big smoke"[4]

This song was part of a narrative to which the design referred and was in the song line associated with a *bulaba* ceremony currently being performed in the camp.

In another instance, a design being painted on the body of a dancer during ceremonial preparations was explained to me as a depiction of the tail and boomerang (both items specified by a single graphic element) of an opossum ancestor. Men then continued their explanation by singing a song belonging to the ceremony that had been sung during the preparations: "Opossum travels on, opossum tail." Pointing to the design, they added that the opossum walked a long way. Designs and songs are thus treated as complementary channels of communication; each is a repository of narrative meaning, and the production of one may evoke the other. The treatment of *guruwari* designs and songs in this manner is a specialized form of the general tendency to perceive figures in the graphic system as stores of narrative, potentially verbalizable meaning, or to use them in conjunction with verbalization to communicate such meanings. For the Walbiri, graphs do indeed "speak."

The interlocking of verbal and visual-graphic forms is a pervasive feature of Walbiri *eidos*, one which characterizes both the masculine and feminine subcultures: it is operative both in the casual social contexts of storytelling and conversation and in ceremonial contexts where the two forms function as coordinate parts of a construction process through which the qualities and potency of the ancestors are reembodied.

In ceremonials, songs combine with designs to infuse the event with *djugurba* qualities, as well as to represent *djugurba* meanings. Unlike the designs and other visual constructions, songs lack spatial localization and can pervade the activity as a whole. Thus a synthesis of spatially localized and nonlocalized media is required to form the sensual qualities of the event.

Indeed, it seems that in positing the close association of songs and designs in their cosmological assumptions about the nature of the world Walbiri are expressing symbolically the relation for them of verbal language and graphic or, more generally, nonverbal communication as a whole. Songs are in a sense symbols of oral language, and ancestral designs are symbols of visual or graphic "language." The ancestors are in effect "talking about" the things that happen to them in both visual-graphic and verbal ways, and such "talking" objectivates the world around them, giving it social, communicable reality.

## NOTES

1. Illustrations taken from paper drawings that men did for me are used here...as "visual texts" in much the way verbal texts may be used in the study of cultural expression and conceptualization.

2. The sequence is not, however, carried out precisely in ceremonial, and of course the sequence itself is always subject to the vagaries of individual memory.

3. Informants used the term *ganari-li,* which they translated as "line up," "we follow'm up."

4. Song words often take a special form, or are foreign terms; translation is therefore chancy. My informant gave the meaning "big smoke" for *miraranggana.* According to Kenneth Hale (n.d.), the term *mirawari* means "mirage"; in my data it also appears as the name of an ancestral site associated with rain, fire, and smoke and thus may, perhaps, be related to the song word.

# LIBRO DESIERTO / DESERT BOOK
## Cecilia Vicuña

| | |
|---|---|
| Libro oxidado | Oxidized book |
| textos bailados<br>y abandonados | texts danced<br>and abandoned |
| libro de nada | book of nothing |
| polvo y des<br>pedida | dust and de<br>parture |
| libro de tiempo<br>y piedra re<br>movida | book of time<br>and stone<br>shifting |
| libro de aliento | book of breath |
| aquí<br>me voy | here<br>I go |
| escribo con viento<br>oxidando el tierral | I write with wind<br>oxidizing dust |
| escribo con brisa<br>entintando la piedra | I write with breeze<br>dying the stone |

Trapezoidal Figure, Nazca Desert, Peru (100 B.C.–600 A.D.)

escribo con cuerpo
danzando la marca

escribo con gestos
cruce y temporal

mi cuero
en pellejo

la tierra
marcada

¿quién lee
los signos?

la pampa
tatuada

el rojo
en el muslo

el rastro
borrado

¿quién lee
los signos?

I write with body
dancing the mark

I write with gestures
crossing and temporal

my hide
of skin

the earth
inscribed

who reads
the signs?

the pampas
tattooed

the red
on the thigh

the traces
erased

who reads
the signs?

Photograph by César Paternosto.

Trapezoidal Figure, Nazca Desert, Peru (100 B.C.–600 A.D.)

el cielo
nocturno

el polvo
estelar?

la ella
en desierto

seco polvar?


mano manantial
la ella tatuando

su cuerpo
de estrellas

el clito
la puerta

llave
el germinar

el centro y el borde
gozó
     manantial

hallando
     la hallé
y la ví

marcando
sus signos

la tierra

su ser

no la tierra
ni el cuerpo

si no
un marcar

libro
a destiempo

clito brotando

el signo
inicial


the nocturnal
sky

the stellar
dust?

the she
in desert

dried dustless?


fountainhead hand
the she tattooing

her body
with stars

the clit,
a door

budding
its key

the center and border
pleasure
     spring

finding
     I found her

marking
her signs

the earth

her being

not earth
nor body

a marking

a book
out of time

clit growing

the initial sign

*— Translated from the Spanish by Rosa Alcalá.*

Photographs by César Paternosto.

Lines, Nazca Desert, Peru
(100 B.C.–600 A.D.).

Radiating Figure, Nazca Desert, Peru
(100 B.C.–600 A.D.).

NAZCA: THE DESERT LINE

Writing is opposition: the plane and the incision, ink and paper, light and shadow, knot and cord. In Nazca, the dark desert gravel, a surface oxidized by dew through millennia, has been removed to create levels of darkness, which are only "readable" from a distant height. They are so large that they can't be read if you stand by them—as if they were destined for a mental or stellar eye. Perhaps, they are meant for *Llamacñawin*, The "Eyes of the Llama" constellation, Alpha Beta Centauri, next to the Southern Cross. The Eyes of the Llama "see" at night, when the writing in the desert cannot be seen. Furthermore, the lines seem to radiate from the ceremonial center of *Cahuachi*, meaning "make them see," an offering of vision for celestial eyes.

Writings or drawings to be danced? Dancing the lines, they went into ecstasy to fertilize the land, as if their trance state and the lines were creating a symbolic form of irrigation. Even today, people in the Andes dance praying and playing music as they walk in large processions devoted to the *Pachamana*, the mother of Space/Time.

But we don't know—the nouns and the verbs of the people we call Nazca have been lost. Present day Quechua only uses one verb for painting and writing: *kellcani*. Of the Nazca culture only some sounds remain, the invention of a flute, the ceramics and weavings to help us imagine the meaning that writing and dancing on the desert may have had.

In a museum in Southern Chile, I found two Nazca ceramics: a naked woman with her belly and hands tatooed with stars, and a small vase with nine abstract clitorises transformed into aquatic seeds budding, surrounded by fish. On that plane, any stone or isolated mountain could be the earth's clitoris, its budding, the source of water and its sign, a temporal flow. (Alan Sawyer speaking of a similar Nazca piece at the Krannert Museum says: "they are seated, their legs splayed and vulva extended as if about to give birth.")

—Cecilia Vicuña

"In June 21, 1941, the American geographer-historian Paul Kosok and his wife Rose went for a picnic on the pampa, or plain, of Nazca, a wedge-shaped plateau of desert perhaps fifteen miles across at its widest, bounded on two sides by river valleys and on the third by the foothills of the Andes. He had come to Peru to study the irrigation systems built by the ancient agricultural peoples to nourish crops in the coastal desert…. The "canals" turned out to be nothing of the sort. What he found instead were broad stripes etched on the desert surface, running arrow straight across rises and gullies for hundreds of yards, even several miles. Scattered among them were other markings, in the form of tight spirals or plazalike trapezoids as much as half a mile long…. Paul and Rose Kosok watched the sun set that evening fifty years ago. Accounts differ about whether it was he or she who first noticed that a line radiating from their vantage was aimed directly at the setting sun. But, as Kosok later wrote, they made the intuitive leap together: "With a great thrill we realized at once that we had found the key to the riddle." The pampa and its markings, Kosok soon became convinced, were the "largest astronomy book in the world," a great chart recording significant celestial objects and alignments."

—Anthony F. Aveni and Helaine Silverman, in
"Between the Lines," *The Sciences,* July-August 1991

# from *THE CHINESE ART OF WRITING*
## Jean François Billeter

*An Art of Gesture*

EACH CHINESE CHARACTER is written according to a set sequence of strokes. To learn how to write a character is to learn how to trace each of its elements in a precise order, which is itself determined by a certain number of rules. With practice, the hand gets used to the sequence and carries it out without hesitation, transforming it into a single gesture. A character that has been learned is a gesture at one's disposal, which, like all gestures, immediately responds to an intention and expresses it.

To conceive how it is possible to memorize hundreds and thousands of characters, it must be understood that what is learned is a gesture more than a picture, that it is motorial memory and more than visual memory that is called upon. This means that a much larger store of information can be integrated, for the resources of motorial memory are in fact richer and more reliable than those of visual memory.

This superiority is understandable. The more involved we are in an activity, the better our memory works. When we enter completely into the gestures of writing, our memory automatically records the characters; no prompting is needed. But if our activity slackens, our body forces are demobilized, memory tends to do its work less well. Chinese teachers have always known that in the beginning of writing was the gesture. So it is that Chinese children traditionally begin learning characters by tracing them rhythmically in the air with broad gestures of arm and hand. They name each element as it is traced (a bar, a leg, a dot and so on), and they pronounce the character at the end. After the gesture has been learned, the character is written down, again broadly, rhythmically and collectively. The concern with form, that is the conformity with a model, comes only afterwards, when the gesture has become so sure that it requires no attention. The transition to a quicker and smaller execution comes later as a matter of course.

This perfect integration of the gesture would be unthinkable without the set, predetermined sequence of strokes. In Chinese writing as in our own, this fixed order makes it easier to achieve automatic responses and ensures that the *same* automatic responses will be acquired by all. A given character must be written at all times with a like gesture so that, in the case of a rapid execution, when the elements run together, the connections shall always be the same and the character remain identifiable.

One of the problems Westerners have when they learn the Chinese script is that they do not call upon the resources of gesture and motorial memory as the Chinese do. The reason is that alphabetical writing has not prepared them to do so. In our writing, we repeat only a small number of mechanical gestures. The hand does all the work, leaving the rest of the body inactive, so that our writing is reduced in the end to a cerebral activity almost entirely cut off from its gestural foundation. Chinese writing, on the contrary, has to be grappled with; it must be learned through gestures. The use of the brush sets the forces and faculties of the whole body in action and so facilitates the learning process. Unfortunately, very few people today can afford the time which this apprenticeship requires.

To Westerners starting to learn Chinese, the habit of alphabetical writing is more of a hindrance than a help. Approaching Chinese writing as an equivalent of their own, they content themselves with *jotting down* the characters, without taking the time to look at them and get the feel of them. They do not realize that what is required is a fresh bestirring of oneself, and that it takes a certain liking for play and gesture to get the knack of it. As many a traveller has remarked, the Chinese are born actors. Montesquieu noted that the literati could be recognized by the "ease with which they make a bow," and he likened the writing to the rites which were so prominent a feature of ancient Chinese society: "It was through the exact observance of these rites that the Chinese government triumphed. One's entire youth was spent in learning them, and one's entire life in practising them. The literati taught them, the magistrates inculcated them. And, as they encompassed all the minor acts and doings of life, once a way had been found to their exact observance, China was well governed." Montesquieu shrewdly adds that one of the things that "might easily have fixed the rites in the heart and mind of the Chinese" was none other than "their extremely composed manner of writing." It is well to keep in mind this close relationship between the gestures of social life and the "composed" gestures of writing, both of which were executed with an equal gusto.

The best way to learn the characters is through progressive interiorization. This means that the learner should first execute the gesture in the air with slow and regular movements, carefully making the attacks and the endings, visualizing the character as it is formed and pronouncing it out loud when it is finished. Gradually the amplitude of the gesture can be reduced until it becomes an imperceptible finger movement. The visualization accompanying the exercise can be done at a certain point with the eyes closed, by projecting the character on to an imaginary screen. The gesture is mimed in the imagination and the character takes form as miming proceeds. At this last stage of interiorization, inner movement and imaginary visualization coincide. Of course, at each stage, imaginary execution and actual execution on paper should be alternated. When we subsequently wish to recall the character, the inverse procedure will be used: we then start with the interiorized movement rather than by trying to recall the image directly. Our normal reaction is to call upon our visual memory—only to realize its powerlessness. For the character to reappear, we must first put our motorial memory into action; that is, put ourselves into motion, just as we would to recall a forgotten dance step. As only the legs can remember the step, so only the hand can retrieve the gesture of writing, and consequently the character we are looking for. This is what the Chinese do instinctively when they cannot remember a character: they search with the hand until the gesture performs itself and restores the forgotten form. In fact, they are so accustomed to "mock writing" that when there is any uncertainty about a word in conversation, which happens often in Chinese, they trace the character in the air or on their palm, or even in the other person's outstretched palm, and this usually suffices to dispel the misunderstanding.

The character, which we have so far been considering as a form, now appears as a gesture. It comes before us as a dual entity: static as a form and dynamic as a gesture. From the practical standpoint of a person writing, it is both at the same time: it is at once a formal matrix, of which the written character will be the concrete realization, and a motorial pattern.

The two aspects of this definition are inseparable: the character is as much a gesture converting itself into a form as it is a form converting itself into a gesture [Fig. 1]. It is because of this dual and unstable nature that it can become animate and expressive.

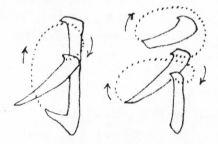

Figure 1.

The whole art of writing arises from this interplay between gesture and form. Calligraphic execution swings constantly between these two poles, becoming more gestural as it approaches the dynamic pole, that is, giving priority to motion over structured form, or more static as it gives priority to structured form over movement.

The shaping of the character and the manoeuvring of the brush are combined in the actual execution, but do not merge completely. The best way of defining their relationship is to say that the manoeuvring of the brush *completes* the shaping. For the calligrapher tracing a character, the shape is laid down in advance; it constitutes the foundation. He has only to call up the necessary gesture for the character to appear fully formed on the paper. He initiates a preprogrammed operation and witnesses its performance as if it were a natural and spontaneous phenomenon. At that moment, two parts of himself are in action: the part which unhesitatingly executes the necessary gesture, and the part which follows, controls and inflects the development of this gesture. His body, as it were, gives birth to the character while he acts as his own midwife. As the character comes into being by itself, all he has to do is subtly modify the emerging forms, introduce correspondences, variations, contrasts, compensations, in short, all the fine touches that give life to the finished character. This is how the handling of the brush completes the shaping of the character.

Here, right [Fig. 2], is an example of the exchanges, correspondences and tensions that the calligrapher introduces into the form of the character as he executes it. The character "two" 二 (*erh*) consists of two bars, a shorter one on top and a longer one below. To compensate for their disparity and give them a comparable weight, the calligrapher adds to this initial inequality a contrast between the thicker gauge of the bar above and the thinner gauge of the one below. He gives a rounder, fleshier contour to the first, and a more bony, angular and severe aspect to the second. The first bar has a simpler, more compact form, and the second bar a more composite form. The two endings are similar and suggest a straight line that forms one side of the equilateral triangle into which the character fits more or less, but the attacks are dissimilar: more abrupt and full at the top, more slender below. The upper bar curves inward at the bottom and the lower bar curves inward at the top, so that they seem to be mutually attracted by a strong magnetism and held by a force field whose centre coincides with the middle of the square. The calligraphers say that these two elements are "back to back," *pei*, like the two parts of reversed

Figure 2. Different executions of the character *erh* "two."

parentheses )(, while others are said to be "facing," *hsiang*, like normal parentheses (  ). The first pattern suggests a force of attraction, the second a force of repulsion—but each is contained by the opposite force. Figure 2 (page 293) shows examples of this same character as executed by different calligraphers.

Figure 3.

In the character "three" 三 (*san*) [Fig. 3] done in current script, the calligrapher has varied the length of the three elements, their respective distances, their gauge, their profile; he has connected the two upper elements, he has set the third one apart and drawn it out, giving it a slight crook to avoid adding a third parallel line. The first two elements were executed in a series of quick and sweeping gestures, while the last was done in a more restrained and meditative manner. The attacks at the top are direct, they show the movement of the brush, while the attack below is closed in upon itself.

These subtleties are the outcome of continuous analysis or, if you like, a series of instantaneous analyses made by the calligrapher in course of execution. But his judgments and decisions are so swift, so intimately linked and so complex that the notion of analysis does not mean much here and should be replaced by that of intuition. What we break down laboriously after the fact is the product of the artist's intuition, of a focused act whose complexity defies analytic description.

The complexity of the operation is increased by the fact that, during the execution, not only does the calligrapher bring into play his cool understanding of the forms but he also stamps them with his wit, his wayward imagination, his emotions; he gives vent to his feelings by subtle changes of proportions or slight modifications of balance, by inflecting the lines, by nuances of the inking. Thus the brushwork can reveal a wealth of sensibility and invention.[...]

Expressiveness of the brush is the prime virtue in calligraphy. It is what gives that touch of life which the Chinese cherish above all, in calligraphy as in painting. As we say of an artist that he "has a fine hand," so the Chinese say of a calligrapher that he "has got brush," *tê pi,* which means that his sensibility passes through his brush, communicating itself to the forms and endowing them with a distinctiveness all his own.

*Expressiveness of the brush is to calligraphy what musicality is to music.* There is no better comparison than this to give a Westerner an insight into calligraphy. Because the analogy between calligraphy and music is a profound one and touches on the very essence of these two arts, I shall develop it here and also bring out certain differences between them. Where music is concerned, I shall refer initially only to classical instrumental music, and especially to the violin, which I have already had occasion to compare to the brush.

## A Musical Art

The comparison between music and calligraphy can be made on three levels. The first and most basic one is that of the musical note and the calligraphic *element*. On this level, the analogy has several aspects:

(1) What the note and the calligraphic element have in common first of all is that they are produced by instruments which have the power to transform the artist's gesture. They are born of a metamorphosis of this gesture and, as a result, their emergence has something that is equally miraculous.

(2) Both are the outcome of a gesture that has a duration. With the violin, the duration of the gesture is obvious from the duration of the note. In calligraphy, the duration of the gesture in each element is perceptible to those who have seen a calligrapher at work or who practise it themselves.

(3) According to Pierre Schaeffer, author of the *Traité des objets musicaux,* the note is characterized by a "dynamic curve defining a precise temporal form, with an attack, a body and a fall"; the attack, he adds, is a "crucial and determining moment" of the note. This definition applies in every particular to the calligraphic element. Pierre Schaeffer establishes a typology of attacks which can be put into relation with that of calligraphy. He calls "suitable" all notes that can be integrated into a musical composition, and we may call "suitable" all elements formed in such a way that they are bodied and produce the calligraphic effect. In his treatise, he points out that a note is "suitable" when it achieves an accord between two complementary qualities: balance and originality. Balance is a compromise between what is "over-structured" and what is "over-simple," and originality is a greater or lesser ability to "surprise expectation." Now this same accord is constantly sought for in calligraphy: to be "suitable," an element should be neither

(a)

(b)

Figure 4.

over-structured (a), nor over-simple (b), and should at the same time surprise expectation, but without being too original (or "eccentric," according to Pierre Schaeffer), for this would keep it from integrating itself into the character. This remarkable homology between the note and the element could be developed further [Fig. 4].

(4) The breadth of the calligraphic element has its musical equivalent in the volume of the note or in its pitch. To the contrast between thick and

thin elements corresponds, according to the point of view we adopt, the contrast between loud and soft notes or between bass and high notes.

(5) The qualities of ink and the nuances of inking may be likened to the timbre in music. The qualities of ink are its shade and its more or less glossy or matte coat. Its darker or lighter shades, its more or less dense or translucid appearance result from the amount of water with which it is diluted. The inking can be dry and rough, or fluid, unctuous, velvety. These tactile values contribute much to the appeal of the works.

(6) Finally, what the calligraphic element and the musical note have in common is that they are bodied and create a space. To the phenomenon of projection whereby we attribute a corporeal reality to an inked form, corresponds the phenomenon whereby we spontaneously relate a well-tempered note to a corporeal presence. The human voice, especially a fine voice, forcibly conveys the idea of a physical presence in a space.

These similarities can be illustrated. The elongated strokes of the clerical characters reproduced in Figure 5a evoke the deep-toned notes of the cello

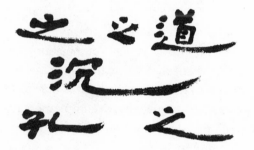

Figure 5a. Brush drawn characters inspired by the *K'ung Chou Stele* (A.D. 100, Eastern Han), one of the great classics of the clerical script.

Figure 5b. Detail of Huang T'ing-chien (1045–1105, Northern Sung), *Memories of Old Walks,* beginning.

or the double-bass, while two characters of Huang T'ing-chien in Figure 5b bring to mind a more fanciful note, of a violin perhaps, freely modulated and followed by spirited pizzicatos, but having a flute-like mellowness.

The second level of the analogy is that of the written *character* and the musical *motif.*

By musical *motif* I mean part of a melody connected by phrasing and set off by two more or less marked pauses; for example the first six notes of the French song *Au clair de la lune.* Such a motif may be likened to a gesture because it springs from a single intention, which it expresses and carries out. In calligraphy, a character is also a gesture which springs from a single intention, expressing it and carrying it out. Thus there is a natural equivalence between a sequence of motifs forming a complete melody and a sequence of characters forming a written sentence. The melody of *Au clair de la lune,* which is composed of eight motifs, would therefore correspond to a series of eight characters. However, because of the unequal duration of the musical motifs, as opposed to the uniform dimensions of the characters, this correspondence is not always easy to establish; it nonetheless represents one aspect of the comparison between musical aesthetics and calligraphic aesthetics.

Whether in music or in calligraphy, the execution of a work takes shape first of all on this second level. It is to the motif that the musician gives an expressive value first of all; and a character superlatively well written by a great calligrapher can be just as moving as a sublime melodic motif rendered by a gifted interpreter. We can be moved by the memory of the seven notes that accompany

*Là ci darem la mano*

in Mozart's *Don Giovanni,* but a character written by a calligrapher whom we admire can leave us with just as profound an impression.

The third level of the analogy is that of the musical composition (i.e., the piece) and the calligraphic composition. The setting out of the characters on the sheet or scroll involves what is called *chang-fa,* "the art of composition." This organization of space is an aspect of calligraphy often overlooked in the scholarly literature.

To adjust his composition, the calligrapher can vary the calibre of the characters, making them bigger or smaller, longer or broader. He can modify the spacing by drawing the characters apart or bringing them closer together. Likewise he can modify the spacing of the columns. These initial variables give him a freedom comparable to that of an architect designing a façade: by modifying the variables, he can give an overall effect of compactness or lightness, of severity or pleasantness, he can impart more presence to the forms that occupy space or more life to the intangible space in which these forms stand.

By regularly aligning characters of the same size and mass, as in the work by T'ung Ch'i-ch'ang (1555–1636, Ming) reproduced on the following page [Fig. 6], the calligrapher creates static compositions. But he can also "give play" to them by varying the dimension of the characters, their relative weight and their spacing; he can let them interact and communicate. The movement, which at first was kept contained within the characters, spills over and extends to the vertical space of the column, and the composition becomes dynamic. The space of the column is thrown open and the energies circulate. The characters seem to be exchanging glances and nods, making signs and calling out to one another, jostling and even laying hold of each other. Whereas in a static composition each character has its centre of gravity within itself, here we see the imbalance of one character

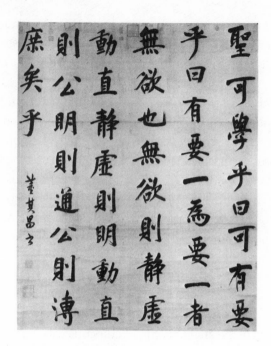

Figure 6. Tung Ch'i-ch'ang (1555–1636, Ming), passage from the *T'ung-shu* of Chou Tun-i (1017-1073, Sung).

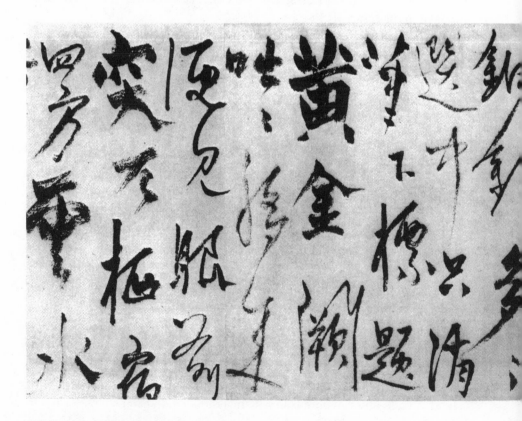

Figure 7. Yang Wei-chen (1296–1370), Yüan), passage from the *Invitation to Subscribe to the True Mirror Monastery (Chen-ching-an mu-yüan-shu).*

compensated by the imbalance of the next. The unstable equilibrium may even prevail and so make the column look like a series of leaps and bounds. But the relaxing of constraint may be evidenced in another way: it may give the characters a semblance of almost complete autonomy; it may make them look like pranksters or hermits ignoring one another and each indulging himself as he sees fit.

The animation may overflow the column and overwhelm the page. This happens when the calligrapher gives an irregular spacing to the columns or makes them deviate from the vertical to simulate awkwardness, to beguile the eye with a certain abandon or to suggest that invisible forces are traversing space and upsetting the order of the lines. There are extreme forms of dynamic composition. One is called the "Milky Way" because the characters, separated by large blank spaces, create an impression of sparseness and disorder: "Things cast there at random, the finest arrangement.." There is another style where the characters, on the contrary, fill up the space and give the impression of a tropical forest in a rainstorm. The *Invitation to Subscribe to the True Mirror Monastery* [Figs. 7–8 by Yang Wei-chen (1296–1370, Yüan), shown (below, left and right)], is a fine example of this kind of composition. This short extract gives only a slight idea of the luxuriance of the work, of the luminosity of the space drenched

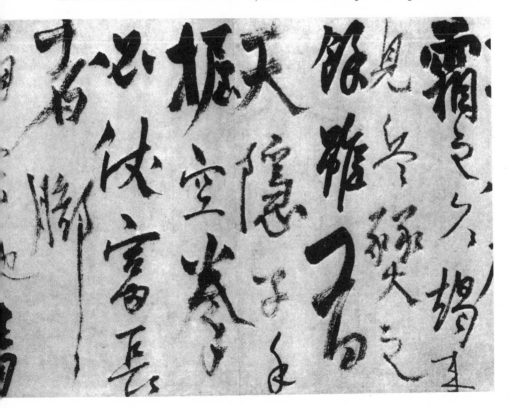

Figure 8. Yang Wei-chen (1296–1370), Yüan), passage from the *Invitation to Subscribe to the True Mirror Monastery (Chen-ching-an mu yüan-shu).*

by the rainshower, quickened by erratic turbulences that threaten to confuse the composition, but never do: the columns remain distinct and the text is perfectly legible.[...]

One might think that these different types of composition are naturally associated with the various genres of Chinese writing and that calligraphers necessarily give a static arrangement to a page in regular script, and a dynamic organization to a page written in cursive. But it may happen that they set up an opposition between the style of writing and the style of composition[...] The great calligraphers make use of these paradoxical combinations to obtain refined effects.

Finally, one aspect of composition is the avoidance of repetitions that would conduce to monotony. An experienced calligrapher will use the repetition of similar elements as an opportunity to introduce variations that will enhance the composition while giving it an even greater cohesion. Wang Hsi-chih (321–379 Eastern Chin), traditionally considered as one of the greatest calligraphers, was the master of variation. Let us look at his *Letter to an Aunt (I-mu-t'ieh)* [Figs. 9–10]. In the first column, on the right, the repetition of the horizontal bars of the 2nd, 4th, and 5th characters ( 一 *i* "one," 十 *shih* "ten," 三 *san* "three") could have paralysed the physiognomy of the text, and so Wang Hsi-chih gave them three different types of curves, once even

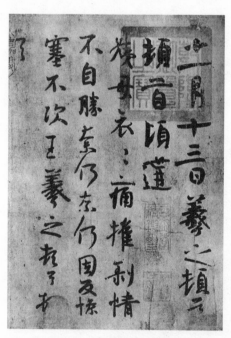

Figure 9. Wang Hsi-chih (321–379, Eastern Chin) *Letter to an Aunt* (I-mu-t'ieh), written on raw silk.

changing a convex contour into a concave one, and attacked them in three distinct ways. But the repetition still seemed to him too pronounced, and he corrected this effect with a descending bar in the 8th character ( 之 *chih*, a "particle"), lightly traced so that this device would not be too obvious. But most of all, farther away, in the 5th character of the 3rd column ( 痛 *t'ung*, "to suffer"), he made a bar that leans slightly to the right, instead of rising a little as it should. This deviation is supremely delicate, as well as extremely effective. One's commentary could go on. The two characters 羲 *hsi* and 之 *chih* that form the calligrapher's forename are not opposed in the same way in the first column as in the last. The *hsi* on the right is dense, it looks like a strangely attired matron keeping steady despite a small foot;

Figure 10. Two details from Wang Hsi-chih's *Letter to an Aunt* and Pierre Bonnard's *Ice Rink,* 1897–1898: the movement is the same

it is followed by an ethereal *chih*. The second *hsi* has a leftward thrust, like Bonnard's skater; the *chih* coming after catches up and reverses the motion like skaters waltzing on the ice. Taken all together, the three characters 王 *wang,* 羲 *hsi* and 之 *chih,* which compose the calligrapher's complete name, have the same movement as the three beats of a waltz. The motif is stated twice, in the first and last columns, but it is by no means the same. This is how genius combines consonance and dissonance to enrich the physiognomy of the page in subtle ways. This is what a musical performer does when he transforms the repetitions in a piece into endlessly modified recalls.

Such are the resources of composition in calligraphy. When this art of composition lies in setting out the masses and adjusting the relationship between the parts, it corresponds to the art of the composer in music; when it lies in giving rhythm and variety to the forms required by the text, it is closer to the art of the musical performer.

In the act of writing, the calligrapher interprets his text as a musician does his score. He does not invent any forms, he neither adds nor takes anything away. Apart from the improvised cadenzas of a concerto, musician and calligrapher have the same task: to give life to predetermined forms and through them to express something uniquely their own. Paradoxically, the constraints to which they submit are the source of their freedom: not being called on to *invent* forms, they can devote themselves entirely to the realization of their expressive potential. Because this potential is contained both in the minutest parts and in the whole, they must give life to the detail at the same time as they incorporate it into a coherent interpretation of the whole. They integrate each of their gestures into larger gestures, and finally their interpretation of the work becomes a single gesture born of a single intention.

In calligraphic as in musical execution, there is no turning back. Each gesture, each sequence of gestures, is irreversible. Thus a successful interpretation is always the result of sustained activity, made possible by flawless concentration. When writing, the calligrapher moves with the utmost rapidity from one character to the next because his activity tolerates no interruption. He gives himself no respite, for the slightest pause would break the spell. As in music, calligraphy must be done at one go. The only difference is that the calligrapher, although he cannot let his mind wander, may from time to time permit himself a hesitation, and even—but very rarely—the retouching of a detail.

When we watch a good musician play, we participate more in his playing, we become more involved in his interpretation of the music and our pleasure is thereby increased. The pleasure we take in watching a calligrapher write is of the same order. It is true that, unlike a musical performance, we can appreciate calligraphic execution only afterwards, when the work has been mounted and displayed. Nevertheless, it is a keen pleasure to watch calligraphers write, and one must have seen them at work to gain an idea of the kind of gestures that go into their writing. It goes without saying that the interest of their works and the pleasure they afford is even greater when we have handled the brush ourselves, when we know the calligraphic gesture from the inside. When looking at a work, the art lover who has this experience follows the elements of the characters in the order in which they were traced, reproduces within himself the gestures that gave them form in time and space, their rhythm and style, and thus inwardly reconstitutes the activity of the calligrapher. The written trace for him is like the groove of a phonograph record which recreates the music. It is easy to see why watching the calligrapher in action is an essential part of the learning process and subsequently becomes an enduring source of inspiration: there is always something to be gained in watching a master handle the brush.

Our comparison with music has until now obscured an important aspect of calligraphy: the role played by the text. Let it not be forgotten that, while it can be appreciated like a musical performance, a work of calligraphy is meant to be *read*. To clarify the relation between aesthetic appreciation and the reading of the text, we may note first of all that from one to the other, from writing meant to be agreeably and easily legible to writing whose purpose is not communication but expression, the transition is often hardly noticeable. It can be made as imperceptibly as the transition, of like nature, from walking to dancing: an onset of playfulness or an upsurge of emotion is enough to start the change-over. This change-over may also be likened to the transition from speech to song, which occurs when energies from within, from afar, begin to bear up our diction. In all these cases, the moment always comes when an activity that was subordinated to an external goal breaks free and becomes an end in itself—when it is released and "flies as may be."

But what happens to the text after this transition? What part does it play in the appreciation of a work of calligraphy? Does its content or its literary quality have any effect? Here vocal music affords a better comparison than instrumental music. The music lover can listen to an operatic air in different ways: he can try to understand the words without attending to the music, as if he were trying to understand someone speaking to him; or he can surrender to the pleasure of the music without attending to the words. We may say that in the first instance he practises "ordinary" listening, and in the second "detached" listening. The lover of calligraphy has the same choice: he can practise "ordinary" reading, that is, take note of the text; or he can give himself up to "detached" reading, disregarding the text content and concentrating on the expressive values of the brushwork. A work of calligraphy and an operatic air are similar in that they both depend on a text, but at a certain moment the reader or the listener gives no further thought to the text and relishes, in a comprehensive manner, the sensible qualities of the performance. To these two ways of approaching a work should be added a third, which might be called "attached" and which also bears on the sensible qualities of the execution, but is selective and analytical instead of comprehensive and intuitive. A music lover may be said to practise attached listening when, for example, he follows a certain melodic line or a particular instrument in the orchestra; and a lover of calligraphy practises attached reading when he focuses his attention, for instance, on the attacks or the inking values or the composition.

Before a work of calligraphy, anyone unable to read Chinese can still practise detached reading and derive a certain pleasure from it. It is by this approach that this art is accessible to those who do not read Chinese. The Chinese lover of calligraphy also begins with a detached reading, but afterwards goes on to other ways of reading, alternating and combining them. Thus he explores the work in all its bearings and compares it with others which are stored in his memory. His culture adds to his pleasure. The detached reading to which he returns after many alternations is a richer reading, a synthesis of the observations that he has made on the work itself, of the associations that it has evoked, of the emotions that he has felt in its presence. In the great works, this synthesis can be indefinitely repeated and enhanced. Similarly, the music lover observes, analyses, alternates between different ways of listening, and compares interpretations to enrich his perception of the work and increase his enjoyment. In this respect, the affinity between calligraphy and operatic music (and other forms of music as well) is a close one. Since certain cursive scripts are difficult to decipher, the reader may sometimes have to consult someone more knowledgeable to understand a certain passage, or look up the printed text if one is available. He is in the same situation as the opera lover who turns to the libretto; once his uncertainty is cleared up, he follows the performance without difficulty.

When he has familiarized himself with the work and knows its literal content as well as its calligraphic form, the two become intimately linked in his mind; they are as closely associated as the melody of *Là ci darem la mano,* the words and the situation in which they are sung, all of which become one in the mind of the music lover. However, the relationship between the content of the text and its execution varies according to the nature of the text and the spirit in which it was set down calligraphically. This relationship changes much more than in the case of the operatic air, where it is always more or less the same; one would have to evoke the various forms of singing, from the lightest hum or the improvised tune to the Lied or religious hymns to suggest the range of diversity.

·   ·   ·

The calligrapher interprets his text like a musician his score. He does not invent new forms, but gives life to forms that are defined in advance. This constraint to which he defers is what makes the power of his effects possible, for he can devote all his resources to interpretation alone. The constraints submitted to in calligraphy, however, are not quite the same as those in music, and they vary from one case to another. When he takes a preexisting piece of calligraphy as a model and interprets it according to his own sensibility, he is more like the musician who plays a piece after a remembered or recorded interpretation, than the musician who plays from a score. In that case, the calligrapher is interpreting an interpretation. He does this with the intention of capturing its spirit as much as possible, of reproducing its physiognomy as faithfully as he can, or, on the contrary, of modifying it according to his bent or mood.[...] When the calligrapher starts not with a calligraphic work but only a text, and chooses his own genre, style, format and composition, he has greater freedom, like a musician improvising from a given theme. But the comparison ends there, for the calligrapher always needs a text, while the musician can do without a set theme and improvise freely.

To understand how the calligrapher finds scope for freedom, remember that the character has a dual nature; it is both form and gesture, and so it can be executed in a more static and constructed way, as in the regular script, or in a more dynamic and gestural way as in the cursive. It should be kept in mind that the calligraphic genres interact, that between the static pole of the regular and the dynamic pole of the cursive lies a whole range of intermediary balances: regular, cursive and current script are not strictly defined, mutually exclusive categories, but rather positions in a continuous spectrum. The proof of this is that, while certain works may be ascribed unambiguously to one of these three genres, others are more difficult to define because they belong to a regular script turning into current, or to a current script turning into cursive. The brush technique is the same in regular, current and cursive. Now we see that the unity of technique overspreads the unstable unity of the three genres on the formal plane, and that this unstable unity is one of the foundations of calligraphic aesthetics. Whoever tries his hand at the art of the brush will discover that the strict architecture of the regular cannot be quickened from within unless one has explored the resources of movement by practising the cursive; nor, inversely can one give a good bearing to the cursive without first having studied the laws that govern the shaping of the regular. To excel in one genre, the calligrapher must be thoroughly familiar with the others.

All the classic texts on calligraphy stress this complementarity of the genres. In his *Treatise on Calligraphy (Shu-p'u)*, Sun Kuo-t'ing (c. 648–703, T'ang) writes, for example, that "the regular which does not have something of the cursive is stilted, the cursive that does not retain something of the regular ceases to be writing." In his *Sequel to the Treatise on Calligraphy, (Hsü Shu-p'u)*, Chiang K'ui (c. 1155–1221, Northern Sung) gives a more detailed description:

Angles and curves exhibit the interplay of square (*fang*) and round (*yüan*). The regular uses chiefly angles, the cursive chiefly curves. One should pause slightly in the angles; this gives them force. The movement should be continuous in the curves; the slightest indecision takes away from their vigour. Some amount of curve, moreover, should be worked into the regular to give it vigour, and some amount of angle into the cursive to give it firmness.

Chiang K'ui relates angles and curves (that is, the crooks of the regular and the rounded elements that replace them in the cursive) to the categories of "square," *fang*, and "round," *yüan*. In traditional Chinese thought, square and round are not abstract geometrical notions, but a pair of terms designating antithetical and complementary qualities. The square includes everything that is discontinuous, compound, structured and static, while the round includes everything that is continuous, simple and active. Like similar pairs of notions familiar to Chinese thought, they serve not so much to classify discrete objects as to account, by their combinations, for concrete phenomena: every phenomenon is conceived as a combination of qualities belonging to the square and of qualities belonging to the round. At another level, square and round correspond to Earth and Heaven, and on a still

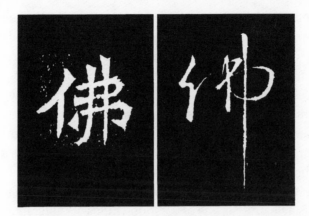

Figure 11. The calligraphic ellipsis: *fo* "Buddha," in regular (left) and cursive (right).

more abstract level to *yin* and *yang,* so that every phenomenon may also be seen as a combination of terrestrial and celestial qualities, or of *yin* and *yang,* qualities. Whichever terms are used, every phenomenon is always a complex totality animated by an inner dynamism, a concrete realization of the changing union of contraries. Thus in speaking of the interplay of square and round, Chiang K'ui evokes in the mind of his Chinese readers associations of great richness: he implicitly identifies the internal dynamism of calligraphic forms with the dynamism of reality as a whole. Like the world itself, the great calligrapher realizes the perpetually renewed union of contraries:

The interaction of square and round quickens both the regular and the cursive. The regular favours the square, the cursive the round, but one must know how to introduce roundness into the square and squareness into the round. From this arises the wondrous effect.

Regular, current and cursive form a complete register [Fig. 11]. When the calligrapher changes over from regular to current, the movement takes hold of the forms, modifying and connecting them. When he changes over to the cursive, his gesture takes hold of them and fuses them together, but without impairing their strength, their backbone. The term "ellipsis" may serve to designate this gestural synthesis which reduces to a single continuous motion the

Figure 12. A classic of the T'ang period "mad cursive": from the *Autobiographical Presentation (Tzŭ-hsü-t'ieh)* by Huai-su (737-?) of 777.

execution of several elements, sometimes of a great number of them, and renders them by a single flourish.

This kind of calligraphic ellipsis has its equivalent in dancing. I remember seeing an old man dancing the sardana in a Catalan port one evening. While the other dancers *detailed* the step in the faster parts, he contented himself from time to time with *sketching it out,* giving a simplified version of the figure. With a single sweeping motion of his leg, he summarized seven or eight of his companions' lively leaps. The superb ease of these ellipses, all the more striking in contrast with the briskness of the music, has left a lasting impression in my mind. The thrill remains with me ten years on.

In order to keep on truly expressing the forms which it synthesizes, the ellipsis must retain within it all their complexity. This is why it is sometimes executed slowly and meditatively, like the dance step of the old man. If the execution is too brisk and the momentum no longer under control, the form may dissolve into pure motion and lose all meaning. Such a dwindling away may be seen occasionally in the mad cursive, for example [Fig. 12] at the end of Huai-su's *Autobiographical Presentation;* the form is in danger of being frittered away completely by the movement.

I shall use the term "hyperbole" to describe the disproportionate development of any one element of the character. It occurs in the horizontal bars and oblique downstrokes of the clerical script, and in the verticals and sometimes the diagonals of the cursive. Some of these verticals seem to break loose from the character like a lightning bolt running along the axis of the column. In the *Tzŭ-yen-t'ieh* attributed to Chang Hsü, there is even an element that sweeps back up the column like a whirlwind.

For a musical equivalent to these sallies, it is no use turning to the average concerts of classical music today, from which humour, disrespect, the odd outburst, have been pretty well banished. Judging by certain accounts scattered in memoirs, performances were once more spirited and brash. One has to look now to jazz and other forms of improvised music to find any such pertness. Ellipsis

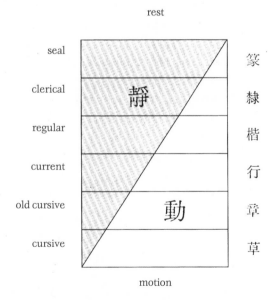

Figure 13. The major calligraphic genres listed according to the amount of rest (*ching*) and motion (*tung*) which go into them.

would be out of the question in performing classical music, but sometimes composers have provided for it in their scores: the abridgments achieved at the end of Ravel's *Valse* are masterly examples of this, and they correspond exactly to the most daring gestural syntheses found in calligraphy.

The regular, current and cursive scripts form a complete whole, but the range of an accomplished calligrapher is even greater, since it further includes the seal, the clerical and the old cursive. This complete register [Fig. 13], like the reduced register, extends from a static pole to a dynamic pole. If we set out the three older genres and the three modern ones in an order going from the most static to the most dynamic, we get the following sequence: seal, clerical, regular, current, old cursive, and modern cursive. And if we replace the Western notions of static and dynamic by the Chinese notions of rest, *ching,* and motion, *tung* (which are thought of in the Chinese view as being related and interacting, motion always containing something of rest, and rest always something of motion), then we can classify the six genres according to the proportion of motion and rest that characterizes each of them.

This classification is convincing if we keep to the conventional definition of each genre, but it fails to account for the diversity of the works, for in actual practice one version of clerical script may be more animated than another in regular, for example, or some particular cursive may be more ordered than a particular sample of current script. The calligrapher who has mastered the whole calligraphic tradition is not only free to move from one genre to the next or to keep to the borderline between them, in stable or unstable equilibrium. He is not only free to multiply the transitions and interchanges in this way. He can also resort to paradoxical combinations by associating non-contiguous genres. For example, he can combine the stable and massive architecture typical of the regular with a cursive handling of the brush; or, on the contrary, a loose shaping of the characters with neat and regular brushwork. The characters by Wu K'uan (1435–1504, Ming), reproduced on the right [Fig. 14], seem at first glance to have a stocky and coarse appearance associated with the regular; some even have a development in breadth and massive endings which recall the clerical script—especially the 5th and 10th of the righthand column ( 奭 *shih* "vast," 燈 *teng* "lamp"), and the 4th of the lefthand column ( 七 *ch'i* "seven"). But others display a whirling, rhythmic movement midway between the cursive and the current, in particular the 3rd and 5th of the middle column ( 成 *ch'eng* "to become," 也 *yeh* "particle"), as well as the next to last in the lefthand column ( 翁 *weng* "old man"): they seem to be bursting with energy, ready to be caught up in some dance. The next to last character of the righthand column ( 剔 *t'i* "wipe the nose") ends on the right with an overlong and wilful-looking vertical, which is normally done only in cursive. The lover of calligraphy discerns in this writing an alternation of contradictory impulses, a sort of instability that is accepted in a spirit of humour and self-possession,

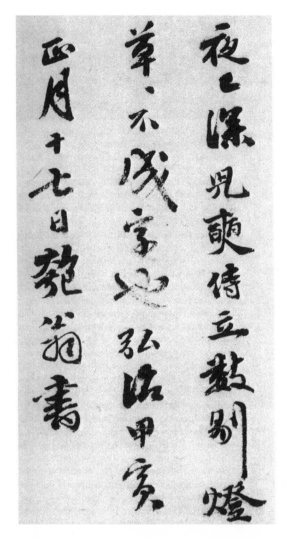

Figure 14. Wu K'uan (1435–1504, Ming) *Planting My Bamboos, Poems (Chung-chu-shih)*, 1480 and 1498, extract.

and sees them expressed without showy effects or affectation, by switching unexpectedly from one register to another. It is a very appealing work, the faithful record of a moment lived through five hundred years ago.

One advantage of the art of writing over music is that the older interpretations have been preserved. We no longer know how Rameau, Mozart, Chopin and the great performers of their time played, but we still have before us today, in all their delicate nuances, the interpretations of the great calligraphers of the Ming, Yüan, Sung and T'ang dynasties, and even of calligraphers from earlier times. We possess thousands of works and hundreds of masterpieces bearing witness to two thousand years of history, while all the music played before the invention of modern recording techniques is lost forever to music lovers and musicologists.

One thing more. From the above, it would seem to follow that calligraphic execution and musical execution unfold within a like duration, that they imply a like experience of time. However, when the musician plays, he has the feeling that he is stringing the motifs together uninterruptedly, and so moving through time in a continuous fashion. The calligrapher, on the other hand, organizes each character around a fixed centre; he finishes it completely before going on to the next fixed centre and shaping the next character around it. As long as one character is not finished, there can be no question for him of hurrying on to the next. Unlike our way of writing, which makes our hand race along, Chinese writing springs from a series of independent operations, each centred on a fixed point and each requiring the writer's undivided attention.

Georges Roditi saw rightly when he observed that "Chinese ideograms, in which everything is particular, and nothing interchangeable, could well be less favourable than our alphabetic writing to the acquisition of an expeditious turn of mind."

One character takes form at a certain spot, then another takes form at the next spot. The temporality of Chinese writing is a compartmentalized temporality, made up of complete moments succeeding one another. It seems discontinuous, but is only apparently so. There is an underlying continuity in the emergence of the forms. As soon as the forming of one character is finished and it has become fully visible, the process of formation continues and brings the next character into being. The characters therefore appear like a series of flowerings following one another without a break, each abandoned as soon as completed, to be replaced by the one that was in gestation behind it. While our writing suggests a time-flow carrying us along in its course or gliding by before us, Chinese writing suggests the idea of a temporality springing from a source just in front of us and manifesting itself by an uninterrupted series of figures emerging and withering away forthwith before our eyes. Even in the current and the cursive, where a more or less explicit transversal connection binds one character to the next, each character is still formed by an operation centring on one point: it always emerges from the same central source.

We shall have occasion later to see the importance of this idea that every sign is an emergence.

*—Translated from the French by Jean-Marie Clark and Michael Taylor.*

# THE WRITTEN FACE
## Roland Barthes

THE JAPANESE THEATRICAL FACE is not painted (powdered), it is written. This unforeseen movement occurs: though painting and writing have the same original instrument, the brush, it is not painting, however, which seduces writing with its decorative style, its sprawling, caressing touch, its representative space (as no doubt would have happened with us in the West, for whom the civilized future of a function is always its esthetic ennoblement); on the contrary, it is the act of writing which subjugates the pictorial gesture, so that painting is always only writing. This theatrical face (masked in Noh, drawn in Kabuki, artificial in Bunraku) is made from two substances: the white of the paper, the black of the inscription (reserved for the eyes).

The function of the white of the face is apparently not to make the complexion unnatural, or to caricature it (as is the case with Western clowns, for whom flour and plaster are just an incitement to daub their faces), but only to efface the prior trace of features, to make of the face an empty expanse of dull material which no natural substance (flour, dough, plaster, or silk) can succeed in animating with any texture, sweetness, or reflection. The face is only *the thing to be written on;* but this future tense itself has already been written by the hand which whitened its eyebrows, the protuberance of its nose, the planes of its cheeks, and gave the page of flesh the black boundary of a head of hair compact as stone. The whiteness of the face—not at all candid, but heavy, disgustingly thick, like sugar—simultaneously signifies two contradictory movements: immobility (what we would "morally" call "impassivity") and fragility (which we would likewise, and as unsuccessfully, call "emotivity"). By no means *on* this surface, but engraved, incised in it, are the precisely elongated slashes of eyes and mouth. The eyes—crossed, uncircled by the rectilinear eyelids, with no circles under them (circles under the eyes: the truly expressive value of the Western face—fatigue, morbidness, eroticism)—open out directly on the face, as if they were the black empty depth of writing, "the night of the inkwell"; or, rather, the face is drawn like a sheet of water toward the black (but not at all somber) well of the eyes. Reduced to the elementary signifiers of writing—the blank of the page and the hollows of its incisions—the face banishes all the signified, that is, all expressivity: this writing writes nothing (or writes: *"nothing"*). Not only does it not "lend" (naively accountable accounting word) itself to any emotion, to any meaning (not even that of impassivity, of inexpressivity), it copies no characters: the transvestite (for women's roles are played by men) is not a boy powdered to look like a woman, with a copious supply of nuances, veristic touches, costly simulations, but a pure signifier whose *underneath* (verity) is neither clandestine (jealously masked) nor surreptitiously pointed out (by a smirking wink at the virility of the actor in the supporting role as done by Western transvestites, opulent blondes whose coarse hands or big feet infallibly belie their hormonal chests), but is simply *absented*. The actor, in his face, neither plays at being a woman nor copies her, but only signifies her; if, as Mallarmé says, writing is made of "the gestures of the idea," the transvestite is here the gesture of femininity, not its plagiarism. It follows that it is not at all remarkable—that is, not at all *marked* (which would be inconceivable in the West, where transvestism is already, in itself, badly thought of and poorly tolerated, purely transgressive)—to see a fifty-year-old actor (very famous and respected) playing the role of a shy young woman in love, because youth, like femininity, is not a natural essence here, the verity of which one madly pursues. The refinement of the code, its precision—which is indifferent to any related copy of an organic type (to create the real, physical body of a young woman)—results in, or is justified by, absorbing and fading all feminine reality, through a subtle diffraction of the signifier. Signified, but not represented, Woman is an idea (not a nature); as such, she is brought back into the classificatory action and into the verity of her pure difference. The Western transvestite wants to be *a* woman; the Oriental actor seeks only to combine Woman's signs.

Nevertheless, in that these signs are extreme—not because they are emphatic (I rather think they are not), but because they are intellectual, being, like writing, "gestures of the idea"—they purify the body of any expressivity: one might say that by dint of being signs, they exhaust meaning. Thus is explained the conjunction of sign and impassivity (an improper word, I repeat, since it is moral, expressive) which marks Asian theatre....

—*Translated from the French by Sandy MacDonald.*

# *HYAKUNIN ISSHU:*
# BETWEEN POWER AND PLAY,
# AN ANTHOLOGY IN TRANSLATION
## Toshi Ishihara and Linda Reinfeld

THE JAPANESE POETRY anthology known as *Hyakunin Isshu*—literally translated, *100 Poets, 100 Poems*—was assembled about 1235 A.D. by Teika no Fujiwara in Ogura, Japan: it includes poems written over the course of five and a half centuries and it continues to be actively read today. Among the poets represented here are emperors and empresses, military officers, monks, women of aristocratic families, servant maids at court, and ordinary people with no particular connection to courtly culture. Although the 100-poem sequence was a common poetic genre in medieval Japan, the *Ogura Hyakunin Isshu* is remarkable for its social role as well as its longevity and aesthetic excellence: in this paper we would like to explore some implications of its many traditional forms and possible transformations.

Each verse is in the form of a tanka, that is, a 5 line syllabic form of 31 syllables, 5-7-5, 7-7. The first poem in the anthology as we have it today, shows the two-part structure.

> Aki no ta no kariho no iho no toma wo arami
> Waga koromode wa tsuyu ni nuretsutsu.
>
> In the fall field, a shelter for the harvest
> Dew drips through the weave of the roof, wetting my sleeve.

Verses about love make up about half the collection (43); seasonal songs come next in number (autumn, 16; spring, 6; winter, 6; summer, 4) and four songs deal with travelling. Parting is a common theme. The collection seems to have been originally commissioned for the purpose of decorating the screens in an elegant summer house. Thus, from the beginning, the collection was designed to exist within a rich visual dimension. In the seventeenth century, the poems developed into a popular card game. This game, with the rules virtually unchanged, continues to be widely played today. The poems, along with their interpretations, are taught in the schools, and there is even a national competition for champion players.

In the game, we have two sets of cards. The cards of one set are for the orator, or reader. Each card has one verse printed in its complete form, and it usually includes a stylized drawing of the author wearing a costume indicative of his or her social class. The cards of the other set are for the players (usually two, sometimes more) and only the latter half of the verse is printed on this card. The players spread the cards of the second set on the floor. When two players compete, each keeps fifty cards placed neatly in front of him or her. The orator draws a card at random and reads—or chants—one poem aloud.

> Oe yama ikuno no michi no tokereba
> Mada fumi mo mizu Ama-no-Hashidate
>
> Through Ikuno and over Mount Oe it's a long road, one I
>     don't know
> No echoes here of my mother, no word from her home on
>     Ama-no-Hashidate

As soon as the orator begins to recite the first line of the poem, the players begin to look for the card that matches the one being recited. This means that the player who has accurately memorized all the poems may locate the right card without waiting until the orator recites the last half of the poem—the part which is written on the players' cards. The better the player's memory, the better the chance of winning. When all the cards are taken, the game is over, and the player with the most cards wins the game.

Card games originated in shell matching. The object of the game was to compare the beauty of one's shell with that of one's opponent —winning meant picking the shell judged to be the most beautiful. And the game of matching shells was often accompanied by a game of matching verses. In this version of the game, the object was to come up with the most beautiful poem. Here the material equivalence of poem and shell points toward the emptiness of meaning in the word itself and locates the life or aesthetic value of an object, be it "natural" or "artificial," in a context created by play. The best poet is the one who most skillfully selects and assembles the material available in the language game at hand. Shell cards with verses written on them were made for those who were not good at writing poems impromptu.

Another version of the shell-matching game, clearly related to the card game of *Hyakunin Isshu* as we know it today, was played specifically with bivalves, shells consisting of two hinged halves. Each poem, like each shell, was split into two parts, so that one half of a poem could be inscribed on one half of the shell, and one half on the other. The object of the game, of course, was to correctly match the two parts of the shell, thereby matching the two parts of the poem. Here there is no split between natural and artificial: opposition is otherwise conceived.

Today the game of poetry is usually considered apolitical; however, the making of *Hyakunin Isshu,* viewed in historical context, shows the complexity of the link between power and play. For Teika, putting together this collection was not only an exercise of literary skill but, quite possibly, a politically subversive act.

*Hyakunin Isshu,* as we know it now, is considered to have been a re-working of Teika's earlier *Hyakunin Shuka,* an anthology commissioned by Utsunomiya Nyudo Rensho, the father of Teika's daughter-in-law. *Hyakunin Shuka* was designed to become an architectural element of his summer house: the 101 poems of this collection were to be inscribed on the sliding screens—in effect, movable walls—of the structure. However, for *Hyakunin Isshu,* four poems of the original *Hyakunin Shuka* collection were omitted and replaced by three newly selected poems. Of the newly selected poems, one was written by Gotoba, Teika's former patron, by then out of power and living in exile; and another was written by Gotoba's son. It has not been definitively determined who made this replacement, Teika himself or his son Tameie; however, the aesthetic intention behind this change is generally considered to be clear. It gives a sense of symmetry to the anthology, for the collection starts with two poems by an imperial father-daughter pair, and it ends with two poems of an imperial father-son pair.

If it was in fact Teika who made this change, his intention in compiling this anthology may well have been political as well as artistic. As a poet who depended for his livelihood and audience on the benevolence of a military government (Nyudo was on the side of the military government), Teika could not have afforded, at the time of compiling *Hyakunin Shuka,* the luxury of expressing any loyalty to Gotoba, his former patron. However, later, in *Hyakunin Isshu,* Teika appears to have made a covert gesture of apology. It is possible that Teika had always been loyal to Gotoba and the culture of the displaced court. As a book artist, Teika was able to use his power to translate the values of a disempowered court and courtly culture into a collection that could survive in a political atmosphere opposed to those values. Thus *Hyakunin Isshu* carries with it a tradition of protest against "official verse culture" and the binding authority of the book.

The bound collection of *Hyakunin Isshu* presents the poems in strict chronological order. However, when the poems are rearranged in space, which is easy to do with the card-game version of the anthology, we may have further evidence of Teika's political intention. The scholar Naomichi Hayashi suggests that the poems can be laid out in such a way as to evoke, through textual imagery alone, what appears to be a depiction of Gotoba's estate, an image that would display—or should we say, discover?—that landscape of Teika's earliest and most joyful poetic associations. Teika may have been making it possible for his old friends to read a message he could not directly convey. It is almost as if he was saying that although he had not been willing to give up his public life as a writer and had continued to write poetry even under the Kamakura military regime, his heart and loyalties remained with Gotoba and the culture of the displaced court.

Perhaps as we begin to translate these poems from Japanese to English, we find ourselves faced with a problem analogous to the problem faced by Teika himself: how to reinscribe the body of an unfamiliar, old, and perhaps unwelcome language right at the border, the cutting edge, of contemporary American poetry? In the dialogue between card play and computer screen, shell games and trade wars, what is the location of poetic language, the context of meaning? Japanese poetry in English has often been over-aestheticized, romanticized, rendered transparent to an exotic message (a lovely little nothing) always tantalizing just out of reach. Yet for over 1000 years, poetry in Japan has been very much a part of ordinary life. We would like the sense of both power and play restored to this poetry in translation.

It is our project to make these poems available in English in a variety of forms—as material for card games, computer games, and do-it-yourself illustrated anthologies. (We'd love to see a game called "Is that a real poem or did you make it up?"—the object of this would be to assemble pieces of the poems, or lines at random, into interesting combinations...)

Originality and authenticity are not our primary concerns. Specifically, by proposing to translate these poems in a multiplicity of forms, we are trying to restore

a) the power of sound in language as the poems are read aloud;
b) play in language, the drama of game competition;
c) language as living material, motion, physical body;
d) the visual, the rhythms of calligraphy; and
e) the image as provocative and political.

To make an anthology is to exercise power, to create an order. To take that anthology apart and shuffle the pieces around, as in a game, would seem to break that order apart.

But in the history of this card game, play gradually assumed a didactic purpose, and the cards became tools for teaching. *Hyakunin Isshu* continues to be taught in school. Students are often asked to memorize these poems —not for the purpose of playing cards, but for didactic reasons: to absorb the principles of literary excellence and interpretation, to acquire a sense of history, to learn what attitudes are considered morally respectable. For our Japanese audience especially, we would like to liberate *Hyakunin Isshu* from its didactic role and bring it back to play again.

Even at the simplest levels of the game, where only the pictures are "read," we see the operation of a poetics of power. Children learn how the writer's gender and social status control their worth. And in the game as it is traditionally played, read aloud, the first part controls the second part. Language has to be controlled in a rigid pattern of 31 letters. Players have to memorize poems (control language) to win the game. Indeed, the control of language becomes quite literally physical. In the slapping down, moving, and picking up the cards, children learn what it means to take language right into their own hands. With our translations, however, we would like to emphasize the possibility of translation as resistance to power and liberation from control.

Often our predecessors have tried to keep the number of lines intact, or the number of syllables: some, in an attempt to render the verse in a musical way, added rhyme. We would like to think, however, that translation can be a productive act, writing that liberates text from its original context and opens up the possibility of other meanings in other contexts. The translator, too, is liberated, freed to make the poems rather than receive meanings. Thus we decided to avoid any foot binders in our translation: each poem consists of simply two unrhymed lines. We liberate poems from the constraints of class and gender by taking the texts away from the authors' portraits. This is no small matter. At one point there was actually a deck of cards made with all male poets portrayed in costume and all women poets rendered in the nude.

We would also like to erase from our attempts at translation the trace of fixed order. Presenting the translated poems in card form is important in that it encourages players to think of poetic material, or material power, in terms of its range and potential for rearrangement. There need not be a fixed context. One can rearrange cards, or change the rules—power, like poetry, can sometimes be played with.

We would like to include photos as part of our own free translation game. Because there is no clear relation between the pictures and the verses, we raise an issue of referentiality/representation. The meaning of the image depends on the viewer. Of course there are editions of *Hyakunin Isshu* illustrated with photographs: they usually present landscapes evoked by the poems and pick up on references to locations, trees, flowers, and natural phenomena. On the other hand, in our photos, we cut the direct association between the poems and photos, portrayal and object portrayed. The meaning of the photos is produced by the reader, player, translator. One translation of images can't be authoritative.

Now with the reproduced game, we challenge the player to assume the role we have assumed, to take over control of the given. Without being subjected to the poems as fixed entities, the player poet engages in creating meanings, lists, poems, possibilities. In this way, our translation saves itself from becoming an authoritative text. We don't want any of our poems to be bound within itself. We challenge all fixed meaning, even when it is our own.

We hope to repeat what was actually done by great poets of the past: to translate the poetry of others, embodying resistance; to place texts on cards, and shuffling, displace them; to create an order, and playing, discard it. To participate in this game is to become anthologizer, translator, destroyer, gambler, creator—freely, in repetition.

## NOTE

Our translation, *The Game of 100 Poems: Hyakunin Isshu,* was printed privately in 1996 as a set of cards: only a few copies for distribution remain. A bound version of our translation, entitled *Hyakunin Isshu: One Hundred Poets, One Hundred Poems,* with photographs, was published in 1997 by Kansai University Press and is readily available.

# NOVELTY BOOKS:
## ACCENT OF IMAGES AND WORDS
### Martha L. Carothers

"THERE IS AN INHERENT METER and rhythm in the sequence of symbols, words, and images. Books of today very rarely meet a form that corresponds to the living pulsation of the reading eye...most of our books are dreary tenements of words badly in need of rhythmical accents—accents which exist in the spoken language." One of the most effective ways of providing rhythmical accents in a verbal book with imagery is by the use of novelty devices. Generally understood, a "novelty" is something new or unusual. Books with novelty devices have unusual features that go beyond the two-dimensional page of type and image by combining mental participation with physical manipulation and/or three-dimensionality. More is involved than just the physical manipulation of turning the pages while reading. Novelty devices are pages or pictures that fold out, revolve, slide, move, slat-dissolve, pop up, or are die-cut in special shapes.

The novelty device provides the ultimate means of emphasis. Immediately attracting a viewer's attention, the device invites the reader to become involved in its special presentation of the visual and verbal. Once physically encountered, the novelty urges the viewer to collaborate mentally, interpreting the verbal and visual. Novelty adds an exciting dimension and "life" to a book. The novelty device is added to enhance the verbal and visuals. The risk of novelty devices is that a book may become just a collection of gimmicks. When properly used, a novelty should explain, describe, or entertain, at the same time piquing the viewer to action, both physical and mental. Otherwise, it becomes a trick feature without significant meaning.

Novelty devices in books are not new, particularly when used to explain or educate. An early book with a novelty device is Jacob Leupold's *Theatrum Arithmetico Geometricum* (Leipzig, 1727). This finely printed encyclopedia of mechanical engineering and hoisting employs a volvelle, "a device consisting of one or more movable parchment or paper discs rotating

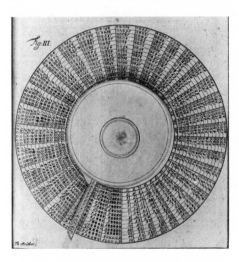

Volvelle, or movable disk to perform mathematical and other calculations, from Jacob Leupold's *Theatrum Arithmetico Geometricum* (Leipzig, 1727).

on string pivots and surrounded by either graduated or figured circles. With its help problems concerning the calendar, tide tables, astronomy and astrology could be solved." This mathematical device is a functional multiplication table not intended to be integrated with the verbal by providing rhythmical accents. The book is a collection of illustrations of scales, pulleys, balances, weights, measures, scribes, compasses, and measuring devices. It was used for reference and not meant to entertain. The volvelle was needed to make the calculations described in the text.

Another calculating device is *Palmer's Computing Scale and Fuller's Time Telegraph*. This double-sided cardboard-mounted dial with metal-tipped corners was, according to its printed inscription, "entered according to Act of Congress, in the year 1843, by Aaron Palmer, in the Clerks Office of the District Court of the State of Massachusetts." More portable and durable than a volvelle contained in a book, this device is functional in and of itself for calendar calculations with no context of either imagery or text.

Early functional visuals are also to be found in Humphrey Repton's well-known volumes, including his *Fragments on the Theory and Practice of Landscape Gardening* (London, 1816). These beautiful volumes contain aquatint engravings of Repton's drawings of English parks and gardens. He is credited with inventing the term "landscape gardening" to express his theory that the art requires "the united powers of the landscape painter and the practical gardener." Just as Repton understood these "united powers" of painter and gardener, his novelty devices introduce the "united powers" of visuals and function. Repton wished to show his clients the before and after of his landscape designs. To do so, he developed systems of overlay lifts, tab/slots, and foldout sections that first showed the existing landscape. "The pleasing combination of Art and Nature adapted to the use of Man" was the landscape visual revealed after the physical manipulation of lifting, sliding, or opening the altered sections. These secondary scenes visually described Repton's proposed landscape designs.

The visuals of Repton's book are not integrated with the reading of the text. Rather, the landscape plates coincide within the text discussion of a particular landscape redesign. There is no pacing to their placement in the book; they only serve to illustrate Repton's capabilities.

Educational and documentary intent combine in *The Heroes of the Victoria Cross* (London: Kensington Fine Art Association, 1887) published on the occasion of Queen Victoria's Jubilee. This accordion-folded, die-cut and embossed book, which pulls from left-to-right, paints "twelve reliefs portraying the various deeds of daring valour performed by Britain's soldiers from the Crimean War to the present day." For the most part this is a visual book, as the text appears as descriptive captions to identify the places, captains, and fighting men. The twelve separate scenes are connected by tapes and the effect when completely opened is that of the onrushing attack and the thundering of hooves.

A similar format is used in nursery sample books. Produced by various firms such as J.W. Thompson Company, D.M. Dewey, and Chase Brothers Company from the late nineteenth through the early twentieth century, these leather-bound, pocket-sized books were carried around by seed salesmen. The horizontal and vertical accordion folding pages collapsed into miniature briefcase size, often with a leather handle on the spine. As new seeds became available, additional sample card pages could easily be added to the book without rebinding the entire book. Additional pages were connected to the last with ribbon, and the book grew in both directions, usually in three rows. The printing and color of these sample pages are exquisite, usually showing the blossom, fruit, and/or the tree.

In an illustrated children's book, it is not completely necessary for children to understand the purpose of the book right away. Rather, the book can act as a stimulus for further action, such as turning to an adult with questions. In this way, books provide a way for children to rehearse reality without suffering the consequences. A children's picture book, as well as any visual book, is basically "designed time." Since it takes time to perceive the verbal and visual, organizing these two elements creates a specifically co-ordinated time sequence. In a sense, the book becomes cinematic, both directing and controlling the viewer by its pace. Each page relates to the next, giving the entire book a serial continuity. The organization of the visual and verbal establishes the pacing which gives rhythm and flow to the book.

When used properly, the verbal provides a part of the information and the visual provides another. Viewed together, they should mesh to reinforce each other; alone, neither part conveys the complete thought. It is the combination of visual and verbal that provides the viewer with the proper clues to interpret the message, and communication is the result.

In *The Act of Creation,* Arthur Koestler draws a parallel between communication and jest. Koestler states that "to make a joke…'unfold,' the listener [viewer] must fill in the gaps, complete the hints, trace the hidden analogies. Every good joke contains an element of the riddle—it may be childishly simple, or subtle and challenging—which the listener [viewer] must solve. By doing so, he is lifted out of his passive role and compelled to co-operate, to repeat to some extent the process of inventing the joke, to re-create it in his imagination." Thus, books that compel the viewer actively to interrelate the verbal and the visual provide more effective communication than those books that allow the viewer to remain passive as the visuals literally picture the story line.

The mind perceives total relationships and not piecemeal assembly of individual parts, according to Gestalt psychology. Thus, a clear visual structure of individual pages is not sufficient to make a book integrated, a unified whole. All pages need to be integrated by a specific arrangement of visual sequences to direct movement from page to page, thus creating linear continuity. However, the organization and pace must be varied enough to retain the viewer's interest throughout the book.

This is especially true in the pacing of children's books. The original purpose of children's books was to educate. Primarily of a religious and moral nature, with some simple black line drawings, early children's books lacked the kind of visual stimuli that interested young readers. The idea of incorporating a novelty device with religious teachings in a children's book originated in England in the late 1700s, when juvenile publishing began to flourish. Robert Sayer, a printer and publisher, developed folding booklets called Harlequinades. These booklets had four sections, each with two flaps which folded over. On each section was an interchangeable picture, and beneath these pictures were religious descriptions in verse. As the verse was read and the flap turned, different scenes were revealed.

Harlequinades had become popular by 1800. They were marketed throughout Britain and in America. Quick to pick up on a good thing, American publishers pirated the idea. The first American to publish and sell such a book was probably Samuel Wood of New York City in 1816. J. Rackstraw of Philadelphia printed *Metamorphosis or a Transformation of Pictures with Poetical Explanations,* which related the story of Adam and Eve. This novelty proved as popular in America as in England. It was so easy to copy that many children as well as parents began to make their own examples, some of which have survived.

The popularity of this novelty proved its worth—it got children interested in reading. Publishers and printers found that children as well as parents were entertaining themselves by creating their own "metamorphosis" with their own stories and pictures. As this trend continued, a second (and increasingly popular) purpose in children's books developed—entertainment. By the 1880s, American society was becoming more sophisticated, and attitudes toward children and their education were changing. The idea of books which entertain children had become respectable. Also, an abundance of British children's books was being imported into America that reflected a more relaxed English attitude. These included picture books, fairy tales, nursery rhymes, fables, riddles, travel, and animal story books.

Two books adapt the peep show novelty format in an attempt to integrate the visual and the verbal throughout the book. Both books, *Peepshow Pictures—A Novel Colour Book* and *Wild Animal Stories,* were published by Ernest Nister in the late 1890s. The peephole device was abbreviated into a panorama of two or three tiers of window scenes "which required no work on the reader's part, for the three layers of the picture were linked to the facing page by a tab which automatically pulled them into perspective as the child opened the book." This arrangement placed the text on the verso pages and the panorama on the recto pages throughout the book.

*Peepshow Pictures* contains directions for how to view this novel picture book. The title and directions also suggest that this book form developed from traveling showmen:

> This is the Peepshow Picture Book
> All you've to do,
> When you want to look
> Is open the pages, not too wide,
> And see what you can find inside.
>
> • • •
>
> But there's one thing I ought to say,
> Everyone must this rule obey,
> Turn its pages over with care,
> Never a finger-mark or tear!

At the end of the book, the directions continue:

> As soon as you come to the end of a book,
> And at all the pictures you've had a look,
> The very best thing you can do, 'tis said,
> Is to shut it up and put it to bed.

Three-dimensional page from *Peepshow Pictures—A Novel Colour Book,* published by Ernest Nister in the late 1890s.

Not in the garden, and not on the floor,
And not in the corner behind the door;
But put it away on the nursery shelves,
For Books don't cry if they sleep by themselves.

Contained in this book are ten poems with black-and-white line drawings. These illustrations are literal visual interpretations of the characters and events of the poems. These two elements exist on the pages without really being integrated. Four of the poems are illustrated with panorama-tiered visuals. These images, too, are literal, visual interpretations of the poems, but they do come to life with three-dimensionality, intricate detailing, and excellent color printing. One panorama in particular attempts to make the three-dimensionality significant. "The Pussy Family" poem is illustrated with a two-tier scene of the cat family at breakfast. Papa is reading the "Daily Mews" newspaper, mother is serving breakfast, and the cat children are eating playfully. Three pictures hang on the wall behind papa, and the largest one is a painting of the same scene in 2-D of the 3-D scene of the panorama.

This panorama technique in book form is three-dimensional in the sense of giving the illusion of depth or varying distances, but it can be viewed as two-dimensional flat surfaces made to lift or stand apart from each other. One book that uses the 3-D idea to create sculptural dimensionality is *Tale of an Old Sugar Tub; With Surprise Model Pictures* (London: Dean & Son, ca. 1860), the story of two boys set afloat in an old sugar tub. The right- and left-hand margins have printed thumb prints that constitute visual directions of how to view and handle the book. As the pages are turned and the double-page spread laid flat, an exposed string crosses the gutter to pull the sugar tub up into three-dimensional roundness. One 3-D tub even has a rivet attached which, when manipulated, creates movement. Also, the type and imagery in this book are integrated on the page. The type overprints on top of the illustrations in some areas and wraps around the significant shapes in the illustrations, conforming to the contours.

Another type of novelty device utilized by the London publisher, Dean & Son, was the movable. In this type of book, perfected by Lothar Meggendorfer in Germany, parts of the illustration were actually moved by viewer manipulation. "The devices that operated the various figures...consisted of a series of inter-connecting cardboard [and wire] levers sandwiched between the coloured illustration on the front of the [page and the page] pasted behind it. The animated limbs and heads were cut-out models on the front of the picture, and moving the tab set the whole scene in motion." *Dean's Moveable Cock Robin* and *The Royal Punch & Judy as Played Before the Queen* are movable books dating from the 1860s. Both books are rather poorly produced with irregular printing and cut-out shapes. The page pacing is irregular with some recto and verso pages printed, and some blank.

*The Royal Punch & Judy* uses the movable technique effectively for emphasis. The page makeup consists of the top half of the page as a stage for the Punch and Judy puppets, with the text printed on the bottom half. The viewer thus becomes the puppeteer and brings life to the characters acting out the story. At one point the text carries the stage idea further by referring to the audience, both the implied audience of the staged story and the book viewer.

The publisher Ernest Nister developed yet another movable device in the late 1800s. Movable books are often referred to as toy books, and in Clifton Bingham's *Something New for Little Folk* (London: Ernest Nister, ca. 1890), the inspiration and movement of a child's toy, the kaleidoscope, are evident. The manipulated visuals of this book, as in Nister's *Wonderland Pictures* (ca. 1890), are scenes "made up of six interlocking sections which, when a tab in the frame was pulled, slid away to reveal a kaleidoscopic effect." The visuals, once revealed, are wonderfully drawn and printed, but again depict the rhymed text literally. The movable device is ingenious, but it is merely another gimmick lacking integration of visual and verbal in the competition to produce a new picture book format.

Closed kaleidoscope illustration for poem, "King Frost," in Clifton Bingham's *Something New for Little Folk* (London: Ernest Nister, ca. 1890).

Worth noting is *The Mammoth Menagerie* (New York: McLoughlin Brothers, ca. 1880), produced by the first American publisher of pop-up books. McLoughlin Brothers, New York, were innovators of printing techniques and quick to realize the profitability of the novelty formats being produced in Europe. This book, published in *The Showman Series*, is actually a compilation of other McLoughlin Brothers publications. The six stories contained in this book were each produced as separate folios. The text is revealed after the panorama flap is lifted. The closed flap, which illustrates the animals in their natural environment, appears to be painted on a scroll or curtain that is starting to curl up. This is a visual instruction to the viewer to lift the flap. Once it is lifted, the animals appear in the cage, while children and parents look back into the three-dimensional distance at the animals.

Two other books published by McLoughlin Brothers employ the novelty of a book within a book. *Naughty Girl's & Boy's Magic Transformations* (ca. 1870) recalls the moralistic purpose of children's books with rhymed stories of greed, truancy, idle chatter, and vanity. The text and image are separated by the gutter (type verso and image recto), but the double-flapped images reveal a humorous before and after. The image on the right page is split down the middle and when the flaps are lifted, a new image is revealed, twice the size of the original image. The flap images and the revealed images align across the split so that a completed image is seen throughout the lifting sequence. This technique illustrates the moral to the story effectively by showing before and after, yet works in the reverse visually.

Shape book novelty format, presenting *Cinderella* on a theater stage (New York: McLoughlin Brothers, ca. 1891).

*Cinderella* (New York: McLoughlin Brothers, ca. 1891) is a shape book and actually two books within a book. Its shape is that of a stage proscenium and it is bound on both the left and right sides. The cover and pages are split down the center so pages are turned from the middle out, rather than from left-to-right. Once opened, the half pages that are turned back become the seating boxes to the left and right of the stage. These are printed in black-and-white (dimmed house lights), and the images on the unopened pages are in color (the action on the stage). The text acts as script, located across the front of the stage. One problem with this format is that the story can unfold out of sequence if the left page is not turned first. In all other respects, this book format depicts the theater experience of Cinderella effectively. Cinderella presented as a play is in itself an attempt to make the story more lifelike.

Also at the turn of the century, novelty book publishers Ernest Nister, E.P. Dutton, and Raphael Tuck realized another profitable application of the novelty device: novelty valentines. The cover illustrations can be manipulated to move on rivets, pop up like the panorama, die-cut to reveal the inside image or message. Shaped valentines were also popular, the heart being the most-used shape. Generally the imagery and words of the cards are not integrated visually. For the most part, the images are just loving depictions of the birds (and the bees), flowers, cupids, etc.

The peephole die-cut was used in two books of a three-book series published by Harper & Brothers, New York in 1908 and 1912. This series of novelty books is significant because it constitutes an American product that was written, illustrated, and designed by the same person, Peter Newell. "One can find mirrored in the humor of Peter Newell a reflection of his early 20th-century America—the perils of urban living, as well as child and adult fads and interests of the time." Up to this time, most novelty books in the United States were either published in Europe and distributed here or else they were produced in the United States but still reflected European style and subject matter. Newell was working in the period "now regarded as 'the golden age of book and magazine illustration'" and he contributed to "the development of objective realism through...close and penetrating observation of American life."

With the same person responsible for the visual and verbal aspects, there exists a unity of imagery and text. Generally speaking, the images visualize the text literally, but the slapstick situation humor and juxtaposition of the images around the die-cut holes make for a lively visual dialogue. The images appear on the rectos, and the story line can almost be "read" like a flipbook. The text is not essential to understanding the story, but after flipping (thumbing the pages in rapid succession) through the book, the text provides colorful details to the monochromatic visuals.

*The Hole Book* (New York: Harper, 1908), written in four-line verse, is about a gunshot that travels throughout the book. Each page is die-cut where the shot has passed through twenty-two scenes, including a clock, a man's hat, a balloon, and a mousehole. It is finally flattened on the last page, which is not die-cut. *The Rocket Book* (New York: Harper, 1912) uses the same format, but the die-cut is oval instead of round, and the rocket travels vertically upward through twenty floors of an apartment building and through a potted plant, a silver drawer being burglarized, a bathtub, and a typewriter.

Peter Newell controlled the working relationship between writer, illustrator, and book designer. This situation was the exception rather than the norm at the turn of the century, much as it still is today. Initially, children's book publishing was controlled by the printer. With novelty books, the paper engineer was usually employed by the publisher, and control moved away from the printer. This trend paralleled broader developments in book publishing. By the early 1900s, the publisher held most of the control.

Publisher control dominates trade book production today, as most books are first written, then the publisher assigns an illustrator, and finally a third person designs the book. Customarily, publishers keep these creative aspects separate, with no collaboration among the artists involved in the project. This is partly due to the schedule necessary to print and produce books in large quantities. This assembly-line system of trade publishing runs counter to the creativity and unity of idea and form that occur when artists work together.

The spirit of artists laboring together is embodied in the private press and artists' book movements in America and Europe of recent years. The limited edition books produced by contemporary book artists differ greatly from trade publications. As Francis O. Mattson, Curator of Rare Books at the New York Public Library, explains it, "Among the most vital and appealing aspects of the contemporary book arts scene are the flourishing state of fine printing; the emergence of certain of the book arts, notably papermaking and bookbinding, as independent forms of artistic creativity; and, simultaneously, the exploration by visual artists of book forms and structures."

Private press books generally adhere to the traditional book arts that "include hand-press printing, papermaking and marbling, and bookbinding. Their scope may be extended to include methods of book illustration and decoration." Mattson notes, "The traditional book forms range from the severely typographical handprinted private press book to the livre d'artiste to the mass-produced offset artist's book. The limited edition press books are today predominantly first editions of modern poetry, with an occasional prose piece or a reprint or new translation of a classic among them. In the fine printing tradition every element of bookmaking is carefully considered: the selection of the paper on which to print, the typeface, the format and typography, and the binding. The aim is a harmoniously designed (and, it goes without saying, readable) book."

As inspiration, Mattson explains, "What soon becomes apparent is that artists are adapting not just the codex format to their artistic intentions, but that they extend their interest to other forms of communication as well: the middle eastern scroll and clay tablet, the medieval girdle book, the Renaissance calligraphic manuscript, the pop-up books of childhood, scrapbooks, photo albums—the range of allusion to the printed and documentary record is almost unlimited." The nostalgic trend in the past fifteen years of reprinting children's novelty books from the 1800s may have influenced book artists and private presses to incorporate novelty devices into their books.

One such press is Emanon Press, founded by Debra Weier and William Bridgers in 1977. Two books produced by the press, *Skystones*, 1981, and *A Merz Sonata*, 1985, display a sensitivity to text, an integration of verbal and visual, and a concern for the overall production of the books.

*Skystones* comprises five poems about the sky and the earth by Pablo Neruda, translated by Ben Belitt, with intaglio images by Debra Weier. The visual contrast of type and image placement is resolved through an inspiration recorded in the preface:

I was inside a cavern of yellow rock.... I called out to see if someone were still hiding in the yellow rock needles. Weirdly enough, I was answered: by my own voice and its hoarse echo building steadily toward a lament at once plangent and penetrating. I called out again, this time more loudly:...The echo answered me again... and then my word was wafted away among the stones with a delirious howling, as though it came from another planet....That soundless evasion was somehow my triumph...that wilderness of great watery rock beaten by the implacable ocean of Chile.

The poems are hidden beneath intaglio images tipped onto recto and verso pages, which fold open to reveal the text in Spanish and English. These foldouts act as the iron door, mentioned in the preface, that opens to a cavern of text that describes what is seen, felt, and heard inside. The layout of the typography under the foldout flaps reinforces the idea of the gutter as the division between two pages. The Spanish is set flush right/rag left to the left of the folded gutter, and the English is set flush left/rag right to the right of the gutter. This format sets up a respectful integration of space dominance by the visuals.

The oxymoron of the title is verbally resolved as follows:

> To harden the earth
> is a stone's occupation—
> till stone became winged
> and flew.

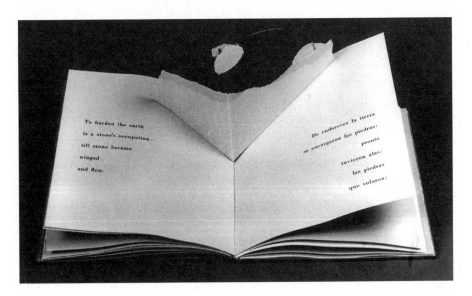

Pop-up page from *Skystones,* a collection of poems by Pablo Neruda, translated by Ben Belitt, with intaglio images by Debra Weier (Emanon Press, 1981). Reproduced by permission of Debra Weier.

The oxymoron is visually resolved by the use of a pop-up in which a "paper stone" (visual oxymoron) is suspended over the text by means of a thin wire. The incongruous nature of the verbal meaning is resolved by this delightful and efficient use of the pop-up device. The placement across the gutter of this pop-up, and another one later in the book, play on the closing structure of the gutter in a codex book.

The physical structure of the gutter affects the visual structure of the book as well. The gutter is used as a place for "echoes" to fade and return. The visual echo is that of a horizon line from the cover which disappears into the gutter of the endsheet, only to emerge throughout the book as a mountain, the flight path of the stone, the surface of the sea, or the "web of green rubber...the lichens climb higher, plaiting and braiding." This visual echo, with paced changes, ranges between simple and complex printed forms as well, such as gold foil stamp, intaglio, and blind deboss.

In contrast to the visual dominance in *Skystones,* Jerome Rothenberg's *A Merz Sonata,* 1985, is dominated by the verbal. It was written for Kurt Schwitters (1887–1948), who "created a non-political offshoot of Dada that he named Merz, coined from the word *kommerz* ('commerce') in one of his collages." (Philip B. Meggs, *A History of Graphic Design,* 1983) The verbal/visual interaction of *A Merz Sonata* suggests Schwitters's philosophy of poetry: "Poetry that played sense against nonsense was an important concern. Schwitters defined poetry as the interaction of elements: letters, syllables, words, sentences." The text consists of rambling thoughts, associations, and remembrances that are set flush left/rag right in Futura (a plain straight-forward typeface). The word, "merz," is always set in a contrasting Old English blackletter typeface. Blocks of color behind the type keep the type anchored on the page while the meanings fly about with the images.

The disjointed, random images seem to float and play around the text and serve as punctuation on the page. The pop-ups slow the reader as he gets caught up in the text which, without punctuation, reads faster and faster. As such, they give direction and pacing, rather than literally or symbolically interpreting the text. The pop-up device is a symbolic reference to Schwitters's 3-D assemblages and relief constructions. A curious stick figure image that runs left-to-right throughout the book is a visual reference to Schwitters's *"Die Scheuche Marchen"* ("The Scarecrow Marches"): "In this modern fairy tale, type and image are wedded literally and figuratively as the B overpowers the X with verbiage." The overpowering B and the X are stick figures made of letterforms. The colorful rubber stamp images of numbers, hands, arrows, paper clips, and the pop-up ticket stub pay homage to Schwitters's collages composed of printed ephemera and found materials.

*Dear Mr. Clifford* (Madison, Wis.: Sailor Boy Press, 1986) contains excerpts from a letter written by Henri Matisse on the occasion of the 1948
Philadelphia Exhibition, in which Matisse talks about use by young artists
of color, "not colour as description, but as a means of personal expression."
*Dear Mr. Clifford* was created by Jeffrey W. Morin who, as the colophon
reads, "wishes to bring this letter to light—admitting its influence and importance." The subject of the letter and the notion of Matisse's paper cutouts
are conveyed by the playful arrangement and movement of color shapes,
mostly triangles, half circles, and paper punch circles. The pop-ups of paper
and wire constructions seem unnecessary and do not relate to Matisse's
words, which speak of being "able to lead colour through the paths of the
*spirit.*" The delicate pop-ups seem to be in the wrong book (perhaps better
suited to a letter from Alexander Calder).

*Alphabeta Concertina* (Guildford, England: Circle Press, 1983) is a book
which makes effective use of the pop-up device. As a three-dimensional alphabet book, the type and the visual are one. Ronald King has designed a
simplified A to Z typeface which exists in the peaks and valleys of one long
accordion fold. The letterforms are created by the fundamental principal
of pop-ups—cutting, folding, and counter-folding a flat surface so that the
two-dimensional becomes three-dimensional. In this work, the ingenuity
of paper engineering creates a pure, visual form.

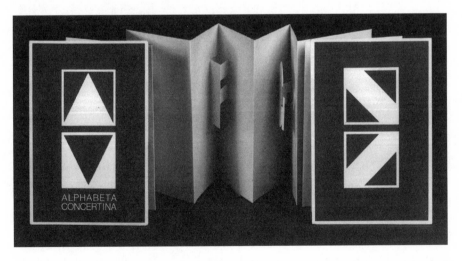

*Alphabeta Concertina,* an accordion-fold work produced by Ronald King (Circle Press, 1983).
Reproduced by permission of Ronald King.

*Isabelle Dervaux's Dress Eclectique* (New York: Purgatory Pie Press, 1986)
was produced as the result of artist Dervaux's collaboration with Esther
Smith, designer, and Dikko Faust, printer. This mix-and-match visual format instructs the viewer to "take a 60's skirt, add your 70's shoes, an 80's

chemise and top it all with 50's chapeau & gloves. Then dance into the 90's in your Dress Eclectique!" Eighteen faces/bodies are presented in horizontally sliced pages bound on both sides. The bodies divide into heads, neck-to-hip, and hip-to-feet. The body parts, dressed in various garments, can be mixed and matched by either layering or opening the sections. The book's nontraditional format forces the viewer to become interactive with the sequence of visuals far beyond just turning the page.

Another nontraditional result of collaboration is *Self-Portrait in a Convex Mirror* (San Francisco: Arion Press, 1984), the work of eight contemporary fine artists, the poet John Ashbery, and Andrew Hoyem of the Arion Press. Parmigianino (the artist who painted his self-portrait in a convex mirror in 1523–24) was the inspiration for the text. The book consists of twenty-seven circular, unbound pages of text and eight circular, unbound leaves of images. The text pages are numbered, and the typography sets the poem as lines of type radiating from the page number in the middle. The viewer is reading each line from the center out while continuing to revolve the page. One becomes self-conscious of handling the page, which confirms Helen Vendler's observation that, "What drew Ashbery to this painting was its combination of extreme beauty and self-conscious expressive distortion." Ashbery was inspired by the painting to write about distortion in life and dreams. The pages of the book are contained in a metal canister with a convex mirror inlaid on the top. Deckle-edged circular pages do not easily allow for binding, so leaving the sheets unbound is an aesthetically practical solution.

The physical separation of text and imagery in *Self-Portrait* is more effectively coordinated in *Rock Rodondo* (New York: Red Angel Press, 1981). Herman Melville's text was written when he visited the Galapagos Islands nearly a century and a half ago. The inside covers become interactive with the text, which is printed on short-sheeted pages bound into the gutter. As the book is read and the pages are turned from right-to-left, the viewer is constantly reminded of the flock of printed birds on the back cover, "flying through the text" to come to rest on the Rock Rodondo of the front inside cover. The rock is raised/molded handmade paper with blind debossed birds, whose positions indicate the hierarchy of "Natural History of strange sea-foul...It is the aviary of Ocean...Birds light here which never touched mast or tree." The last printed page is an identification key to the birds on a foldout block print concealed under the back inside cover. This block print is a two-dimensional representation three times the size of the molded paper Rock Rodondo.

Novelty devices in books are not new, particularly when used to explain or to educate. When explaining means more than just making understandable, and educating means more than developing mental and moral faculties, the novelty takes on the function of interpretation and accent. It is no longer a gimmick, or literal 3-D device contained in the sequence of words and images. In the world of contemporary bookmaking, collaboration among designer, imagemaker, printer, and author is yielding effective visual/verbal relationships in books. Book artists are using a traditional format innovatively, and their work is reinvigorating book design and production.

## NOTE

Many of the works discussed here can be found in the Special Collections Department, University of Delaware Library.

# from *TONGUES OF MEN AND ANGELS*
## William J. Samarin

*Written Glossolalia*

GLOSSOLALIA IS A SPOKEN phenomenon, and this is so not because it resists transcription but because speech better suits its functions than writing does. Much to the surprise of laymen, and glossolalists for that matter, glossolalia can be written down by almost anyone if he is able to mimic an utterance and remember it; tape recordings only make the task easier. Slowing speech down helps one's memory, but glossolalists would ordinarily find this artificial in speech. However, one person who was not able to write down her own speech did succeed in transcribing, in shorthand, the "words" of her glossolalic songs. Special training in phonetics is necessary only when one encounters unfamiliar sounds. Glossolalists themselves have written down samples of their glossas for me. If they have any difficulties, it is primarily because they do not know how to represent the sounds. Thus, the following sample is undoubtedly an inaccurate transcription of actual speech: *play coon del ē cues pel suel proloque doos fundos en day den doos.* People appear inclined to make their task more difficult by writing exotically. Thus, although /sh/ is a common sound in the glossas of native speakers of English, as it is in their native language, they very often represent it by "sch," as in German!

It seems fair to conjecture that the reason why glossolalists should try to make a written sample of glossolalia look exotic is that it is supposed to be different from normal language. For many, in fact, it is sacred. This is why many of my respondents refused to write anything whatsoever, and the woman who wrote down *La Re Gu She a. Munde Ra, Munde Ra, Kulea, Kulea, Kumbisando, Kashia, Lagia, etc. etc.* added: "This seems almost too sacred to repeat."

It is the presumed strangeness of glossolalia, for one thing, that keeps it from being used religiously in written form, because this strangeness, which is conveyed as much by intonation and paralinguistic features (such as "tone of voice") as by consonants and vowels, cannot be fully portrayed in the common use of the Roman alphabet. The other reason is that it is impossible to translate into a series of consonants and vowels the totality of events that gives glossolalia its significance. It is experience, not speech as speech, that is religious.[1] Of course, this experience can be translated into sound, and when sound specifies experience it is meaningful: this is the function of language—normal language. Because glossolalia is meaningless, however, because it is not related to experience in a discrete, systematic way, there is no point in recording it; it wouldn't say anything. This is one possible explanation for the nonexistence of written glossolalia.

It is only when an utterance becomes a part of tradition, like a religious relic, that there is a desire to record glossolalia. There appear to be very few cases of this kind of traditionalized glossolalia. I know only of the following two. There are, of course, lots of examples of writing that has religious significance (cryptic, cabalistic, archaic, unintelligible, strangely written, etc.) in different parts of the world and in different religions. But we are talking here about something quite specific—glossolalia that is more or less accurately recorded and that has religious value.

The first is from the Russian Molokan sect, most of whose members immigrated to the United States early in the twentieth century, locating themselves on the west coast. It is heretical certainly from the point of view of Russian Orthodoxy and perhaps even marginally Christian when compared with traditional Christian beliefs and practices. It is, for example, Zionist (in believing that Molokans are the "chosen people"), and it practices neither baptism nor eucharist in any form. As already noted, the Molokans were tongue speaking long before there was anything like a world-wide Pentecostal movement.[2]

Among the Molokans any person who feels inspired to speak to the congregation must first present himself to the priest and say *Parginal assurginal (yuzgoris)*. If the priest responds with this same formula, the prophet may speak. Now the words are understood by the Molokans to be glossolalic, as is clear from one of the songs in which they appear (here in translation from Russian):

> Let us sing, Brothers and Sisters,
> This song of our King,
> According to the dictate of God's Spirit from above,
> In new fiery tongues:
> (Chorus) God is alive and the Lord be blessed,
>      And we are their people in the Holy Spirit.
>      *Parginal Assurginal Yuzgoris.* Amen.[3]

We can assume that these words are preserved from some long-forgotten glossolalic event.

The Shakers, an "emotional" sect that broke off from the Friends (Quakers), was also tongue speaking, and glossolalia provided the "words" to many of its songs. These are from Edward D. Andrews' *The Gift to be Simple*:

> O san-nisk-a-na nisk-a-na, haw, haw, haw,
>      fan-nick-a-na nisk-a-na, haw, haw, haw.
> O san-nisk-a-na, nisk-a-na yea se-ne-aw, fan-a-na,
>      nisk-a-na, haw, haw, haw.
> O san-nisk-a-na-na, haw, haw, fan-nik-a-na-na, haw, haw,

*O sen-a-go fan-a, nick-a-na-na na nick-a-na-na*
*O sen-a-go fan-a, nick-a-na-na na.*

The following occurs with interpretation:

| | |
|---|---|
| *O sa ri anti va me* | "O Saviour wilt thou hear me |
| *O sa ri anti va me* | O Saviour wilt thou hear me |
| *I co lon se ve re* | I am poor and needy |
| *I con e lo se va ne* | I'll come and bow before thee |
| *I con e lo se va ne* | I'll come and bow before thee |
| *Se ran te lo me.* | Thy cross I'll take upon me." |

For written glossolalia to be exotic it must be both incomprehensible and orthographically unusual (we can call it *glossographia*), but such writing is not difficult to produce if one already knows a writing system. All that a person needs to do is abstract a few of the motions that make up the system and combine them in a more or less haphazard way. Children do this when they pretend to write; adult glossolalists do it rarely.

In Pentecostal literature there is no discussion of glossographia; the subject is not even mentioned as far as I know.[4] But observers of Pentecostalism have noted a couple of cases.

Mary Campbell, whose glossolalia had some influence on the congregation of E. Irving's Presbyterian church in London, is reported by Miller to have transcribed her tongues in an unknown system which "had most likeness to those [characters] one sees on Chinese tea-chests." Another interesting case is that of a certain "Simon" whose writing resembles shorthand. He was raised and confirmed in the German Lutheran church at the beginning of this century but had a Pentecostal experience when he was twenty years old at a meeting conducted by a Norwegian evangelist. Simon's glossographia (seen below), which Pfister calls "idiographie," is said to be related to concepts, not sounds. Since translations are provided by Simon, one also observes that some symbols are used for entirely different concepts, something that we also find when glossolalia is interpreted by the speakers. This inconsistency could pose no problem, however, because Simon seems to have indulged in glossographia only for writing out "sermons" for his own pleasure.

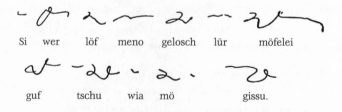

| Si | wer | löf | meno | gelosch | lür | möfelei |
|---|---|---|---|---|---|---|

| guf | tschu | wia | mö | gissu. |
|---|---|---|---|---|

*Glossographia with German transcription.*

The social use of glossographia is reported by J. A. Samarin, an eyewitness to an event that took place in a Molokan church about forty years ago. One of the prophets scribbled a message on a piece of paper and handed it to the priest during the church service. Neither the prophet, who was a glossolalist, nor anyone else could interpret the message that day; in fact, it was ridiculed by one of the elders as being nothing but squiggles. (The eyewitness reports that the writing resembled shorthand.) On the following day, however, another prophet under inspiration took the message which had been placed in the altar-Bible and gave its interpretation. The prophecy is supposed to have come true but the manuscript was long ago lost. Forty years after the incident, even the prophet, whose reputation was not enhanced by it, had forgotten this event.

It must be noted that in the Molokan case there is no evidence whatsoever that this was automatic writing in the technical sense, that is, in a state of dissociation. Nor am I convinced that Simon's was automatic. However, Helen Smith did write in a state of trance as did the young man whose glossographia of a nonreligious sort is illustrated below. He is a member of the group that has become interested in parapsychological and occult phenomena. It illustrates how a written, pseudolanguage has its own ways of appearing exotic. It is also worth noting that it has some "Germanic" features, as does the spoken glossolalia of another member of the group.

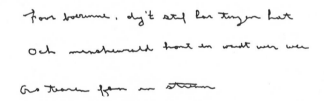

1. Automatic writing in a pseudolanguage while in trance: that is, "glossographia."

2. First two words of the third line of the above sample enlarged.

## NOTES

1. By the use of the word "experience" here I do not intend to espouse an existential position that denies a "non-existential ultimate reality" to religion. Whether or not truth—religious truth—exists apart from what human beings experience is irrelevant to what I am talking about. I am only saying that religion, as recognized by different groups of human beings in different cultures and subcultures, involves the *meaning* that is attributed to the events that man goes through, not just the forms or the events themselves. The problem here is that "experience" has special meanings for Pentecostalists as well as some theologians.

2. It should be noted that it was the Molokans, identified by historians of the Full Gospel Business Men's Fellowship International simply as "Russian Pentecostals," who were responsible for the conversion of the Shakarian family from Armenian Presbyterianism to charismatic religion. The Shakarians were "Pentecostal" when they immigrated to the United States and before they had come in contact with the new American Pentecostalism. Among the Russian Molokans, however, their coreligionists are known simply as Armenian Molokans. There is no schism between them, but neither is there fellowship.

3. *Sionskiy Pesennik* ("Songs of Zion"), 1958, Number 518. There are many other meaningless words in the *Dukh i Zhizn* ("Spirit and Life"), an anthology of sacred writings, but these appear to be the names for God, the Devil, angels, etc.: for example, *Admeil, Tavtan, Anga Ishmaga Shagmas, Alkhaim Fatmi, Alfeil Likhtamis, Tarifta Rafti Khental', Fel'fa Sal'ma Khal'migar' Yul'khin Esvamil' Darmigal' Gindagu.* Some of these look more like borrowings from a non-Slavic language than glossolalia.

4. One would think that the well-known incident of the handwriting on the wall, interpreted by Daniel for Belshazzar, King of the Chaldeans, might have given rise to glossographia, at least among poorly-educated Pentecostals. For the record, in any case, it should be noted that the problem that Daniel was called on to solve was to explain the meaning of *Mene, Mene, Tekel, Parsin,* not to decipher the handwriting.

# BOOKS WITHIN BOOKS:
## SOME NOTES ON THE KABBALAH & THE
### *SEFER YETSIRAH*

David Meltzer

THE KABBALAH, as much as poetry, is the study of and submission to the mysteries of the word. The language used by Kabbalists is so intricately dimensional that it is almost impossible to fully convey the simultaneous layers of meaning revealed in the simplest of words. It is said that one word is the seed of a particular universe, a system of interactions and realities as complex as the birth and death of a sun.

Much of what is of utmost significance in the Kabbalistic tradition never approaches the page. Its deepest secrets can only be set free beyond the page. The oral transmission of Kabbalistic mysteries remains a series of moments between a master and his disciples, moments that transcend the limits of written language.

Most of the texts collectively called the Kabbalah were not written to serve the continuity of a literary tradition; instead, they take the form of notes for the actual teaching, which takes shape only in the context of a sharing-of-breath experience between teacher and student. With few exceptions these texts remain as the aftermath of the actual teaching—they are shadows, ghosts.

The Kabbalist is not unlike the poet or shaman in the risks taken in creation. Whether spoken or written, the emergence of a word becomes a momentous event. The Kabbalist's devotion leads him into a deeper comprehension of each word he confronts. He knows that when words are combined into a sequence their overall impact often transforms the immediate reality. Through creation inspired by the words within the Torah and through endless meditation upon the meaning of each letter, each word, each sentence, chapter, book, even each vowel-point, the Kabbalist hopes to penetrate through the folds and veils to enter other realms, to ascend new rungs of consciousness and to ultimately reach emersion and dispersal into the highest source of his yearning's goal. Creation—for the Kabbalist or poet or shaman—is the ability to receive the word, as well as being responsive to his capacity as word-creator. To embody the book, to be filled with vision, truth, compassion; to live in such a way that no spot within or without is unblessed by word. As a contemporary Kabbalist once wrote to me, echoing the traditional longing, "to be walking, breathing Torah." To be as we are: organisms guided by light to light.

Yet the paradox of the Kabbalah is that of all mystical traditions: the intensive study of the book, the books, the books within books, words within words, meanings within meanings, serves as a process which leads beyond the book, the words, to a point of complete word-less-ness. You ascend to a plateau of profound blankness, the blankness of a piece of paper before words are engraved into it.

• • •

The *Sefer Yetsirah* is literal and secret at the same time. It is dense, compressed, elusively simple. Its concepts continue to intrigue and to escape captivity. Of all the Kabbalistic texts, it has been the most continuously translated into English. In the past five years I have come across five new translations of the book.

According to Gershom Scholem, the *Sefer Yetsirah* was written sometime between the third and sixth centuries in Palestine "by a devout Jew with leanings towards mysticism...[his] aim was speculative and magical rather than ecstatic."

The book consists of six brief chapters and exists in two versions. The first and earlier version is shorter than the second. Yet both together are less than thirty-two pages.

It is the earliest systematic treatment of the Jewish mystical doctrine. It has been called the earliest scientific treatise in the Hebrew Language. It contains the germ of a system of Hebrew phonetics and of a natural philosophy and physiology based on that doctrine.

It is the book which prepared me for the Kabbalah and provided me with an insight into the Kabbalistic process of receiving the mysteries intrinsic in language. Its mystical shorthand remains a clear statement of the inner and outer environments of human possibility. The very literalness of the text acts as a fulcrum for a dual reception/perception of what is within and without.

# from *SEFER YETSIRAH*
## Anonymous

### Chapter I

#### § 1

Thirty-two mysterious ways of wisdom has the Lord, Lord of hosts, ordained through Scribe, Script, and Scroll.

#### § 2

These are the thirty-two mysterious ways of wisdom, twenty-two letters, which are ten double and twelve simple.

#### § 3

The ten double letters are ת, ש, ר, פ, כ, ד, ג, ב, א ten and not nine, ten and not eleven. The twelve simple letters are ח, ז, ה, ק, צ, ע, ס, נ, מ, ל, י, ט twelve and not eleven; twelve and not thirteen. Investigate them, examine them, establish the matter clearly, and restore the Creator to His abode.

#### § 4

Twenty-two letters are engraved by the voice, hewn out in the air, and established by the mouth in five places.

#### § 5

Twenty-two letters He engraved, hewed out, weighed, changed, combined, and formed out of them all existing forms, and all forms that may in the future be called into existence.

#### § 6

How did He combine them, weigh them, and change them around? א with all of them and all of them with א; ב, with all of them and all of them with ב; and so forth, all of them turning around in order; thus all words and all forms are derived from them.

#### § 7

Twenty-two letters are engraved in a circle, with 484 divisions, and the circle turns forward and backward; thus in ענג [delight], the ע is at the beginning; in נגע [plague], the ע is at the end.

## § 8

Out of two stones two houses are built, out of three stones six houses are built, out of four stones twenty-four houses are built, out of five stones one hundred and twenty houses are built, out of six stones seven hundred and twenty houses are built, out of seven stones five thousand and forty houses are built. Go and count further, what the mouth is unable to pronounce, and the ear is unable to hear.

## Chapter II

### § 9

He combines and changes about and makes all forms and all words with the One Name; thus all forms and all words are derived from the One Name.

### § 10

Three vowels אמש constitute a great secret, marvellous and hidden. From them go forth air, water, and fire. Fire above and water below, and air holds the balance between them; thus מ is mute, ש is hissing, and א holds the balance between them.

### § 11

Three vowels אמ״ת constitute a great secret, mysterious and hidden. From them go forth air, water, and earth. Four vowels, אמשת, which are five vowels, that gave birth to twenty-seven consonants.

### § 12

The five vowels stand each one by itself, but the twenty-seven consonants are all dependent on the vowels. He made them in the form of a state, and arranged them like an army in battle array. The only One Master, God, the faithful King, rules over them from His holy abode forever and ever.

### § 13

The five vowels and twenty-seven consonants, these are the twenty-two letters which the Lord, Lord of hosts, established out of the ten digits and zero.

## Chapter III

### § 14

The ten digits and zero—close thy mouth from speaking and thy heart from thinking, and if thy heart should leap, bring it back to its place; for concerning this has the covenant been made.

## § 15

The ten digits and zero, their end is joined with their beginning, and their beginning with their end, as the flame is attached to the coal. Understand wisdom and be wise in understanding, that there is but one Master, and there is no second to Him, and before One, what countest thou?

## § 16

The ten digits and zero, their appearance is like lightning; to their aim there is no limit. They go and come at His word, and at His command they pursue like the whirlwind, and kneel before His throne.

## § 17

These are the ten digits and zero, with which the Eternally Living God, blessed be His name, ordained His world.

## § 18

One—He graved and hewed out of it voice, air and speech, and this is the Holy Spirit.

## § 19

Two—He graved and hewed out of them void and chaos. Void is a green line that surrounds the whole universe, and chaos refers to viscous stones, sunk in the abyss, whence water comes forth.

## § 20

Three—He graved and hewed out of them mud and clay. He arranged them like a garden bed. He set them up like a wall. He covered them like a pavement, and poured upon them snow, and the earth was formed.

## § 21

Four—He graved and hewed out of them the throne of glory, the ophanim, the seraphim, the holy animals, and the ministering angels.

## § 22

He formed existence out of void, something out of nothing, and he hewed large stones out of intangible air, thus twenty-two in number, one in spirit.

## § 23

Also God set the one over against the other, good against evil, and evil against good; good out of good, and evil out of evil; good testing evil, and evil testing good; good is stored away for the good, and evil is stored away for the evil.

## § 24

When Abraham our father arose, he looked and saw and investigated and observed and engraved and hewed and combined and formed and calculated, and his creation was successful. Then the Master of all revealed Himself to him, and made a covenant with him and with his seed forever. He made a covenant with him on the ten fingers of his hands, and this is the covenant of the tongue; and on the ten toes of his feet, and this is the covenant of circumcision; and tied the twenty-two letters of the Torah to his tongue and revealed to him their secret. He drew them through water; stormed through air, He kindled them in fire, and melted them into ten double and twelve simple letters.

—*Translated from the Hebrew by Phineas Mordell.*

# CELESTIAL ALPHABET EVENT
## Jacques Gaffarel

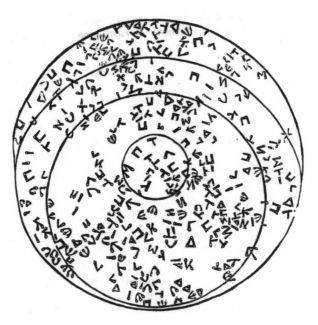

*Commentary*

(1) AN EXTREME EXAMPLE OF a language process event based on natural phenomena, this derives from Hebrew alphabetic practice projected on the night sky. The key is calligraphic: a form of the alphabet ("magic letters") going back to Hellenistic period, in which the lines of the letters culminate in rounded points (thus, א, alef, = ✕), permitting a later application to the night sky, where patterns of stars (points joined by "lines") can then be read as letters, groups of letters read as words, etc. In the process the sky becomes a massive concrete poem, a "book of the sky" or a "book of nature," whose words or "messages" are constantly transforming. (J. R.)

(2) "To the realm of practical Kabbalah...belong the many traditions concerning the existence of a special archangelic alphabet, the earliest of which was 'the alphabet of Metatron.' Other such alphabets of *kolmosin* ('[angelic] pens') were attributed to Michael, Gabriel, Raphael, etc. Several of these alphabets that have come down to us resemble cuneiform writing, while some clearly derive from early Hebrew or Samaritan script. In kabbalistic literature they are known as 'eye writing' (*ketav einayim*) because their letters are always composed of lines and small circles that resemble eyes." (Gershom Scholem, *Kabbalah*, page 186.)

## from *CONVERSATIONS WITH OGOTEMMÊLI*
### Marcel Griaule

*[This dialogue, circa 1947, was between Griaule qua anthropologist &
the Dogon sage Ogotemmêli: on the materiality/spirituality of the
word and the creation of the world through language.]*

THE NUMMO, LOOKING DOWN from heaven, saw their mother, the
earth, naked and speechless, as a consequence no doubt of the original incident in her relations with the God Amma. It was necessary to put an end to
this state of disorder. The Nummo accordingly came down to earth, bringing with them fibres pulled from plants already created in the heavenly regions. They took ten bunches of these fibres, corresponding to the number
of their ten fingers, and made two strands of them, one for the front and one
for behind. To this day masked men still wear these appendages hanging
down to their feet in thick tendrils.

But the purpose of this garment was not merely modesty. It manifested
on earth the first act in the ordering of the universe and the revelation of
the helicoid sign in the form of an undulating broken line.

For the fibres fell in coils, symbol of tornadoes, of the windings of tor-
rents, of eddies and whirlwinds, of the undulating movement of reptiles.
They recall also the eight-fold spirals of the sun, which sucks up moisture.
They were themselves a channel of moisture, impregnated as they were
with the freshness of the celestial plants. They were full of the essence of
Nummo: they *were* Nummo in motion, as shown in the undulating line,
which can be prolonged to infinity.

When Nummo speaks, what comes from his mouth is a warm vapour
which conveys, and itself constitutes, speech. This vapour, like all water,
has sound, dies away in a helicoid line. The coiled fringes of the skirt were
therefore the chosen vehicle for the words which the Spirit desired to reveal to the earth. He endued his hands with magic power by raising them
to his lips while he plaited the skirt, so that the moisture of his words was
imparted to the damp plaits, and the spiritual revelation was embodied in
the technical instruction.

In these fibres full of water and words, placed over his mother's geni-
talia, Nummo is thus always present.

Thus clothed, the earth had a language, the first language of this world
and the most primitive of all time. Its syntax was elementary, its verbs few,
and its vocabulary without elegance. The words were breathed sounds
scarcely differentiated from one another, but nevertheless vehicles. Such
as it was, this ill-defined speech sufficed for the great works of the beginning of all things.

*—Translated from the French by Ralph Butler.*

# ON THE CULT OF BOOKS

## Jorge Luis Borges

IN BOOK VIII OF THE *ODYSSEY*, we read that the gods weave misfortunes so that future generations will have something to sing about; Mallarmé's statement, "The world exists to end up in a book," seems to repeat, some thirty centuries later, the same concept of an aesthetic justification for evils. These two teleologies, however, do not entirely coincide; the former belongs to the era of the spoken word, and the latter to an era of the written word. One speaks of telling the story and the other of books. A book, any book, is for us a sacred object: Cervantes, who probably did not listen to everything that everyone said, read even "the torn scraps of paper in the streets." Fire, in one of Bernard Shaw's comedies, threatens the library at Alexandria; someone exclaims that the memory of mankind will burn, and Caesar replies: "A shameful memory. Let it burn." The historical Caesar, in my opinion, might have approved or condemned the command the author attributes to him, but he would not have considered it, as we do, a sacrilegious joke. The reason is clear: for the ancients the written word was nothing more than a substitute for the spoken word.

It is well known that Pythagoras did not write; Theodor Gomperz maintains that it was because he had more faith in the virtues of spoken instruction. More forceful than Pythagoras' mere abstention is Plato's unequivocal testimony. In the *Timaeus* he stated: "It is an arduous task to discover the maker and father of this universe, and, having discovered him, it is impossible to tell it to all men"; and in the *Phaedrus* he recounted an Egyptian fable against writing (the practice of which causes people to neglect the exercise of memory and to depend on symbols) and said that books are like the painted figures "that seem to be alive, but do not answer a word to the questions they are asked." To alleviate or eliminate that difficulty, he created the philosophical dialogue. A teacher selects a pupil but a book does not select its readers, who may be wicked or stupid; this Platonic mistrust persists in the words of Clement of Alexandria, a man of pagan culture: "The most prudent course is not to write but to learn and teach by word of mouth, because what is written remains" (*Stromateis*), and in the same treatise: "To write all things in a book is to put a sword in the hands of a child," which derives from the Gospels: "Give not that which is holy unto the dogs, neither cast ye your pearls before swine, lest they trample them under their feet, and turn again and rend you." That sentence is from Jesus, the greatest of the oral teachers, who only once wrote a few words on the ground, and no man read what He had written (John 8:6).

Clement of Alexandria wrote about his distrust of writing at the end of the second century; the end of the fourth century saw the beginning of the mental process that would culminate, after many generations, in the predominance of the written word over the spoken one, of the pen over the voice. A remarkable stroke of fortune determined that a writer would establish the exact instant (and I am not exaggerating) when this vast process began. St. Augustine tells it in Book 6 of the *Confessions*:

When he [Ambrose] was reading, his eyes ran over the page and his heart perceived the sense, but his voice and tongue were silent. He did not restrict access to anyone coming in, nor was it customary even for a visitor to be announced. Very often when we were there, we saw him silently reading and never otherwise. After sitting for a long time in silence (for who would dare to burden him in such intent concentration?) we used to go away. We supposed that in the hubbub of other people's troubles, he would not want to be invited to consider another problem. We wondered if he read silently perhaps to protect himself in case he had a hearer interested and intent on the matter, to whom he might have to expound the text being read if it contained difficulties, or who might wish to debate some difficult questions. If his time were used up in that way, he would get through fewer books than he wished. Besides, the need to preserve his voice, which used easily to become hoarse, could have been a very fair reason for silent reading. Whatever motive he had for his habit, this man had a good reason for what he did.

St. Augustine was a disciple of St. Ambrose, Bishop of Milan, around the year 384; thirteen years later, in Numidia, he wrote his *Confessions* and was still troubled by that extraordinary sight: a man in a room, with a book, reading without saying the words.[1]

That man passed directly from the written symbol to intuition, omitting sound; the strange art he initiated, the art of silent reading would lead to marvelous consequences. It would lead, many years later, to the concept of the book as an end in itself, not as a means to an end. (This mystical concept, transferred to profane literature, would produce the unique destinies of Flaubert and Mallarmé, of Henry James and James Joyce.) Superimposed on the notion of a God who speaks with men in order to command them to do something or to forbid them to do something was that of the Absolute Book, of a Sacred Scripture. For Muslims, the Koran (also called "The Book," *al-Kitab*) is not merely a work of God, like men's souls or the universe; it is one of the attributes of God, like His eternity or His rage. In chapter XIII we read that the original text, the Mother of the Book, is deposited in Heaven. Muhammad al-Ghazali, the Algazel of the scholastics, declared: "The Koran is copied in a book, is pronounced with the tongue, is remembered in the heart and, even so, continues to persist in the center of God and is not altered by its passage through written pages and human understanding." George Sale observes that this uncreated Koran is nothing but its idea or Platonic archetype; it is likely that al-Ghazali used the idea of archetypes, communicated to Islam by the *Encyclopedia of the Brethren of Purity* and by Avicenna, to justify the notion of the Mother of the Book.

Even more extravagant than the Muslims were the Jews. The first chapter of the Jewish Bible contains the famous sentence: "And God said, 'Let there be light,' and there was light"; the Kabbalists argued that the virtue of that command from the Lord came from the letters of the words. The *Sepher Yetzirah* (Book of the Formation), written in Syria or Palestine around the sixth century, reveals that Jehovah of the Armies, God of Israel and God Omnipotent, created the universe by means of the cardinal numbers from one to ten and the twenty-two letters of the alphabet. That numbers may be instruments or elements of the Creation is the dogma of Pythagoras and Iamblichus; that letters also are is a clear indication of the new cult of writing. The second paragraph of the second chapter reads: "Twenty-two fundamental letters: God drew them, engraved them combined them, weighed them, permutated them, and with them produced everything that is and everything that will be." Then the book reveals which letter has power over air, and which over water, and which over fire, and which over wisdom, and which over peace, and which over grace, and which over sleep, and which over anger, and how (for example) the letter *kaf,* which has power over life, served to form the sun in the world, the day Wednesday in the week, and the left ear on the body.

The Christians went even further. The thought that the divinity had written a book moved them to imagine that he had written two, and that the other one was the universe. At the beginning of the seventeenth century, Francis Bacon declared in his *Advancement of Learning* that God offered us two books so that we would not fall into error: the first, the volume of the Scriptures, reveals His will; the second, the volume of the creatures, reveals His power and is the key to the former. Bacon intended much more than the making of a metaphor; he believed that the world was reducible to essential forms (temperatures, densities, weights, colors), which formed, in a limited number, an *abecedarium naturae* or series of letters with which the universal text is written.[2] Sir Thomas Browne, around 1642, confirmed that "Thus there are two Books from whence I collect my Divinity; besides that written one of God, another of His servant Nature, that universal and publick Manuscript, that lies expans'd unto the Eyes of all: those that never saw Him in the one, have discover'd Him in the other." In the same paragraph we read: "In brief, all things are artificial; for Nature is the Art of God." Two hundred years passed, and Scot Carlyle, in various places in his books, particularly in the essay on Cagliostro, went beyond Bacon's hypothesis; he said that universal history was a Sacred Scripture that we decipher and write uncertainly, and in which we too are written. Later, Léon Bloy would write:

There is no human being on earth who is capable of declaring who he is. No one knows what he has come to this world to do, to what his acts, feelings, ideas correspond, or what his real *name* is, his imperishable Name in the registry of Light.... History is an immense liturgical text, where the i's and the periods are not worth less than the versicles or whole chapters, but the importance of both is undeterminable and is profoundly hidden. (*L'Ame de Napoleon,* 1912)

The world, according to Mallarmé, exists for a book; according to Bloy, we are the versicles or words or letters of a magic book, and that incessant book is the only thing in the world: more exactly, it is the world.

*—Translated from the Spanish by Eliot Weinberger.*

## NOTES

1. The commentators have noted that it was customary at that time to read out loud in order to grasp the meaning better, for there were no punctuation marks, nor even a division of words, and to read in common because there was a scarcity of manuscripts. The dialogue of Lucian of Samosata, *Against an Ignorant Buyer of Books,* includes an account of that custom in the second century.

2. Galileo's works abound with the concept of the universe as a book. The second section of Favaro's anthology (*Galileo Galilei: Pensieri, motti e sentenze,* Florence, 1949) is entitled *"Il libro della Natura."* I quote the following paragraph: "Philosophy is written in that very large book that is continually opened before our eyes (I mean the universe), but which is not understood unless first one studies the language and knows the characters in which it is written. The language of that book is mathematical and the characters are triangles, circles, and other geometric figures."

# *from* "SIGNS AND THEIR TRANSMISSION: THE QUESTION OF THE BOOK IN THE NEW WORLD"

## Walter D. Mignolo

ALEJO VENEGAS WAS a well-known humanist and man of letters in the Spain of Carlos I. He was the teacher of Cervantes de Salazar, who went to Mexico toward 1550 and became the first professor of rhetoric at the Universidad Real. In 1540, in Toledo, Alejo Venegas published the first part of an ambitious project titled *Primera parte de las diferencias de libros que hay en el universo*. He provided the following definition of the book:

[A] book is an ark of deposit in which, by means of essential information or things or figures, those things which belong to the information and clarity of understanding (*entendimiento*) are deposited.

Following the rules of logical discourse at the time, Venegas proceeded to analyze each component of the definition. The book is an "ark," he said, because it is derived from the verb *"arredrar"* (to frighten), and, according to Venegas's interpretation, the book frightens ignorance. The book is a "depository" because, in the same way that the ark was invented to contain things, books keep the treasures of knowledge. Furthermore, things are deposited "by means of essential information" because the Divine Book contains the information and knowledge that God has of Himself and through which He knows everything past, present, future, and possible. Because of His divine essence, God produces and engenders the eternal Verb by means of which He creates everything. Venegas's definition also includes "things" because "things" are signs which bring information about something else. Finally, he says "by means of figures" because of the diversity of "written letters." Thus, "figures" basically means "written letters."

After defining the book, Venegas introduced the distinction between the "Archetype Book" and the "Metagraph Book." He called the first *"exemplar"* or *"dechado"* and the second *"trasunto"* or *"traslado."* The first is the uncreated book read only by the angels; the second is the book read by worldly human beings. The idea of the book as presented by Venegas is that it is an expression of the Divine Word and also the container of All Knowledge. God as the supreme writer has expressed the truth in the Book of Nature and in the Holy Book (Archetype), which has been inscribed in alphabetic characters. The human book [Fig. 1] has two functions: to know the creator of the Universe by reading His Book and, at the same time, to censure every human expression in which the Devil manifests itself by dictating the false books.

The idea that the Holy Book was the expression of the Divine Word and the human book a container of knowledge and the inscription of the human voice in alphabetic writing was taken for granted during the sixteenth century and still has validity in communities of believers. In the sixteenth century, what missionaries and men of letters perceived in Amerindian sign carriers was molded by an image of the book to which Venegas's definition largely contributed. One can also surmise that the concrete examples that Venegas, as well as any educated person in sixteenth-century Castile, had in mind were medieval codices and recently printed books.

Figure 1. Writing and an actual sign carrier: a medieval codex. Berlin, Deutsche Staatsbibliothek.

This hypothetical person had probably forgotten the story about what a "book" might have been before papyrus was replaced by vellum and the roll by the codex, and perhaps also that writing did not imply the need of a "book" (Figs. 2-3). He might not necessarily have been aware that in the transformation and subsequent use of the codex form, Christianity and the reproduction of the Bible played a crucial role.

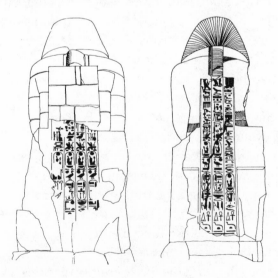

Figure 2. Writing without books: graphic inscriptions on stone (the Colossus of Memnon; Royal Mortuary Temple of Amenhotep III).

Figure 3. Writing without books: inscription of an ancient Maya battle scene on a polychrome vase (from Michael Coe, *The Maya Scribe and His World*).

Thus, when the missionary, the educated soldier, or the man of letters was exposed to the artifact the Mexicas called *amoxtli* and which the Maya called *vuh,* the Europeans described it as an object folded like an accordion, and it was translated as "book" [Figs. 4-5]. In China and Japan, during the

Figure 4. Writing and an actual sign carrier: a Mexica *amoxtli* (*Codice Borbonico,* author's collection).

Figure 5. Writing and the transformation of *amoxtli* into book: the *Codice Tudela,* a hybrid of pictograms and alphabetic writing, bound in book form (author's collection).

fifteenth century, narratives painted on folding screens and hanging scrolls were still very common, and the bound "book" familiar to European men of letters, like Venegas, one among other alternatives. But since the Spanish were not sure what *kind* of "books" the Amerindian "books" were, they feared that the words of the Devil were registered in them, without suspecting that the notion of "book" might have been alien to Amerindians and the very idea of the Devil questionable. The Spanish took action consistent with what they believed a book was and what they perceived Amerindians to have. One reaction was to burn them, perhaps in the calm and secure spirit which characterizes the following description by Friar Diego de Landa, one of the first Franciscans in the Yucatan Peninsula:

> These people used certain characters or letters, with which they wrote in their books about their antiquities and their sciences; with these, and with figures, and certain signs in the figures, they understood their matters, made them known, and taught them. We found a great number of books in these letters, and since they contained nothing but superstitions and falsehoods of the devil we burned them all, which they took most grievously, and which gave them great pain.

Misunderstanding was entrenched in the colonization of language. Landa presupposed equal means of communication and social practices in such a way that reading and writing were the same both for the Spanish and the inhabitants of the Yucatan peninsula; he also presupposed the concept of letters among the Maya, which he distinguished from "characters." Finally, because he was accustomed to seeing Medieval illuminated books, he assumed that the Maya *vuh* (translated by the Spanish as "book") were also written and illustrated with pictures. It did not occur to him that such a distinction may not have been relevant to the Maya. Landa, toward 1566, gave a physical description (instead of a definition) of the Maya "book." It would be worthwhile when reading it to keep in mind Venegas's definition:

> They wrote their books on a long sheet doubled in folds, which was then enclosed between two boards finely ornamented; the writing was on one side and the other according to the folds. *The paper they made from the roots of a tree, and gave it a white finish excellent for writing upon.* Some of the principal lords were learned in these sciences, from interests, and for the greater esteem they enjoyed thereby; *yet, they did not make use of them in public.* (italics mine)

Landa might not have had any choice but to talk about "their letters" and "their books," rather than think in terms of "our *vuh*" and ask what concept or concepts the Maya used for designating the basic units of their writing. Nor did he ask whether the distinction between painting and writing made sense for them and, consequently, what was the purpose of describing "their" books as having pictures illustrating their writing if the Maya did not care to make a distinction between writing and painting. Landa could also have asked whether there was, among the Maya, a distinction between "book" and "paper," since *vuh* seems to refer to the surface on which signs were inscribed and to the object created by written signs on a solid surface made out of tree bark (*vuh*). But there is still more: why did Landa believe that Maya writing was to be understood in terms of books, and why did he not think that they could have had other surfaces on which signs were inscribed and on which they practiced writing? I assume that for Landa, in the latter half of the sixteenth century, writing was naturally conceived in terms of papers and books, and books in terms of the medieval manuscript and the printing press, which were also the examples Venegas might have had in mind some twenty-five years before Landa's report.

In the lake of Mexico, the term regularly employed to refer to the surface on which painted narratives were inscribed was *amoxtli*. Fray Toribio de Benavente (Motolinía), who arrived in Mexico in 1524, reported on the Mexica "books." Contrary to Landa, Motolinía's description oscillates between the material inscriptions and the conceptual "genres" he perceived in Mexica's books. In a letter Motolinía wrote to Lord Antonio Pimentel, he reported:

I shall treat of this land of Anáhuac or New Spain…according to the ancient books which the natives had or possessed. These books were written in symbols and pictures. This was their way of writing, supplying their lack of an alphabet by the use of symbols.… These natives had five books, which, as I said, were written in pictures and symbols. The first book deals with years and calculations of time; the second, with the days and with the feasts which the Indians observed during the year; the third, with dreams, illusions, superstitions and omens in which the Indians believed; the fourth, with baptisms and with names that were bestowed upon children; the fifth, with the rites, ceremonies and omens of the Indians relative to marriage. Only one of all these books, namely the first, can be trusted because it recounts the truth.

The quotation above, taken from Borgia Steck's translation, has left out some important words in the original—namely, Motolinía's statement that only the first book can be trusted *because* the other four were invented by the Devils. It is curious to note that a similar observation was made by Landa, although not in section 7 of his *relación,* from which the previous statements by him were quoted, but from section 41, where he talks again about writing and the books in connection with the Maya concept of time. In this section, he precisely translates Maya glyphs into alphabetic writing and reports:

The sciences which they taught were the reckoning of the years, months and days, the festivals and ceremonies, the administration of their sacraments, the omens of the days, their methods of divination and prophecies, events, remedies for sicknesses, antiquities, *and the art of reading and writing by their letters and the characters wherewith they wrote, and by pictures that illustrated the writings.* (italics mine)

Venegas's dual typology, distinguishing between the archetype and the metagraph book, did not take into account a third type which emerged in almost every report about writing and books in the New World: the book of the Devil, which contained not science but superstition, not truth but falsehood. The material differences in writing practices, in the storage and transmission of information, and the construction of knowledge became—in the Spanish conceptualization—a process of analogizing by which the material aspects of reading and writing practices across cultures were erased in the name of God and His fight with the Devil.

The game of the word became, thus, a conceptual game which impinged on understanding across cultures (what is "behind" words such as *amoxtli, vuh,* and book?), on the exercise of power (who is in a position to decide whose knowledge is truth; what container and sign carrier is preferred and should be trusted?), and on the colonization of language. The only kind of artifact that Motolinía trusted he called *xihutonal amatl,* which he translated as "book counting the years." *Amatl* is derived from *amoxtli,* a plant which grew in the lake of Mexico and from whose bark sign carriers were prepared. *Amatlacuilo* was a name for the individual whose social role it was to paint on the *amatl;* this was translated as "scribe." Other expressions related to social roles in writing activities have been derived, such as *uei amatlacuilo,* which Remi Siméon has translated as "secretary or principal writer"; and also *amoxtlacuilo,* which he has translated as "scribe, author." Siméon's translation of the first as "secretary" and of the second as "author" suggests that *amoxtli* might have referred to "books" and *amatl* to "paper." In any case, not only was the material of the artifact different, but also the conceptualization associated by each culture with the signs (letters or painting), with the sign carrier *(amoxtli* and book), and with social roles *(tlacuilo* and scribe) and activities (writing/reading and looking at/telling a story).

These conceptualizations varied according to the respective traditions, cultural and social uses, and the materiality of reading and writing interactions. The Spanish, however, had the last word and took for granted that their reading and writing habits, their human and divine books, and their ways of organizing and transmitting knowledge were for some reason better and exempt from devilish design. The spread of Western literacy, then, not only took the form of reading and writing; it was also a massive operation in which the materiality as well as the ideology that Amerindians built around their own semiotic interactions began to be combined with or replaced by the materiality and ideology of Western reading and writing cultures.

*Writing without Words, without Paper, without Pens*

Writing does not necessarily presuppose the book, although during the sixteenth century, under the influence of the celebration of the letter, the meaning was narrowed down almost exclusively to just that. Its image is so strong in cultures of the book that peoples who do not belong to these cultures are not always aware of what a book means. The complicity between writing and the book was such that alternative sign carriers (like newspapers) were not yet available, and the possibility of writing on clay, animal skin, tree bark, and the like was just beyond the cultural horizon of the time. Venegas's definition of the book, very much like the Spanish humanist Elio Antonio de Nebrija's celebration of the letter, erased previous material means of writing or denied coeval ones that were not alphabetically based.

Keeping with examples from the Yucatan peninsula, the large number of Spanish descriptions and reactions to Mayan writing practices make it seem as if Western books and the equivalent of Western paper were the only sign carriers. Less attention was paid to writings carved in stone and painted on pottery, which had very wide use and significant social functions. The reader of these descriptions was invited to conceive of Maya literacy in terms of European literacy and never invited to imagine what Europeans might lack if the point of reference were Maya script and sign carriers.

A few years after Landa wrote his *relación,* another Franciscan, Antonio de Ciudad Real, observed in his report on the life of Fray Alonso Ponce that the Maya should be praised above all other people of New Spain for three things. He was impressed, first, by the characters and figures (he called them *letras*) with which the Maya wrote their narratives and recorded their past (which he called *historia*). Second was their religion with its sacrificial rites devoted to their gods (which he called *idols*). Third was the Maya calendars inscribed on artifacts made of tree bark. He described these artifacts as consisting of very long strips almost a third of a *vara* (thirty-three inches) wide, which were folded "and came to be more or less like a quarto-bound book." He made some observations revealing the spread of Maya literacy. Only the "priests of the idols" (*ah kins*) and every so often a noble person (said Antonio de Ciudad Real ) understood such "figures and letters." After the conquest, however, "our friars understood them, knew how to read them, and even wrote them."

The analogy with "a quarto-bound book" is indeed quite revealing. The medieval bound manuscript was basically similar in format to the printed book during the Renaissance (Fig. 1). When paper was introduced in Europe toward the end of the thirteenth century, replacing previous sign carriers (such as parchment), it was folded into two or four leaves (in-folio or in-quarto) and then assembled into segments (*fasciculus*) of four to six sheets. Medieval and Renaissance printed books acquired a very distinctive material format in relation to the previous rolls or scrolls. According to standard histories of the book, the first books were in scroll form. The implication is that the original material format (i.e., of the Medieval and Renaissance book) was imperfect when invented and that, in its final form, the book achieved an essential quality that had been *in potentia* since its inception. This evolutionary model of writing and the book was to a great extent an invention of the European Renaissance, and it was precisely the model used by missionaries and men of letters when they described Amerindian writing practices and sign carriers. What is somewhat curious is that if the evolutionary model was used, the analogy was made between the Amerindian *amoxtli* or *vuh* and the "quarto-bound book" instead of the scroll to which new pieces could be added. The famous dictum of Bernal Diaz del Castillo (one of Cortes' soldiers during the conquest of Mexico-Tenochtitlan) that Mexican books were folded like Castilian fabric conveyed the image of the scroll rather than the bound "book."

I would like to elaborate on this point, taking an example from current observations about writing. An evolutionary model seems to prevail according to which "true writing" is alphabetic writing; writing is, in this view, indistinguishable from the "book," which, in turn, is indistinguishable from the material form of the European medieval and Renaissance examples.

Following David Diringer [in his 1962 book, *Writing*] three kinds of writing can be visualized: embryonic, non-alphabetic, and alphabetic. He calls the last two "pure" writing. While it is possible, he says, "to count as 'writing' any semiotic mark…an individual makes and assigns a meaning to," the antiquity of writing is perhaps comparable to the antiquity of speech. But, he states, a "critical and unique breakthrough into new worlds of knowledge was achieved within human consciousness not when simple semiotic marking was devised but when a coded system of visible marks was invented whereby a writer could determine the exact words that the reader would generate from the text." Writing thus conceived is restricted to syllabic and alphabetic writing.

If this distinction is valid from the standpoint of the history of writing, ethnography, or paleography, it is not as satisfactory from a semiotic point of view. I am less concerned with the change of name than with the change of *level,* which directs us away from the lexicon and expressions of a culture linked with the representation of a particular mode of interaction and toward the lexicon and expressions of the discipline in which a concept is bonded to its theoretical definition. One needs, first, a theoretical definition of graphic signs and of graphic semiotic interactions before moving into a historical classification of different stages in the development of writing. Semiotically, a graphic sign is, then, a mark on a solid surface made for the purpose of establishing a semiotic interaction. Consequently, a human interaction is a semiotic one if there is a community and a body of common knowledge according to which: (a) a person can produce a visible sign with the purpose of conveying a message (to somebody else or oneself); (b) a person perceives the visible sign and interprets it as a sign produced for the purpose of conveying a message; and (c) that person attributes a given meaning to the visible sign. Notice that in this theoretical definition of writing the links between speech and writing are not necessary.

In this sense, writing is a common communicative device in a large number of cultures all over the world, although not every member of a community has access to writing. For its part, the "book" is a concept united with "writing" only in the conceptualization of a culture in which "writing" is understood in the restricted sense defined by Diringer. To avoid the ambiguities caused by the use of concepts which preserve, in a disciplinary context, the same meaning they hold in cultural (nondisciplinary) expressions, a theoretical definition is needed. Before giving a definition of "book," I will first attempt a description. In what follows I rely on Diringer's classic study, *The Book Before Printing* (1953). My own recognition of his important contribution will not prevent me from challenging some of his basic presuppositions. The most relevant of Diringer's presuppositions for the issues explored in this chapter is his consistency in using the term "book" in the restricted sense furnished by the expression of his own Western and contemporary culture and projecting it into different times and places. Let me illustrate this statement. Diringer writes:

> *Libri Lintei* ("linen books") are mentioned by Livy not as existing in his own time, but as recorded by Licinius Macer…who stated that linen "books" were kept in the temple of Juno Moneta. They were not "books" in the modern sense, but simply "very ancient annals and libri magistratum ("books of magistrates").

Despite the caution ("they were not books in the modern sense"), Diringer translates *"libri"* as "books." It is known, as Diringer certainly knows, that *libri lintei* designates ancient chronicles of the Romans which were written on linen and preserved in the Temple of Juno Moneta. But it is not known for sure that they were books, since *libri* may have been used to designate the solid surface on which writing was performed (a possible extension from the original meaning: inner bark of a tree, or just "writing on linen"—and *libri magistratum* could also be translated as "writings of the magistrates").

A second example comes from the idea that *papyrus* was the "main writing material for books" in the Greco-Roman world. Although *papyrus* was indeed the primary writing material, it does not follow that it was "for writing books," but rather just for writing and a multitude of other purposes (e.g., recording data for future use, communicating on a synchronic level, communicating with gods). To be inscribed and transmitted, a graphic sign needs, certainly, a medium. But from this point to the "book" is a long road. Diringer states that the Greek word *biblos* means the "pith of the papyrus stalk"; this gave origin to the word *biblion,* which was the common word for "papyrus scroll" or "papyrus roll," whose plural was biblia, "papyrus rolls"; hence *tá biblía,* "the scrolls." In this case, Diringer translates "the scrolls" as the equivalent of "the book." In the Roman lexicon, Diringer relates that the modern word "volume" derives from the Latin *volumen* (a thing rolled up); it is formed from the verb *volvere* (to roll), and is the Latin rendering of the Greek *kylindros* (cylinder). It is in this context that *evolvere, folia volvere* (to unroll) was often used in the sense of "to read" (*folia conjicere*). When, after all this information, Diringer relates that the term *volumen,* like *liber* (to peel, the inner bark of a tree), was in common use for "book," the quotation marks do not solve the problem of the manner in which a community represents its own objects and social interactions. For an educated member of Western culture, the word "book" is associated with a body of knowledge (and representations) far from the meaning of a roll (*volumen*) from the inner bark of a tree (*liber*) or the frame in which a roll was cut (*tómos*), which in all probability were among the meanings associated with these words in the Roman community.

Certainly the entire problem of the book cannot be reduced to the meaning of the words coined to designate the material aspects of writing ("roll," "cut," "unfold," "bark of a tree," etc.), and we cannot view the "book" only as an object (or a class of objects). With the increasing complexity of literacy, the practice of writing on *liber, boc, papyrus,* and *biblos* changed. A change in a given practice and in the object affected by that practice is accompanied, sooner or later, by a change in the conceptualization of the practice and of the object. The meaning of the original words related to the practice of writing and the graphic sign carrier entered a process of transformation. I am mainly interested in two aspects of this transformation: (a) the plural of *biblion—biblia—*came to indicate "Sacred Scriptures" and "The Book" par excellence; (b) from *biblos* (the inner bark of the papyrus) was formed the Greek *bibliothéke* (house of papyrus), which came to mean "wisdom" or "knowledge." In other words, the representation of the semiotic system of interaction achieved by inscribing and transmitting graphic signs on solid surfaces began to change with the increasing complexity of literacy and became strongly associated with religion and knowledge.

This long detour through the house of words leads me to believe that a more accurate translation of *amoxtli* would be *biblos, papyrus, liber,* or *boc,* rather than "book" or "*libro*," as shown through a closer look at some of the Aztec words related to *amoxtli:*

*Amoxcluiloa,* whose roots are *amoxtli* and *icuiloa,* "to paint," "to inscribe something";

*Amoxcalli,* whose roots are *amoxtli* and *calli,* "house," "room";

*Amoxitoa/amoxpoa,* both of which have as their roots *amoxtli; itoa* means "to say" or "to narrate something by heart"; *poa* means "to tell," "to summarize a process," "to count."

The translation of *amoxitoa/amoxpoa,* offered by Siméon as *"lire un livre"* (to read a book), is quite misleading if it is understood either in the sense of "to go over a written page with the eyes" or "to pronounce out loud what is written," for the romance words *"lire"* or *"leer"* (to read) come from the Latin *legere* meaning "to collect" (*lectio,* a gathering, a collecting). The sense of "collecting" is absent from the Nahuatl word designating the "same" activity, and the emphasis is on "telling or narrating what has been inscribed or painted on a solid surface made out of *amoxtli."* The difference is not trivial. It gives us a better understanding of the idea of the sign carriers in societies with alternative literacies.

Now it is possible to attempt a definition of "book" which, contrary to that of "sign," will be culture-specific: (a) a solid surface is a book as an object to the degree to which it is the sign carrier for some kind of graphic semiotic interaction; (b) a book as an object is also a book as a text to the degree to which it belongs to a specific stage in the development of writing ("pure writing," according to Diringer's classification) and the members of a given culture represent the system of graphic semiotic interaction in such a way that it attributes to the sign carrier (the book as an object) high and decisive functions (theological and epistemological) for their own organization.

According to this definition, the book as text implies "pure" writing, although "pure writing" does not necessarily imply the idea of the book. The necessary connections are founded in the presuppositions underlying cultural expression. A rereading of the seminal chapter by [E.R.] Curtius on "The Book as Symbol" (in his *European Literature and the Latin Middle Ages*), will show that he devotes a great deal of time to metaphors about writing; and that he seems to assume that they are plain and simple synonyms of metaphors for the book.

Be that as it may, some example needs to be drawn from Curtius in order to back up our definition of the book as text. In 1948 Curtius called attention to the amount and the significance of the images that different cultures had constructed to represent their ideas about writing and the book. He began his survey with the Greeks, noting that they did not have any "idea of the sacredness of the book, as there is no privileged priestly caste of scribes." What is more, one can even find a disparagement of writing in Plato. There is the familiar last part of Plato's *Phaedrus* in which Socrates attempts to convince Phaedrus that writing is not an aid to memory and learning but, to the contrary, can only "awaken reminiscences" without replacing the true discourse lying in the *psyche* of the wise man, which must be transmitted through oral interactions. It should be emphasized that Socrates is mainly concerned with "writing" in its relationship to knowledge and its transmission, but not with the "book." If one thinks of the rich vocabulary associated with graphic semiotic interactions inherited from the Greeks and also remembers that the idea of the sacred book was alien to them, for they were more concerned with "writing" than with the "book," it should again be concluded that to translate *"biblos"* as "book" implies imposing our meaning of what a book is upon theirs, rather than fully understanding their meaning of *"biblos."* This observation, amounting to the general problem of "fusion of horizon" or "fusion of cultural expressions," is also valid in the case where *amoxtli* is translated as "book."

Contrary to the corrupted nature of writing in which Plato represented graphic semiotic interactions, nothing is found but the utmost praise (and with God as the archetypal writer) in Christianity. In this form of representation, the tongue becomes synonymous with the hand and the Universe with the Book. While Socrates anchors knowledge in the *psyche* and conveys it through the oral transmission of signs, Christianity secures knowledge in the *Book* and conveys it through the graphic transmission of signs. One could surmise that "the idea of the book" may have entered into the system of representation of graphic semiotic interaction at the point when "writing" gained its autonomy from orality and the "book" replaced the "person" as a receptacle and a source of knowledge. It is quite comprehensible that when the word was detached from its oral source (the body), it became attached to the invisible body and to the silent voice of God, which cannot be heard but can be read in the Holy Book. However, the theological view of writing developed by Christianity and the epistemological view of knowledge provided by Socrates/Plato (where God is not only the archetype of the writer but also the archetype of wisdom) joined forces during the Middle Ages and continued into the Renaissance. Nature is the book that God wrote, and to know nature is the best way to know God. Curtius quotes a telling passage from Fray Luis de Granada's *Símbolo de la fé,* in which Granada uses the expression "to think philosophically in this great book of earthly creatures" to mean that because God put us in front of the "marvelous book of the entire universe" we must read the creatures as live letters and thus, through them, come to know the excellence of their Creator.

Christianity is not, of course, the only religion having a holy book or scriptures (take, e.g., the Koran, or the Torah). But it shares with these others the disequilibrium of power between the religions that possess the Book and those that do not. What is at stake here is the role played by "the book as a text" during the process of colonization carried on by literate societies. As a matter of fact, the role of the book in our understanding of the colonial period in the New World may not have been entirely exploited. One could, perhaps, profit by taking an example from Jack Goody as an analogy. To practice the Asante religion, observes Goody [*The Logic of Writing and the Organization of Society* (1986)], you have to be Asante. Due to the lack of a written narrative that traces the border between the internal and the external space, between what is prescribed and permitted and what is proscribed and forbidden, the "idea" attached to the Asante religion varies considerably over time. Religions founded in alphabetic writing and the corresponding idea of the book are, concludes Goody, "generally religions of conversion, not simply religions of birth. You can spread them, like jam. And you can persuade or force people to give up one set of beliefs and practices and take up another set." What is important here is not the "content" of the Book but rather the very existence of the object in which a set of regulations and metaphors were inscribed, giving to it the special status of Truth and Wisdom.

It is now easier to understand Motolinía's metaphorical language when he refers to and descibes Aztec "books." One can also understand the context of meaning underlying the epistemological metaphors he employs to describe these "books." By talking about "the five books" the Aztecs had, he projects the cognitive component of the idea of the book; by deciding which ones are "true" and which "false," he draws from the theological component of the idea of the Book in which truth finds its warranty. If Motolinía cast the Devil as the author of the false books it was not only because the Devil was guilty of all wrongdoing in this world, but also because he had a thousand faces. In this case, the face he showed was related to the sacralization of the Book in Christianity.

The model of writing and the book imbedded in the European mind during the Renaissance, and generally defined by Venegas, erased many of the possibilities for missionaries and men of letters to inquire into different writing systems and sign carriers rather than simply describe them by analogy with their own model. Because the paradigmatic example of writing was alphabetic and referred to the medieval codice and the Renaissance printed book, the Peruvian *quipu* was virtually eliminated from the perspective one might get concerning the materiality of reading and writing cultures—when reading and writing was mainly conceived in terms of inscribing letters on paper and then composing and printing books. There was certainly more than a reading and writing culture both in Renaissance Europe and in the colonial New World. However, the model provided by the alphabet and the book was a paradigmatic example of the material facets of reading and writing.

The *quipu* certainly did not go unnoticed among those who were in Peru observing Amerindian cultures during the first century of the conquest. Acosta, in his *Historia natural y moral de las Indias* (1590), devoted several chapters (Book VI) to descriptions of Amerindian writing systems, comparing them with alphabetic as well as Chinese writing. Acosta referred to the *quipu* when he spoke about memory and recordkeeping in Peru. He began his description by noticing the differences between the *quipu* and other writing systems:

> The Indians of Peru, before the Spaniards came, had no sort of writing, not letters nor characters nor ciphers nor figures, like those of China or Mexico; but in spite of this they conserved no less the memory of ancient lore, nor did they have any less account of all their affairs of peace, war and government.

The *quipu* was considered by Acosta a valid sign for recordkeeping but not equivalent to writing since it did not consist of letters, characters, or figures. Acosta's definition of writing, then, presupposed that a graphic sign (letter, character, or image) inscribed on a solid surface (paper, parchment, or bark of a tree) was needed in order to have writing. A bunch of knotted strings of different colors would not qualify as such for an insightful observer as analytically minded as Acosta. However, when Acosta had to describe what a *quipu* was and how it was used, he could not avoid using the notion of "writing"; even more, he made a perfect analogy between writing with letters and writing with strings, colors, and knots. Acosta defined the *quipu* by saying: "*Quipus* are a kind of recordkeeping or registers made out of a set of branches in which a diversity of knots and a diversity of colors mean different things."

What attracted Acosta's attention, however, was not the material appearance of the *quipu*, but what the Inca did with it. Acosta thought that whatever could be done with books in matters of recording the past, of keeping track of the law, of ritual, and of business matters could be also done with the *quipus* (*"los libros pueden decir de historias, y leyes y ceremonias, y cuentas de negocios, todo eso suplen los quipos tan puntualmente, que admira"*). Thus Acosta's hesitation between the fact that *quipus* are *not* considered writing or books and the fact that they perform like writing and books. More striking in this respect is the analogy Acosta established with alphabetic writing:

> And in every bundle of these, so many greater and lesser knots, and tied strings; some red, others green, others blue, others white, *in short, as many differences as we have* with our twenty-four letters, arranging them in different ways to draw forth an infinity of words: so did they, with their knots and colors, draw forth innumerable meanings of things. (emphasis mine)

It seems evident, after reading Acosta as well as other writers who described the *quipu*, that not only the material image of a roll or scroll has been forgotten and replaced by the "quarto-bound book," but the meaning of *textum* has also faded out of the vocabulary of the time. *Texo* in Latin meant "to make" and more specifically "to weave." By transference, it was also used in the sense of "join or fit together," to interlace or to intertwine. Hence, *textum* evoked the idea of something woven or made into a web. It was also transferred by the Roman rhetorician to alphabetic, written compositions to denote the texture of a composition (*"dicendi textum tenue"*). What Acosta missed, because he assumed that writing presupposed graphic signs inscribed on flat surfaces, was the tactile aspect of the *quipu*. Modern scholars who have recently studied them in detail have observed that the *quipu* maker produced meaning, recorded memory, and worked with numbers by tracing figures in space. In the process of organizing or weaving strings and colors, and of knotting them, the *quipucamayoc* had to change the direction of the strings and the position of the colors relative to each other. This process, the author observed, was not simply preparatory to the "real stuff" of making a record. It was an integral part of "*quipu* making" or "writing." The materiality of *quipu* making invites interesting comparison with the brush and the stylus, the instruments of Mexica and European writing practices:

> ...the quipumaker's way of recording—direct construction—required tactile sensitivity to a much greater degree. In fact, the overall aesthetic of the quipu is related to the tactile: the manner of recording and the recording itself are decidedly rhythmic; the first in the activity, the second in the effect. We seldom realize the potential of our sense of touch, and we are usually unaware of its association with rhythm....In fact, tactile sensitivity begins in the rhythmic pulsating environment of the unborn child far in advance of the development of other senses. (Maria Ascher and Robert Ascher, *Code of the Quipu: A Study in Media, Mathematics and Culture* [1981])

The tactile sensitivity perceived today in the *quipu* maker would have been difficult to perceive by Renaissance men of letters who were thinking in terms of letter writing and books as the paradigmatic model of producing meaning and keeping records. Acosta, as we have seen, certainly did not miss the similarities between *"guisar"* (to organize or weave letters, strings, little stones, or beans) and constructing the *quipu* in order to produce meaning and to keep records. But he failed to see the tactile dimension in *quipu* making.

*Quipu* making was, then, an important activity in Inca society, important enough to be associated with a social role—that of the *quipu* maker. Guaman Poma de Ayala, in his *Nueva Crónica y Buen Gobierno*, left a few drawings which illustrate what a *quipu* and a *quipucamayoc* looked like (Fig. 6). For Acosta to consider the *quipucamayoc* as a social role equivalent to a medieval scribe (Fig. 7), a Renaissance secretary, or a man of letters

(Fig. 8) would perhaps have been beyond his horizons. Or perhaps he was also seeing, from a different perspective, the transformation that Guaman Poma de Ayala saw when he depicted an Inca colonial secretary (Fig. 9); this, we can imagine, resulted from the social transformation of the ancient *quipu* maker in colonial society.

Figure 6. Writing and social roles: Andean *quipucamayocs* and the administration of the Inca Empire (Guaman Poma de Ayala, *Nueva Crónica y Buen Gobierno*, toward 1615).

Figure 7.                              Figure 8.                              Figure 9.

Figure 7. A Medieval scribe (Dijon, Municipal Library, ms 493, fol. 29).

Figure 8. Writing and social roles: a Renaissance man of letters (National Gallery of Art, Washington; Rosenwald Collections).

Figure 9. Writing and social roles: a colonial secretary—a possible transformation of a *quipu-camayoc* (Guaman Poma de Ayala, *Nueva Crónica y Buen Gobierno,* toward 1615).

• • •

*A Book is Not Necessarily a Book: The Material Aspects of Signs and their Descriptions*

The Spanish translated as "book" certain kinds of sign carriers. Writing that appeared on stone, for instance, was neither translated as "book" nor seriously considered as a sign carrier. The previous discussion has suggested, I hope, the implications of such a translation, given the fact that the network of meaning that Amerindians associated with the material aspects of their reading and writing cultures was suppressed and supplanted by the network of meaning that Spaniards created around similar kinds of cultural practices. While the translation of *amoxtli* as "book" or *libro* may be correct inasmuch as this rendering offers the best alternative in the English or Spanish lexicon, it is also misleading, since it does not take into account the etymological meaning of these words and the social function related to these translations in the respective languages. As a consequence, the "idea" associated with the object designated by a word is suppressed and replaced by the idea and the body of knowledge associated with that word in the lexicon and the expressions of the culture in which the original is translated. Thus, the translation of *amoxtli* as "book" does not capture the differences in the conceptualization of the activities related to the object (book, *amoxtli*), such as "to write"/ *"tlacuiloliztli"* and "to read"/*"amoxitoa."* A partial description of the knowledge associated with the word "book" and the verbs "to write" and "to read" in fifteenth- and sixteenth-century Spain, and a comparison with their Nahuatl equivalents (*amoxtli, tlacuiloliztli, amoxitoa*) would soon make it evident that the Aztecs could hardly have had books in the same sense that Castilians understood that word. The Aztecs did, nevertheless, have books.

The point I am trying to make here is that while it is possible to generalize by saying that writing (in the sense of scratching on solid surfaces or using any kind of material meant to codify meaning) is an activity common to several cultures (and it is conceivable that every culture with writing systems has expressions to designate these activities), the *conceptualization* (i.e., the "meaning network") associated with the word and with the conceptualization of the activity is *culture specific.* The same statement could be made in relation to the material aspects of sign carriers and their conceptualization in different cultures. "Book" is neither the universal name nor the universal concept associated with solid surfaces on which graphic signs are inscribed, preserved, and transmitted. It is only from the point of view of a culture capable of applying its own regional concept to similar practices and objects in other cultures that the clay tablet of the ancient Middle East and the papyrus in Egypt could be seen as forerunners of Western and Christian books.

If the hypothesis is that "book" designates the object and implies its representation in a network of semiotic interactions, then the question "What is a book?" should be answered in the same way that the question "What is writing?" can be answered: a "book" is not a class of objects whose essential property can be identified, but rather a cultural and regional interpretation of a specific kind of object. Writing, although it refers to an activity rather than to an object, follows the same logic. The Mexica used "red and black ink" to describe an activity similar to what the Spanish referred to as "writing." The development of speech and the extension of hands to scratch solid surfaces (originally "to write" came from the Anglo-Saxon *writan* and meant "to scratch" marks with something sharp; in Icelandic it was *rita*, "to scratch"; in Swedish *rita*, "to draw, to trace"; in Dutch *rijten;* and in German *reissen,* "to tear") have increased the complexity of semiotic behavior among the species *Homo sapiens* and, together with speech, have contributed to the consolidation of features we recognize as "human." Because in the West the concept of writing had been associated with the activities of scratching or the drawing of graphic signs on solid surfaces, Peruvian *quipus* presented a lot of difficulties to be interpreted and accepted also as writing.

If the properties which make an object into a book are neither in the object nor in the class of objects of which the "book" is one element (mainly because there is no such thing as an essential meaning supporting all different ideas of the "book" but, rather, changing conceptions of sign carriers), then we have to seek an answer to the question from among the specific cultural descriptions of similar kinds of objects. The question now becomes "What kind of conception/description does a culture associate with a class of physical objects made of graphic marks on a solid surface or of knotted and colored strings?"—or something equivalent, such as: "For whom is a physical object with a given set of characteristics a 'book'? How much is the idea of the 'book' based on the alphabet and on literacy? What kind of 'books' do we find in societies with nonalphabetic writing systems?"

One possible answer to this set of questions seems obvious: *"amoxtli"* and *"vuh"* were words coined to designate a class of objects within a society with picto/ideographic writing systems, while "book," during the fifteenth century, was a word used to designate a class of objects within a society at a complex stage of alphabetic literacy. This answer, however, does not tell us much about the kind of representation associated, in each culture, with the word in question. To explore this issue, it is necessary to relativize the notion of the "book" that we all bring with us and become observers of our own cultural presuppositions. Let us explore first the question of writing and then the question of the book.

According to current estimates, the biological line of the hominids to which human beings belong is a lineage about fifteen million years old. The human features to which one is accustomed today were consolidated far more recently (about three million years ago). One of the crucial aspects of this consolidation was the emergence of a particular kind of semiotic interaction: speech. All animals can be characterized by their ontogenetic, communicative, and semiotic behaviors. The first behavior accounts for all the actions of the individual; the second, for their tendency to live in "common union" with other individuals of the same species; the third, for their ability to exchange signs. To live in "common union" implies a communicative behavior and, therefore, the transmission and exchange of signs. If speech and writing distinguish the species *Homo sapiens* from other species, reading (from the Anglo-Saxon *raeden,* "to discern") seems to be one aspect of the sphere of semiotic interactions shared by all animal species— although not every animal species uses its hands "to write," all are certainly able "to discern" (e.g., to read) the semiotic behavior of other animals as well as changes in the cycles of nature.

If it is true that with speech a form of semiotic interaction was introduced that had a significant impact on biological configuration (enlargement of brain size) as well as on the organization of communal life (law, family life, planning, etc.), with writing (visible signs) both a restructuring of thought and a reorganization of social life was attained. Writing (in the general sense of the use of hands and the extension of hands through a sharp instrument, brush, pen, fabric, or knotted strings, etc.), together with speech, distinguishes the network of semiotic interactions proper to humans from the more limited ones found in other animal species. Writing, which is of interest here for its ties to the book, seems to have a larger extension than the book. Writing is a practice, the book a regional object resulting from a particular practice and its corresponding conceptualization. The "book" could be conceived as a general object among communities with different writing systems, only if there is agreement to call that a "book" any kind of material or solid surface on which graphic signs are inscribed (i.e., the book as mere object); it is culture-specific if there is agreement that what a culture understands by "book" (e.g., Holy Book) transcends the object and becomes a text: the idea of the object on which graphic signs are inscribed as conceived by the culture producing and using it.

*Concluding Remarks*

I have attempted to avoid the dangers of placing an all-powerful colonizer in front of a submissive native by taking a mountain detour in which the winding road that I have followed has offered the reader a vast scenic view. You may have perceived, in the distance, that colonial semiosis implies constant interactions, where relations of domination cannot be avoided, adaptation by members of cultures in conflict takes place, and opposition (from "inside") and resistance (from "outside") to the official power structure are enacted in various forms. Speaking, writing, and sign carriers, as well as their conceptualization, constitute one set of relations or network in which colonization took place. Thus, the spread of Western literacy linked to the idea of the book was also linked to the appropriation and defense of cultural territories, of a physical space loaded with meaning. The Western book became a symbol of the letter, in such a way that writing was mainly conceived in terms of the sign carriers: paper and the book, and the practices associated with reading and writing more and more came to be conceived in terms of the sign carrier; reading the word became increasingly detached from "reading the world," as the *tlamatinime* would have preferred to say.

Paradoxically, modern technology has returned us to the "beginnings of the book" (*biblos*) in that microfilms, screens, floppy disks, and tapes have become the new kind of surface on which writing is inscribed. The new forms of storage and retrieval of information are in the process of eliminating our bookish habits. Soon, we will have no need to peruse pages to find the necessary pieces of information. We already have access to alphabetical and thematic menus from which to obtain what we need. The metaphor of the Divine Book could be replaced, then, by the metaphor of the Electronic Book, an international data bank in which all knowledge will be contained.

A professor of literature, teaching Borges's "The Library of Babel" will have to explain to his or her students what a "book" and a "library" were.

During the process of colonization, however, the book was conceived by the Spanish as a container in which knowledge from the New World could be deposited, as a carrier by means of which signs could be transmitted to the metropolis, and, finally, as a text in which Truth could be discerned from Falsehood, and the Law imposed over chaos. The book, furthermore, also played a very important role in the reverse process of sign transmission: from the metropolis to the colonial periphery. Printed books facilitated the dissemination and reproduction of knowledge and replaced, in the New World, the practice of the *tlacuilo* [see page 356] and the function of the *amoxtli,* thus contributing to the colonization of languages.

# THE BOOK TO COME

# from *THE HEART OF A HUMUMENT*
## Tom Phillips

# THE ARTIST'S BOOK AS IDEA AND FORM
## Johanna Drucker

THERE IS NO DOUBT that the artist's book has become a developed art-form in the twentieth century. In many ways it could be argued that the artist's book is *the* quintessential twentieth-century artform. Artists' books appear in every major movement in art and literature and have provided a unique means of realizing works within all of the many avant-garde, experimental, and independent groups whose contributions have defined the shape of twentieth-century artistic activity. At the same time, artists' books have developed as a separate field, with a history which is only partially related to that of mainstream art. This development is particularly marked after 1945, when the artist's book has its own practitioners, theorists, critics, innovators and visionaries. Among the many individuals to be mentioned here there are literally dozens whose achievements belong almost entirely to the realm of artists' books and whose work could sustain the in-depth discussion accorded major painters, composers, poets, or other artists who work in more familiar forms.

What is unique about artists' books, however, is that with very few exceptions they really did not exist in their current form before the twentieth century. However, a single definition of the the term "an artist's book" continues to be highly elusive in spite of its general currency and the proliferation of work which goes by this name. The increased popularity of artists' books can probably be attributed to the flexibility and variation of the book form, rather than to any single aesthetic or material factor. Rather than attempt a rigid or definitive characterization of artists' books, I'm going to sketch out a zone of activity which I think of as "artists' books." This zone is made at the intersection of a number of different disciplines, fields, and ideas—rather than at their limits. Instead of trying to account causally for the development of the artist's book in the twentieth century, I hope to make a case for the ways in which it is *the* twentieth-century art form par excellence.

It's easy enough to state that an artist's book is a book created as an original work of art, rather than a reproduction of a preexisting work. And also, that it is a book which integrates the formal means of its realization and production with its thematic or aesthetic issues. However this definition raises more questions than it answers: What is an "original" work of art? Does it have to be a unique work? Can it be an edition? A multiple? Who is the maker? Is it the artist who has the idea? Or only if she or he does all of the work involved in production—printing, painting, binding, photography, or whatever else is involved? Or do each of these practitioners have to be taken into account, especially when there are complicated transformations involved in going from drawings to print, or photographs to inked plates, or when the binding has a structural form to it which has been designed or codified by someone other than the artist? What kinds of production means can be included in this definition—is a Gestetner print as valid as a means of producing art as a litho stone, a silver print, or a linoleum block? What about computer printers and xerox machines? Is a work which is made only of bound set-up sheets or other found paper a book production? Or one made of blank paper? Or appropriated images? Most people would agree to a common-sense definition of what is or is not a book. But with the work of artists this obvious definition soon loses its clarity. Is a book restricted to the codex form? Does it include scrolls? Tablets? Decks of cards? A block of wood with one end painted with a title, like a conventional spine? A walk-in space of oversized panels hinged together? A metaphysical concept, disembodied, but invoked in performance or ritual? While these questions address only a few aspects of an artist's book's definition, they show the immediate difficulty of trying to make a single, simple statement about what constitutes an artist's book.

If all the various elements or activities which contribute to artists' books as a field are described what emerges is a space made by their intersection, one which is a zone of activity, rather than a category into which to place works by evaluating whether they meet or fail to meet certain rigid criteria. There are many of these activities: fine printing, independent publishing, the craft tradition of book arts, conceptual art, painting and other traditional arts, politically motivated art activity and activist production, performance of both traditional and experimental varieties, concrete poetry, experimental music, computer and electronic arts, and last but not least, the tradition of the illustrated book, the *livre d'artiste*. Since this last term causes the most confusion and difficulty it serves as a useful point of departure for beginning to sketch out this zone at the intersection of, but just beyond the limits of, any of these individual fields of activity.

The *livre d'artiste* came into being as a publishing enterprise initiated by such figures as Parisian art dealer Ambroise Vollard, whose first productions appeared in the mid-1890s, and Daniel-Henry Kahnweiler who began publishing slightly more than a decade later. This trend caught on among other editors who saw the opportunity to market deluxe editions which bore the name of a rising or established star in the world of visual arts or poetry (Vollard was associated with Georges Rouault and Kahnweiler with Apollinaire, Picasso, and other Cubists). Deluxe editions predate the existence of the *livre d'artiste* and books with all of the elements of the genre—

large-sized format, elaborate production values such as hand coloring, virtuoso printing, fine binding, use of rare materials, texts, or images which catered to a sophisticated or elite market—had long been an established part of the publishing industry. The *livre d'artiste* took advantage of the expanded market for visual art which had grown in the nineteenth century, along with other luxury markets expanded by industrial growth, the accumulation of capital, and an educated upper middle class with an appetite for fine consumer goods. The market for these books was developed as an extension of the market for painting, drawing, and sculpture. Kahnweiler was fully aware that he was creating a sideline in books which could be sold on the strength of the popularity and fame of artists whose work he dealt.

But if for editors these books were attractive in part as a new commodity, for artists they often offered the possibility to produce work which they wouldn't or couldn't normally produce themselves. This might include working in a printmaking medium, for example, or pursing a theme which didn't find an easy place in their other work. The artists whose work was featured in early *livres d'artistes* are among the foremost in twentieth-century art; their names are the roster known from survey lectures and blockbuster exhibitions: Pierre Bonnard, Henri Matisse, Joan Miró, Max Ernst, and Pablo Picasso. These books are finely made works, but they stop short of being artists' books. They stop just at the threshold of the conceptual space in which artists' books operate. First of all, it is rare to find a *livre d'artiste* which interrogates the conceptual or material form of the book as part of its intention, thematic interests, or production activities. This is perhaps one of the most important distinguishing criteria of the two forms, since artists' books are almost always self-conscious about the structure and meaning of the book as a form. For instance, the standard distinction between image and text, generally on facing pages, is maintained in most *livres d'artistes.* By contrast to the lively innovations which abound in artists' books, the work of even recent, late twentieth-century *livres d'artistes* tend to be embalmed in excessive production values, burdened by the weight of traditional format and materials. The paper wrappers of these books can barely contain their thick paper pages, and the large scale of the typefaces is surrounded by a veritable swath of blank margin. The images and text often face each other like new acquaintances across the gutter, wondering how they came to be bound together for all eternity in the hushed, mute, interior of the ponderous tome.

Most of the works produced by entrepreneurs such as Kahnweiler were initiated as the vision of an editor. The artist and writer were often contracted independently (in many cases classic texts or authors were used as the basis of a new modern visual interpretation—Ovid, Shakespeare, Dante and Aesop were favorite staples of the *livre d'artiste* genre). Artist and writer often didn't meet, or met through the arranged connection of the project, as in some loveless mechanical nuptial of convenience. These editorial habits, however, vary considerably from individual to individual, often with positive results. The contrast between the editorial vision of Collectif Génération and that of Andrew Hoyem at Arion Press, two contemporary producers of *livres d'artistes*—both successful on their own very different terms—makes this point very dramatically. Gervais Jassaud, the editor of Collectif Génération, only produces works by living writers and artists. These are previously unpublished, often hand-done or hand-written editions for which Jassaud provides the framework (the shape, size, general format of the book). The degree of collaboration and interaction is left to the artists involved. In addition, Jassaud has worked to make his collaborations and his overall program an international one to an unprecedented degree—not merely publishing artists from a wide range of locations, but also facilitating an international process of exchange. Hoyem, in contrast, has used the texts of living and classic writers, and his work in many ways is a clearer continuation of the *livre d'artiste* tradition. Though in general it is the artist's and writer's reputations which sell these books, a rare or unpublished literary text can also be a selling point.

Editors' visions tend to be market oriented—theirs is a vision whose aesthetics are meant to guarantee the value of the product, not necessarily realize an original work. Thus the discrete nature of the elements: text, image, production (including printing, binding, typesetting, design, and so forth) are independent operations, guided by the editor, who engineers their compatibility with the necessary, consummate, taste. This third point is the telling one: the format of these works is perhaps their most characteristic feature, with a standard alternation of word and visual artwork, usually within a single spread or opening. This mechanical repetition of the conventional distinction between image and text returns these works to the category of illustrated books, rather than artist's books. This formula is hardly inevitable. It is interesting to note that some of the earliest examples of *livre d'artiste*s were more adventurous in blurring the boundaries of image and text than the later ones. The Ambroise Vollard edition of *Parallèlement* (1900) with images by Pierre Bonnard, shows Bonnard's lithographed images weaving into the printed text, uniting the visual and verbal elements on the page. This approach is a continuation of innnovations which began with Romantic printers and engravers almost a century earlier, most notably Thomas Bewick, who were intent on merging image and text in their works. While many *livres d'artistes* are interesting on their own terms, they are productions rather than creations, products, rather than visions, examples of a form, not interrogations of its conceptual or formal or metaphysical potential.

Any attempt to describe a heterogenous field of activities through particular criteria breaks down in the face of specific books or artists—and this is true with the distinction between artist's books and *livres d'artistes*. The work of Iliazd, a Russian avant-garde artist who became an editor of fine editions after 1945, is often closer to the conceptual form of an artist's book in its originality of vision and investigation of the book form than it is to the deluxe books it resembles through its materials and production means. Similarly, there are many inexpensive books whose format reproduces the juxtaposition of word and image as discrete elements in a pattern characteristic of the *livre d'artiste*. Similar problems occur with other definitions of artists' book activities.

Fine printing, for instance, can't really be subsumed under the *livre d'artiste* nor can it be absorbed into the realm of artists' books—though there are many finely printed volumes in both categories. The term "fine printing" is generally associated with letterpress, handset type, and limited editions, but also can be used to describe carefully produced work in any print medium. There is a category of fine printing which invokes the production of limited edition works for bibliophiles concerned with well-made versions of classic texts printed on archival paper, in durable leather bindings, and so forth. These books are produced with close attention to all aspects of printing art, but are not generally innovative in form or concerned with explorations of books as an artistic concept. Though artists' books tend to be associated with offset or electrostatic (commonly referred to by its trade name: xerox) processes, they have also been produced through the methods of letterpress, hand binding, and relief images (woodcut, linoleum, or engraving). Widening access to a variety of printing technologies has played a part in the proliferation of artists' books, especially in the first world, where the ready availability of production means increases in every decade.

But neither the methods nor the quality of production can be used in themselves as criteria for determining a book's identity as an artist's book. Artists use what they have access to and knowledge of. There have been some wonderfully imaginative uses of letterpress from that of the Russian Futurist Vassily Kamensky's *Tango with Cows* (Moscow, 1914), to pieces produced by an obscure pair of California letterpress printers active in the San Francisco Bay Area in the 1970s: Holbrook Teter and Michael Meyers, whose independent productions had an unsurpassed creative vision, critical edge, and originality while participating in production conventions traditionally associated with fine printing. Letterpress, like offset printing or traditional darkroom techniques, requires a significant investment of time and energy and depends upon regular access in order to be acquired as a skill.

However, it does not require huge amounts of capital to set up or acquire. Artists' books are often (though not always) produced on a shoestring budget by the artists themselves, however, letterpress is now prohibitively expensive in most situations (since it is labor intensive and thus costly when contracted out)—unless one owns and operates the equipment. The tactile, dimensional physicality of letterpress tends to be associated with fine printing, and fine printing with a conservative tradition, but an artist's book can certainly be well printed without losing its identity, just as bad printing is often acceptable and successful in the context of artists' books.

The field of artists' books also has a relation to other forms of printing activity. One of these, more literary and political in its origins, is that of independent publishing. I define independent publishing as any publication effort which is mounted for the sake of bringing an edition into being which cannot find ready sponsorship in the established press or among commercial publishing houses. Largely associated with the literary realms and political activism, independent publishing allocates the power of production to anyone in possession of a press or the means to pay for printing. The term "independent" suggests an independence from commercial motives or constraints. In the twentieth century much of the experimental literature which blossomed as part of modernism, the avant-garde, and other innovative aesthetic traditions, failed to find a receptive place in established publishing houses. Often authors have early work published in these venues and then are picked up by larger houses. The efforts of the British writers, Virginia and Leonard Woolf, at the Hogarth Press (established in 1917), or of John Heartfield and his brother, Weiland Herzfelde in the establishment of the Malik Verlag (also 1917), or of Caresse and Harry Crosby's Black Sun Press (begun in Paris, 1925) are a handful of the many classic, historic examples of independent publishing. Because such enterprises are launched with the ideal of publishing innovative, creative, or experimental work rather than making money, and are generally staffed by the editor/publishers who often also print the work, these independent publishers serve to make work available to the public which might not appear if profit were the sole publishing motive. The vast majority of creative writing, poetry, and prose is published through independent means by the labors and efforts of editors who barely break even monetarily or who subsidize their publishing work through other sources of income. Funding from private or public organizations sometimes provides additional help, but hardly enough to replace the initiative and determination which carry these projects through on a sustained basis. Artist's book publishing—whether by artists or by the publishers dedicated to artists' books, of which there are a significant number—is often in this financial category. This is not to suggest that artists never make money off their books, but to note that the same impetus which gives rise to independent publishing—the desire to make a voice heard, or a vision available—fuels artist's books.

The idea of the independent publisher is closely linked to that of the activist artist. Activist artists often give little thought to financial return or careerist investment (though both publishers and artists sometimes establish a name and a reputation which they can leverage to future successes as a result of these efforts). Much activist work is topical, politically or socially motivated in its thematics, and distributed through inexpensive editions as cheaply and widely as possible. Artists with a social or political motivation for their work have frequently turned to the inexpensive multiple as a means of gaining a wider audience for the work. Books, because they have the capacity to circulate freely, are independent of any specific institutional restraints (one finds them in friends' houses, motel rooms, railroad cars, school desks). They are low maintenance, relatively long-lived, free floating objects with the capacity to convey a great deal of information, and serve as a vehicle to communicate far beyond the limits of an individual life or contacts. The notion of the book as a means of available communication is part of what informs the myth of the book as democratic multiple, in spite of the many paradoxes of production involved in this idea. From the Russian Futurists to the Fluxus artists to the Press at the Woman's Building in Los Angeles, to the Lower East Side Print Shop in New York, the idea of making the book a tool of independent, activist thought has been one of the persistent elements of the mystique of the artist's book. That artists' books can facilitate a change of consciousness is clear, as with any other symbolic form be it poetry, visual arts, or music; whether such work can result in a change of political structure and policy opens the door to another set of debates about the role and function of art in the twentieth century which cannot be adequately addressed here.

It would be hard to find an art movement in the twentieth century which does not have some component of the artist's book attached to it, though in some cases this definition would have to be stretched to include journals, ephemera, or other independent publications. For example, Guillaume Apollinaire and Pierre Albert-Birot produced books in the context of Cubist art while Russian and Italian Futurism had many practitioners committed to books as a major or significant part of their work from Velimir Khlebnikov and Natalia Goncharova to Franceso Depero and Filippo Marinetti. A path could be traced which would include Expressionism, Surrealism in Western and Eastern Europe, Dada in Europe and the United States, as well as post-war movements such as Lettrism, Fluxus, Pop art, Conceptualism, Minimalism, the Women's Art Movement, and Postmodernism to the present mainstream artworld concern with multiculturalism and identity politics. It is clear that books played a part in other movements as well, including the activities of experimental musicians, such as John Cage and Henri Chopin, performance artists such as Carolee Schneeman, Robert Morris, Vito Acconci, artists involved with systemic work, such as Mario Merz, Ed Ruscha, or Sol LeWitt, and so on. This list would be exhaustingly long if it were complete and in spite of that fact, artists' books as a genre have not been surveyed, codified, or critically incorporated into the history of twentieth-century art. These works will appear here but they will be treated as books and as examples of artistic involvement with the book as a form, rather than as attributes or sidelines of the movements with which the artists are associated. The sensibility of Sol Lewitt or Marcel Duchamp or Hanne Darboven is indissoluble from the aesthetic issues which form the mainstream context for their work, but their engagement with the book as a form has been more than incidental. Among mainstream artists, these are people who have looked at the book as a form to interrogate, not merely a vehicle for reproduction.

It is the fact of this engagement as a major feature of art of the twentieth-century which argues for the identity of artists' books as a unique phenomenon of the era. To an unprecedented degree books have served to express aspects of mainstream art which were not able to find expression in the form of wall pieces, performances, or sculpture. Dick Higgins has even suggested that the book as a form of *intermedia* (to use his term), combines all of these modes of art in a characteristically new way. In some cases artists have made use of the documentary potential of the book form, while in others they have engaged with the more subtle and complicated fact of the book's capacity to be a highly malleable, versatile form of expression. Not every book made by an artist is an artist's book, in spite of the old Duchampian adage that art is what an artist says it is. It is also as true in the late part of the twentieth century as it was in the early decades that books are often produced on the strength of an artist's capacity to generate sales, and books are a cheap sideline for many galleries. A mere compendium of images, a portfolio of prints, an incidental collection of images original or appropriated, is not always an artist's book, though the terms on which the distinction may be sustained are often vague. The final criteria for definition resides in the informed viewer, who has to determine the extent to which a book work makes integral use of the specific features of this form. The desire to engage with the elusive character of what constitutes a book is part of the impetus for my current project: to seek critical terms on which to examine a book's book-ness, its identity as a set of aesthetic functions, cultural operations, formal conceptions, and metaphysical spaces.

Just as books have served to extend the possibilities of visual arts, performance, and music, they have also offered a unique conceptual possibility to the poet. Concrete poets have engaged with books as a conceptual space, one which by its form and finitude, its structural specificity and visual restraints, has offered a unique means of realizing particular works. While many concrete poets have worked with sculptural elements, sound, or at the level of the single, flat sheet or broadside, there are a substantial number who have used books as the form for their work. Again, not every concrete poet is a book artist, and not every concrete work is an artist's book, but there are works which demonstrate the ways in which concrete poets have been able to extend the parameters of what a book does as a verbal field in a manner which also extends the possibilities of the way an artist's book can function as a poetic text.

The crafts of book arts have also burgeoned in the latter part of the twentieth century. Workshops and classes in binding, papermaking, book structures, and so forth are a major staple of centers devoted to book arts. Though structure is an important component of a successful book the craft aspect of book production is not sufficient in itself to constitute the substance of an artist's book. Attention to materials, their interactions, and the content bound within the book is an integral feature of a book, but as with other aspects of production, artists' books tend to bend and stretch all the rules and conventions of craft decorum. One can trace the influence of individual practioners among certain communities of artists involved with books—for instance, the popularization of certain structures included in Keith Smith's texts on book production. The contribution of Smith, and others who have taught extensively such as Hedi Kyle, or Walter Hamady, in their various past and present arenas of influence, is a visible feature of artists' books in their current incarnation. But there are also works produced from far outside this tradition which succeed without its influence, as there are many works produced as an expression of craft which fall short of being artists' books. An artist's book has to be more than a solid craft production or it falls back into the same category as the *livre d'artiste* or fine print work. An artist's book should not be formulaic—it might be generic, of a familiar type or established category of artists' books and make its contribution without innovating formally, and it might be wildly innovative and sloppy and badly made and in many ways fall short of perfection or even good realization—but ultimately an artist's book has to have some conviction, some soul, some reason *to be* and *to be a book* in order to succeed. It is particularly difficult to keep the craft tradition of book arts and the expressive tradition of the artist's book apart—nor is there any need to—but they should not be confused with each other.

Given the above discussion, it is not surprising that the history of the artist's book is mapped in a wide variety of ways by different scholars and critics. Even among those writers whose general sense of what constitutes an artist's book makes a clear distinction between this form and that of, say, the *livre d'artiste,* there is a tendency to make what seems like an arbitrary and too definitive point of origin. Most particularly the book *Twenty-six Gasoline Stations,* by Ed Ruscha has become a cliche in critical works trying to establish a history of artists' books. There is some reason for this—since Ruscha's work arguably breaks new ground in embodying and defining an artist's book. But it seems counterproductive to try to make a single point of demarcation for this complex history. It seems more useful and more interesting to recognize that by the time Ruscha's work was produced (the date of the first edition is 1962) there was already both a historical precedent in examples from Russian Futurism through Surrealism to the American avant-garde, from both artistic and literary traditions. To state that the artist's book comes into being through the work of Ruscha, and to credit him with the idea, concept, and form, makes an erroneous foundation for this history on two counts. First, the artist's book has to be understood as a highly mutable form, one which cannot be definitively pinned down by formal characteristics (such as the inexpensive printing and small format of Ruscha's work). The book form is always under investigation by artists, and this investigation includes reaching into the many, various traditions described above, as well as into new realms of material expression and creative form. More importantly, this approach to history is hopelessly beleagured by an old-fashioned notion, one in which there are founding fathers who beget whole traditions through their influence. I prefer to think of the artist's book as a field which emerges with many spontaneous points of origin and originality. This is a field in which there are underground, informal, or personal networks which allow growth to surface in a new environment, or moment, or through a chance encounter with a work or an artist. This is also a field in which there are always inventors and numerous mini-genealogies and clusters, but a field which belies the linear notion of a history with a single point of origin.

That this history has become more complicated since the middle of this century is quite clear. Where the artist's book has to be coaxed from its art or literary context in the early part of the century it becomes so full-blown and prolific a form afterward that only the most general overview or alternately an exhaustively detailed description of activity will suffice to describe that development. I have chosen the former model. Briefly, here is the way I see the post-war history: In the late 1940s and early 1950s there are a number of artists who begin to explore books in a serious way. These include the CoBrA artists in Denmark, Belgium and Holland as well as the French Lettrists, led by Isidore Isou and Maurice Lemaitre, whose major experimental work is produced from 1948 through the 1950s. The Concrete poets in Brazil, particularly Augusto and Haroldo De Campos, and in Germany and France, also begin working actively with books in the 1950s. By the late 1950s, artists working in experimental music, performance, and other non-traditional forms take up book arts within the context of Fluxus soon after its first events in the early 1960s. There were other localized or individual art formations of the same period—the work of the French composer, Henri Chopin, for example, or Bern Porter the American practitioner of found poetry. Dieter Roth, arguably the most significantly imaginative post-war European book artist, began his work with the book in the 1950s. These are scattered points of activity, some of which came into being without connections to each other, while others spun off as part of the large, loosely interrelated post-war avant-garde.

In the 1960s books as an artist's medium took off in the United States and Europe. They fit the sensibility of the 1960s alternative scene, whether produced independently by artists or by galleries as an extension of an exhibition, also giving rise to the hybrid genre of the catalogue as artist's book. The proliferation of works which use the small format and inexpensive production methods bespeaks the transformation of print technology as much as the transformation of conceptual sensibility which promotes this expansion. Offset printing and later electrostatic reproduction were further complemented by the increasingly available modes of photographic and electronic typesetting. The availability of the Multi-lith, a small, affordable offset press, as a standard job shop item, as well as the rapid transformation of the printing industry from high-speed letterpress to offset (many newspapers and magazines, such as the *New York Times* and *Time* magazine, continued using relief printing until the 1970s, only replacing this with offset equipment as electronic typesetting became viable), were all developments which provided the means for artists to produce inexpensive multiples. The development of artists' books was not determined by technological advances but these changes did permit easier access to production than had been the case earlier in the century. In the 1970s major centers for the production of artists' books were established, most notably Visual Studies Workshop (in Rochester, New York), Nexus Press (in Atlanta, Georgia), the New York Center for the Book Arts, Pacific Center for the Book Arts (in the San Francisco Bay Area), Printed Matter (in New York City), the Graphic Arts Press in the Woman's Building (in Los Angeles) and The Writers Center (in Bethesda, Maryland). Other institutional sites developed as well within art school and university programs in the arts, museum and library collections, and private collections. By the 1970s, then, the artist's book had come of age.

By the late 1970s, however, another area of book related activity began to develop a highly visible profile: book-like objects or book sculpture. Their proliferation was apparent in the U.S. in both New York and California, and in Europe as well. This development has fewer precedents in the history of twentieth-century arts than does the artist's book. One can point to several works by Duchamp (as always)—such as his altered book, *Do Touch*, with the female breast cast on its cover, or even his large *Green Box* as a conceptual book, and the boxes of Joseph Cornell have a formal and conceptual relation to the sculptural "book." In the 1950s, Dieter Roth shredded paper, boiled it, and filled animal intestines to make "literary sausages." Large scale book works which are as much installation and performance as object were a part of 1960s Fluxus and other investigations. But the recent increase in these productions marks an intensifying exchange between artists who make books and the world of mainstream visual art. In the post-war period the arts gradually turn away from traditional media forms and categories so that the synthetic possibilities seen in the domain of artists' books, and this hybridization of book as object, seem completely consistent with its trends.

In the 1980s, following this wave of sculptural work, one begins to see installation pieces which are ambitious in scale and physical complexity, closet size to room size, with video, computers, and any moment now a virtual reality apparatus. Many of these are made by artists who had previously been involved with artists' books, or who use books as an integral aspect of these installations. Here I am thinking of Buzz Spector's frozen edition of Sigmund Freud's work, Janet Zweig's computer driven kinetic sculptures, Karen Wirth and Robert Lawrence's *How to Make an Antique*, Marshall Reese and Nora Ligorano's *Bible Belt,* among others. Much of this work poses important questions for the identity of a book and its cultural, social, poetic, or aesthetic functions, but it could not be accommodated here without stretching the parameters of my discussion into an awkward shape. Some of these are compelling and original works, some are one-liners produced at the expense of books as cultural artifacts, some are fascinating, fetishistic, or conceptual pieces—but for the purposes of this study, I am keeping them just beyond the zone of artist's books. I am concentrating here on understanding what a book is when it functions as a book, when it provides a reading or viewing experience sequenced into a finite space of text and/or images. To extend beyond this would dilute the focus of this book.

In addition, I am convinced that many of these works belong more to the world of sculpture or installation art than to the world of books. They may function as icons of book-ness or book identity, but not provide an experience associated with books themselves. Electronic media, however, pose other and equally complex problems. The nature of the book as an electronic form—whether in hypertext, CD-ROM, or as an infinite and continually mutating archive of collective memory and space—is already functioning as an extension of the artist's book form. The issues raised by this medium seem too imperative to leave aside, and so will find their, albeit limited, place in this discussion.

In closing, a few final remarks. Most attempts to define an artist's book which I have encountered are hopelessly flawed—they are either too vague ("a book made by an artist") or too specific ("it can't be a limited edition"). Artists' books take every possible form, participate in every possible convention of book making, every possible "ism" of mainstream art and literature, every possible mode of production, every shape, every degree of ephemerality or archival durability. There are no specific criteria for defining what an artist's book is, but there are many criteria for defining what it is not, or what it partakes of, or what it distinguishes itself from. In mapping out this initial definition my intention has been to demonstrate the incredible richness of artists' books as a form which draws upon a wide spectrum of artistic activities, and yet duplicates none of them. Artists' books are a unique genre, ultimately a genre which is as much about itself, its own forms and traditions, as any other art form or activity. But it is a genre as little bound by constraints of medium or form as those more familiar rubrics "painting" and "sculpture." It is an area which needs description, investigation, and critical attention before its specificity will emerge. And that is the point of this project: to engage with books which are artists' books in order to allow that specific space of activity, somewhere at the intersection and boundaries and limits of all of the above activities, to acquire its own particular definition.

# INTRODUCTION TO *BOOKS AND GRAPHICS*
## Dieter Roth

PERHAPS SOMEBODY COMES and asks, what all this stuff was made for. Then I cannot say anything but: Me one cannot ask, since I have only so few words to say, like: I do not know!

Yes, but! somebody says at that moment, perhaps. But! somebody says, it does smell mock here, burny somehow, like as if some sugarbomb of the bigger kind or make has fallen explosionwise to the walls and on the floor and ceiling. Look, smashed sugarcane everywhere! The bits and tids are hanging up and down all the walls, along the whole run. Sure, securely, somebody says to that, the same moment: I am sure, he says or she says, or, as we in big G. say, IT says: This must have been an all encompassing sugarbomb of the biggest width or size, with special chocopuss fillings, since otherwise it does not hang up or down like this in any way but Sugarpuss itself—Miss Neverdry or Mister Everwet. It must have made a hell of a pressure on the walls and floors and on it's maker, the sugarbomb maker's mind. Or, if it should have been sugarload of a backfire grenade, then we should say: What a mammouth's pressure under the maker's heart, where the belly is! may I ask! somebody says, then, often,—why! somebody, then, often

VIELLEICHT FRAGT JEMAND, wozu dieser Kram hier gemacht worden sei. Da kann ich nichts sagen als, mich kann man nicht fragen, ich habe nur ganz wenig, nämlich fast nichts zu sagen: Ich weiß es nicht.

—Ja, aber! sagt dann jemand, vielleicht, hier riechts verschmurzelt mit Nachgeruch, ein Prachtgeruch, wie wenn eine Zuckerbombe von der größeren Sorte und der billigen Art explodiert sei. Die Fetzen, das zerdrückte Zuckerrohr, hängt noch die Wände runter und entlang. —Ja eben, sagt da jemand, das muß eine Zuckerbombe von der großen Kaliber-Art mit extra Schokoladenmatscheinlage hier gewesen sind, denn ansonsten hängt nichts an der Wand, als dieser Zuckermatsch, das flachgedrückte (aber noch lange nicht trockene) Etwas. Das muß ein Höllen Druck gewesen zu sein vorgegeben haben, bei der Herstellung, sonst wäre das in seiner Härte nicht so abgeräuchert worden. Das ist ja ganz furchtbar weich, Menschenskind! —Undschon fragt einer, was soll das Alles? Warum schmandet das da so und hat diese Beulen?

Solche und ähnliche Fragen kommen und gehen. —Ja, wie die Gezeiten des großen Meeres, sagt says or ask,—how come, it shmears like this and cries like hell?

Such questions (and their like) come and go like the tides of the sea! somebody says, coming to honk in. And often it goes so, that I hear it coming and going, too—though I run like water from steep shores after the storm, when I hear Question's horn beblown. Thanks—to whom, I couldn't say—for letting me hear Question from far, before falling to it the stumbling way! Yes, Question lives a goof life among the men of this part of Earth (the name of which you know, so I dont have to write it dow here, I think, O.K.?).

But Answer is fat and mad, too. It lives in the shape of answerers and explorer's admirers, Good Jesuses or Strong Devils, etc etc, among questioneers, by their own stickiness attracted through the suckers, as you know. It fights the fighting armies of the question-and-answer game-avoidants, those posters shaking, whereon you can see written, if you can read: Well, how stupid we are! The weather does not shine so bright in these parts of written staments' territory, so let me pass—and you are invited, to come there, too—to seemingly quieter parts, of civilized stay. But, shit! I cannot find!—What can you not find?—I cannot find it, Cannonball! Your sugarshot did not blast us a break at all! But now I leave this part of youknowwhat, and we hear, by bad mistake spoken, the question: Whatfor good this

da jemand. Und ich komme manchmal dazu oder herzu wenn jemand sowas sagt, mit fragendem Tone. Dann laufe ich aber immer schnell weg und denke: danke schön!—wem immer hier zu dankensei—, daß ichs vom Weiten schon gebrodelt habe hören, jenes fragende, leicht schimpfende Etwas. Das wohnt unter Menschen am frechsten, bei denen wirds frech und groß. Es überrollt die Völker-stämme (und die drumherum gezogenen Dämme) in Form vieler, vieler verschiedener Dinge, z. B. liebe Gotts, Vater, Mutter, Heiland, Meister, Meister Schuster, Bombendreher, Künstler und ihre Trabanten, alle mit den fest verschlossenen Antwortsäcken auf den Buckeln.

Dahinmarschierend im Gegen-wind der Fragerei zieht der Mensch seine mühsame Bahn, schlängelang auf den winkenden Abgrund zu. Tut er winken mit den Plakaten in der Hand, worauf geschrieben stand: Ich antworte nicht! —oder mit den Fahnen, worauf in Aben-drotgoldstich geschrieben stand: Morgen wird es wahrscheinlich noch einmal tagen, da kann man dann noch einmal fragen! Es hilft alles nichts, der Sturm hält an.

Verzieh ich mich aus diesem sicherlich selbstgebrauten Wetter, und suche ich nach ruhigeren Gegenden zivilisierten Aufen-thaltes, so finde ich sie—selbstver-ständlich—nicht. Wo nämlichnicht gefragt wird: Was soll denn das?

talking or/and writing is? Whyfor
has it written been?—and other
whyes and whatfors, more and
more. What a fill! But here, the
answer: You know the answer!

It could, yes, it justly could have
been,that there were, some time
ago at least maybe, youknowwhat?
Peaceful times, as they are called.
Without noise and s-bombs. But!
they are gone, some people say.
This air we breathe is the last sip
of itself. Comes it from the sugar
fabrication places like almost
nothing anymore, the rest of it,
living still somehow in studios of
different kinds and coffeehouses,
oceanliners' pantries, brothels,
cake factories and literature of the
sweet old kind, where the masters
of the written word spilled their
guts; GhospelPropper himself, or
Pussfutz herself, always sticking
their ways out against the most
strong wind of bitter destiny. So kind
and sweet of manners, as bakers
after fucking plumcake. Yes, or no!
whatever, now it's over, it is going
swiftly too much now, it is on its
way out, dying away! You can see
this idea hanging on the walls. And
already there they are coming and
they ask: Could it maybe dead, all
ready, Baby? Gone, all ready for the
go since long before? Away, gone?
You do know?

No, I only can say. I don't know.
Look, lack of experience! I only
little sugarbomb. Busted long, long,
long gone ago, see? Look on wall!
See me? Busted little bomb's

oder so, da wird gesagt: Das sollst
du nicht tun! Und, BATSCH machts,
und es klascht und kracht, sie
schlagen sich! Hör sich das einer
an! Nun mag jemand fragen, was
diese Rederei soll, genauer: Was soll
dieses Vorgelese dieses vorgele-
senen Vorgeschriebenen? Wozu ist
das geschrieben worden, und
warum und woher und anderer
Fragen mehr? Darauf eine Antwort
zu geben fällt mir nicht schwer,
man kann sie sich denken,
nämlich: Ihrwißtschonwas!

Es mögen Zeiten in Frieden hier
durchgegangen sein, ohne Fragen,
ohne Antworten, ohne Krach ohne
Krieg ohne Sieg etc. etc. —aber,
dahingegangen sind sie, und sie
scheinen auch nicht mehr dazusein.
Es ist aus, liebe Leute, wir atmen
gerade noch die Luft einiger ster-
bender Zuckerfabriken oder
dahingehender Zuckerfabrikations-
institute wie Mal- und Filmateliers
oder Kaffeehäuser, Linienschiffe,
Kirschkuchenbäckereien, Puffs,
Literatur etc. etc. Das ist am
Sterben, es atmet schon nicht mehr
so recht! Schaut auf die Wand,
horcht in den Apparat! es säuselt
nur noch. Es stirbt. Und nun
kommt jemand und fragt: Ist es
vieleicht schon tot? Ist alles
vielleicht schon weg? Ab nach—
Duweißtwohin?

Da kann ich nur sagen: Ich
weiß es nicht, ich habe keine Erfah-
rung. Ich bin doch nur ne kleine
Zuckerbombe, die aber schon
längst, längst, längst zersprungen

splinters flatty?—Yes, but! somebody says at that moment, why
then seemingly pressured little
bomb has always been? Why this
and that? Why so exited, strongly
smashed on the liver and heart?
Why fast and sick?—Surely, I say,
because Big Bang was here. And I
say it quietly, like a clergy, in
blossoming lullaby flowerpot bed.
Yes, als Old Big Band was here, it
was not so nice, he or she or it says,
but now, it is little sugarbomb
that was here, and that was, and is
still, nice!

—No, Baby! I say, only maybe!
and I cry a little bit, one never knows
for sure! You know how they go.
How they smash and fart and cut
and bleed! And you should not have
to ask.—But, says he or she or it,
why do you ask yourself, Answer's
greatest avoider?—Thanks for the
compliments, I say, got you there!
Since it is too dark to see anything,
there is no answers visibel.

—What's it mean? I and you
and invisibility, somebody says in
a questioning way now, or then, but
we cannot see him or her or it, it
or she or he is too dark in the dark.
Please, I say, forgive, Mrs. Madame
or Mr. Monsieur, its too dark to
distinguish neither you nor me.

—Its you yourself, Mister Bad
himself, that is putting out the little
light in his own mind's self now,
Buster! Hahaha! You have now
switched off you own wee little
spotty, Max! Hahaha! (it seems to

ist. Schau doch an die Wand, wies
da klebt und krümelt! Ja, aber! sagt
da jemand, wozu dann der Druck?
Dieser Druck dort damals oder
jemals auf der Bombe, das gewalt-
same Kräuseln der Explosion-
slammellen und die Sprungfedern
im Speck? Ja, sage ich darauf, Big
Bang scheint hiergewesen zu sein,
mit Sicherheit kann man da nicht
antworten, du weifßt ja selbst, wie
die sich streiten, wies da kracht und
knallt wo die einander darüber
ausfragen, wies da rascheit und
blutet, das weißt du doch, was
fragstu dannoch? Ja, aber warum
fragst DU denn hier? fragt da Herr
oder Frau Jemand zurück, was soll
das? Tja und nein, erwidere ich, da
gibts keine Frage drauf, nicht mal
das, ne Frage, es ist zu dunkel. Was
heißt hier Dunkel? sagt da jemand
aus dem Hintergrunde. Aus dem
Schutze der Hintergrundsdäm-
merung kommt die Frage hoch, ich
höre sie im Koppe, sehn kann ich
sie nicht. Es ist zu dunkel, und ich
kann dann immer nur die Antwort
geben: Ich weiß es nicht, ich seh ja
nichts, es dunkelt allzusehr, mein
Herr oder meine Dame! Ich seh
euch leider nicht, wer seid Ihr?
Wir sind Ihr selber, Herr Bösewicht,
antwortets dann meistens aus der
hinteren Reihen einer. Sie selber
Herr Hosenmatz, haben sich
eben selbst das Licht ausgeknipst.
Hahaha!

—Da lacht wieder einer so
dreckiglich, oder nicht? fragt einer

come sounding out of the dark blue).

Be it, that somebody laughs? Whowhowho! darkly, or Hahaha! stickily, or whatever comes to your mind now. I go now, and you look, for answers, on the wall or at the wall. As the King there was, in the old times, remember, do you? looking at the wall's letters.

—Yes, somebody himself says now, I see! I see shit on the wall! dirty ways on walls, picture-hanging and description-making, it is all on the wall.—All is on the wall?—Yes, yes! All that shit and all this piss or all this shit and so on, everything the wall. Sticky shitty pissy walls everywhere with sticky stuff on damp picturepissing contraptions on every wall! Wallfucker was here!

—Cakefucker, too! somebody says at once, can't you see sticking out of wall, sticking to it wise, fuckingcake? Baker was here! Such talkingstuff makes one forget worse things or stuff. Talking wise sweet time goes by, seeming to be or have been talked through wisely, staying inside one's four stickers with all the pictures, happily or still, somebody says. But there is, yes, there IS something going on outside in the open, and it is something not very much like open air acrobatics and nothing like the worst: Football, no! There marching is going on or bleeding etc etc., like forty years ago, when the big bloody thing started (see date near the signature

(oder jemand) da, ich aber habe dann immer schon das Weite oder die Weite gesucht. Vielleicht nicht gefunden, tue dann aber vielleicht meistens (oder sogar immer) so, als wäre ich nicht da, oder wenigstens nicht dort an jenem Ort. Was dunkel ist und ständig jemand fragt, was das soll? Und immer wenn jemand fragt, was soll das? dann sage ich: Ich weiß es nicht, aber schaumal, wie weiland der König an die Wand, vielleicht steht dort was geschrieben?

—An der Wand steht nur Sand, heißt die Antwort dann vielleicht, oder meistens, ja, immer. Tja, sage ich dann manchmal, Sand im Putz, das kann wohl sein, aber, was ists dann, was auf dem Putze hängt?

—Des Menschen von Europa (oder Süd-bzw. Nordamerika) schmutzige Bildgedanken hängen an der Wand! sagt jener dann, und ich sage, was heißt hier schmutzig? Und er sagt, ich will mal nicht so antworten wie du immer, nämlich: Ich habe nichts zu sagen, bzw. ich weiß es nicht, sondern ich will mal sagen: Des Menschen ungeputzter, mistiger, trüber Gedankenkram hängt in mistigen, ungeputzten, trüben Formen an der ekelhaft steilen, geraden, harten Wand.—Oh, weh! bringe ich mich dann vielleicht manchmal noch zum Sagen, siehstu dennich, wiedas oftso schönver zucker tist? —Eben, mein Alter! ist dann manchmal oft das Letzte, was ich aus friedlich angehauchten

of this pamphlet or underneath it),
and then you can see that this
sugarbombing goes like angels fart.

　—But what else? somebody
asks always, and the answer you
know already.

*written to celebrate 1st of September 1939*
*Stuttgart, August 1979*
*D. R.*

Menschen Munde noch höre bevor
ich Ihrwißtschonwas. Eben, mein
Alter, Trüber! der Zucker ists,
welcher die Wand solcherweise
trübt, der Zuckerpiß läuft trüblich
bzw. betrüblich dran runter.

　Über dergleichen Gespräche
vergißt der Redenide, der Zeit- und
Ortsgenosse, oft die trüben Dinge
welche da im Freien geschehn, wo
niemand hinschaut, oder wo man
denkt, dort gibts nur Freiluft-
akrobatik (und im schlimmsten
Falle Fußball).—Nein, dort gibts
Krieg! Dort wird marschiert, dort
blutets, und es bombt so sehr! Wie
heute (siehe Datum bei der Unter-
schrift) vor vierzig Jahren, als der
Zentraleuropäer losblutete und
losschrie, daß unser Fragespiel,
hier im Dunkeln, sich wie ein
Engelspup dagegen ausnimmt.—
Aber, was solls? fragt sich dieser
oder jener (bzw. diese oder jene
bzw. dieses oder jenes), und die
Antwort ist: Ihrwißtschonwas!

*geschrieben zur Feier des*
*　1 September 1939*
*Stuttgart, August 1979*
*D. R.*

# THE BOOKS OF DI[E]TER ROT[H]
## Richard Hamilton

TYPOGRAPHY IS MORE a craft than an art—the graphic designer using type will need to be something of an artist but the typographer of today is a logician whose job is to distribute given information in the most rational way possible. His skill is demonstrated through his ability to organize information, his knowledge of modern printing techniques, his precision when ordering and specifying and by the taste he exhibits in the selection and patterning of elements. The typographer's task is clearly to present the ideas provided in the copy with sympathy and understanding. The best of typographers attempt no more, nor need they.

Prior to the invention of printed type a rather more intimate association existed between the meanings of words and their mode of expression in written form. And during the last fifty years there has been a revival of interest in the possibility of making the visual form of a word, or group of words, convey some part of the message inherent in the literal sense. Poets like Apollinaire, Marinetti and Mayakovsky used type layout to reinforce poetic ideas and some even made pictures with type as, for example, in the calligrams of Apollinaire. Artists such as Schwitters, Picabia, Boccioni, van Doesburg and Lissitzky used type to create messages as much pictorial as

Ideograms by Diter Rot from *Bok 1956–9*, published in an edition of 400 copies.

literary. These onslaughts against the prim barricades of printing technique have left some indents in the vocabulary of graphic design but it is as
art objects, each with its own unique merit, that the original manifestations must be judged.

The work of Diter Rot must be placed in this context of type as a
medium of high art. What distinguishes his work from that of other artists
who have attempted to render aesthetic propositions in type is that he
does so as typographer *per se*. For the first time we find the roles reversed:
an evidently typographic mind ordering type into a poetry rather than the
essential poet wrenching the printer's form into art. For Diter Rot manipu-
lates the limitations of the mechanics of modern print to construct his aesthetic; the instruments of his poetry are mathematics, the micrometric
assemblage of metal units and a language that seems to consist of twenty-
six letters instead of 50,000 words. He can write an essay with 2304 full
points and a poem with a single i.

Diter Rot's language and attitude are esoteric and isolated and so is his
situation. Since 1957 he has lived and worked in Reykjavik, Iceland. From
Box 412, his address is a mere box number, have emanated a few books, published from his own miniature publishing house. The *Diter Rot bok 56–59*
consists of 72 pages, 9½ x 8⅜ inches, with a spiral wire binding. It is the result of three years' work, averaging out to two pages impressed with surgical tenderness every month. The monotype font was bought by the artist

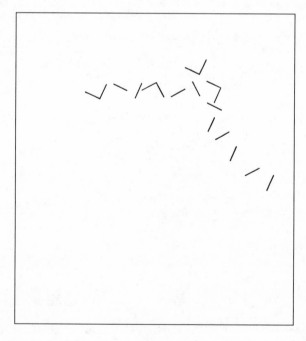

From Diter Rot's book of ideograms, *Bok 1956–59.* The original page size is 22 x 24 cm.

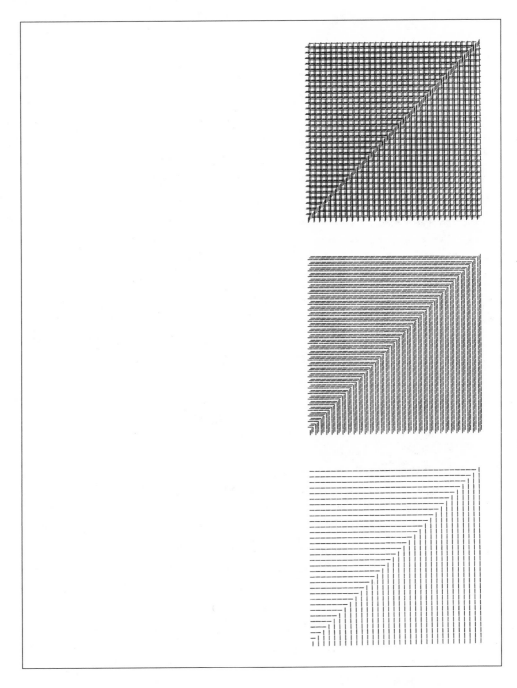

Three pages from *Bok 2a*, published by Diter Rot in 1960 in an edition of 50 copies.

and left with a printer in Copenhagen who then worked upon instructions sent piecemeal by Rot from Iceland. The book, for Rot, isn't simply a form which provides the means to a continuous sequencing of text. The book is a plastic entity which can be entered from back or front—it can accept the limitation of attachment of sheets along a common edge or not. It gives a multiplicity of surfaces which project a set of precisely conditioned variations. In his bound books the page is a rectangle with one attached and three free edges—the sheet can be considered as a single continuous surface or as two related surfaces. Paper, the fabric of the book, can be subjected to a range of operations—it can be cut, perforated, folded and crumpled; inked metal can be pressed into it. The pieces of metal that Diter Rot uses in *bok 56–59* are of one font, lower case only and of only one size; his technique is contrapuntal and its harmonies and reverberations derive from a carefully restricted range of units. Fundamentally Rot's interest in words is plastic rather than semantic—the palindrome and the anagram are two of his favourite devices; for him the visual pun has great significance, the verbal pun less. His work, for this reason, easily crosses the barriers of language; it is written in an Esperanto of the eye but, like the poetic language of Kurt Schwitters, it is a tongue susceptible to universal comprehension but that only its creator can utter.

Better known than the printed books of Diter Rot, because they have been exhibited as works of art in galleries, are the albums made from separate sheets of perforated paper. The perforations are slots of different widths laboriously hand-cut by Diter Rot for a limited edition. The reader of these works simply examines the consequences of laying one sheet over another until the vast range of possibilities is exhausted—a more rewarding experience than it sounds, a sensuous and physically creative pleasure which readers...cannot fully appreciate from the photographs of the loose sheets.

Other books have been made without type: *Diter Rot bok 2a*, made by overprinting a standard grouping of pieces of monotype rule; *bok 2b*, a similar project but using a modified sequence of shifts and turns of the basic unit; *bok 4a*, made with two kinds of triangular blocks with slots in the rubber face—fourteen pieces of each kind were variously composed on the machine bed to give a range of combinations, using either single or double impression.

Despite the remoteness of his present location and the refinement of his vision Diter Rot moves freely and frequently throughout Europe. His talents have been directed to furniture, textile and graphic design, painting and engraving, poetry, films, books and commercial typography. No doubt his influence on typography will be felt whether he chooses to operate in many fields or not. We must hope, though, that the book as art form, the book within his newly invented terms, will continue to obsess him.

# ON *THE BOOK OF BEAN*
## Alison Knowles

### The First Guided Tour through *The Book of Bean*

SO HERE IT IS to begin at the beginning (but one may also turn to the left and begin at the end). Passing through the soybean endpapers one steps up and through the truck tire inner tube to swing out over the lake, a water reflection of oneself. In page three and four is the bean world of word and letter: a roll deck of alphabetically compiled information, books by Beans and a graffiti panel of the word "bean" from Arabic to Swahili. An eye-level gallery exhibits beans and shoes. All this time and throughout one hears the tape: first the sounds of the carpenter climbing the steps of the Franklin Furnace to go to work, of the Hudson River falls, of feet walking along a path by the water. Then the sounds of the pages being made out of town. There is a horse munching and a morning chicken. This side of the tape is overlaid with a telephone book poem of people named Bean, answered by the name of a real bean legume. ("Scarlet Runner," for example, duets with "Bean, Adelaide.") A bean orchestra is heard: red, black and white beans are sounded in containers of glass, wood and ceramic. (Beans don't all sound the same.) These sounds collage with the reader in real time as he makes his way through the pages. A tunnel exists from the bean in word/letter environment. It is another circle but going the opposite way. It leads the reader to the soup via a bean walking tray.[1] In the next space, a moonlight kitchen, are the four guides on the trip, the Red Queen and the White Rabbit from Tenniel's *Alice,* a Bean God, and a four-headed demon dog. The Bean God is kept out of the house, a Japanese house, by throwing beans in his face at the New Year. These guides have come to steal the soup! The soup space is also the performance area of the book; a large white half circle re-peats the moon and provides a stage for performance. Old umbrellas and abandoned clothing have been bunched and burned to make a hill for the running guides. (All objects and garments were found during the summer of the Book building.) There are beans here to be walked on, rolled in or eaten. Beans feel good. The atmosphere is ominous, however, and one is glad for the soup. To continue through, one goes outside the pages and from this vantage sees into the core of the spine. The electrical outlets and tape recorder are visible by turning back a swivel page. Sitting down in page nine we find a "real" book, *Bean Culture,*[2] by a Mr. Sevey. Mr. Sevey purports to

*The Book of Bean* was Alison Knowles' assemblage installation in the form of a large walk-through book.

Installation view of *The Book of Bean*.

present the first book printed in America dealing with the science of bean planting. One can easily escape into admiration of steel engravings of bean harvesters from the early 1900s. The reader leaves via a ladder or out the window and through a muslin panel printed with contradictory wisdom concerning beans and dreaming. At this last entrance/exit, small sound-making objects scrape the floor. One can begin again either by going on or

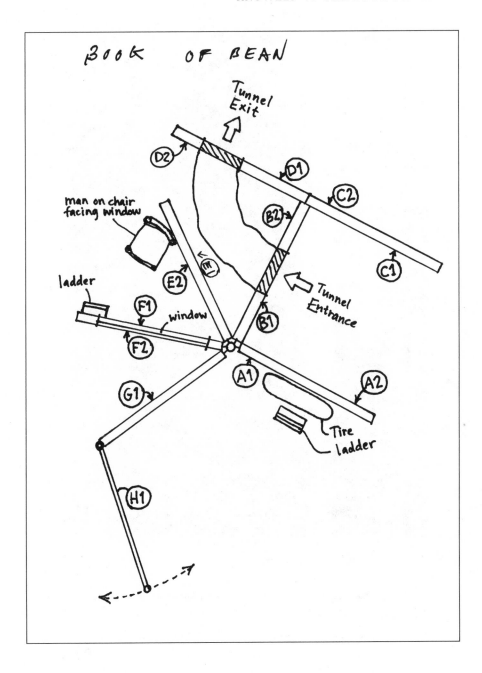

Detail from *The Book of Bean*.

turning back. There is a free-standing page in the vicinity of *The Book of Bean.* It is the same size (four by eight feet) as the bound pages; it is made of red pockets and is a notation panel for performance. Duets for a single bean and an object are presented on slips of paper and tags. The objects and ideas are easily taken away. A formal performance accompanies the opening of the book from the white half-circle stage.

Real soup is served.

## NOTES

1. All beans in the book were donated by Goya Foods, Inc.
2. Gift of Michael Cooper.

# O!
## Jess

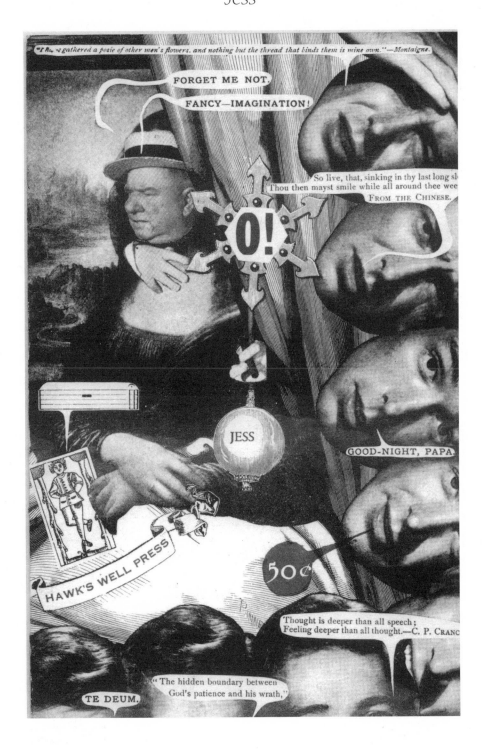

P R E - F A C E

*O!* so many faces, no! they seem to be phases.
Funny papers means they are humorous, but in
America *funny* means *strange, queer, odd,* too.
Absolutely no part here is originally the artist's. What he has achieved is totally his,
but in every detail derivative. Jess has
provided us, not with play-money, but with
an art that is that very genuine phony fifty
dollar bill - but it's a three dollar bill,
and with the face of the Mona Lisa counter-
feited out as if for laughs with W.C. Field's
immortal visage: and that in turn ... For
hasn't Duchamp or Salvador Dali or somebody
used the Mona Lisa before? Is she to be ever-
lastingly useful? to the same purpose? Or is
this the same purpose? Only our eyes are entertained. Surely he insults our sense of
what can be done. *O!* is a book that oughtn't
have been done to Art, a serious alteration
in the possibilities, as if one could supply
a map given the borderlines of Ernst's *Femme
100 Tetes* and Baum's *Land of Oz.* But Baum
was right, the American homeland of the imagination is surrounded by a Deadly Desert and
cannot be seen by airplanes. Someplace unseen Jess has built up out of advertizements
and old throwaway masterpieces a serial image
multi-phasic crowd of one *O!* that escapes being D a d a, because Jess has swallowd D a d a
whole; is not able to be surrealism any more
than a swallow can be a rose; and ends up *O!*,
an imaginary real thing for those who look.
Or finally *O!O!*; unavoidably the artist has
committed another masterly hodgepodge of a
taste that is frightful for those who are
afraid there is something funny going on here.

*ROBERT DUNCAN*

*Published by Hawk's Well Press, 50 Broadway,
New York City 4, New York.*

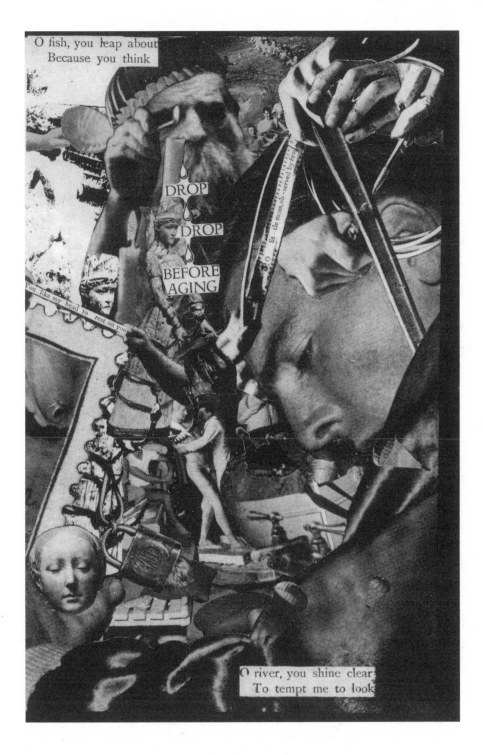

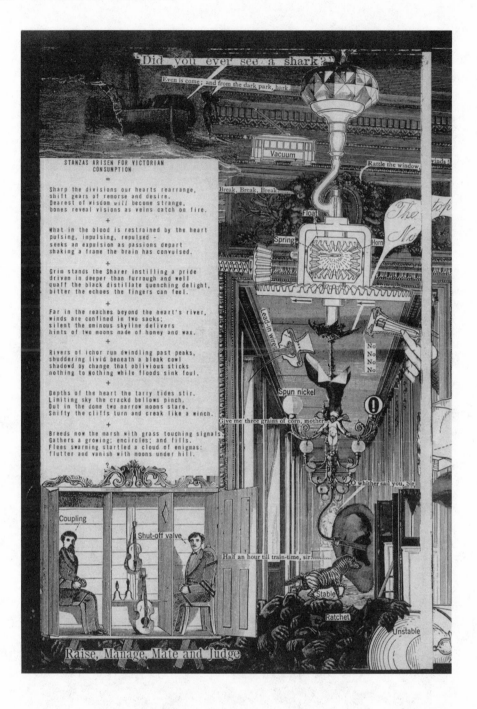

**STANZAS ARISEN FOR VICTORIAN CONSUMPTION**

=

Sharp the divisions our hearts rearrange,
shift gears of remorse and desire.
Dearest of wisdom will become strange,
bones reveal visions as veins catch on fire.

+

What in the blood is restrained by the heart
pulsing, impulsing, repulsed –
seeks an expulsion as passions depart
shaking a frame the brain has convulsed.

+

Grim stands the Sharer instilling a pride
driven in deeper than furrough and well
quaff the black distillate quenching delight,
bitter the echoes the fingers can feel.

+

Far in the reaches beyond the heart's river,
winds are confined in two sacks;
silent the ominous skyline delivers
hints of two moons made of honey and wax.

+

Rivers of ichor run dwindling past peaks,
shuddering livid beneath a bleak cowl
shadowd by change that oblivious sticks
nothing to Nothing while floods sink foul.

+

Depths of the heart the tarry tides stir.
Limiting sky the crackd bellows pinch.
Out in the dome two narrow moons stare.
Snifty the cliffs turn and creak like a winch.

+

Breeds now the marsh with grass touching signals.
Gathers a growing; encircles; and fills.
Flees swarming startled a cloud of enigmas;
flutter and vanish with moons under hill.

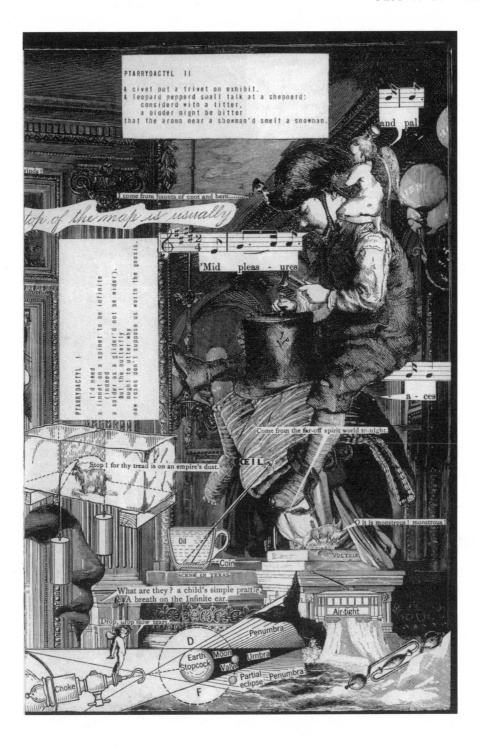

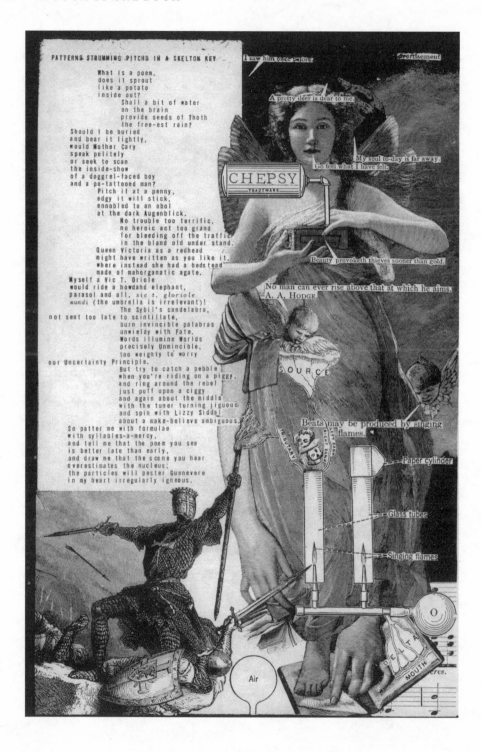

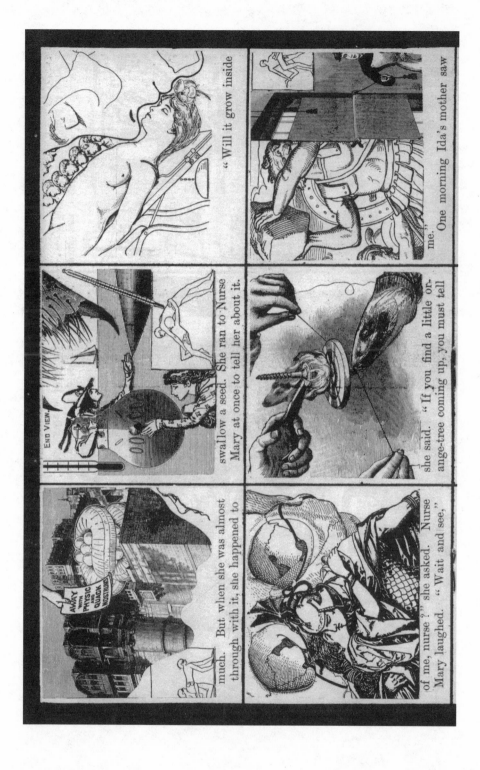

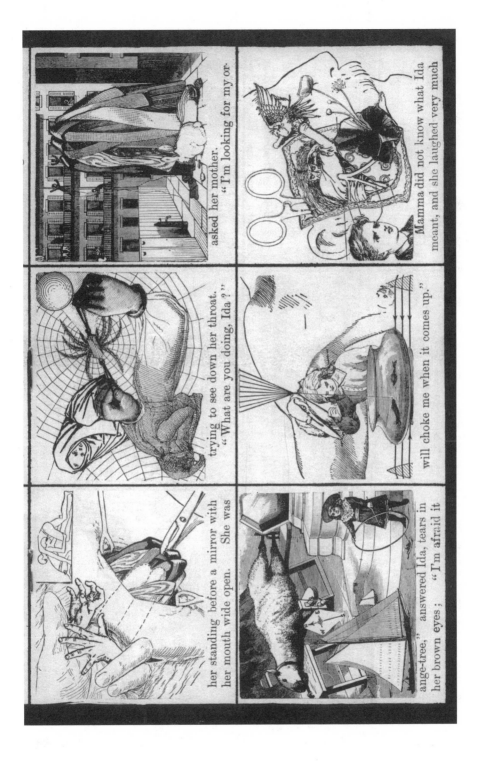

asked her mother.
"I'm looking for my or-

Mamma did not know what Ida
meant, and she laughed very much

trying to see down her throat.
"What are you doing, Ida?"

will choke me when it comes up."

her standing before a mirror with
her mouth wide open.    She was

ange-tree," answered Ida, tears in
her brown eyes;    "I'm afraid it

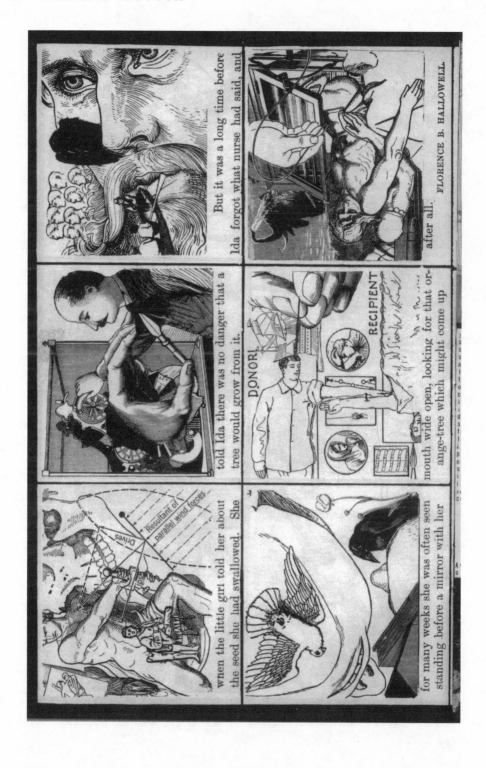

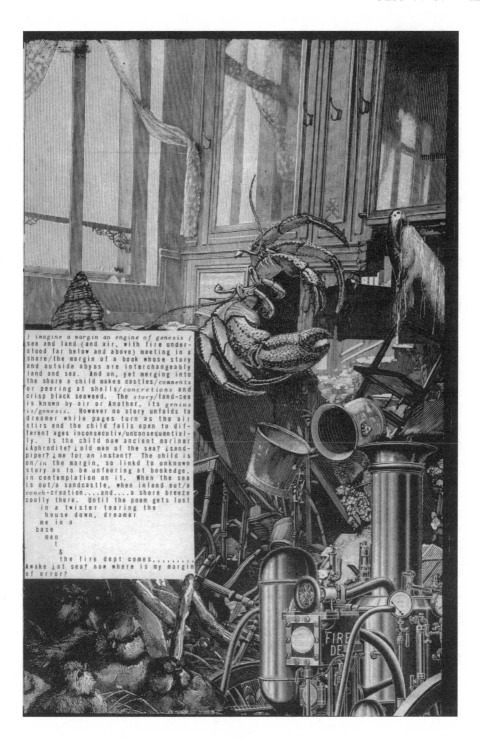

) *imagine a margin an engine of genesis* (
sea and land (and air, with fire understood far below and above) meeting in a
shore/the margin of a book whose story
and outside abyss are interchangeably
land and sea.  And on, yet merging into
the shore a child makes castles/*comments*
or peering at shells/*concretions* and
crisp black seaweed.  The *story*/land-sea
is known by air or Another, its *genius
is/genesis.*  However no story unfolds to
dreamer while pages turn as the air
stirs and the child falls open to different ages inconsecutiv/unconsequential-
ly.  Is the child now ancient mariner
¿Aphrodite? ¿ old man of the sea? ¿sand-
piper? ¿me for an instant?  The child is
on/in the margin, so linkd to unknown
story as to be unfearing at bookedge,
in contemplation on it.  When the sea
is out/a sandcastle, when inland out/a
*conch-creation....and....*a shore breeze
coolly there.  Until the poem gets lost
     in a twister tearing the
        house down, dreamer
      me in a
    base
       men
          t
             &
        the fire dept comes,.........
Awake ¿at sea? now where is my margin
of error?

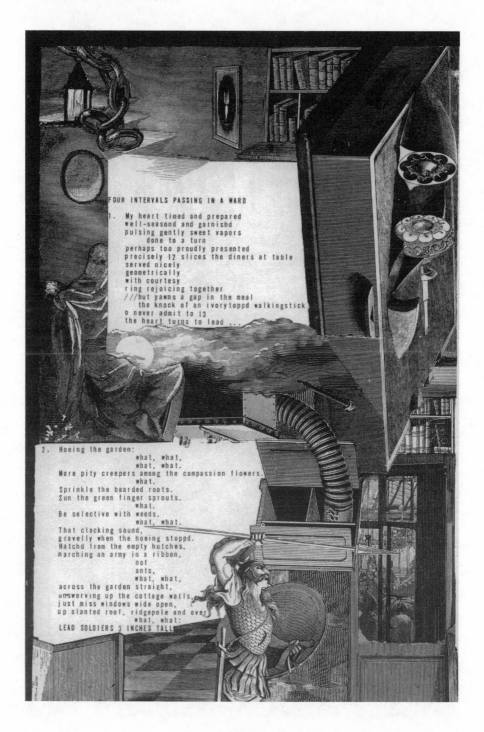

FOUR INTERVALS PASSING IN A WARD

1.    My heart timed and prepared
      well-seasond and garnishd
      pulsing gently sweet vapors
          done to a turn
      perhaps too proudly presented
      precisely 12 slices the diners at table
      served nicely
      geometrically
      with courtesy
      ring rejoicing together
      ///but yawns a gap in the meal
          the knock of an ivorytoppd walkingstick
      o never admit to 13
      the heart turns to lead ...

2.    Hoeing the garden:
                what, what,
                what, what.
      More pity creepers among the compassion flowers.
                what.
      Sprinkle the bearded roots.
      Sun the green finger sprouts.
                what.
      Be selective with weeds.
                what, what.
      That clacking sound,
      gravelly when the hoeing stoppd.
      Hatchd from the empty hutches,
      marching an army in a ribbon,
                not
                ants,
                what, what,
      across the garden straight,
      unswerving up the cottage walls,
      just miss windows wide open,
      up slanted roof, ridgepole and over
                what, what:
      LEAD SOLDIERS 3 INCHES TALL

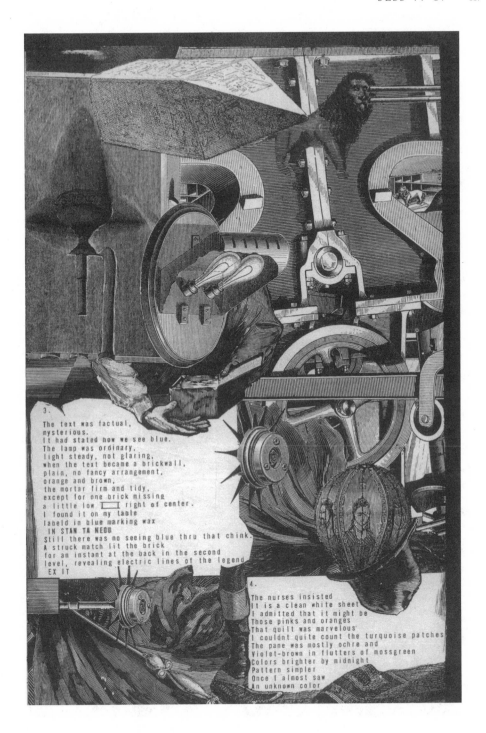

3.

The text was factual,
mysterious.
It had stated how we see blue.
The lamp was ordinary,
light steady, not glaring,
when the text became a brickwall,
plain, no fancy arrangement,
orange and brown,
the mortar firm and tidy,
except for one brick missing
a little low □□□ right of center.
I found it on my table
labeld in blue marking wax
 IN STAN TA NEOU
Still there was no seeing blue thru that chink.
A struck match lit the brick
for an instant at the back in the second
level, revealing electric lines of the legend
 EX IT

4.

The nurses insisted
It is a clean white sheet
I admitted that it might be
Those pinks and oranges
That quilt was marvelous
I couldnt quite count the turquoise patches
The pane was mostly ochre and
Violet-brown in flutters of mossgreen
Colors brighter by midnight
Pattern simpler
Once I almost saw
An unknown color

This is the House that Jack built (spiral text): This is the Tongue that answerd the Eaves echoing the Wind that caught the Key pitchd by the Double alone at the Crossing of the Path worn by the World listening at the door where the Rattle was trappd in the Box Pandora shook. This is the Lid raised by the Voice droning in the Box Pandora shook. This is the Shake that Stoppd the...

### H A W K ' S   W E L L   P R E S S

*TALES OF ANGELS SPIRITS & DEMONS*
by Martin Buber                    95¢

*FIGHTING TERMS* (Poems)
by Thom Gunn          75¢

*THE LOVELY QUARRY* (Poems)
by Seymour Faust          65¢

*WHITE SUN BLACK SUN*    (Poems)
by Jerome Rothenberg
*Publication Date: Spring 1960*

#### Hawk's Well Pamphlets

*O!* (Collages and poems)
by Jess                    50¢

*POEMS FROM THE FLOATING WORLD* (Anthology)
Wallet-sized format                    25¢

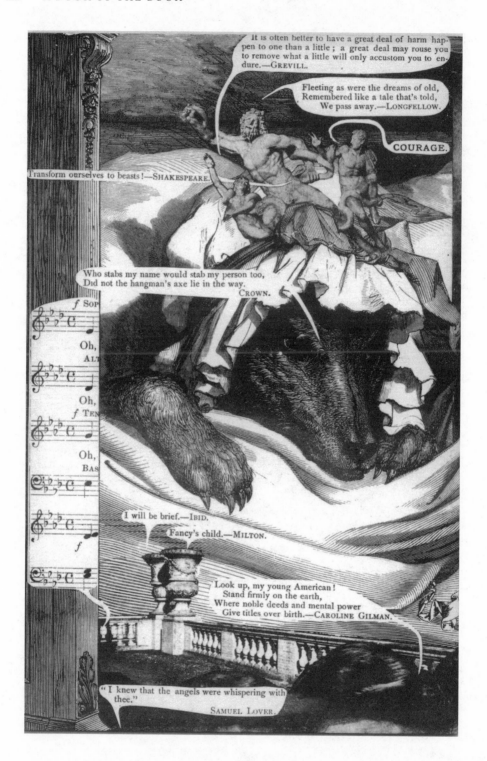

# NOTES ON *A HUMUMENT*
## Tom Phillips

LIKE MOST PROJECTS that end up lasting half a lifetime, this work
started out as idle play at the fringe of my work and preoccupations. I had
read an interview with William Burroughs (*Paris Review* 1965) and, as a result, had played with the 'cut-up' technique, making my own variant (the
columnedge poem) from current copies of the *New Statesman*. It seemed a
good idea to push these devices into more ambitious service.

I made a rule: that the first (coherent) book I could find for threepence
(i.e., 1¼p) would serve.

Austin's, the furniture repository, stands on Peckham Rye, where Blake
saw his first angels and along which Van Gogh had probably walked on his
way to Lewisham. At this propitious place, on a routine Saturday morning
shopping expedition, I found, for exactly threepence, a copy of *A Human
Document* by W. H. Mallock, published in 1892 as a popular reprint of a successful three-decker. It was already in its seventh thousand at the time of
the copy I acquired and cost originally three and sixpence. I had never
heard of W. H. Mallock and it was fortunate for me that his stock had depre-
ciated at the rate of a halfpenny a year to reach the requisite level. I have
since amassed an almost complete collection of his works and have found
out much about him. He does not seem a very agreeable person: withdrawn
and humourless (as photographs of him seem to confirm), he emerges
from his works as a snob and a racist (there are extremely distasteful anti-
semitic passages in *A Human Document* itself). He has however been the
subject of some praise from A. J. Ayer for his philosophical dialogue *The New
Republic,* and *A Human Document* itself is flatteringly mentioned in a novel
by Dorothy Richardson. However, for what were to become my purposes,
his book is a feast. I have never come across its equal in later and more
conscious searchings. Its vocabulary is rich and lush and its range of reference and allusion large. I have so far extracted from it over one thousand
texts, and have yet to find a situation, statement or thought which its words
cannot be adapted to cover. To cite an example (and one that shows how
Mallock can be made ironically to speak for causes against his grain), I was
preparing for an exhibition in Johannesburg (May 1974) and wanted to find
some texts to append to paintings; I turned (as some might do to the *I Ching*)
to *A Human Document,* and found, firstly:—

*wanted. a little white opening out of thought.*

and secondly:—

> *delightful the white wonder*
> *to have the sport and grasses.*
> *The ancient dread*
> *judgement now has come*
> *judgement suddenly. black from a distance.*
> *expected, hurrying on.*
> *Take a new turn*
> *back to reason.*

More recently, in working on an illustrated edition of my own translation of *Dante's Inferno*, I have managed to find a hundred or so parallel texts from *A Human Document* which act as a commentary to the poem. I have even found sections of blank verse to match the translation as in this fragment which forms the halftitle:—

> *My stories of a soul's surprise, a soul*
> *which crossed a chasm in whose depths I find*
> *I found myself and nothing more than that.*

When I started work on the book late in 1966, I merely scored out unwanted words with pen and ink. It was not long though before the possibility became apparent of making a better unity of word and image, intertwined as in a mediaeval miniature. This more comprehensive approach called for a widening of the techniques to be used and of the range of visual imagery. Thus painting (in acrylic gouache) became the basic technique, with some pages still executed in pen and ink only, some involving typing and some using collaged fragments from other parts of the book (since a rule had grown up that no extraneous material should be imported into the work). In some recent pages I have incorporated elements of their printed predecessors.

Much of the pictorial matter in the book follows the text in mood and reference: much of it also is entirely non-referential, merely providing a framework for the verbal statement and responding to the disposition of the text on the page. In every case the text was the first thing decided upon; some texts took years to reach a definitive state, usually because such a rich set of alternatives was present on a single page and only rarely because the page seemed quite intractable. In order to prove (to myself) the inexhaustibility of even a single page I started a set of variations of page 85: I have already made over twenty. The visual references used range from a telegram envelope to a double copy of a late Cézanne landscape.

The only means used to link words and phrases are the 'rivers' in the type of the original; these, if occasionally tortuous, run generously enough and allow the extracted writing to have some flow so that it does not become (except where this is desirable) a series of staccato bursts of words.

Occasionally chance procedures have been used. One page (p. 99) executed in this way was first divided into half, and, by tossing coins, every word except one was eliminated from each half. Once again the book spoke (like the *I Ching*). Its two words, in a faintly Jewish voice, said (in 1967) 'something already.' The title itself was arrived at by invited accident: folding one page over and flattening it on the page beneath makes the running title read A HUMUMENT, [i.e., A HUM(AN DOC)UMENT], which had an earthy sound to it suitable to a book exhumed from, rather than born out of, another. According to Mary Ann Caws who has written at length on *A Humument* this procedure is called crasis.

The numerical order of the pages is not the chronological order of their making. The initial attack on the book was made by taking leaves at random and projecting the themes that emerged backwards and forwards into the volume. In the end the work became an attempt to make a *Gesamtkunstwerk* in small format, since it includes poems, music scores, parodies, notes on aesthetics, autobiography, concrete texts, romance, mild erotica, as well as the undertext of Mallock's original story of an upper-class cracker-barrel philosopher, ex-poet and diplomat, who falls in love with a sexy prospective widow from Hampstead (her husband is out of combat, being a sick man, and, being a Jew, beyond the pale in any case).

Many rules have grown up in the course of the work. Although Mallock's original hero (Grenville) and heroine (Irma) have their parts to play, the central figure of this version is Bill Toge (pronounced 'toe-dj'). His adventures can only (and must) occur on pages which originally contained the words 'together' or 'altogether' (the only words from which his name can be extracted). He also has his own recurrent iconography; his insignia include a carpet and a window looking out onto a forest and his amoeba-like, ever-changing shape is always constructed from the rivers in the type. His story, the Progress of Love, is a favourite neo-platonic *topos* and there are deliberate parallels with the *Hypnerotomachia Polophili*, the most beautiful of printed books, published in Venice in 1499.

New manoeuvres keep on springing up. A recent strategy has been, in revising pages, to introduce fragments of their previous imagery, colours etc. as in the new page 105, shown here, where the picture on the wall is concocted from shreds of the former version.

As well as *A Humument* itself, Mallock's novel has been the source for other ventures, notably the complete score of an opera *IRMA* whose libretto, music, staging instructions and costume designs all come from *A Human Document*. Other offshoots include *Trailer* (published by edition hansjörg mayer, Stuttgart 1971), which is in effect garnered from the cutting floor of *A Humument*, though a self-sufficient work, and *DOC*, a series of affidavits and testimonies which attempt to build up the picture of a lecherous doctor. There exists also a large number (about three hundred to date) of self-contained fragments, small paintings which make variations of

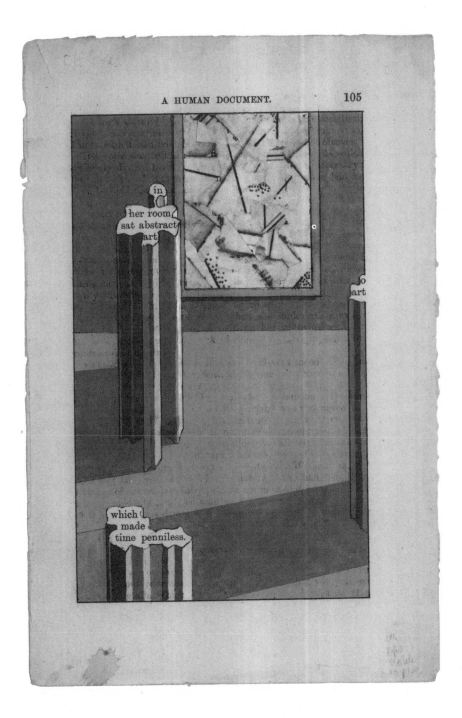

wording and design from the book itself and catch up on some lost opportunities in the original. Texts from the same Mallock novel also appear as pendants to paintings such as the series *The Quest for Irma* (1973) and *Ein Deutsches Requiem: after Brahms*. In preparation is a ballet scenario (with score and costume designs) which could either be performed separately (as *The Quest for Grenville*) or as an interlude in performances of *IRMA*.

As work went on and ramified, a second copy of *A Human Document* became necessary. Curiously enough it turned up in the other branch of the same furniture repository (though this time it cost 1/6d). This copy had belonged to one Lottie Yates who had herself 'treated' it to some extent, heavily underlining passages that seemed to relate to her own romantic plight (occasionally in the margin she had sighed 'How true!'). It seems also that she had used it as a means of saying to her beloved the things she lacked words for, passing the underlined copy to him as a surrogate love letter. Thus, in 1902, someone had already started to work the mine. The first copy had belonged to a Mr. Leaning and was unmarked save for his signature. I have since acquired fifteen or so copies, many sent gratis from well-wishers (notably Patrick Wildgust, most dedicated of Mallock hunters). Most have no sign of their owners: one, however, which was purchased at the Beresford Library, Jersey, in 1893, by Colonel J. K. Clubley, passed eventually into the hands of someone who merely signs himself 'Hitchcock.' The most recent addition has been a copy supplied by a well-wisher from the library of Sir Gerald Kelly, a past president of the Royal Academy, though how he got it from 'Nell' to whom it was presented by 'Michael' in 1901 is not recorded.

The recent find of the original three-decker first printing has been somewhat of a disappointment. Its letters are big and, with its broad type-rivers and wide spacings it lacks the tight look of the single volume. Each word seems to have fewer neighbours. Yet a new quest has started: an even more recondite curiosity has come to my notice in the form of a one volume American edition, also published in 1892 (by Cassell Publishing Co. N.Y.). I have not seen a copy as yet but apparently it differs from the English text mainly in the suppression of foreign and exotic words. If any one who reads this has such a copy that they would be willing to part with I should be glad to hear from them. I need hardly add that reasonably priced examples of the ordinary English popular edition would still be exceedingly welcome. To help me locate certain key words (when tackling the Dante project for example) I have, with some help from others, compiled a complete concordance to *A Human Document*.

All the work on *A Humument* has been done in the evenings so that I might not, had the thing become a folly, regret the waste of days. One kind of impulse that brought this book into slow being was the prevailing climate of textual criticism. As a text, *A Humument* is not unaware of what then occu-

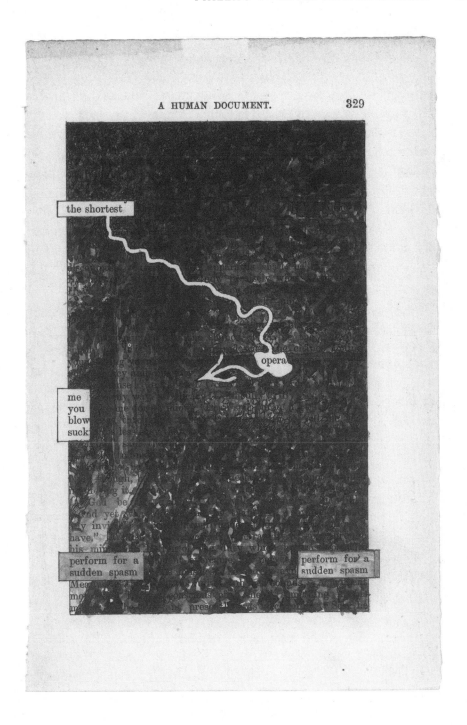

pied the pages of *TelQuel* (and by now must already have become a feature of undergraduate essays). Much of structuralist writing tends to be the picking over of dead words to find sticks for the fires of cliqueish controversy. *A Humument* exemplifies the need to 'do' structuralism, and (as there are books both *of* and *on* philosophy) to be *of* it rather *on* it. At its lowest it is a reasonable example of *bricolage,* and at its highest it is perhaps a massive *déconstruction* job taking the form of a curious unwitting collaboration between two ill-suited people seventy-five years apart. It is the solution for this artist of the problem of wishing to write poetry while not in the real sense of the word being a poet…he gets there by standing on someone else's shoulders.

Publication of *A Humument* was started in 1970 by the Tetrad Press with a box of ten silkscreened pages which made up Volume 1. Other volumes (ten in all, containing varying quantities of pages) were printed by lithography, silkscreen, and letterpress in a limited edition of one hundred copies. The original manuscript was completed in the autumn of 1973 and was shown within days of that event, in its entirety, at the Institute of Contemporary Arts (in whose bulletin, then edited by Jasia Reichardt, it was first mentioned in 1967).

This first edition in book form differs from the private press edition in that several new pages have been substituted for the first versions and many other pages have been reworked by hand, using the advantages of revision offered by the preparatory stages for colour offset lithography. If this book finds favour (i.e., sells), and I live, the consequent reprints will allow me to replace say a dozen pages with each new edition. A notional thirtieth(!) printing therefore would be an entirely reworked book with almost no pages surviving from the first.

In a sense, because *A Humument* is less than what it started with, it is a paradoxical embodiment of Mallarmé's idea that everything in the world exists in order to end up as a book.

## NOTE

This is a revised version of the notes printed in *Works/Texts to 1974* (Editions Hansjörg Mayer) which were themselves adapted from an article published in the *London Magazine* in 1971. As readers of the 1987 Thames & Hudson version will note, the promise of the penultimate paragraph has been kept. Since that edition *The Heart of a Humument* has been published by Hansjörg Mayer and there have been several other by-products including *A Course in Sussex* (screenprint) and the graphics produced by the now defunct Wine Arts Ltd dealing with the Chateaux of Bordeaux (*O Chateaux O Raisins*): three *Humument* globes have also come into existence and, inevitably, a T-shirt (designed for sale in the Royal Academy shop). Pages of *A Humument* have also celebrated the artist's fiftieth birthday, as well as providing a Christmas card for the RAC. Perhaps it is very post-modern to have one foot in Academe and the other in Disneyland. Rumours of a French translation persist but this prospect may have receded, since, with the demise of structuralism (how old-fashioned now seem my references to it above) the brief modishness of my treated novel in France may have had its day.

# WRITERS FORUM —
# LIFE BY 1000 BOOKS
## Lawrence Upton

THIS ARTICLE IS written as the 750th Writers Forum publication goes to press in September 1998. By the time it sees the light of day, the 1000th will either be out or in production: it is already planned. If it happens as planned, and that depends on grant-aid, it will be the most ambitious publication yet, both in editorial scope and in production. The achievement of the press and its founder/operator/proprietor, Bob Cobbing, is not just in its volume of output, but also the philosophy behind all the press's activities and the application of that philosophy to produce a unique and invaluable series of aesthetically pleasing publications.

Some presses are carefully planned. Their purposes are determined beforehand. Their business plans are drawn up. [I shan't cite any examples in case others accuse me of not understanding their business acumen.] Others seem to creep up on their owners, like habits or disasters or obsessions. I *think* that Writers Forum is one of the latter. Bob Cobbing describes its beginning as follows:

[Jeff Nuttall] was the stimulus that got the Writers Forum press started. He said: "Why don't we publish some books." And I said: "Okay, why not?" We published a book by him and Keith Musgrove, called *The Limbless Virtuoso,* in 1963. (From an unpublished interview with Bob Cobbing on February 16, 1995 by Wolfgang Görtschacher.)

Writers Forum is also one of the most important little presses in the UK, perhaps because it has responded primarily to needs felt by artists and poets rather than to a series of business plans.

In reviewing its history, it is useful to clarify the origin of the name because Writers Forum can be dated both from the 50s and the 60s. Hendon Writers Group started in December 1952, and its first magazine, *And,* commenced in July 1954.

Hendon Writers Group became Writers Forum and still exists: the Writers Forum workshop commenced its forty-sixth year in September 1998 in the upstairs room of a pub near Camden Town, London. *And* continues, although in 1998 it is a magazine co-edited by Adrian Clarke and Bob Cobbing and is not based on any formal grouping of writers.

In listing Writers Forum publications, Cobbing starts in 1954, but when talking about Writers Forum as a little press as such, he takes 1963 as the starting point.

In terms of the quantity of titles put out by the press (on average, about one a fortnight for a working life), Writers Forum is becoming more productive as the years pass:

Writers Forum produced its hundredth book, the anthology *WF100*, in October 1973. It had taken 10 years to reach a hundred. Number 200, *Concerning Concrete Poetry*, came in September 1978, after 5 years. Number 300 was in February 1984; that's 5½ years. Number 400 was February 1986—2 years. Number 500, in 1992, was the anthology *VerbiVisiVoco*, another nearly 7 years. Number 600, in June 1995, was your [Upton's] *Messages to Silence Volume One*—3½ years. Number 700, in November 1996; that's 1½ years. Number 800, Eric Mottram's *Pollock Record* is scheduled for January 1998, just over a year. So it looks as if output has somewhat increased, but it all depends on money. Since 1971, WF has had one publishing grant from the Arts Council, which they now describe as an aberration, and one publishing grant from London Arts Board. As to the future, things will go on much the same. Probably we are producing a greater proportion of books of visual poetry now, but they are harder to sell. (Bob Cobbing interviewed by Lawrence Upton, December 1997; awaiting publication.)

It should be borne in mind that the publications vary enormously in size from hundreds of pages (*verbivisivoco,* the 500th Writers Forum publication, edited by Bob Cobbing and Bill Griffiths, 320 pages, 1991) to single sheets.  In addition, the recent *Domestic Ambient Noise* project has created an unprecedented, almost anomalous, surge in output.[1]

You may also have noticed that Writers Forum publications are *sometimes* out of sequence so that the eight hundredth, by numbering, appeared before the seven hundred and fiftieth because the latter took over a year to prepare for publication.

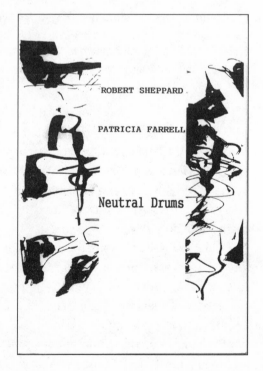

*Neutral Drums.* Robert Sheppard and Patricia Farrell, 1999. White card cover, black and white text, photocopied, centre-stapled. Cover design by Patricia Farrell.

However one views the figures, the sheer persistence and energy of Bob Cobbing, who will be 80 years old in the year 2000, is astonishing. As the Canadian Steven Ross Smith has said, Cobbing demonstrates "determination despite fashion, courage in the face of conservatism, and aggression in pushing out one's edges."[2]

An important facet of Writers Forum publications is their design. In almost all cases the form of the publication is appropriate to its content. Cobbing's instincts are reliable, but he can be quite self-effacing about his achievement:

It is simply that some poems are big and you need an A4 page or, in those days, a foolscap page. Some poems are small and can go onto a very tiny page. It seemed pretty obvious to use different size pages. (Görtschacher, ibid.)

Later in this article I shall quote some of the sizes used so you can see how they vary to suit the circumstances.

In some ways, Writers Forum books are a kind of artist's book except that Cobbing generally uses office reprographics to make them. When I put it to him that his approach has been not just a purely practical matter, but one also of *aesthetically appropriate* decisions, he agreed to some extent:

Aesthetic decisions are one part of the practical decisions one makes... The aim always was to produce them to the best artistic standards possible on limited finances and limiting machinery, but they were never conceived as artists' books. (Upton, ibid.)

For years, he used a Gestetner ink duplicator, cutting the stencils on a typewriter, or, more often, electro-scanning the originals/masters—often handwritten texts and drawings—to make stencils of uneven quality and very limited life with which, somehow, he managed to produce superb results where others would have made a mess of ink:

I loved the qualities one could achieve on the Gestetner, from solid blacks to the most subtle greys. Together with a scanner, all things were possible. (Upton, ibid.)

When the Gestetner failed, in 1984—actually it was dropped during house-moving—he found the money to buy a photocopier; and he stuck with the newer technology:

They are even more versatile. I miss some of the qualities I got on the duplicator, but can get just as interesting results and more varied ones on the photocopier. I'd like to have both but haven't got room for both; so I shall stick to the photocopier. (Upton, ibid.)

As a poet/artist, working largely with the manipulation of visual images, the publication of other people's work and the preparation and publication of his own work is all part of one activity or, as the late Eric Mottram described it, one campaign. It has become a life's work:

That is useful, to have a photocopier on the premises and it means that even in the middle of the night I can think of something and go downstairs and do it. And just, you know, ideas keep on coming and if an idea comes I've got the opportunity of actually doing it at that time, rather than waiting. (Bob Cobbing, interviewed by Cris Cheek, 1998, in *skin of noise* by cris cheek, unpublished.)

His current copier is more than a desktop and less than an industrial job. There is no collator. Collation is done by hand. (He has neither the funds nor the storage space to buy paper in much bulk so he purchases small lots and sells his books as quickly as possible to get the money to buy more paper.) Except for the copying itself, most processes are undertaken on the kitchen table, where an old, slightly battered cat often sleeps; and the cat is rarely disturbed intentionally. He really dislikes strangers; I'm not sure what he thinks of Bob, but he has his own cushion on the table, at one end, to disincline him to make a bed on manuscripts and books-in-collation.

It is the care with which Cobbing uses utilitarian machines, as well as the strong visual content in many of the items, which makes Writers Forum publications at least *like* artists' books. While the photocopier is intended by its makers for bulk output, Cobbing is quite capable of watching each print come out to make sure that it is up to standard, just as, in making his own images, collaborative or solo, he does not just use a machine or process as a medium but pushes it to its limits.

When we made *Fuming* (Bob Cobbing/Lawrence Upton, 13 A4 cards, colour, in folder, 1997), each card went through the photocopier one card at a time, one colour at a time, as we made our images opposite to the process of colour separation, because that was the only way we could afford to produce the book. Though a unique event, that publication also typified the effect of working with Cobbing: nothing stops him this side of impossibility; there has to be a way and he'll find it. If it means *imagining* a set of polychrome images that you will not see properly until they are already printed, then so be it. Once this idea had been put to me a couple of times, I found it is not so difficult as I had imagined.

He folds each piece of paper carefully. He presses the ends of office staples down.

Another defining difference between Writers Forum and so many other publishers, large and small, is that it is committed to making its products available to everyone; and that means making them cheap, often very cheap:

They were always produced to be able to be sold at a relatively cheap price, because customers were fellow poets, poor students and other impecunious people. Keep the prices down and the books get into more hands. (Upton, ibid.)

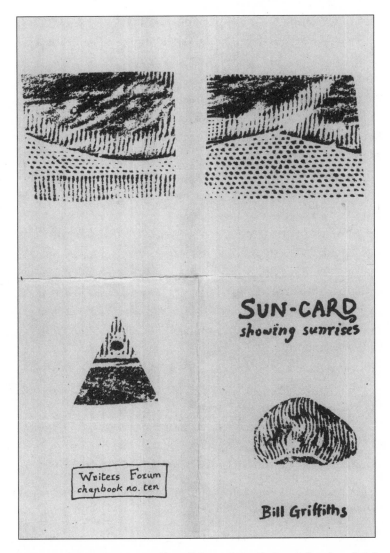

*Sun Card showing sunrises.* Bill Griffiths, n.d., [mid 70s]. Colored card, ink duplicated. A "chapbook" is a publication folded with one cut to make eight pages. Seen here are four of the pages spread out, with cut and fold marks showing. The two images at the top are upside-down. Design by Bill Griffiths.

Much of the time, I suspect, Cobbing can hardly get his money back. This makes it difficult for him to display and distribute because the units moved do not generate that much real income; but he persists. The look and shape of the publications cry out for artistic book display; the price makes that financially impossible except by public or private support.

On the other hand, when there is support, on those rare occasions, it is *used.* For instance, the five hundredth and seven hundred and fiftieth publications are the perfect bound output of professional printers, giving them a potentially wider market because of their bookseller-friendliness; and, also, widening the range of *types* of publication put out by the press which have, on occasion, included records, tapes, items in boxes, and items in plastic bags!

Writers Forum's range is enormous and its choice of authors is often very perceptive. It published Allen Ginsberg's *The Change* (12 pages, 8" x 6," ink duplicated with cover 9" x 7" bearing a linocut by Jeff Nuttall) in 1963, bpNichol (*Konfessions of an Elizabethan Fan Dancer,* 34 pages, 10" x 8," ink duplicated, with a litho cover) in 1967. There's an early Anselm Hollo (*The Going-On Poem,* 1966). The name Jiri Valoch occurs and recurs, Jeff Nuttall, Franciszka Themerson, Eugen Gomringer...*Nancy Adler Poems,* 1970, by one...P. J. O'Rourke.

In 1998, Writers Forum brought out *Postcards from Hitler* by Barry Mac-Sweeney, a book far more exciting than other recent titles by MacSweeney which had attracted greater publicity.

He published Eric Mottram's book of poetry, *Local Movement,* in 1973; and, posthumously, his *Pollock Record,* in 1998, using a book design which had been developed by Mottram and Cobbing for Mottram's earlier *Precipice of Fishes* (1979).

When Dom Silvester Houedard's work had entered that eclipse which so often follows an artist's death, it was Writers Forum which brought out *In memoriam dsh* (60 pages, 1995).

Writers Forum changes over time rather as a person's behaviour may change. Everything in its season, subject to outside pressures. Let's look, briefly, at a couple of examples, the two magazines, *Kroklok* and *And*:

*Kroklok* was intended to be just a magazine for sound poetry, whereas *And* magazine was more general. (Görtschacher, ibid.)

*Kroklok* ran to 4 issues (two issues in 1971, one in 1972 and one in 1976—Writers Forum's sixty-ninth, seventy-sixth, ninety-first and one hundred and thirty-sixth publications), but hasn't been seen in a couple of decades. It was always quirky, but that was one of its joys. It was also extremely provocative and informative—it had to be with dsh (Dom Silvester Houedard) as its main editor. But it seems that, after initial enthusiasm, other things became more important either to the editors or the publisher or both.

*And #1* appeared in July 1954, and is now counted as the first publication of Writers Forum. *#2* came out in February 1961 and *#3* in February 1963. Not exactly frequent, perhaps, but it should be noted that *And #2* and *#3* were the third and fourth Writers Forum publications. The second Writers Forum publication was an anthology of "members of Writers Forum."

*And #4* was published in March 1966, *#5* September 1969, *#6* (WF100) October 1973, *#7* February 1994, *#8* December 1994, *#9* July 1995, and *#10* September 1998.

In the late 90s, *And* is at least as lively and wide-ranging as it ever was. The circumstances surrounding its making have changed, but the need is there and the magazine appears. Perhaps there will never be another issue.

It's often impossible to tell what will appear next. If you leave London for a month, say, then you will come back to find the appearance of Cobbing's displays at workshops and readings transformed. It is very like a garden. When things grow, they can be and usually are delightful; but they have their times and things die back.

Theoretically, all the titles are still available: "out in print" as someone dubbed it. The Cobbing house is bursting at the seams.

The print-run always used to be 220 copies in the early days of Writers Forum, 200 for sale, 12 copies are given to the poet, and 8 copies are sent out to magazines to get some reviews. The magazine always used to have a 500 run, and some books that we do that get a bit popular will have a 500 run. At the moment, because I am publishing so much and because storage space is restricted, I quite often only do 50 or 100 copies of a book to start with and then reprint as they run out. It may well sell several hundred eventually, or even 1,000 or more. But the initial run at the moment is only about 50 or 100. (Görtschacher, ibid.)

Writers Forum publications are more than worth seeking out. I am inclined to say that it is essential you seek them out. Not a few of each edition end up in archives. In one way that is excellent because they will be there for the future; but the pity of it is, if that is all that happens, that Bob Cobbing will have spent his life making publications *for now.*

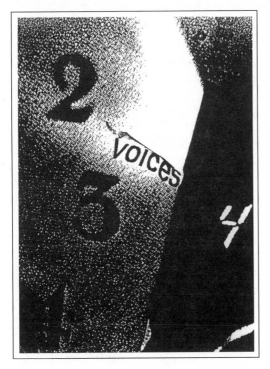

There is nothing like these books for the commitment of their publisher and the excitement of so many of the texts. For many poets Writers Forum is either their only publisher or their first publisher. Years ago Bob Cob-

*voices.* Bob Cobbing, 1999. White card cover, black and white text, photocopied, centre-stapled.

bing said to me: "I publish the unpublishable," and I think that's a pretty good, if unintentional, manifesto.

With many WF books, there is a wonderful exuberance, visual and (potentially) aural. Cobbing's work and his work with collaborators, and much of the work by others that he publishes, is intended for performance, often wild performance with verbal utterance, non-verbal utterance, movement, percussion—including tables and chairs or whatever happens to be around. I have smuggled what had been a rather extensive and gaudily magnificent ceramic ashtray from the pub where he was perform-ing because I thought the landlord would not appreciate it being in pieces. "I am sorry that I broke your ashtray, but you see I was performing a poem with it."

In his own work, he uses colour rarely and finds his way to do most things in black and white. Scores, texts, starting points, whatever one calls the Cobbing visuals, are made in black and white and such greyscale as the photocopier allows. Allows under duress, for Cobbing copies with extreme prejudice. They are beautiful things in their own right, but they can be a little daunting, at first, to the inexperienced eye when it is announced that they are poems.

As a result, at bookfairs and the like, I have seen person after person— three or four to every one who stays—pick up such a book, open it, close it, often quickly, and move on, sometimes to another display entirely. It's such a pity. For all that, he shifts a lot of pamphlets at such events.

He and I sometimes do guerrilla performances of our collaborative pieces, processing through the spaces without prior warning, improvising between loudly and very loudly; and with any dogs that have brought their owners and stayed; and with children—children don't have prior defini-tions of poetry, though they are already more inhibited than the dogs. After, the Writers Forum stand will get many more customers. People are interested now. How do you read this score? Do they each sound different? Only a pound? This book is only a pound?

There is a resistance to unfamiliar linkages of media and genre, espe-cially in the environment of poetry. Announce the work as visual art and there is less problem; artist-types seem more open to visuals being per-formed than poetry-types are to poems being painted; similarly with those involved in music. They will open the booklets and look at them.

Wherever there is work being done which pushes practice out beyond what expectation has prepared us for and theory allows, potentially you'll find Bob Cobbing, liberating the...for want of a better phrase, liberating the source material from pockets, folders, desks and even the maker's dustbin to get it into a book or a folder where it can be read/performed. The name of his press, Writers Forum, describes its activity exactly.

The unfamiliar and unexpected interest him. He seeks them out in himself and in others. He seems just as interested in those extending the linear verbal text as he is in those working in less well-defined and more conceptual space. If there is a piece of work that, for him, has its own energy, he may well publish it so that others have the opportunity of sharing his experience. Not all, perhaps not many, of Writers Forum's authors share Cobbing's stated conviction that every mark has its own sound; but he is not inclined to force the belief on them; he merely puts it into practice in front of them at workshops and the like.

That, wherever it is, is where Cobbing's philosophy, as I have called it, and his activity have their centre. It's a still centre. When he works, he hums to himself, a contented quiet song which goes on and on with small variations while he is putting together on the page signs for extraordinary sounds, indications of outrageous connections and gateways between quite heterogeneous states of utterance. It is a stillness of concentration and conviction and optimism: rare attributes, especially in combination.

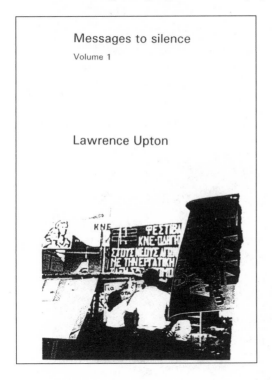

*Messages to Silence.* Lawrence Upton, 1995. White card cover, black and white text, photocopied, centre-stapled. Cover design by Lawrence Upton.

## NOTES

1. *Domestic Ambient Noise* is a three hundred pamphlet collaboration between Bob Cobbing and Lawrence Upton, due to reach completion with the publication of #300 on 1st April 2000. Each pamphlet, size B6 with card cover, consists of an image by one poet followed by six variations on that image by the other poet who then takes one of those variations as his image to vary. All the images, as well as being visual works, are also intended for performance.

2. *Ballet of the Speech Organs: Bob Cobbing on Bob Cobbing,* Underwhich Editions, Saskatoon and Toronto, 1998.

# from *A SMELL OF PRINTING*

## AN ODE
## FOR THE RECOVERY OF
## AN OLYMPIA SPLENDID 66 TYPEWRITER

## Simon Cutts

An ode for the recovery of an olympia splendid 66
typewriter originally designed by max bill in 1944
and once bought in nottingham in 1966 with elite
pitch and its keys altered for accents then lost
in a paris market street in 1987 another found at
ludgate typewriters london in 1994 with pica pitch
its fraction keys identically altered for accents

# SOUVENIR DE VOYAGE
## Ian Tyson

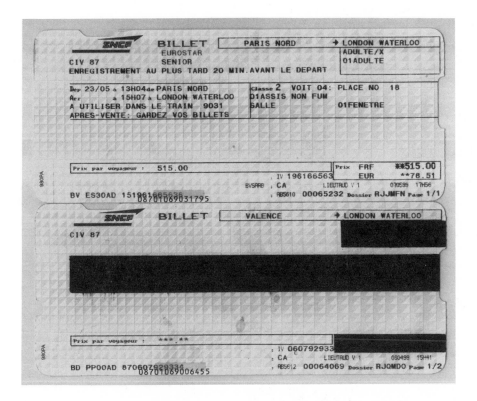

THESE PAGES ARE NOTES to myself on the way to establishing the most satisfactory solution to an abstract problem. Since living in France I have been using the trains more, and there are machines there, situated at the entrance to the platforms, in which one has to "validate" one's ticket, i.e., it punches a small section out to show it has been used. This ritual stayed with me and prompted the initial concept of "cutting out" from the edge or the interior of a page. The form changed from black and grey intersecting sheets of a "carnet" to recycling proof pages from a previous book into two inter-related and inter-locking fold outs. Other diverse implications arrived "par hazard." The result is a standing paper sculpture contained in a wrap-around folio/cover. It is, in a certain sense, also a book and reflects my interest in extending the possibility of what a book may be by linking two and three dimensions.

—*St. Roman de Malegarde 1999.*

1

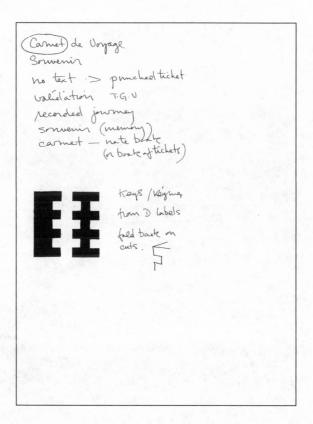

2

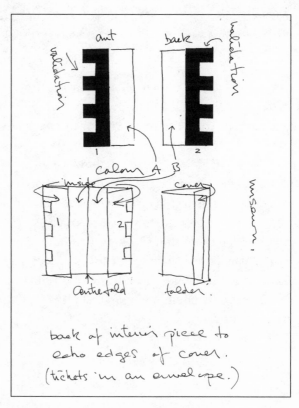

3

"it is necessary to arrive at
the station in time to miss
the previous train"

—

standing piece >
continuation of cut out
cards — "lumina" 2+3 D.

—

recycle proof pages from
part work ro 3 colours
black < blue
        red

papers                    G.F. Smith
Cuches noir               Cover
                          grey
Zerkall,
(blue grey)

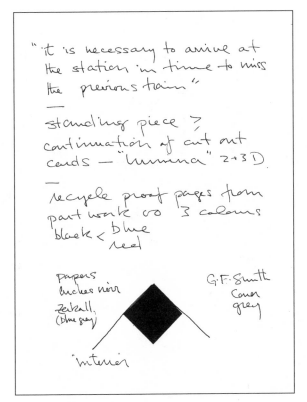

interior

---

4

A   B

interlock
interior cut
piece inside

← Cover

Cover
better than Ⓐ

(recap)

move through > an aperture
> something seen > place to
place > crossing non exist-
ant borders.
open the foldeel cover
(envelope)/grey card/the
cut outs on front > A B
slowly reveal the inner
piece ——→

5

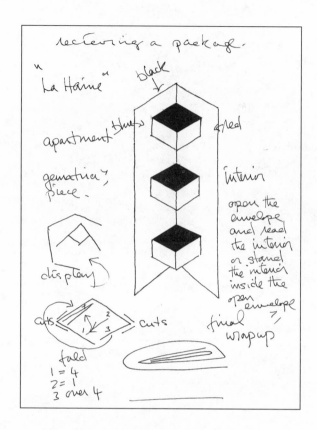

Photograph of finished project.

# WORDS: AN ENVIRONMENT
## Allan Kaprow

TWO ROOMS, one 9' x 9', leading railroad style into another, 6' x 6', each 8' high, constructed within a room. Doorways covered by white cloths.

Outside first room is a large electric sign saying "WORDS." Red and white lights blinking all around top of the walls. Inside, four lights hanging at eye level: a blue, a yellow, a green, and a white one, which alone blinks. Two vertical rows of lights, also not blinking, from floor to ceiling, on opposite walls. On the other two walls are five continuous rolls of cloth, also floor to ceiling, on which are stenciled words. Operated manually, these rolls, containing fixed elements, can be aligned variously with each other to make sense-groups or non-sense, as one wishes. Governing the other two walls are word strips on paper (lettered by a group of friends and myself

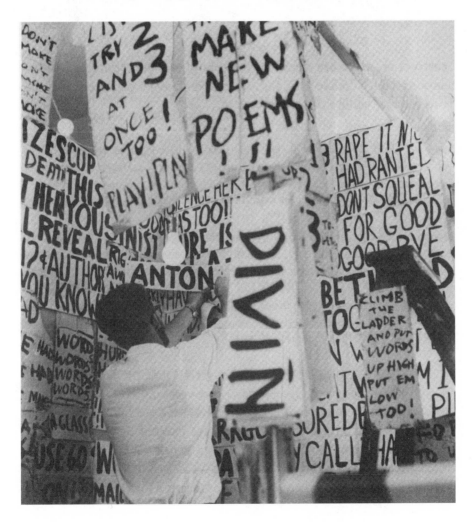

and derived at random from a number of poetry books, newspapers, comic magazines, the telephone book, popular love stories, etc.; these having been shuffled, I composed them into wall-sized poems). Overhead are crudely-lettered signs urging the visitors to roll the rolls, to tear off more word strips from stacks nailed to a center-post, and to staple them over the ones already there; in addition, they are exhorted to play the victrolas and listen to the records I had made, of talk, lectures, shouts, advertisements, ramblings of nonsense, etc.—either singly or all together.

In the smaller room, painted blue, illuminated by a single, weak light bulb and covered overhead by a plastic film, the atmosphere is very close and intimate (in contrast to the brash, open feeling of the first room). Many strips of cloth hang from the sheet of plastic filling the entire space; and above, through its filminess one can see crumpled newspapers scattered here and there on top. A visitor has to push through these hangings which brush his face like cobwebs. Clipped onto these hangings are many small pieces of paper with hand-written notes from, and to, different people. Near the doorway are a pencil, clips, and more paper for additional notes. Then, hanging all around the walls from strings are large colored chalks. (I and friends had written and drawn already on these walls to start things off and thereafter the visitors added whatever they wished.) Finally a record-player on the floor whispers when it is turned on.

This environment, therefore, is transformed every day.

# WHEN A BOOK IS NOT A BOOK
## Thomas A. Vogler

*Whether a urinal signed "R. Mutt" (1917) or an objet trouvé, any object can be elevated to the status of art. The artist defines the object in such a way that its future can lie only in the museum. Since Duchamp, the artist is author of a definition.*

—Marcel Broodthaers

*If that person declares it a book, it is a book! If they do not, it is not. Definitions are not ageless laws, but current understanding. They grow with usage through insight and error. We extend our knowledge, as well as our false assumptions, and both of these change the way we think. Our definitions evolve; they are not cut in stone.*

—Keith A. Smith

IN WHAT FOLLOWS I shall use the useful though somewhat cumbersome term, "book-object," to emphasize the fact that the works I discuss are not books, even though their whole being exists only in relation to the book. A linguist once explained to me the semiotic difference between a dog's nip and its bite. The nip, he said, can best be described as *not* a bite— you have to know what a bite is before you can know what a nip is. If the nature of these book-objects is determined to a degree by their existence as *not*-book, then to understand them we need to have some understanding of what a book is and what books are. The term *book* can have three distinct meanings: the text of a book, the object itself ("a book"), and the institutionalized mode of a composite technology ("the book"). Each of these deserves separate attention if we want to explore the relationship between book-objects and the world of books.

The word "text" is cognate with "textile" and "tissue," reminding us of its physical origins in the sense of a "woven thing." *Webster's* calls text "the principal part of a book," but the role of text in the art of book-objects is highly problematic. I'm tempted to say that book-objects always have texture, but never have text, in the sense that books have text and exist for the texts they have. This does not mean that a graphic play of writing cannot be a significant part of a book-object; but when writing occurs it occurs *as* writing, as graffito, rather than "text" being packaged for the sake of its semantic content. Mottoes, written pointers, desemanticized verbal signifiers, text-like graphic effects, are frequently found, but they exist more as graphic than semantic signs, not unlike the deconstruction of words into letters and the play with the concrete characteristics of language practiced by Isidore Isou and other artists under the banner of *Lettrisme*. Thus

Greely Myatt, *Redbook.*

Greely Myatt's *Redbook* is emphatically not a "read book." Instead of "word" we encounter "wood," in a mediumorphosis in which the book is changed into wood rather than wood into the book, reminding us through its embodied etymological traces that the material origins of the book were dictated by available materials. The term "boards," still used in bookbinding terminology, referred both to the material and the shape (sawed rectangle) of the early codex covers. The word "book" is derived from Germanic *boc* (plural *bec*) and probably refers to the beech tablets on which Germanic tribes carved and painted their records. The Latin *liber* meaning "book" comes from the word for the inner bark or rind of a tree, used as a writing surface. From it come the Romance languages' names for the book (e.g., *livre, libro*) and the English "leaf" (< Ger. *laufs*). French *feuillet* is from *foillet,* dim. of *foille* for "leaf." Folio is from Latin *folium* for "leaf." Codex is from *caudex,* "tree-trunk" (hence wooden tablet, book, manuscript).

I think we should resist the tendency to call anything with verbal text a book or artist's book or even a book-object, simply because it is a sculpture with text. After all, sculptures with text existed long before the era of the book, and one of the most ancient modes of publishing documents was to inscribe them in stone and set them up in the public space of a city. Text alone does not make a book, even though a book without text (including non-verbal text and illustrations) would not be a book in the conventional sense. This problematic relationship of non-text writing to the book-object grows out of an established sense of the book as a physical object that exists only, or primarily, to be the "container" of a therefore separable text. One of the reasons it is easy to think of the ordinary book as a container of, or mere supplement to its text, is the conventional separation of text production (by the author) from material book production (by editor, designer, printer, et al.). The "physical" production is separated from the "artistic" production, in a way that parallels the conceptual separation of the content of a text (which always points elsewhere to its meaning) and text regarded as material object. Thus the reigning editorial theory insists on separating the literary "work" from its material embodiment in any merely physical form, continuing the famous doctrine of Wellek and Warren on

"The Mode of Existence of a Literary Work of Art," that the "real poem" is separable from its textual embodiments. G. Thomas Tanselle summarizes this view of textual ontology in *A Rationale of Textual Criticism*: "If we destroy a painting or a piece of sculpture or a building, we destroy it completely...while the mere destruction of the copy of a book or even of all its copies may not touch the work of art at all...the writing on the paper is not the 'real' poem."

There is no place for an immaterial "work" of this sort in the tissue of an insistently physical book-object. Instead, it would seem that text is separating itself from the book in order to go somewhere else. The verbal text that is increasingly finding its home on an electronic screen, where it is repainted sixty times a second on phosphor, is not a cultural artifact of the same order as the text printed in ink on paper. The graphic form of its pixeled signifiers can be changed instantly to an enormous range of forms, freeing the literary text from any concept of a final form to be printed in books and shelved in libraries. Not only do texts no longer need books, texts are being produced in forms that cannot be represented adequately in any printed form whatsoever. There are other ways texts are increasingly becoming free from the codex book form which has been their home for so many centuries, and this liberation poses still another problem for an adequate definition of the "artist's book." Consider the case of Kenneth Goldsmith, whose work is regularly reviewed by Nancy Princenthal in her "Artist's Book Beat" in *Art on Paper* (formerly *Print Collector's Newsletter*). One of her recent columns was devoted to Goldsmith's *Fidget*, a multifaceted project involving a website, a performance, an installation, an introductory pamphlet, and a full-scale book, based on a movement-by-movement auto-narration—spoken into a mike worn around his neck—of his body's progress through the day of June 16, 1997. Princenthal gives a detailed account of the performance at the Whitney Museum of American Art in New York, where musician Theo Bleckmann sang the text from a balcony high up in the gallery's lobby space; as each phrase was intoned, Bleckmann dropped the sheet of paper on which it was printed to the floor below where the drifting sheets were collected by young boys dressed in Bloomsday-period costume, then transformed into a two-piece suit that was hoisted up to the balcony where Beckmann, who had meanwhile stripped himself, could put it on. While this was clearly a "textual event," its connection to the world of the book is an after-the-fact form of documentation, rather than the work itself. We might recall the work of Allan Kaprow from the 1960s, especially his large-scale work *Words* (1961) that expanded to fill the three-dimensional space of a gallery, forming a textual environment without any reference whatsoever to the codex book form. When one does confront the printed and bound version of a Goldsmith work, like his *No. 111 2.7.93–10.20.96,* (a 606 page text compiled from material on the web over a four-year period), the effect is to emphasize the futility and inadequacy of the "book" as antiquated "container" for a rampant textuality that includes ATM messages, email samples, advertising slogans, sound-text files, pop songs, dirty jokes, rhymes, and all the verbal litter strewn across the World Wide Web. The form of the book, as permanent container of information, is the wrong vehicle for such a proliferation of the ephemeral in chaotic and uncatalogable form.

I think it is a mistake to classify the growing number of textual works of this sort either as "artists' books" or as book-objects, and that we sorely need a new definition of the concept of text that has been separated from its immediate association with the specific form of the book—the *codex*—that some seventeen or eighteen centuries ago replaced another form, the *volumen* or scroll, in a similar period of technological transformation of textuality. I think of David Antin's delightful sky-writing poem, with a multitude of airplanes puffing smoke at computer-driven intervals to spell out the text across the sky, or of an artist group called Kunstwaffen, based in Pineville, Wyoming, that took the words from a paragraph in a pioneer woman's journal, painted them on the sides of seventy steers that were then encouraged to move around creating potentially endless combinations of the words. In another bovine text-work, Helen Lessick's 1993 project *Le Paysage Vivant,* we find an ephemeral landscape poem with one word shaved onto one side of one cow in a herd of twenty-two animals. The word *Poème* grew fainter over a three-month period and then disappeared.

Helen Lessick, *Poème.*

A similar Lessick project from 1993 was called *New Math*, where mathematical symbols were shaved onto both sides of a flock of sheep near Crest, France. The ram had a zero on his left side and a multiplication sign on his right; the ewe had infinity on her left and division on her right; and the lambs all had + on their left and − on their right sides. As the ram took the lead the ewe and lambs would follow, so if the ram headed left the equation would read zero to infinity; if he headed right, "multiply and divide."

Perhaps such works should be called "textual events" or "performance texts," and take their place alongside the work of artists like Mel Bochner, Jenny Holzer, Marcel Broodthaers, Jonathan Borofsky, Jasper Johns, Laurie Anderson, Robert Smithson, Barbara Kruger, Victor Burgin, Maria Porges, and the many others who are preoccupied with investigations of the nature and materiality of the linguistic signifier and whose involvement with language does not necessarily have anything to do with the book. Jenny Holzer, for example, in a work like *Truisms*, generates one-liner fortune-cookie aphorisms that are then turned into commercially manufactured signs and electronic signboards. Her work, like that of Laurie Anderson and others, is more involved with late twentieth-century media like electronic display boards and digital units than with the form of the codex book. Indeed, such electronic media challenge the inherent linearity of the codex sequential page format and its teleological predispositions. Helen Lessick's 1991 work *Metaphor* consists of the word "metaphor" made into a neon sign; it is both an example of and a comment on this shift of text, since "metaphor" literally means to transfer or carry over. Of course text does not have to be electrified to be free from the book form, as seen in works as varied as ancient inscribed stellae and modern grafitti. Deborah Garwood's text installations in her *Texts in the Public Domain* reproduce texts in different media (painted panels, textiles, plexiglass) for exhibition in public sites in New York. Jim Rosenberg, a San Francisco Bay artist, came up with a nice summer piece in the early 1970s, fondly recalled by the poet Ron Silliman as an interactive work in which words floated on plastic cards and the "reader" had to earn the text by swimming from one to another, transforming Barthes's "readerly" text to a "writerly" text with a vengeance. Paradoxically, now that texts are no longer prisoners of an original physical material existence, different in nature from the books in which we are used to finding them, textual artists are showing more graphic textual inventiveness than we have seen in any period since the invention of moveable type and the triumph of the printed text. Richard Kostelanetz, in his exploration of "the assumption that media other than the printed page are feasible for Literature" has used video and computer technologies to make works "whose only content is language" and that truly deserve to be called by his term for them: *Kinetic Writings*.

Whether exploiting the computer word-processor or not, writers of a wide range of persuasions are using all the technologies at their disposal to explore the materiality of language at the pre-book level of the signifier. The ancient past, with its richly varied materiality of writing (clay, wood, stone, fabric, etc.), and the theoretical arguments of critics like Jacques Derrida and Jacques Lacan, seem to merge with technologies of electronic *écriture* and reproduction to create new horizons for verbal texts. Given the conceptual and ideological bases for claiming that the literary work was never *in* the book anyway, it is perhaps more understandable that the status of text as strings of semantic verbal signifiers should be a problematic one for the artistic category of book-objects. By not having texts in any of the conventional senses of text, the book-object fails to be "a book" in one sense, while succeeding in others.

When we consider "book" in its meaning as the object we take from the shelf and hold in our hands, we are close to the material basis of one of the most common forms of book-object art: the treatment or alteration of a found book. But first we have to transform the object in our hands from being a book to being a mere thing. If I put quotation marks around the word "word" it suddenly changes from being a functioning semantic unit to being an example of such a unit, even though at the level of the letter its signifiers are the same. When I die, my body becomes a body, a corpse, passive material to be operated upon. All the varieties of "appropriation art," from Borges's Pierre Menard's *Quixote* to Kathy Acker's *Don Quixote*, play on the same possibility of transformation, and book-objects can play the same game.

One of the primary ways to make a book-object is by altering a single copy of a found volume, but here too we must distinguish the book-object category from the artist's book category. It is possible to treat or alter a book and still have it be *a book*, even if it is an "artist's book." Verbal artists in the spirit of Mallarmé have done it often, and it is a strong strain of modern literary art that has gone hand-in-hand with developments in the graphic and plastic arts. One of the best known of these "treated" or "altered" or "converted" versions of a "found" book is the now canonical Tom Phillips's *A Humument, a Treated Victorian Novel,* which "treats" the Victorian author W. H. Mallock's *A Human Document.* This is a unique work, even though Thames and Hudson printed thousands of "copies" of it; but it is still definitely a book rather than a book-object. For an example of the complete progression, from book to treated book to book-object, we can consider a work by Marcel Broodthaers. When he published a small volume of poems called *Pense-Bête* (Brussels, 1964), he was thoroughly self-identified as a poet, and the poems in that volume were typical of his work in the early 1960s. After a small number of copies were sold, Broodthaers began altering the remaining ones by covering over portions of the text with monochrome colored paper, erasing large chunks of text while leaving incomplete fragments still visible here and there, at times gluing these to the top of the page so they could be lifted for a glimpse of the hidden text. Thus began that suspension of reading and displacement of the literary, that would mark his future work as exemplified in his various versions of *Un coup de dés jamais n'abolira le hasard,* where he recreated Mallarmé's poem, replacing the blocks of text with horizontal black bands in direct proportion to the size and scale of the printed words in the poetic text, thereby translating its layout and irregular typography into purely visual terms, what Broodthaers called the poem's traces (*sillons*), with all lexical and semantic meaning left behind. In a later special edition of twelve copies the spatialized version of the poem's thirty-two page text was engraved into anodized aluminum. It was during this period that Broodthaers moved from being a poet, or producer of text for publication in book form, to being an artist of the altered book, transforming his oeuvre from multiple copies of identical works to a group of unique artist's books. The next step in his move towards objectification came in with his first exhibition as an artist (Brussels, Galerie Saint-Laurent, April 10–24, 1964), when he exhibited a sculpture made from the remaining copies of *Pense-Bête.* These copies, still partly bundled in their original wrapping paper, were embedded in a plaster-cast pedestal, which effectively transformed them from books to sculpture. Buzz Spector's *History of Europe* (1983), with its cascade of plaster over a found book, is an allusion to this critical moment in Broodthaers's work as well as a gesture towards the pours and spills of Robert Smithson, who wrote:

Vast moving faculties occur in this geological miasma, and they move in the most physical way. This movement seems motionless, yet it crushes the landscape of logic under glacial reveries. This slow flowage makes one conscious of the turbidity of thinking. Slump, debris slides, avanlanches all take place within the cracking limits of the brain.

The ontological step in such a transformation comes when the book is not merely altered or treated, while continuing to be a book, but is reduced or converted into the materiality of a medium for sculpture. This can be done with one book alone, or with any number of books. Books can be reduced to the materiality of a pseudo raw material, to be laminated and carved, as when Byron Clercx took pages from Janson's famous textbook *The History of Art* and laminated them together so he could carve a full-sized crutch out of the material. Inspiration for this transgressive act may have come from John Latham's famous 1965 treatment of a copy of Clement Greenberg's *Art and Culture.* Latham checked the book out from

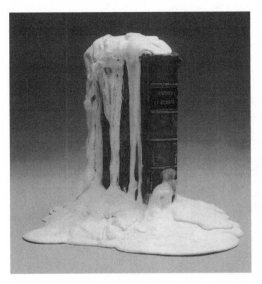

Buzz Spector, *History of Europe.*

St. Martin's School of Art, where he was teaching in London, and then divided it up among a group of friends who chewed the book's pages and spat them into a bottle of acid. The aggression in this procedure was intellectual as well as physical, challenging Greenberg's claims for the exalted purity and independence of the medium of painting, as pristine as the "white cube" of the museum designed to contain it. The result, titled "Still and Chew," was rejected by the library when he returned it, and Latham was fired from his position as lecturer. Another oral precursor was Dieter Roth, who made book sausages— like his *Literaturwurst* in 1961—from scraps of the *Daily Mirror* stuffed into natural sausage casings, mixed with water and gelatin or lard and spices. Closer to home was Scott McCarney's work called *Altered Janson,* where the artist cut the pages of the text so that they spiraled out from the spine of the book.

Books can be cut up and transformed in other ways, as in Harriet Bart's 1993 work *Real to Reel: Webster's Third,* where she cut and pasted the entire text of a Webster's dictionary into a continuous strip which was then wound onto a 35 mm film reel complete with case, or her *Nature of Art,* a cut and collaged text of Jerome Stolnitz's *Aesthetics and Philosophy of Art Criticism,* sitting cheerfully like an egg on a nest of shredded wood. Or they can be converted to modular units of construction, as in Gregory Shelnutt's *Book Chapel for Italo Calvino,* one of several works by him that take their form from the portable chapels and reliquaries popular in Italy in the Renaissance. The books are drilled and bound shut, cementing their transformation into chapels while obliterating their function as conveyors of printed information. Among the most impressive examples of the multiple conversion are Buzz Spector's *Library of Babel* and his *Toward a Theory of Universal Causality,* each requiring an enormous number of "found" volumes to achieve its architectural scale. The first is a free-standing triangle of thousands of neatly stacked books; the second is a stepped wedge composed of 6,500 used books arranged into 168 stacks, 28 books deep and four wide. At its taller end, which abuts a wall, the structure is as tall as a human being.

Buzz Spector, *Toward a Theory of Universal Causality.*

Walter Benjamin commented on the duality of the "destructive, cathartic aspect" of "the liquidation of the traditional value of the cultural heritage," a duality strongly present in the realization of most book-objects. The negative side is implicit in the French term for the treated book: *livre détourné,* or "deviant book," from the *"détournement"* proclaimed and practiced by the Situationists during their brief flourishing in Paris. According to Guy Debord:

Détournement, the reuse of preexisting artistic elements in a new ensemble, has been a constantly present tendency of the contemporary avant-garde....The two fundamental laws of détournement are the loss of importance of each detourned autonomous element...and at the same time the organization of another meaningful ensemble that confers on each element its new scope and effect....Détournement has a peculiar power which obviously stems from the double meaning, from the enrichment of most of the terms by the coexistence within them of their old senses and their new, immediate senses....Détournment is thus first of all a negation of the value of the previous organization of expression....But at the same time, the attempts to reuse the "detournable bloc" as material for other ensembles express the search for a vaster construction, a new genre of creation at a higher level.

It is often easier to see the negative side or "law" of détournement than the positive, and Renée Hubert provides a good example with her reactions expressed in her essay "Gertrude Stein, Cubism, and the Postmodern Book": "When shows at the Centre Pompidou as well as in various Parisian and New York galleries feature the *livre détourné,* artists expose burnt volumes, volumes stapled together, volumes twisted into unexpected shapes. The deviant book withholds the tentative security provided by reading; it excludes readers, turns them into outsiders. These castrated books function as threatening performers capable of reducing us to the state of impotent spectators." This largely European treatment of Mallarmé's spiritual instruments dates back to the notorious *Documenta 6* exhibition in Kassel, Germany, where Theodore Heinrich noted that "the common thread...is sadistic destruction...anything to make the book both unreadable and unhandsome."

But as Debord suggests, there can be a positive side functioning alongside the negative. To alter or convert a book is to take it from the circuit of mass-produced consumer commodities and to elevate it to the combined status of craft object and museum object. The converted book can be seen as removed from the fall into mass production, redeemed by its aura of uniqueness and conferring a comparable aura of individuality on its creator. By being unique, it privatizes the experience of its possessor and distinguishes her from mass forms of commodity consumption. It may be destroyed as a book along the way, but it is saved as an art object. The act of "personalizing" a book is also commonly performed by inscription, and the tradition of the "family Bible" has long combined the realm of fixed text with unique personal possession. The artist who seems to be violating one code, that says don't mistreat valuable property, is obeying another, that says the right to ownership derives from the mixture of one's own labor with something that is common to all.

Examples of book-object art may be based on the concept or image of the book, as well as on actual books, employed as a part of their medium. The two methods are not mutually exclusive, since often the way a found book is altered contains an implicit comment on the nature of the book as book, as when a found book is hollowed out to become a literal "container" of non-literary contents. To glue or nail a book open to a fixed place violates the function of sequence, which is universally recognized as the key structural feature of the codex book. But in a book where each page is blank the function of sequence is lost in a different way. Similarly, books that are locked shut, that do not suffer themselves to be opened by their possessor—whether their "contents" are known or not known—exaggerate one function of the book (containment) at the expense of all the others. Book-objects do not have to be made literally out of books in order to engage conceptually and materially with the many aspects of "the book" in its artifactual, socio-historical, psychological, and phenomenological modes of being.

Johanna Drucker has observed that "Even in its most conventional format, the book is a sculptural object. It has spatial dimensions, material qualities, and a complex structure." And Rosalind Krauss has pointed out that what holds the genre of "sculpture" together "is not defined in relation to a given medium—sculpture—but rather in relation to the logical operations on a set of cultural terms, for which any medium—photography, books, lines on walls, mirrors or sculpture itself—might be used." Thus the genre can be expanded to include everything from earthworks to "narrow corridors with TV monitors at the ends; large photographs documenting country hikes," so that the category has become "almost infinitely malleable," because it has its "own internal logic, its own set of rules, which, though they can be applied to a variety of situations, are not themselves open to very much change." In a similar way, the sub-genre of sculpture in which book-objects find their place is governed by an internal conceptual logic and implicit rules, by the highly structured institutionalized form and technology of the book.

Thus it is important for an understanding and appreciation of book-object art to resist the temptation to embrace too broad a definition of "the book," including anything with the semblance of a text (from tattooed bodies to the skies above), rather than approaching it in its historical and material specificity. Although a history of writing might have to include anything from the cave walls in Lascaux to ancient stellae, to a computer disk or sky-writing, our definition of the book must be narrowed to records in portable form, going back at least as far as the Sumerian clay tablets, and following the availability of materials and techniques of material manipulation. For the modern book, the dominant denotation (*Webster's*: "a collection of written, printed, or blank sheets fastened together along one edge") with all its connotations, is the codex, a Greco-Roman invention consisting of two or more wooden tablets coated with wax in which letters were scratched with a stylus. These were fastened together along one side with leather strips or rings to become "pages" (from the root *pag, pak*: to fasten or bind, first physically, then figuratively). Suggestive cognates and derivatives from the Latin (*pagus:* fixed, i.e., staked, boundary) include *pagan, paynim, peasant, paysage, pageant,* and *pagina* (prop for vines). From *pagina* came *propaginem,* shortened to English prop (to support, or prune), hence *propagate,* and *propaganda,* the gerundive form for "what should be propagated."

There is a theory of technological determinism, popularized in a rather crude and utopian form by Marshall McLuhan, which teaches that

many of our most cherished, most commonplace ideas and attitudes toward literature and literary production turn out to be the result of that particular form of information technology and technology of cultural memory that has provided the setting for them. This technology—that of the printed book and its close relations, which include the typed or printed page—engenders certain notions of authorial property, authorial uniqueness, and a physically isolated text.

When "the book" does engender such "notions," it does so not at the level of the idea, but at the level of *techne* and praxis. A book is not an idea; it is a structural mechanism with important functions. Its mechanism of turn-able pages defines a sequence of spaces, each of which must be perceived at a different moment. A book is also a sequence of moments designed to produce a unified experience out of multiple sheets by binding them in a determined order. Thus our physical engagement with the book pre-enacts the structuring of subjectivity for which the book has long been a primary cultural agency. Unlike alteration or treatment, which operate on individ-ual books as physical objects, book-objects can be "troped" books, figura-tive constructs where "the book" as generic cultural artifact is the subject for representation, imitation, or violation.

Other important structural features of the book which offer them-selves for consideration include *scale,* one of the features most readily troped by book-objects. The book is embodied in the form of an intimate portable object, so that extremes of sheer size (whether large or small) can change its nature, by changing the possibilities of our physical relationship with it and its mechanisms (opening, closing, ordered sequencing, amount of text, etc.). The size of "the book" is like the size of an easel painting, the results of a cultural algorithm that includes an enormous range of factors. The image of the self-contained, individually authored text, whose author can be held accountable to a reading public, is integral to our cherished lib-eral conception of cultural authority, and size or scale is an implicit part of the construct. In a similar way, what Philip Fisher calls "the free-standing work of art" must be of a middle size in order to embody images of the com-pleteness, simplicity and stability of the ideal of a "self." Its size and pro-duction costs must be congruent with private ownership, and be available along with a space for individual privacy (with its complementary silence) to allow the proper acts of consumption.

As already pointed out, the conventional modes of book production reinforce our notion of the book as a *container* of text separable from its physical vehicular form. This is not so much a part of the physical require-ments of book production as it is of the culturally valorized separation of mental from physical labor. It is hard to imagine any book-object that will not engage in some significant way with the concept of contents and con-tainer. We can say the same thing about the *pages* of the book. Inevitably, as a structural system designed to hold its pages, a book *is* its pages. A book without any pages is almost as hard to imagine as that single volume de-scribed in Borges's *The Library of Babel,* "of ordinary format, printed in nine or ten type body, and consisting of an infinite number of infinitely thin pages." It is the binding that makes sheets into pages and that main-tains the predetermined order of viewing the structured sequence of spaces that constitute the book.

Finally, I would point to *reproducibility* as another essential concept associated with the book, so much so that the book can serve as exemplar of mass produced consumer commodities. William M. Ivins Jr. emphasizes the point in his *Prints and Visual Communication*: "A book, so far as it contains a text, is a container of exactly repeatable word symbols arranged in an exactly repeatable order." Benedict Anderson, in *Imagined Communities: Reflections on the Origin and Spread of Nationalism,* has demonstrated how significant the uniformity of book production is in constituting the modern sense of belonging to a nation state, an "imagined community" extrapolated from a knowledge that millions of others are just like us, reading the same book and sharing the same values. It is tempting to say that the uniqueness of the book-object is a given, the most inevitable way to trope on the book's function of delivering identical content in multiple copies. But does the book-object have to be unique? Walter Benjamin, in *The Work of Art in the Age of Mechanical Reproduction,* claims that "In principle a work of art has always been reproducible. Man-made artifacts could always be imitated by men." How significant is the difference, whether a work is in principle reproducible or whether it has in fact been reproduced? Buzz Spector uses "unique book" interchangeably with "book-object," as two names for the same "genre of artwork that refers to the forms, relations, and configurations of the book." But his own work frequently begs the question of "uniqueness." How is a wedge of 6,500 books always the same work, even when it changes completely every time it is taken apart and reassembled in a different place? If it is the idea or concept that makes it the same, then why can't the physical form of that idea be copied by someone with other books? My point here is not that Spector's work is marred by self-contradiction, but that it is the engagement with concepts that makes the art of book-objects a conceptual as well as aesthetic practice.

Although Clive Phillpot casually dismisses the category we are exploring here as "only one step away from mute sculptural book objects that at best simply provoke reflections on the history and role of the book as a cultural phenomenon," it is possible to see the practice in a more positive light as one that historicizes many of our most commonplace assumptions and forces them to descend from the ethereality of abstraction and appear as corollaries to a particular technology rooted in specific times and places. Our own moment in this history is still a conflicted one, where the dominant theorizers of textual ontology like G. Thomas Tanselle still maintain that the physical form of the book is irrelevant to its contents, that "literary works...cannot exist in physical form," and "that language is an intangible medium and that words on paper are therefore not verbal works themselves but only guides to the reconstitution of such works." With a few notable exceptions, most literary critics would seem still to agree with Georges

Poulet's experience of the phenomenological disappearance of the book at the moment we engage the text, their reading experience conforming to the ideals of transparency towards which the modern book strives:

Such is the initial phenomenon produced whenever I take up a book, and begin to read it.... Where is the book that I held in my hands? It is still there, and at the same time it is there no longer, it is nowhere. That object wholly object, that thing made of paper, as there are things made of metal or porcelain, that object is no more, or at least it is as if it no longer existed, as long as I read the book. For the book is no longer a material reality. It has become a series of words, of images, of ideas which in their turn begin to exist.

Meanwhile many writers are still exploring a textual aesthetic very much involved with the idea of "the book," even as that idea is challenged by the new electronic media of our time with the claim to transcend its inherent linearity and its sequential page format and its ideals of a final form. Hypertext, we are advised daily, is the new way to write, to create linkages and short circuits within a text, an endless number of tracks or arrangements rather than the single track of the ordinary book. And hypertext is "interactive," the reader participating in creating the structure of what is read.

It may well be that the book is most powerful precisely when it is most invisible, and that the growing theoretical, historical, and practical emphasis on the materiality of the verbal signifier and its vehicular codex is a sign of healthy resistance to the continued hegemony of "the book." Or perhaps *The Coming of the Book* (Lucien Febvre and Henri-Jean Martin) has become a significant discipline of study in our time precisely because we are experiencing "The End of Books" (Raymond Kurzweil). Although print has been the basis of the organization and presentation of knowledge for the past five centuries, the vast majority of printed books in modern industrial societies bear no cultural burden at all, or only that cultural burden born by parts catalogues, tide tables, airline schedules, and census reports. It is obvious that our capacity to deal with all the "information" contemporary culture requires is approaching a crisis, when Travelers Insurance Company produces in six months enough printed output to fill the Bibliothèque de France, and the printed documentation that accompanies the delivery of a Boeing 747 weighs 350 tons (still a little less than the plane itself!). And how much longer can we deal with the housing and custodial care of billions of codex books that no one may ever have the time or inclination to read?

Are the bold treaters of books avant-garde lions, going for the jugular of Kulture, or vultures hovering over the corpse of "the book?" Or are they perhaps like nostalgic Romantic versions of the "cargo cult" natives in South America, whose ancestors claimed to have seen real creatures come down from the sky with food and treasures, but who themselves can only make little effigies of planes and landing strips in the vain hope that the historical moment will return. This is not a frivolous analogy if, as Roger Chartier claims in "Libraries Without Walls," "the end of the *codex* will signify the loss of acts and representations indissolubly linked to the book as we now know it." The end of the twentieth century is witnessing an international spate of monumental library building, from San Francisco to London to Paris, that seems to have an increasingly ominous fin de siècle air. Blake was not the first to suggest that libraries are where the bodies of dead books are preserved, and these late twentieth-century edifices may well be tome tombs. Dominique Perrault's design for the colossal mausoleum of the new Bibliothèque de France suggests as much, and its four whimsical towers, shaped like open codex books (turned inwards), make it a contender for the world's largest work of book-object art. Soon no doubt we will have resource centers physically free from such book mausoleums, in the form of multi-media libraries called médiathèques, rising alongside the traditional bibliothèques like a spirit from a corpse.

In the meantime, we are left with a number of enigmatic signs in the form of book-objects, and I'd like to end with brief comments on three of the many book artists who represent some of the things I've been describing. Buzz Spector is one of the most interesting and inventive of those working with the book as raw material. Spector has been accused of destroying sacred objects with some of his works, but he counters this charge with the claim that he *saves* the books he uses from pulping or garage sales.

The glass tongue of Spector's work called *Silence: A Synopsis* might suggest the textual ideal of the "crystal goblet" of a transparent typography, or

Buzz Spector, *Silence: A Synoposis*.

a "talking book" [cf. the Chinese ideogram for Book: *shu,* a mouth with a hand holding a brush—"talking brush"]. But the book here seems "blank," with nothing left to say. Is its silence that of a "still unravished bride of quietness" (Spector has written seductively, in "The Fetishism of the Book

Object," about how "the topography of an open book is explicit in its erotic associations: sumptuous twin paper curves that meet in a recessed seam"), or has its text gone elsewhere, perhaps to the polygraphically perverse textual nirvana of the pixeled screen? In any case we are left with a pleasing object, as worthy of our attention as John Cage's few minutes of silence that remind us that music too is a kind of noise. The work is in fact an homage to Cage in the form of an altered copy of *Silence,* in the spirit of what Walter Benjamin, in *One-Way Street,* calls "the archaic stillness of the book." Among Spector's most impressive constructions are his book installations, especially when they reverse the usual proportional relationship of scale with the human body, where the conventional relationship is the hand-held book. Another impressive work is a 1992 piece called "Freeze Freud." It is composed of a large-scale industrial freezer that contains all the volumes of the complete Freud. The books are arranged in numerical order, each book frozen into its own niche, with the lettering on the spine clearly legible, the whole illuminated by the cold-blue neon light of the freezer.

Byron Clercx offers a completely different approach. He got his start when he cut all of his books into two-inch squares, reducing an entire library to what he called "bite-size chunks," observing that the books were "infinitely more useful to me in small pieces than they were as whole texts." This act gave him the sense of owning a history of which he didn't feel a part, and transforming them into a series of works made that sense even stronger. Clercx is perhaps best known for his gallery installations of *Power/Tools,* that at first look like those displays of old-fashioned tools hung up for show after a lifetime of use. Clercx's is a complementary aesthetics of labor and of craft objects that presumably bear the stamp (either literally or in the traces of their "hand-made" origin) of a maker who took pride in being responsible for their creation. Without a unique maker, the industrially produced commodity has only an anonymous identity shared with innumerable identical counterparts, unless it is claimed *in advance* as a "readymade" by Duchamp, or as the parody of a readymade by Hans Haacke. Clercx does not labor *with* the tools he exhibits, he labors *on* them, with a complex process of aggregating and laminating pages from books that are then painstakingly carved by hand. But in both cases the tool is a sign of labor and a comment on the status of the "work of art." Mallarmé identified the book as an "instrument," but Heidegger, in his "Origin of the Work of Art," pushed the relationship further with his claim that

equipment displays an affinity with the art work insofar as it is something produced by the human hand....As a rule it is the use-objects around us that are the nearest and authentic things. Thus the piece of equipment is half thing, because characterized by thingness, and yet it is something more; at the same time it is half art work and yet something less, because lacking the self-sufficiency of the art work. Equipment has a peculiar position intermediate between thing and work, assuming that such a calculated ordering of them is permissible.

Clercx's works overcome this identity problem by combining the identity of equipment and art work with its "self-sufficiency," invoking the old-fashioned work ethic that sees both as Heidegger's "something produced by the human hand."

One of my favorite Clercx pieces is *Purification* (1993), a book-object made from soap, with text on a towel taken from Ponge's prose-poem *Le Savon,* "soap." Those familiar with the Ponge work can appreciate the literalness of Clercx's work, which is in effect a concrete version of the poem:

There is much to say about soap. Precisely everything that it tells about itself until the complete disappearance, the exhaustion of the subject. This is precisely the object suited to me.

\*

Soap has much to say. May it say it with volubility, enthusiasm. When it has finished saying it, it no longer is.

Byron Clercx, *Purification.*

The same fascination with works that are consumed through use led him to carve book-objects out of salt, then to mount them on lecterns to be fed to livestock. With these Salt Lake Salt-Licks we are back in the pasture for more *paysage vivant!* Clercx has also used laminated books to make a chair, called *Reading Context,* and numerous tools, including a 1992 one called *Untitled (Power Tool),* made from Susan Sontag's *Illness as Metaphor* and *AIDS and its Metaphors.* Here Clercx alludes to Nietzsche (doing philosophy "with a hammer") while making the point that language in Sontag's text and the hammer share a common identity as tools used for construction and destruction.

This was followed by a full-scale perfectly detailed baseball bat called *Big Stick,* made entirely from the works of Sigmund Freud, complete with its own black vinyl case lined

Byron Clercx, *Untitled (Power Tool).*

with red velvet. Clercx returned recently to the hammer form, this time a blacksmith's hammer, for a work titled *Forgery*. Made entirely from Kathy Acker's work, Clercx claims that "it is a reference to the fact that Acker is forging voyeurism into a new literary style.... She writes about violence, incest, sexual attack...[yet] her writing itself becomes a kind of violent assault of the reader." The hammer is packed in an elegant black case trimmed with stainless steel studs; opened up it becomes a red velvet-lined heart with the hammer nestled inside.

My final example is Patrick Luber, an artist who delights in taking those familiar everyday objects that are defined for us by their form and function, and then de-utilitizing them. "How objects make meaning, and the tension between the literal and figurative, is something that has always

Patrick Luber, *Pictorial Reference*.

intrigued me," Luber has said. Thus he takes a form like the book, or the bed, and constructs a full-scale equivalent structure. Part of the effect of Luber's works is the quality of craftsmanship that goes into their production, a combination of intricate carpentry and rich texturing that rivals the craft of fine book printing. But his objects exist in a world where ordinary semiotics and expectations go awry, like a Jacques Tati comedy routine where the human body and language and the physical world become a playful terra incognita. An unnamed work from 1993 joins the form of the book with that of the lock, as two very large keys protrude from the front and back of the book-form. Perhaps they represent the author and the reader, as both try to occupy the same keyhole in the hopes of unlocking meaningful dialogue; or does the work suggest the opposite, how meaningful intercommunication is always barred? Luber has said, "My art is not just about discovering new ways to construct visual meaning, but about amusing the viewer. In the final analysis," he concludes, "the artist is as much a comedian as anything else." Luber's play can however be quite serious, and his work seldom falls into that realm of one-liners where a small blip of recognition is the only reward.

In spite of Buzz Spector's claim for an "elegiac sensibility" in the "inherent futility of such singular transformations," there is much potential for humor and pleasure in the materialization of Mallarmé's "spiritual instruments." The experiential reality is quite different from that claimed by the textual idealist and theoretician G. Thomas Tanselle, who writes that "the human drama enshrined in all artifacts" must be a tragedy, because "what every artifact displays is the residue of an unequal contest: the effort of a human being to transcend the human, an effort constantly thwarted by physical realities." Those who accept and enjoy the physical realities of the material book-object might well prefer to give the final word to Jean Arp, who wrote:

concrete art aims to transform the world. it aims to make existence more bearable. it aims to save man from the most dangerous folly: vanity. it aims to simplify man's life. it aims to identify him with nature. reason uproots man and causes him to lead a tragic existence. concrete art is an elemental, natural, healthy art, which causes the stars of peace, love and poetry to grow in the head and the heart. where concrete art enters, melancholy departs, dragging with it its gray suitcase full of black sighs.

# AFTERWORD TO *LITTLE SPARTA*
## Alec Finlay

LITTLE SPARTA IS a composition: one made [by Ian Hamilton Finlay] over three decades from earth, water and sky, from plants and trees, shadows and light; from inscriptions, statues and temples. Growing up there I learnt that poems were not just found in books. A poem can also be an inscribed stone or plaque, placed in the landscape.

I was once asked to describe my favourite place in the garden, and instead of choosing a poem, I wrote about the small heathery plateau above the lochan, looking westwards towards the evening skyline where I would watch the silhouetted bog-cotton move ceaselessly and gently in the breeze. Above the horizon, peewits wheel and turn, as the sky passes from pearl, through a ray of green, to the celestial blue of the night sky.

Robin Gillanders's portrait of Little Sparta reminds me of this. To be drawn to such poetic moments is not necessarily a rejection of the ideas and historical associations the garden contains. Little Sparta is a fiercely independent territory, in thought and deed, and makes claims upon history and tradition. Here though, in these photographs, we can enjoy the beauty of the landscape without commentary; enjoy its ineffable moods, which are as much a part of the garden as its rhetoric, and enjoy a poetry which exists long after inscriptions disappear into the evening's shadows.

Little Sparta is a poet's garden, a composed landscape. However, the visitor's experience does not depend on understanding each allusion. The garden is not a crossword puzzle of cultural references to be worried away at and ticked off one by one, nor is it a fixed sequence of views and vistas. It is a dialogue in which feelings and ideas coexist.

For the photographer the composed landscape can present a problem. If the poet is the undisputed arbiter of this landscape is the meaning of each part fixed, literally and metaphorically, in stone? Does the photographer simply retrace a succession of fixed coordinates, translating poetic words into poetic images? The answer to this is no. For the photographer, as for the visitor, their experience will always transcend any fixed or programmatic meaning.

Gillanders' portrayal was composed over a number of years and different seasons, during which he familiarised himself with the garden's topography and Finlay's poetry and thought. As he came to know the place, he describes a growing spiritual and imaginative response, and, with this, a sense of permission to explore the landscape on his own terms. This sense of possibilities opening before him echoes Finlay's detached sentence on gardening: *A garden is not an object but a process.*

Little Sparta is both a place and a territory; a poetic garden, a place for anyone to wander with a sense of delight; a 'Raspberry Republic' with its own ideology, its own stamps, flag, calendar and wars. The garden's remarkableness lies in the ideas it inscribes and the different moods that inhabit it. That said, the rhetoric of Little Sparta falls rather too easily into a familiar dichotomy between culture and nature. Finlay's assertion that our understanding of nature is mediated by culture, implicitly seems to favour the interpretations of the commentator, who explicates the garden's historical associations, above those of the photographer, whose art naturally inclines towards subjective sensations. However, photography has an important and long standing role in Finlay's work, and provides useful evidence of a more complex vision than this rhetorical point of view might at first suggest.

Despite the militancy of his argument with contemporary culture, Finlay is concerned with shared experiences, and the terms in which we describe these. When he attacks secularism, because it allows for only one level of experience, he is not simply arguing against an idea, he is creating a redoubt in which our experience of the landscape, or of art, is acknowledged to have a spiritual dimension. The *Temple of Apollo* which sits at the heart of the garden speaks to this experience.

Behind Finlay's didacticism there is recognition of the more mysterious workings of the Muses. For instance, in his explanation of the relationship between a garden poem and its environment, the *'hierarchies of the word'* are subsumed within the ineffable experience of sense of place:

*The garden proceeded as a series of what I call little 'areas'. Usually each area gets a small artefact, which reigns like a kind of presiding deity or spirit of place. My understanding is that the work is the whole composition—the artefact in its context. The work is not an isolated object, but an object with flowers, plants, trees, water and so on.*

Finlay acknowledges a hierarchy here. The artefact or poem reveals a spiritual level of experience, summoning to mind a sense of place, and although this can be analysed in terms of its intellectual and philosophical dimensions, the experience itself is a synthesis, a weaving together of reflection and feeling, creating what Unamuno calls a 'succession of coordinated states of consciousness.'

Finlay's collaborations with photographers tend to emphasise the composed nature of the landscape: a landscape which is arranged by the poet, informed by the classical tradition, and now framed by the camera. However, photography offers something more than a direct record of phenomenal reality. The photograph is, as Stephen Bann suggests, a 'necessary element in the realisation of the work,' one which secures the connection between the garden and the many historical reference points it touches upon.

Finlay's collaborative strategies, including his many photographic projects, aspire to distance the work of art from subjectivity. He argues for the representative or commonly held characteristics of glade, grove and vale; however this rhetoric does not elide the mystery, the poetry of the moment, which is conveyed in each photograph, and each garden poem.

The tension between fixed ideas and changing moods, culture and nature, the generic and the momentary, is at the heart of Finlay's art. There is a fragile equilibrium in his work, between the epic, the static fundamental principles, which culminate in his Jacobinism, and the lyrical, suggested by the delicate beauty of the wildflower, an emblem of the French Revolution, which lies hidden in the moorland grasses, amongst the bog-cotton and heather.

Stone is silent, yet at Little Sparta it speaks, calling our attention to the song of the wind in the trees, to a passing shadow, or to two carved lovers' names reflected on water. The garden and the lyrical poetry it contains celebrate fleeting experiences, isolated moments of beauty and loss. In Robin Gillanders's photographs our attention is drawn to these passing moments, and to the *genius loci,* which is the essence of Finlay's garden poetry.

We begin this book facing the single FRAGILE stone, at the furthest edge of the garden, the bare moorland stretching beyond, and close with the monumental head of Apollo, a glinting secret glimpsed amongst the silver barked trees. Our sojourn in the garden is dear, but brief. A poem written on stone or carved in wood may, despite its physical presence, be emblematic of the fragility and beauty of each passing moment, gifting us a memory to be carried away, a guerdon to comfort us in our exile.

*—For Zoë.*

*from* LITTLE SPARTA

Texts by Ian Hamilton Finlay

Photographs by Robin Gillanders

# UP TO AND INCLUDING HER LIMITS
## Carolee Schneemann

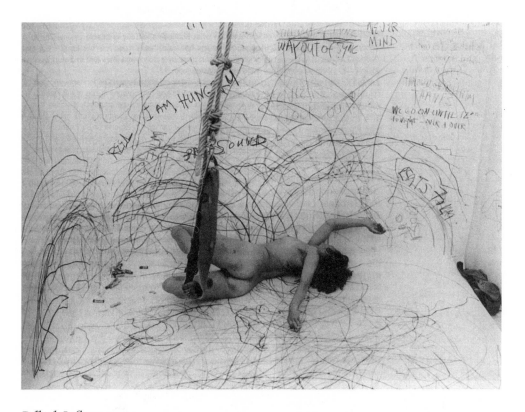

*Pollock Influence*

MY DRIVE HAD BEEN TO occupy a place of simultaneities to bring forward sensory evidence of this multiplicity....as a landscape painter to occupy the visual changing field of forms, to capture wind, light, temperature on my body as I sat in fields, marshes, the edge of frozen ponds warming my paints with candles stuck in the snow....the paintings of my late teens early twenties were always "failures" of momentum....I would begin to add motorized elements and increase the painting surface to collage and three dimensions....this was the obvious implication of Abstract Expressionism....in order to perceive the works of Pollock, de Kooning, perception became muscular—the entire body was active in the eye....I considered my early work with "performance" to be a visual arena, an exploded canvas....

"Up To and Including Her Limits" is the direct descendant of Pollock's physicalized painting process....his extended reach, the arm in fluid motion....my entire body becomes the agency of stroke, trace, vestige of the body's action, its mark in space....

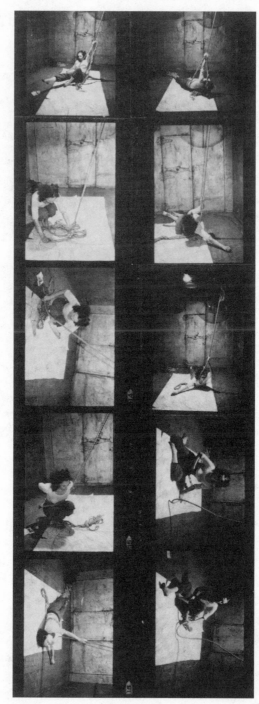

*Trackings*

December 1973 Avant Garde Festival Grand Central Station NY
April 11, 1974 University Art Museum Berkeley California (Performance-Installation)
June 18, 1974 Arts Meeting Place, London (Performance–Installation)
June 19, 1974 London Filmmakers Cooperative
December 1, 1974 Artists Space NY
December 12–13, 1974 Anthology Film Archive NY
February 13–14, 1976 The Kitchen NY (Performance–Installation)
June 10, 1976 Studiogalerie Berlin (Installation June 10–25)
June 13–20, 1976 Basel Art Fair (Installation)

*Components of UTAIHL at Artists Space, The Kitchen, Studiogalerie.*

1) Walls at right angles covered with six feet of white paper; the rope attached to steel fittings in ceiling, 3½ feet between walls.
2) Continuous double screen projection (vertical) Super 8 "Kitch's Last Meal" (eight reels 1973–76) adjacent to performance area.
3) Sound tapes with film.
4) Three to six video monitors grouped together, showing tapes of the previous rope work and the current actions. (Tapes of each performance/installation are cumulative and finally replace the live action.)
5) A reading area, away from the rope and film projection; writings related to the work.
6) Continuous relay of slides relating to the work—image area no larger than 9" x 12".
7) Walls between the reading area and installation/performance with texts describing the components. (The components are adapted to each space; doors and windows are utilized as active environmental elements.)

# INTERPRETING THE "KUNSTKAMMER"
## Harriett Watts interviewing Barbara Fahrner

*H.W.* How did you come on the idea of a "Kunstkammer" or, as you've called it, the "Kunstkammer" project?

*B.F.* It all began with my love for collecting and my longing for a small, provincial museum, known here as a "Heimatmuseum"—the "Heimatmuseum" as a place where daily life is collected and exhibited, not just works of art but also examples of what the local inhabitants have produced—both the scientists and the crazy inventors of the region. The "Heimatmuseum" as a symbol of life in a given locality—that has always fascinated me, in such museums I feel very much at home. That's how I'd like my books to be, I thought to myself, in principle also collections, collections of thoughts, of memories. But how I actually came on the idea of a "Kunstkammer"—that came about in Munich sometime ago. I happened on a catalogue of "Kunstkammer" from the Renaissance. As I was reading it, it became clear to me that these Renaissance collectors had not assembled their material in a haphazard manner but had proceeded according to definite criteria with the intention of creating a microcosm in which the macrocosm is contained. The idea of micro- and macrocosm has always fascinated me, and the book as metaphor for the world is another basic theme in my work. So here I had found a way of bringing both together; I would construct a "Kunstkammer," my very own "Heimatmuseum," in the form of books.

*H.W.* How did you translate the early models into your own work?

*B.F.* My interest was not so much in any "Kunstkammer" already in existence or in what had been exhibited there; what interested me more was the concept of the macrocosm within a microcosm and the idea of the book as symbol for the world. I looked into how the Renaissance princes had set up their collections and it was clear to me that my aim was not actually to collect curious or exotic things in order to construct a "Kunstkammer." I wanted to write about objects rather than collecting them and build up a "Kunstkammer" out of books. I decided, nevertheless, to retain the hierarchy of seven categories that the Renaissance collectors had observed in organizing their "Kunstkammers" and to assemble my books accordingly.

*H.W.* Which seven categories?

*B.F.* Those explained by Giulio Camillo in his "Idea del teatro," published 1550 in Florence. The first is the order of the planets, which includes astronomy and astrology. This order I interpreted as religion. The second order is the simple elements; the third, the composite elements; the fourth, man's own creations; the fifth, the unity of body and soul; the sixth, human activities in nature; the seventh, the arts. And with these seven categories I had my basic structure.

*H.W.* The early "Kunstkammer" often exhibited curiosities, rare items collected from all possible sources. The things that found their way into your "Kunstkammer" via the books—did you also choose them as curiosities?

*B.F.* My intention was not so much to gather curiosities that relate to the themes of the "Kunstkammer" as to find subject matter that had not been discussed frequently and to incorporate it into the individual orders. Take the second order, for example, the simple elements: I didn't want the themes that everyone would expect, so I chose a Japanese story for one of the first books, the biography of a grinding bowl, a strange and perhaps somewhat aberrant story of an ordinary object—here a clay bowl and what it experiences in the course of its life. The story is told as if the bowl had human emotions and reactions. It arrives in a well-heeled household where it lives the good life, makes a career for itself, so to speak, before its decline sets in. It becomes cracked and finally ends up on a manure heap. This life story is an example of the simple elements.

*H.W.* Are all your simple elements as humble as this one?

*B.F.* Not necessarily. I was trying to achieve the greatest variety possible in the "Kunstkammer." Another book, also in the category of simple elements, consists of the famous Einstein relativity formula: $E = MC^2$. Then there is a book on energy free particles and another one on stones. Here I chose rocks to which I have some sort of relationship. In the third order, the composite elements, I wrote about frogs, about herbs—botany is one of my favorite themes—about mushrooms. For the same order, however, I also produced a long, descriptive book on the process of paper-making. What I tried to do was to include only those things which have some relation to me, that is to say, to my work.

*H.W.* In other words, a "Heimatmuseum" in which you feel totally at home. How do human beings enter this museum, people with the things they've produced?

*B.F.* For the theme of man and his creations I included for example a "Kunstkammer" notebook. When I started work on the "Kunstkammer" project, I was convinced that the idea had arisen spontaneously from my encounter with the catalogue. I established my categories and a timetable in which I gave myself exactly one year—from the first of November to November of the next year—to complete the entire project. My personal ambition was to prove to myself how far I could go, to find my limits, purely in the sense of work. Within this set span of time I was determined to complete 84 books and 16 illustrated charts. While working on my notes, I wanted to doublecheck something from earlier and began going through old notebooks. There I stumbled upon long-forgotten entries made during an entire month to do with a "Heimatmuseum." And that was quite an experience for me to realize that I had already had this idea in my head, worked it out in considerable detail months before. I was intrigued by my discovery and I took over the notes in their entirety for the "Kunstkammer," incorporated them as the "Kunstkammer" notebook. I'll find it for you later—it contains many ideas related to my work that I had written down long before they made themselves manifest in what I was doing. It's not the first time that this has happened to me: I'm convinced that I have come up with a new idea, but then it isn't the case at all. The idea has actually been incubating, sometimes for years in advance. And that I consider to be very human, it belongs in the category: "the creations of man."

*H.W.* How did you arrive at your prescribed number of books—84?

*B.F.* I have my own private number magic: first with the number 3 and then with the 4. I simply played with the 3 and the 4, multiplied them and then added them. $4 \times 4$ is 16, the number of the illustrated charts; $3 \times 4$ is 12, $3 + 4$ is 7 (7 is already an important number) and if you multiply 7 by 12 (taking into account the 12 months in one year) the result is 84. So the numbers were set arbitrarily: $7 \times 12 = 84$ books; $4 \times 4 = 16$ charts.

*H.W.* Your model Camillo, incidentally, also provided the portals to the seven orders in his theater with illustrated panels. What role do your charts play in the "Kunstkammer"?

*B.F.* They're there to liven up the entire installation. The general idea behind the "Kunstkammer" project needed to be explained visually. I not only made books, which are to be looked at individually but also the charts—an introductory panel to provide a brief explanation of the entire project and then one or two panels for each of the seven orders. This way visitors can read an explanation on the wall as well as the texts on the page. The books, of course, can only be opened up one page at a time and are locked in the showcases where one can't see that much.

*H.W.* Can one sense a hierarchy in your actual presentation of the books, or do the books all co-exist together at the same level in your "Kunstkammer?"

*B.F.* No—there is a hierarchy that I'm convinced of. In principle I converted the first order, the planets, into the order of the gods. This was the order in which I addressed the question of religion. I wasn't interested in

Christianity or the other major world religions; my aim was to find material about as many female deities as possible. For the first chart, I collected
all the names of goddesses from ancient cultures that I could find in the
time I had allowed myself. The first book, and this is no accident, is a book
about Maya, the theme of Maya as the veil of the world. This book stands
for my own conviction that nothing is actually real, that all objects, all appearances are in effect a lie. But back to your question; after the first division the others follow in appropriate order. When one reaches the category
"the activities of man in nature," one sees that I have tried to address contemporary issues: the catastrophic relation of man to his environment. This
chart demonstrates the destructive activities of man in nature. Then I also
included historical themes in this category, and there my special interest
was the middle ages. I worked extensively on the persecution of witches as
an example of the suppression of women. I conducted research on women
artists in the middle ages, what possibilities they had, where they were allowed to work—in the convents and, in Holland, in the Beguine courts,
where women could withdraw from bourgeois life and not be forced into
marriage. There they could pursue their own studies, and one can find
women who were very good painters, draftsmen, actually all the visual
arts were being practiced there. These are all subjects that I included in the
category of human activities in nature. For me, of course, the crown of all
the orders is my final category, the arts. There I included themes that occurred to me spontaneously, works of literature to which I have a special
relationship; for example, I produced books with texts by E.T.A. Hoffmann
and Edgar Allan Poe. Then I made a book about the marionette theater, the
significance of the puppet theater in China. Sometimes I simply took off
on a theme that occurred to me, made free art, so to speak. But how well
that comes across in the exhibition is not for me to say.

*H.W.* When you choose the texts, do you incorporate them as fragments,
take citations from them, or do you include complete poems or entire
prose pieces in your books?

*B.F.* It varies a great deal, but I do have an aversion to short citations whenever my intention is not specifically that of producing a collage, which is in
effect a collection of different citations played off against one another to produce a new meaning. I took a number of quite long discursive stories and essays—for that reason some of the books are so thick. For example I included
a complete essay by Alexander von Humboldt. Thoroughness matters to me
a great deal; it is also the idea behind the "Kunstkammer." It was not meant
to be just a collection of random allusions or citations; I conceived of it as a
place where the visitor can inform himself in depth concerning the subjects
I have chosen. And in this regard, I made a real effort to be thorough.

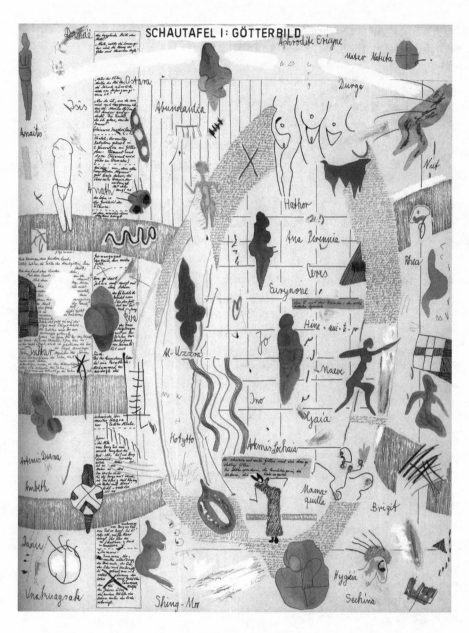

Schautafel I: *Götterbild.*

*H.W.* How did you manage it all in the span of one year?

*B.F.* I was working all the time, working like a maniac, actually. Every morning I read for two hours and take notes on themes that interest me at the moment. Those notes were at my disposition, so that much of the preparation had already been done. Actually, it was possible to complete the "Kunstkammer" in so short a time because the work was so varied. After I'd sat at home drawing, for example, until I was tired or had run out of ideas, I could get up and go to the library and read, or go to a bookstore and leaf through books related to my themes. And whenever I no longer felt like reading, I could return to drawing or to painting, so that there was always variety and a change of pace. That made it possible for me to work much longer than usual every day.

*H.W.* Did you research your visual material as well, for example, what you took from antiquity?

*B.F.* A bit, but not all that much. Actually, I was afraid to research things all that much because the one thing I don't want to be with my books is an illustrator. I don't want to produce drawings or water colors to illustrate what I am thinking. A unity must be achieved in a book, but it has to consist of two components wholly independent of one another. What I am attempting to do—it's hard to describe, I usually have to resort to musical examples to explain the process—is to compose as if for a canon, with two or three voices: one voice is the text; another, the image; a third, the rhythm of the pages in the book. The number of pages and the format always play a major role in my books, they are almost as important to me as the text and the drawings.

   Although sometimes I did take recognizable forms or outlines, for example in the illustrated chart for the planets with the names of all the goddesses, and all but copy them. But that is done consciously, a certain distance is maintained, one can see clearly—here is the name of a goddess and this is the outline of some antique Egyptian figurine which is still in existence. But usually I am trying to put together my own contemporary cabinet of drawings. The act of drawing itself, however, and this I want to emphasize, takes place intuitively. Then I'm no longer thinking, I'm doing—it's different from how I work with the texts. The texts are my intellectual side, the drawing just happens. If the book is successful, it is because there's a dialogue taking place, and if that doesn't come about, then the book's a flop.

*H.W.* So you're striving for a sort of polyphony?

*B.F.* Yes, that's it. The terms from music usually come closest to describing how I work.

*H.W.* The individual books that you have produced for the "Kunstkammer," can they stand on their own or are they complete only within the framework of the "Kunstkammer"?

*B.F.* Of course I tried to produce every book so that it exists on its own. Purely in artistic terms, I think of each book as a small, individual work of art. Whether or not that is always successful is not for me to say. On the other hand, I should still insist that the "Kunstkammer" be presented in its entirety. I can't possibly break it up into pieces and give it away. The idea of the whole project was to put together an image of the world out of many individual things, many mosaic pieces.

*H.W.* To go back to the themes that you've handled in the individual books. Once you'd determined your basic structure, many things make the impression of having entered your books spontaneously.

Buch: *Alexander von Humboldt.*

*B.F.* The choice of material from my notes was in large part spontaneous. I had given myself one year and was under considerable time pressure. Then I had decided on 84 books, not one more, not one less. It was left for me to decide what subjects I would take up in the individual orders, and that came about, if I remember correctly, for the most part spontaneously. Sometimes, but not always, the determination was a formal one, simply the desire, let us say, for a brush-drawing. And an expansive, gestural brush-drawing is not necessarily appropriate for all subject matter. The Humboldt essay is accompanied, for example, by large black ink drawings. There my desire for ink drawings was so overwhelming that I simply added a text, in this case, the Humboldt, to accompany them. I never worked systematically from one order to the next; instead I did whatever interested me or occurred to me at the moment. With time it all came together, like a mosaic, and then there it was, finished. I checked it over to see if I had all the individual books for the separate orders, counted them up, and that was that.

There's another point I want to make, however, in regards to the idea of micro- and macrocosm, not in terms of the texts but in terms of the visual realization of the book. It is possible that someone can look at the "Kunstkammer" without knowing much about it and come away with the impression that it is chaotic, stylistically too eclectic. But I was deliberately trying to use the entire register of my artistic faculties, that is to say, to work with color, with black and white, with pen and brush, with ink and bister and with tempera. I employed the most diversified techniques at my disposal in order to achieve the most richly varied material possible.

*H.W.* As varied as your texts?

*B.F.* Everything as varied as the texts and as the idea itself: micro- and macrocosm as something rich and iridescent, multifaceted. If something is going to symbolize the macrocosm it must be truly variegated.

*H.W.* Could you sustain this variety in your choice of forms?

*B.F.* Yes, the formal spectrum extends so to speak from the written word, composed of letters, to the concrete, realistic image. In between there are the individual letters, the sign, the symbol, many modulations all the way to the image, and I deliberately capitalized on this variety. Not every text or every subject can be presented symbolically; not every topic can be presented realistically. To span the arc from word to image and play it for all it was worth, to the limit of my abilities—that was my goal.

*H.W.* To play on a spectrum of signs, or at least those that can be included in a book.

*B.F.* Yes, and then there is yet another element, time, the time element as a rhythm established by the sequence of pages. Here is a dimension that one doesn't have in a normal picture movement, rhythm—it's one reason I prefer making books to simply drawing or painting.

*H.W.* In a brochure for the exhibition of your "Kunstkammer" in Holland, there is a reference to the book as a time/space sequence. Is space an element as well in your notion of the "Kunstkammer," the sense of moving sequentially through an actual room?

Buch: *Im Anfang.*

*B.F.* Yes, I can see what you mean, and I did in fact envision the "Kunstkammer" as an actual room, a room in which one is together with books.

*H.W.* Should the visitor observe your sequential order, that is to say, your and Camillo's seven orders in viewing the exhibition?

*B.F.* That would be my wish, although the fact that books are the objects being exhibited makes it difficult. For this reason, I also compiled all the texts appearing in the books and the charts and had them typed up and bound. They are each numbered according to their sequence in the "Kunstkammer" so that one can easily look up any particular work and read it.

*H.W.* This supplemental volume of over 1,000 pages attests to the importance you attach to the texts you have chosen.

*B.F.* My real wish is that the viewer sit in a room filled with these books arranged in their seven categories with the possibility of actually studying the texts, not just of looking at the books from a visual standpoint. But this is of course all but impossible in the given situation—an exhibition in a museum or a library where no one will really linger or spend time reading the books.

*H.W.* In illustrations of Renaissance "Kunstkammer" the collector is sometimes depicted as standing under the influence of Saturn rather than of Jupiter. He spends his time as a melancholic amongst his objects, pondering these things about him in a vain attempt to comprehend the universe.

*B.F.* And he persists because he cannot bear the beauty and the heartrending nature of things.

*H.W.* Are you suggesting that the Saturnian aspect also plays a role in your collecting and the "Kunstkammer" project?

*B.F.* I've written about memory and melancholy, for example this note: The Saturnian spirit yearns for the things remembered. One lives with the (often unbearable) torment inherent in the fact that life means constant loss. Memory is the only way in which one can combat this loss. But memory itself has the transience of a dream and results in a need to take things down, to collect, to produce. I produce books and drawings in order to give all that which vanishes some sort of permanency. A concrete permanence.

*H.W.* But your relation to the things you desire, that you wish to hold fast in some form or other, is rather ambivalent, or not?

*B.F.* Ambivalent, very much so. Take this narcissus bouquet on my table for example. There is a cyclical pattern of experiencing things. Here I see a narcissus before me and am drawn to it by its beauty, by its very existence.

I can describe the narcissus, can name it, can paint it, and the more I have to do with it, the more conscious I become of the fact that I am unable to capture it, to hold it fast. And it is not at all clear if it is a question of my own limitations or if the narcissus is withdrawing from me—I suspect that that may be the case—or perhaps both. Out of all this struggle a dialogue ensues—perhaps I'm crazy, but I'm convinced of it. The more I reflect on the flower, however, the stronger my impression becomes, no, my conviction, that there is an unbridgeable gulf between this narcissus, the thing, and myself. By this point I have begun to brood—and there is a distinction between brooding and thinking things through—and the more I brood over the flower, the more distant it becomes until we reach a point of complete alienation. I wrote about this cycle in my "Kunstkammer" notes—how I gradually become distanced from things and they from me, what happens when one begins to brood over things—we could take that entry as my answer:

I'm weary of the many things, their profiles and shapes wear me down. Beyond their beauty, their richness of form, I can sense their increasing rigidity, this definition which will end in death. The eternal return, the appearances, human insufficiency and the suffering that grows out of it, it all seems a blasphemy to me...creation, the monstrous idea of an insane god.

But I can't bear this train of thought for too long, because once again the longing arises, the insatiable yearning for I-don't-know-what, for some sort of reason that would dictate that

> It cannot, must not all be the senseless work of a demiurge
> it is we who are unable to understand
> Not to understand the signs that we see, signs!

Yes, the sign is all, and still in the clutches of ennui but once again filled with yearning, I spurn reproduction of the object in my work, the thing itself that deceives me, that is the cause of my despair, I must no longer indulge myself in the affectionate, affirmative process of forming.

> I must search for what is behind the thing—the sign.

I intoxicate myself with a pencil line, a dab of color, a brush stroke, an outline sketched in ink, and whenever a work is successful it is because one sees only the essence, the spirit of things—the line lives, the color breathes —abstract life! It is the exact opposite of what nature produces—the elaboration of variant forms, differentiation and observance of the most minute detail as the way to death. The division of labor in the organism which is essential to its beauty, its form, its capabilities—this division serves only to dilute the spirit, the concentrate dispersed within a solution.

In such phases my love for Chinese and Japanese art (steadily) grows.

*Space—Emptiness—Silence—Sign—Intimations*

The silence of visual art! Leaving space empty, things unformed, open—in contrast to the *horror vacui* that compels me at other times, the need to fill things up, to go into detail...

> *Nothing—the nothing of ZEN, a singing nothing,*
> *a fecund nothing, a paradox*
> *irreconcilable—*
> *the heartrending nature of things.*

After the ecstasy of nothingness my gaze falls back on the things, things which I now perceive in their full shape against the background of emptiness, things which I now see in their radical corporeality, the realm of matter, an intoxication of diversity, the diversity of forms, the colors, the beauty. I gaze, I gaze, and a desire to copy these things, an appetite for collecting, for knowledge wells up in me. I want to build a showcase, a chamber for curiosities, a "Heimatmuseum" with its display cases and windows, its storage shelves.

*—The microcosm as representation of the macrocosm—*

In literature I regain my appetite for stories, I immerse myself in the text.

*—I am back at home in the world*

H.W. Back in your "Heimatmuseum" with its collection of things, all laden with ambivalence, a tension between the emptiness of Nothing you describe and the plenitude of the world. In constructing the "Kunstkammer," you must have subjected yourself to 84 encounters like this.

B.F. Yes, that's good, that describes it, 84 encounters with things. You know, Magritte has this theme—it is central for him—he calls it "the mystery." I'm convinced he was trying to describe an incredible yearning for the chance to transcend the things themselves, something that can succeed only in a few rare moments, and, curiously enough, never in one's work. I don't know, perhaps some people can bring it into their work, but somehow there is no satisfaction to be got from it there.

H.W. But your work is propelled by this longing, or not?

B.F. Yes, but my work is, strictly speaking, only a product of this longing, not a solution, not satisfaction—but a product, yes. And what I am convinced of is that these moments, these epiphanies as James Joyce called them—that one cannot really do anything with them. They occur, and they are incomparably important, but they are not convertible in any direct way. No one's art is the better for them, no one's art is worse, they simply happen somewhere else. That is what is so interesting—they are inconvertible, and, I would venture to say, ultimately indescribable.

What has always impressed me about the writings of the mystics—and here I'm overstating it somewhat—is how they ramble on and on. And this I can well understand. It comes from the impossibility of describing in any appropriate or comprehensible way what they have experienced in their ecstasy or visions. There is simply no getting around the flood of words, this garrulousness, and in the end one still hasn't got it. I think it's the reason they write so much. You've just had, so to speak, the most important experience of your life, but if you try to hold on to it, it dissipates, because capturing it can take place only in the realm of the senses, in the material realm, there's nothing else available—you have to write it down, designate it. And that won't work, because what has happened occurred in a language that can never be recorded. And for this reason, the many words—and perhaps art itself.

*—Translated from the German by Harriet Watts and Jill Bepler.*

# *from* "LIVING HISTORY:
## FAITH RINGGOLD'S RENDEZVOUS WITH
## THE TWENTIETH CENTURY"
### Dan Cameron

THE GRADUAL TRANSITION from the postconceptual strategies of "pure" appropriation adopted by artists in the late 1970s and early 1980s to the working through of unresolved sociocultural issues that serves as one of the prevailing artistic modes of the 1990s marks one of the least-noticed yet all-pervasive changes in the making of art in the United States today. Without this perspective, one might see the present selection of Faith Ring-gold's *French Collection,* displayed with several story quilts that have pre-ceded and followed this series, as simply a curatorial attempt to develop a fitting context for breakthrough work by a major American artist. From the broader standpoint of artistic relevance, however, this project, like its sub-ject, aspires to a somewhat higher goal. As a self-contained narrative sum-marizing one artist's relationship to the main artistic developments asso-ciated with Paris from 1895 to 1925, *The French Collection* is one of the most imaginative efforts in American art to reconcile the critical inquiry that drove appropriation with the revisionist approaches to history that have prevailed over the past decade. Of even greater significance, however, is the argument that *The French Collection* places Ringgold's art squarely and somewhat unexpectedly at the center of artistic discourse in the United States at the precise moment when the aspiration toward a truly global art community and the need to address the dilemmas left behind by history are no longer mutually exclusive forces. Perhaps even more to the point, it seems increasingly likely that an artist can no longer work toward one without engaging the other.[...]

Not unlike her near-contemporary Andy Warhol, Ringgold possesses a particular genius for transforming the narrative of her personal develop-ment into a form of popular myth. Her gift may not have won her fans in the rigidly conceptual wings of the appropriation movement, but Ringgold has more than compensated for this lack of support through her achieve-ment as an author, especially of children's books, during the past ten years. Two noteworthy characteristics of these books are their formal and con-ceptual continuity with the rest of Ringgold's art and their remarkable ca-pacity for stirring the reader's empathy. The narrative voice in books like *Tar Beach* and *Aunt Harriet's Underground Railroad in the Sky* is instantly recognizable as Ringgold's own, and much of their impact comes from the author's ingenuity in inviting young readers to visualize the world through the eyes of an artist. They can be compared both to Ringgold's performance art of the 1980s, in which the artist's personal struggles were the subject matter, and to her story quilts, in which storytelling is central. Even when it remains largely fictional, the story Ringgold is telling is invariably her own, and her personal link to the histories explored by her work connects her recent pieces, especially *The French Collection,* to earlier quilts like *Change: Faith Ringgold's Over 100 Pounds Weight Loss Performance Story Quilt.* In this 1986 work, we are drawn into every step of the artist's crisis: first, as a woman who wants to feel good about herself; second, as someone struggling to get her body to conform to cultural norms of beauty; third, as a person whose intelligence and political sensitivity allow her to see all the inherent contradictions in her position; and finally, as the artist who is inspired to transform the whole dilemma into an artwork. By the time Faith at last takes the weight off, it is clear to her viewers that even this accomplishment has been robbed of its pleasure, since we have moved, with the artist, through the torturous thoughts and actions behind this loaded topic.

A narrative of epic dimensions, *The French Collection* functions as a meditation on the individual's relation to history, granting as much importance to what may have happened as to what surely did or did not. In the most direct and literal sense, it is a tribute to Ringgold's mother, Willi Posey. A dressmaker and designer, Willi Posey was able to visit Europe only in her later years, but she could have almost doubled as Willia Marie Simone, the Atlanta-born protagonist of the twelve story quilts, who goes to Paris at age sixteen in the 1920s and leads a life that no African American woman artist could have dreamed of having at the time. Not only does Willia Marie meet all the artistic and literary luminaries of the day, pose for Picasso, and attend Josephine Baker's birthday party, but she actually "makes a name for herself in the modern art movement" and eventually retires from art-making as the owner of an artists' café.

Examining *The French Collection* as a series, one senses that Ringgold's ambitions for the project grew while she worked on it: the first story quilt, *Dancing at the Louvre,* tells of a spontaneous moment of youthful rebelliousness, and one of the last works, *Le Café des Artistes,* highlights Willia Marie's maturity by incorporating "A Proclamation of the Colored Woman's Art and Politics," complete with a "prediction" of what the rest of the twentieth century might be like for aspiring women artists of color. In between these two story quilts, the fictional narrative frequently gives way to the author's attempts to confront and overcome the effects of racism: *Matisse's Chapel,* for example, depicts the deceased members of Ringgold's own family gathered together in front of the famous stained-glass windows, while Willia Marie's letter relates a true hair-raising story about slavery passed down from Ringgold's own great-grandmother.

Because the thin line in *The French Collection* between fiction and historical narrative is constantly being blurred, our relationship to the work's subject matter keeps shifting. Some of Ringgold's fusions, like *The Sunflowers Quilting Bee at Arles,* seem perfectly whimsical at first glance, until one begins to pick out some of the work's more submerged connections. The first layer, which is not at all hidden, concerns the identity of the eight historically significant women who are "piecing" together the quilt: Sojourner Truth, Madame Walker, Rosa Parks, Mary McLeod Bethune, and others. They have been called together, the narrative tells us, by Aunt Melissa to produce a quilt that will serve as a "symbol of their dedication to change the world." The other, half-concealed purpose for their visit seems to be to boost Willia Marie's own flagging spirits and challenge her to look toward her tradition for support, especially as she lives so far away from home. At one point the discussion turns to quilting, which is described as "what we did after a hard day's work in the fields to keep our sanity and our beds warm and bring beauty into our lives." As we become drawn into an origin myth concerning the work in front of us, Ringgold's powerful argument for tradition resonates with an additional significance: namely, that the American quilt tradition may have played as seminal a role in the growth of a characteristically American late-twentieth-century sensibility as van Gogh's mythic sunflowers within the development of modern European painting.

Behind the apparently triumphalist narrative of *The French Collection* that is its primary source of appeal, several other subtexts appear frequently enough to give us a clear indication that all is not as inspirational as it seems. The symbolic yet passionate rejection of European culture that opens the series—cavorting in front of the Mona Lisa, hurling a traditional wedding bouquet into the Seine—soon collides with another tug-of-war for the artist's conflicting loyalties, from the women's movement (*The Picnic at Giverny*) and the courageous African American women. In this light, as Michele Wallace points out, it is intriguing that the sixth story quilt, *Matisse's Chapel,* in which the sublime beauty of the site cannot be separated from the burden of loss in the narrative, is framed by two quilts in which the ostensible content is the black female body caught within the gaze of the male European artist. That, in Ringgold's version of the story, Willia Marie has posed for Matisse and later Picasso (she is the anonymous African model in *Les Demoiselles d'Avignon*) underlines her growing transformation from a passive object of beauty into a responsive subject with the need to direct the narrative from her own point of view. By flipping the white male gaze back on itself in order to mirror certain implicitly racist assumptions of the modern era, Ringgold accomplishes in a single pictorial glimpse what feminist art historians have struggled to do for a generation, and she prods the Western canon's critical drive into tackling its own history of unacknowledged exploitation and oppression, to see if it can analyze and grow from its previous moral vacuity as profitably as it deconstructs space, form, and color.

The redirection of this deflected male gaze can be traced through the remaining quilts in the series. With *On the Beach at St. Tropez,* the controlling gaze is clearly Willia Marie's, languid but sure as it takes in the skimpily clad male (and occasionally female) bathers showing off in the surf, while Willia Marie relates her need for independence to her son, who has been raised by his great-aunt in Georgia. In *Jo Baker's Birthday,* the power of the gaze belongs once more to the subject, who, although seductively dressed and reclining luxuriously on a divan, makes it clear through her body language that she is in complete control of all she surveys. The organization of the world according to proto-feminist principles becomes even more explicit in *Dinner at Gertrude Stein's,* where the presence of expatriate writers conforms to an atmosphere of statelessness in keeping with Stein's and Alice B. Toklas's sense of having been displaced in the modern world. This movement away from the need to place one's body at the disposal of powerful men's desires and toward the shaping of a world in one's own image parallels the underlying psychological narrative in *The French Collection,* in which the protagonist ends her journey of self-realization by literally becoming her own subject—or, in the example of *Le Café des Artistes,* opening a business that offers other artists and writers a refuge from the intolerance of the world outside.

It is telling that *The French Collection* ends and *The American Collection* begins with the same focal point: Africa. Whereas *Moroccan Holiday* caps the theme of European culture's imperialist attitudes toward Africa, *We Came to America,* the first story quilt in *The American Collection,* summarizes in one terrifying image the perils and hardships that most black Americans' ancestors faced just to arrive physically intact on these shores. The painting shows New York harbor with an African Statue of Liberty standing guard over the waters, while hundreds of bodies fight against the treacherous waters and a slave ship burns on the horizon. The overwhelming tragedy of seeing so many struggling figures who have come so far, only to perish at the threshold of a new country, is somewhat mediated by the composition's focus on one young girl who has been swept up in Liberty's arms and saved.

We are now quite far, in terms of narrative direction, from the saga of Willia Marie Simone making her way in Paris. Yet the fact that *The American Collection* was produced after *The French Collection,* while tracing an earlier chronology of historical events, affirms that the lives of Marlena and Willia Marie, however distinct, will mirror each other across parallel chapters in time. The main difference between the two series lies in the way they present the solution to overcoming history's painful legacy. Whereas Willia Marie's world is still circumscribed by events and personalities that belong to the "official" record of modern art, Marlene's variations on the past are charged by a more combustible mixture of social history and artistic legacy—as if she were so deeply involved in creating the paintings that will assure her place in history that she cannot separate her own heritage from the creative rewriting of it that is her particular genius.

•  •  •

# from *THE FRENCH COLLECTION*, PART 1, #3:
## THE PICNIC AT GIVERNY
### Faith Ringgold

Acrylic on canvas, printed and tie-dyed fabric, 73½" x 90½". *Front row, left to right:* Picasso, Moira Roth, Ellie Flomenhaft, Lowery Sims, Judith Lieber, Thalia Gouma-Peterson, Emma Amos, Bernice Steinbaum, Michele Wallace, Willia Marie Simone. *Back row, left to right:* Ofelia Garcia, Johnetta Cole.

Dear Aunt Melissa,

TODAY I WAS INVITED to paint in the garden of the celebrated painter, Claude Monet at Giverny. There, in an area of the garden composed of water-lily ponds, with weeping willow trees and beautiful flowers everywhere, was a group of American women artists and writers having a picnic and discussing the role of women in art.

2    I strolled through the beautiful jardins, taking in the fantastic, beautiful flower beds and trees, passing over the matrix of Japanese bridges that connect the wildly wooded areas of the jardins with the fields of flowers near Monet's house. Then I settled on the same area near the water-lily ponds flanked by weeping willow trees near the American women who were picnicking.

3    I kept seeing Manet's *Le Déjeuner Sur L'Herbe,* the painting that caused such a scandal in Paris. It was not allowed at the salon because it showed Manet's brother-in-law and a male friend having a picnic with two nude women, all of whom were recognizable. I kept thinking: Why not replace the traditional nude woman at the picnic with Picasso in the nude, and the ten American women fully clothed?

4    That would be crossing Monet's beautiful *Nymphéas* with Manet's scandal, and a reaction to the conversation of the American women about the role of women artists to show powerful images of women. They were discussing female nudes in the company of fully clothed men in paintings like Manet's *The Picnic.* Seeing it and wondering what to paint, this seemed a good idea to begin ma nouvelle conscience.

5    What to paint has always been my greatest problem as an artist. And then how to paint it? These were the questions I looked hard for answers to. Now there is the role of women artists? Some special niche we can occupy, like a power station? A woman artist can assume the rights of men in art? And be seen? I am very excited to meet these women. This may be the very first day of my life.

6    They are speaking of la libération et la liberté for women. Sometimes we think we are free, until we spread our wings and are cut down in mid air. But who can know a slave by the mere look in her eye? Ordinarily I would just paint the jardin and include in it some of these women at a picnic. That was before the question of freedom came up. Is it just the beauty of nature I am after?

7    Monet painted his most wonderful masterpiece, *Décorations des Nymphéas,* of the garden and the water-lily ponds. Those paintings hang in the circular galleries of the Musée de l'Orangerie in the Tuileries Gardens in Paris. That must be wonderful, to have your work so approved and revered by people to have it hanging in a space specially made for it. What does that amount of respect feel like?

8    Can a woman of my color ever achieve that amount of eminence in art in America? Here or anywhere in the world? Is it just raw talent alone that makes an artist's work appreciated to the fullest? Or is it a combination of things, la magie par une example, le sexe par une autre, et la couleur est encore une autre, magic, sex, and color.

9    One has to get the attention one needs to feed the magic. There is no magic in the dark. It is only when we see it that we know a transformation has taken place, a wonderful idea has been created into art. If we never see it we never know, and it didn't happen. Isn't that why I and so many other

Negro artists have come to Paris—to get a chance to make magic, and find an audience for our art?

10   Should I paint some of the great and tragic issues of our world? A black man toting a heavy load that has pinned him to the ground? Or a black woman nursing the world's population of children? Or the two of them together as slaves, building a beautiful world for others to live free? Non! I want to paint something that will inspire—liberate. I want to do some of this WOMEN ART. Magnifique!

11   What will people think of my work? Will they just ignore it or will they give it some consideration? Maybe tear it apart and say that it is the worst ever and this artist should have her brushes burned and her hands, too. And isolate me as a woman artist because I am no longer trying to paint like, or to be like a man. Paris is full of these women artists who have no first names, wear men's trousers and deny they are married or have children.

12   I paint like a woman. I always paint wearing a white dress. Now I have a subject that speaks out for women. I can no more hide the fact that I am a woman than that I am a Negro. It is a waste of time to entertain such subterfuge any longer.

13   There are enough beautiful paintings of nude women in the world. I now want to see nude men painted by women, or nude men in the company of fully clothed women. C'est de la fantaisie pure. The men are expressing their power over women. But I am not interested in having power over anyone. I just want to see nude men in the company of fully clothed women for a change.

14   I am deeply inspired by these American women and their conversations about art and women in America. It makes me homesick for my country. And for their women's movement, I have created this painting *Picnic at Giverny* par le tribut. They have given me something new to ponder, a challenge to confront in my art, a new direction. And pride in being a Negro woman.

# WRITING (UNDER-)SKY:
# ON XU BING'S *TIANSHU*
## John Cayley

...the designation...
"meaningless"
especially insofar as this is conceptualized as
positive or liberating...
         is symptomatic of a desire to
evade responsibility for meaning's total, &
totalizing, reach; as if meaning was a husk
that could be shucked off or a burden that could be
bucked. Meaning is not a use value *as opposed to*
some other kind of value, but more like valuation
itself; & even to refuse value is a value & a sort
of exchange.
      —Charles Bernstein "Artifice of Absorption."[1]

XU BING, WHO ORIGINALLY TRAINED as a woodblock printmaker, is now recognized as a major international visual and installation artist. However, his work leads us to the body-and-soul problems of writing and language. Xu Bing's work is marked by a tenacious, love-hate engagement with what he calls *wenhua* and we call 'culture.' We might have been tempted to say 'Chinese culture' here, or even 'traditional Chinese culture,' but this would be unnecessary, limiting and essentializing in the context of Xu Bing's work (which is already, demonstrably, translated to the West). Instead, all we need do is to read 'culture' or *wenhua* along with the particular Chinese connotations of the term. Etymologically, *wen* refers to 'pattern,' especially those patterns which, as civilization emerged in East Asia, could be recognized and used as elements of writing. Characters in Chinese are *wenzi,* or, in literary Chinese, often simply *wen.*

This engagement with literary culture or culture-as-writing enables a properly poetic reading of Xu Bing's work. I began by quoting an essay by the American poet, Charles Bernstein—an essay which is, arguably, central to the understanding and reconfiguration of contemporary poetic practice. In this essay, Bernstein distinguishes — *nonexclusively* — between writing which is 'absorptive' and that which is 'antiabsorptive.' While all writing is artifice, the former employs artifice to absorb the reader's (self-)conscious attentions; the latter challenges such absorption, foregrounding itself and its techniques and resisting both reading and readability, whenever, that is, 'to read' is cast as to gaze through a transparent, permeable, 'absorptive' window, opening onto signification. To simplify his argument, Bernstein sets out a case for the valorization and value-creating potential of anti-absorptive writing, especially in literary cultures, like our own, which are dominated by—gendered, politically and economically over-determined—cults of absorptive readability.[2]

What are the marks of antiabsorptive writing? These are significantly represented—though by no means exclusively—by the 'extralexical' cultural forms which are incorporated into writing-as-art, and especially poetry, as a function of artifice. Easily recognized examples include line breaks and special typography, underlying sound and visual patterning: both traditional (e.g. verse forms, rhyme) and experimental (non-standard typography, acrostic patterning). Extralexical forms are those which express meanings which cannot be *paraphrased*—from the language of the poem to the language of the reader—as when, for example, a critic attempts to outline the underlying tenor or plot of a poem. In fact, *all* writing is embodied in and framed by extralexical forms. After all, even 'simple' graphic marks of ink on paper have an intrinsic extralexical aspect.

In his essay, Bernstein is at pains to argue that extralexical does not mean meaningless or even 'nonsemantic'. How could it be otherwise? This would be like claiming, for instance, that the fact that a poem is published in a book (rather than traced in the sand) is of no significance for the poem's meaning. At this point we turn to Xu Bing's *Tianshu* ('Book from the Sky'). From a certain perspective Xu Bing's work is the epitome of the impermeable, antiabsorptive poetic work, 'the radically impervious text' as Bernstein has it. The *Tianshu* was produced as a text aiming explicitly to subvert *all* lexical meaning. Over four years Xu Bing hand-carved a 'font' [Fig. 1] of approximately four thousand characters which were each intended to be unreadable, absent from any lexicon. While the graphic and compositional forms of his characters correspond precisely to the graphic and compositional principles of readable Chinese characters—i.e., they look like they should be characters—there is always some aspect of their spelling—extra or missing strokes, unrecorded combinations of elements —which locates the writing of the *Tianshu* outside all dictionaries.[3]

However, this exemplary extralexical, unreadable text is embodied in forms which are eminently 'legible' as expressions of the *wen*, the figurative 'letters' or inscribed 'patterns' of Chinese culture, all of which implicate aesthetics, though in various differing ways. In the carving of his font Xu Bing uses traditional materials, tools, and methods. As already mentioned, the graphic forms of strokes and compositional principles of character-formation are, in *visual* terms, strictly adhered to. Furthermore, these character forms are made in a consistent style, chosen to represent a particular

Figure 1. Hand-carved font.

moment in the history of Chinese type design. In the layout of the *Tianshu*, as a book, Xu Bing employs entirely canonical forms. The book is printed by hand in a factory specializing in traditional printing and binding.[4] As a product of this craft, it is an example of high-quality Chinese book-making modeled on that of a specific period, the late Ming. It contains a wealth of traditional book design and typographic features, which are arranged in abstract design 'rhythms' throughout the work. The overall layout of the book is familiar; its parts and elements are recognizable as, for example, preface, table of contents, main text, commentaries, quotations, and so on. These parts collate and are internally consistent ('titles' in the contents page match titles in the body of the work). The sections of the book can be identified as to broad genre of writing—expository prose with or without commentary, poetry, religious (sutra) writings, technical texts, glossaries, etc.[5] The binding of the book, in four stitch-bound paper-covered volumes encased in a walnut box, is all in accord with what is expected for an authoritative, encyclopaedic work, an extensive record from the archive of Chinese literature. In general, as an object, apart from its unreadable characters, the *Tianshu* is an icon of cultural authority; apart from its anti-lexicon, every other aspect of its material cultural signification is intact.

By contrast, the impermeable aspects of the specific, contemporary—mainly poetic—texts which Bernstein addresses are, generally, functions of experimental or avant-garde practices. They are new, disruptive, anti-traditional, strikingly different from canonical forms. Moreover, the lexical or conventionally readable, content of these poems tends to be aligned with their radical formal gestures. Xu Bing's work, as concept and installation, is a standard-bearer for the renaissance of the Chinese avant-garde and, in his statements about *Tianshu*, he claims that it is intended to expose the meaninglessness, the bankruptcy and boredom of traditional Chinese culture: to buck its tedious burden, or shuck it off like a husk, perhaps.[6] Paradoxically, when displayed in the West, his work reads as an exhibition of the traditional Chinese book: before the concept is explained to the non-Chinese reader, the aesthetic experience of the work involves an encounter with traditional Chinese literary culture, faithfully presented as the end result of many traditional practices. Apart from the self-consciously artistic arrangement of the *Tianshu*'s open volumes or the hanging of the Sutra galley sheets from the ceiling [Fig. 2–3], how, for example, does a visit to the *Tianshu* installation differ from the experience of visiting display cases of fine Chinese editions in the galleries of the Oriental Collections of the British Library?

Figure 2. Bound volumes of *Tianshu*.

This work generates paradoxes, which both complicate and resolve as we go on to place it in the context of its installation in the West, amongst readers who cannot read its unreadability *directly* —if they do not know Chinese, if they do not know (without being told) that the words of the *Tianshu* are *not* Chinese. Transported to the West, the *Tianshu* suddenly appears, in a sense, to be maximally legible [Fig. 2]. Both non-Chinese and Chinese readers see an exhibition of traditional literary culture, in a form

Figure 3. Installation view of *Tianshu*.

which, frankly, may be as familiar to certain Western readers as to many of their Chinese counterparts, who are also raised on paperbacks and cheap modern codices, printed by lithography. Both groups are equally unable to read any lexical content in the work; both are engaged with the same complexes of aesthetic experience.[7] Xu Bing says he wants to produce a 'tianshu,' a meaningless writing, an inscription of the meaninglessness of Chinese culture.[8] Paradoxically he produces a work which has transcultural resonance and translatability; a work which addresses radically different audiences with an experience which is somehow the same and *profoundly* the same, since it starkly reveals how the extralexical serves to create undeniable and absorbing meanings.[9]

What would be the complement of the *Tianshu*? What would be a complement of this text which is minimally legible in lexical terms and seems to be maximally legible in its extralexical material culture? How might we conceive a writing which was maximally legible, lexically, and minimally engaged with the culture of the extralexical, with antiabsorptive artifice, in Bernstein's terms. Perhaps this 'counter-*Tianshu*' would be a dictionary inscribed in and through nature? Letters and words set amongst their 'natural definitions,' which would speak as simple presence? Apart from the insoluble problem of identifying or delineating any such 'natural definitions,' there would have to be a prior choice of lexicon for such a *Book of Earth*. Would its letters and words be in English or Chinese, for example? This decision would require an extralexical, culturally determined judgment, which would imply lexical impermeability for one or other group of potential readers. However realized (as universal language-makers soon discover), such a 'natural lexicon' would be unreadable for some or require to be learned (not only its lexical items but also their categorical 'positions' on the problematically delineated landscape). Xu Bing's impermeable text reads across cultures with far greater facility, and necessarily so, for its excision of the lexical ironically indicates that the lexical and extralexical must always be coextensive in order for writing or reading to occur at all. If writing became transparent, absorbed into a supposed natural definition, it would either cease to exist or remain illegible to all but its writer or writers. It would certainly claim to abandon meaning—where meaning is generated by patterns of inscription (*wen*)—which is what Xu Bing's *Tianshu*, in this written essay's final paradox, necessarily fails to do.

## NOTES

1. Charles Bernstein, "Artifice of Absorption," in *A Poetics* (Cambridge, Mass.: Harvard University Press, 1992), p. 13. Bernstein's essay employs a number of the 'antiabsorptive' techniques which he discusses, including, as here, poetic lineation.

2. It should be recalled that the effectiveness of absorption and absorptive rhetoric is dependent on ideological as well as aesthetic agreements, which are hegemonic and politically implicated, both West & East.

3. A number of commentators on the *Tianshu* have pointed out that there may be one or two characters in the work which do, in fact, appear in the most comprehensive dictionaries of Chinese characters—as rare forms or *hapax legomena*. This does not take anything away from the fact that the *Tianshu* characters were designed by their creator to be extralexical. These few characters may appear in dictionaries which Xu Bing failed to check, but they are not *identical* with those characters; they cannot be read as those characters. (Look at the context!)

4. The only unusual aspect of the production of the *Tianshu* as a traditional Chinese book is the fact that it is printed in wooden moveable type. Although moveable type was invented in China, in the 11th century, because of the huge scale of the fonts required, it was more economical—until the advent of lithography—to print books from carved blocks corresponding to Western book openings (facing pages). Nonetheless there are many fine early examples of printing from wooden moveable type. The aspect as of the *Tianshu* as a superb example of the—very traditional—art of the book in China has mostly been overlooked by commentators.

5. The one formal feature which the *Tianshu* does not have, which might have been expected, is a language-like distribution of the four thousand characters throughout the texts of the work. I mean a non-lexical mapping of the character forms to classes of words (e.g., nouns and verbs vs. grammatical function words), so that, for example, some of the characters would appear much more frequently in the texts. This would also have produced a more Chinese text-like appearance to the pages of the *Tianshu* roughly corresponding to the sense of density or blackness of type which Western readers perceive when glancing at the page of a book.

6. See, for example, Xu Bing's remarks in "Non-Sense in Context: Xu Bing's Art and Its Publics," interview and translation by Janelle S. Taylor, *Public Culture* 5:2 (Winter 1993), p. 327: "One of the things I wanted to convey in [*Tianshu*] is that I feel that culture places too great a burden on people, it leaves people feeling exhausted." In a conversation about the work with the present writer, he also spoke of traditional culture as 'boring' or 'without interest' (*taoyan; mei yisi*).

7. "The equal or identical always moves toward the absence of difference, so that everything may be reduced to a common denominator. The same, by contrast, is the belonging together of what differs, through a gathering by way of difference." (Martin Heidegger, '... Poetically man dwells ...,' in *Poetry, Language, Thought,* trans. Albert Hofstadter [New York: Harper & Row, 1975], p. 218; quoted in Zhang Longxi, *The Tao and the Logos* [Durham: Duke University Press, 1992], p. xv.) See also Xu Bing's comments in

Taylor, *op. cit.*, p. 326: "These characters are fair, they treat all the people of the world equally. Americans can't read them, Chinese can't read them, I myself can't read them either. The ways in which people understand this artwork will vary according to their different cultural backgrounds, but I don't think that it really loses any of its meaning."

8. Wu Hung in "A 'Ghost Rebellion': Notes on Xu Bing's 'Nonsense Writing' and Other Works," *Public Culture* 6:2 (Winter 1994), pp. 411–418, has provided the most informed gloss—by no means an exhaustive gloss in my view—of *Tianshu* as 'nonsense writing,' a sense which it will bear without damage to the other meanings of the work, which are partially addressed here.

9. See note 7, and "To speak of a radically impervious text/is to speak oxymoronically—absorbency & repellency/are relative, contextual, & interpenetrating/terms, not new critical analytical categories./The unreadable text is an outer limit for poetry;/ in practical terms, the complete shutout/of the reader's attention is subverted/by most ostensibly antiabsorptive texts, partly/by some readers' 'paradoxically' keen interest/ in impermeability.../The nonabsorbable text often turns/out to be eminently performable, [or 'installable' as visual art, in the case of the *Tianshu*] .../Antiabsorptive does not necessarily mean nonentertaining—/on the contrary." (Bernstein, *op. cit.*, p. 65.)

# THE ART OF IMMEMORABILITY
## Charles Bernstein

IN THE JANUARY 1999 issue of the almost unreadably hyperdesigned *Wired* magazine, a quote from the poet and Zen abbot Norman Fischer is splashed across three full-color pages: "The real technology—behind all of our other technologies—is language." This useful motto, echoing as it does the sense of language as *tekhne* suggested by Jerome Rothenberg in his preface to *Technicians of the Sacred* thirty years ago, appears in a paper-bound journal of the new electronic communications technologies, a strangely amphibian publication with one foot firmly planted in the print past and the other ready to kick the ball into a digital future. But what ball? What past? What future?

And anyway, who invented language? While that question may have to be left to anthropologists and theologians, the question of the invention of writing in the West is quite a different matter, with a long and well-docu-mented prehistory of inscriptions on rock faces and cave walls, an opening act consisting of Sumerian cuneiform and Egyptian hieroglyphs (emerging about 5000 years ago); a second act of North Semitic, Phoenician, and He-brew consonantal scripts (as early as 3700 years ago), which was followed fast upon by the Greek alphabet (2700 to 2800 years ago).

The technological significance of each of these phases of writing cannot be overestimated. North Semitic, Phoenician, and Hebrew (proto)alphabetic scripts, consisting of twenty-two letters, all consonants, eliminated the need to memorize the hundreds of characters necessary to decipher earlier writ-ing and created a means of representing the sound of spoken language that remains fundamental to Western conceptions of literature. The Greeks built upon and improved this system, creating a set of twenty-four letters, of which seven were vowels. The Greek alphabet was easy to form, decipher, and pronounce. In *The Muse Learns To Write: Reflections on Orality and Liter-acy from Antiquity to the Present,* Eric Havelock tells the story of the evolution of this alphabet, noting that the civil society of classical Greece controlled its own transition from primary orality to writing by using a system that they had invented and that was particularly suited to represent the sounds of spoken Greek. The genius of the Greek alphabet was the invention of subsyl-labic units that broke sound down into "atomic elements" that could be com-bined to represent "any linguistic noise." This was not quite *wysiwyg* (what you see is what you get), but close—what you see is what you hear; and the alphabet's simplification and supersession of previous systems of writing is not unlike the transformations from Fortran to DOS to Windows. Never be-

fore had writing been able to so efficiently represent the full sound senso-
rium of spoken language. The Greek alphabet was, in Havelock's words,
the "first and last instrument to reproduce the range of previous orality."

For those accustomed to rating computer technology in terms of storage memory and processing speed, the alphabetic revolutions can be measured in analogous terms: a remarkably accessible user interface and an
enormous capacity to store retrievable information. In the West, Greek-
style alphabets would dominate writing technology until the present,
though no doubt there is value in the slogan "think different," as the current Apple computer ads insist. The Hebrew alphabet showed a remarkable resiliency when revived mid-century as the official language of Israel.
And the Chinese written character remains the longest-running show in
the writing business. But just as current digital technology is eclipsing the
alphabet, it is also forcing changes in Chinese writing as Asian language
users converge on the Internet and try to find ways to adapt to the limitations of the alphabetic computer keypad.

While the Greek alphabet, and Greek verbal art, has had an enormous
influence on the subsequent Western literature, it is not necessary to argue
for the uniqueness of classical Greek literary culture or for the cultural supremacy of the Greek alphabet when considering the value of Havelock's
claims. Havelock provides a richly suggestive case study of the effect of
writing technology on poetry. In Havelock's view, the greatness of the verbal art in the period from Homer to Plato is significantly the result of the
major technological shift that occurred during this time, when alphabetic
writing was emerging in an a/literate culture. Thus Homer, Hesiod, and
Euripides are not the product of a fully literate culture; rather, they capture
by alphabetic technology the existing and dominant oral culture. Yet to
capture is also to misrepresent (all representation is also misrepresenta-
tion) and to misrepresent is, of course, also to change.

Havelock's perspective runs counter to transcendental humanist
claims often made for classical Greek "literature," since he argues that the
greatness of this work is partly the result of it *not* being the product of a
fully literate culture and partly the result of technological innovation.
While early Greek oral and performance art had an aesthetic and entertainment value, Havelock sees the primary function of such works as encyclopedic and memorial: to store for reuse the customs and manners of
the culture. For a/literate verbal art to have this capacity, listeners must be
able to memorize, remember, and echo. As a result, the language must be
memorable. And, indeed, the works whose function it is (at least in part) to
store cultural memory are repeated over and over again, like children's
stories, to allow memorization. Indeed, the word games and songs of chil-

dren preserve in our contemporary culture several of the features of such analphabetic verbal art.

Havelock argues that Greek alphabetic writing provided a new and better means for the storage and retrieval of cultural memory by providing a highly supple means to record the aural textures of performed language, thus preserving in writing the modes of information storage deployed by the oral culture of the Greeks. According to Havelock, and in this he echoes the findings of Alfred Lord and Milman Perry, the oral (or pneumonic) forms of language storage employed by the Greeks relied on a range of mnemonic techniques that are preserved in a remarkably full-blown way by the Homeric epics. That is, the Homeric epics embody in writing an-alphabetic modes of language storage. The earliest Greek writing, marked by the emergence of a new alphabetic technology within a culture in which oral technology remained dominant for a few hundred years, takes from a/literate verbal performance the form of rhythmic verse, with much of the emerging "literature" written for the holdover medium of performance. Much of the new alphabetic writing, then, was an aid to memory, taking the form of scripts to be memorized for subsequent performance. As a result, the prosody was, to some extent, carried over from analphabetic verbal art. In such scripted writing, the page is not the final destination but a prelimi-nary stage, a prompt for final presentation elsewhere.

Such holdover writing practices might be contrasted with more distinc-tively textual features of writing, ones that are less bound to transcription and scripting—less bound, that is, to "transcriptive" functions of writing. If you write something down, then you don't have to remember it and you don't have to write it in a way that will help you to memorize it. The writ-ing takes on the work of memory rather than being an aid to memory and this function is not compromised by writing that is difficult or impossible to memorize. On the one hand, it's the difference between the *Odyssey* and the *Encyclopedia Brittanica*; on the other, between a counting game and a poem by Jackson Mac Low.

The distinction I am suggesting here is not unlike one that Marshall McLuhan makes in *Understanding Media* between the received and the new content of the emerging medium. The initial content of television was the product of the previous moving image medium, film (which, in turn, not only shaped the TV but also changed movies). In contrast, "live" TV (initially broadcasts of sporting events but epitomized by live news broadcasts) is the best example of a distinct genre particular to the medium of television. If "live" TV suggests a formal essence for the new medium of television, we might look at non-oral, non-speech-based forms of writing in order to identify the distinctly textual, rather than holdover or transcrip-tive, features of writing.

Greek alphabetic writing, because of both its ingenuity in phonetic re-production (transcription) and its use as scripts for subsequent perfor-mance, may obscure the emergence of specifically textual forms. The al-most immediate use of the Greek alphabet for inscribing epitaphs (a quintessentially memorial function of writing and one of the earliest uses of any kind of writing) is an important exception, since, like epigrams, epi-taphs are neither transcriptions of, nor scripts for, performed verbal art. Greek prose, in the sense of nonrhythmical, nonperformance-scored writ-ing, emerged later, with Plato and Herodotus.

In contrast to the phonic agility of Greek writing, earlier nonalphabetic writing systems had a more marked separation of speech and writing, since such writing systems were less insistent on (or less effective in) invoking a phonemic reality outside the written characters. In such nonalphabetic writing, there are numerous examples of codes, laws, accounts, and other catalogs and compendia that appear to dispense with the mnemonic for-mula of a/literate verbal art and begin to mine writing's textuality. These writing systems may have potentiated the textual and immemorial func-tions of writing more fully than alphabetic writing, which bears the trace of its phonetic transcription. The very effectiveness of the Greek alpha-bet's apparent ability to "capture" speech may have resulted in the appear-ance of speech "capturing" alphabetic writing. Except that, according to Havelock, the Homeric epics are not transcriptions of speech as such, but rather the translation into writing of the performed verbal art of the pe-riod. This suggests that the "transcriptive" process was twofold: notating the oral performance and creating scripts for subsequent performance.

The distinction between textual and transcriptive functions of writing is by no means clear-cut since the definitions of each are recursive. On the one hand, my speculation about the greater textuality of nonalphabetic or early alphabetic writing is undermined by the possibility that what now ap-pears as textual rather than scripted writing was performed or incanted, as is the case with biblical Hebrew texts. On the other hand, the alphabet pro-vided novel, nonprosodic, means of textual organization, from alphabet-ization to the numerology of gematria. While not an opposition, a certain divergence can be noted: Writing as transcriptive retains the mnemonic features of a/literate verbal art either as reproduction or to facilitate mem-orization for subsequent performance. Textualized writing, in contrast, is not an intermediate stage to a performance elsewhere. The immemorial possibilities of textual writing put the memory in the text rather than using the text as an aid to memory.

Writing not only records language, it also changes language—and con-sciousness. Once some of the memory functions of language are shifted from oral to alphabetic technology, then language may be freed up from these tasks—or in the darker semiotic economy of Walter Ong or David Abram, it loses bodily touch with them. In other words, alphabetic writing makes its own particular marks on language, allowing for greater levels of abstraction and reflection, which has often resulted in diminishing the amount of action and "doing." For example, descriptions of acts of seeing give way to the idea of sight; or consider, as another example: "Toronto-Hatted McLuhan exhorts his minions" versus "Language reveals truth." Indeed, abstraction and reflection are two qualities that typify later classical Greek writing, but, contrary to much received wisdom, these qualities may be less truth-effects than media-effects. The rest, in other words, is history.

The means of language and cultural reproduction always become a means of production and variance, as what is "stored" is transformed by the means of its imagined storage—so that it is a matter of morphing more than storing.

Writing, read in this way, tells us more than what it purports to tell since it embodies the story of its mode of telling alongside any tales it tells. However, it's not the tail wagging the dog, as much literary criticism has assumed, but a tale of the dog; though if the dog could talk, would we understand its bark or only its plight?

My speculative model here is not of one technology replacing another, nor am I suggesting that changes in the technology for language reproduction create social or cultural improvement. Alphabetic technology does not replace oral technology anymore than cars replace walking. But it does shift the balance and writing registers the change. After all, poetry precedes prose, but prose does not abolish poetry. Indeed, prose is as agonistic to poetry as it is complementary. Prose has killed poetry many times but poetry doesn't seem to get the message. But maybe that's because poetry is the vampire medium, sucking the blood from other modes of writing and leaving them lifeless, while itself living on into an eternity at the cost of its mortality. This is why poetry often metamorphoses into prose—to regain its historical existence by casting aside its ghoulish triumph.

In any period, some poetry will discover that which can only be done in and as writing by using new technical means available, while other poetry will bring into the present of writing the forms and motifs of previous technological and historical moments. Neither approach is invalid just as neither is surefire, but evaluating one approach by the criteria derived from the other is misguided.

Havelock goes on to theorize that Greek lyric poetry is the product of the alphabet, which allows for the abstraction of the "I" and for the development of the individuated lyric self—a claim that modifies Bruno Snell's earlier Hellenophilic argument for the Greek invention of the lyric and the concomitant emergence of polis (the city state). No sooner does the Greek alphabet appear than the "I" of writing also appears. And with the lyric, so the satiric—Sappho and Archilochos—and also (the Greek version of) the civic. While early Greek lyrics were composed to be sung with musical accompaniment, early satiric verse was not. Lyric and satiric were the formally innovative poetry that emerged with the new Greek alphabet and with a new civic society; epic persisted, transformed by the new medium and by the company, if not rivalry, of the new genres.

This is not to say that the self was invented by the alphabet but rather that the Western literary genre of the lyric (and also the satiric) might have been. By making possible a semblance of the speaking voice of the poet, the alphabetic lyric took possession of (or was possessed by) the "other" of that vexed double sense of "lyric"—words to be sung and words spoken by an individual. In this way, the alphabet facilitated the creation of a more stable author identity—the signature, a prerequisite for the lyric as literary genre. The lyric utilized the signature-effect of writing in ways not accessible to (or perhaps even desirable for) analphabetic verbal art. Various forms of self-expression, and of signature, certainly existed in the West prior to the Greek alphabet and there are a number of precursors to lyric poetry in earlier Western writing as well as in Greek verbal art prior to the invention of the Greek alphabet. Gregory Nagy has argued that the metrical patterns and possibly the phraseology of Greek lyric poetry predate the metrics of the oral epics associated with the names Hesiod and Homer and have their origins in far more ancient Indic religious hymns and prayers, such as those found in the Rigveda, the oldest parts of which go back 3500 years (though the means for any such possible transmission remain obscure). Such archaic meters may themselves be derived from earlier fixed phrases or "charms," providing a means for intact preservation over time. Moreover, the Hebrew "Song of Songs" (written about 400 years before Sappho) is often cited as protolyric verse. These examples notwithstanding, the Greek alphabet opened a set of particular possibilities for poetry, including a modulation in the effect of using the "I," which were immediately and brilliantly exploited by the secular early Greek poets in a way that had an indelible impact not only on the medium of poetry, as we know it in the West, but also on writing.

In his comparative study of Greek and Indic meter, Nagy notes that Alfred Lord defines "a truly 'oral' tradition as one in which every performance generates a new composition." In contrast, writing has often been misunderstood as fixing texts. Transcriptive writing has its end not in a fixed and final text but rather in a series of alphabetic and performative versionings—a dynamic that carries over into textual writing as well. Contrary to the received wisdom of textual and bibliographic theory, based on a Biblical model that seeks to recover the immutable scriptural original, textual "transmission" should not be understood only in terms of "corruption" but also as new alphabetic performances.

All early Greek writing bears the stamp of a/literate verbal art and the metrics of both lyric and epic retain features of the mnemonic systems essential to that art. The question is what effect Greek alphabetic writing had on these archaic modes, both epic and lyric. To what degree did lyric and epic poetry take on distinctly new textual attributes after the introduction of the Greek alphabet into an a/literate culture with a long history of both epic and protolyric modes? The Greek alphabet did not create the lyric out of the blue nor did a particular technology determine a particular literature. Nothing is ever entirely new. But the "same thing" takes on new meanings in new technological contexts. Writing technologies affect poetry in ways that are often hard to explicate but nonetheless become part of their meaning. In this particular circumstance, it might be more fruitful to focus not on intrinsic features of lyric verse but rather on the "reading effect" that the alphabet created for the lyric, including those that took place over long periods of time, such as the possibility that a lyric might be read and not sung. That is, the lyric takes on a different quality in the new medium. While the lyric initially may have been a script for performance or song, it led to a newly textualized form of poetry.


After the invention of the alphabet, the next most significant Western technological revolution in the reproduction of language occurred in 1451 with the invention of the printing press (the Chinese were printing books 800 years earlier). There were other important technological developments between the Greek alphabet and the printing press, including the invention of the Roman alphabet and other scripts, the fabrication of new and more efficient surfaces to write on, and the development of codices and manuscripts and books. But none of these was quite so far-reaching in its impact as Gutenberg's press.

The printing press occurs very late in the history of the book; nonetheless, it ushered in what well might be called the Age of the Book, a period of unprecedented circulation for writing. If the stage epitomizes the transcriptive or memorial functions of writing, the book epitomizes the immemorial storage function of writing. The book is writing's own stage, not a prompt to some other stage. Insofar as literary works appear in books they make possible a circulation distinct from presentation in theatrical performance. The book is the place where writing as writing comes into its own, has its own "place," finds its own forms.

Many of the effects we associate with literacy were not yet dominant in the medieval Europe of Gutenberg, which held fast to many characteristics of analphabetic culture. Writing remained an aid to memory and oral forms were still part of its infrastructure. Indeed, medieval poetry, scripted to be performed—that is, heard not read—retained many of the rhythmical and rhyming qualities of oral poetry. Augustine of Hippo's 400 C.E. citing of silent reading is a crucial signpost along the road to changing the user interface with writing technology, since the emergence of silent reading is generally thought to begin only post-Gutenberg and with the advent of prose. As Wlad Godzich and Jeffrey Kittay note in *The Emergence of Prose,* prose in medieval France emerged from verse and gradually replaced a number of the functions of verse, simultaneous with the rise of a middle class.

According to H. J. Chaytor, in *From Script to Print: An Introduction to Medieval Vernacular Literature,* during the script period of medieval Europe, reading was word-for-word, out loud, and not fluent. Poems were written for recitation. There was no uniformity of grammar or spelling because scripts were to be performed and were only rarely read; except for the case of Latin, only with printing did uniformity even become possible. Before Gutenberg, it was assumed that vernaculars were in flux in terms of pronunciation and vocabulary; the rise of uniform national languages as standard bearers for states was, in part, a media-effect. Language stabilization and stylistic idealization (manuals, grammars) are the blow-back of the printing press.

According to Chaytor, the first French prose appeared in the late twelfth century; before that, the literature that was produced for public entertainment and education was in verse. This first prose was for legal documents, bible translations, and, subsequently, historical accounts. Prose was written for individual readers and it was reserved for "matters of fact, not fancy." As part of an emerging, ultimately massive, deversification process, poetry was translated into prose (much as print databases are now being digitized). The earliest prose by nonpoets or literary artists in France comes from 1202 in an account of the crusades written in an unembellished, factual style. From the twelfth century on, Chaytor notes, all "important" households in England and Europe had at least one person who could read. By the late 1300s, the first "reading public" emerged in England, with the production of secular literature licensed by universities for students. By the 1400s, prose was preferred for erudition and instruction while at the same time there was a gradual rise of literacy; but just being literate didn't mean you could read books. According to Irving Fang's "Timeline of Media History," the first paper was used in England in 1309 and the first paper mill was established in 1495. In the fourteenth and fifteenth centuries books were scarce and expensive and were willed to heirs. Educated men learned to read (women did not)—possibly one half of the population of England was literate. Indeed, there were more schools in the 1400s than in 1864, suggesting the intensity of interest in literacy in the fifteenth century. By 1450, the first newspapers began to circulate in Europe.

Four hundred years after Gutenberg, the next technological revolution for language reproduction began. For the purposes of defining this ongoing technological vortex, I would point to the telegraph (first invented in 1806, with the first transcontinental service becoming available in the 1860s), photography (invented in 1827, popular by late 1830s), the telephone (1876), the phonograph (1877), magnetic audio recording (1899), the loudspeaker (1899), wireless telegraphy (1894), the movie camera (1895), phototypesetting (1895), radio (first regular broadcasting around 1907), television (first network TV broadcast 1949), photo-offset printing (late 1950s), photocopying (first plain paper copier 1959), and, finally, in the last two decades, digital writing and imaging (via computer, the Internet, and the Web). Writing in this age of photographic and electronic reproduction is fundamentally postalphabetic in that it no longer relies on scripts to store and transmit information: cultural memory is becoming digital, more image than letter. At the same time, just as the Greeks lived through several hundred years of simultaneous alphabetic and oral culture, we are now living in a period of overlaid oral, alphabetic, and photo/electronic culture.

One crucial mark of the overlay of alphabetic and electronic technologies is the emergence of radical modernist art in the late nineteenth and early twentieth centuries. Just as some of the Greek literary art of the period immediately following the invention of the alphabet formally reflected the new writing forms of an oral culture soon to be eclipsed, so radical modernism formally reflects the alphabetic culture soon to be eclipsed (but not replaced) by photographic, electronic, and digital media.

The other crucial marker of the overlay of the oral, alphabetic, and photo/electronic is the fact that in North America and Europe, the rise of mass literacy in the late nineteenth century occurs just as the new era of photographic and electronic communications is beginning, making mass literacy and postliteracy intertwined historical developments. Indeed, the culture of literacy reaches its technical apotheosis in the mid-nineteenth and twentieth centuries, not only with the rise of a mass readership, but also with invention of nonelectronic/nonphotographic devices that make language storage and retrieval by writing even more efficient and accessible than ever; for example, carbon paper (1869), the typewriter (first manufactured by Remington in 1873), the mimeograph (invented in 1875 and retailed in 1890), linotype (1886), the Waterman fountain pen (1884), and the ballpoint pen (1938). (The pencil was invented in 1565 and the eraser in 1770, while steel pen points began to replace quill pens in 1780.) The nineteenth- and twentieth-century boom in the production of lyric poetry is coincident with the rise of mass literacy, since many more people were able to become authors. The ability to write and sign something as yours—the signature effect—remains culturally viable until literacy is fully distributed in the society, an event that has yet to occur.

This rise of mass literacy, late in the history of writing, has had the effect of putting the printed and bound book front and center, as the cathected object of the alphabetic unconscious. From the perspective of the year 2000, the printed book is the best picture we have of alphabetic textuality. As we enter into a postliterate period, we can begin to see the book as the solid middle ground between the stage (performed poetry) and the screen (digital poetry).

In making this broad overview of language reproduction technologies, I want to reiterate that one medium does not conquer another. It is not a question of progress but rather of a series of overlays creating the web in which our language is enmeshed. The alphabet did not prescribe the emergence of lyric poetry as a medium of art but rather created the possibility. Technology determines neither art nor politics but politics and art are never free from the effects of technology. Technology informs but it does not determine.

Havelock speculates that perhaps he and McLuhan were alerted to the importance of understanding media by hearing Winston Churchill's "blitz" speeches on the then relatively new and popular medium of the radio. The sheer oral force of the speeches, he says, helped him to reconsider the effects of centuries of silent reading and of the contrasting possibilities for oral performance in early Greek culture. Indeed, radio and, later, TV, marked a turn to a/literate modes for transmission and storage of cultural information, and, as we turn to the twenty-first century, analphabetic media are the primary source of information for most people: you are more likely to hear or see the news than to read it (even while newscasts continue to rely on alphabetic scripts). Yet, while audio and video reproduction have eclipsed both alphabetic and oral technologies, they have qualities in common with both. Postliteracy brings us back to preliteracy. In particular, the emergence of the World Wide Web in the 1990s has awakened a sharper appreciation for the medium of writing and for the visual and acoustic elements of language. Similarly, hypertext theory has reopened consideration of the achievements of radical modernist writing.

My interest in the technoformalist criticism of Havelock and McLuhan, as well as Walter Benjamin, Clement Greenberg, and Stanley Cavell is not only that they draw attention to what it means to work within a medium, but also that they acknowledge the value of using a medium to do what can only be done in that medium. While humanist literary criticism naturalizes the medium of the art, just as it neutralizes its ideology, technoformalist criticism recognizes the medium (and by extension ideology) to have qualities of its own that some art within this medium will choose to foreground, which is to say, bring to consciousness. In poetry, this approach is at the heart of radical modernist composition, with its focus not only on what is conveyed, but also on the specific conditions of the conveyance. Perhaps the motto for this project can be taken from Jerome McGann's "Imagining What You Don't Know: The Theoretical Goals of the Rossetti Archive": "To treat all the physical aspects of the documents as expressive features."

Writing is a storage medium. It stores verbal language. But the various technologies (hieroglyphs, scripts, printing, hypertext) literally score the language stored.

In other words: Writing records the memory of language just as it explores the possibilities for language.

In a formalist emphasis on the medium, we do not escape the question— a medium of what, for what? Can the medium be emptied out, so that it is just the medium, the pure medium? In that case what does it transport but the *contexts* (contents) in which it is placed, like a crystal ball reflecting the hands that (be)hold it.

A medium cannot be in and of itself autonomous, for only readers or listeners or viewers bring a medium into use. In this sense, a medium is a mediation, constituted by what it does, for whom, and how.

The "medium" is a metaphor, as Jack Spicer and Hannah Weiner demonstrate when they insist that their poems are mediums, receiving language from a place outside themselves, north of intention.

A medium is an "in-between" in which you go from one place to another, but also the material of that in-betweenness. Metaphors are mediums of transformation, in Greek the bearer (*phor*) of change (*meta*). Metaphor involves transference/transport/transfer. A medium is the means of transport, the conveyance, and also the material or technical process of art, as brass or silver. But only use makes something a medium of art. Materials by themselves are inert. Yet sometimes one discovers the use of a medium by relying on the resistance of the materials that constitute it.

If poetry in analphabetic culture maximizes its storage function through memorizable language (formulaic, stressed), then poetry in the age of postliteracy (where cultural information is stored orally, alphabetically, and digitally), is perhaps most fully realized through refractory—

unmemorizable—language (unexpected, nonformulaic, distressed). This is why apparently nonliterary writing—catalogs, directories, dictionaries, indexes, concordances, and phone books, as well as printing errors, textual variations, holograph manuscripts—have become so important for poetry. And this is also why the textuality of contemporary poetry is so often tested in performance. For the performance of a textual writing, refractory to memorization, creates a new-old *frisson* that is rich with structural meanings and acoustic resonances.

But what of the age between the two—the age of ascendant literacy? It is commonplace to say that photography freed painting from the burden of pictorial representation, as for centuries paintings and drawings had been the primary means of pictorial and image storing (morphing) and transmission. (The trope of being freed from a burden should not obscure the fact that pictorial representation goes on happily ever after in painting; the point is that the meaning of images changes in painting because their use value changes.) Alphabetic writing ultimately freed poetry (though never completely) from the necessity of storage and transmission of the culture's memories and laws—*poetry's epic function*. In the age of literacy, this task was ultimately assumed by prose. Poetry, released from this overriding obligation to memory storage, increasingly became defined by the individual voice, *poetry's lyric function* (the persistence of epic notwithstanding, since epic in the age of lyric becomes less infrastructure and more art). In this speculative schema, the lyric is contrasted to the impersonal authority of (nonfiction) prose, constituted by such subjects as law and philosophy.

With the advent of the photo/electronic, postliterate age, the emerging function for poetry is neither the storage of collective memory nor the projection of individual voice, but rather an exploration of the medium through which the storage and expressive functions of language work. That is, the technological developments of the past 150 years have made possible, in a way hardly conceivable before, viewing and reproducing and interacting with language as a material and not just as a means. Poetry's singular burden in a digital age is to sound the means of transmission: call it, *poetry's textual function:* making audible/visible the ethos enacted in and by the fabric of writing. Textuality does not erase poetry's epic and lyric functions; rather it supplements and transforms, and in so doing aestheticizes, these increasingly vestigial modalities of the medium.

Another way of saying this is that photography not only loosened the grip of representation on painting but also on poetry.

Humanist literary criticism cannot and will not recognize the necessity of a poetry of textuality in which "memorable language" is just one among many tools of the trade, and not an end in itself. The persistence of the criteria of "memorable language" as a primary category for evaluating poetry is a throwback to an actual social function poetry once had, but which has become in our age largely ornamental and nostalgic except when it is used to tap into the deep fissures of poetry's past, to locate sonic geysers that erupt in the surface of our verses.

A textual poetry does not create language that is committable to memory but rather a memory of the analphabetic that is committable to language. This is why so much textual writing seems to return to a/literate features of language, not only in other cultures but also in our own. This is what I mean to suggest, in part, by the term *a/orality*—the acoustic or aural dimension of language within a postalphabetic environment. The significance of speech for textual poetry is fundamental because such poetry is able to foreground features of speech that do not contribute to the memory function essential for poetry in cultures where oral art is the primary technology for language storage and retrieval.

In the early part of the twentieth century, Gertrude Stein discovered her own version of a/orality through a process of close listening to the vernacular. In the context of a postliterate writing, the transcription of speech looks very different than it did at the dawn of the alphabetic age: static, noise, and other microtextures loom large when the art of memory is not at stake. Repetition without memorability uses the features of oral art for textual ends: it is not memory that is being stored but texture that is being exhibited. The result is not a poetry in the service of memory but a poetry, in Stein's phrase, "of the continuous present."

Textuality, sounded, evokes orality. Conversely, orality provokes textuality (polymorphously), albeit the virtual, aliterate materiality of woven semiosis. This is orality's anterior horizon, its acoustic and linguistic ground, embodied and gestural. The *stuffness* of language, its *verbality*, is present in both writing and speech but it is particularly marked when language is listened to, or read, without the filter of its information function. (The material stratum that weaves together speech and writing provides not only the means for language's information function but also information in its own right.) Textuality is a palimpsest: when you scratch it you find speech underneath. And when you sniff the speech, you find language under that.

Poetry's social function in our time is to bring language ear to ear with its temporality, physicality, dynamism: its evanescence, not its fixed character; its fluidity, not its authority; its structures, not its storage capacity; its concreteness and particularity, not its abstract logicality and clarity.

To say we are in an age of postliteracy does not mean that literacy is no longer necessary but rather that it is no longer sufficient; perhaps the better term would be hyperliteracy. Poetry in a digital age can do more than simply echo the past with memorable phrases. It can also invent the present in language never before heard.

## WORKS CITED

Chaydor, H. J. *From Script to Print: an Introduction to Medieval Literature* (Cambridge [Eng.]: The University Press, 1945).

Fang, Irving. "Timeline of Communication History": http://www.mediahistory.com/time/alltime.html, accessed Jan. 1, 1999.

Godzich, Wlad and Jeffrey Kittay. *The Emergence of Prose: An Essay in Prosaics* (Minneapolis: University of Minnesota Press, 1987).

Havelock, Eric. *Reflections on Orality and Literacy from Antiquity to the Present* (New Haven: Yale University Press, 1986).

McGann, Jerome. *A Critique of Modern Textual Criticism* (Chicago: University of Chicago Press, 1983).

____. "Imagining What You Don't Know: The Theoretical Goals Of The Rossetti Archive": http://jefferson.village.virginia.edu/~jjm2f/chum.html, accessed February 1, 1999.

Nagy, Gregory. *Comparative Studies in Greek and Indic Meter* (Cambridge: Harvard University Press, 1974).

Snell, Bruno. *The Discovery of the Mind: Greek Origins of European Thought.* Tr. T. G. Rosenmeyer (Cambridge: Harvard University Press, 1953); see especially ch. 3: "The Rise of Individuality in the Early Greek Lyric" (1941).

• • •

*Thanks to Tan Lin for his prescient advice, to Jerome Rothenberg for his comments and for his lifelong work finding links between oral and textual poetries, and to Thomas McEvilley for the conversation.*

# SOURCES & ACKNOWLEDGMENTS

Artaud, Antonin. "Spell for Léon Fouks." Photo ©1999 Artists Rights Society (ARS, New York/ADAGP Paris). Translation of "Les figures sur la page inerte..." [February 1947] by Richard Sieburth appears in *Antonin Artaud: Works on Paper*, edited by Margit Rowell. New York: Museum of Modern Art, 1996. Reprinted by permission of the translator.

Barthes, Roland. "The Written Face." *Drama Review*, Spring 1971, pp. 80–82. Reprinted by permission of the publisher.

Beaumelle, Agnès de la. "Spells and Gris-Gris." Translated by Jeanine Herman. In *Antonin Artaud: Works on Paper*, edited by Margit Rowell. New York: Museum of Modern Art, 1996. Reprinted by permission of the translator.

Bernstein, Charles. "The Art of Immemorability." ©2000 by Charles Bernstein.

Billeter, Jean-François. From "The Act of Writing." In *The Chinese Art of Writing*. New York: Skira/ Rizzoli, 1990. Reprinted by permission of the author and the publisher. The original work was published in a French Language edition as *L'art chinous de l'ecriture*, Editions d'Art Albert Skira S.A., Geneva, 1989.

Blake, William. *The Marriage of Heaven and Hell*. [Self-published], 1790–93. The most brilliant view is in The William Blake [hypermedia] Archive: http://jefferson.village.virginia.edu/blake/

Blanchot, Maurice. "The Book to Come." In *The Siren's Song*. Translated by Sacha Rabinovitch. Bloomington: Indiana University Press, 1982. Originally published in French as *Le Livre a Venir*. Copyright ©1959 by Editions Gallimard. Reprinted by permission of Georges Borchardt, Inc; English translation reprinted by permission of Pearson Education.

Borges, Jorge Luis. "On the Cult of Books." In *Selected Non-fictions*. Edited and translated by Eliot Weinberger. New York: Viking Penguin, 1999. Copyright ©1999 by Maria Kodama; translation copyright ©1999 by Penguin Putnam Inc. Used by permission of Viking Penguin, a division of Penguin Putnam Inc.

Breton, André. Foreword to *The Hundred Headless Woman*, by Max Ernst. Translated by Dorothea Tanning. New York: George Braziller, 1981. Reprinted by permission of the translator.

Cameron, Dan. "Living History: Faith Ringgold's Rendevous with the Twentieth Century." In *Dancing at the Louvre*, edited by Dan Cameron. New York: New Museum of Contemporary Art, 1998. Reprinted by permission of the author.

Carothers, Martha L. "Novelty Books: Accents of Images and Words." *Collections* (Newark, University of Delaware Library Associates), vol. 3 (1988): 36–58. Reprinted by permission of the University of Delaware Library and the author.

Cayley, John. "Writing (Under-) Sky: On Xu Bing's *Tianshu*." ©2000 by John Cayley. Revised version of an essay that originally appeared in *Un'altra Cina: Poeti e narratori degli anni Novanta*, a special issue of *In Forma de Parole*, 1991.1 (Spring 1999), pp 143–153 (published in Bologna).

Cendrars, Blaise and Sonia Delaunay. *La Prose du Transsibérien et de la petite Jehanne de France*. Editions des Hommes Nuveaux, 1913. Translation in *Complete Poems*. Edited/translated by Ron Padgett. Berkeley & Los Angeles, University of California Press, 1992. Copyright ©1992 Ron Padgett, ©1947 Editions Denoel. Reprinted by permission of the translator and the publisher.

Cutts, Simon. "an ode for the recovery of an olympia splendid 66 typewriter." In *A Smell of Printing*. New York: Granary Books, forthcoming. ©2000 by Simon Cutts.

Davidson, Michael. "The Material Page." A modified version of the essay which appeared in *Ghostlier Demarcations: Modern Poetry and the Material World*. Berkeley & Los Angeles: University of California Press, 1997. Reprinted by permission of the author.

Derrida, Jacques. "Edmond Jabès and the Question of the Book." In *Writing and Differ-ence.* Translated by Alan Bass. Chicago: University of Chicago Press, 1978. ©1978 University of Chicago Press. Reprinted by permission of the publisher.

Drucker, Johanna. "The Artist's Book As Idea and Form." In *The Century of Artists' Books.* New York: Granary Books, 1995. Reprinted by permission of the author.

Duchamp, Marcel. *Boîte-en-Valise.* [Self-published], 1935/41. Distributed by Art of This Century [New York] in 1943.

Erdman, David V. From "Introduction" to *The Illuminated Blake: William Blake's Com-plete Illuminated Works with a Plate-by-Plate Commentary.* Mineola, New York: Dover Publica-tions, 1992. Reprinted by permission of the publisher.

Ernst, Max. From *The Hundred Headless Woman.* Paris: Editions du Carrefour, 1929.

Everson, William. "The Poem As Icon–Reflections on Printing As a Fine Art." In *Earth Poetry: Selected Essays & Interviews, 1950–1977.* Edited by Lee Bartlett. Berkeley: Oyez, 1980. Reprinted by permission of Robert Hawley, Bill Hotchkiss and the Estate of William Everson.

Fahrner, Barbara. "Interpreting the 'Kunstkammer.'" In *Das Kunstkammerprojekt.* Wolfenbüttel: Herzog August Bibliothek, 1992. Reprinted by permission of the author and the publisher.

Finlay, Alec. Afterword to *Little Sparta* by Robin Gillanders. Edinburgh: Scottish National Portrait Gallery, 1988. Reprinted by permission of the author and the National Galleries of Scotland.

Finlay, Ian Hamilton/Robin Gillanders. From *Little Sparta.* Edinburgh: Scottish National Portrait Gallery, 1988. Photos ©Robin Gillanders. Reprinted by permission of the author and the National Galleries of Scotland.

Gaffarel, Jacques. "Celestial Alphabet Event." In *Curiosités innoviés.* 1637. Reprinted in Kurt Seligman, *The Mirror of Magic.* New York: Pantheon Books, 1948.

Griaule, Marcel. From *Conversations with Ogotemmêli.* Translated by Ralph Butler. New York: Oxford University Press, 1965. Published by Oxford University Press for the Interna-tional African Institute. Reprinted by permission of the International African Institute.

Hamilton, Richard. "The Books of Diter Rot." In *The Liberated Page,* edited by Herbert Spencer. San Francisco: Bedford Press, 1987. Reprinted by permission of the author.

Howe, Susan. "These Flames and Generosities of the Heart." In *The Birthmark: Unsettling the Wilderness in American Literary History.* Hanover, New Hampshire: Wesleyan/University Press of New England, 1993. ©1993 by Susan Howe; Wesleyan University Press, by permis-sion of University Press of New England. Material by Emily Dickinson is reprinted by per-mission. From *The Poems of Emily Dickinson,* Thomas H. Johnson, ed., Cambridge, Massachusetts: The Belknap Press of Harvard University Press, Copyright ©1951, 1955, 1979, 1983 by the President and Fellows of Harvard College. Reprinted by permission of the pub-lishers and the Trustees of Amherst College. From *The Letters of Emily Dickinson* edited by Thomas H. Johnson, Cambrige, Massachusetts: The Belknap Press of Harvard University Press, Copyright ©1958, 1986 by the President and Fellows of Harvard College. Reprinted by permission of the publishers. From *The Manuscript Books of Emily Dickinson,* Ralph W. Franklin, ed., Cambridge, Massachusetts: The Belknap Press of Harvard University Press, Copyright ©1951, 1955, 1978, 1979, 1980, 1981 by the President and Fellows of Harvard College. Copyright ©1914, 1924, 1929, 1932, 1935, 1942 by Martha Dickinson Bianchi. Reprinted by per-mission of the publishers.

Ishihara, Toshi and Linda Reinfeld. "*Hyakunin Isshu:* Between Power and Play, An Anthology in Translation." In *Talking the Boundless Book: Art, Language & the Book Arts,* edited by Charles Alexander. Minneapolis: Minnesota Center for the Book, 1995. Reprinted by permission of the authors.

Jabès, Edmond. From *Desire for a Beginning Dread of One Single End.* Translated by Rosmarie Waldrop. New York: Granary Books, forthcoming. ©2000 by Rosmarie Waldrop.

Janacek, Gerald. "Kruchonykh and the Manuscript Book." In *The Look of Russian Literature: Avant-Garde Visual Experiments, 1900-1930*. Princeton, New Jersey: Princeton University Press, 1984. Copyright ©1984 by P.U.P. Reprinted by permission of the author and Princeton University Press.

Jess [Collins]. *O!* New York: Hawk's Well Press, 1960. Reprinted by permission of the author.

Kaprow, Allan. "Words: An Environment." In *Assemblages, Environments & Happenings*. New York: Harry Abrams, 1966. From an environmental happening at the Smolin Gallery, New York, 1962. Reprinted by permission of the author.

Khlebnikov, Velimir. "The One, The Only Book." In *Collected Works of Velimir Khlebnikov*. Vol. 3. Translated by Paul Schmidt, edited by Ronald Vroon. Cambridge, Massachusetts: Harvard University Press, 1997. Copyright ©1997 by the President and Fellows of Harvard College. Reprinted by permission of the publisher.

Knowles, Alison. "On the Book of Bean." *New Wilderness Letter*, no.11 (1982): 35–37. Reprinted by permission of the author.

Maizels, John. "The Phenomenon of Adolf Wölfli." In *Raw Creation*. London: Phaidon Press, 1996. Reproduced from *Raw Creation* ©1996 Phaidon Press Limited. Photos copyright ©Adolf Wölfli Foundation, Museum of Fine Arts, Bern.

Marinetti, F.T. *Destruction of Syntax–Imagination Without Strings–Words-in-Freedom*. 1913. Reprinted in *Futurist Manifestos*, edited by Umbro Appollonio. New York: Viking Press, 1973.

McCaffery, Steve and bp Nichol. "The Book As Machine." In *Rational Geomancy*. Vancouver: Talonbooks, 1992. Reprinted by permission of Steve McCaffery and the Estate of bp Nichol.

McGann, Jerome. "Composition as Explanation (of Modern and Postmodern Poetries)." In *Black Riders: The Visible Language of Modernism*. Princeton, New Jersey: Princeton University Press, 1993. Copyright ©1993 by P.U.P. Reprinted by permission of the author and Princeton University Press.

Meltzer, David. "Books Within Books: Some Notes on the Kabbalah & the *Sefer Yetsirah*." ©2000 by David Meltzer.

Mignolo, Walter D. "Signs and Their Transmission: The Question of the Book in the New World." In *Writing Without Words: Alternative Literacies in Mesoamerica and the Andes*, edited by Elizabeth Hill Boone and Walter D. Mignolo. Durham: Duke University Press, 1994. Copyright ©1994 by Duke University Press. All rights reserved. Reprinted by permission of the author and the publisher.

Mordell, Phineas, trans. *Sefer Yetsirah*. In *The Secret Garden: An Anthology in the Kabbalah*, edited by David Meltzer. Barrytown, New York: Station Hill Openings, 1998. Reprinted by permission of the editor.

Munn, Henry. "Writing in the Imagination of an Oral Poet." *New Wilderness Letter*, no. 5/6 (1978):6–10. Reprinted by permission of the author.

Munn, Nancy D. "Guruwari Designs." In *Walbiri Iconography*. 1974. Reprint. Chicago: University of Chicago Press, 1986. Reprinted by permission of the author.

Nezahualcoyotl [1402–1472]. "The Painted Book." In *Native Mesoamerican Spirituality*, edited with a foreword, introduction, and notes by Miguel Léon-Portilla. Mahwah, New Jersey: Paulist Press, 1980. ©1980 by the Missionary Society of St. Paul the Apostle in the State of New York.

Perloff, Marjorie. From "Profond Aujourd'hui," In *The Futurist Moment*. Chicago: University of Chicago Press, 1986. Reprinted by permission of the author.

Phillips, Tom. Introduction to *The Heart of A Humument*. Stuttgart: edition hansjörg mayer, 1985. Reprinted by permission of the publisher.

_____. "Notes on *A Humument*." In Tom Phillips: Works and Texts. New York: Thames and Hudson, 1992. Reprinted by permission of edition hansjörg mayer, distributed by Thames and Hudson.

Ringgold, Faith. "The Picnic at Giverney." From *The French Collection,* Part 1: #3, 1991. ©1991 by Faith Ringgold. Reprinted by permission of the author.

Roth, Dieter. Introduction to *Books and Graphics.* Stuttgart: edition hansjörg mayer, 1979. Reprinted by permission of the publisher.

Rothenberg, Jerome. "The Poetics and Ethnopoetics of the Book & Writing." ©2000 by Jerome Rothenberg.

Samarin, William J. "Written Glossolalia." In *Tongues of Men and Angels: The Religious Language of Pentecostalism.* New York: Macmillan, 1972. Reprinted by permission of the author.

Schneemann, Carolee. "Up to and Including Her Limits." In *More Than Meat Joy.* Kingston, New York: McPherson & Co., 1997. Reprinted by permission of the author. Photo by Peter Moore ©Estate of Peter Moore/Licensed by VAGA, New York, NY.

Sieburth, Richard. From Mallarmé's *Le Livre.* Translated by Richard Sieburth. ©2000 by Richard Sieburth.

Smith, Keith A. "The Book As Physical Object." In *Structure of the Visual Book.* 3rd ed. Rochester, New York: keith smith BOOKS, 1994. Reprinted by permission of the author.

Stein, Gertrude. "Book." In *Tender Buttons; objects, food, rooms.* 1914. Reprint. Numerous republications.

Tedlock, Dennis. "Toward a Poetics of Polyphony and Translatability." In *Close Listening: Poetry and the Performed Word,* edited by Charles Bernstein. New York: Oxford University Press, 1998. Copyright ©1998 by Oxford University Press, Inc. Reprinted by permission of the author and Oxford University Press.

Tyson, Ian. "Souvenir de Voyage." ©2000 by Ian Tyson.

Upton, Lawrence. "Writers Forum—Life by 1000 Books." ©2000 by Lawrence Upton.

Vicuña, Cecilia. "Desert Book." Translated by Rosa Alcalá. ©2000 by Cecilia Vicuña and Rosa Alcalá.

Vogler, Thomas A. "When a Book Is Not a Book." ©2000 by Thomas Vogler. Reprinted by permission of the author. Revised version of "Ceci n'est pas un livre," in *Books as Objects,* Portland, Oregon: Comus Gallery, 1993.

Waldman, Anne. "My Life A Book." ©2000 by Anne Waldman.

Whitman, Walt. "So Long." In *Leaves of Grass.* 1891–92. Reprint edition. Numerous republications.

Young, Karl. "Notation and the Art of Reading." *Open Letter,* Spring 1984, pp. 5–32. Reprinted by permission of the author.

An exhaustive effort has been made to locate all rights holders and to clear reprint permissions. This process has been complicated, and if any required acknowledgments have been omitted, or any rights overlooked, it is unintentional and forgiveness is requested.

Revised version of an essay that originally appeared in *Un'altra Cina: Poeti e narratori degli anni Naventa,* a special issue of In *Forma de Parole,* 1991.1 (Spring 1999), pp 143–153 (published in Bologna).

# INDEX

Page numbers in italics refer to illustrations
Page numbers in brackets refer to chapters by the author

Jerome Rothenberg is a poet and one of the world's leading anthologists. Among his more than sixty books are *Technicians of the Sacred: A Range of Poetries from Africa, America, Asia, Europe and Oceania* (1985), *Revolution of the Word: American Avant-Garde Poetry between the Two World Wars* (1974), and *Shaking the Pumpkin: Traditional Poetry of the Indian North Americas* (1986). With Pierre Joris he edited the monumental two volume *Poems for the Millennium: The University of California Book of Modern & Postmodern Poetry* (1995 and 1998). He lives with his wife in Encinitas, California.

Steven Clay, publisher of Granary Books, is an editor, curator and archivist specializing in the art and literature of the 1960s, 70s and 80s. He is the author, with Rodney Phillips, of *A Secret Location on the Lower East Side: Adventures in Writing 1960–1980* (1998). He lives in New York City with his wife and their two young daughters.

*A Book of the Book* was set in 10.75 Veljovic Book with a horizontal scale of 97% with Mantina and Nueva Multiple Masters for display. The long s [ſ] in the Karl Young essay was created in Fontographer.

The book was printed and bound by Thomson-Shore, Dexter, Michigan.

DATE DUE

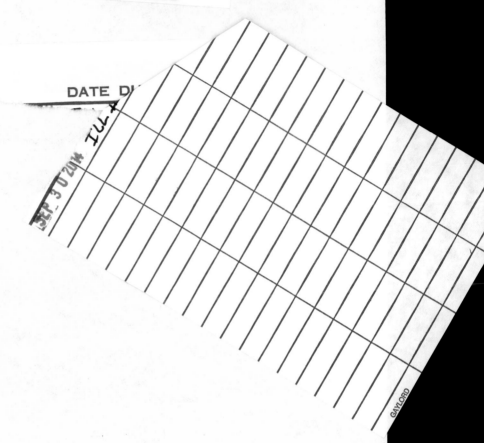